EAT: **LOS ANGELES** 2012
The Food Lover's Guide to Los Angeles

PROSPECT PARK MEDIA

PROSPECT
· PARK ·
BOOKS

EAT: **LOS ANGELES** is a trademark of Prospect Park Media.

Published by Prospect Park Media
prospectparkmedia.com
eat-la.com

Distributed to the trade by
SCB Distributors
scbdistributors.com

SPECIAL SALES
Bulk purchase (10+ copies) of EAT: Los Angeles is available to companies,
organizations, mail-order catalogs and nonprofits at special discounts, and
large orders can be customized to suit individual needs. For more information,
contact Prospect Park Media.

Library of Congress Control Number: 2011934243
The following is for reference only:
Bates, Colleen Dunn
            Los Angeles / Colleen Dunn Bates
                    p.cm.
            Includes index.
            ISBN: 978-0-9844102-8-6
            1. Los Angeles (Calif.) – Guidebooks. 2. Los Angeles County (Calif.)
    – Food / Restaurants.
            I. Bates, Colleen Dunn. II. Title.

Fourth edition, first printing

Production in the United States of America.
Design by Joseph Shuldiner.
Printed in China by Imago Group.

EAT: **LOS ANGELES 2012**
The Food Lover's Guide to Los Angeles

EDITOR
Colleen Dunn Bates

CONTRIBUTING EDITORS
Jean T. Barrett
Linda Burum
Miles Clements
Jenn Garbee
Amelia Saltsman
Pat Saperstein
Elina Shatkin
Joseph Shuldiner

PROSPECT PARK MEDIA

[TABLE OF CONTENTS]

[ABOUT THE AUTHORS]

COLLEEN DUNN BATES (editor and publisher) was the American editor of the Gault Millau guides (including *The Best of Los Angeles*) and the restaurant critic for *L.A. Style*. Now she writes about restaurants for *Westways* and heads up Prospect Park Media, which publishes *EAT: Los Angeles*, the *Hometown* books, *Helen of Pasadena*, *Celebrating with Julienne*, *The Spa Less Traveled* and other titles, sites and apps. A sixth-generation Southern Californian, Colleen lives in Pasadena.

JEAN T. BARRETT is a food and wine writer whose articles have appeared in the *Los Angeles Times*, *Westways*, *Sky* and *Wine Spectator*, among other publications. The Hollywood Hills resident has also co-authored three books with Colin Cowie, including *Colin Cowie Weddings* (Little, Brown).

LINDA BURUM is the author of *A Guide to Ethnic Food in Los Angeles* (Harper Collins) among other books, and she writes regularly about L.A.'s culinary world—with a particular focus on ethnic cuisines—for the *Los Angeles Times* and *Los Angeles* magazine. She lives in Santa Monica.

MILES CLEMENTS writes about food for the *Los Angeles Times* and others. The Long Beach-area resident (and native) also roams the South Bay—and, indeed, all of L.A.—for his blog, *Eat Food With Me*.

JENN GARBEE reports on all things ingestible for the *Los Angeles Times*, *Squid Ink* (the *L.A. Weekly*'s food blog) and Tribune Media's national food and beverage wire. She is the author of *Secret Suppers* (Sasquatch Books) and co-author of *Hometown Santa Monica* (Prospect Park Books). This former pastry chef sidelines as a food stylist and kid's cooking teacher.

AMELIA SALTSMAN is the author of *The Santa Monica Farmers' Market Cookbook* (Blenheim Press). The L.A. native and longtime Santa Monican also writes about cooking, markets and food for such magazines as *Bon Appetit* and is a regular guest on Evan Kleiman's *Good Food* show on KCRW.

PAT SAPERSTEIN is the intrepid eater behind *Eating L.A.* (eatingla.com), one of L.A.'s most respected food blogs. The South Pasadena resident is also a senior editor at *Variety*.

ELINA SHATKIN was born in the Ukraine, educated at UCLA, and has worked as an entertainment-industry reporter/editor and food writer. She currently writes about food and drink for the *L.A. Weekly* and *Squid Ink*.

JOSEPH SHULDINER is *EAT: Los Angeles*'s art director and a contributor to Eat-LA.com. An L.A. native, this artist and former *Los Angeles Times* designer is also a passionate cook. He produced the hit cookbook *Celebrating with Julienne* and is about to publish his own book, *Pure Vegan* (Chronicle).

[THE REST OF THE TEAM]

CONTRIBUTORS: Darryl Bates, Troy Corley, Nealey Dozier, Sandy Gillis, William Goldstein, Lennie LaGuire, Mary Arranaga Landis, Susan LaTempa, Melody Malmberg Skylar Sutton & Julia Wong

ART DIRECTOR: Joseph Shuldiner

EDITORIAL ASSISTANTS: Laura Derr, Gina Magnuson & Natalie Weinstein

PROOFREADER: Nancy Roberts Ransohoff

DATABASE DESIGNER: Anton Anderson

IT DIRECTOR: Darryl Bates

WORDPRESS GURUS: Jesse McDougal & John Stephens

MARKETING DIRECTOR: Caroline Purvis

DISTRIBUTOR: Aaron Silverman, SCB Distributors

[PLEASE CHECK OUT EAT: LOS ANGELES'S WEB SITE AT: Eat-LA.com]

[AND LISTEN TO EAT LA ON 89.3 KPCC'S SHOW OFF-RAMP]

[AND GET YOUR EAT LA IPHONE & IPAD APPS AT THE ITUNES STORE!]

SPECIAL THANKS to L.A.'s passionate and interconnected food-journalism community, especially the Chowhounds; the Yelpers; the *Los Angeles Times* Food section; Jessica Gelt and the gang at the *Times*'s Daily Dish; Jonathan Gold, Amy Scattergood and friends at the *L.A. Weekly* and its blog, *Squid Ink*; Patrick Kuh and Lesley Bargar Suter at *Los Angeles* magazine; Evan Kleiman and *Good Food* (KCRW); *Tasting Table*; Merrill Shindler; the *Hometown* books and their authors; Citysearch.com; and the many great blogs, including EatingLA.com, LA.Eater.com, FoodGPS, la.foodblogging, Rameniac.com, GreatTacoHunt.com, *Vegetarians in Paradise* (vegparadise.com), *Tuna Toast* (tokyoastrogirl.com), GastronomyBlog.com and *L.A. & O.C. Foodventures*. Finally, heaps o' gratitude and an extra hot dog to our radio partner, John Rabe at 89.3 KPCC.

[ABOUT EAT: LOS ANGELES 2012]

THE LAST YEAR WAS A BIG ONE for *EAT: Los Angeles*. We sold out of books by July, became radio partners with KPCC, launched an iPhone and iPad app, added Elina Shatkin to our writing team, and generally had one hell of a good time eating and drinking our way across Los Angeles. Like countless Angelenos, we delighted in the explosion of places serving and/or making craft beer. We reveled in the juxtaposition of opposing trends: on the one hand, pork was *everywhere*, and on the other, vegan cooking came into its own. We told each other about our finds: a sandwich place in Highland Park, a pizzeria on Beverly, an outdoor café in South Pasadena, a gourmet market in Brentwood, a soda fountain in Canoga Park, a Vietnamese gastropub in Alhambra, a casual wine bar Downtown, an accomplished restaurant in Malibu.

So now we're sharing all those finds in this new book, which has been thoroughly updated and enriched with new discoveries. And after hearing so many of you ask us, "What's your favorite restaurant?" we've added a new section called Favorites, which is basically short lists of our team's personal favorites in all sorts of areas, from brunch to beer.

This 2012 edition may be updated and improved, but it is still by no means a comprehensive guide—that would be so massive you couldn't lift it. *EAT: Los Angeles* is, however, a broad-ranging book, in terms of geography, cuisines and price points. Most of all, it's a discerning one—we don't have every single restaurant in Koreatown, for instance, but we point you toward our favorites. Our goal is to give you interesting, thoughtful, delicious choices in every category across L.A. County. And we explore the food world far beyond restaurants, because if you like to eat, you want to know about worthwhile cheese shops, caterers, taco trucks, farmers' markets and everything that has to do with living a gustatorily rewarding life in Los Angeles.

Here you'll find the Why, What and Who for L.A.'s best food sources, from restaurants and coffeehouses to ethnic markets and bakeries. But we don't know it all, not by a long shot. So if we've missed your favorite Thai market or Italian trattoria or American breakfast café, please let us know at Eat-LA.com.

Colleen Dunn Bates
Editor

P.S. DESPITE OUR BEST EFFORTS . . .

Please forgive us if a business has closed, if prices have been raised or if your experience does not match ours. We labored mightily to verify every scrap of information in this book, but some places will close, change or misbehave, and we can't do a thing about it.

HOW WE DECIDE WHAT TO INCLUDE: *EAT: Los Angeles* has about 1,300 listings, but of course the L.A. Basin has gazillions more places to eat, drink and shop. Our job is to steer you to the best. If we don't like a place, we simply don't include it.

Most importantly, we celebrate the places that are mom 'n' pop in spirit—individual businesses and local chains with hands-on owner-ship and enthusiasm for whatever is being cooked, sold or served. So you'll find loads of smaller cafés, shops and bistros, but you won't find every high-end hotel restaurant, say, or the sort of MBA-managed club-restaurants that run rampant in Hollywood.

A NOTE ABOUT CHAINS: In general, we eschew corporate chains. This isn't because we think they're inherently evil—we'll confess to a weakness for Houston's, and our families would starve without Trader Joe's—but everyone knows about them, and you don't need us to help you find the Cheesecake Factory. Occasionally we'll make an exception, as with Peet's, which has an indie sensibility and is some-times your only choice for good coffee in certain parts of town.

FAVORITES + FOOD TRUCKS: Our new first section starts with eclectic yet helpful short lists of the writers' personal favorites—where we return to again and again for sandwiches, breakfast, tacos, cocktails, late-night dining and more. We also dish about our favorite food trucks and food-truck gatherings around town.

GOOD FOOD NEIGHBORHOODS: This chapter brings you 12 pro-files of food-lovers' neighborhoods. Some are walkable and some re-quire driving, but each has a strong sense of place and a vibrant food community. Once you explore them all, you'll be a true Angeleno.

ESSENTIALLY L.A.: In each chapter, we recognize some places as "Essentially L.A." Perhaps it serves exceptional food, or does a bet-ter job of selling wine or making coffee than others, or stocks the best selection of cheese or Chinese ingredients in town. Or perhaps its food isn't exactly remarkable, but its atmosphere or history or people are, well, essentially L.A.

DESTINATION DINING: Immigrant groups naturally congregate in certain areas, and therefore immigrant restaurants do the same thing. So accept, for instance, that you will not find great Chinese food on the westside—you need to go to the south San Gabriel Valley to get the real thing. Other cuisines are well represented in many areas but have a particular intensity in one community. You'll find good Armenian food, for instance, in Hollywood and Pasadena, but Glendale has by far the largest Armenian population in the region.

[HERE'S WHERE TO FIND REGIONAL SPECIALTIES]

ARTESIA:
Indian

BRENTWOOD:
Italian trattorias
(no one knows why, but tons are here)

CHINATOWN (NORTH DOWNTOWN):
Chinese and Vietnamese, though not as much as
in the San Gabriel Valley

EAST L.A.:
Mexican and Central American

EAST VALLEY:
Thai

GLENDALE:
Armenian & Middle Eastern

HOLLYWOOD (EAST):
Mexican & Central American

HOLLYWOOD (EAST-CENTRAL–THAI TOWN):
Thai

KOREATOWN (CENTRAL L.A.):
Korean

LITTLE TOKYO (NORTH DOWNTOWN NEAR CITY HALL):
Japanese & a little Korean

LONG BEACH (NORTH):
Cambodian

SAN GABRIEL VALLEY (SOUTH):
Chinese & Vietnamese

SAWTELLE & CENTINELA, WEST L.A.:
Japanese

STUDIO CITY:
Japanese/sushi bars

TORRANCE:
Japanese

[THE REGIONS]

It's not easy to break massive L.A. County into manageable chunks, and it requires some semi-arbitrary decisions. Here's how we did it:

CENTRAL CITY: The city of L.A.'s modern core, encompassing Los Feliz, Hollywood, Koreatown, Hancock Park, Beverly/Third, the Mid-City area, Melrose, Miracle Mile, Fairfax and West Hollywood.

EASTSIDE: The city's original core: Downtown, East L.A., Highland Park, Echo Park, Silver Lake, Eagle Rock and environs. Okay, fussy folks, we know it's sacrilegious to some to call Silver Lake "eastside," but that's the way things are evolving in L.A., and we're going with the flow.

SAN GABRIEL VALLEY: A huge swath of the east county, ranging from Monterey Park almost to Pomona and encompassing Pasadena, San Gabriel, Sierra Madre and beyond. Yes, we know Glendale and La Cañada aren't technically in the SG Valley, but for simplicity's sake, we're pretending they are.

EAST VALLEY: The San Fernando Valley from Burbank to Sherman Oaks, including Studio City and North Hollywood.

WEST VALLEY: From Encino and the 405 way out northwest and west to the Ventura County line.

WESTSIDE: CENTRAL: The heart of the westside, including Beverly Hills, Culver City, Century City, Rancho Park and Westwood; the 405 is the western border.

WEST OF THE 405: Pretty self-explanatory. Brentwood to the Palisades, Malibu to Venice.

SOUTH BAY TO SOUTH L.A.: Another huge swath of the county, from the South Bay beach towns (Playa del Rey, Manhattan, Redondo), along the coast from Torrance to Long Beach, and across the south basin from Downey to Inglewood.

PRICE SYMBOLS ARE BASED ON AVERAGE ENTREE PRICES:

$	$11 & under
$$	$12-$17
$$$	$18-$25
$$$$	$26-$34
$$$$$	$35 & up

Favorites + Food Trucks

Yes, every place in this book is a favorite of one or several of the Eat LA team of food journalists. But every day we are asked for our real favorites, so in this new edition of the book we're adding short lists of the places we find ourselves returning to over and over again. For more detailed listings sorted by neighborhood, see the Index by Neighborhood at the end of the book. And note our Essential L.A. places at the start of each chapter.

As for Food Trucks, see the end of this chapter for our favorites.

[FAVORITES]

ADVENTURE
The Bazaar at SLS Hotel, Beverly Hills (PAGE 53)
Java Spice, Rowland Heights (PAGE 104)
LudoBites, location varies (PAGE 50)
New Chong Qing, San Gabriel (PAGE 108)
Omar, San Gabriel (PAGE 109)
Pondok Kaki Lima, Duarte (PAGE 266)
Renu Nakorn, Norwalk (PAGE 175)
Tara's Himalayan, Palms (PAGE 140)
Tashkent Russian Deli, North Hollywood (PAGE 292)
Totoraku Teriyaki House, Century City (PAGE 141)
Udupi Palace, Artesia (PAGE 177)

BREAKFAST
3 Square, Venice (PAGE 221)
Auntie Em's, Eagle Rock (PAGE 208)
BLD, Beverly/Third (PAGE 204)
Ed's Coffee Shop, West Hollywood (PAGE 205)
John O'Groats, Rancho Park (PAGE 220)
Jongewaard's Bake N Broil, Long Beach (PAGE 226)
North End Caffé, Manhattan Beach (PAGE 227)
Shaky Alibi, Beverly/Third (PAGE 207)
Square One, East Hollywood (PAGE 208)
Sweet Butter Kitchen, Sherman Oaks (PAGE 218)
Village Bakery & Café, Atwater (PAGE 306)

SPECIAL OCCASION

Bouchon, Beverly Hills (PAGE 130)
Drago Centro, Downtown (PAGE 82)
Drago Ristorante, Santa Monica (PAGE 146)
Lucques, Melrose (PAGE 64)
Mélisse, Santa Monica (PAGE 153)
Piccolo, Venice (PAGE 156)
Providence, Melrose (PAGE 69)
Urasawa, Beverly Hills (PAGE 141)
Vincenti, Brentwood (PAGE 160)

TO TAKE OUT-OF-TOWNERS

Ammo, Hollywood (PAGE 51)
Coast, Santa Monica (PAGE 222)
Fuego, Long Beach (PAGE 166)
Gjelina, Venice (PAGE 148)
Hollywood Farmers' Market (PAGE 338)
Jitlada, East Hollywood (PAGE 62)
La Serenata de Garibaldi, Boyle Heights (PAGE 86)
Lotería Grill, Hollywood (PAGE 64)
Saddle Peak Lodge, Calabasas (PAGE 127)
Santa Monica Farmers' Market (PAGE 341)
Six Taste Tours (PAGE 364)
Spago, Beverly Hills (PAGE 139)
Street, Melrose (PAGE 73)

A GOOD SANDWICH

Angelo's Italian Deli, Long Beach (PAGE 278)
Artisan Cheese Gallery, Studio City (PAGE 291)
Bay Cities importing, Santa Monica (PAGE 275)
Brent's Delicatessen, Northridge (PAGE 125)
Cemitas Poblanas Don Adrian, Van Nuys (PAGE 270)
Cook's Tortas, Monterey Park (PAGE 99)
Euro Pane, Pasadena (PAGE 213)
Fiore Market Café, South Pasadena (PAGE 213)
Food + Lab, West Hollywood & Silver Lake (PAGES 205 & 210)
Havana Sandwich Company, El Segundo (PAGE 280)
Langer's Deli, Westlake (PAGE 211)
Mendocino Farms, Downtown (PAGE 259)
Schodorf's Luncheonette, Highland Park (PAGE 261)

TACOS ON THE RUN

El Chato, Mid-City (PAGE 251)
El Parian, Pico-Union (PAGE 257)
El Pique Taco Truck, Highland Park (PAGE 257)
Lotería Grill Farmers Market, Fairfax District (PAGE 252)
Plancha, A Taco Joint, Beverly/Third (PAGE 253)
Poquito Mas, Studio City (PAGE 269)
Taqueria La Mexicana, Long Beach (PAGE 283)
Yuca's, Los Feliz (PAGE 255)

BEER

Angel City Brewery, Downtown (PAGE 183)
Blue Dog Beer Tavern, Sherman Oaks (PAGE 191)
Eagle Rock Brewery, Glassell Park (PAGE 186)
The Golden State, Fairfax District (PAGE 180)
Library Alehouse, Santa Monica (PAGE 197)
Local Peasant, Sherman Oaks (PAGE 192)
Steingarten, West L.A. (PAGE 198)
Surly Goat, West Hollywood (PAGE 182)
The York, Highland Park (PAGE 188)

JUST PLAIN COOL

Anzen Hardware, Little Tokyo (PAGE 342)
Bar Keeper, Silver Lake (PAGE 343)
Central Library Culinary Collection, Downtown (PAGE 333)
Farmers Market, Fairfax District (PAGE 357)
Galco's Soda Pop Shop, Highland Park (PAGE 357)
Guidi Marcello, Santa Monica (PAGE 358)
Lindy & Grundy, Hollywood (PAGE 349)
South Pasadena Farmers' Market (PAGE 341)
Surfas, Culver City (PAGE 345)

VIEWS

The Beachcomber, Malibu (PAGE 143)
Hotel Shangri-La, Santa Monica (PAGE 197)
The Lobster, Santa Monica (PAGE 152)
Nelson's, Palos Verdes (PAGE 201)
Perch, Downtown (PAGE 187)
Tower Bar, West Hollywood (PAGE 75)
WP24, Downtown (PAGE 94)

PLACES THAT TIME FORGOT
Dal Rae, Pico Rivera (PAGE 164)
Fosselman's, Alhambra (PAGE 308)
Musso & Frank, Hollywood (PAGE 181)
Original Pantry, Downtown (PAGE 89)
Pacific Dining Car, Downtown (PAGE 89)
Philippe the Original, Chinatown (PAGE 260)
Pie 'n' Burger, Pasadena (PAGE 310)
Smoke House, Burbank (PAGE 122)
Taylor's Steakhouse, Koreatown (PAGE 74)

BURGERS
26 Beach Café, Venice (PAGE 142)
Bill & Hiroko's, Van Nuys (PAGE 270)
Blue Dog Beer Tavern, Sherman Oaks (PAGE 191)
Father's Office, Santa Monica & Culver City (PAGES 196 & 194)
Hungry Cat, Hollywood (PAGE 61)
Lazy Ox Canteen, Little Tokyo (PAGE 187)
Rustic Canyon, Santa Monica (PAGE 157)
Umami Burger, East Hollywood & Miracle Mile (PAGE 75)

SUSHI
Bar Hayama, West L.A. (PAGE 143)
Echigo, West L.A. (PAGE 147)
Kiwami, Studio City (PAGE 118)
Noma Sushi, Santa Monica (PAGE 155)
R23, Downtown (PAGE 90)
Sushi Go 55, Little Tokyo (PAGE 92)
Sushi Nozawa, Studio City (PAGE 123)
Sushi Zo, Palms (PAGE 140)

VEGANS & CARNIVORES CO-EXIST
Bloom Café, Mid-City (PAGE 204)
Forage, Silver Lake (PAGE 83)
Four Café, Eagle Rock (PAGE 210)
Inn of the Seventh Ray, Topanga (PAGE 150)
Local, Silver Lake (PAGE 211)
Mohawk Bend, Echo Park (PAGE 88)
Tender Greens, Hollywood, Culver City & beyond (PAGES 208 & 140)
Tony's Darts Away, Burbank (PAGE 192)

QUIET ENOUGH TO TALK BUT NOT DULL

AKA an American Bistro, Pasadena (PAGE 95)
Jar, Beverly/Third (PAGE 61)
La Cachette Bistro, Santa Monica (PAGE 151)
La Cava, Sherman Oaks (PAGE 119)
Le Saint Amour, Culver City (PAGE 134)
Locanda Portofino, Santa Monica (PAGE 153)
Lou, Hancock Park (PAGE 181)
Raphael, Studio City (PAGE 121)
Savory, Malibu (PAGE 158)

COCKTAIL CRAZE

1886 Bar, Pasadena (PAGE 189)
Caña Rum Bar, Downtown (PAGE 184)
The Edison, Downtown (PAGE 186)
La Descarga, Hollywood (PAGE 181)
Ray's & Stark Bar, Miracle Mile (PAGE 182)
The Tap Room, Pasadena (PAGE 190)
The Varnish, Downtown (PAGE 188)

PIZZA

Casa Bianca PIzza Pie, Eagle Rock (PAGE 79)
The Coop Pizza, Cheviot Hills (PAGE 272)
Eatalian Café, Gardena (PAGE 165)
Mother Dough, Los Feliz (PAGE 66)
Olio Pizzeria, Beverly/Third (PAGE 207)
Pizzeria Mozza, Melrose (PAGE 69)
Pavich's Brick Oven Pizzeria, San Pedro (PAGE 281)
Vito's Pizza, West Hollywood (PAGE 255)

BRUNCH

Café del Rey, Marina del Rey (PAGE 144)
Campanile, Miracle Mile (PAGE 54)
Canelé, Atwater (PAGE 79)
Cliff's Edge, Silver Lake (PAGE 81)
Culina at Four Seasons, Beverly Hills (PAGE 131)
Delphine, Hollywood (PAGE 57)
Fig, Santa Monica (PAGE 147)
Firefly Bistro, South Pasadena (PAGE 101)
Hugo's, West Hollywood & Studio City (PAGES 206 & 217)

Jar, Beverly/Third (PAGE 61)
Joe's, Venice (PAGE 150)
Mas Malo, Downtown (PAGE 87)
The Park, Echo Park (PAGE 90)
Petrossian, West Hollywood (PAGE 68)
Tavern, Brentwood (PAGE 159)

HAPPY HOURS WITH FOOD

Allston Yacht Club, Echo Park (PAGE 183)
Chaya Brasserie, West Hollywood (PAGE 55)
Chaya Downtown (PAGE 80)
Chaya Venice (PAGE 145)
L'Epicerie, Culver City (PAGE 221)
Rush Street, Culver City (PAGE 194)
Vertical Wine Bistro, Pasadena (PAGE 190)
The Yard, Santa Monica (PAGE 199)

24-HOUR

Du-par's, Fairfax District & Studio City (PAGES 205 & 216)
El Puerto Escondido, Inglewood (PAGE 165)
Fred 62, Los Feliz (PAGE 59)
Hodori, Koreatown (PAGE 61)
Izzy's Deli, Santa Monica (PAGE 224)
The Kettle, Manhattan Beach (PAGE 169)
Original Pantry Café, Downtown (PAGE 89)
Pacific Dining Car, Downtown (PAGE 89)

GUILTY PLEASURES

Bludso's BBQ, Compton (PAGE 278)
Carmela Ice Cream, Pasadena (PAGE 307)
Churros Calientes, West L.A. (PAGE 318)
Donut Man, Glendora (PAGE 307)
Fab Hot Dogs, Reseda (PAGE 271)
Hawkins House of Burgers, Watts (PAGE 280)
Honey's Kettle Fried Chicken, Culver City/Compton (PAGES 273 & 280)
Jerry's Soda Shoppe, Canoga Park (PAGE 313)
Little Flower Candy Co., Pasadena (PAGE 309)
Littlejohn's English Toffee, Fairfax District (PAGE 302)
Sweet Rose Creamery, Santa Monica (PAGE 320)

[FOOD TRUCKS]

L.A. has a rich history of roving tamale, corn and champurrado vendors, taco tables and food trucks, but in the last few years, the scene has gone upscale. Sporting funky names and bold graphics, these nouveau trucks live and die by Twitter. They serve more elaborate food than traditional taco trucks (with prices to match), offering everything from classic American comfort food to all manner of fusion fare. Here's the relatively short list of our current favorites. (Note that they can come and go as rapidly as political sex scandals.)

[Auntie's Frybread] @auntiesfrybread, auntiesfrybread.com
"Native American fusion" doesn't sound promising, but the golden discs of freshly fried dough prove otherwise. Savory versions are topped with barbecued beef or a mild chili, but a classic, dinner-plate-size frybread, with airy pockets of dough rising from the surface and cinnamon sugar amassing in the valleys, may be the best $3 you can spend at any truck.

[Barbie's Q] @BarbiesQ, barbiesq.com
This rider on the mobile-truck bandwagon makes solid, respectable barbecue, notably the brisket and pulled-pork sandwiches, the faux-pork vegetarian sandwich and the baby-back ribs.

[Border Grill Truck] @BorderGrill, bordergrill.com
One of the city's best-known food trucks does a lot of private events, but it also hits the usual truck hot spots; it's also at the Santa Monica Farmers' Market the first Saturday and second Wednesday of the month. Border Grill's quesadillas and excellent tacos (Yucatan pork, potato, Baja-style fish) are our faves.

[Buttermilk Truck] @buttermilktruck, buttermilktruck.com
Comfort food doesn't get any more comfortable than on the Buttermilk Truck, where the mobile kitchen dishes out breakfast sliders, fantastic homemade cake doughnut balls, bite-size buttermilk pancake balls, red velvet cupcakes and Hawaiian-bread cinnamon french toast sticks. It all tastes just as good, if not better, at 9 p.m. as it does at 9 a.m.

[Canter's Truck] @CantersTruck, canterstruck.com
Langer's pastrami on rye may tower above rival Canter's, but the mobile version of Canter's is pretty darn satisfying when you're nowhere near Deli-land. The oversize pastrami and corned beef sandwiches are smaller on the truck, which means they're just the right size, and also more reasonably priced at $8.50.

[Coolhaus Ice Cream Truck] @coolhaus, eatcoolhaus.com
All-natural, homemade, terrific ice cream sandwiches shaped vaguely like modern houses come in varieties including Frank Behry (sugar

cookie and strawberry ice cream) and Mintimalism (chocolate cookie and mint chip ice cream).

[Dosa Truck] @dosatruck, dosatruck.com
While this might seem like just another trendoid truck, Indian street food really is ideally suited to serving out of a catering truck. This one specializes, of course, in dosa (crisp sourdough rice-and-lentil cakes), cooked to order and topped with chutneys or things like eggs, masala (curried potatoes), caramelized onions, mushrooms and cheese.

[Frysmith] @frysmith, eatfrysmith.com
This fancy-pants truck serves up hand-cut Kennebec and sweet potatoes, fresh-fried and smothered with, as they say on the website, "stuff": beer- and chocolate-flavored chili fries, kim chee and Kurobuta pork-belly fries, vegan chili fries, steak, poblano and caramelized onion fries, and tomatillo-tamarind chicken and cashew fries, all of which can be paired with craft sodas. Weekly specials are just as dynamic—after finding a (temporary) supply of good, fresh cheese curd, they quickly developed their own poutine, much to the delight of the French-Canadian ex-pat hipster community.

[Get Your Lardon] @getyourlardon, getyourlardon.com
Welcome to the cuisine of gluttony, which can be hard to resist, especially when it rolls up to your doorstop smelling of smoky Nueske bacon. Everything on this truck is bacon-based: breakfast burritos, sandwiches, French toast, even the brownies. The signature item is the baco (pronounced "bock-oh"), a reverse taco with strips of bacon woven into a shell and fried around a chunky potato hash. Not for the faint of heart.

[Global Soul Truck] @globalsoultruck, globalsoultruck.com
This pan-ethnic truck, formerly of San Francisco, approaches food with a gleeful "more is more" abandon, like shrimp in garlic coconut curry, or hot links with onions, peppers, bacon, a fried egg and chipotle crema. Prepare for a messy meal that's sweet, savory and strange.

[Green Truck] @Green_Truck, greentruckonthego.com
These sustainable twists on the roach coach, fueled by recycled vegetable oil, cruise Culver City, Santa Monica and the Wilshire/La Brea area on weekdays. Your ahi poke tacos, vegan sesame-tofu wraps and sweet potato fries are served in biodegradable packaging to lots of creative-industry workers.

[Grilled Cheese Truck] @grlldcheesetruk, thegrilledcheesetruck.com
It seems crazy that there's always such a long line for cheese and bread, but this truck has mastered the art of this seemingly simple sandwich. Chef Dave Danhi's most famous creation is the Cheesy Mac & Ribs, a sandwich with a slice of baked mac 'n cheese, smoked

rib meat, onions and more cheese; we're partial to the harvest grilled cheese with butternut squash, roasted leeks and balsamic.

[Heirloom LA] @wpheirloomla
Devoutly organic, this offshoot of a catering company brings a farm-to-plate aesthetic to the mobile-cuisine scene, serving classy California fare, with prices to match: market-fresh green peas atop a brisket hash, waffles in real blueberry sauce. They're famous for the lasagne cupcake, sheets of pasta dexterously layered in a cupcake form and wrapped around an artichoke confit or short ribs and cipollini onions.

[Jogasaki] @jogasakiburrito
A clever mashup of Japanese sushi and L.A. street food, this place makes sushi burritos that are big and filling, stuffed with rice and some version of sushi (though it's usually of a non-traditional, deeply fried and mayonnaise-soaked variety) wrapped in a large flour tortilla or a thin sheet of soy paper that falls apart at first bite.

[Kogi BBQ] @kogibbq, kogibbq.com
The icon of the nouveau food truck scene, Kogi has a legion of imitators but still makes the best Korean taco in L.A., and the hungry masses are eating it up. Wherever one of the five Kogi trucks parks, there's bound to be a line for their trademark mix of short ribs or spicy pork and house-made kim chee in taco, burrito or quesadilla form.

[Komodo] @komodofood, komodofood.com
Like Kogi, Komodo uses tortillas as a delivery system for Asian-influenced flavors, but instead of kim chee you'll taste things like peanut sauce (on the soy tempeh salad), citrus-soy (in the Asian marinated chicken with stir-fried rice and mandarins) and cucumber (atop the Indonesian beef rendang). Bright flavors, quality ingredients and prices on the high side, but not unfairly so.

[Nacho Truck] @nachotruckla, nachotruckla.com
What's so special about nachos? Nothing, unless they're made from freshly fried triangles of flour tortillas and topped with lamb and goat cheese or chili, bacon and house-made cheese sauce. Stoner food hits new heights.

[South Philly Experience] @southphillyexp, southphillyexperience.com
Run by a couple of Philly transplants, these two trucks do one thing—the cheese steak—and they do it right. "Wit wiz" or witout, this is a pile of thinly sliced, grilled beef on bread shipped from Amoroso's in Philadelphia. To complete the experience, they also sell Tastykakes.

[Vizzi Truck] @VizziTruck, vizzitruck.com
The Vizzi Truck goes beyond the usual food-truck haute junk food, with flatbread sandwiches, skillfully seasoned grilled chicken and beef

and garlicky chickpea sliders. House-made mango salsa or powerful chimichurri tops the fresh, healthy dishes. On the side, there's
pimento-spiced popcorn—an unusual yet inspired touch.

FOOD TRUCK LOTS

With the proviso that truck gatherings change faster than Lady Gaga
changes shoes, here are some good ones.

[7th + Fig]
WHERE: 7th and Figueroa Plaza, Downtown
WHEN: Monday–Wednesday 11 a.m.–2 p.m., tinyurl.com/7thandfig

[Altadena]
WHERE: N. Lake Ave. (behind Webster's), Altadena
WHEN: Friday evenings, @WebstersPharm

[Automobile Driving Museum]
WHERE: 610 Lairport St., El Segundo
WHEN: Friday lunch, theadm.org

[Century City]
WHERE: 5985 W. Century Blvd., (in the back lot), Century City
WHEN: Tuesday 11 a.m.–3 p.m., tinyurl.com/centuryblvd

[Glendale]
WHERE: 121 W. Lexington Dr., Glendale
WHEN: Monday, Wednesday, Friday 11 a.m.–2 p.m.

[Hollywood Production Center]
WHERE: 1149 N. Gower St., Hollywood
WHEN: Monday–Friday, 11 a.m.–3 p.m., tinyurl.com/hpclot

[LA Mart]
WHERE: 1933 S. Broadway Ave., Downtown/Fashion District
WHEN: Monday–Friday 11 a.m.–3 p.m., tinyurl.com/lamart

[Main Street]
WHERE: 2612 Main St., Santa Monica
WHEN: Tuesday 5:30 p.m.–10 p.m., tinyurl.com/mainstlot

[The Truck Stop]
WHERE: 1520 N. Cahuenga Blvd., Hollywood
WHEN: Monday–Friday 11:30 a.m.–2:30 p.m., @truckstop1520

[Westside Food Truck Central]
WHERE: 10601 W. Washington Blvd., Culver City
WHEN: Lunch Monday–Friday, 11 a.m.–2:30 p.m., dinner Monday &
Wednesday 5–9 p.m., westsidefoodtruckcentral.com

GOOD FOOD NEIGHBORHOOD
[3rd Street]

IN THE HEART OF LOS ANGELES, 3rd Street has been a food destination since the summer of 1934, when a group of farmers gathered at 3rd and Fairfax to sell their produce. Today the L.A. Farmers Market hosts millions of tourists annually while remaining a popular gathering spot and food source for locals. The section of 3rd Street extending about a mile west from the market has evolved into one of the city's top shopping rows, with plenty of food shops, restaurants, cafés and wine bars in the mix.

Start your tour at the Farmers Market, of course, with coffee and a bear claw at **BOB'S COFFEE & DOUGHNUTS**. It's a superlative fried-dough experience coupled with unsurpassed people watching: sugar-buzzed screenwriters, tables of elderly regulars on their third cup of decaf and bemused out-of-towners on a bus tour. Nearby, **HUNTINGTON MEATS** sells Harris Ranch beef as well as an impressive array of house-made sausages and a hamburger blend ground to chef Nancy Silverton's specifications. Huntington is next to **MONSIEUR MARCEL GOURMET MARKET**, which aims to satisfy all cravings, from anchovies to Zinfandel; the adjacent café serves authentically French salade de chèvre chaud and poulet rôti.

Just steps away is **LITTLEJOHN'S CANDIES**, an old-fashioned candy shop where visitors can watch the confectioners make their justly famous English toffee. At the other end of the market is **MARCONDA'S MEATS**, a butcher shop that custom-cuts meats to the most demanding standards and offers its own meatloaf blend in ready-to-bake pans. If it's time for lunch, head to **LOTERÍA GRILL**, a Mexican counter spot that serves superb tacos (try the cochinita pibil, carne asada or a vegetarian option).

There are many other worthy options here, but with 3rd Street beckoning, head west to **AOC**, a wine bar and dinner-only restaurant owned by Suzanne Goin and Caroline Styne, where you can pair tastes from one of L.A.'s most interesting wine lists with delicious appetizers and roasted items from the wood-burning oven (reservations advised). Craving a burger? Drop into **BURGER KITCHEN**, an informal, family-owned joint offering a lengthy list of well-made burgers and plenty of inexpensive wines by the glass and craft beer on tap. A block west is **TASCA**, a very good wine bar (only open for dinner), specializing in Spanish and Italian-style tapas.

On the same side of the street is the ultra-charming, pricey, open-air restaurant **THE LITTLE DOOR**, but we prefer its companion café/market, **LITTLE NEXT DOOR,** a virtual replica of a Paris sidewalk café (including French-speaking customers) offering excellent pastries, a bistro menu and a wide selection of gourmet items, from house-made preserves to cheeses and charcuterie.

PLANCHA, A TACO JOINT, a new spot ably run by Poquito Mas veteran Pete White, is a beacon of good value and great flavor in the neighborhood (try the shrimp tacos or the $5 taco trio). You'll need more than a fiver, though, on the next block at **JOAN'S ON THIRD**, a café, bakery, gourmet-to-go and caterer that offers one of the city's best selections of epicurean items. And now that you're really hungry, grab a seat at the bar or at the communal table at **SON OF A GUN**, the new small-plates seafood restaurant from the owner/chefs of Animal. Temptations abound, but don't miss the lobster roll, a miniature (yet perfectly executed) version of the New England classic and certainly one of the tastiest treats on 3rd Street.

—Jean T. Barrett

IN THE FARMERS MARKET AT 3RD AND FAIRFAX:

Bob's Coffee & Doughnuts
323.933.8929

Huntington Meats
323.938.5383

Littlejohn's Candies
323.936.5379

Lotería Grill
323.930.2211

Marconda's Meats
323.938.5131

Monsieur Marcel Gourmet Market
323.939.7792

ALONG 3RD:

AOC
8022 W. 3rd St., 323.653.6359

Burger Kitchen
8048 W. 3rd St., 323.944.0503

Joan's on Third
8350 W. 3rd St., 323.655.2285

The Little Door
8134 W. 3rd St., 323.951.1210

Little Next Door
8142 W. 3rd St., 323.951.1010

Plancha, A Taco Joint
8250 W. 3rd St., 323.951.9911

Son of a Gun
8370 W. 3rd St., 323.782.9033

Tasca
8108 W. 3rd St., 323.951.9890

GOOD FOOD NEIGHBORHOOD
[Abbot Kinney, Venice]

JUST BLOCKS FROM THE OCEAN, the six-block strip of Abbot Kinney Boulevard epitomizes the sun-drenched, lazy-afternoon surfboard vibe of Venice Beach. Though parking can be tight, you can usually find a spot; if not, try the valet at Joe's. Either way, you won't need a car to explore the cafés, upscale restaurants and funky shops.

Start on the northwest end of Abbot Kinney near Westminster and enjoy a leisurely weekend patio brunch or lovely lunch at **JOE'S**, the neighborhood pioneer known for its stellar Cal-French food, reasonable prices and hospitable chef-owner Joe Miller. Next door at **PRIMITIVO WINE BISTRO**, fans of less formal dining can have a glass of Riesling and a petite salad for lunch, a glass of Bordeaux and steak frites for dinner or a glass of Vin Santo and the warm bread pudding with Calvados, caramel, and vanilla bean ice cream at any time. A few doors down at **LILLY'S FRENCH CAFÉ**, the ethereal île flottante (caramel-drizzled floating meringue islands atop crème anglaise) is reason enough to linger in the lush outdoor garden, but the reasonably priced croque monsieurs, heaping bowls of moules frites, and good-value happy hour don't hurt, either.

Those with heartier appetites can head across the street to **GLENCREST BAR-B-QUE**, where the smoky pork ribs are best taken to go for a picnic, unless you can nab one of the rickety stools. Don't bother with the sides; instead save room for dessert. **N'ICE CREAM** provides you with excellent gelati and sorbets, made fresh daily by a lovely Danish couple. Made with organic milk and fresh fruits, all the flavors are creative and delicious.

One block further on you'll find **HAL'S BAR AND GRILL**, an artists' hangout where the menu is packed with solid California salads, pastas and grilled meats. But it's the massive 40-foot bar that's the real draw. Order a round of cocktails made from freshly squeezed juices and a platter of fries to share, and take in the scene—on Sunday and Monday nights there's even live jazz.

If you're more in the mood for caffeine, cross the street again and head down one block to **ABBOT'S HABIT** for a strong cup of java (skip the food). Next door is **ABBOT'S PIZZA**, the beloved home of the self-named "bagel crust" pizza. New Yorkers, don't knock the California-inspired pizzas laden with such ingredients as spinach and sun-dried tomatoes. Toss back a slice at the tiny stand-up counter, or order a whole pie to go.

You might be needing a sugar pick-me-up by now, so try to score a table in the back walled patio at ultra-cool **GJELINA** and order the astonishing butterscotch pudding with sea-salt caramel. Come back another time for a relaxed lunch or romantic dinner.

If it's happy hour at **WABI-SABI**, where the sundown specials are too good to pass up, order some sake and a round of spicy tuna rolls. If you spend the evening doing some more serious drinking at **THE BRIG**, watch for the rotating roster of hipster food trucks that park out front—from Kogi to the Grilled Cheese Truck, they all stop here sooner or later.

But wait… on your way home, stop at **MARKET GOUR-MET**, which not only has its own parking but is a treasure trove of goodies to take home: cheeses, chocolates, sauces, grains and lots more, including a refrigerator case stocked with fresh pasta, pumpkin-seed pesto and puff pastry.

— *Jenn Garbee*

Abbot's Habit
1401 Abbot Kinney Blvd.,
310.399.1171

Abbot's Pizza
1407 Abbot Kinney Blvd.,
310.396.7334

The Brig
1515 Abbot Kinney Blvd.,
310.399.7537

Gjelina
1429 Abbot Kinney Blvd.,
310.450.1429

Glencrest Bar-B-Que
1146 Abbot Kinney Blvd.,
310.399.9641

Hal's Bar and Grill
1349 Abbot Kinney Blvd.,
310.396.3105

Joe's Restaurant
1023 Abbot Kinney Blvd.,
310.399.5811

Lilly's
1031 Abbot Kinney Blvd.,
310.314.0004

Market Gourmet
1800 Abbot Kinney Blvd.,
310.305.9800

N'Ice Cream
1410 Abbot Kinney Blvd.,
310.396.7161

Primitivo Wine Bistro
1025 Abbot Kinney Blvd.,
310.396.5353

Wabi-Sabi
1637 Abbot Kinney Blvd.,
310.314.2229

GOOD FOOD NEIGHBORHOOD
[Boyle Heights]

JUST OVER THE BRIDGE FROM DOWNTOWN L.A.,
Boyle Heights combines traditional Mexican flavors with East L.A.-style Chicano traditions. It's close enough for downtown workers to head over for lunch, but the bustling carnicerias and crowded tamale shops are a world away. This neighborhood, which now boasts light-rail service from Downtown and Pasadena via the Gold Line extension, is clearly L.A.'s next in line for gentrification. Though the area's a bit rough around the edges, it's perfectly safe for shoppers and diners, and the rewards are many.

Start on East Cesar Chavez Avenue by stopping for breakfast, lunch or dinner at **LA PARRILLA**, which specializes in parrillada grills with meats and seafood and guacamole prepared tableside.

A stop at longtime L.A. hangout **EL TEPEYAC** is a must, for gargantuan Hollenbeck or even more huge Manuel burritos. Also on Cesar Chavez is **GUISADOS**, a gourmet taco shop run by the owners of East L.A.'s delicious Cook's Tortas. Choose from complex and spicy tacos with beef, chicken or vegetable fillings stewed with a dizzying array of spice and chiles.

Where Cesar Chavez Avenue meets Indiana Street is called Five Points, or Cinco Puntos. At **LOS CINCO PUNTOS** meat market, all the makings for an authentic feast are ready to be assembled, starting with corn tortillas made while you watch, prepared carnitas and other meats, and cactus salad, guacamole and salsa in bulk.

Cross over to East 1st Street and head east to **TERESITA'S**, where home-style dishes like albondigas soup, *costillas* (ribs) and enchiladas are served with homemade tortillas. Heading back toward Downtown on 1st Street, stop in at **TAMALES LILIANA**. Take home a bag of freshly made tamales or try chilequiles or *huevos divorciados* (eggs "divorced" by a row of beans down the middle) for breakfast at this homey diner, which also makes menudo on weekends.

Just down the street is **EL MERCADO**, a marketplace that's similar to Downtown's Grand Central Market, but with the addition of mariachis and margaritas at the upstairs restaurants. Stalls sell everything from chiles and seafood to toys and cowboy hats. Further west on 1st Street, the large, colorful **EL RINCONCITO DEL MAR RESTAURANT** is the place for seafood cocktails of shrimp or octopus and hearty seafood stews called *caldos*.

Heading south toward Whittier Boulevard, pick up a snack at **LA MASCOTA**, one of L.A.'s best Mexican bakeries. Choose heavenly smelling bolillo rolls fresh from the oven, pan dulce pastries or tamales.

Finish your walk or drive at **MARIACHI PLAZA**, the closest thing to a Boyle Heights meeting point, on East 1st Street near Boyle Avenue. Mariachi musicians hoping to be hired for parties gather in the small park, which includes a charming old-world bandstand. Near the plaza is the area's most upscale restaurant, **LA SERENATA DE GARIBALDI**, where diners often spot the mayor and other politicos. The handsome place (which now has two westside offshoots) emphasizes creative preparations of Mexican seafood and offers valet parking. Finish off the evening at **EASTSIDE LUV**, a sure sign—along with the new Metrolink station right outside—that the neighborhood is on the rise. The wine bar/music venue is livening up the neighborhood with everything from burlesque shows to Chicano art exhibits.

— *Pat Saperstein*

Eastside Luv Wine Bar
1835 E. 1st St., 323.262.7442

**El Mercado
de Los Angeles**
3425 E. 1st St., 323.268.3451

**El Rinconcito
Del Mar Restaurant**
2908 E. 1st St., 323.269.8723

El Tepeyac Cafe
812 N. Evergreen Ave.,
323.267.8668

Guisados
2100 E. Cesar E. Chavez Ave.,
323.264.7201

La Mascota Bakery
2715 Whittier Blvd.,
323.263.5513

La Parrilla Restaurant
2126 E. Cesar E. Chavez Ave.,
323.262.3434

**La Serenata
De Garibaldi**
1842 E. 1st St., 323.265.2887

**Los Cinco Puntos
Mexican Foods**
3300 E. Cesar E. Chavez Ave.,
323.261.4084

Tamales Liliana
3448 E. 1st St., 323.780.0839

Teresita's Restaurant
3826 E. 1st St., 323.266.6045

GOOD FOOD NEIGHBORHOOD
[Culver City]

EVEN THOUGH THIS ENTERTAINMENT STUDIO HUB
turned foodie mecca is losing a bit of its star power thanks to the
ascendancy of Downtown L.A., it's as packed with good-food destina-
tions as ever, and now it's less crowded. It's divided into two areas,
with the hot restaurants on Culver Boulevard to the west, where Park
and Lock should be renamed Park and Nosh, and the Helms Bakery
home-furnishings complex to the east, where you can grab a hot
dog or toss back a pint while shopping for that perfect loveseat. Plan
ahead (translation: bring an ice-filled cooler) and you can cart home
everything from takeout fried chicken to roasted vegetables.

   Start off with a lunchtime quest for inner peace—or at least darn
good star anise–ginger short ribs with parsnip purée—at **AKASHA**,
part of the new wave of sustainable restaurant/bakery/bars. If after
achieving clarity you'd like to celebrate with a nice drink, stop into
BOTTLEROCK wine bar for a glass of your favorite grape and an order of bacon-wrapped dates. Grab a bottle to take home while you're
there, then head around the corner to **FRAICHE** for an herb-infused
homemade absinthe cocktail. Stay to enjoy the lamb *spezzatino*
(stew) with ricotta gnocchi, or, if you're vegetarian, head around the
corner to **TENDER GREENS**, a vegetable-lover's cafeteria with organic
fare galore, plus wine, beer and desserts. A few doors down you can
get your carnivore fix with the cured meat platters at **FORD'S FILLING
STATION**, where Harrison's son Ben turns out stellar appetizers and
flatbreads; the mains take second stage. Or revel in the charms of
a pitch-perfect French bistro at **LE SAINT AMOUR**, where the soup
is onion and the moules have frites. And consider the lively scene,
great bar and excellent, upscale pub grub at Chicago import **RUSH
STREET**. Before you leave Culver, consider stopping into **HONEY'S
KETTLE** to pick up some amazing fried chicken for later, and by all
means stop into the new **L'EPICERIE MARKET**, home to hard-to-find
French products (mustards, candies, cheeses) to take home, croissants to nibble on for breakfast, and a good tapas happy hour.

   Next, hop in the car and head down Washington to the Helms
complex—or walk to work up an appetite, because it's only three-
quarters of a mile. Alas, Beacon has closed, but there's still **LA
DIJONAISE**, where you can get a lovely, reasonably priced French-style
breakfast or café lunch. At **FATHER'S OFFICE**, you'll find the same

famous grilled onion–blue cheese bacon burger as at the Santa Monica original, with a bonus: This one has a larger menu and a heck of a lot more space, though that doesn't mean the line to nab a seat is any shorter. If you're lucky, the **LET'S BE FRANK** cart will be parked across the street, serving its grass-fed beef dogs with caramelized onions on freshly baked buns to tide you over. Or get a four-pack to take home for later.

Just a bit east of the Helms complex is a new spot, **SUB-LIME FOOD LOUNGE**, notable for an excellent happy hour featuring half-price flatbreads; we're partial to the one with burrata, cippolini onions and guanciale. If you haven't had your daily dose of carbs 'n' fat yet, try the macaroni and cheese—it's worth it.

Wrap up the gloriously gluttonous day with a shopping spree at **SURFAS** on the bustling corner of Washington and National. It's a cook's Disneyland, filled with hard-to-find kitchen items you didn't know you needed and ingredients you've only read about. Make sure to pick up some of the delicate little canelés from the café for tomorrow's breakfast.

— *Jenn Garbee*

Akasha
9543 Culver Blvd., 310.845.1700

BottleRock
3847 Main St., 310.836.9463

Father's Office
3229 Helms Ave., 310.736.2224

Ford's Filling Station
9531 Culver Blvd., 310.202.1470

Fraîche
9411 Culver Blvd., 310.839.6800

**Honey's Kettle
Fried Chicken**
9537 Culver Blvd., 310.202.5453

La Dijonaise
8703 W. Washington Blvd.,
310.287.2770

L'Epicerie
9900 Culver Blvd., 310.815.1600

Le Saint Amour
9725 Culver Blvd., 310.842.8155

Let's Be Frank Dogs
Helms Ave. parking lot
across from Father's Office,
415.515.8084

Rush Street
9546 W. Washington Blvd.,
310.837.9546

Sublime Food Lounge
8631 Washington Blvd.,
310.287.2093

Surfas
8777 W. Washington Blvd.,
310.559.4770

Tender Greens
9523 Culver Blvd., 310.842.8300

GOOD FOOD NEIGHBORHOOD
[Koreatown]

EVEN IN THE '70S, WHEN KOREAN BUSINESSES began
to put down roots near Vermont and Olympic, you could smell garlicky broiling meat wafting down the streets after dusk. Today the aroma is even more intense. About 700 restaurants and markets cluster
along Olympic, Wilshire, 8th and 6th from Crenshaw to Alvarado.
Every kind of Korean specialty is represented, from noodle shops to
octopus soup joints. The simplest way to get an overview of K-town's
riches is to hit the food courts at two malls, each anchored by a
supermarket. The eateries are family run, not corporate chains. Start
at the **KOREATOWN GALLERIA** at Olympic and Western. The **Food Gallery** on the top level offers city views and juicy handmade dumplings
or cold buckwheat noodles at **SEO KANG MYUN OAK** (323.373.1717).
There's no English menu; simply point at the pictures. Next door,
FOOD PICNIC DAY (323.735.7030) sells Korean-style bento boxes,
while **JIN SU SUNG CHAN** (323.766.9292) serves traditional stews
(seafood with black cod, hearty short-rib soup) and stone pots filled
with *bibim bap*, rice topped with matchstick-cut veggies and an
egg. Two blocks north on Western is **KOREATOWN PLAZA**, whose
dozen or so vendors include the traditional **PLAZA KOREA HOUSE**
(213.480.0203), known for its meal-in-a-bowl soups, especially spicy
yue kae jang beef. **TOWN NOODLE** (213.388.5280) serves noodles,
while **SOON TOFU HOUSE** (213.383.3781) makes fine fresh tofu in
spicy broth (choose your heat level) and **PAOJAO** (213.385.1881) is
known for dumplings and stuffed buns. Driving north on Western,
you come to **BCD TOFU HOUSE**, a branch of a popular soon-tofu
chain that's open very late. Continue west and you'll hit **FENG MAO
2**, whose signature cumin- and chile-laced grills and kebabs gained
fame at its more modest Olympic Blvd. restaurant. Next, head over
to Wilshire and Harvard, where you'll find **MYUNG DONG KYOJA**, a
stylish, spacious 24-hour *kal gooksu* (knife-cut noodles) specialist also
known for *bibim naeng myun*, cold, chewy northern-style noodles in
spicy sauce. On 8th at Harvard, you'll see **DONG IL JANG**, a classic
grill house known for quality meats and beautifully made, abundantly
served *panchan* (side dishes). Traveling east on 8th, you get to **HON-
EY PIG**, a pork-belly barbecue house that also serves about a dozen
more meats, including wild boar. You grill these on cast-iron domes
and eat bites wrapped in thin rice noodle sheets and lettuce. Farther

east on Vermont is **YOUNG SUSAN**, a rare northern restaurant where elegant prix fixe menus are served in private rooms. Also on Vermont is **HODORI**, a 24-hour Korean comfort-food diner that really gets jumping after 2 a.m., when the clubbing set comes in to refuel. Back to Olympic and you'll discover **WIEN KON-DITOREI UND CAFÉ**, a Euro-Korean patisserie/tea room behind bougainvillea-draped lattices. Order excellent coffee or tea and a French tart, Asian-style refined breads or croissant sandwich. Or head to Western for the best all-you-can-eat barbecue in town at **ROAD TO SEOUL**, where a meal of brisket, short ribs, pork belly and loads of carefully made panchan comes in at under $18. Back to Olympic again and, heading west, you'll notice what looks like a giant chia pet. It's actually the ivy-covered **CHOSUN GALBEE,** one of K-town's most popular traditional restaurants, with a bar, seductively tented patio and waitresses dressed in hamboks. Of course they serve grilled meats, but the menu also proffers classic stews, soups and a fine version of the cold buckwheat noodle dish, *naeng myun*.
— *Linda Burum*

Koreatown Galleria
3250 W. Olympic Blvd.,
323.733.6000

Koreatown Plaza
928 S. Western Ave.,
213.382.1234

***

BCD Tofu House
869 S. Western Ave., #2,
213.380.3807

Chosun Galbee
3330 W. Olympic Blvd.,
323.734.3330

Dong Il Jang
3455 W. 8th St.,
213.383.5757

Feng Mao 2
414 S. Western Ave.,
213.388.9299

Hodori
1001 S. Vermont Ave., #102,
213.383.3554

Honey Pig
3400 W. 8th St.,
213.380.0256

Myung Dong Kyoja
3630 Wilshire Blvd.,
213.385.7789

Road to Seoul
1230 S. Western Ave.,
323.731.9292

Wien Konditorei und Café
3035 W. Olympic Blvd.,
213.427.0404

Young Susan
950 S. Vermont Ave.,
213.388.3042

GOOD FOOD NEIGHBORHOOD
[Little India]

ALIVE WITH THE COLOR OF BRILLIANT SILK SARIS, the aroma of a hundred curries and the rhythms of Bhangra-inspired folk hits pouring out of music shops: This is Pioneer Boulevard, the heart of Little India. It sits in the middle of Artesia, a suburb north of Long Beach just off the 91 Freeway—which, conveniently for the widely dispersed Indian community (and the rest of us in L.A.), connects to the 405, 110, 710 and 605. Most restaurants serve regional specialties and street foods, and more than half are vegetarian, reflecting the way most Indians eat. A short stroll down this lively street brings total immersion into the varied cuisines of the Subcontinent.

Start at **WOODLANDS** on the northeast corner of Artesia Boulevard and Pioneer. The Karnataka-style southern vegetarian cuisine is so diverse and complex it renders meat irrelevant. From humble grains and legumes come crisp crepes, crunchy fritters, thick pancakes and breads, all eaten with dozens of curries and dipped into fresh coconut chutney. Across the street, the northern-style **AMBALA DHABA** gets it name from the funky roadside spots in the Punjab region. But this is a comfortable restaurant, offering beer and wine along with a lengthy menu of chicken, lamb, goat and vegetarian specialties. Still further south, **LITTLE INDIA GRILL**, an ultra-casual order-at-the-counter spot, turns out bargain northern-style combo meals and a wonderful array of breads, like keema naan stuffed with spiced, minced lamb.

Casual snack sellers known as *chat* shops are everywhere, and each has its own character and specialties. **PIONEER SWEETS & SNACKS** carries all the famous southern vegetarian items, such as dosas, parathas and a wide range of sweets. But its five different *thalis*—essentially combo meals—make ordering easy. A few shops further south, the separately owned **AMBALA SWEETS** sells an array of *namkeen*—crunchy, savory tidbits made from flours, lentils and nuts. You eat them plain or in salad-style dishes topped with tamarind and cilantro chutneys. Among the sweets here are *rasmalai* and *cham cham*, spongy milk-based balls in sweetened cream or syrup.

At the center of Little India, on 186th Street just east of Pioneer, is **SURATI FARSAN MART**, an elegant Gujarat-style snack shop. Worth a stop for the beautiful gift boxes alone, the café serves stellar chat and sweets. The *pani puri*, crunchy fried ping-pong ball–size orbs you fill with beans and minty water, are a must-try.

Close to 186th is **FARM FRESH**, where you can stock up on lentils, beans and spices, as well as masala dosa mix. Nearby is **SHAN**, serving the meat-intensive cuisine of Hyderabad. The central Indian city, long a crossroads, takes a smattering of flavors from many regions. There are 17 lamb curries in addition to five tandoor-cooked lamb items—yet the ruggedly spicy vegetable dishes are among the best on the street. A few steps south, the neat-as-a-pin **UDUPI PALACE,** named for the southern temple city in Karnataka state, makes dosas as long as baseball bats. Its *kadi* (little fritters) come submerged in sumptuous coconut curry.

You come to the end of Little India at the Little India Village mall. Upstairs sits the neo-moderne **TIRUPATHI BHIMAS**, serving the classic vegetarian fare of Andhra Pradesh state. The *thalis* and *tiffins*—multi-dish meals served on a tray—are the way to go. Follow these delights at **SAFFRON SPOT**, where Indian-style ice creams come in spectacular flavors, and the ice cream–topped rose or saffron milk drinks are studded with cooling basil seeds.

— *Linda Burum*

Ambala Dhaba
17631 Pioneer Blvd.,
562.402.7990

Ambala Sweets
18433 Pioneer Blvd.,
562.402.0006

Farm Fresh
18551 Pioneer Blvd.,
562.865.3191

Little India Grill
18383 Pioneer Blvd.,
562.924.7569

Pioneer Sweets & Snacks
18413 Pioneer Blvd.,
562.402.1155

Saffron Spot
18744 Pioneer Blvd.,
562.809.4554

Shan
18621 Pioneer Blvd.,
562.865.3838

Surati Farsan Mart
11814 E. 186th St.,
562.860.2310

Tirupathi Bhimas
18792 Pioneer Blvd., 2nd fl.,
562.809.3806

Udupi Palace
18635 Pioneer Blvd.,
562.860.1950

Woodlands
11833 Artesia Blvd.,
562.860.6500

GOOD FOOD NEIGHBORHOOD
[Little Tokyo]

LITTLE TOKYO STARTED OUT AS the hub of L.A.'s early-1900s Japanese immigrant community, complete with temples, movie theaters and traditional restaurants. Japanese-Americans have mostly spread across L.A. or moved to the Torrance area, but this neighborhood has retained its roots while adding energy from residents of new lofts. Although many Downtown streets are sparsely populated at night, Little Tokyo—also called J-Town by some Angelenos—is jumping, especially on weekends.

Starting at the Japanese American National Museum, walk west on 1st Street, the area's most historic block. The Chinatown-era neon Chop Suey Café sign is a landmark for generations who celebrated family occasions there. Have a drink at the adjacent **FAR BAR** lounge, but eat somewhere else. **SUEHIRO CAFÉ** serves Japanese diner food until 3 a.m. on weekends, including sturdy bowls of nabeyaki udon and bargain combination dinners. Nearby, **DAIKOKUYA** draws raves and crowds for deeply flavored pork-broth ramen.

Japanese Village Plaza is a short car-free block full of unique flavors. **MITSURU CAFE**'s well-worn imagawayaki molds have been turning out crispy, lightly sweetened red bean cakes for several generations. Also in the Plaza, **MIKAWAYA** invented the ice cream–filled mochi that are found all over now, but there are more flavors here. Try the red bean, coffee and peanut butter flavors, or the Italian gelato with a light Japanese touch. Next door, the compact **NIJIYA MARKET** is jam-packed with Japanese items and even a Hawaiian products department.

Near San Pedro and 1st Street, Weller Court is a modern office plaza full of restaurants. Spice lovers will appreciate **OROCHON RAMEN**, where steamy bowls of noodles come in seven levels of heat, with the bravest diners opting for the "hyper" and "extreme" levels. Around the corner, the Kyoto Grand Hotel is home to a lovely Zen garden and Little Tokyo's only tempura bar at the **THOUSAND CRANES** restaurant.

Japanese restaurants are usually categorized by their specialties, and 2nd Street is home to top-quality sushi, shabu-shabu and izakaya—small plates of cooked food that go well with beer. **HARU ULALA** is a fun izakaya where diners watch the chef grill fish and vegetables. Had enough sushi? **SPITZ** features Turkish doner kebabs and a carefully selected beer and wine list. And the ultra-hot **LAZY OX CANTEEN** mixes a pub vibe with seriously good modern American cooking. A bit farther east on 2nd Street, Honda Plaza is home to **SUSHI GEN**, one of the area's most beloved, and crowded, sushi bars. If you continue east on 2nd to Alameda, you'll find the Little Tokyo Shopping Center, housing the Korean-owned **LITTLE TOKYO GALLERIA** supermarket, which stocks a wide selection of Asian ingredients; the bento boxes make a quick and tasty lunch. Other worthy spots in the indoor mall include **SUSHI GO 55** and an outlet of the Beard Papa cream-puff empire.

Across Alameda Street on 3rd Street is **WURSTKÜCHE**, which is packed with young customers sampling Belgian brews in a dimly lit, high-style beer hall that serves a wacky array of sausages, including alligator and rattlesnake. To recover from your sausage and beer, you can caffeinate a couple of doors down at the **NOVEL CAFÉ**, the coffeehouse that's become the hub for this increasingly inhabited loft neighborhood.

— *Pat Saperstein*

Daikokuya
327 E. 1st St., 213.626.1680

Far Bar
347 E. 1st St., 213.617.9990

Haru Ulala
368 E. 2nd St., 213.620.0977

Lazy Ox Canteen
241 S. San Pedro St., 213.626.5299

Little Tokyo Galleria
333 S. Alameda St., 213.617.0030

Mikawaya
333 S. Alameda St., 213.613.0611

Mitsuru Café
117 Japanese Village Plaza, at 1st St. and Central Ave., 213.613.1028

Nijiya Market
124 Japanese Village Plaza, at 1st St. and Central Ave., 213.680.3280

Novel Café
811 E. Traction Ave., 213.621.2240

Orochon Ramen
123 S. Onizuka St., 213.617.1766

Spitz
371 E. 2nd St., 213.613.0101

Suehiro Café
337 E. 1st St., 213.626.9132

Sushi Gen
422 E. 2nd St., 213.617.0552

Sushi Go 55
333 S. Alameda St., 213.687.0777

Thousand Cranes
Kyoto Grand Hotel, 120 S. Los Angeles St., 213.253.9255

Wurstküche
800 E. 3rd St., 213.687.4444

GOOD FOOD NEIGHBORHOOD
[San Gabriel Valley]

DRIVE A FEW MILES EAST OF DOWNTOWN on the 10 Freeway and you'll hit the south San Gabriel Valley, which Taiwanese and Hong Kong venture capital has turned into the largest, splashiest suburban Chinatown in North America. Monterey Park was the first enclave, but as the Chinese population has escalated, this new-era Chinatown has spread like peanut butter into Alhambra, San Gabriel, Arcadia and Rowland Heights, bringing us the largest collection of regional Chinese restaurants outside the motherland.

How to find your way around? Simply imagine a grid. The two main drags run east and west, parallel to the 10 Freeway: Valley Boulevard on the north end and Garvey Avenue on the south. Several north-south commercial streets intersect: Atlantic Boulevard, Garfield Avenue, and San Gabriel and Rosemead boulevards.

The multi-level Focus Plaza at Valley and Del Mar in San Gabriel, nicknamed the Great Mall of China, is crammed with restaurants, noodle shops, boutiques and a huge 99 Ranch supermarket. **DONG TING SPRING**, a Hunanese spot, serves dishes incorporating grand quantities of chiles and funky condiments. Must haves: stir-fried smoked pig's ear and dried tofu steamed with fresh garlic tops. At the north end, **GOURMET VEGETARIAN** may have the most sophisticated food of all, with dishes like fried rice noodles tossed with shredded pumpkin, or Sichuan tofu, radish and egg pancake.

Further west on Valley Boulevard is **101 NOODLE EXPRESS**, home to the Shandong-style beef roll: miraculously spiced beef wrapped in lightly crisped Chinese pancakes that people drive across town to eat. Still further west, turn south on Atlantic Boulevard and you'll find a row of restaurant-laden malls. In the Mar Center is **OCEAN STAR**, one of the best traditional live seafood and dim sum halls. The cavernous room, with ladies steering burnished dumpling carts, is preferable after noon, when they roll out the more exotic items. Further south is **DUCK HOUSE**, home to the best Beijing duck in the valley. For fancier, more au courant dim sum ordered from a menu, nearby **ELITE RESTAURANT** will serve you Thai-style papaya salad garnished with goose tendons and luscious steamed live shrimp with their roe. Returning north to Atlantic and Garvey, you'll find the northern-style **LITTLE SHEEP**, which reveals just how diverse Chinese cuisine can be. Shabu shabu–style dining is taken to extraordinarily spicy heights, and lamb comes in dumplings, pancakes, meatballs and more.

Traveling east on Garvey you'll come to **SEAFOOD VILLAGE**, a Chiu Chow spot serving such ethereally flavored dishes as duck soup with pickled lemon. Meals can be made of the appetizers: crisp-fried shrimp balls, oyster omelet, whole cold crab. Keep heading east to **MAMA LU'S** dumpling house, where the *xiao long bao* (soup dumplings) and the won tons are as good as anything you'll find in Hong Kong. Still further east is the not-to-be-missed **CHINA ISLAMIC**, with its multi-layered sesame breads, spectacular lamb hot pots and hand-shaved noodle dishes. Continue east to San Gabriel Boulevard and go north to **CHUNG KING**, our favorite down-home Sichuan restaurant, famous for its dry-chile-covered diced chicken with peanuts. Finally, if you keep traveling north you'll get to Las Tunas, a once-sleepy street that's starting to rival Valley—don't miss the famous lobster palace **NEWPORT SEA-FOOD** and, after Las Tunas becomes Main, **KING HUA**, a new contender for best dim sum in the SG Valley.

—Linda Burum

101 Noodle Express
1408 E. Valley Blvd., Alhambra, 626.300.8654

China Islamic Restaurant
7727 E. Garvey Ave., Rosemead, 626.288.2426

Chung King
1000 S. San Gabriel Blvd., San Gabriel, 626.286.0298

Dong Ting Spring
Focus Plaza, 140 W. Valley Blvd., San Gabriel, 626.288.5918

Duck House
501 S. Atlantic Blvd. Monterey Park, 626.284.3227

Elite Restaurant
700 S. Atlantic Blvd., Monterey Park, 626.282.9998

Gourmet Vegetarian
Focus Plaza, 140 W. Valley Blvd., San Gabriel, 626.280.5998

King Hua
2000 W. Main St., Alhambra, 626.282.8833

Little Sheep
120 S. Atlantic Blvd., Monterey Park, 626.282.1089

Mama Lu's Dumpling House
153 E. Garvey Ave., Monterey Park, 626.307.5700

Newport Seafood
158 W. Las Tunas Dr., San Gabriel, 626.289.5998

Ocean Star
145 N. Atlantic Blvd., Monterey Park, 626.308.2128

Seafood Village
684 W. Garvey Ave., Monterey Park, 626.289.0088

GOOD FOOD NEIGHBORHOOD
[Sawtelle]

THE WESTSIDE'S "LITTLE OSAKA," along a three-block stretch of Sawtelle west of the 405, throbs with nightlife and the sort of restaurants you're likely to see in modern Tokyo. This enclave between Olympic and Santa Monica boulevards was once farmland for immigrants and later drew Japanese-Americans returning from internment camps. Today, apart from a few extant bonsai nurseries, Sawtelle is all about anime shops, izakaya and noodle bars.

At the southern end in the Olympic Collection complex sits ultra-casual **YAKITORI-YA**, serving nothing but skewered chicken parts grilled over imported hardwood charcoal. Its neighbor is **KIRIKO SUSHI**, where the house-smoked salmon salad with mango lures a devoted clientele, who also rave about the house-made ice creams.

Across the street, the Sawtelle Place Mall holds many delights. **NIJIYA**, a small supermarket, carries goods that seem plucked from the Tokyo suburbs: fresh cut sashimi, bento meals to go, Japanese cookware and Pocky sticks. A few doors down, two delightful bakeries are shoehorned into a single shop: international cream-puff chain **BEARD PAPA** and **MOUSSE FANTASY**, which turns out elegant cakes and light takes on French pastries. The Sawtelle Centre strip mall across the street holds **MANPUKU**, a *yakiniku* house (the Japanese version of a cook-at-your-table Korean barbecue). Walk north to **BLUE MARLIN**, where the walls shimmer with an underwater seascape and the menus offer *youshoku*, popular "foreign" dishes tailored to Japanese palates. The pastas are al dente, the chicken free-range and the curries sing with flavor. A few steps more get you to **2117 RESTAURANT** a small, pleasant space where Japan's love affair with French food is aptly demonstrated with light modern fare emphasizing organic ingredients: elegant pastas, duck confit and soft-shell crab—and a pretty good wine list, too.

Across the street is the casual izakaya **FURAIBO**, whose jocular style attracts young families and college kids for pub-style small dishes and tebasaki chicken fried to a crackling crispiness and washed down with shochu. Nearby is the venerable **HIDE SUSHI**, the bar that introduced many boomers to sushi; its bargain prices and pristinely fresh fish ensure a wait.

Further north, chef Hideo Yamashiro (of Shiro in South Pasadena) offers sophisticated renditions of izakaya at the sleekly minimalist

ORRIS, where you can order a platter of charcuterie along with tempura with house-made curry powder and choose from a beautifully edited wine selection. In the same complex, Mako Tanaka, former Chinois chef and proprietor of Mako in Beverly Hills, brings his modern take on Japan's traditional grill houses at **ROBATA YA**. The small, casual space emphasizes pristine ingredients; grilled skewers include several cuts of *wagyu* (Kobe-style) beef, along with hot and cold small plates. In the next space is **MIZU 212**, a modern shabu-shabu bar, where you poach your meal of thinly sliced beef, pork or chicken to dip in the kitchen's outstanding sauce of freshly ground sesame seeds.

Cross the street and walk toward Santa Monica Boulevard to find **BAR HAYAMA** in a converted cottage with a bamboo shaded patio, fire pit and two sake bars. Here graduates of the California Sushi Academy turn out lovely *kozara* (equivalent of tapas) that go beyond standard sushi and sashimi to the likes of beef tartare with quail egg and yellowtail sashimi with myoga.
— *Linda Burum*

2117 Restaurant
2117 Sawtelle Blvd., 310.477.1617

Bar Hayama
1803 Sawtelle Blvd., 310.235.2000

Beard Papa
2130 Sawtelle Blvd., 310.479.6665

Blue Marlin
2121 Sawtelle Blvd., 310.445.2522

Furaibo
2068 Sawtelle Blvd., 310.444.1432

Hide Sushi
2040 Sawtelle Blvd., 310.477.7242

Kiriko Sushi
11301 Olympic Blvd., 310.478.7769

Manpuku
2125 Sawtelle Blvd., 310.473.0580

Mizu 212
2000 Sawtelle Blvd., 310.478.8979

Mousse Fantasy
2130 Sawtelle Blvd., 310.479.6665

Nijiya Market
2130 Sawtelle Blvd., 310.575.3300

Orris
2006 Sawtelle Blvd., 310.268.2212

Robata Ya
2004 Sawtelle Blvd., 310.481.1418

Yakitori-Ya
11301 Olympic Blvd., 310.479.5400

GOOD FOOD NEIGHBORHOOD
[Silver Lake]

ONE OF L.A.'S MOST QUICKLY changing neighborhoods, Silver Lake is a mix of young musicians, writers and creative types, film-business workers, and professionals who enjoy the hilly streets lined with architecturally significant homes and the proximity to Downtown L.A. In the past few years, the neighborhood has gained still more gourmet food shops, under-the-radar restaurants and funky boutiques.

Start a walking tour of Silver Lake at Sunset Junction, the area starting around Sunset Boulevard and Sanborn Avenue, where several tasty shops are close together. **INTELLIGENTSIA COFFEE & TEA**, which originated in Chicago, kicked up the local coffee competition by several notches; its shady terrace is a great place for lingering over carefully drawn lattes. After fueling up on coffee, stop by the **CHEESE STORE OF SILVERLAKE**, one of the city's top cheesemongers, and stock up on cheeses, condiments, charcuterie, olives and wine for your pantry.

For a leisurely dinner, dine next door to the Cheese Shop at **CAFÉ STELLA** for pricey French bistro food in a bohemian sidewalk-café atmosphere, or go across the street to Silver Lake's order-at-the-counter eatery of the moment, **FORAGE LA**, where the chicken is Jidori, the produce is from local backyard farmers, and the baked goods are incredible. If ice cream is more your dessert style, walk next door to **PAZZO GELATO**, which carries unusual flavors of hand-crafted gelati. And the block has more! **BERLIN CURRYWURST** has brought a taste of Germany's favorite street food to the area, and **SPICE STATION** is a destination for serious cooks, its walls lined with hard-to-find herbs and seasonings. Or head east on Sunset to pick up some salted caramels or red velvet cupcakes at the dainty **LARK CAKE SHOP**.

While the area is more ethnically diverse than it once was, it's still rich in Latino culture and food, and you'll see lots of Mexican restaurants. Try the fish tacos at the popular **EL SIETE MARES** taco stand; for lighter, updated Mexican dishes, a tasty mole and good vegetarian choices, head to **ALEGRIA ON SUNSET**. And if it's a drink you're after, you'll find margaritas and a killer tequila selection at **MALO**, a hip hangout whose drinks are better than its food.

Breakfast is the favorite meal for a certain sort of Silver Lake resident. Late sleepers favor grungy old-school diner **MILLIE'S**, while

Francophiles order omelets or quiches at a sidewalk table at **MADAME MATISSE**. People who want room to spread out in a booth with the newspaper settle in at **DUSTY'S BISTRO**, which has a full bar and French-Canadian specialties. If Dusty's is packed, try the new **FOOD + LAB**, where the food has a Viennese slant.

Vestiges of the area's scruffier past can be found at **CAFÉ TROPICAL**, a Cuban café serving up café con leche, fresh-squeezed juices and baked goods, like the iconic guava cheese pastry. Or dig into a bowl of steaming pho noodle soup into the wee hours at **PHO CAFÉ**, a Vietnamese mini-mall spot with a modern décor but no sign out front.

As you leave the area, head north onto Silver Lake Boulevard to check out **LA MILL**, a high-style coffee emporium with baroque brewing methods and top-notch food conceived by Michael Cimarusti, chef of Providence. Continue along the Silver Lake reservoir to Glendale Boulevard to find **SILVERLAKE WINE**, where regular tastings (as well as the every-Thursday appearance of the Let's Be Frank truck) draw enthusiastic crowds of oenophiles.

— *Pat Saperstein*

Alegria on Sunset
3510 W. Sunset Blvd., 323.913.1422

Berlin Currywurst
3827 W. Sunset Blvd., 323.663.1989

Café Stella
3932 W. Sunset Blvd., 323.666.0265

Café Tropical
2900 W. Sunset Blvd., 323.661.8391

Cheese Store of Silverlake
3926 W. Sunset Blvd., 323.644.7511

Dusty's Bistro
3200 W. Sunset Blvd., 323.906.1018

El Siete Mares
3131 W. Sunset Blvd., 323.665.0865

Food + Lab
3206 W. Sunset Blvd., 323.661.2666

Forage LA
3823 W. Sunset Blvd., 323.663.6885

Intelligentsia
3922 W. Sunset Blvd., 323.663.6173

LA Mill
1636 Silver Lake Blvd., 323.663.4441

Lark Cake Shop
3337 W. Sunset Blvd., 323.667.2968

Malo
4326 W. Sunset Blvd., 323.664.1011

Millie's
3524 W. Sunset Blvd., 323.664.0404

Pazzo Gelato
3827 W. Sunset Blvd., 323.662.1410

Pho Café
2841 W. Sunset Blvd., 213.413.0888

Silverlake Wine
2395 Glendale Blvd., 323.662.9024

[South Pasadena]

QUAINT SOUTH PASADENA HAS DONE ITS UTMOST
to preserve its leafy, small-town flavor, and the arrival of the Metro
Gold Line cemented its pedestrian-friendly status. Just a few blocks
long, the charming Mission Street area is rich with food-centric
places, as well as boutiques and antiques shops; shady El Centro
Street, one block south, is also part of this district.

Starting at the Gold Line's Mission station, walk north across Mission to find **HEIRLOOM BAKERY**, the neighborhood's best breakfast
place, with sturdy coffee, homey baked goods, generous egg dishes
and a large patio. If you just want coffee, stop at quirky **BUSTER'S**,
which also has Fosselman's ice cream.

At the corner of Mission and Meridian you'll spot **RADHIKA**, an
Indian restaurant with lightened-up dishes as well as beer and wine.
A few doors down, **MY SWEET CUPCAKE** has won cupcake competi-
tions with flavors like key lime and peanut butter. Across Mission,
MIX N' MUNCH draws tots to college students with build-your-own
cereal bowls and a dozen kinds of grilled cheese sandwiches. Cyclists
and schmoozers hang out at **GREAT HARVEST BREAD CO.**, with Peet's
coffee and pastries and bread made with whole-grain flour milled on
the premises.

Next, walk south a block to El Centro, a pretty little street that
parallels Mission. It's even more French here—the first place you'll
see, right next to the tracks, is **NICOLE'S GOURMET FOODS**, run by
the *charmant* Nicole Grandjean. A wholesaler of French cheeses and
goodies, she also has a retail store and café complete with a flower-
lined patio. The store opens early for *cafés et croissants* and makes
lunchtime sandwiches (try the prosciutto, pecorino and arugula).
Nicole's also stocks hard-to-find baking items, kitchenware and frozen croissant dough and tarte shells. **BISTRO DE LA GARE** completes
the block's French theme, with indoor and outdoor dining on such
traditional French fare as steak frites, onion soup and roast chicken.

A few steps east on El Centro is **KALDI**, the antithesis of chain
coffeehouses, with funky couches and chairs, free WiFi and good
cappuccino. Also on El Centro is **FIREFLY BISTRO**, a quintessentially
Californian spot whose dining "room" is a tented, twinkle-lit patio. The
eclectic menu draws from the South (shrimp and grits), the Mediterranean (grilled calamari with olives, pine nuts and arugula) and the

modern American playbook (a great BLT for lunch, crab hash for brunch). Note that if you plan your visit for a Thursday afternoon, you'll find El Centro taken over by the small but very good weekly **FARMERS' MARKET**, a fine fate for a food lover!

Head north a block back to Mission and stop in at friendly **MISSION WINE**, which pours tasting flights every day and also has beer on tap. Its selection of small-production wines includes some good values. If it's time for dinner, choose from **MIKE & ANNE'S**, which has a lively bar, delicious upscale comfort food (get the sweet potato fries) and yet another lovely patio, or **BRIGANTI**, a convivial Tuscan trattoria with an excellent burrata caprese salad and grilled fresh fish. The old-timer of the neighborhood is **SHIRO**, a modern space with imaginative French-Japanese cooking; its sizzling whole catfish with ponzu is legendary.

Just make sure to fit in an old-fashioned sundae or milkshake at the historic corner **FAIR OAKS PHARMACY**, complete with an antique soda fountain and counter.

— *Pat Saperstein*

Bistro de la Gare
921 Meridian Ave., 626.799.8828

Briganti
1423 Mission St., 626.441.4663

Buster's Ice Cream & Coffee Shop
1006 Mission St., 626.441.0744

Fair Oaks Pharmacy
1526 Mission St., 626.799.1414

Firefly Bistro
1009 El Centro St., 626.441.2443

Great Harvest Bread Co.
1019 Mission St., 626.441.4786

Heirloom Bakery & Café
807 Meridian Ave., 626.441.0042

Kaldi
1019 El Centro St., 626.403.5951

Mike & Anne's
1040 Mission St., 626.799.7199

Mission Wine
1114 Mission St., 626.403.9463

Mix n' Munch
1005 Mission St., 626.441.8808

My Sweet Cupcake
954 Mission St., 626.441.4010

Nicole's Gourmet Foods
921 Meridian Ave., 626.403.5751

Nicole's Maison et Objet
950 Mission St., 626.403.0601

Radhika
966 Mission St., 626.744.0994

Shiro
1505 Mission St., 626.799.4774

South Pas Farmers' Market
El Centro St. & Diamond Ave., Thurs. 4-8 p.m.

GOOD FOOD NEIGHBORHOOD
[Ventura Boulevard, Studio City]

WE'LL ADMIT IT: VENTURA BOULEVARD lacks the cachet of such other important streets "over the hill" as Wilshire and Sunset. The main surface artery through the San Fernando Valley has long, utterly forgettable stretches lined with strip malls, auto dealerships and low-end motels. However, as Ventura heads into Studio City, it's studded with some of the Valley's best food finds—ones that are even worth a drive over the hill. Start around the corner from Universal City at **MANTEE**, a small Lebanese place serving an extensive Middle Eastern menu filled with unusual specialties, notably *mantee*, a casserole of succulent toasted ravioli in a creamy, garlicky yogurt sauce.

Just up the boulevard in a dark corner of a Marshall's strip mall is newcomer **RAMEN JINYA**, a great pit stop on a chilly L.A. day (pork belly fanciers, go for the tonkotsu ramen). Across the street is the celebrated **SUSHI NOZAWA**, which anchors the eastern end of Sushi Row, the section of Ventura named for its sushi restaurants. Chef Kazunori Nozawa, aka the Sushi Nazi, offers a distinctive style of chef's-choice omakase ("trust me" is his motto) to cowed but doting customers (he also operates Sugarfish in Brentwood and Marina del Rey). In the same strip mall is the humbler but more hospitable **DA-ICHAN**, a hole-in-the-wall that serves excellent homestyle Japanese dishes, such as udon noodles, poki bowls, curries and tempuras.

A few blocks west on Ventura is **RAPHAEL**, an upscale spot that expanded last year, got a full liquor license and welcomed chef Adam Horton, formerly of Saddle Peak Lodge. Steak tartare and pan-roasted Scottish salmon are top picks, and we love that they offer more than 50 wines by the glass. Close by is chef Katsuya Uechi's original **SUSHI KATSU-YA**, the beachhead of what is now a sushi empire. It specializes in elaborate cut rolls and intricate presentations, and if you can swing a reservation it's a fun evening for a small group. Not far away you'll find Uechi's **KIWAMI**, an elegant, contemporary spot for sushi connoisseurs to savor omakase or nosh less formally on soba noodles, tempura and miso-marinated black cod. If you're on an expense account, head across the boulevard to **ASANEBO**, known for superb sashimi and a range of imaginative cooked dishes; omakase starts at $75 per person and ascends from there.

Since man does not live by yellowtail alone, climb to the second floor of the mall at Ventura and Laurel Canyon to sample terrific tacos and Mexico City specialties at chef Jimmy Shaw's **LOTERÍA GRILL**, a branch of the well-known Farmers Market stand and its Hollywood Boulevard spinoff. The **ARTISAN CHEESE GALLERY**, located across Ventura, purveys handmade cheeses from all over the world, as well as Fra' Mani salumi and superb sandwiches (try the duck confit with fig jam and Le Marechal cheese). On Sundays, Ventura Place behind the Cheese Gallery is home to the **STUDIO CITY FARMERS' MARKET**, a small, high-quality market that is hugely popular with the locals (parking can be a challenge). A block west of Laurel Canyon you'll find a chic little bakery called **BIG SUGAR BAKESHOP.** Every day the bakers create a different lineup of temptations, from red velvet cake and tender scones to some of the best lemon bars we've tasted (check the website, bigsugarbakeshop.com, to see what's just come out of the oven). Last, for a relaxing capper to this culinary crawl, stop in at **FLASK FINE WINES**, which has been satisfying local needs for premium bottlings for more than four decades. After all, pounding the pavement in search of good eats is thirsty work.

—Jean T. Barrett

Artisan Cheese Gallery
12023 Ventura Blvd., 818.505.0207

Asanebo
11941 Ventura Blvd., 818.760.3348

Big Sugar Bakeshop
12182 Ventura Blvd., 818.508.5855

Daichan
11288 Ventura Blvd., 818.980.8450

Flask Fine Wines
12194 Ventura Blvd., 818.761.5373

Kiwami
11920 Ventura Blvd., 818.763.3910

Lotería Grill Studio City
12050 Ventura Blvd., 818.508.5300

Mantee
10962 Ventura Blvd., 818.761.6565

Ramen Jinya
11239 Ventura Blvd., 818.980.3977

Raphael
11616 Ventura Blvd., 818.505.3337

**Studio City
Farmers' Market**
Ventura Place at Ventura Blvd.,
Sunday 8 a.m.-1 p.m.

Sushi Nozawa
11288 Ventura Blvd., Ste. C,
818.508.7017

Sushi Katsu-Ya
11680 Ventura Blvd.,
818.985.6976

Restaurants

In these pages you'll find nearly 500 of L.A.'s most interesting restaurants, from the humblest to the *haute*-est. Look for more good eating in Food That's Fast, Breakfast + Lunch, Drink + Eat, Gourmet-to-Go and Bakeries + Sweets.

[ESSENTIALLY L.A.]

CENTRAL CITY

Angeli Caffé, Melrose (PAGE 51)
Animal, Fairfax District (PAGE 52)
AOC, Beverly/Third (PAGE 52)
Campanile, Miracle Mile (PAGE 54)
Canter's Deli, Beverly/Third (PAGE 55)
Chosun Galbee, Koreatown (PAGE 56)
Harold & Belle's, Mid-City (PAGE 60)
Hatfield's, Melrose (PAGE 60)
Hungry Cat, Hollywood (PAGE 61)
Jar, Melrose (PAGE 61)
Jaragua, East Hollywood (PAGE 62)
Jitlada, Hollywood (PAGE 62)
Lotería Grill, Hollywood (PAGE 64)
Lucques, Melrose (PAGE 64)
Osteria Mozza & Pizzeria Mozza, Beverly/Third (PAGES 67 & 69)
Providence, Melrose (PAGE 69)
Soot Bull Jeep, Koreatown (PAGE 73)
Street, Melrose (PAGE 73)
Taylor's Steakhouse, Koreatown (PAGE 74)
Umami Burger, Miracle Mile (PAGE 75)

🏛 ESSENTIALLY L.A. ☺LATE ♥ROMANTIC 🍽 VALUE 🔈QUIET ♻ SUSTAINABLE

[ESSENTIALLY L.A.]

EASTSIDE

SAN GABRIEL VALLEY

VEGETARIAN KID FRIENDLY PATIO DINING DELIVERY PRIVATE PARTY

[ESSENTIALLY L.A.]

EAST VALLEY

WEST VALLEY

WESTSIDE: CENTRAL

CITYWIDE

🏛 ESSENTIALLY L.A. ☺ LATE ♥ ROMANTIC 🍽 VALUE 🔊 QUIET ♻ SUSTAINABLE

[ESSENTIALLY L.A.]

WEST OF THE 405

SOUTH BAY TO SOUTH L.A.

VEGETARIAN ☺ KID FRIENDLY ☼ PATIO DINING 🚗 DELIVERY 🏛 PRIVATE PARTY

CITYWIDE

[LudoBites] 🔒 ludolefebvre.com. $$$ - $$$$ **WHY** You never know where it'll pop up or what's on the menu, and that's the fun of it. **WHAT** Good luck getting a reservation at L.A.'s (and now the nation's) premiere pop-up restaurant. (So many people want in, the online reservation system usually crashes soon after it opens.) Ludovic Lefebvre is a classically trained French chef, but he doesn't let that hinder him. Cornichon velouté, Thai choucroute, foie gras doughnuts as big as Humvees—anything and everything is in play. The food is wildly inventive, which is why fans flock to LudoBites wherever it pops up next. **WHO** Culinary thrill seekers, *Top Chef Masters* fans, chef groupies, food bloggers and restaurant critics who have traveled all the way across the country for this one meal.

CENTRAL CITY

[8 oz. Burger Bar] 7661 Melrose Ave., Melrose, 323.852.0008, 8ozburgerbar.com. L & D daily. American. Full bar. AE, MC, V. $$ **WHY** The short-rib griiled cheese, which is every bit as heavenly as it sounds; the high-quality build-your-own burgers, made with grass-fed beef or a blend of Angus steak, tri-tip, chuck and short rib; and the light, wonderful onion rings. **WHAT** This upscale burger bar occupies the former Table 8 space and shares the same owners. The feel is more casual than when it was Table 8, but it's still chic, with wainscoting and a handsome bar. The surprise is why it's not more crowded, given the surprisingly moderate prices and very good burgers. 🖼 🍴

[Ackee Bamboo] 4305 Degnan Blvd., Leimert Park, 323.295.7275, ackeebamboojacuisine.com. B, L & D daily. Jamaican. BYOB. MC, V. $ **WHY** Zingy Jamaican food in a casually hip Leimert Park café. The daily specials are a mere $6.95. **WHAT** Close your eyes and the sea of L.A. concrete outside might just morph into the blue Caribbean, thanks to the vividly flavorful, bargain-priced Jamaican cooking at this friendly neighborhood spot. If you like spicy, have the classic jerk chicken; if you like it mellower, try the beef stew, meat patties, barbecued ribs or the namesake ackee (the meat of a Jamaican flower) with salt cod, the traditional Jamaican breakfast dish. 🖼 ☼

[Ago] 8478 Melrose Ave., Melrose, 323.655.6333, agorestaurant.com. L Mon.-Fri., D nightly. Italian. Full bar. AE, MC, V. $$$ - $$$$$ **WHY** For celebrity cachet and hearty, South Beach–friendly Tuscan meals of salads followed by delicious bistecca fiorentina, flattened chicken or veal chops with rustic beans. **WHAT** The star power burns bright at this manly (and pricey) Tuscan trattoria, where the ingredients are good and the plastic surgery is better. **WHO** With co-owners like Robert De Niro and the Weinstein brothers, it's no surprise that the place is packed with famous faces and wannabes day and night.

🔒 ESSENTIALLY L.A. ☽ LATE ♥ ROMANTIC 🖼 VALUE 🍴 QUIET ☼ SUSTAINABLE

[Amalia's Guatemalan] **751 N. Virgil Ave., East Hollywood, 323.644.1515. B, L & D daily. Guatemalan. No booze. MC, V. $**
WHY For an unexpected taste of Latin America. **WHAT** A graceful dining room inside an old bungalow serves Guatemala's national turkey dish, *kakik de pavo*, a mole-like thick soup, and pollo en crema, rich and sharp with the tang of buttery cultured cream. Enchiladas topped with a tower of shredded beef, beet salad, and aged white cheese bring salty, sweet, crunchy and meaty sensations into mind-bending harmony. Breakfast offers plates with meats, eggs, beans, plantains and cream, or *sopa de huevo*, two eggs poached in an herbal broth.
WHO Discriminating Guatemalans and well-traveled foodies.

[Amarone Kitchen & Wine] **8868 W. Sunset Blvd., West Hollywood, 310.652.2233, amarone-la.com. D Mon.-Sat. Italian. Beer & wine. AE, MC, V. $$$ - $$$$ WHY** It's like escaping to Florence right there on Sunset Boulevard. **WHAT** While the rest of the Sunset Strip screams for attention, this doll house of a ristorante is happy to be invisible — its clientele cares more about food, service and charm than being noticed. Couples and friends reminisce about their last trip to Italy while the young Bolognese chef sends out grilled octopus with white beans, squid-ink spaghetti with seafood, risotto with porcini and parmigiano and flawlessly cooked *spigola* (a sea bass cousin of branzino).
WHO Handsome people old enough to be the parents (grandparents?) of the crowd in front of the Viper Room down the block. ♥ 🌱

[Ammo] 🔖 **1155 N. Highland Ave., Hollywood, 323.871.2666, ammocafe.com. L Mon.-Fri., D Mon.-Sun., brunch Sun. American/Mediterranean. Full bar. AE, MC, V. $$ - $$$$ WHY** Some of the most boldly flavorful modern American cooking in town, plus a decent chance that you'll see a famous face or two, although you'd never be so gauche as to act like you cared. **WHAT** This former takeout café reinvented itself so profoundly that it's now one of L.A.'s best restaurants. Stylish and modern without being trendy and noisy, it's home to the Italian- and Moroccan-tinged modern American cooking of chef Daniel Mattern: meticulously constructed salads, hand-cut pastas with heavenly and hearty ragus, simple but sublime roasted fish dishes, and homey desserts. Try the Sunday family-style feast if you can. **WHO** Music-industry folks, screenwriters, actors and other moneyed creative types. ✿

[Angeli Caffé] 🔖 **7274 Melrose Ave., Melrose, 323.936.9086, angelicaffe.com. L Tues.-Fri., D Tues.-Sun. Italian. Beer & wine. AE, MC, V. $ - $$$ WHY** Wonderful pizzas, panzanella, perfectly dressed salads and toothsome pasta dishes. Delivery, too! **WHAT** Back in the early days of Melrose, Evan Kleiman set the L.A. standard for casual, affordable *trattorie* serving robust and delicious food. Today Angeli continues to be a standard-bearer. An L.A. treasure, and a great place to have a private party. **WHO** Old-time Melrosers sporting L.A. Eyeworks glasses and only the subtlest of tattoos. 📷🍃☼🚚🏛

🍃 VEGETARIAN ⊙ KID FRIENDLY ☼ PATIO DINING 🚚 DELIVERY 🏛 PRIVATE PARTY

[Angelini Osteria] **7313 Beverly Blvd., Beverly/Third, 323.297.0070, angeliniosteria.com. L Tues.-Fri., D Tues.-Sun. Italian. Beer & wine. AE, MC, V. $$$ - $$$$ WHY** Rich oxtails, braised artichokes, green lasagne and other delicious pastas, and wonderful branzino. **WHAT** There are fancier Italian restaurants in town, but few with better food than this one (and chef Gino Angelini's other restaurant, La Minestraio). The minimalist storefront is packed a little too tightly, and the room's a little too loud, but that only seems to make the food taste better. If only it wasn't so expensive, we'd eat this Italian soul food every week. **WHO** A sophisticated crowd that cares more about the cooking than the scene, although there is a bit of a scene anyway.

[Animal] 🗎 **435 N. Fairfax Ave., Fairfax District, 323.782.9225, animalrestaurant.com. D nightly. Modern American. Beer & wine. AE, MC, V. $$$ - $$$$ WHY** Bacon in your salad, bacon for your main course, bacon in your dessert. **WHAT** This foodie sensation is a bare-bones room crammed with people who aren't even mad that they had to wait 45 minutes... with a reservation. It helps that the staff is remarkably kind, but really it's because who can stay mad when the food is so damn good? The smart way to go is to share plates, so you don't OD on the rich squares of pork belly with kim chee. Owner/chefs Jon Shook and Vinny Dotolo, the "2 Dudes" of brief TV fame, are indeed dudes, but they are not slackers—they work hard to make sure you will be happy with your kale salad with pecorino, polenta with slow-cooked bolognese, crisp-tender pork ribs with a balsamic glaze, and bacon-chocolate crunch bar. If you're a pescatarian, check out their new Son of a Gun. If you're a vegetarian—well, sorry, they can't help you. **WHO** A thundering herd of handsomely tousled carnivores. ☺

[AOC] 🗎 **8022 W. 3rd St., Beverly/Third, 323.653.6359, aocwinebar.com. Brunch Sat.-Sun., D nightly. Mediterranean/wine bar. Full bar. AE, MC, V. $$ - $$$ WHY** AOC has an NYC bistro feel with excellent wines by the glass and perfectly ripe cheeses—and staff members who know more than just their name. The Cal-Mediterranean food is always reliable, if a smidge less so than at sister restaurant Lucques. **WHAT** Anything vegetable (or animal, for that matter) is coddled by the cooks at this oh-so-hot wine bar and small-plates restaurant—even cod haters will be converted by the fritters with citrus salad and aioli. Don't skip dessert—all the better to linger with a glass of Muscat and take in the nuevo-bistro feel, complete with the requisite high-decibel chatter. **WHO** D girls, agents and food-and-wine lovers traveling from the Palisades and Pasadena. 🍸

[Atlacatl] **301 N. Berendo St., East Hollywood, 323.663.1404. L & D daily. Salvadoran. Beer & wine. Cash only. $ WHY** Wonderful and wonderfully inexpensive Salvadoran home cooking: pupusas, empanadas with cream, *sopa de res* (a stew-like beef soup) and thick Salvadoran-style horchata. **WHAT** In a faded cottage on a worn stretch of Beverly lies a wonderful Salvadoran café, staffed with incredibly nice women who deliver hefty pupusas filled with cheese and *loroco* (flower buds reminiscent of asparagus) or beans, cheese and *chicharroón* (pork); tender-crisp-sweet fried plantains; and complimentary sides of *curtido*, the tangy Salvadoran cole slaw. **WHO** Neighborhood families, including many Salvadorans, who don't mind waiting 20 minutes for a table, and who keep an eye on soccer on the TV while they wait.

[The Bazaar at SLS Hotel] **465 S. La Cienega Blvd., West Hollywood, 310.246.5555, thebazaar.com. Tea & D daily, brunch Sun. Spanish/ modern American. Full bar. AE, MC, V. $$$$ - $$$$$ WHY** For a Vegas-style experience, complete with over-the-top food by celebrity chef José Andrés and a jaw-dropping décor by Philippe Starck. **WHAT** In two adjoining über-chic tapas bars, famed Spanish chef Andrés serves small dishes unlike anyone else's: cotton candy foie gras lollipops (amazing, trust us), Philly cheese steaks with "air bread" (really mini bread-like shells toped with Kobe beef that pops open to reveal melted cheese) and an ever-changing menu of don't-try-this-at-home creations. Brunch, afternoon tea or nibbling at the separate (and fantastic) patisserie are good lower-priced options if you haven't hit the jackpot. The sexy Bar Centro makes cocktails that may be expensive but are wildly creative yet balanced (think a Manhattan with a "liquid" cherry that explodes in your mouth) and so big they count as two. This is no place for the scene-averse, and service can be dreadful, but if you can live with that, you'll have quite an adventure. **WHO** A fascinating mix of the young and the mature (though no less primped)—think the *The Hills* meets *Real Housewives*. They don't skip dessert, particularly Andrés's magical flan with cloud-like vanilla cream.

[Beverly Soon Tofu House] **2717 W. Olympic Blvd., Koreatown, 213.380.1113. L & D daily. Korean. Beer & wine. AE, MC, V. $ WHY** For the *soon dubu jjigae*, a spicy, garlicky stew of fresh tofu that bubbles like volcanic lava in its individual iron pot. The superheated dish cooks a raw egg that the server cracks in at your table. Seafood or bits of meat add extra flavor to the extravaganza. **WHAT** Rivals of this 25-year old café—including a well-known chain—may seek to encroach on its long-held supremacy, but we're drawn back for the cloud-like texture of its tofu, the spot-on balance of its broth and the charming rusticity, with tables fashioned from sliced trees.

[BLT Steak] **8720 Sunset Blvd., West Hollywood, 310.360.1950, bltsteak.com. D nightly. American/steakhouse. Full bar. AE, MC, V. $$$$$ WHY** NYC chef Laurent Tourondel understands the true meaning of the Holy Trinity: meat, potatoes and pastry. **WHAT** There are a lot of things to like about BLT: sauces that are actually worthy of the top-quality steaks (three-mustard, chimichurri); non-beef mains that are often even better than the excellent steaks; potatoes nine ways (the gratin is so worth the calories); the huge popovers; and too many tempting caramelized/souffléd/creamed desserts to choose from. Save big bucks (you are *not* going to skip dessert here) with the daily blackboard menu, a $60 prix-fixe three-course dinner. **WHO** At these prices, and with the Sunset Boulevard location, a celebrity or two is inevitable, and Bentleys are parked three deep at the valet stand. 🏛

[Buddha's Belly] 7475 Beverly Blvd., Beverly/Third, 323.931.8588, bbfood.com. L Mon.-Sat., D nightly. Asian/Californian. Beer & wine. AE, MC, V. **$$ WHY** The perfect middle-of-L.A. spot to meet friends from across town for lunch, with a menu that has something for everyone. **WHAT** The quintessential L.A. café, Buddha's Belly has a bright, bamboo-lined indoor-outdoor space, an appealing and affordable pan-Asian menu and good service, and we find it handy when needing a central spot to meet people. Good salads, edamame, pad thai, bento boxes and other modern L.A. standards. A loyal friend. **WHO** Casual business lunchers and lithe yoga moms and their families. 🌀🗝☺☼

[Bulan Thai Vegetarian Kitchen] 7168 Melrose Ave., Melrose, 323.857.1882, bulanthai.com. L & D daily. Thai/vegan. No booze. MC, V. **$ WHY** Truly delicious vegan Thai cooking, served by nice people in a homey setting—and free delivery, too! **WHAT** Bulan serves good Thai food first—the vegan part seems almost secondary. Faux chicken and shrimp dishes are specialties; try the satay, the green curry and the pad kee mao noodles. **WHO** Vegans bringing their carnivorous mates, who always leave happy. 🗺🌀🗝🚐

[Burger Kitchen] 8043 W. 3rd St., West Hollywood, 323.944.0503, burgerkitchenla.com. L & D daily. American. Beer & wine. AE, MC, V. **$ - $$ WHY** Sometimes you just want a burger. **WHAT** This family-owned spot serves burgers made from Harvey Guss's Wagyu beef, as well as such alternatives as lamb or turkey burgers, vegetarian (chickpea, portobello mushroom) burgers and seafood patties. Burgers are mostly in the $10 to $12 range and fries are extra, but the sweet potato fries with aioli are worth the additional $3.50. There's also a nice selection of craft beers and relatively inexpensive wines by the glass. **WHO** An eclectic, mostly younger crowd. 🗝

[Campanile] 🏛 624 S. La Brea Ave., Miracle Mile, 323.938.1447, campanilerestaurant.com. L Mon.-Fri., D nightly, brunch Sat.-Sun. Californian/Mediterranean. Full bar. AE, MC, V. **$$$ - $$$$$ WHY** For Mark Peel's mastery of simple grilled meats, for the desserts, for Thursday grilled cheese night and for the handsome, old-L.A. setting that makes everyone happy. **WHAT** Lucques may be the Campanile of the new millennium, but that doesn't mean Campanile peaked in the '90s. It remains the perfect L.A. restaurant, the sort of place that doesn't make us want to up and move to San Francisco or Portland, like so many of our scene restaurants do. Owner/chef Mark Peel loves bold, rustic flavors that are carefully built but not complicated—a California-

Mediterranean cuisine that focuses on exceptional ingredients. If you haven't been here in ages, come back—you won't be sorry. **WHO** Business folks at lunch, stylish families on Thursdays for grilled cheese night and, for dinner, longtime regulars. ♥☺☜☼

[Canter's Deli] 🏠 419 N. Fairfax Ave., Beverly/Third, 323.651.2030, cantersdeli.com. B, L & D 24 hours. American/deli. Full bar. AE, MC, V. **\$\$ WHY** No-nonsense deli sandwiches stacked high—don't be afraid to get your hands messy. **WHAT** This L.A. landmark has been around since 1931 and is open 24 hours. The endless menu boasts breakfast food, soups and salads, but it's the sandwiches you want, even if they are pricey. It's not quite Langer's, but Canter's serves one of the better pastrami sandwiches in town, though classics like tuna melts, roasted turkey and brisket are also good. Sides like fresh pickles, potato salad and cole slaw bring back memories of what mom used to make. **WHO** Longtime regulars, yuppies seeking a midnight snack and the occasional celebrity walking in from nearby CBS studios. ☺ ☺

[Carlitos Gardel] 7963 Melrose Ave., Melrose, 323.655.0891, carlitosgardel.com. L Mon.-Fri., D nightly. Argentinean. Beer & wine. AE, MC, V. **\$\$\$ - \$\$\$\$ WHY** First-rate Argentinean wine and food: beef empanadas, matambre, sausages, remarkable french fries and, of course, the baked garlic to squish over your bread. **WHAT** Less showy than the Brazilian churrascarias that are currently the rage but every bit as devoted to delicious grilled meat, Gardel's has been L.A.'s go-to Argentinean restaurant for years. Good service, a reasonably priced wine list, a romantic setting and, in case your loved one is a vegetarian, tasty meat-free pastas. **WHO** Carnivores. ♥

[Chameau Delibar] 339 N. Fairfax Ave., Fairfax District, 323.951.0039, chameaurestaurant.com. L & D daily. Moroccan. Beer & wine. AE, MC, V. **\$ - \$\$ WHY** A handy place for a quick bite with a dash of modern Moroccan style. **WHAT** Chameau has been transformed into Chameau Delibar, and though some are mourning the flaky duck b'stilla, Delibar has its own appeal. Gourmet sandwiches and salads bear a hint of the restaurant's Moroccan past, such as the zingy eggplant purée, a traditional Moroccan carrot salad and spicy harissa sauce on the sandwiches. Merguez sausage with tapenade on a baguette is a taste of the Mediterranean, and even tuna salad on a pretzel bun packs plenty of flavor. Cheese and charcuterie plates and beer and wine make Delibar a good spot for an informal supper, or pick up a roast chicken and some salads to take home.

[Chaya Brasserie] 8741 Alden Dr., West Hollywood, 310.859.8833, thechaya.com. L Mon.-Fri., D nightly. Asian/French. Full bar. AE, MC, V. **\$\$\$ - \$\$\$\$ WHY** It's an L.A. pioneer that set the standard for French-Japanese-American cooking that's inventive but not silly. And it has a great and affordable bar menu. **WHAT** It's too easy to forget about this chic bistro near Cedars-Sinai, and indeed we did forget it in our last edition. But we were sorry: It's a quintessential L.A. restaurnt with consisnetly good food and a cool vibe. Excellent lunchtime salads and dinnertime burgers and miso-marinated sea bass. **WHO** Agents, writers and such stars as Zac Efron and David Byrne. 🏚

[Cheebo] **7533 W. Sunset Blvd., Hollywood, 323.850.7070, cheebo.com. B, L & D daily. Italian/Californian. Beer & wine. MC, V. $$ - $$$ WHY** For a robustly flavorful, modestly priced salad-and-pizza meal after an ArcLight movie. And they deliver! **WHAT** This noisy, cheerful café has something for everyone—breakfast burritos, panini, chopped salads, vegan lentil soup, a kids' menu—but we're most partial to the rectangular pizzas. **WHO** A boisterous crew of young folks. 📋💧🗑🕐🚗

[Chosun Galbee] 🏚 **3330 W. Olympic Blvd., Koreatown, 323.734.3330, chosungalbee.com. L & D daily. Korean. Full bar. AE, MC, V. $$$ - $$$$ WHY** Groups can mix orders of short ribs, sliced beef, chicken, shrimp and pork and then help servers tend to the meats on the grill in the center of the table, creating a fun and interactive meal. **WHAT** This stylish, modern setting is more upscale than the typical Korean barbecue restaurant, with a sleek, chic décor, a lovely outdoor patio and private rooms that are often packed with business groups or parties. A Koreatown must. **WHO** Upscale Korean couples on dates, large celebratory groups. 🗑⚙🏚

[Cobras & Matadors] **7615 Beverly Blvd., Beverly/Third, 323.932.6178. D nightly. Spanish. Beer & wine from the neighboring shop. AE, MC, V. $$ - $$$ WHY** One of the best sangrias in town, and some tasty (if inconsistently prepared) little dishes to have with it, including the addictive socca cakes with a cilantro dipping sauce. Save room for the churros with chocolate sauce. **WHAT** One of the first ventures by restaurateur Steven Arroyo, this original Cobras & Matadors (the East Hollywood one is now a Umami Burger) is as cramped as ever, but at least now it takes reservations. Pick up a bottle of wine from Arroyo's shop next door and dabble in the mostly good small-plate dishes: grilled octopus, grilled prawns with garlic, asparagus with Manchego cheese, and *pa amb tomàquet*, tomato-rubbed toast with jamón serrano. **WHO** Locals who seem to come here weekly.

[Comme Ça] **8479 Melrose Ave., West Hollywood, 323.782.1104, commecarestaurant.com. L & D daily, brunch Sat.-Sun. French. Full bar. AE, MC, V. $$$ - $$$$ WHY** Good classic French bistro fare: bouillabaisse, steak frites (great), sole meunière. The cheese bar is a dairy addict's heaven. **WHAT** Dubbed a slice of Paris in L.A., David Myer's place is really a Paris brasserie gone Hollywood, with slick Marilyn Monroe–white booths and old-school bartenders making excellent drinks. Some regulars come just for the duck confit; others come for the gorgeous cheese counter, the charcuterie plate or the desserts, although we've

🏚 ESSENTIALLY L.A. 🕐 LATE 💜 ROMANTIC 📋 VALUE 🔇 QUIET ♻ SUSTAINABLE had some dessert disappointments. And some service issues, too. Nonetheless, this is a fun place with generally terrific food and lots of atmosphere. **WHO** David Myers fans who miss Sona. ♥

[Cube Café] **615 N. La Brea Ave., Melrose, 323.939.1148, cubemarketplace.com. L & D Tues.-Sat. Italian/modern American. Beer & wine. AE, MC, V. $$ - $$$ WHY** For the complimentary Prosecco and cheese to "toast" your arrival, as well as the In-the-know staff, eager to pair the perfect Barbera with your tagliatelle with Fatted Calf sausage ragú. Oh, and for the spiffy upscale market. **WHAT** This intimate neighborhood café, cheese bar and marketplace serves a pricey Italian-driven menu rich with farmers' market produce, house-made pastas, an evolving selection of more than 85 varieties of cheese, and salumi from Salumi Salame, the Fatted Calf and Pio Tosini, to name a few. **WHO** Attractive, youthful Hollywood people, including a pop starlet or two. Don't be afraid to sit at the bar and mingle with the knowledgeable bartender and cheese guru. 🍸

[Delphine] **W Hotel, 6250 Hollywood Blvd., Hollywood, 323.798.1355, restaurantdelphine.com. B, L & D daily, brunch Sat.-Sun. French. Full bar. AE, MC, V. $$$ - $$$$ WHY** South of France–inspired dining morning, noon or night in a pretty Côte d'Azur setting. **WHAT** Hollywood's glitzy W Hotel may seem an improbable place to find a bright brasserie seemingly transplanted from Cannes, but this bustling, white-tiled, marble-floored spot is good for business meetings, visitors touring Hollywood and post-clubbing late meals. The menu is seafood-intensive, with towers of oysters and crab claws, but you can also get such bistro classics as croque monsieurs and roast chicken. Breakfast starts early—and with a full bar, why not add a mimosa? **WHO** Business travelers, Hollywood dealmakers and their high-heeled hotties, girls'-night-out gaggles. 🍸

[Dominick's] **8715 Beverly Blvd., West Hollywood, 310.652.2335, dominicksrestaurant.com. D nightly, brunch Sat.-Sun. Italian. Full bar. AE, MC, V. $$ - $$$ WHY** The steal is the $15 three-course Sunday supper with $12 bottles (yes, whole bottles) of house wine. Brilliant? No. Fun and economical? You bet. Dominick's is a great place to take out-of-towners. **WHAT** An old-school Rat Pack hangout restored to its original red-sauce Italian splendor with black and white photos lining the walls and plenty of filling Italian dishes to share. Ask for a seat on the back patio near the fireplace and cozy up with some meatballs. 🍽

[Don Dae Gam] **1145 S. Western Ave., Koreatown, 323.373.0700. L & D daily. Korean. Beer & wine. MC, V. $$ WHY** Modern Korean barbecue with an emphasis on all things porcine. **WHAT** Owned by the same folks as the beloved Park's, Don Dae Gam boasts a modern feel and high-quality meats. Though beef is available, this place is really for pork lovers, with choices like pork belly, pork neck, short ribs and

---

🌿 **VEGETARIAN** ☉ **KID FRIENDLY** ✿ **PATIO DINING** � **DELIVERY** 🍸 **PRIVATE PARTY**

pork diaphragm. The meats sizzle over charcoal grills, but with a powerful ventilation system, it's not as smoky as at other Korean spots. Design a combination meal with such appetizers as crispy, rich kim chee pancake or spicy pork and baby squid stew. Got little ones? There's a play area with cartoons and toys. **WHO** Korean families and students, adventurous pork lovers. ☺

[El Cholo] **1121 S. Western Ave., Mid-City, 323.734.2773, elcholo.com. L & D daily, brunch Sun. Mexican. Full bar. AE, MC, V. $$ WHY** To experience an L.A. landmark, drink a large, sweet margarita and, in season, have green corn tamales. **WHAT** If you're a native Angeleno, you've been to El Cholo at least once. It's a formula but a fun one: Waitresses in hokey Mexican get-ups swoop through the many stuccoed, frescoed, Mexican-kitsch rooms taking orders for margaritas, substantial plates of enchiladas ("Careful! The plate is hot!"), smoke-spewing fajitas and the famed sweet green-corn tamales. It's not the best Mexican food you'll ever have, but it's an essential L.A. Cal-Mex experience. **WHO** Big groups of friends celebrating birthdays, tourists, families that have been coming here for generations. 📷☺🛏

[Eva] **7458 Beverly Blvd., Beverly/Third, 323.634.0700, evarestaurantla. com. L Fri., D Tues.-Sat. Modern American. Full bar. AE, MC, V. $$ - $$$ WHY** For talented, gregarious chef Mark Gold, and for the Sunday brunch and dinner. **WHAT** Cozy, minimalist Eva has two faces: the more restrained cuisine, such as udon noodles with clams and scallops served at lunch and dinner most days, and the heartier Sunday dinners. The Sunday four-course prix-fixe meals are a great value, with free-flowing wine and haute-meets-homey dishes like wonderful fried chicken, meatloaf, short ribs and apple pie. Gold makes an enthusiastic host, though some of his dishes, like the popular burrata ravioli, are almost too delicate to be satisfying.

[Fat Fish] **3300 W. 6th St., Koreatown, 213.384.1304. L Mon.-Sat., D nightly. Japanese/sushi. BYOB. MC, V. $$ WHY** For surprisingly good *kaiten* (conveyor-belt) sushi at exceptionally low prices, and a fun, Jetsons-in-2012 setting. **WHAT** Sleek, chic and more modern than an *Austin Powers* movie set, Fat Fish is a Koreatown hot spot even though it lacks that critical liquor license. Sushi floats past you on a conveyor belt, a gimmick to be sure, but with prices so low (lunch is a total bargain) and the sushi so good, who cares? **WHO** Young folks stuffing themselves on the bargain rolls and sashimi. 📷

[Feng Mao] **3901 W. Olympic Blvd., Koreatown, 323.935.1099. L & D daily. Korean/Chinese. Beer & wine. MC, V. $ - $$ WHY** Addictive tabletop-grilled skewers that blur the boundary between Korean and Chinese cooking. **WHAT** Feng Mao is a hybrid, its kitchen preparing the Korean-Chinese cuisine of China's Jilin province. Accordingly, you're as likely to spot platters of the Korean blood sausage *soondae* here as you are bowls of mapo tofu. But the fusion is at its best with its signature mutton kebabs: Lean cubes of meat and strategic strips of fat are threaded onto skewers and charred at tabletop grills, blackened first on a lower rung then moved above the fire to soak up some smoke. The mutton is dusted with the mix of ground cumin, sesame seeds and chile powder that flavors all of the kebab menu, from simple chicken wings to all kinds of offal. **WHO** Koreatown locals congregating for family dinners and Hite-fueled benders. ☺

[Figaro] 1802 N. Vermont Ave., Los Feliz, 323.662.1587, figarobistrot. com. B, L & D daily. French. Beer & wine. AE, MC, V. $$ - $$$ **WHY** Honest French-bistro charm, a civilized breakfast, a dreamy chocolate soufflé and a good happy hour, with $5 Kirs and wine and tasty small plates. **WHAT** The service is often problematic, the kitchen can be slow, and the prices could be lower. But we still love Figaro, which bursts with Parisian charm, from the sidewalk tables to the zinc bar to the terribly romantic chandelier room. The excellent onion soup and a glass of Côtes du Rhône make for a perfect supper. ☺ ♥ ☼

[The Foundry] 7465 Melrose Ave., Melrose, 323.651.0915, thefoundryonmelrose.com. D nightly. Modern American. Full bar. AE, MC, V. $$$$ **WHY** Because the food is much better than at most Hollywood scene restaurants. Extras are the good bar menu (tater tot fondue!) and the live jazz. **WHAT** Owner/chef Eric Greenspan may be rumpled, exuberant and sometimes annoyingly loud, but his cooking is elegant. He set out to create a destination restaurant that combines serious food and professional service with an informal conviviality and good jazz. And he has succeeded. The details snap: a terrific, fairly priced wine list, one of the best cheese plates in town, and smart service. **WHO** A remarkably normal crowd — sure, they're attractive, but they're all ages and don't look overly Botoxed and lip-plumped. ☼

[Fred 62] 1850 N. Vermont Ave., Los Feliz, 323.667.0062, fred62.com. B, L & D 24 hours daily. Californian. Beer & wine. AE, MC, V. $ - $$ **WHY** Postmodern diner food (White-Trash Tuna Sandwich), served 24 hours a day in comfy booths at modest prices. **WHAT** Not only is Fred's one of the few 24-hour eateries in L.A., but it also achieves that rare state of being all things to all people. High school kids looking to share after-school chili-cheese fries? Check. Eddie Bauer–clad boomers looking for a movie-night Chardonnay 'n BLT? Check. Pierced-tongued twentysomethings looking for an after-midnight hangout to slurp udon noodles? Check. Hip grandmas taking the grandkids out for Sunday-morning waffles? Check. The prices are low, and the setting is bright and retro-diner, with booths, counter stools and a too-cool-for-you staff. **WHO** Everyone who's anyone in Los Feliz. ☺ 🖼🥢☺ ☼

[Girasole] 225 1/2 N. Larchmont Blvd., Hancock Park, 323.464.6978, girasolecucina.com. L Tues.-Fri., D. Tues.-Sun. Italian. BYOB (no corkage).

🍃 VEGETARIAN ☺ KID FRIENDLY ☼ PATIO DINING 🚐 DELIVERY 🏛 PRIVATE PARTY

AE, MC, V. $$ WHY Pillowy spinach or pumpkin gnocchi, various pastas with a rich homemade ragú, and a sublime linguine with shrimp, tomato and olive oil. **WHAT** This tiny, family-run storefront trattoria is one of the best-kept secrets on Larchmont. Sweet people, low prices and delicate yet flavorful pastas. Our only regret is the limited hours. **WHO** Hancock Park couples who like the modestly romantic vibe and the fact that they can bring their own wine. ♥ 🗺 🔖

[Go Burger] **6290 Sunset Blvd., Hollywood, 323.327.9355, goburger. com. L & D daily (to 12:30 a.m. Fri.-Sat.). American. Full bar. AE, MC, V. $ - $$ WHY** Quality burgers and good drinks, right next door to the ArcLight. **WHAT** This isn't the cheapest burger in town, but as long as you avoid the prime steakhouse burger, it's a good deal for this happening neighborhood. The meat is a mix of sirloin, short rib, chuck and brisket, and it's properly cooked and dressed, packed in a glossy brioche bun. Respectable turkey and veggie versions and, for those trying to bulk up for football season, alcohol-infused milkshakes and the Ultimelt, a burger whose "bun" is actually two grilled-cheese sandwiches. **WHO** Moviegoers and tourists. ☉ 🔖 ☺

[Guelaguetza] **3014 W. Olympic Blvd., Koreatown, 213.427.0608, guelaguetzarestaurante.com. B, L & D daily. Mexican/Oaxacan. Full bar. AE, MC, V. $$ WHY** Intensely flavorful, stick-to-your-ribs Oaxacan food served in a sunny yellow room by nice people. Live marimba music most nights. **WHAT** Only loosely affiliated with the better Guelaguetza in Palms (they're owned by siblings, but the restaurants themselves aren't related), this one is still a good and authentic Oaxacan place serving moles of every color, enchiladas, camarones and other tasty things, all in hefty portions. 🗺 ☺

[Harold & Belle's] 🏛 **2920 W. Jefferson Blvd., Mid-City, 323.735.9023, haroldandbellesrestaurant.com. L & D daily. Soul food/ Creole. Full bar. AE, MC, V. $$ - $$$$ WHY** New Orleans heaven: gumbo, jambalaya, soft-shell crab, crawfish etouffée and, most of all, the fried chicken. **WHAT** A landmark on a battered stretch of Jefferson, Harold & Belle's is home to L.A.'s best Cajun and Creole cooking. This is not the funky dive some people expect given the neighborhood—it's a nice restaurant with a full bar, valet parking, an expensive menu and sometimes-slow service—but hey, you don't want to rush over this rich food anyway. Relax, have a drink, take your time over your etouffée and fried chicken, and if you hope to have room for the famed bread pudding, don't clear your plate (portions are huge). **WHO** Dressed-up folks out for a splurge.

[Hatfield's] 🏛 **6703 Melrose Ave., Melrose, 323.935.2977, hatfieldsrestaurant.com. D nightly. Modern American/Californian. Full bar. AE, MC, V. $$$$ - $$$$$ WHY** For the innovative $59 four-course tasting menu ($49 for vegetarians) matched with stellar sommelier Peter

🏛 ESSENTIALLY L.A. ☉ LATE ♥ ROMANTIC 🗺 VALUE 🔖 QUIET ☺ SUSTAINABLE

Birmingham's wine pairings. **WHAT** After stints in San Francisco and at a smaller home in L.A., chefs Quinn and Karen Hatfield have settled beautifully into the dramatic dining room and sexy bar that once housed Citrus. The food is plenty entertaining—creative yet dodging the follies of the molecular gastronomy fad and borrowing from Moroccan, Greek and Spanish kitchens. Their now-famous croque madame of yellowtail-filled brioche is still a favorite, but there's also horseradish-dusted beef ribs paired with juicy hangar steak; grilled prawns over a creamy risotto spiked with preserved lemon; and Karen's ever-imaginative desserts and pastries. **WHO** Those who appreciate Hatfield's attention to flavor over novelty. ♥

[Hodori] **1001 S. Vermont Ave., Koreatown, 213.383.3554. Daily 24 hours. Korean. No booze. MC, V. $ WHY** Decent and cheap Korean standards served 24/7. **WHAT** The short list of L.A. restaurants open 24 hours a day includes this Koreatown diner, and you could do far worse at 3 a.m. than Hodori's bibim bap or bulgogi. Parking's a pain, and the service and setting are basic, but the hours and price are right. ☺ 🍴

[Hungry Cat] 🔷 **1535 N. Vine St., Hollywood, 323.462.2155, thehungrycat.com. L & D daily. Seafood/modern American. Full bar. AE, MC, V. $$$ - $$$$ WHY** A pristine raw bar, impeccable New England seafood dishes and a smart wine list—and it's all served until midnight, with the raw bar open until 1 a.m. **WHAT** Always full of hungry hep cats sharing oversize seafood platters, this glass-and-metal bistro may not be L.A.'s most elegant seafood restaurant, but it might be its most accomplished. It keeps the formula simple: You come here for New England-style seafood (or one of the best burgers in town), a good glass of wine and one killer dessert, the chocolate bread pudding. **WHO** Post-ArcLight filmgoers. ☺ ✿

[Itacho] **7311 Beverly Blvd., Beverly/Third, 323.938.9009, itachorestaurant.com. L Mon.-Fri., D Mon.-Sat. Japanese. Beer & wine. AE, MC, V. $$$ WHY** Lovely small dishes—Japanese fried chicken, crab claws with cucumber, black cod with miso, braised eggplant—at reasonable prices given the quality. **WHAT** Years ago, in its original low-rent Hollywood location, this restaurant introduced *izakaya* (small plates) to Angelenos, who followed the place when it moved to this more stylish industrial space on Beverly. What's on the menu? Classical Japanese preparations of whatever the chefs decide is right for the moment—along with some very good sushi, too. **WHO** Japanese and non-Japanese business people and date-nighters. 🍴 ✿

[Jar] 🔷 **8225 Beverly Blvd., Beverly/Third, 323.655.6566, thejar.com. D nightly, brunch Sun. Modern American/steakhouse. Full bar. AE, MC, V. $$$ - $$$$$ WHY** Superb steaks and chops, succulent side dishes (duck fried rice, Japanese purple yams with crème fraîche) and comfort foods (pot roast, coq au vin). Oh, and a Sunday brunch that *Los*

🌿 VEGETARIAN ☺ KID FRIENDLY ✿ PATIO DINING 🚗 DELIVERY 🎁 PRIVATE PARTY

Angeles Magazine has twice declared the city's best. **WHAT** This retro-contemporary (think *Mad Men*) chophouse run by star chef Suzanne Tracht delivers a superior dining experience in a civilized yet comfortable setting. Entrées can be pricey, but the meltingly tender coq au vin and the chopped sirloin burger with a fried egg and green peppercorn sauce are both bargains at $21, and you can sample small dishes at the bar for less. Side dishes are exceptionally good. **WHO** Well-dressed residents of the nearby hills, who consider Jar their country club, along with younger hipsters who like the cocktails and the cool vibe.

[Jaragua] 4493 Beverly Blvd., East Hollywood, 323.661.1985. L & D daily. Salvadoran. Beer & wine. MC, V. $ **WHY** Perhaps the most beautifully executed Salvadoran food in the city. **WHAT** The rich golden paint on this corner restaurant on a shabby stretch of Beverly lets you know that the place has ambitions, and boy, does it achieve its ambitions. Inside the even-more-colorful dining room, happy regulars attack plates of expertly made pupusas (try the rice-flour one with squash and cheese, or the *chicharron* (pork with a corn crust); gorgeous shrimp cocktails; medium-rare grilled rib-eye; plantains every which way; and a massive sandwich made of fresh-roasted turkey rubbed with herbs and spices. **WHO** East Hollywood immigrants and adventurous eaters from Hancock Park and Los Feliz.

[Jitlada] 5233 1/2 Sunset Blvd., East Hollywood, 323.663.3104, jitladala.com. L Tues.-Sun., D nightly. Thai. Beer & wine. AE, MC, V. $$ **WHY** Such amazing specialties as the *yam priaw dawng* (pickled crab salad), soft-shell crab curry and crispy morning glory stems with shrimp and fried shallot slices. **WHAT** Over the last few years Jazz Singsanong and her chef brother, Suthipom, have turned one of Thai Town's better restaurants into a destination dining spot, thanks to her devotion to making her customers happy, and his devotion to the dishes of Pak Panang, their home region in southern Thailand. The menu is huge, so ask for Jazz's advice—or know that you won't be sorry with the mango salad with fresh coconut, shrimp, nuts and chile, the jungle curry, the whole fried sea bass and the famous rice salad (*khao yam*). Warm service and a nicer dining room than the Thai Town norm. **WHO** Chefs and food lovers from across the country.

[Katana] 8439 W. Sunset Blvd., West Hollywood, 323.650.8585, katanarobata.com. D nightly. Japanese/sushi. Full bar. AE, MC, V. $$ - $$$ **WHY** The Sushi Roku of robata, this place serves reasonably authentic skewers of tasty meats and veggies at prices that reflect the neighborhood and the scene. **WHAT** "Our food comes from three kitchens," the waiter will explain to first-timers dining at this trendsetting West Hollywood spot ensconced in a stunning 1920s-era Mediterranean structure. Nibble on grilled robata foods speared on slender skewers, long-simmered homestyle dishes in miniature, or sushi—or a little of each. **WHO** Little-black-dress women and the men who chase them.

ESSENTIALLY L.A. LATE ROMANTIC VALUE QUIET SUSTAINABLE

[Kobawoo House] **698 S. Vermont Ave., Ste. 109, Koreatown, 213.389.7300. L & D daily. Korean. Full bar. MC, V. $ - $$ WHY** Because there's more to Korean food than barbecue. **WHAT** Mimicking a Korean tavern with its charming faux country-style décor, Kobawoo serves dishes that best accompany frosty beers or soju. Its tremendous lineup of savory pancakes includes a pizza-size, seafood-stuffed one called *haemul pajun*. A color-drenched salad of clear acorn noodles, *jangban gooksoo*, comes tossed with masses of leafy herbs, julienned veggies and a spicy-sweet dressing. *Bosam*—pork belly with spicy condiments to wrap burrito-style in paper-thin white radish slices or napa cabbage—is fun to construct at the table. **WHO** Nostalgic Koreans who know they can count on a well-cooked taste of home.

[KyoChon Chicken] **3833 W. 6th St., Koreatown, 213.739.9292, kyochon.com. L & D daily. Korean. No booze. MC, V. $$ WHY** They really mean it when they say "super-spicy" fried chicken. Or take a safer route and order the soy-marinated crispy chicken. **WHAT** It's fried chicken, but it's not fast. In fact, they don't start cooking it at this stylish Korean café until you order it, which can mean a wait of 25 minutes or so. But the payoff is a deeply flavorful bird accompanied by a refreshing side dish of pickled white radishes.

[La Morenita Oaxaqueña] **3550 W. 3rd St. , Koreatown, 213.365.9201. L & D daily. Oaxacan/Mexican. No booze. MC, V. $ - $$ WHY** For the enormous, flopppy-crusted *tlayuda con todo*, Oaxaca's answer to pizza, the red mole, and the delicate, delicious Oaxacan-style empanadas filled with things like *huitlacoche* (a mushroom-like fungus) or *flor de calabaza* (zucchini flower)—or even *chapulines* (grasshoppers). **WHAT** The vibrant colors inside this strip-mall café hold the promise of equally vibrant cooking, and La Morenita delivers on that promise. A few dishes disappoint, notably the expensive mixed grill and the bland mole amarillo, but most everything else here is richly redolent with the spices and sophistication of good Oaxacan cooking. Don't miss the *coloradito*, a red mole that shines with the open-faced enchiladas al gusto. **WHO** Mexican-American families and young singles from the neighborhood. 🗓️☺️

[La Paella] **476 S. San Vicente Blvd., West Hollywood, 323.951.0745, usalapaella.com. L Mon.-Fri., D Mon.-Sat. Spanish. Beer & wine. AE, MC, V. $$$ WHY** Catalan warmth and hospitality and outstanding paellas. Try the squid-ink one or the paella marinara, with saffron and seafood. *Los Angeles* magazine proclaims this the best flan in town. **WHAT** An intimate (read: make reservations) and fetching cottage with a devout following for its delicious paellas. The tapas aren't anything to shout about, but the paellas—and the romantic charm of the place—are worth a trip. **WHO** Spaniards, Argentineans and couples reliving that trip to Spain they took two years ago. ♥ 🍸

🌿 **VEGETARIAN** ☺ **KID FRIENDLY** ☼ **PATIO DINING** 🚚 **DELIVERY** 🏛 **PRIVATE PARTY**

[Little Dom's] 2128 Hillhurst Ave., Los Feliz, 323.661.0055, littledoms.com. B, L & D daily. Italian. Beer & wine. AE, MC, V. $$ - $$$ **WHY** Red-sauce Italian, served with modern flair and a wink of the eye. The three-course Monday Night Supper is a steal at $15, with house wine for just $12 a bottle. **WHAT** A lot of people consider this handsome, booth-lined trattoria to be a bargain, which we don't quite get—starters are $10 to $15, a burger's $15, and sides are $8, which ain't cheap in our book. On the other hand, the food shares well, so a group can have a tasty and affordable meal if they order carefully, particularly if they add one of the good pizzas into the mix. Share a sweet focaccia for dessert. **WHO** Mod Los Feliz families. ☺ ☼

[Lotería Grill Hollywood] ⌂ 6627 Hollywood Blvd., Hollywood, 323.465.2500, loteriagrill.com. B, L & D daily. Mexican. Full bar. AE, MC, V. $$ - $$$ **WHY** One of the best Mexican restaurants in Southern California, and superb margaritas, too. **WHAT** Jimmy Shaw may look like an Irishman, but he cooks like the Mexico City native he is, and after building a rabid following at his little Farmers Market stand, he's hit the big time with this Hollywood restaurant and his newest place in Studio City. The menu is similar to the one at the stand—tacos, tostadas, sopes and burritos with richly flavorful fillings like cochinita pibil, nopalitos and shrimp with spicy morita salsa—only here you get great cocktails and a proper restaurant setting. If you can't make up your mind, get the fantastic 12-mini-taco sampler platter and try 'em all. **WHO** Aficionados of real Mexico City cooking. ☼

[Lucques] ⌂ 8474 Melrose Ave., Melrose, 323.655.6277, lucques.com. L Tues.-Sat., D nightly. Mediterranean/modern American. Full bar. AE, MC, V. $$$ - $$$$ **WHY** For the farm-fresh ingredients that shine with just the right amount of chef behind them. The beloved family-style Sunday Supper brings gorgeous home-style cooking for $45 per person. **WHAT** Relaxed and beautiful, homey yet elegant, with just-attentive-enough service that's never pretentious, Lucques is the reigning Chez Panisse of Los Angeles. It's one of the best patio dining spots in town, but being inside by the fireplace is pretty nice, too. Suzanne Goin's dishes—ricotta dumplings with garbanzos and summer squash; grilled whole fish with Asian greens and yellow-tomato confit; grilled club steak for two with the amazing potatoes parisienne—end up being copied around town later, so come here first. Indulge in Caroline Styne's wine list, and don't pass up the pastry chef's remarkable desserts, perhaps profiteroles with seasonal fruit or warm chocolate cake with dulce de leche. **WHO** Attractive but not plastic people who really care about what goes into their mouths. ♥ ⌂ ☼

[Luna Park] 672 S. La Brea Ave., Miracle Mile, 323.934.2110, lunaparkla.com. L Mon.-Fri., D nightly, brunch Sat.-Sun. Modern American. Full bar. AE, MC, V. $$ - $$$ **WHY** Modern comfort food (goat cheese fondue, grilled chicken with cornbread pudding, make-your-own s'mores) at modest prices in a funky-chic setting. Miracle Mile locals can get it delivered, too. **WHAT** Vintage mismatched chandeliers, curtained booths and deep colors lend an air of shabby-chic romance to this lively San Francisco transplant, which serves affordable modern comfort food and cocktails that make everyone happy. Dinnertime is generally packed and noisy, but lunch is quieter—and weekend brunch is a well-kept secret. **WHO** Girlfriends meeting for lunch, lively groups of friends at night. ♥ 🖼️ 🧺 �bus

[M Café de Chaya] 7119 Melrose Ave., Melrose, 323.525.0588, mcafedechaya.com. B, L & D daily. Modern American/vegetarian. No booze. AE, MC, V. $ - $$ **WHY** Macrobiotic, organic, vegetarian and/or vegan cooking that's better than you might think is possible. **WHAT** Shigefumi Tachibe, founding chef of the late lamented La Petite Chaya and executive chef of Chaya Venice and Chaya Brasserie, became an avid student of macrobiotic cooking years ago, and his studies finally paid off with this chic little restaurant and deli, which has spawned a larger offshoot in Culver City. His menu eschews red meat, poultry, dairy, eggs and refined sugar—and yet it's full of delicious things to eat. A fine place for a lovely, light meal. 🌿 🧺 ☼ 🚌

[Madeo] 8897 Beverly Blvd., West Hollywood, 310.859.4903. L Tues.-Fri., D nightly. Italian. Full bar. AE, MC, V. $$$ - $$$$ **WHY** Carpaccio, simple roast veal carved tableside, light gnocchi with pesto and Tuscan fish soup, served with deference at a quietly A-list Hollywood canteen. **WHAT** Well-dressed, middle-aged folks with business to discuss feel very much at home in this traditional ristorante, where the service is smooth and the food is consistently satisfying. It's the kind of place that people come to every week for years and always order the same thing. **WHO** Agents, producers, movie stars, studio execs and doctors from Cedars-Sinai. ♥ 🕊️

[Mario's Peruvian & Seafood] 5786 Melrose Ave., Hollywood, 323.466.4181. L & early D daily. Peruvian/seafood. No booze. MC, V. $ - $$ **WHY** Ceviche, the seafood platter and the chicken or shrimp *saltado*, a stir-fry with red onions and tomato served with a heap of very good fries (potatoes come from Peru, after all). **WHAT** There's usually a wait at Mario's, and for good reason—its food is drop-dead delicious, and inexpensive to boot. The strip-mall setting is basic, and the parking lot is always full, but you won't be sorry for your trouble. Great for takeout, too. **WHO** A studio lunch crowd and, on weekends, fans who drive here from all over. 🖼️ ☼

[Meals by Genet] 1053 S. Fairfax Ave., Fairfax District, 323.938.9304, mealsbygenet.com. D Wed.-Sun. Ethiopian. Beer & wine. MC, V. $$ **WHY** Diverse Ethiopian flavors elevated for a white-tablecloth world. **WHAT** Proprietor Genet Agonafer's restaurant is the only one of its kind in Little Ethiopia, a serious, almost formal place unlike its more casual neighbors. But Meals by Genet isn't stiff—it's homey and warm and alive with spice. The menu is succinct, consisting of a half-dozen stews and accompanying small plates of vegetables. *Doro-wot* is essential, chicken stewed in a red pepper sauce alight with ginger and clove. Equally pleasing is *yebere siga tibs*, beef sautéed with onions and green chiles. But just as important are those vegetables: tender orange split peas; puréed sunflowers with jalapeño, onion, olive oil and lemon juice; and green lentils fortified with Ethiopian mustard. **WHO** African food fans and vegetarians seeking serious flavor. 〰 🥢

[Mother Dough] **4648 Hollywood Blvd., Los Feliz, 323.644.2885, motherdoughpizza.com. D Tues.-Sun. Pizzeria. Beer & wine. AE, MC, V. $ - $$ WHY** True Neapolitan-style pies in a pleasant sit-down space with beer and wine. **WHAT** According to the menu, Neapolitan-style pizza is meant to be enjoyed without excessive toppings. The thin, chewy crust has a distinct sourdough tang, while the tomato sauce is bright and fresh. Pies are simply topped with buffalo mozzarella, a scattering of fennel sausage slices or proscuitto and arugula. Snack on marinated olives or bacon-wrapped dates while the pizzas are painstakingly prepped for their quick tour in the wood-burning oven. A notch up from most of the area's casual pizza places, the menu is almost deceptively simple—but the pies are the real deal. **WHO** Couples plotting their next glass of wine at Bar Covell down the street. 🥢

[Natalie Peruvian Seafood] **5759 Hollywood Blvd., Hollywood, 323.463.8340. L & D daily. Peruvian/seafood. No booze. MC, V. $ - $$ WHY** Peru's Chinese influence is evident in the wonderful fried-rice dishes; also try the fried calamari and classic pescado saltado with french fries, and wash it down with an Inca Kola. **WHAT** This rival to Mario's goes a little easier on the chiles but turns out Peruvian food that's still powerfully flavorful. It's a pleasant little café that doesn't get as crowded as Mario's, although the parking's no better. Delicious food, low prices. 📷 ☺

[Natraliart] **3426 W. Washington Blvd., Mid-City, 323.737.9277 , natraliart.com. L & D Tues.-Sat. Jamaican. No booze. MC, V. $ WHY** For the city's best jerk chicken grilled over wood and for Jamaican-style vegetarian meals. **WHAT** Decorated with murals of island beach scenes, this funky but tidy place adjoins a Caribbean market. Pick up your cassava flour or yams or carry out the richly filled stuffed patties (like empanadas). Beans and rice are cooked in fresh coconut milk and braised oxtails fall from the bone. Sometime there's akee or butter-tender stewed chicken and always vegetable soup, fresh juices and homemade ginger beer. **WHO** Jamaicans. There's hardly a one who doesn't know about this near-legendary spot. 📷 ☺

[Night + Market] **9043 Sunset Blvd., West Hollywood, 310.275.9724, nightmarketla.com. D nightly. Thai. Beer & wine. MC, V. $ - $$ WHY** A

🏛 ESSENTIALLY L.A. ☺ LATE ♥ ROMANTIC 📷 VALUE 〰 QUIET ☘ SUSTAINABLE

fun, open-till-midnight option on the touristy Sunset Strip with a serious devotion to real Thai street food flavors. **WHAT** Owner Kris Yenbamroong's family has run Talesai in front for 25 years. After living in Thailand as a teenager, he wanted to bring more authentically spicy and pungent tastes to this stylish, modern room, which also features an excellent wine list. Sour fermented Isaan sausage is a must, as is the subtly perfumed catfish "tamale" steamed in a banana leaf. On a Hollywood bar crawl? Try crab-fried rice or drunken noodles to sop up the damage. For dessert, a Thai-style ice cream sandwich features coconut ice cream and condensed milk on a sweet roll. The music is good, and they screen classic films (sound off) on the walls. **WHO** Young clubbers and Talesai fans ready to branch out. ☺

[Nishimura] 8684 Melrose Ave., West Hollywood, 310.659.4770. L Tues.-Fri., D Mon.-Sat. Japanese/sushi. Beer & wine. AE, MC, V. $$$$$ **WHY** Sushi, sashimi and cooked dishes of tremendous beauty and flavor. **WHAT** The classicist's sushi served in this serene and minimalist space is not for the faint of wallet, and neither is it for the person looking for a scene. Hiro Nishimura is very serious about his food, and that's exactly how his fans like it. You can easily drop $200 for a meal here. **WHO** Fans who would follow chef Nishimura to Panorama City if necessary but are much more at home in WeHo. ♥ 🍴

[Osteria Mamma] 5732 Melrose Ave., Melrose, 323.284.7060, osteriamamma.com. L Mon.-Fri., D Mon.-Sat. Italian. Beer & wine. AE, MC, V. $$ - $$$ **WHY** For handmade pasta made by a real Italian mamma. **WHAT** When Filippo Cortiva split with his partner at nearby Osteria La Buca to open his own place, he brought his mother, Loredana, with him, and now she's a partner and chef. When she's not making fresh pasta, she cruises the relaxed, high-ceilinged trattoria to say hello to the many regulars. Do what they do and skip the pricey meat and seafood entrées, instead choosing from the generous, lightly dressed salads, Neapolitan-style pizzas and fresh pastas; choose the light gnocchi or the tagliatelle bolognese over the too-wet carbonara. **WHO** Hollywood hipsters and Hancock Park householders. ☺

[Osteria Mozza] 🏠 6602 Melrose Ave., Melrose, 323.297.0100, mozza-la.com. D nightly. Italian/modern American. Full bar. AE, MC, V. $$ - $$$$ **WHY** The mozzarella tasting plate, grilled octopus with potatoes, celery and lemon, orecchiette pasta with sausage and swiss chard, pan-roasted sea trout with Umbrian lentils—in fact, pretty much everything. **WHAT** The frenzy that built around the opening of this joint venture between Mario Batali, Joe Bastianich and Nancy Silverton may have subsided, but getting a table in this simply handsome dining room is still not easy. Happily, it's well worth the effort, thanks to the terrific pastas, hearty Batali-style main courses and a lavish array of cheese-based nibbles made in front of the dozen people who managed to score seats at the mozzarella bar. The (pricey) wine list is a whirlwind tour of Italy, from Alto Adige to Sicilia. **WHO** Batali and/or Silverton groupies, celebrities, and the L.A. elite. 🍷🍴

[Papa Cristo's] **2771 W. Pico Blvd., Mid-City, 323.737.2970, papacristo.com. L Tues.-Sun., early D Tues.-Sat. Greek. Beer & wine. AE, MC, V. $ - $$ WHY** Savory, straightforward Greek classics at very low prices. **WHAT** Founded as a market in 1948 by Sam Chrys, this funky, rambling place is run by Sam's son, Chrys Chrys, who grew it into a restaurant in the early '90s, in time to cash in on the *My Big Fat Greek Wedding* phenomenon. You order at the chaotic counter, look for a table (in the big dining room, the market or out on the covered patio), and soon you'll be served plates heaped with lamb souvlaki or roast chicken. Thursday is the Big Fat Greek dinner, complete with Greek dancing. **WHO** Students and teachers from Loyola High, folks from the neighborhood's many little warehouses, and Downtowners escaping the overpriced joints in their office buildings. 🍽🐟🌙☼

[Park's BBQ] **955 S. Vermont Ave., Koreatown, 213.380.1717, parksbbq.com. L & D daily. Korean/barbecue. Beer & wine. MC, V. $$$ - $$$$ WHY** A particularly lavish and beautiful array of *panchan*, the small appetizers that accompany traditional Korean barbecue, and meat of very high quality. **WHAT** As far in atmosphere from smoky, funky barbecue joints like Soot Bull Jeep as you can get, Park is spare and industrial-chic, with a gorgeous and fairly formal serving staff and powerful ventilation whisking away smoke from the tabletop grills. It's an investment to cook your own meat here, but it's a worthwhile one: the prime short ribs, bulgogi, pork belly and Kobe-style beef are all superb. **WHO** Businesspeople and well-heeled couples.

[Paru's] **5140 W. Sunset Blvd., Hollywood, 323.661.7600, parusrestaurant.com. L Sat-.Sun., D nightly. Indian/vegetarian. Beer & wine. AE, MC, V. $ - $$ WHY** Richly flavorful southern Indian cooking that is all vegetarian with many vegan choices, too, served on an atmospheric secret patio. **WHAT** Paru's has a speakeasy feel to it—you have to be buzzed in, and there's a hidden tree-filled garden in back—which lends it an aura of romance that is continued with the cooking. The tasty (and vegetarian) dosas, samosas, *sambar* (potato-squash soup) and lassi drinks are fun to share, and the prices are more than fair. **WHO** Family groups and vegetarian date-nighters getting cozy in the twinkle-lit garden patio. ♥🍽🐟🌙☼

[Petrossian] **321 N. Robertson Blvd., West Hollywood, 310.271.6300, petrossian.com. L & D daily, brunch Sat.-Sun. Russian/French. Beer & wine. AE, MC, V. $ - $$$ WHY** The happy hour (Monday to Saturday from 4 to 7 p.m.) is a hell of deal—the $5 specials include luscious Petrossian country pâté with toast points, eggplant caviar à la russe and those charming almond sweetmeats from Provence. An equal bargain is the monthly caviar tutorial and tasting (with Champagne or vodka) for

$35. **WHAT** This Euro-moderne outpost of the Parisian fancy food emporium has a caviar-and-crème fraîche décor and a surprisingly terrific restaurant—even if you can't afford the Caspian caviar. Chef Giselle Wellman makes the classics (spectacular scrambled eggs with caviar) and some modestly inventive dishes (Scottish salmon with lentils and bacon), and her brunch has a devoted following. **WHO** Well-dressed people having a civilized lunch. ♥

[Pizzeria Mozza] 🔒 **641 N. Highland Ave., Melrose, 323.297.0101, mozza-la.com. L & D daily. Italian/pizzeria. Beer & wine. AE, MC, V. $$ - $$$ WHY** Dough of perfect flavor and bite, paired with superb toppings; the margherita is simple the way E=MC2 is simple. **WHAT** Is Mozza's pizza the second coming of Christ? You'd think so with all the hullabaloo around this pizzeria and its celebrity-chef parents, Nancy Silverton and Mario Batali. But the result is something more earthy than celestial—heaven on earth, we'll call it. The food, and not just the pizzas (try the bruschetta, roasted brussels sprouts and salads), really is worth all the fuss. The at-the-counter deal at lunch and in the late evening ($20 for pizza, dessert and a glass of wine) is awesome. **WHO** Groupies thrilled to have scored a tiny table or counter seat. 🔵🔌🏛

[Playa] **7360 Beverly Blvd., Beverly/Third, 323.933.5300, playarivera. com. D Mon.-Sat., brunch Sat.-Sun. Latin American. Full bar. AE, MC, V. $$$ - $$$$ WHY** Modern Latin American cuisine that's at once traditional and playful. **WHAT** John Sedlar's sequel to Rivera follows much the same model as his Downtown restaurant, a handsome place showcasing a vast array of Latin American flavors. Cocktails are almost universally excellent, devised as at Rivera by Julian Cox. Plates are large (to humor Sedlar's proclivity for making art pieces of his food) but portions are small. Still, there are some great flavors. A delicate corn custard embraces the very essence of the vegetable. Duck confit crackles with expert technique. Skate wing streaked with a tamarind-cinnamon gastrique is impressive, if skimpy. Tacos are, for whatever reason, nominally transformed into "maize cakes" and topped with things like hibiscus-pickled cauliflower, fresh burrata and black garlic and olive "soil." **WHO** Food scene floaters and cocktail hounds.

[Providence] 🔒 **5955 Melrose Ave., Hollywood, 323.460.4170, providencela.com. L Fri., D nightly. Seafood. Full bar. AE, MC, V. $$$$$ WHY** It's one of best fine-dining seafood restaurants in the United States. Okay, maybe it is *the* best. **WHAT** Michael Cimarusti's seafood dishes are constructed as carefully as paintings, and they're as delicious to eat as they are to gaze upon. He's been cooking in this serene and appropriately elegant space for so long and so well that it's almost forgotten that Patina lived here. All the details—service, wine, tableware—are seamlessly tended to so diners can feel as important as they think they are, or actually are. Every dish is worthwhile, even if it's not seafood—the foie gras a la plancha, for instance, is divine, and

🔪 **VEGETARIAN** 👁 **KID FRIENDLY** 🌸 **PATIO DINING** 🚐 **DELIVERY** 🏛 **PRIVATE PARTY**

the cheese selection is among L.A.'s finest. **WHO** Expensively dressed captains of industry and food lovers (chefs, journalists, aficionados) from around the country, checking it out while they're in town. ♥ 🍸

[Public Kitchen & Bar] **Hollywood Roosevelt Hotel, 7000 Hollywood Blvd., Hollywood, 323.769.8888 , thompsonhotels.com. L Mon.-Fri., D nightly. American. Full bar. AE, MC, V. $$$ WHY** The gorgeous old hotel, the fabulous setting, the appetizers and the beautiful people. **WHAT** Atmosphere oozes out of this new dining room in the historic Roosevelt: tufted leather banquettes, burnished woods, marble tables, painted ceilings and aproned waiters who really know what they're doing. Everyone gets the squishy Parker House rolls and samples the terrific cocktails. As for the food, we adore the starters—chicarrones, cheeses, diver scallops with zucchini risotto, charred octopus, crab-cakes—but have been disappointed with entrees (dry pork schnitzel, ordinary steak frites). Desserts are rich and all-American. **WHO** Before 9 p.m., a diverse mix of foodies chat over relaxed meals; by 10, it's all beautiful twentysomethings shouting over blasting music. ☺ 🍸

[Rahel Ethiopian Veggie Cuisine] **1047 S. Fairfax Ave., Miracle Mile, 323.937.8401, rahelveggiecuisine.com. L & D daily. Ethiopian/ vegetarian. BYOB. AE, MC, V. $ - $$ WHY** Hearty stews made from chickpeas and lentils accompany plenty of vegetable side dishes, like greens with garlic or tomatoes with green pepper, while the fluffy in-jera bread adds healthy touches like flax, sunflower seeds and sesame. Flaxseed and barley also make appearances in smoothie-like drinks. **WHAT** Most of the Ethiopian restaurants on Fairfax serve meat dishes, but this one is all vegan, with dishes cooked in olive oil instead of butter. The simple, colorful room is decorated with messob tables, and a traditional Ethiopian coffee ceremony finishes the meal. 🌱 🍸 ☺

[Red Corner Asia] **5267 Hollywood Blvd., East Hollywood, 323.466.6722, redcornerasia.com. L & D daily. Thai/Asian. Beer & wine. AE, MC, V. $$ WHY** RCA's signature dishes, including flaming whole volcano chicken, crispy catfish with apple salad, fish cakes on lemon-grass skewers and spicy shrimp with cashews and fried basil leaves. **WHAT** This clean, modern addition to the Thai Town dining scene has a user-friendly menu and a devoted clientele, thanks in part to its late hours (until 2 a.m. most nights). Prices are a little higher than the Thai Town norm, but the food and setting are worth it. ☺ 🍸 ☼

[Red O] **8155 Melrose Ave., Melrose, 323.655.5009, redorestaurant. com. D nightly. Mexican. Full bar. AE, MC, V. $$$ WHY** To try Rick Bay-less's famed Mexican cooking without having to fly to Chicago. **WHAT** It's hard to know why überchef Rick Bayless thought he should bring his upscale Mexican cooking to L.A., where Mexican food from every region is plentiful, but he did, and mobs of people have flocked to this great-looking place since opening day. His cooking is serious, running to such things as pork belly sopes with black beans, salsa negra and sesame, and his Chicago restaurants are swell, but this one... it's fine, but we don't really see the point. **WHO** Scenemakers.

[Roscoe's House of Chicken & Waffles] 1514 N. Gower St., Hollywood, 323.466.7453, roscoeschickenandwaffles.com. B, L & D daily. Southern. Beer & wine. MC, V. $ - $$ **WHY** Fried chicken and big waffles, of course. **WHAT** The name pretty much says it all. The original location of this small chain of gut-busting L.A. soul-food cafés, Roscoe's is a Hollywood institution, and it's a haven for people who can't bear one more vegan scramble or nonfat chai latte. The fried chicken, waffles and other Southern standards are high-fat, high-sugar and all-around bad for you—in a very good way. **WHO** Music-industry folks, African-American families and the young 'n hungry. 🖼️☺

[Ruen Pair] 5257 Hollywood Blvd., East Hollywood, 323.466.0153. L & D daily to 4 a.m. Thai. No booze. Cash only. $ **WHY** Don't miss the papaya salad and authentic dishes like shredded fish salad, fried rice with Chinese sausage and stir-fried morning glories. **WHAT** The homey, reasonably priced restaurant is cash only with no liquor, but it's worth it for excellent, cheap Thai dishes, which are served until 4 a.m. **WHO** Locals and, in the midnight hours, the post-club crowd. ☺ 🖼️🍴

[Sake House Miro] 809 S. La Brea Ave., Miracle Mile, 323.939.7075, sakehousemiro.com. L Mon.-Fri., D nightly. Japanese. Beer & wine. AE, MC, V. $ - $$ **WHY** Beer and sake happy-hour specials, serviceable sushi and a fun selection of izakaya small plates. Korean bibim bap is surprisingly good here. **WHAT** Koreatown hipsters and Miracle Mile office workers populate the heavy wooden tables at this spot that reveals the Japanese fascination with '50s-era Tokyo memorabilia. A faux alley at the rear of the bar is lined with replicas of old storefronts, signage and posters, while Asian movie one-sheets grace the dining room walls. Multiple menus offer satay-like skewers of grilled kushiyaki, sushi rolls, fruit juice–laced shochu "martinis" and the kind of quick-bite snack food found everywhere in urban Japan. **WHO** Young women with streaked hair in denim microskirts and bobby socks and their Blackberry-toting dates. ☺

[Salt's Cure] 7494 Santa Monica Blvd., West Hollywood, 323.850.7258, saltscure.com. L & D Wed.-Mon., brunch Sat.-Sun. Modern American. Beer & wine. AE, MC, V. $$$ - $$$$ **WHY** Carefully sourced meats, poultry and fish, smoked and cured by hand. **WHAT** Salt's Cure does its own thing. In fact, it does virtually everything: smoking its own fish, curing its meats without nitrates, and pickling a vast array of vegetables. Chefs Chris Phelps and Zak Walters preside over the tiny, tall dining room from a minuscule open kitchen ringed by a few barstools. The menu is limited and not inexpensive but studded with must-haves, including potted pork in a wee glass jar, house-made

🍴 VEGETARIAN ☺ KID FRIENDLY ☼ PATIO DINING 🚚 DELIVERY 🎉 PRIVATE PARTY

charcuterie and succulent smoked fish. Not everything works; pork tongue has novelty value in a Reuben sandwich, but it's not nearly as good as corned beef, even with house-made sauerkraut. **WHO** WeHo hipsters and *bourgeois bohèmes*.

[Sanamluang Café] 5170 Hollywood Blvd., East Hollywood, 323.660.8006. L & D daily to 4 a.m. Thai. No booze. Cash only. **$** **WHY** Noodle dishes are the stars—standouts include *pad see euw* (drunken noodles) and boat soup noodles, and they're served every night until 4 a.m. **WHAT** This venerable spot offers a late-night Thai fix that's hard to beat, despite the bare-bones atmosphere and crowded parking lot. Good food at a great price, and it tastes even better after midnight. **WHO** The after-hours club crowd, along with hospital workers from nearby Kaiser and Children's. ☉ ⑤

[Sapp Coffee Shop] 5183 Hollywood Blvd., East Hollywood, 323.665.1035. B, L & D Mon.-Tues. & Thurs.-Sun. Thai. No booze. Cash only. **$** **WHY** Thai food cooked for the Thai palate. **WHAT** At this 20-year-old Thai Town luncheonette (open through dinner as well), the full-throttle onslaught of capsicum heat in its *po-tak* soup, stir-fried pork or chicken reminds Thais and the rest of us how food tastes in the homeland. **WHO** Anyone jonesing for a spicy chile fix plentifully served at bargain-basement prices. ⑤

[Simon/L.A.] Sofitel, 8555 Beverly Blvd., West Hollywood, 310.358.3879, simonlarestaurant.com. B, L & D daily. Modern American. Full bar. AE, MC, V. **$$$$** **WHY** The fantastic, funky outdoor patio, the great Bloody Mary and the junk food platter (the pastry chef's version of Ding Dongs and Ho Hos) are an odd combo, but secretly you've got to love it for brunch. **WHAT** As the restaurant for the trendy Sofitel hotel, Simon/L.A. is a bit over the top, but there's no doubting the appeal of chef Kerry Simon's modern comfort food. If you've got the bucks, go early for the food—like truffle mac 'n cheese or tuna with crab and red chile aioli—and leave before the young Hollywood crowd takes over. **WHO** Uber-trendy hotel guests and Kardashian wannabes. ☼

[The Smokin' Joint] 8486 W. 3rd St., West Hollywood, 323.655.7427, thesmokinjointbbq.com. L & D Tues.- Sun. Barbecue. Full bar. AE, MC, V. **$$$ - $$$$** **WHY** For Q that rivals meats at the best steakhouses. **WHAT** This tiny, casual restaurant serves only grass-fed organic meats and uses farmers' market produce for sides like hand-cut fries, fried onion loaf and roasted vegetables. Chef Shari Teremotos brines the meats in apple juice and then adds spice rubs before smoking them over wood. Brisket and tri-tip take about 15 hours, resulting in a deep penetration of smoke flavor. Baby backs, though lean, remain juicy. House-made desserts—chocolate cake and flaky, bourbon-infused pecan pie—could be proudly served at the fanciest of tables. **WHO** Music-industry and Hollywood acolytes.

🏛 **ESSENTIALLY L.A.** ☉ **LATE** ♥ **ROMANTIC** ⑤ **VALUE** 🔊 **QUIET** ♻ **SUSTAINABLE**

[Son of a Gun] **8370 W. 3rd St., Beverly/Third, 323.782.9033, sonofagunrestaurant.com. L Mon.-Fri., D nightly. Modern American. Full bar. AE, MC, V. $$ - $$$$ WHY** Because you never know when the urge for a terrific, if Lilliputian, lobster roll (creamy and a bit spicy, stuffed into a warm, butter-grilled roll) will hit. **WHAT** This seafood-centric spinoff of Animal is tiny and generally mobbed, so it's nice that a long communal table as well as a few seats at the bar are set aside for walk-ins. Small plates of extremely tasty stuff fill the menu, including Sriracha-spiked shrimp toast, Pernod-scented mussels with tarragon, and a surf 'n turf of a Niman Ranch hanger steak with fried oysters. A few dishes made us feel underserved; linguini with clams surely was never meant to be doled out in one-cup portions. The wine list is dominated by Champagne, which goes great with the cuisine, but we're unsure if folks will pop for $100-plus bottles of bubbly in a place that uses Ball jars as water glasses. **WHO** A smattering of celebs among the foodies.

[Soot Bull Jeep] 🏛 **3136 W. 8th St., Koreatown, 213.387.3865. L & D daily. Korean/Barbecue. Beer & wine. MC, V. $$ - $$$ WHY** For the quintessential grill-your-own Koreatown experience — it's a great place to bring out-of-towners. **WHAT** You'll smell like meaty smoke all night after dinner here, and you won't mind a bit. It's one of Koreatown's best-known places, a dive with brusque service and a constant wait for a table. The *panchan* (side dishes) aren't as complex and interesting as at some of its competitors, but the mesquite-fueled tabletop grills are the real thing, and the meat you cook over that mesquite is satisfying in a deeply primal way. **WHO** Korean businesspeople, hungry young folks and Koreatown explorers. 🛢☺

[Spicy BBQ Restaurant] **5101 Santa Monica Blvd., East Hollywood, 323.663.4211. L & D Mon.-Tues. & Thurs.-Sun. Thai. BYOB. Cash only. $ WHY** To taste rarely found northern-style Thai cooking at its best. **WHAT** A super talent plies the stoves at this minuscule northern-style restaurant hidden in a strip mall next to a falafel place. The specialties listed toward the back of the menu include *gaeng hung lae*, pork curry spiked with whole garlic cloves and ground peanuts, *nam prik num*, an explosively hot roasted chile and eggplant dip, *nam prik oom*, the milder tomato pork dip, and *khao sawy*, the north's impossibly delicious curry noodle dish. **WHO** Homesick northern Thais and in-the-know Thai food lovers. 🛢

[Street] 🏛 **742 N. Highland Ave., Melrose, 323.203.0500, eatatstreet. com. L & D daily, brunch Sun. International. Beer & wine. AE, MC, V. $$ - $$$$ WHY** For its celebration of street foods from around the world, it's L.A.-hip patio and the skill and enthusiasm of owner/chef Susan Feniger. **WHAT** Celebrity chef Susan Feniger (Border Grill, Ciudad, *Too Hot Tamales*) is a warm-hearted Midwestern gal whose culinary passions are truly global, and at her solo venture she shares all those

🍃 VEGETARIAN ☉ KID FRIENDLY ☼ PATIO DINING � DELIVERY 🏛 PRIVATE PARTY

passions, from Burmese lettuce wraps to Egyptian basbousa lime cake. Now that it's matured a little, Street has hit its groove, and almost everything is terrific: amazing slow-cooked Moscow-style eggplant, chicken soup with spoonbread dumplings, coconut Kaya toast, even a traditional Hawaiian plate lunch. **WHO** Feniger's chef pals, tattooed hard-body moms with adorable babies, and aging foodies who sport L.A. Eyeworks glasses and drive Priuses. 🔖 ☺ ☼

[Talésai] **9043 Sunset Blvd., West Hollywood, 310.275.9724, talesai. com. L Mon.-Fri., D nightly. Thai. Full bar. AE, MC, V. $$ - $$$ WHY** A sane and serene retreat in the heart of the Sunset Strip, with beautifully presented and delicious Thai food. **WHAT** This Thai pioneer has a new lease on life, thanks to a major renovation and the energy and good cooking of young Kris Yenbamroong, grandson of the 27-year-old restaurant's original chef. In a stylish black-and-white room, regulars share pretty, artfully spiced Thai classics, with a few modern twists: beef larb, salmon steamed in banana leaf, and fried chicken with sticky rice and *noom* (a Thai salsa); make sure to start with the Hidden Treasures, heavenly little bites of crab, shrimp and calamari. **WHO** Musicians, actors and other longtime residents of the Hollywood Hills who've been coming here for years. 🍷 🚗

[Taylor's Steakhouse] 🏛 **3361 W. 8th St., Koreatown, 213.382.8449, taylorssteakhouse.com. L Mon.-Fri., D nightly. American/ steakhouse. Full bar. AE, MC, V. $$ - $$$$ WHY** Effortlessly retro steakhouse classics, old L.A. atmosphere and good cocktails. **WHAT** This 1953 matriarch is a genuine outpost of all we know and love about steakhouse ambience and cuisine: red Naugahyde booths, the dimmest possible lighting, iceberg wedges smothered with blue cheese, icy martinis, generous and perfectly satisfying steaks for less than $30. **WHO** Angelenos who remember when Sam Yorty was mayor. 📷 🍷 🏛

[Tere's Mexican Grill] **5870 Melrose Ave., Hollywood, 323.468.9345. B, L & D Mon.-Sat. Mexican. No booze. MC, V. $ WHY** Homemade Mexican food that's anything but generic in a generic strip-mall setting. There's no beer to drink, but you can have a Mexican Coke, made with cane sugar instead of corn syrup. (That Coke alone draws a loyal clientele.) **WHAT** Although the bare-bones, order-at-the-counter setting isn't much, Tere's cooking provides all the atmosphere you need. Robert and Maria Teresa Melgar make everything from scratch: the soft tortillas, the chunky, fantastic guacamole, the light, almost pungent verde sauce on the enchiladas, the hearty fideo soup, the savory chorizo-filled empanadas, and more. **WHO** Paramount folks and Hancock Park families getting takeout. 📷 ☺ ☼

[Terroni] **7605 Beverly Blvd., Beverly/Third, 323.954.0300, terroni.ca. L & D daily. Italian. Full bar. AE, MC, V. $$ - $$$ WHY** Thin-crust pizzas in the individual Italian style, topped with gorgonzola, pears and walnuts

🏛 ESSENTIALLY L.A. ☺ LATE ♥ ROMANTIC 📷 VALUE 🍷 QUIET ♻ SUSTAINABLE

or spicy Italian sausage, and a wide selection of pastas, perhaps with shrimp and asparagus or with homemade Italian sausage. **WHAT** The stylish import from Toronto brought a lively café to a neighborhood hungry for mid-priced, casual Italian. From the Eames chairs, to the open shelving and sidewalk tables, to the extensive menu (salads, panini, pastas, mains), Terroni is a perfect L.A.-style trattoria. 🍷☼

[Tower Bar] **Sunset Tower, 8358 W. Sunset Blvd., West Hollywood, 323.848.6677, sunsettowerhotel.com. B, L & D daily. French/modern American. Full bar. AE, MC, V. $$$$ - $$$$$ WHY** The elegance, the view, the impeccable service run by famed maître d' Dimitri Dimitrov... and the food's good, too. **WHAT** Is it a movie set or a restaurant? This restaurant atop the Sunset Tower Hotel is a little of both, a dazzlingly glamorous set with equally dazzling city views; outside is a separate operation, the Terrace, a poolside boîte that's filled with *Entourage* types. Back inside, you'll be served special-occasion French and modern American dishes (shrimp cocktail, caviar, steak frites, poulet rôti) that's better than it needs to be, given that Olive Garden food could sell in such a setting. **WHO** Anniversary and birthday celebrants, well-heeled tourists and some famous faces. ♥ 🍷 ☼ 🏛

[Trattoria Farfalla] **1978 Hillhurst Ave., Los Feliz, 323.661.7365, trattoriafarfalla.com. L Mon.- Fri., D nightly. Italian. Beer & wine. AE, MC, V. $$ - $$$ WHY** Penne alla Norma, insalata Farfalla (a salad on a pizza crust), thin-crust pizza with pesto and goat cheese, and good (if pricey) wine by the glass. **WHAT** A pioneer in the makeover of Los Feliz, Farfalla has been slinging pasta and Chianti to a constant crowd of regulars for many years, and it's every bit as good as it was in the early days—and every bit as packed. The kitchen knows how to get a ton of flavor into a very simple dish: say, tagliolini with shrimp or gnocchi with pesto. **WHO** Actors, writers, Los Feliz families. 🚚

[Tropicalia] **1966 Hillhurst Ave., Los Feliz, 323.644.1798, tropicaliabraziliangrill.com. L & D daily to midnight. Brazilian. Beer & wine. AE, MC, V. $ - $$ WHY** To sample Brazilian food in a cheerful room warmed with Brazilian music, or out on the terrace overlooking the Los Feliz parade. **WHAT** Owned by the neighboring Trattoria Farfalla, Tropicalia serves its own take on the vibrant, flavorful cooking of Brazil. There's *moqueca de peixe*, a wonderful coconut-milk-based sauce served with shrimp or white fish, and classic grilled marinated steak and chicken, but also California-influenced salads, like the delicious *salada brasileira*, with quality greens, hearts of palm, avocado and a heap of sautéed shrimp. Fun food at modest prices. **WHO** Los Feliz locals who need a break from Farfalla and Mexico City. ☺ ☼

[Umami Burger] 🏛 **850 S. La Brea Ave., Miracle Mile, 323.931.3000; 4655 Hollywood Blvd., East Hollywood, 323.669.3922; umamiburger.com. L & D daily. American. BYOB ($5 corkage fee). MC, V. $ WHY** For what is

---

🌿 **VEGETARIAN** ☺ **KID FRIENDLY** ☼ **PATIO DINING** 🚚 **DELIVERY** 🏛 **PRIVATE PARTY**

possibly the best burger in town. Sorry, Father's Office. **WHAT** Adam Fleischman takes burgers very, very seriously. He grinds the beef from flap steak and short ribs, gets soft, shiny yet sturdy buns from a Portuguese bakery, and offers such toppings as grilled onions, parmesan cheese crisps and shiitake mushrooms. The signature Umami burger has a rich savoriness; other choices include the Triple Pork, the Turkey Miso, the Hatch (chile), the Truffle Cheese and the Earth (veggie). It's just too bad the service so often falls short. More locations in Santa Monica and Hollywood. **WHO** Young, hungry foodie men. 📷😊☼

[Vegan Glory] **8393 Beverly Blvd., Beverly/Third, 323.653.4900, veganglory.com. L & D daily. Vegan/Thai. Beer & wine. MC, V. $ - $$** **WHY** A consistently good vegan Thai-American café with very good fake chicken, fish and meat dishes; pass on the vegan burger in favor of the vegan tacos, three-flavor fish, pad Thai, curries and coconut ice cream. **WHAT** At this bright and cheerful strip-mall spot near the Beverly Center, the only shortcoming is the lack of parking, although there is a valet option. Other than that, it's a godsend for vegans and the people who love them, because they can eat well, too. **WHO** Devout regulars, including some famous vegans. 📷🍴🚗

[Vermont] **1714 N. Vermont Ave., Los Feliz, 323.661.6163, vermontkitchenandbar.com. L Mon.-Fri., D nightly. Modern American. Full bar. AE, MC, V. $$$ - $$$$ WHY** Chic elegance in a neighborhood more known for casual bistros. Check out the lobster bake on Wednesdays. **WHAT** Now that the cocktail-lounge action has moved out back to the adjacent Rockwell VT, Vermont is more about the dining experience. Stephane Beaucamp's food is as elegant as the space: warm Medjool date salad, prime flat-iron steak with black peppercorn sauce, crispy whitefish with a watercress-basil sauce. A lovely date-night destination that's not cheap but not as expensive as it could get away with being—especially on Sundays and Mondays, when a three-course dinner is just $28. **WHO** A tastefully beautiful gay and straight crowd—if they've had work done, you'd never be able to tell. 💗

[Xiomara] **6101 Melrose Ave., Melrose, 323.461.0601, xiomararestaurant.com. L Mon.-Fri., D Mon.-Sat. Cuban. Full bar. AE, MC, V. $$$ - $$$$$ WHY** The lunch-only cubano sandwiches are delightful, especially the *pan con lechón* (shredded pork with Spanish peppers). And the Cuban club is a tasty fusion of marinated turkey breast with applewood-smoked bacon on sourdough. **WHAT** This is no ordinary sandwich joint—although they do serve them, elegantly, and garnished with microgreens, no less. Xiomara Ardolina's Nuevo Latino eatery is high-style all the way, from the house-pressed sugarcane juice in the mojitos to the Christofle silverware. The cream of L.A.'s Cuban crop.

[Yai Restaurant] **5757 Hollywood Blvd., Hollywood, 323.462.0292. L & D daily. Thai. Beer & wine. Cash only. $ WHY** Jungle curry, a subtly

📖 ESSENTIALLY L.A. ☺ LATE 💗 ROMANTIC 📷 VALUE 🔇 QUIET ♻ SUSTAINABLE

spicy, coconut-milk-based seafood stew; grilled beef salad with Chinese broccoli; pad Thai with a fiery spiciness instead of an American sweetness; and the succulent BBQ beef appetizer. **WHAT** Thai Town has lots of fine cafés, but this one stands out. You don't come here for the setting: Formica tables jammed into a brightly lit room in a grimy mini-mall. You come for the fabulous, and fabulously cheap, food. And believe it or not, you also come for the service, provided by friendly young women who are happy to introduce this cooking to newcomers. **WHO** Local Thais and adventurous food explorers. 🍴🥢

[Yai's on Vermont] **1627 N. Vermont Ave., Los Feliz, 323.644.1076. L & D daily. Thai. No booze. Cash only. $ WHY** Spicy papaya salad, minced chicken with red curry and fried trout are recommended; make sure to specify your desired spice level. **WHAT** On the easternmost end of Thai Town with ample free parking, this offshoot of the original offers a chance to try authentic Thai dishes without the grunge factor of the Yai on Hollywood Boulevard. **WHO** A mix of Thai families and bargain-seeking Los Feliz hipsters. 🍴🥢☺☼

EASTSIDE

[Aburiya Toranoko] **243 S. San Pedro St., Little Tokyo/Arts District, 213.621.9500, toranokola.com. L & D daily. Japanese. Full bar. AE, MC, V. $$ - $$$ WHY** A forward-thinking izakaya for the Downtown set. **WHAT** Aburiya Toranoko, it has been said, is the hip-hop equivalent of its rocking sister restaurant, Lazy Ox. It fits that description in soundtrack and style, but the kitchen hews closely to traditional izakaya cooking. There's *sumiyaki* (every conceivable bit of chicken as well as vegetables and white balsamic–marinated foie gras threaded onto skewers and grilled) plus a section of soupy oden highlighted by a pillowy Hanpen fish cake. The *kakuni* (braised pork belly) should find its way onto every table, as should a few pieces of the well-crafted sushi. There is, of course, a smart selection of seasonal cocktails, too. **WHO** Young lofties and Arts District elders. ☺

[Birriería Jalisco] **1845 E. 1st St., East L.A., 323.262.4552, birrieriajalisco.com. B, L & D daily. Mexican. No booze. MC, V. $ WHY** This 35-year-old institution turns out Southern California's most refined birria. **WHAT** Unlike most birrierías specializing in Guadalajara's famous roasted kid specialty, *birria*, this place doesn't hedge its bets by serving combination plates or other entrées. The drill is simple: You pile soft shreds of the sweet roasted meat onto a fresh tortilla and moisten the crispy-edged flesh with an accompanying broth that's the color of sun-drenched terra cotta and as complexly seasoned as Oaxacan mole. Six meat cuts are listed in Spanish on a card at every table: No. 1, the surtida, includes leg, rib and back meat. No. 2, leg and back alone, is the leanest, while No. 3, the rib and leg, offers lots of wonderful gelatinous cartilage to gnaw. The homemade desserts and iced drinks are also wonderful. **WHO** Connoisseurs of kid and Mexican ex-pats for whom the dish is pure comfort food. 📷

[Blair's] 🔒 2903 Rowena Ave., Silver Lake, 323.660.1882, blairsrestaurant.com. D nightly. Modern American. Beer & wine. AE, MC, V. $$$ **WHY** Owner/chef Marshall Blair, ex of Water Grill, is not only adept at preparing seafood (don't miss the tuna tartare with spiced ginger vinaigrette), but he's also got a way with meat and pastas, like the dreamy braised Colorado short ribs with polenta and leeks. **WHAT** Blair's has everything an L.A. restaurant needs to be a hot spot: a Silver Lake location, a dimly lit, romantic atmosphere, an artistically attractive clientele, a clever list of boutique wines and au courant modern comfort food. What it doesn't have, fortunately, is the attitude, noise and scene that you might expect of such a stylish bistro. **WHO** The same eastside intelligentsia you see at Canelé. ♥ 📷

[Border Grill] Union Bank Plaza, 445 S. Figueroa St., Downtown, 213.486.5171, bordergrill.com. L Mon.-Fri., D nightly. Latino. Full bar. AE, MC, V. $$ - $$$$ **WHY** Great margaritas and mojitos (which taste better during the great-value happy hour), winning tacos and the $35 pre-theatre prix fixe dinner, which includes a free shuttle to the Music Center. **WHAT** Mary Sue Milliken and Susan Feniger finally gave up on their Ciudad concept and turned this space into a Border Grill, with the same menu and happy-hour focus as their hit Santa Monica place. Try the lamb tacos, the Peruvian tostaditas, the tres leches cake and, of course, the margaritas, either classic or creative. **WHO** Suits from the Downtown towers and a lively happy-hour crowd. 🌙📷

[Bottega Louie] 🔒 700 S. Grand Ave., Downtown, 213.802.1470, bottegalouie.com. B Sat.-Sun., L & D daily. Italian. Full bar. AE, MC, V. $$ - $$$ **WHY** Crisp, puffy-edged pizzas, delicious salads and seemingly hundreds of fun small plates. **WHAT** In a vast, open space with white marble floors, white walls and a white ceiling way up high, an army of well-trained staff serve solidly satisfying trattoria fare to a constant crowd. It's one of Downtown's hottest hot spots, roiling with noise and conviviality. Weekend breakfast is both quieter and very good, and Downtown dwellers frequent the long, gleaming deli for prepared dishes, sandwiches and cookies to take home or back to the office. **WHO** After-work professionals and Hancock Parkers meeting their Pasadena friends before a show at the Music Center or Club Nokia, even though none of them can hear each other talk. 📷

[Bulan Thai Vegetarian Kitchen] 4114 Santa Monica Blvd., Silver Lake, 323.913.1488, bulanthai.com. L & D daily. Thai/vegan. No booze. MC, V. $ **WHY** Truly delicious vegan Thai cooking, served by nice people in a homey setting—and delivery, too! **WHAT** This Silver Lake outpost of the Melrose vegan destination has found the success of its sibling—even though vegan restaurants are as plentiful as tattoos in

Silver Lake and Los Feliz, few are as good as this place. **WHO** Vegans bringing their carnivorous mates, who always leave happy. 🚚🌀🌿🚐

[CaCao Mexicatessen] **1576 Colorado Blvd., Eagle Rock, 323.478.2791, cacaodeli.com. B, L, D Tues.- Sun. Mexican. BYOB. MC, V. $ - $$ WHY** Warmth, a strong sense of neighborhood and a serious approach to food—and, more importantly, to Mexican chocolate in all its forms. **WHAT** The name was a poor choice—everyone stumbles over it—but everything else about this richly colorful café/deli/market succeeds. You order at the counter to eat in the café or out on the patio, or to take out; there's also a fine coffee bar that adds Mexican chocolate drinks to the usual mix. Try the cochinita pibil tacos, Tijuana-style Caesar salad, tortilla soup, cubano torta and the cheese plate. Some balk at the $2.75 tacos, but this is not a truck, this is a nice café with table service and flowers on the table, and you can bring your own wine. **WHO** Eagle Rock people flocked from day one, including vegetarians grateful for the good choices. 🌿☺☼

[Café Pinot] 🍴 **700 W. 5th St., Downtown, 213.239.6500, patinagroup.com. L Mon.-Fri., D nightly. Modern American/French. Full bar. AE, MC, V. $$$ - $$$$$ WHY** Sitting under the olive trees in front of the L.A. Central Library, sipping a Viognier and eating the famed mustard-crusted rotisserie chicken with fries, is one of Downtown's greatest pleasures. **WHAT** When the weather's good, book a table on the terrace at this chic bistro owned by celebrity chef Joachim Splichal. If the weather's not good, you'll still have a very fine French-Californian bistro meal in the concrete-and-glass dining room staffed by skilled waiters. The $40 Sunday prix-fixe menu is a great deal. **WHO** Well-dressed attorneys, bankers and real estate brokers, often entertaining clients. 🍴🌿☼🏛

[Canelé] **3219 Glendale Blvd., Atwater, 323.666.7133, canele-la.com. D Tues.-Sun., brunch Sat.-Sun. Modern American/French. Beer & wine. AE, MC, V. $$ - $$$ WHY** The most extraordinary plain omelet in town, served in a casual, open-kitchen room alongside a short list of really good French-American-Mediterranean dishes. Great brunch, too. **WHAT** Owner/chef Corina Weibel cooked at Campanile and Lucques, but her style at Canelé is more modest: it's a convivial neighborhood bistro serving quality Cal-French-Mediterranean food at modest prices. Her cooking is simple and robustly flavorful, particularly notable for the meats (lamb chops, beef bourguignon), fish (whole roasted branzino) and desserts. Be prepared for cheek-by-jowl seating, and enjoy the we're-in-on-the-secret eastside vibe. No reservations, so come early or late. **WHO** Everyone here looks like an artist, writer, software developer or actor-on-an-HBO-series, and they probably are. 🌿

[Casa Bianca Pizza Pie] 🍴 **1650 Colorado Blvd., Eagle Rock, 323.256.9617, casabiancapizza.com. D Tues.-Sat. Italian/pizzeria. Beer &**

🌿 **VEGETARIAN** ☺ **KID FRIENDLY** ☼ **PATIO DINING** 🚐 **DELIVERY** 🏛 **PRIVATE PARTY**

wine. Cash only. $ - $$$ **WHY** The crust is thin, the cheese and sauce are in fine balance, and the vintage sign out front still calls it a "Pizza Pie." **WHAT** The pizza is an L.A. legend, but this funky Eagle Rock landmark is no place for a quick bite; waits are fearsome, and even ordering a to-go pie can take an hour. The payoff is a thin crust, New York-style pizza with a flavor that makes you forget how long it took to get seated (try it topped with eggplant). Smart regulars place their order when they put in their name for a table, so the pizza's ready when they sit down. The rest of the basic Italian food is fine but forgettable. **WHO** Old-school Eagle Rock and the entire pizza-loving populations of Pasadena and Glendale. 📷🔖☺

[Chaya Downtown] 525 S. Flower St., Downtown, 213.236.9577, thechaya.com. L Mon.-Fri., D nightly. Asian/French. Full bar. AE, MC, V. $$$$ **WHY** Terrific L.A.-style Euro-Asian food, a swinging happy hour, four hours of free parking and a free shuttle to the Music Center. **WHAT** The youngest member of the great Chaya family is a hit. The serene, Asian-accented space has an impressive art-glass chandelier in the bar and comfy outdoor booths that, on a warm summer evening, make you forget you're in a sterile office-tower neighborhood. The kitchen is adept at seafood dishes, the Kobe beef short ribs melt in your mouth, and the happy-hour menu boasts $5 cocktails and great-value sushi and appetizers. **WHO** Business folk who think McCormick & Schmick's is too stodgy and the Standard is too annoying. ♥🍸☼🏮

[Chichen Itza] Mercado la Paloma, 3655 S. Grand Ave., USC, 213.741.1075, chichenitzarestaurant.com. B, L & D daily. Mexican/Yucatán. No booze. AE, MC, V. $ **WHY** Seductive dishes from the Yucatán: robust, citrus-spiked soups; panuchos with shredded turkey, tomato, pickled red onion and avocado; cochinita pibil; and wonderful tamales, including the colado, with chicken and achiote. **WHAT** Terrific Yucatán cooking is served at this order-at-the-counter café in the nonprofit Mercado la Paloma, also home to Mo-Chica. The flavors are rich, with such ingredients as black beans, fried plantains, pickled red onions, achiote and citrus. Excellent pork dishes, and tasty vegetarian fare, too. **WHO** Local Latino families and SC folks. 📷🔖☺

[Church & State] 🏛 1850 Industrial St., Downtown, 213.405.1434, churchandstatebistro.com. L Mon.-Fri., D nightly. French. Full bar. AE, MC, V. $$ - $$$ **WHY** The first-rate execution of French bistro classics, at more than fair prices. **WHAT** This too-loud, brick-walled restaurant lost chef Walter Manzke, who made it an L.A. culinary destination, but so far the kitchen seems to be running like a top without him. They're still making his charcuterie, procuring pristine oysters, preparing a mean bouillabaisse and knowing enough not to tinker with such classics as moules marinière, steak frites and an elegant omelet (all terrific). Be warned that the ultra-flaky Alsatian-style tarts are huge and best shared with a group, and the onions on the tarte flamiche are caramelized to the point of ultra-sweetness (heaven for some, too sweet for others). Also a big hit with the regulars are the tasty, reasonably priced French wines and that milk of modern yuppiedom, absinthe. Service is not always as good as the food, but no one seems to care. **WHO** Chic lofties from the block and visitors from Pasadena and the Palisades. 📷 ☼

[Cliff's Edge] **3626 W. Sunset Blvd., Silver Lake, 323.666.6116, cliffsedgecafe.com. D Mon.-Sat., brunch Sat.-Sun. Italian/modern American. Full bar. AE, MC, V. $$ - $$$ WHY** For the most beautiful outdoor dining on the eastside, with food that suits the setting; try the leek and onion tart with an arugula salad, the rigatoni with wild-boar ragú, and the warm seafood salad. Brunch is lovely, too. **WHAT** We'd eat Arby's fare in this setting—a hidden walled garden built around a massive ficus tree, with levels and nooks and, at night, flickering candles—so we're all the more grateful that the food is good. The shocker is that the staff is actually nice—a place like this about ten miles west would be dripping with attitude. What was once an indoor dining room is now a bar lit by Moroccan chandeliers and fueled by cucumber margaritas. **WHO** TV directors keeping a low profile and production assistants splurging on a big night out. ♥ ☼

[Cole's] **118 E. 6th St., Downtown, 213.622.4090, colesfrenchdip.com. L & D daily. American. Full bar. AE, MC, V. $ - $$ WHY** Whether the french dip sandwich was invented here or not, lots of thought has gone into the redo of this historic spot. **WHAT** Chef Neal Fraser consulted on the menu when the oldest public house in L.A. re-opened after a restrained remodel, featuring red leatherette booths and historic black and white photos. Everyone gets hand-sliced dip sandwiches of beef, pork, turkey and lamb with au jus and "atomic" pickle spears, paired with sides including bacon-potato salad and mac 'n cheese.

[Colori Kitchen] **429 W. 8th St., Downtown, 213.622.5950, colorikitchen.com. L Mon.-Fri., D Wed.-Sat. Italian. Beer & wine. MC, V. $ - $$ WHY** Because it's one of the best-value restaurants in Downtown L.A. **WHAT** This is the kind of simple neighborhood Italian place you've seen everywhere *but* Downtown. Past a fairly grim-looking doorway in a transitional block (over here, $750,000 lofts, over there, a shabby residence hotel) is a charming room with brick walls and an open kitchen, where the owner/chef turns out delicious Italian classics at modest prices, including lunch combos (salad, pasta, drink) for $12 or less, a terrific chicken-pesto sandwich for $9 and, at dinnertime, a range of tasty pastas for $15 or less. **WHO** An interesting Downtown mix: fire captains and lawyers sitting next to loft-dwelling screenwriters and fashion-district hipsters. 📷 🍴

[Domenico] **1637 Silver Lake Blvd., Silver Lake, 323.661.6166, domenicoristorantesilverlake.com. L & D daily. Italian. Wine.. AE, MC,**

V. $$ - $$$$ **WHY** Elegant Italian dishes in a relaxed sidewalk café with excellent service. **WHAT** Tiny and white inside, with a spacious front patio, this neighborhood restaurant is culinarily ambitious for the neighborhood. Handmade pastas—think lasagne with oxtails, beet tortelli or Peruvian blue-potato ravioli—and hearty, creative mains like braised rabbit make it a sophisticated alternative to the area's profusion of pizzerias. It's pricier than we'd like, but it's delivering the goods. **WHO** Date-night couples; a smattering of local actors. ☼

[Drago Centro] 🏛 **525 S. Flower St., #120, Downtown, 213.228.8998, dragocentro.com. L Mon.-Fri., D nightly. Italian. Full bar. AE, MC, V. $$$$ - $$$$$ WHY** For the best Italian cooking east of Santa Monica. **WHAT** We can't remember the last time we thought any dish was worth $44, but our investment in fresh spaghetti with truffles here was money very well spent. This modern office-building ristorante has a New York vibe in the best sense: big-city, urbane, sophisticated but not trendy. It offers both great value—the elegant happy hour with $5 drinks and $4 mini pizzas—and a worthwhile splurge—the gorgeous $75 six-course tasting menu or the $85 bone-in rib-eye for two. It's a star in a Downtown scene that keeps getting better. **WHO** Downtown power people, theater-goers and celebrants. ♥ 🍴 🏛

[El Puerto Escondido] **3345 N. Eastern Ave., El Sereno, 323.909.1008. L & D daily. Mexican/seafood. Beer & wine. MC, V. $ WHY** Ultra-fresh Mexican-style seafood, including Happy Oysters, freshly shucked and topped with a vibrant chopped shrimp cocktail, and *caldo de siete mares*, a light soup generously stocked with Alaskan crab legs, mussels and shrimp. **WHAT** This branch of the Inglewood original serves the seafood dishes of Mexico's Pacific Coast beach towns, and while it's not open 24/7 like the mothership, it has the same terrific shrimp cocktails, *camarones al mojo de ajo*, ceviches and whole fried fish. Excellent seafood at low prices. **WHO** El Sereno blue-collar workers and South Pas surfers pining for Cabo. 🍴 ☺

[El Taurino] 🏛 **1104 S. Hoover St., Pico-Union, 213.738.9197. B, L & D daily to 4 a.m. Mexican. Beer & wine. Cash only. $ WHY** Juicy carne asada burritos, tacos al pastor, famously fiery salsa roja, a divey bull-fighting decor, and a 4 a.m. closing time. **WHAT** Some complain about the long lines and the fact that they charge 40 cents for the salsas, but this is just petulant whining. El Taurino is a gift to Angelenos, and not just because of its late-night hours and parking. The meats (carne asada, barbacoa, al pastor, carnitas, lengua) are all excellent and the salsas addictive (get the verde instead of the roja if your mouth isn't coated in flame retardant). **WHO** USC students, Koreatown residents and, late at night, the post-party crowd. ☺ 🍴

[El Tepeyac] **812 N. Evergreen Ave., Boyle Heights, 323.267.8668. B, L & D Mon.- Sat. Mexican. BYOB. MC, V. $ WHY** Machaca burrito, guacamole and taquitos, all in massive portions. **WHAT** This venerable L.A. dive is famed for its monstrous burritos, especially the Hollenbeck, which we find dull. Try the machaca instead, and plan to share it with another hungry soul. You can bring your own beer or sip a good horchata. **WHO** Almost always a line of college students, working men and families from the Valley having an adventure. 🗺 ☼

[Elf] **2135 Sunset Blvd., Echo Park, 213.484.6829, elfcafe.com. D Wed.-Sun. Vegetarian. BYOB ($5 corkage). Cash only. $$ - $$$ WHY** Homey vegetarian fare (mac 'n cheese, vegetable tarts, tagines) served out of a tiny, charming Sunset Boulevard storefront. **WHAT** The owners of this candlelit chocolate box of a café are folk musicians who turn out organic fare with a retro feel from a minuscule kitchen. Mediterranean-inspired vegan and vegetarian dishes (roasted tomato-feta tarts, kale salad, delicious chickpea crêpes with chèvre butter) taste like earnest home cooking. With friendly service, Elf captures the groovy vibe of the new Echo Park. **WHO** Bearded musicians, hot yoga babes, pierced parents pushing designer strollers. 🗺 ♻ 🍷 ☺

[Empress Pavilion] **988 N. Hill St., Chinatown, 213.617.9898, empresspavilion.com. L & D daily. Chinese/dim sum. Full bar. AE, $$** **WHY** The best dim sum in Chinatown, and good Hong Kong–style seafood for dinner, too. **WHAT** Chinatown's most elegant restaurant, Empress Pavilion is packed for weekend dim sum; we prefer coming during the week. It's lesser known for dinner, but the more than respectable cooking (steamed Dungeness crab with flat noodles in garlic sauce) and professional service make it a good place to know about, especially for groups. **WHO** Businesspeople, large family groups and, on weekends, friends from around L.A. meeting for dim sum. ☺ 🏛

[Forage] 🏛 **3823 W. Sunset Blvd., Silver Lake, 323.663.6885, foragela. com. L & D Tues.-Sat. American. No booze. AE, MC, V. $ - $$ WHY** All things good and local are found at this modestly sized temple to tempting baked goods, bursting-with-flavor vegetables and ever-changing menus. **WHAT** The quintessential Silver Lake café turns out some of the area's best home-style,locally sourced cooking, from the pork belly sandwich to superb daily quiches, many involving produce from nearby backyard farmers. At dinner, the selection changes nightly, with highlights such as braised brisket lasagne and slow-roasted pork loin stuffed with chorizo. Every day, diners can count on Jidori roast chicken, bright-tasting seasonal salads (don't miss the beets with citrus) and a well-curated array of tarts, crumbles and cookies. Despite tight seating and no alcohol, Forage is one of the neighborhood's hottest cafés. **WHO** Vegetarians and omnivores — scruffily fashionable Silver Lakers of all ages. ♻ 🍷 ☺

[Gingergrass] **2396 Glendale Blvd., Silver Lake, 323.644.1600, gingergrass.com. L & D daily. Vietnamese. Beer & wine. AE, MC, V.**

$ - $$ WHY Vast bowls of delicate noodles crowned with flowering basil tops and mint; char-grilled meats arranged over hillocks of raw greens; shrimp rolled around sugarcane sticks; sweet-tart jackfruit salad with pickled lotus roots; and more such crowd-pleasing dishes. **WHAT** Vietnamese cafés are hip and happening—the light, intensely colorful, vividly flavorful food perfectly suits the L.A. aesthetic, and with nearly a half million Vietnamese-Americans living in California, there's no shortage of skilled chefs. Gingergrass is a perfect example of the trend, an always-jammed spot fragrant with the aromas of mint, basil, grilled meat and pickled vegetables. It's great fun with a group, though you'll have to shout to be heard at the other end of the table. **WHO** A Silver Lake–eclectic mix of families and friends packed tightly into the high-ceilinged, glass-walled, noisy space. 📷🦪☺

[Gobi Mongolian BBQ House] **2827 W. Sunset Blvd., Silver Lake, 213.989.0711, gobimongolianbbq.com. L & D daily. Mongolian. Beer & wine. AE, MC, V. $ - $$ WHY** Design-it-yourself one-bowl meals that are a couple of notches above the norm at most low-budget Mongolian barbecue joints. **WHAT** This style of cooking is neither Mongolian nor barbecue—it's really a melding of Japanese teppanyaki cooking and Taiwanese flavors. Many of us Angelenos of a certain age remember the late great Col. Lee's, where hungry twentysomethings in the '80s could stuff themselves silly for a few bucks. Gobi is the hip new version of that, moved a couple of miles east on Sunset. You pay a flat price to load up your bowl from the buffet—meats (often organically raised), vegetables (some from the farmers' markets), sauces and seasonings (oyster and chile sauces, Asian pesto, lemongrass, garlic oil) and cooked noodles. Grill cooks sauté it up and add a basket of soft sesame bread. Part of the fun is watching big hungry boys heap their bowls to precarious heights before handing them to the cooks. **WHO** Hungry young men, families and middle-aged people reliving the Mongo BBQ feeds of their youth. 📷🦪☺

[Golden City Seafood] **960 N. Hill St., Chinatown, 213.253.2660. L & D daily. Chinese. Beer & wine. AE, MC, V. $ - $$ WHY** To discover that Chinatown's food isn't always lame. **WHAT** Before its expansion, this busy Cantonese café was the central-city grail for won ton lovers. Now, without the wedding-hall ambience often found at similar San Gabriel spots, a lengthy menu offers well-wrought classics: minced squab in lettuce cups, clams or scallops with black bean sauce, lobsters and meaty mushrooms with chicken cooked in a rice-filled stone pot. **WHO** Lunching City Hall employees and noodle soup devotees who crave a warm won ton potage with duck meat or seafood. ☺

[Good Girl Dinette] **110 N. Ave. 56, Highland Park, 323.257.8980, goodgirlfoods.com. L Fri.-Sun., D Tues.-Sun. Vietnamese/American. BYOB. Cash only. $ WHY** Vietnamese-American comfort food in a stylishly barren Highland Park café. **WHAT** Why a place calls itself a dinette and chooses not to serve lunch during the week is beyond us, especially because the Grandma's Pho, pork baguette sandwich, spicy fries and delicious curry chicken pot pie are great lunch dishes. Oh well, we're happy to come for dinner, especially because we can bring our own wine. **WHO** Tatted new-era Highland Parkers. 🖼️🕯️☺

[Hawaiian Chicken] **686 N. Spring St., Chinatown, 213.626.1678, hawaiianchicken.com. L & D Mon.-Wed. & Fri.-Sat. Hawaiian. Beer & wine. MC, V. $ WHY** Sensational grilled chicken for those who can't wait for farmers' market day to roll around. **WHAT** This family-run restaurant expands on the Hawaiian *huli huli* (literally, "turn turn") concept that's made its rotisserie chicken a hit on the farmers' market circuit. The birds roast over mesquite-like *kiawe* charcoal, and in this Chinatown location, you can get such fusion dishes as grilled chicken in guava-chile sauce. Call ahead for takeout if you don't want to wait. 🖼️☺

[Izakaya Haru Ulala] **368 E. 2nd St., Little Tokyo/Arts District, 213.620.0977. D nightly (to 2 a.m. Fri.-Sat.). Japanese. Beer, wine & sake. AE, MC, V. $$ WHY** Tasty dishes to accompany sake or beer: noodles, yellowtail with daikon, slow-cooked Kurobuta pork belly, shiitake tempura and robata-yaki, served until midnight during the week and 2 a.m. on weekends. **WHAT** Whimsical menus written in crayon set the tone at this casual space dominated by a U-shaped counter around the open robata-style kitchen, where several chefs work grilling yakitori, steaming vegetables, stuffing eggplant and bell peppers and charring bananas for dessert. **WHO** A business and jury-duty crowd at lunch and, in the wee hours, clubgoers looking to refuel. ☺

[JR Bistro] **750 N. Hill St., Chinatown, 213.620.0838. L & D daily. Chinese. Beer & wine. MC, V. $ WHY** Chinatown restaurants can seem all too similar, but JR stands out for hot pots, lobster specials and well-prepared standards. **WHAT** The same owners' JR Restaurant was one of the westside's top Chinese restaurants, and faithful customers will find many of the same favorites at this slightly slicker updated spot with white tablecloths, beer and wine and flat-screen TVs playing Chinese movies. Sweet and addictive orange-peel beef, spicy-salt calamari and XO string beans are all satisfying choices. Lunch combos are a bargain and popular with Downtown workers. 🖼️☺☼🏮

[Kagaya] 🍴 **418 E. 2nd St., Little Tokyo/Arts District, 213.617.1016. D Tues.- Sun. Japanese. Beer & wine. MC, V. $$$$ - $$$$$ WHY** Real shabu-shabu made with exceptional ingredients, notably the Wagyu beef. Best of all: When you finish cooking and eating your meat, seafood and veggies, they take the pot back to the kitchen and turn the now-rich broth into a heavenly thick soup with rice or udon. **WHAT** It's a modest-looking place, and shabu-shabu (meat, seafood and vegetables cooked at the table in bubbling broth) is typically pretty ordinary stuff here in the U.S. But Kagaya has brought it up a few notches, thanks to exceptional meats (including Kobe and Wagyu beef) and the elegant touches the Japanese do so well, like the lovely appetizers and the chrysanthemum leaves in the mounds of seasonal greens to cook in the pot. You pay dearly for this — $43 to $128 per person for a fixed-price meal — but it's worth a splurge, especially if you get the good beef. **WHO** Expense-account adventurers and beef lovers. 🍸

[La Parrilla] 3129 W. Sunset Blvd., Silver Lake, 323.661.8055; 1300 Wilshire Blvd., Westlake, 213.353.4930; laparrillarestaurant.com. B, L & D daily. Mexican. Full bar. AE, MC, V. $ - $$ **WHY** Smoky, aromatic *parrilladas*, where you grill meat (Cornish hens, steak, pork chops) on tabletop grills. **WHAT** Going back 30 years and now boasting four lo-cations, La Parrilla is known for its *parrilladas* (grills) and brochetas, but the rest of the food is good, too. Try the *pollito en pipian* (young chicken with pumpkin seeds). Good happy hour, and the Wilshire lo-cation has a patio that would be right at home in Ensenada. 🍸☺☼🏛

[La Serenata de Garibaldi] 🏛 1842 E. 1st St., Boyle Heights, 323.265.2887, laserenataonline.com. L & D daily, brunch Sat.-Sun. Mexican/seafood. Beer, wine & agave margaritas. AE, MC, V. $$ - $$$ **WHY** Beautiful Mexican seafood in a landmark Boyle Heights setting, with kind service. Try the shrimp gorditas for lunch and a fresh-fish special for dinner. **WHAT** An L.A. treasure, La Serenata serves care-fully prepared, sometimes elegant Mexican seafood dishes to a loving and longtime clientele. It now has two branches on the westside, and they're fine, but this is the holy ground. Seafood is the focus, but veg-etarians are tended to, as are people who insist on having beef tacos. Take the Gold Line — a Metro stop is across the street! **WHO** Politi-cians, depressed *L.A. Times* staffers, leaders in the Latino community and really smart tourists. 🍸☺🥂☺

[La Taquiza] 3009 S. Figueroa St., USC, 213.741.9795. B, L & D daily. Mexican. No booze. AE, MC, V. $ **WHY** The mulita, a sort of taco-quesa-dilla hybrid made with two fresh corn tortillas encasing meat, cheese, guacamole and salsa — the L.A. sandwich of your dreams. **WHAT** Tor-tillas are made fresh here all day, and the al pastor is slow-roasted on a vertical spit... clearly this is more than your typical strip-mall Mexican dive. Everyone gets the mulita, but the tacos, burritos and combina-tion plates are also terrific, as are the horchatas. **WHO** A wonderful multiethnic and cross-class mix of Angelenos, including lots of USC students and staff. 🍸☺

[Lamill] 1636 Silver Lake Blvd., Silver Lake, 323.663.4441, lamillcoffee.com. B, L & D daily. Modern American. No booze. AE, MC, V. $$ - $$$ **WHY** The food is conceived by Providence chef Michael Cimarusti, with imaginative desserts by Providence pastry chef Adrian Vasquez. Eggs with crab, an Asian BLT made with pork belly, and a deconstructed sweet potato pie are standouts. **WHAT** This elegant, high-design coffeehouse and restaurant features deluxe coffee preparations as well as breakfast, lunch and dinner. This is surely the most ambitious coffeehouse food in town, annoyingly pretentious to some and welcomed by others. ☼

[Larkin's] 1496 Colorado Blvd., Eagle Rock, 323.254.0934, larkinsjoint. com. L & D Wed.-Sun., brunch Sat.-Sun. Soul food/Southern. Beer & wine. MC, V. $$ **WHY** Skillet-fried chicken and other Southern comfort dishes served in an atmospheric old home. **WHAT** Everyone loves the charm of the restored Craftsman house, but opinion is divided on Larkin Mackey's Southern cooking. Portions are small by soul-food standards, waits for tables can be painful (no reservations), and service is typically lax. But the chicken is skillet-fried the right way, and the banana pudding is comfort in a crock. Worth checking out for eastsiders. **WHO** Tastefully tattooed parents with gorgeous multiethnic toddlers, and other modern-era Eagle Rockers. ☺ ☼

[Mae Ploy] 2606 W. Sunset Blvd., Echo Park, 213.353.9635. L & D daily. Thai. Beer & wine. AE, MC, V. $ **WHY** All the Thai stalwarts (try the chicken with mint leaves) are well prepared, as are the special dishes, like crab noodles and eggplant salad. **WHAT** Straddling the Silver Lake/Echo Park dividing line, this long-established eatery delivers tasty home-style Thai food throughout the area. You can also eat this delicious food in-house and accompany your meal with Thai beer served in a frosty mug. 🖩🔖☺🚗

[Mas Malo] 515 W. 7th St., Downtown, 213.985.4332, masmalorestaurant.com. L Mon.-Fri., D nightly, brunch Sat.-Sun. Mexican. Full bar. AE, MC, V. $$ - $$$ **WHY** A multi-purpose, festive Mexican spot with killer tequila selections in Downtown's cocktail gulch. **WHAT** Silver Lake favorite Malo has spawned a bigger Downtown sister location in a cavernous historic jewelry store. Hide out in the '70s flashback basement lounge, or sip rare tequila in the tiny vault tasting room tucked away in back. Weekend brunch, lunch and dinner are served in the large, cacaphonous main dining room, including Malo's signature ground beef and pickle tacos, seafood, great Mexican brunch dishes, and a perfectly balanced organic margarita. **WHO** Downtown bar crawlers, office workers, tequila aficionados and, thanks to a great kids' menu, some families. ☺

[Mo-Chica Peruvian] 🏠 Mercado la Paloma, 3655 S. Grand Ave., USC, 213.747.2141, mo-chica.com. L & D Mon.-Sat. Peruvian. No booze. MC, V. $ **WHY** What may be the best ceviches in town. **WHAT** Mercado la Paloma may technically be a food court, but this is no Westfield mall. For one thing, the place is a nonprofit, designed to help small local entrepreneurs. For another, it's home to this Peruvian café, where former sushi chef Ricardo Zarate turns out scallop ceviche with sweet potato, toasted corn and seaweed; lamb shank with white canary beans and cilantro sauce; and a refined *lomo saltado* (a stir-fry of beef and vegetables with fried potatoes) that's almost French in execution and flavor. He's busy at his new westside restaurant, Picca, but he's still making sure the food rocks here. **WHO** Pilgrims eager to explore Peruvian food in greater depth. 🖼️☺🚗

[Mohawk Bend] 🏛️ 2141 W. Sunset Blvd., Echo Park, 213.260.0265, mohawk.la. D nightly (lunch coming). American/vegan. Full bar. AE, MC, V. $ - $$$ **WHY** In a vintage, 10,000-square-foot theater space, Mohawk Bend boasts an enviable selection of craft beers and one of the nicer patios in this part of town. **WHAT** A slew of vegan and vegetarian dishes—like polenta with leeks and broccoli, fire-roasted artichokes and pizzas made with seitan and faux mozzarella—are seamlessly integrated into a wide-ranging menu that includes bison meatballs, Carlsbad mussels and the famous "dork" burger: duck + pork, served on a house-made English muffin. Get the matchstick fries while they're hot—they're delicious. **WHO** Beer freaks, vegans, burger lovers, hungry neighborhood residents and, naturally, hipsters. ☺ 🌀🐚🌼

[Moles la Tia] 🏛️ 4619 E. Cesar Chavez Ave., East L.A., 323.263.7842, moleslatia.com. B, L & D daily. Mexican. No booze. AE, MC, V. $ - $$$ **WHY** There's more than the usual Mexican bill of fare here—this spot elevates sauces to the main attraction. **WHAT** Red, green and black moles are just the beginning of the rainbow of dishes here. Neither divey nor fancy, it's the perfect informal place for a party or group dinner, the better to experience dozens of flavors of moles, including coffee, hibiscus and tequila. Mole sauces are paired with chicken, quail, pork and fish, while the non-mole fare (including a good cochinita pibil) is just as carefully prepared. Homemade tortillas and several flavors of flans round out the menu. **WHO** Culinary explorers ready to explore Boyle Heights. 🖼️☺

[Moreton Fig] USC, Ronald Tutor Campus Center, 3607 Trousdale Pkwy., USC, 213.821.3441, moretonfig.com. L & D Mon.-Fri. (closed summers). American/Californian. Full bar. AE, MC, V. $ - $$$ **WHY** For a "real" restaurant with good modern American cooking and a worthy happy hour, smack in the middle of the USC campus. **WHAT** For proof that college campuses are now luxury resorts, check out this sleek place in the lavish new student center at USC. With a cozy bar, a chic dining room, a huge patio around the eponymous tree, and the modern American classics of star chef Bradley Ogden, Moreton Fig is surprisingly reasonably priced for the quality of food and drink. Try the burger, the seasonal salads, the pan-seared fish of the day on a bed of baby lentils, and the butterscotch pudding, and enjoy the campus people-watching. **WHO** Professors, administrators and a surprising number of students, given the posh setting—but this is USC. 💙🐚🌼

[Noé Restaurant & Bar] Omni Los Angeles Hotel, 251 S. Olive St., Downtown, 213.356.4100, noerestaurant.com. D nightly. Modern American. Full bar. AE, MC, V. $$$$ - $$$$$ **WHY** Excellent cocktails, a superb happy hour, a big-city vibe—and they know how to get you out in time for the curtain. **WHAT** Noé's sophisticated menu has won the hearts of many Downtowners. The food is delicious and elegantly served, running to such things as smoked pancetta tart with quail egg, yellowfin sashimi salad, bouillabaisse and Kurobuta pork chops with seasonal trimmings. The adjacent lounge opens to a patio with firepits and city views. Noé is a great meeting spot before performances at Disney Hall and the Music Center. 🍴🏛

[Original Pantry Café] 877 S. Figueroa St., South Park/Fashion District, 213.972.9279, pantrycafe.com. Daily 24 hours. American. No booze. Cash only. $ - $$ **WHY** For the wait staff, the history and the breakfasts, served 24/7. **WHAT** Do we love the Pantry? Yes. Is the food really good? No. Well, former mayor Dick Riordan loved it so much he bought the place, but he likes plain, filling chow, and that's what the Pantry has delivered, 24 hours a day, since 1924. During prime times the line can last for 30 or 45 minutes; we prefer to visit in the quieter wee hours for steak and eggs or pancakes. Every Angeleno has to eat here at least once in his or her life. **WHO** USC students, tourists, Downtown workers and connoisseurs of the American diner. 🍴☺

[Otomisan] 2506 E. 1st St., Boyle Heights, 323.526.1150. L & D Mon.-Sat. Japanese. Beer & wine. MC, V. $ **WHY** When you're in Boyle Heights but *don't* want Mexican food. **WHAT** You'll feel like you're walking into the film *L.A. Confidential* when you pull open the screen door to this diner, which has just five stools and three leatherette booths. It's a vestige of when Boyle Heights was a hub of Japanese immigrants, before World War II, but it's not just a relic—the sweet couple that own it do a fine job. She handles service, and he handles both the cooking (made-from-scratch miso, good old-school sukiyaki, cold udon, classic teriyaki) and the dishwashing. It's a mom 'n pop in the best possible sense. **WHO** A few elderly Japanese-Americans who've lived in the neighborhood for 50 years and their Mexican-American neighbors. 🍴

[Pacific Dining Car] 🏛 1310 W. 6th St., Westlake, 213.483.6000, pacificdiningcar.com. B, L & D 24 hours daily. American/steakhouse. Full bar. AE, MC, V. $$$$ - $$$$$ **WHY** For delicious, expensive steaks, satisfying, expensive breakfasts, 1920s elegance and food served 24 hours a day. Great for serious business meetings and gleeful middle-of-the-night splurges. **WHAT** Dating to 1921, this added-upon former railroad dining car on the fringes of downtown is as beloved as Musso & Frank and even more—but the food's a lot better. Steaks are the specialty, and they're terrific if someone else is buying; stick with breakfast if you're buying. Note that the room temp is akin to a meat locker, so dress warmly. The Santa Monica branch is less noteworthy. Wednesday is free-corkage night. **WHO** L.A.'s power brokers, writers trying to channel the ghost of Raymond Chandler (who ate here), the rich and elderly and, at 3 a.m., the young, drunk and bleary. ☺ ♥ 🍸

[The Park] 1400 Sunset Blvd., Echo Park, 213.482.9209, thepark1400sunset.com. L Tues.-Fri., D Tues.-Sun., brunch Sat.-Sun. Modern American. Beer & wine. AE, MC, V. $ - $$ **WHY** Jidori chicken, cornmeal pancakes with grilled shrimp and chipotle cream, Mexican Coke and bargain wines. **WHAT** One of the leaders of the Echo Park boom (it's not evil gentrification, it's a *renaissance*!), the Park is stylish in a barren, homespun way, with empty frames on stark walls and a simple patio that's the place to be for weekend brunch. Young chef/owner Joshua Siegel serves eminently affordable modern home cooking — composed salads, artful burgers, pot pies, roast chicken — that is just the thing for this era of modest consumption. **WHO** Carefully scruffy young families and silver-haired Silver Lake adventurers. 🍽☺

[Patina] Walt Disney Concert Hall, 141 S. Grand Ave., Downtown, 213.972.3331, patinarestaurant.com. D Tues.-Sun. Modern American. Full bar. AE, MC, V. $$$$ - $$$$$ **WHY** For fine dining in the French Laundry style, but in the dazzling Walt Disney Concert Hall instead of the Napa Valley. **WHAT** Seafood is a focus at this elegant Joachim Splichal flagship restaurant, with dishes like diver scallops carpaccio with kumquat liquid sphere and black truffle, or a Mediterranean loup de mer with spring minestrone and pesto crouton. Those headed for a concert typically have a two-course meal; destination diners celebrating for an occasion are wise to choose the often-extraordinary seven- or eleven-course tasting menus — assuming, of course, that their net worth is sufficient to allow for the investment. **WHO** Concert-goers, high-end business-lunchers and anniversary celebrants. ♥ 🍸 🏛

[Pete's Café & Bar] 400 S. Main St., Downtown, 213.617.1000, petescafe.com. L & D daily. American. Full bar. AE, MC, V. $$ - $$$ **WHY** Well-prepared modern American comfort food — mac 'n cheese, Caesar salad, flat-iron steak with blue-cheese fries — at fair prices in a swell old building. **WHAT** High ceilings, old tile floors and burnished wooden tables give Pete's a look usually more associated with San Francisco or New York. This is a fine place for a weekend lunch after a MOCA visit or gallery crawl; it's also a comforting haven for a drink and a Hellman burger after a long day of lawyering. Check out jazz night on Tuesdays. **WHO** Businesspeople, artists, families — a rumpled-stylish Downtown mix. ☺ ☺

[R23] 🏛 923 E. 2nd St., Downtown, 213.687.7178, r23.com. L Mon.-Fri., D nightly. Japanese/sushi. Beer & wine. AE, MC, V. $$ - $$$$ **WHY** Dungeness crab salad, grilled yellowtail collar, simple and ultra-fresh sushi and rolls. **WHAT** Find your way to this all-but-hidden space off a gritty loading dock in the warehouse district east of downtown, and you'll be transported into an almost cinematically perfect loft/gallery scene (huge paintings, exposed brick walls, Frank Gehry–designed cardboard chairs) with impressively fresh sushi and well-prepared grilled dishes. Service can be slow but is always thoughtful and friendly. **WHO** Media and business types mingle with loft-dwellers, artists and musicians. (That *was* Leonard Cohen at the next table, right?)

[Rambutan Thai] 2835 W. Sunset Blvd., Silver Lake, 213.273.8424, rambutanthai.com. L & D daily. Thai. Beer & wine. AE, MC, V. $$
WHY Delicious Thai tapas—such small plates as Thai rolls, crab rolls, larb and fried shrimp cakes—along with good sakes and Asian beers.
WHAT A grim mini-mall is home to this sleek and stylish Thai boîte, whose adjacent nightclub is a weekend scene. Avoid the too-sweet mee krob, but try all the rest of the small plates; the happiest people come with a group, so they can try more delectable little dishes. Come for lunch or early dinner if you want to talk to your companions.
WHO Silver Lake sophisticates—quiet by day, lively by night. ☺ 🥡�

[Reservoir] 1700 Silver Lake Blvd., Silver Lake, 323.662.8655, silverlakereservoir.com. D Tues.-Sun., brunch Sun. Modern American. Beer & wine. AE, MC, V. $$$ **WHY** Open-face lasagne with pork, roasted tomatoes and braised artichoke. **WHAT** The site of the former Netty's is now a clean-lined, almost Craftsmanish bistro with elbow-to-elbow tables but not too much noise. Owner/chef Gloria Felix's menu is a little odd—the core is simple grilled salmon, steak or tofu that you pair with your choice of "setups," a structure more suited to a country-club restaurant than a Silver Lake spot. Pass on those in favor of the better salads, pastas and burger. Reservoir hasn't yet lived up to its potential, but we're hopeful that it's moving in the right direction.
WHO Handsome Silver Lakers who might still be pining (just a little bit) for Netty's. ♥ ☼

[Rivera] 1050 S. Flower St. , South Park/Fashion District, 213.749.1460, riverarestaurant.com. L Mon.-Fri., D nightly (to 1 a.m. Thurs.-Sat.). Latino/modern American. Full bar. AE, MC, V. $$$ - $$$$ **WHY** For the inventive (if pricey) cocktails, the suave Staples-convenient setting and some pretty wonderful flavors. **WHAT** We're mixed about this swank South Park spot, where '80s wünderchef John Sedlar has resurfaced—on the one hand, it's a sophisticated space with a good bar and some very good cooking. On the other hand, the portions are wee, and there's a pretentiousness to Sedlar's style, most visually evident in his spice stencils. If you come, try the ahi ceviche, the Basque lamb chops, the Kurobuta pork chop in mole, and the Donjai (basically a pomegranate margarita); feel free to skip the desserts. **WHO** Expense-account studs on a tequila-tasting adventure. ☺

🥡 **VEGETARIAN** ☺ **KID FRIENDLY** ☼ **PATIO DINING** 🚐 **DELIVERY** 🎪 **PRIVATE PARTY**

[The Spice Table] 114 S. Central Ave., Little Tokyo/Arts District, 213.620.1840, thespicetable.com. L & D Mon.-Sat. Vietnamese. Beer & wine. AE, MC, V. $ - $$ **WHY** The perfect place for a Downtown dinner date, where modern Vietnamese food meets seldom-seen Singaporean specialties in the middle of Little Tokyo. **WHAT** A vintage brick building has been transformed into two rooms of rustic style, with filament bulbs in Vietnamese birdcages in the dining room and a buzzing bar scene up front. The menu melds small plates like pâté and terrific fried cauliflower with street food like banh mi and noodle dishes. You'll also find such homey main courses as chicken curry and oxtail stew perfumed with Asian spices. There's house-made soft-serve ice cream for dessert, and a well-edited beer and wine list. **WHO** Savvy Downtown dwellers and citywide visitors. 🗺️

[Suehiro Café] 337 E. 1st St., Little Tokyo/Arts District, 213.626.9132. L & D daily to 1 a.m. (to 3 a.m. Fri.-Sun.). Japanese. Beer & wine. MC, V. $ - $$ **WHY** For good, inexpensive Japanese comfort food, especially udon, served late into the night. **WHAT** A Little Tokyo icon, Suehiro is a simple, affordable café that serves satisfying udon noodle soups, cold soba noodle dishes, bento-box meals and katsudon bowls. Extras include friendly service and a library of Japanese fashion magazines and manga. **WHO** City Hall and *L.A. Times* people at lunch, MOCA visitors on weekends and, late at night, bar scene folks. ☺ 🗺️☺

[Sushi Go 55] 333 S. Alameda St., Ste. 317, Little Tokyo/Arts District, 213.687.0777, sushigo55.com. L & D daily. Japanese/sushi. Beer, wine & sake. AE, MC, V. $$$ **WHY** High-quality sushi that's a bargain at lunch—the $11.50 special gets you miso soup, five pieces of sushi and a blue-crab hand roll; many regulars opt for the chirashi sushi box for $17. **WHAT** Owned by a pioneering family who started the second sushi bar in the U.S. and has been running restaurants in Little Tokyo for six decades, Sushi Go 55 is profoundly traditional—this is not a rock 'n roll sushi joint. Chefs are focused and quiet, and the emphasis is on very fresh, very good food. Reasonable prices, by sushi standards. **WHO** A primarily Asian crowd at lunchtime and a more diverse Downtown mix at night. 🗺️

[Teresita's] 🏛️ 3826 E. 1st St., East L.A., 323.266.6045, teresitasrestaurant.com. B Sat.-Sun., L Tues.-Sun., D Tues.-Sat. Mexican. Beer & wine. MC, V. $ - $$ **WHY** Wonderful, traditional Mexican cooking: goat stew on weekends and always-good daily specials, like albondigas on Monday, pork ribs in chile negro sauce on Wednesdays and pozole on Fridays. **WHAT** This East L.A. landmark family restaurant serves simple home cooking. Weekend breakfasts are worth rolling out of bed for. **WHO** Politicians and police officers. 🗺️☺

[Tiara Café] 127 E. 9th St., South Park/Fashion District, 213.623.3663, tiara-cafe-la.com. L Mon.- Fri. Modern American. Beer & wine. AE, MC, V.

$ - $$$ WHY Panache, casual glamour and Downtown's best pizza. **WHAT** Owner/chef Fred Eric (Fred 62) has always known what a certain sort of stylish Angeleno wants to eat, and he's hit the nail on the head here: fab pizzas, lovely salads and great vegan dishes, all as organic, healthful and sustainably produced as possible. The setting suits the Fashion District: massive columns, pink walls studded with huge fake jewels, and a gregarious and campy staff. **WHO** A lunchtime mob of fashion industry folks. 📷🚲🍸

[Traxx] **Union Station, 800 N. Alameda St., Downtown, 213.625.1999, traxxrestaurant.com. L Mon.-Fri., D Mon.-Sat. Modern American. Full bar. AE, MC, V. $$$ WHY** To eat a good meal in the splendor of L.A.'s Union Station. **WHAT** Chef/owner Tara Thomas serves a concise, appealing menu of modern American dishes (with Asian and Latino influences) in a great-looking streamline moderne dining room or out on the "patio" under the painted beams of Union Station. The separate bar is one of L.A.'s best-kept bar secrets—atmospheric and generally uncrowded. **WHO** Business lunchers, upscale train travelers and couples enjoying the romance of Union Station. ♥ 🍸 ☼

[Viet Noodle Bar] **3133 1/2 Glendale Blvd., Atwater, 323.906.1575. L & D daily. Vietnamese. BYOB. Cash only. $ WHY** A hip scene with respectable noodles and a fun communal table for solo diners. **WHAT** This minimalist modern setting offers communal tables (for groups and singles) and a shelf of intellectual tomes to peruse while eating. The menu's also minimalist, with vegetarian and fish noodle dishes hailing from southern Vietnam, Vietnamese coffee and restorative pennywort juice. **WHO** The coolest of the cool kids. 🍸

[Wat Dong Moon Lek] **4356 Fountain Ave., 323.666.5993, watdongmoonlek.com. L & D daily. Thai. No booze. Cash only. $ WHY** For a taste of au courant Thai cooking followed by fine-dining-caliber desserts. **WHAT** A stylish storefront noodleteria where noodles are just a start. The *kàp klâem*—bar-snack-like small plates—reflect the urban Thai culinary trends inspired by owner Billy Jalanugraha's visits to his native Bangkok. Don't miss the house version of *larb tod:* the fried ground chicken and herbs are a vivid intertwining of sweet, salty, tart and a zing of heat. Desserts created by Jalanugraha's wife, Somjai, who trained as a pastry chef, are the bomb. **WHO** Hedonists, Thai and otherwise. 📷🍸

[Water Grill] 🏛 **544 S. Grand Ave., Downtown, 213.891.0900, watergrill.com. L Mon.-Fri., D nightly. Seafood/Modern American. Full bar. AE, MC, V. $$$$ - $$$$$ WHY** For A-list service, a beautiful setting and elegant, thoughtfully prepared seafood. Splurge on the chilled seafood platter if you can afford it. **WHAT** Although the Water Grill's cooking no longer has foodies in New York buzzing, it's still very, very good. Chef David LeFevre makes things like striped bass ceviche

🍸 VEGETARIAN ⊙ KID FRIENDLY ☼ PATIO DINING 🚲 DELIVERY 🏛 PRIVATE PARTY

with mint, pineapple, candied black beans, butternut squash and achiote oil, or the slightly less complicated seared wild big-eye tuna with beluga lentils and pear-celery root purée. His talent with flavors, along with the high-quality ingredients, swank interior and excellent service, make the prices less painful than they otherwise might be. **WHO** Downtown's movers and shakers, wearing good suits and carrying well-fed Platinum cards. ♥ 🔊 🏛

[Wood Spoon] 107 W. 9th St., South Park/Fashion District, 213.629.1765, woodspoonla.com. L & D Tues.-Sat. Brazilian. BYOB. MC, V. $ - $$ **WHY** For a short, delicious menu of Brazilian dishes, including a fabulous (and massive) chicken pot pie made with hearts of palm, corn, roasted potatoes and olives. **WHAT** The bright, minimalist space in the heart of the Fashion District is warmed with yellow flowers, the rich flavors of Brazil and the presence of the owner/chef, an engaging woman who makes a mean pot pie, an addictive pork burger and great sweet potato fries. **WHO** Fashion-industry workers at lunch, loft-dwellers at dinner. 🕵🍴

[WP24] 🏛 Rtiz-Carlton Hotel, 900 W. Olympic Blvd., South Park/Fashion District, 213.743.8824, wolfgangpuck.com. D nightly. Asian. Full bar. AE, MC, V. $$$$$ **WHY** It's a special occasion. Or your boss is paying. Or you're coming before 7 p.m. for the light $24 three-course meal, great for pre-theater. **WHAT** Glide through the Ritz-Carlton lobby, ascend 24 floors heavenward, make your way through the hubbub of the lounge and prepare to enjoy some of the best food ever served in a "view restaurant." Wolfgang Puck has long had a knack for Asian fare (witness the nearly three-decades-old Chinois on Main) and at his eyrie overlooking the city, the sky's the limit—literally. Prix fixe menus start at $80 for three courses and go up to $170 for ten; you can order à la carte in the lounge. Don't miss the Sichuan lobster, which is almost as good as what you'll find in Monterey Park. Smart diners arrive before sunset to savor a well-made cocktail and watch the traffic creep along below, bathed in the roseate glow. **WHO** The moneyed. ♥ 🔊 🍴 🏛

[Xoia Vietnamese] 1801 W. Sunset Blvd., Echo Park, 213.413.3232, xoiaeats.com. L & D Tues.-Sun. Vietnamese. No booze. Cash only. $ **WHY** Echo Park mixes it up with a winning combo of reasonable prices and modern Vietnamese food that incorporates a nod to the neighborhood's Latin American roots. **WHAT** Tacos get a burst of rich flavor from pho-style beef, while dishes like Vietnamese crêpes, *mi quang* (a rice noodle dish with shrimp and pork) and banh mi sandwiches filled with pork, chicken, beef or tofu are classic Vietnamese. Steaming bowls of chicken, beef or vegetarian pho will warm a winter night. The owner's modern art decorates the sleek space, which also has a small sidewalk patio. Despite its modern style, Xoia has a real neighborhood feel. **WHO** Echo Park oldtimers, neighborhood activists, the new hipoisie. 🕵🍴☺☼

🏛 ESSENTIALLY L.A. ☺ LATE ♥ ROMANTIC 🕵 VALUE 🔊 QUIET ☼ SUSTAINABLE

[Yang Chow] 819 N. Broadway, Chinatown, 213.625.0811, yangchow.com. L & D daily. Chinese. Beer & wine. AE, MC, V. $ - $$ **WHY** It may be Chinese food designed for white people, but it's still seriously tasty, and for many people, addictive. **WHAT** Two simple rooms are permanently packed with regulars who have been coming here for 20 years and always order the same things: sweet-spicy slippery shrimp, hefty pan-fried dumplings, dried-fried string beans with pork, and cashew-rich cashew chicken. This is not diet food—it's the sort of place you take Grandpa for his birthday, and he has to loosen his belt buckle afterwards. **WHO** Always jammed with noisy tables of downtown businesspeople, Dodgers-bound friends and big family groups celebrating birthdays. Don't come without a reservation. ☺

[Yxta Cocina Mexicana] 601 S. Central Ave., Downtown, 213.596.5579, yxta.net. L Mon.-Fri., D Mon.-Sat. Mexican. Full bar. AE, MC, V. $$ - $$$ **WHY** For 40 years, Jesse Gomez's family has been turning out "careful-the-plate-is-hot" Mexican food at El Arco Iris, an old-school hub of Highland Park life. Now Gomez has created a new-school, loft-like place serving regional Mexican dishes, as well as twenty-some tequilas and what may well be the best margarita Downtown. **WHAT** This is not Jesse's father's Cal-Mex cooking—the reasonably priced menu is filled with things like squash blossoms with Oaxacan cheese, an artfully composed and delicious tostada with sashimi-grade ahi, and camarones with garlic and cilantro-lime rice. But it also has the comfort-food standards we Angelenos sometimes require to make it through another day: enchiladas suizas, carnitas (juicy and tender) and, of course, tacos. **WHO** Youngish after-work folks drinking margaritas and sharing tastes of the food.

SAN GABRIEL VALLEY

[888 Seafood] 8450 E. Valley Blvd., Rowland Heights, 626.573.1888. L & D daily. Chinese/dim sum. Full bar. AE, MC, V. $ - $$$ **WHY** High-quality Chiu Chow dim sum, and lots of it. Don't miss the taro and the exceptionally juicy sui mai. **WHAT** This vast and grand restaurant is famed for the incredible range of its dim sum—60 choices most weekdays and 80 on weekends—and its Chiu Chow expertise also extends to dishes like the whole perch poached in broth and a succulent braised goose. ☺🕍

[AKA An American Bistro] 41 Hugus Alley, Old Pasadena, 626.564.8111, akabistro.com. L daily, D Mon.-Sat. Modern American. Full bar. AE, MC, V. $$$ **WHY** The crispy portobello fries with truffle aioli. Did we mention the fries? **WHAT** Veteran Rose City restaurateur (Bistro 45) Robert Simon moved his St. Helena restaurant, AKA, to One Colorado in Old Town, and Pasadena is stoked to have a local boy making good in the midst of the chain eateries. The eclectic menu starts with batter-fried slices of portobello mushrooms and moves

🥬 **VEGETARIAN** ☺ **KID FRIENDLY** ☼ **PATIO DINING** �. **DELIVERY** 🕍 **PRIVATE PARTY**

to an array of temptations, from PEI mussels with chorizo to seared Scottish salmon, a tender Angus burger with house-cured bacon, a Snake River Kobe flat-iron steak and a terrific Prairie Fresh pork chop. There's one heckuva fry cook in the kitchen; in addition to the 'shroom fries, the buttermilk onion rings are killer. **WHO** Everyone who's anyone in Pasadena, and visiting shoppers. ♥ ☼ ⋔

[Arroyo Chop House] **536 S. Arroyo Pkwy., Pasadena, 626.577.7463, arroyochophouse.com. D nightly. American/steakhouse. Full bar. AE, MC, V. $$$$ - $$$$$ WHY** New York strip, spinach with caramelized sweet onions, well-mixed drinks, and, for those who save room, chocolate soufflé. **WHAT** The setting is retro-modern—rich mahogany, white linens, etched glass, Craftsman-influenced light fixtures—and the fare is reliable comfort food for the captains-of-industry set. Prime steak is a specialty, along with simple and carefully prepared sides (asparagus, garlic mashed potatoes). **WHO** Well-dressed, Jaguar-driving professionals. ♥ ⋒ ⋔

[Azeen's Afghani Restaurant] **110 E. Union St., Old Pasadena, 626.683.3310, azeensafghanirestaurant.com. L Mon.-Fri., D nightly. Afghani. Beer & wine. MC, V. $ - $$$ WHY** A fascinating cuisine; squint at the menu and you'll recognize derivatives (or ancestors) of such Indian, Pakistani, Persian and Chinese dishes as pakoras, curries, dumplings, kebabs and pilafs. **WHAT** An elegant, white-tablecloth restaurant with a restful, welcoming atmosphere, Azeen's is just a block from the Old Pas swarms. Share a sampler plate of appetizers followed by tender beef kebabs or *quabili pallaw* (lamb with carrots and raisins). Sweet, translucent butternut squash (*kadu*) is a delicious side. ⋒

[Babita Mexicuisine] ⌂ **1823 S. San Gabriel Blvd., San Gabriel, 626.288.7265. L Tues.-Fri., D Tues.-Sun. Mexican. Beer & wine. AE, MC, V. $$ - $$$ WHY** Great Oaxacan food from a serious and attentive chef. **WHAT** It looks like a dive from the outside, but inside it's inviting and charming—the perfect setting for owner/chef Roberto Berrelleza's outstanding regional Mexican cooking with an Oaxacan focus. The standouts include seriously good Yucatecan cochinita pibil, filet mignon with pimiento-mint sauce, and habañero-blazed camarones topolobampo. The food can be slow to appear, but that's because of Berrelleza's personal attention to each dish. The flan just might be the best anywhere. **WHO** Some people drive across town just for the chiles en nogada—a fall-only pork specialty. ⋒

[Bashan] **3459 N. Verdugo Rd., Montrose, 818.541.1532, bashanrestaurant.com. D Tues.-Sun. French/Modern American. Beer & wine. AE, MC, V. $$$$ WHY** Burrata and wild arugula salad, seared scallops with chorizo and fingerling potatoes, the midweek prix-fixe menu and the Sunday-night burger bargain. **WHAT** Chef Nadav Bashan (Providence, Michael's) and his wife, Romy, have created a welcom-

---

⌂ ESSENTIALLY L.A. ☼ LATE ♥ ROMANTIC ⋑ VALUE ⋒ QUIET ⋔ SUSTAINABLE

ing, modern eatery serving exceptionally refined cuisine that's at the level of the best restaurants in L.A.—yet it's far from the *Entourage* crowd, on a leafy street in a north Glendale suburb. It's not cheap, but you'd pay more for food this good in Santa Monica. **WHO** Food lovers who can't believe a place of this quality exists in Montrose.

[Basil Thai] **411 E. Huntington Dr., Monrovia, 626.447.8845. L Mon.-Fri., D nightly. Thai. Beer & wine. MC, V. $ - $$ WHY** A rare family-owned café in the heart of chainland, serving tasty and healthy Thai food. **WHAT** Not only is this stylish little strip-mall café a friendly family operation, but it's a great value—both the regular menu and the $6.95 lunch buffet. Chef Poki's cooking is several notches above the suburban strip-mall standard—vegetables are crisp and fresh, flavors are skillfully balanced, and chiles are used for flavor, not just to make your face sweat. Try the *tom yum* (spicy-sour) soup with shrimp, the stir-fried chicken with cashews and onion and the *yum pla muek* (a vibrant salad of fresh greens, grilled squid, lime and chile). 🍷🥢☺

[Beijing Pie House] **846 E. Garvey Ave., Monterey Park, 626.288.3818. L & D Tues.-Sun. Chinese. No booze. Cash only. $** **WHY** For golden-crusted north Chinese pastries, flaky flatbreads, meat pies, stuffed buns and dumplings. **WHAT** Probably the first *xian bing* (meat pie) place in SoCal, this tiny café makes irresistible versions, filled with beef, lamb or veggie mixtures—like leeks with egg or wild mushrooms. Don't miss the multi-layered homeland meat pie—filled with juicy seasoned beef, it's the size of a cookie sheet and makes an instant banquet for several hungry souls. **WHO** Mostly Chinese nationals, for whom these goodies are pure comfort food. 🍷☺

[Bistro 45] **45 S. Mentor Ave., Pasadena, 626.795.2478, bistro45.com. D Tues.-Sun. French/modern American. Full bar. AE, MC, V. $$$ - $$$$$** **WHY** Exemplary wine list; creative and confident cooking. **WHAT** This is certainly a contender for the title of Best Upscale Restaurant in the San Gabriel Valley. The patio's the place for lunch; for dinner, the suavely modern dining rooms beckon. Standouts include the superb bouillabaisse and the grilled beef tenderloin. There's usually a bread pudding on the dessert menu, and you should order it. **WHO** Pasadena's beautiful people. ♥ 🍷 ☼ 🏮

[Bistro de la Gare] **921 Meridian Ave., South Pasadena, 626.799.8828, bistrodelagare.com. L & D Wed.-Sun., brunch Sat.-Sun. French. Beer & wine. AE, MC, V. $$ - $$$ WHY** Great setting in a lively neighborhood, steps from the Gold Line station that inspired its name. **WHAT** This lovely red-walled space features a traditional French bistro menu and charm galore. Service can be slapdash and the kitchen uneven but the crowds of spirited locals packing the small bar and dining rooms don't seem to mind. **WHO** Well-dressed locals, farmer's market foodies and Francophiles. ☼

🥬 VEGETARIAN ☺ KID FRIENDLY ☼ PATIO DINING 🚚 DELIVERY 🏮 PRIVATE PARTY

[Briganti] 1423 Mission St., South Pasadena, 626.441.4663, brigantisouthpas.com. L Mon.-Fri., D nightly. Italian. Beer & wine. AE, MC, V. $$ - $$$ **WHY** Seafood salad, burrata with pesto and roasted tomatoes, ethereal thin-crust pizzas, classic pastas, excellent fresh-fish specials. **WHAT** Briganti is the sort of lively Tuscan trattoria that's common on the westside but rare on the eastside, and South Pasaden-ans can't get enough of it. The joint is always jumping, with noise bouncing off the brick walls of the enclosed patio (ask for a table in the main room if you want a quieter conversation). Be warned that the service can be slow and distracted. **WHO** An over-40 crowd from Pasadena, South Pas and San Marino, many of whom know each other from Junior League or Little League. ☼

[Café Spot] 500 W. Valley Blvd., Alhambra, 626.308.3233. L & D daily. Chinese/coffee shop. Beer & wine. MC, V. $ **WHY** A spirited scene, plus lots to choose from on the long menu. **WHAT** One of the San Gabriel Valley's many Hong Kong–style coffee shops, Café Spot stands out for the quality of its food. This is the place to go for dishes like Grand Mom's braised pork belly and the Hong Kong–style waffle. 🖫

[Carousel] 304 N. Brand Blvd., Glendale, 818.246.7775, carouselrestaurant.com. L & D Tues.-Sun. Lebanese/Middle Eastern. Full Bar. AE, MC, V. $$ - $$$ **WHY** Lebanese *mezzas* (small plates) galore, including creamy hummus, spicy muhammara, fattoush salad and frogs legs with lemon and garlic. Plus, it's just steps from the Alex Theatre. **WHAT** Delicious food, speedy service and an attractive décor make Carousel one of Brand Boulevard's most reliable and reward-ing dining options. Don't miss the *fatteh oberjhin* (toasted pita and eggplant appetizer) and the many versions of *kebbeh*, Lebanese steak tartare. For main courses, there are succulent grilled kebabs (lula is excellent) and schwarma. Late on Friday and Saturday evenings, the place jumps to live music and belly dancing with a prix-fixe dinner menu. **WHO** Local Lebanese families and a pre-theater crowd. ☺

[Celestino] 🏛 141 S. Lake Ave., Pasadena, 626.795.4006, calogerodrago.com. L Mon.-Fri., D Mon.-Sun. Italian. Full bar. AE, MC, V. $$ - $$$$ **WHY** The pastas are terrific. **WHAT** This is the San Gabriel Valley's most consistently excellent Italian restaurant, combining warm service, a serious wine list and downright delicious food. Don't miss the baby lettuces with roasted peppers, eggplant and goat cheese; the black and white tagliolini with scallops and saffron sauce; and the whole grilled branzino. **WHO** Madison Heights neighbors running into each other. 🍷 ☼ 🏛

[Central Park] 219 S. Fair Oaks Ave., Old Pasadena, 626.449.4499, centralparkrestaurant.net. B, L & D daily. American. Full bar. AE, MC, V. $$ - $$$ **WHY** A convenient, moderately priced café just south of the Old Town madness—with free parking! **WHAT** Part of a small chain that also owns Wild Thyme, this place feels generic, and yet it fits the bill in many ways. The short-rib hash, Thai beef salad, pizzas and brick-flattened chicken are of the moment and actually quite satisfying—think a better-value Smitty's. **WHO** Writers and the self-employed for breakfast, business people for lunch, seniors for the early-bird bargain dinner menu, and families for a nice after-soccer meal. 🍷 🍴 🦃 ☺

[Chang's Garden] 🏠 **627 W. Duarte Rd., Arcadia, 626.445.0606. L & D daily. Chinese/Shanghai. Beer & wine. MC, V. $$ WHY** Eat like a Shanghai connoisseur, starting with wonderful lotus-leaf-wrapped pork ribs. **WHAT** Chef Henry Chang's cooking represents both the ethereal and earthy sides of Shanghainese food. The shrimp sautéed with Dragon Well tea has the fresh tastes of spring, and his delicate Westlake soup of shredded yellowfish in a pale broth captures the essence of fresh fish. Opposite in style and flavor are the savory caramel-sauced clay pot chicken smothered in roasted chestnuts and a dish called Famous Poet Su Tung Po's Pork, a book-size rectangle of ultra-slow-red-cooked pork belly. A fold-out Chinese-only portion of the menu lists regional dishes made famous at Louwailou, a renowned Hangzhou restaurant that dates back to the 1840s. ☼

[Chung King] **1000 S. San Gabriel Blvd., San Gabriel, 626.286.0298. L & D daily. Chinese/Sichuan. Beer. Cash only. $ WHY** Hot, hot, hot—just like back in Sichuan province. **WHAT** This plain little café sizzles with exceptionally fiery dishes. Go for the Sichuan standards: beef hot pots, Chinese bacon with leeks, spareribs with Sichuan peppercorns, fried chicken with hot peppers. A little less spicy but still delicious are the dry-fried soybeans and the fried potato shreds. Cool down like a Sichuan native with a few of the cold dishes from the buffet. 🍷

[Cook's Tortas] 🏠 **1944 S. Atlantic Blvd., Monterey Park, 323.278.3536, cookstortas.com. B, L & D Mon.-Sat., brunch Sun. Mexican. No booze. AE, MC, V. $ WHY** For a different take on the ubiquitous Mexican sandwich, served in a minimalist, casually stylish café. **WHAT** Cook's—which takes its name from the discoverer of the Sandwich Islands—takes sandwiches to a new plane with soft, house-baked rolls and a rotating menu selected from hundreds of filling choices. Traditional tortas like the fiery ahogada are executed with more flair than the corner torta shops, while original varieties like *bacalao* (Spanish cod and garlic), chicken mole verde and pork mojito create a fiesta of flavors. Refreshing aguas frescas in a rainbow of fruit flavors and imaginative sides and baked goods are also standouts. **WHO** Students from East L.A. City College and culinary explorers. 🍷 ☺

[Daisy Mint] **1218 E. Colorado Blvd., Pasadena, 626.792.2999, daisymint.com. L & D daily. Asian. BYOB. AE, MC, V. $$ WHY** Brightly flavored and affordable Korean-Thai-Chinese dishes, from addictive Shanghai-style soup dumplings and Thai noodle dishes to savory

🥬 VEGETARIAN ⊙ KID FRIENDLY ❀ PATIO DINING 🚐 DELIVERY 🏠 PRIVATE PARTY

Korean rib-eye. **WHAT** This modern mom 'n pop—he's Korean and she's Thai—is decorated with empty flea-market frames and vintage chandeliers, and it's filled to the brim with the kind of people you'd see shopping for those exact same items at the Rose Bowl swap meet. Wine lovers adore the no-corkage policy, and everyone likes the family-style Asian-fusion dishes to share. **WHO** A hip Pasadena crowd from Art Center, the Playhouse and Caltech. 📷🔋◔☼

[Din Tai Fung] 🏛 1108 S. Baldwin Ave., Arcadia, 626.574.7068, dintaifungusa.com. L & D daily. Chinese. No booze. AE, MC, V. $
WHY Drop-dead amazing dumplings. **WHAT** Be prepared to wait in line, but don't expect to mind the minute you bite into your first dumpling. (That said, nothing is worth a 90-minute wait, so try to come outside of prime hours, when the wait might be just 20 minutes.) This American branch of a Taipei dumpling house is famed for its Shanghai-style soup dumplings, whose mix of broth, pork and crab explodes in your mouth. But all the dumplings, from the vegetarian to the shrimp-and-pork sui mai, are dreamy. **WHO** A never-ending stream of Angelenos from every walk of life. 📷🔋◔

[Dip's Grill] 1412 E. Valley Blvd., Alhambra, 626.284.3477, dipsgrill.com. L & D Wed.-Sun. Vietnamese/American. Beer & sake. MC, V. $ - $$
WHY To check out SoCal's first Vietnamese-American gastropub.
WHAT Happy-hour specials and a half-dozen brews on tap pair with beer-friendly food that mirrors the everyday flavors most Vietnamese-American kids grow up eating—with a slightly creative twist. Good examples include the grilled mini skewers of curry-marinated chicken or beef and the sliders on Hawaiian buns (pulled pork, crispy chicken and more). The pork-belly buns rock; the Vietnamese spicy beef soup will clear your sinuses; and the egg rolls and curry-filled rice-paper rolls are a gustatory extravaganza. **WHO** A plugged-in, hip Asian crowd, including young families.

[Duck House] 501 S. Atlantic Blvd., Monterey Park, 626.284.3227, pearlcatering.com. L & D daily. Chinese/Beijing. Beer & wine. MC, V. $$
WHY One word: duck. **WHAT** There are lots of good things to order (scallion pancakes, beef with garlic, the mountain yam jelly called *konnyaku*) but it's really all about the three-course duck dinner, a great feast to share with friends. It starts with a platter of crisp, salty-sweet skin and moist meat to wrap in pancakes with a bit of scallion and a smear of hoisin, then proceeds to stir-fried duck with bean sprouts and concludes with an aromatic and wonderful duck soup. Note that you must call at least an hour ahead to order your duck. **WHO** Lots of birthday-party and other celebratory groups. 📷◔

[Elements Kitchen] 37 S. El Molino Ave., Pasadena, 626.440.0044, elementskitchen.com. D Tues.-Sun., brunch Sat.-Sun. Modern American. Full bar. AE, MC, V. $$ - $$$$ **WHY** To enjoy delicious food and drink in an elegant room without a hint of stuffiness. **WHAT** The team behind Elements Café & Catering operates this attractive white-table-cloth restaurant in the charming, Spanish-style Pasadena Playhouse complex. With a menu organized around key ingredients ("elements") that change with the seasons, this is a fun restaurant for foodies, and the cooking is creative (don't miss the duck confit eggrolls). The adjacent lounge is a great spot for a bite to eat and a cocktail. **WHO** Most of Pasadena, it seems. Not the spot for a clandestine meeting. 🦢

[Elena's Greek-Armenian Cuisine] 1000 S. Glendale Blvd. , Glendale, 818.241.5730, elenasgreek.com. L & D Mon.-Sat. Armenian/Greek. No booze. AE, MC, V. $ - $$ **WHY** Terrific homemade stuffed grape leaves, gyros and kebabs for cheap. **WHAT** How can a tiny restaurant in an out-of-the-way Glendale location with no parking thrive for more than three decades? By offering satisfying, tasty food at unbelievably low prices. We are addicted to Elena's version of stuffed grape leaves, but occasionally fall off the wagon to indulge in the generous gyros or shish kebab platters. You really have to work hard to spend more than $15 per person. At these prices, don't expect a fancy décor—the dining room is basically a patio enclosed with canvas and clear plastic. **WHO** Budget-conscious folks who love to eat. 🚚😊

[Elite] 🏛 700 S. Atlantic Blvd., Monterey Park, 626.282.9998, elitechineserestaurant.com. B, L & D daily. Chinese/dim sum. Beer & wine. MC, V. $ - $$ **WHY** The best dim sum in town, and a superb Cantonese dinner menu, too. **WHAT** The San Gabriel Valley's reigning dim sum house eschews the rolling carts in favor of a large menu of beautiful dumplings and small dishes: deep-fried peanut and sesame cake, flawless sui mai, Macau roasted pork, Macau egg custard pies and many more. The shame is that so many of its dim sum fans never think to return for dinner, when attentive waiters deliver such wonderful things as roast squab, seafood soup with bitter melon and ham, steamed live prawns, and Maine lobster with butter, black pepper, garlic and ginger. **WHO** A crowd of devoted fans, especially for weekend dim sum. 🏛

[Firefly Bistro] 1009 El Centro St., South Pasadena, 626.441.2443, eatatfirefly.com. D Tues.-Sun., brunch Sat.-Sun. Modern American. Beer & wine. AE, MC, V. $$ - $$$$ **WHY** Hip and friendly, with a sangria and tapas menu on Thursdays, when the bustling local farmers' market comes to life outside its door. **WHAT** This tented bistro is bright by day and romantic at night, with an always-interesting and usually wonderful menu of multiethnic offerings, from red chile vegetable egg rolls to warm spinach salad, grilled pork chop with bacon-wrapped asparagus to famed shrimp and grits. The lunchtime salads are excellent, and the wine list is creative and affordable. ♥☼🏛

[Gale's Restaurant] 452 S. Fair Oaks Ave., Pasadena, 626.432.6705, galesrestaurant.com. L Tues.-Sat., D Tues.-Sun. Italian. Full bar. AE, MC,

---

🌿VEGETARIAN ☼KID FRIENDLY ☼PATIO DINING 🚚DELIVERY 🏛PRIVATE PARTY

V. $$ - $$$$ **WHY** Gorgeous lunch salads and very good dinnertime pastas. **WHAT** Run by hometown girl Gale Kohl and her husband, Rene Chila, Gale's features a talented Italian chef, warm atmosphere and professional wait staff. Favorite dishes include mussels with white wine and garlic, caprese salad, Caesar salad and rosemary lamb chops. But for the best eating, check out the specials menu; the salads are particularly excellent. **WHO** Pasadena's connected people: politicians, volunteers, community leaders.

[Giang Nan] 306 N. Garfield Ave., Monterey Park, 626.573.3421. L & D daily. Chinese/Shanghai. BYOB. MC, V. $$ **WHY** Skinny fried eel with shrimp are crunchy and addictive, and the braised pork knuckle is among the best in town. **WHAT** Even during the Cultural Revolution, dignitaries always seemed to eat beautifully at the Jin Nan Guest House in Shanghai, where, before the mid-'90s wave of high-end restaurants, chef Hongwei Kong worked the stoves. Now he is at this modest restaurant, nearly invisible at the back of a large mini-mall. And while most dishes are casually served, the occasional stylish presentation reveals his skill, as with the fingers of yellowfish in their airy tempura-like coating seasoned with salty crumbled seaweed, a dish that melts like cotton candy on the tongue. **WHO** Homesick Shanghaiese flock here for the marinated crab appetizer and the comforting soupy fish head casserole afloat with wide rice noodles. 🖺

[Golden Deli] 815 W. Las Tunas Dr., San Gabriel, 626.308.0803, goldendelirestaurant.com. L & D Mon.-Tues. & Thurs.-Sun. Vietnamese. No booze. Cash only. $ - $$ **WHY** The fresh, light banh mi sandwiches and those fabulously crisp spring rolls. **WHAT** This no-frills diner packs 'em in with fresh, appealing and cheap Vietnamese food: oniony pho, shrimp paste on sugar cane, myriad noodle dishes and justly popular spring rolls accompanied by a fragrant heap of fresh green herbs. Also consider the related Vietnam Restaurant down the street. 🖺 ☺

[Green Street Tavern] 69 W. Green St., Old Pasadena, 626.229.9961, greenstreettavern.net. L Mon.-Fri., D nightly, brunch Sat.-Sun. Modern American. Beer & wine. AE, MC, V. $$$ - $$$$ **WHY** A pretty little restaurant off the Old Town chain highway, with personality and a great Wednesday deal ($20 for an entrée and glass of wine). **WHAT** Not to be confused with Green Street Restaurant, this cozy, upscale little boîte is sculpted with art nouveau curves and holds just a couple of booths, a few tables and a small backlit bar, which pours a good selection of wines and beers. Service is attentive, ingredients are quality (often organic and/or local), and the cooking is accomplished. **WHO** Pasadena date-nighters in on the secret. ♥ ☼

[Happy Sheep] 227 W. Valley Blvd., San Gabriel, 626.457.5599. L & D daily. Chinese/dumplings/noodles. Beer & wine. MC, V. $ - $$ **WHY** Tasty, make-it-your-way hot-pot soups, low prices and a convivial, family-friendly vibe. **WHAT** A chain of hot-pot emporiums popular through-out Asia, this place specializes in a bubbling broth perfect for a foggy winter day. Order chile-red spicy broth or clear mild for the burner in the middle of the table, then check off a variety of soup additions such as meats, vegetables, tofu or noodles. Lamb dumplings and scallion pancakes make good side dishes to the main-attraction hot pots. **WHO** Large Chinese groups with soup-slurping toddlers. 📷😊

[Hunan Seafood] **8772 E. Valley Blvd., Rosemead, 626.280.8389. L & D daily. Chinese/Hunan. Beer & wine. MC, V. $$ - $$$ WHY** To spice up your seafood restaurant list. **WHAT** The Hunan province may be inland, but the restaurant's name isn't an oxymoron. The vast Dong Ting Lake and Yangtze River tributaries supply fish, shrimp, frogs and turtle, all of which are on the menu at this modern chrome-and-glass spot. Also here is Chairman Mao's favorite red-cooked (braised) pork, whose buttery flesh is infused with nearly caramelized sweet garlic and a rice wine–kissed sauce. The house specialty, Hunanese ham, smoked duck and fish braised together for hours, comes steeped in irresistible, spicy juices. **WHO** A loyal Chinese clientele and curious Sinophiles who love the thrill of a capsicum rush.

[Hunan Style] 🏛 **529 E. Valley Blvd., Ste. 108A, San Gabriel, 626.288.0758. L & D daily. Chinese/Hunan. Beer & wine. AE, MC, V. $$ WHY** Our vote for the best Hunanese cooking in Southern California. **WHAT** A chile-emphatic menu offers carefully cooked Hunan dishes without the usual vats of oil. The toss-fried lamb, glowing like an electric-powered Christmas tree, is a powder keg of a dish lit up with a quartet of chile styles: fresh diced, dried whole, flaked in oil and pickled. Similarly spiced are frog's legs, pork belly and cuttlefish with pig stomach—this place doesn't hold back. Spice-loving vegetarians have a whole page of peppery delights to choose from. Don't let the cryptic menu descriptions deter you—the manager-owner is fluent in English, but you may have to convince him you can take the heat. **WHO** Mostly Asian chileheads. 🏛

[Indo Kitchen] **5 N. 4th St., Alhambra, 626.282.1676, indokitchenalhambra.com. L & D daily. Indonesian. No booze. MC, V. $ WHY** Pretend you're voyaging through Indonesia and order the *nasi pecel leme*—deep-fried catfish with a dried shrimp-chili sambal. **WHAT** Indo's nasi campur combination plates, which might include barbecued pork, chicken and a variety of garnishes, are some of the best bargains this side of Jakarta. They're also delicious, as are the *longtong cap goh me* (a creamy chicken curry over cubes of rice and green jackfruit) and the *nasi rames* plate with Sumatran beef curry. 📷

[Japon Bistro] **927 E. Colorado Blvd., Pasadena, 626.744.1751, japonbistro-pasadena.com. L Tues.-Fri., D Tues.-Sun. Japanese. Beer & wine. MC, V. $$ - $$$ WHY** A lively sushi bar, an engaged staff and very good Japanese food, including lots of appealing vegetarian choices. **WHAT** Don't let the home-lettered signs and uninviting, tunnel-like space dissuade you from discovering this fine and eclectic spot. The knowledgeable staff can't wait to introduce you to the live sea urchin, the exotic sake collection and the terrific izakaya menu (salmon carpaccio, Hawaiian-style poke, beef kushiyaki). **WHO** Caltech foodies discussing nanotechnology and black holes. 🈂️🦑

[Java Spice] 1743 Fullerton Rd., Rowland Heights, 626.810.1366. L & D Tues.-Sun. Indonesian. No booze. MC, V. $ **WHY** The nasi bungkus at Java Spice is a magnificent Indonesian meal, a picnic banquet swathed in fresh-cut banana leaf that looks something like a pregnant shoe box. Inside are generous chunks of coconut-infused chicken, smoldering chile-laced beef rendang, brightly spiced jackfruit curry, chunky fish cake, tofu nuggets and a blazing scarlet sambal-topped egg, all atop a rice plateau that soaks up the flavors. **WHAT** If you can't make it to this generic-looking strip-mall place on weekends for nasi bungkus, not to worry—the regular menu during the week is rich with aromatic, spicy-sweet Javanese classics, including the amazing fried chicken; shrimp and egg fried rice; elegant butter-sautéed frog's legs with caramelized shallots; and beef rendang and rice disks floating on an amazing coconut-chile broth. **WHO** Lively multi-generational Indonesian families fill the place on weekends for the nasi bungkus feasts. 🈂️☺

[JTYH Restaurant] 9425 Valley Blvd., Rosemead, 626.442.8999. L & D Wed.-Mon. Chinese/dumplings/noodles. Beer & wine. MC, V. $ - $$ **WHY** For the delicious thrill of expanding your pasta connoisseurship. **WHAT** The house specialties, three northern Chinese noodle styles, open a window onto the earliest forms of noodle: *dao xiao mian*, absorbent ribbon-like noodles that are cleaver-shaved from a stiff dough roll resembling a yule log; cat's ears, little dumpling-like blobs; and dumpling knots, spaetzle-like wet dough tossed into boiling water (ask about #6 and #7 under "snacks," written in Chinese). The shaved noodles come in various soups, stir fries and, by request, tossed with superbly seasoned sauces that cling to their uneven texture. Savory pastries (leek cakes and beef rolled in pancakes), dumplings and mostly spicy stir-fries complete the menu. **WHO** Pasta addicts and the Asian food-blogging brigade. 🈂️☺

[La Cabañita] 🏠 3447 N. Verdugo Rd., Montrose, 818.957.2711. L & D daily. Mexican. Full bar. AE, MC, V. $$ **WHY** Very good food, plus the tasty (but strong) margaritas and sangria. **WHAT** La Cabañita is a cheerful, crowded neighborhood café offering superb food. It's expanded to nearly twice its original size, causing some old-timers to grouse about kitchen consistency, but we think it's as wonderful as ever, especially the beans, the green mole, the sopes compuestos and the chicken soup. **WHO** Locals, plus salsa-to-go customers from Echo Park and beyond. 🈂️☺

[La Caravana] **1306 N. Lake Ave., Pasadena, 626.791.7378. L & D daily. Salvadoran. No booze. MC, V. $ WHY** This is the place to get your fill of pupusas and empanada-like meat-filled pepitos. **WHAT** Plush booths and Central American art and woodwork create a handsome setting for sampling hearty, tasty Salvadoran specialties like savory chicken sautéed with onions and potatoes. 🍽 🎵 ☺

[La Grande Orange] **260 S. Raymond Ave., Pasadena, 626.356.4444, lgostationcafe.com. L & D daily. Modern American. Full bar. AE, MC, V. $$ - $$$ WHY** Although it's the kind of restaurant that MBAs, not chefs, create, Grande Orange an undeniably winning place, especially the bar, the Caesar salad, the burgers and the excellent pizzas emerging from the wood-burning ovens in the adjacent pizzeria. **WHAT** The owners of this spot in the handsomely restored 1925 Santa Fe Depot at Del Mar Station have thought of everything. Good-value happy hour? Check. Retro-hip mac 'n cheese? Check. Grilled ahi tacos? Check. It's got it all, from name-dropping martinis to a thoughtful kids' menu, so all of Pasadena is showing up. **WHO** Early-bird seniors on the patio, young families and middle-aged friends in the dining room and a younger after-work crowd in the bar. 🍽 ☺ ☼

[The Luggage Room] **260 S. Raymond Ave., Old Pasadena, 626.356.4440, lgostationcafe.com. L Fri.-Sun., D nightly. Pizzeria. Full bar. AE, MC, V. $$ WHY** La Grande Orange's casual sibling is a busy pizza specialist in the same historic Pasadena train station. **WHAT** Gourmet toppings like fig and blue cheese or sausage with shaved fennel top chewy sourdough crusts from a wood-burning oven. Crab legs, salads like the Green Day and a few other appetizers complete the menu; plenty of beers and wines are available. Like La Grande Orange, flavors are often on the sweet side, and the room gets cacaphonous. But it's a lively scene, and that crust is worth a wait. Also good for takeout pizza; the valet guys will watch your car while you run in. **WHO** Families with small kids on the outdoor patio; festive groups indoors. ☺ ☼

[Lunasia] **500 W. Main St., San Gabriel, 626.308.3222, lunasiachinesecuisine.com. L & D daily. Chinese/dim sum. Beer & wine. AE, MC, V. $$ WHY** Well-crafted dim sum by day and well-executed upscale Chinese cooking by night, served in an attractive dining room for surprisingly modest prices. **WHAT** The dim sum gets more attention at this swank Cantonese place on Alhambra's auto row, but we think the dinner is equally worthy. As is the trend now in your classier joints, dim sum is made to order so it's fresher than the norm. But consider the dinner menu: whole, crisp-skinned Beijing Duck served with fat pancakes, stir-fried prawns in tea sauce, fresh lobster with black pepper and butter (a bargain at $28), a first-rate kung pao chicken, delicious and vibrantly green pea shoot tips with garlic, and, for groups of about ten, a celebratory whole roast suckling pig ($18). **WHO** Large, prosperous Chinese-American family groups. 🍽 ☺ 🏮

🌿 **VEGETARIAN** ☺ **KID FRIENDLY** ☼ **PATIO DINING** 🚗 **DELIVERY** 🏮 **PRIVATE PARTY**

[Luscious Dumplings] 🏛 **704 W. Las Tunas Dr., San Gabriel, 626.282.8695. L & D Tues.-Sat. Chinese/dumplings. No booze. Cash only. $ WHY** Pan-fried pork dumplings that will have you eating far more than propriety or good health demand. **WHAT** Given the amount of competition, particularly in these parts, it takes a lot of chutzpah to call yourself "Luscious Dumplings," but this simple café's wares deserve the appellation. Each dumpling's covering sports a different decorative pleating that indicates its filling type. Steamed pork dumplings hold the requisite pool of interior broth to suck out before polishing off the rest. Empanada-shaped, golden fried dumplings balance chive, pork, egg and crunchy bits of dried shrimp; a modicum of savory pork brings fish and napa cabbage together for an ethereal filling. Be warned: The early bird gets the dumpling—a small line often forms when it opens, and the kitchen sometimes runs out of the most popular ones. **WHO** Devotees who eat here as often as possible. 🗺 ☺

[Malbec] **1001 E. Green St., Pasadena, 626.683.0550, malbeccuisine.com. L & D daily. Argentinean. Beer & wine. AE, MC, V. $$ - $$$ WHY** Good, honest Argentinean cooking and wines at modest prices. **WHAT** This friendly Argentinean, with its comfortable booths and tasty, affordable Argentinean wines, serves well-prepared classics at more-than-reasonable prices: empanadas, *matambre* (rolled meat stuffed with vegetables and herbs), garlic fries, handmade pastas and such hearty entrées as grilled short ribs (great flavor but too chewy), skirt steak chimichurri (delicious) and grilled salmon. **WHO** Everyone who's anyone in Pasadena, often coming with friends, who then run into their friends. 🗺

[Mandarin Noodle House] **701 W. Garvey Ave., Monterey Park, 626.570.9795. L & D daily. Chinese/Dumplings/noodles. No booze. Cash only. $ WHY** Those "thin onion pancakes"—scallion-laced, layered and crunchy, and the cha-jiang mien noodles. **WHAT** Come here for the food, not the ambience. You'll soon forget the harsh light and less-than-nurturing service when you start slurping a steaming bowl of Family Handmade Noodle Soup with hand-cut noodles and lots of other tasty stuff. The pan-fried dumplings and the pork or shrimp soup noodle are good, too. 🗺 ☺

[Max's of Manila] **313 W. Broadway, Glendale, 818.637.7751, maxschicken.com. L & D daily. Filipino. Beer & wine. AE, MC, V. $ - $$ WHY** The *chicharrón de pollo* (deep-fried chicken skin) sets the gold standard. **WHAT** Mildly seasoned chicken, fried whole to keep it juicy, is the house specialty at this branch of the Filipino chain. You can order it spicy, too, and the palm vinegar dip that accompanies both versions is garlic-studded and terrific. 🗺 ☺

[Mei Long Village] **301 W. Valley Blvd., San Gabriel, 626.284.4769. L & D daily. Chinese/dumplings/noodles. Beer & wine. MC, V. $ - $$**

WHY Go for the Shanghai-style dumplings filled with crab and pork and the light, pastry-style dumplings filled with sautéed leeks—but also try the Shanghai spareribs and the jade shrimp with a spinach purée. **WHAT** Originally known as Dragon Villages, this was one of the first formal restaurants to introduce Shanghai-style cooking to Los Angeles. The main draw for regulars these days: the beloved dumplings—crab, pork and steamed vegetable—and pot stickers. 📋 🍴 ☺

[Merry's House of Chicken] **2550 E. Amar Rd., Ste. A5, West Covina, 626.965.0123. L & D Tues.-Sun. Indonesian. No booze. MC, V. $$**
WHY Classic Javanese cooking and crisp fried chicken. **WHAT** The history of Merry Istiowati's namesake restaurant traces back to her culinary academy in the Indonesian city of Surabaya. Here in a West Covina strip mall, her cooking is indebted to that past. There is, of course, *ayam goreng kremesan*, Indonesian fried chicken covered in crunchy rice-flour crumbles and dabbed with sambal and lime juice. But there's more than simply chicken. The sautéed water spinach is perfect simplicity, the leafy green dressed with a salty fermented soy paste, garlic and flecks of bell pepper. There are soups, including *rawon buntut* (an oxtail soup flavored with the earthy, tarry seed of the kepayang tree), but ultimate convenience comes in the combination plates. Unwrap a banana leaf to find the *nasi bungkus*: steamed rice, curried chicken, beef rendang, a hard-boiled egg dipped in sambal, and jackfruit all packed up for portability. **WHO** Indonesian ex-pats from across the San Gabriel Valley. 📋

[Mezbaan Indian] **80 N. Fair Oaks Ave., Old Pasadena, 626.405.9060, mezbaan.net. L Mon.-Fri., D nightly, brunch Sun. Indian. Beer & wine. AE, MC, V. $ - $$$ WHY** Great lunch buffet. **WHAT** One of the original Old Town eateries, Mezbaan offers tandoori, benghan bharta, palak paneer and distinctive curries that diners can spice on a sliding scale of one to ten. Hyderabad specialties (like the delicious lamb pasinda) also are served. Live Indian music on Friday and Saturday nights, too. ☺

[Mike & Anne's] **1040 Mission St., South Pasadena, 626.799.7199, mikeandannes.com. B, L & D Tues.-Sun. Modern American. Full bar. AE, MC, V. $$ - $$$ WHY** The lovely rosemary-lined patio and the refreshingly uncomplicated modern American food: grilled sandwiches, crisp-skinned chicken, a terrific burger, and its decadent deep-fried trio of delight: sweet potato fries, french fries and the best onion rings in Pasadena. **WHAT** South Pasadena has become a really good town to be hungry in, and this place is one of the foodie focal points. The sunny-by-day, twinkle-lit-by-night patio is the place to be in good weather, but we also like the bar and the brick-walled dining areas. The kitchen stocks its larders from the local farmers' markets, including the Thursday one across the street. **WHO** A typical South Pas mix—Republican Junior Leaguers next to Koi-clad artists. ♥ ☺ 📋 ☺ ☼

🌿 VEGETARIAN ☺ KID FRIENDLY ☼ PATIO DINING 🚚 DELIVERY 🎩 PRIVATE PARTY

[New Chong Qing] 120 N. San Gabriel Blvd., Ste. J, San Gabriel, 626.309.0836. L & D daily. Chinese. No booze. Cash only. $ - $$ **WHY** A place for chileheads to give their palate a thrill ride. **WHAT** Light years beyond kung pao, the Sichuan fare at this nicely designed little storefront is the winning contender for capsicum artistry in a city filled with peppery stir fries and incendiary noodles. The fresh fish hot pot has a fan club, but don't let it obscure the other mouth-tingling goodies, like fried chicken cubelets — as crunchy as chicharones and spicier than jalapeño kettle chips, buried under an inch-deep blanket of dry-fried chiles. **WHO** Serious fans of western Chinese cuisine of every age and nationality. ☼

[Newport Seafood] 518 W. Las Tunas Dr., San Gabriel, 626.289.5998, newportseafood.com. L & D daily. Chinese/Vietnamese. Beer & wine. AE, MC, V. $ - $$$ **WHY** A glistening mountain of lobster, sautéed with lots of garlic, scallions and ginger. Superb giant clams, too. **WHAT** Occupying a bright former coffee shop, Newport is handsome enough to attract business lunchers by day and upscale celebrators by night. And because the house specialties are four- to six-pound lobsters, as well as crab and aptly named elephant clams, this is a place for celebrating. (The lobsters are a far sight cheaper than at, say, the Palm, but they're still an investment.) Don't bother with the glutinous hot and sour soup, and don't feel compelled to try the Vietnamese dishes; just stick with the lobster, clams and excellent vegetables (especially the pea sprouts), and you'll have a memorable meal. who A well-dressed mix of Chinese, Vietnamese and Occidental diners out for a seafood splurge. **WHO** A well-dressed mix of Chinese, Vietnamese and Occidental diners out for a seafood splurge. ⌐

[Oba Sushi Izakaya] 181 E. Glenarm St., Pasadena, 626.799.8543, obasushi.com. L Mon.-Sat., D nightly. Japanese/sushi. Beer, wine & sake. MC, V. $$ - $$$ **WHY** Pasadena's best izakaya: fish cake tempura, an incredible poke salad, the Oba roll with cucumber, avocado, jalapeño and paper-thin beef, and carefully prepared sushi and sashimi, notably the organic farm-raised hamachi. **WHAT** Pasadena's newest Japanese is one of its best — and with a Mexican sushi chef, no less. The strip-mall space has held a few Japanese places, but none that looked this good, and certainly none that tasted this good. You can sit at the sake/wine bar, the small sushi bar or in one of two dining areas, and you'll be well served by very nice people. Lunchtime bento boxes are a good value. ⌐ ⌐

[Ocean Star Seafood] 145 N. Atlantic Blvd., Monterey Park, 626.308.2128. L & D daily. Chinese/Hong Kong seafood. Full bar. AE, MC, V. $$ - $$$$ **WHY** Don't-miss dishes like salt-and-pepper shrimp, whole steamed fish and crab in black bean sauce. **WHAT** Vast and glossy, this reliable Cantonese restaurant is chaotic for dim sum and a bit more refined at dinner. The fresh and varied dim sum is served from rolling carts, and the seafood is consistently excellent. A seafood feast in a private room makes for a great party. ☺🏛

[Omar] **1718 New Ave., San Gabriel, 626.570.9778. L & D Wed.-Mon. Chinese/Islamic. No booze. Cash only. $ - $$ WHY** For the little-known Muslim fare of Xinjiang, China's autonomous far western region. **WHAT** The food at this homey café, a mesh of Chinese elements and central Asian nomad cooking, likely bears little resemblance to anything you've eaten in L.A. Sure, Xinjiang lamb kebabs are well known, but owner Munire Omar brings out *zhuafan*, a rice creation reminiscent of an Afghan pilaf with caramelized julienne carrots and slivers of cumin-laced lamb. The strangely named Xinjiang meatloaf sandwich is actually a juicy meat pie with a crackly potato-chip-thin crust. Omar hand pulls her thick, chewy noodles, which are wonderful with the braised dish called big-plate chicken. **WHO** Taiwanese and Hong Kong ex-pats who fell in love with this cuisine at home, where it's popular. 🐿

[Palate Food & Wine] 🍷 **933 S. Brand Blvd., Glendale, 818.662.9463, palatefoodwine.com. L Fri. & Sat., D nightly. Modern American/French. Full bar. AE, MC, V. $$ - $$$ WHY** Little crocks of "porkfolio" (a charcuterie plate including a suave pork pâté), gorgeous cheeses, pickled vegetables (and fruits!), Valrhona chocolate pudding and terrific wines poured by the half-glass, glass or bottle. The three-course Sunday Supper is $35, a relatively good buy. **WHAT** Ah, Palate, we will always love you, but you've let us down lately. Neglectful service, inconsistent preparation, a bit of smugness... and yet, we remain fans of Octavio Becerra's robust, simple, reasonably priced (very) small plates, which are served with exuberant wines. Everything either comes from a local farmers' market, a small-scale craftsman (as with the cheeses) or is made in-house: house-churned butter, handmade pasta, house-cured prosciutto. In back is a retail wine store with a tasting area, a gorgeous oversize table for parties and a culinary library. Pastas can disappoint; stick with the meat dishes and anything potted. **WHO** A devoutly loyal crowd of hybrid-driving foodies (and wine geeks) from north Glendale, Atwater, Silver Lake and Pasadena. ☺🏛

[Parkway Grill] **510 S. Arroyo Pkwy., Pasadena, 626.795.1001, theparkwaygrill.com. L Mon.-Fri., D nightly. Californian. Full bar. AE, MC, V. $$$$ WHY** It's the Spago of Pasadena. **WHAT** Its California pizzas, organic vegetables, open kitchen and inventive cookery made a big splash in once-stodgy Pasadena when it opened in 1985, and the Parkway Grill remains an appealing destination today. Classic dishes—roasted-beet salad, lobster-filled cocoa crêpes, superb short ribs with parmesan mashed potatoes, seasonal fruit crisps—are the way to go. There's a good wine list and the bar is great, particularly on the weekends, when live jazz is on the menu. **WHO** Well-dressed local power people. ♥🏛

🍃 VEGETARIAN ◎ KID FRIENDLY ☼ PATIO DINING 🚐 DELIVERY 🏛 PRIVATE PARTY

[Penang Malaysian Cuisine] 987 S. Glendora Ave. , West Covina, 626.338.6138. L & D daily. Malaysian. No booze. MC, V. $ WHY For hard-to-find Malaysian classics, from satays and curries to coconut rice and ice *kacang*, a red-bean shaved-ice dessert that's more delicious than you might think. **WHAT** This plaza café turns out Indian griddle breads (*roti canal*) and scalding Indo-Malay *rendangs*, long-simmered chicken, lamb or beef cooked in a thick coconut cream infused with massive quantities of curry spices. Noodle dishes and rice plates are best for single diners, while specials such as spicy Thai sauce shrimp and stir-fried eggplant with *belacan* are more suitable for groups to share. **WHO** Malaysian food buffs who drive a long way, and locals brave enough toook beyond their usual Thai joint. ☺

[Phoenix Inn] 208 E. Valley Blvd., Alhambra, 626.299.1238, phoenixfoodboutique.com. L & D daily to 1 a.m. Chinese/Cantonese. Beer & wine. MC, V. $ - $$ WHY Top-notch ingredients and consistently high quality cooking. Try the boneless chicken, a deceptively simple but fabulous chicken-soy stir-fry. **WHAT** Cantonese cooking is the house specialty, and hearty dishes like lo mein and spareribs with salt and pepper are particularly good. Bonus fun fact: Local legend says this place is haunted by a woman ghost who sits at various tables and admires what you're eating. ☺ 🗺☺🏠

[Plate 38] 2361 E. Colorado Blvd., East Pasadena, 626.793.7100, plate38.com. B & L daily, D Tues.-Sun. (to 1 a.m. Fri.-Sat.). American. Beer & wine. AE, MC, V. $$ WHY Better-than-you'd-think cooking in a no-frills café. **WHAT** Owner Robert Humphreys brings his classical training (at Patina and elsewhere) to his funky, everyday café, and the result is a gift for East Pasadenans. There's good coffee in the morning, worthwhile and affordable wines and beers at night, and one of the best burgers in Pasadena. Also terrific are the breakfast scrambles and pastries, the Cobb salad and the buttermilk-fried Cornish game hen. If only the dining room was warmer and more attractive. **WHO** Caltechers, families, young date-nighters. ☺ 🗺🐟☺☼

[Porto Alegre] Paseo Colorado, 260 E. Colorado Blvd., Pasadena, 626.744.0555, portoalegre-churrascaria.com. L & D daily. Brazilian. Full bar. AE, MC, V. $$$ - $$$$ WHY One of the best churrascarias around, with a generous and beautiful buffet (salads, roasted vegetables, prosciutti, cheeses, garlic rice, bananas fritas) and quality meats. **WHAT** Hidden on the second floor of the Paseo, where P. F. Chang's and Yard House get all the attention, this Brazilian barbecue place is more subdued than the wacky Gaucho's Village, has better food than Picanha in Burbank and is less expensive than Fogo de Chão in Beverly Hills—making it a fine choice for a carnivorous feast. Handsome men carve glistening meats tableside until you cry uncle; just make sure to get one of the lamb chops before you quit. **WHO** Special-occasion celebrants. ♥ 🍷☺

🏛 ESSENTIALLY L.A. ☺LATE ♥ROMANTIC 🗺 VALUE 🍷QUIET ☼ SUSTAINABLE

[Radhika] **966 Mission St., South Pasadena, 626.799.2200, radhikas.com. L & D daily. Indian. Beer & wine. AE, MC, V. $$ WHY** Good, straightforward Indian cooking with a few not-too-trendy modern touches, including Indian-inspired tacos. Excellent-value lunch menu. **WHAT** Radhika calls itself a "modern Indian bistro," which sounds gimmicky but is actually quite accurate. The interior is cozy, done in deep colors. Service is attentive and kind. There's a good list of wines and beers. And as for "modern," well, the menu has Indian tacos. But while they might be an attempt to jump on the LA. trendwagon, they really are good: warm corn tortillas filled with tandoor-style chicken, pickled onions and Indian seasonings. You'll also find delicious baby-back ribs, which aren't exactly an Indian staple. As for the classics, they're mostly well above average: stews (chicken tikka masala, lamb curry) with rich, complex flavors; *saag paneer* (a spinach and cheese dish) with the lightness and flavor of a good soufflé; and perfect garlic naan. Only the generic side vegetables disappoint. **WHO** Office workers and medical folks at lunch; date-nighters at dinner. 🌿🦞

[Robin's Wood-Fire BBQ] **395 N. Rosemead Blvd., East Pasadena, 626.351.8885, robinsbbq.com. L & D Tues.-Sun. American/barbecue. Full bar. AE, MC, V. $$ - $$$ WHY** When the 'cue zealots start debating who does it best, Robin's usually ranks among the finest. **WHAT** There's Pabst Blue Ribbon on tap, a kitschy Americana décor and a swell lineup of side dishes (blueberry cornbread, pecan cole slaw) but those are just supporting players to the deservedly popular meats, smoked over mesquite and hickory and appropriately tender and full of flavor. There are some good deals, too, including Sunday "family feasts" and half-price kids' dishes on Tuesday and Sunday. **WHO** Convivial families. 🍽️☺

[Royce] **Langham Huntington Hotel, 1401 S. Oak Knoll Ave., Pasadena, 626.568.3900, roycela.com. D Tues.-Sat. American/French. Full bar. AE, MC, V. $$$$$ WHY** WeHo chic in old-money Pasadena. **WHAT** This glam white-on-white restaurant doesn't look one bit like Pasadena, and we admire the Langham Huntington for pushing the envelope. (It's always entertaining to see San Marino men in Brooks Brothers blazers trying to figure out what to do with that precious morsel of lobster that appears to be the main course.) Handsome chef David Feau is a serious cook, and his modern French dishes are expertly prepared and flavorful, matched with a wine list of breadth and ambition. Is it worth the significant investment? Only you and your banker can answer that. For us, we'll wait to return until we close that three-picture deal. **WHO** Date-nighters and upscale business travelers. ♥🌿🍸

[Saladang] **363 S. Fair Oaks Ave., Pasadena, 626.793.8123. L & D daily. Thai. Beer & wine. AE, MC, V. $$ WHY** Some of the best Thai food in the SG Valley. **WHAT** Saladang's dining room is chic and modern— with exposed ducts, colorful table settings and handsome rattan

🌿VEGETARIAN ☺KID FRIENDLY ☼PATIO DINING 🚗DELIVERY 🏛PRIVATE PARTY

chairs—and its food deliciously fresh and well-presented. The yellow curries, satays, light fried calamari and spinach-and-duck salad are all excellent. The menu is thoughtfully laid out with lots of vegetarian-friendly options and the service is quick and professional. 🎐🦞

[Savoy Kitchen] 138 E. Valley Blvd., Alhambra, 626.308.9535. L & D daily. Chinese/coffee shop. No booze. Cash only. $ **WHY** Twenty-six years of creating first rate comfort food. **WHAT** Come early to eat at this popular but tiny Hong Kong–style coffee shop. Tables are hard to come by, but when you get one, order the generous and tasty Hainan-style chicken, which almost every table orders. Other standouts include the shrimp rolls, curries and the smoked duck salad. 📷☺

[Sea Harbour] 🏛 3939 N. Rosemead Blvd., Rosemead, 626.288.3939. L & D daily. Chinese/Hong Kong seafood. Full bar. AE, MC, V. $$ **WHY** Seafood selections such as shrimp-stuffed eggplant, tofu rounds topped with scallops and shrimp and shark fin dumplings are stand-outs. **WHAT** Dim sum doesn't roll on carts at this temple to tea snacks; instead the jewel-like dumplings, noodles and other refined small plates are pictured on the extensive, often-changing menu. Hard-core foodies choose the crunchy fried chicken knees and gelatinous chicken feet. Finish the meal with dessert-like dim sum, such as fried durian puffs, flaky egg tarts and the unusual lowfat milk bun. Waits can be long, but reservations and private rooms are available. ☺🏛

[Shamshiri] 122 W. Stocker St., Glendale, 818.246.9541, shamshiri. com. L & D daily. Persian. Beer & wine. AE, MC, V. $ - $$ **WHY** Abundant, interesting and delicious Persian food at low prices. Try the *fesenjon*, a sort of Persian mole, rich and complex, with pomegranate and wal-nuts. **WHAT** The kindly service can be erratic at this Glendale Persian, but it's easy to forgive when you taste the food—and even easier to forgive when you pay the bill. Very good kebabs and stews, with dill, mint and saffron-scented garnishes keeping the plates beautiful and the palate refreshed. 📷☺

[Shanghai Restaurant] 140 W. Valley Blvd., San Gabriel, 626.288.0991. L & D daily. Chinese/Shanghai. Beer & wine. MC, V. $$ **WHY** Ambitious cuisine for discriminating eaters. **WHAT** In its coveted spot—the second floor of the huge Chinese Focus Plaza—Shanghai could probably get by serving the usual cold wine chicken, spicy cold beef tendon and a few pedestrian hot pots. Those are on the menu, but the kitchen turns out more sophisticated fare, such as poached dumpling-like rolled tofu sheets stuffed with meat and the Chinese green *chi-tsai*. Tender, savory custard with clams is another wonder. And those fond of assertive flavors might try a thin fish fillet coated in deep red wine lees (an inspiration from Fujian to the south). But avoid the braised pork knuckle with soy sauce, a sad mound of con-gealed fat. 📷☺

[Shiro] 🏛 **1505 Mission St., South Pasadena, 626.799.4774, restaurantshiro.com. D Wed.-Sun. French/Japanese. Full bar. AE, MC, V. $$$$ WHY** The signature whole sizzling catfish with ponzu sauce, but don't stop there—it's all delicious. For a memorable experience, ask Chef Shiro to surprise you. **WHAT** Chef Hideo Yamashiro knows his seafood and the menu reflects it, with lots of fresh, interestingly sauced fish offerings. As competition has intensified in increasingly food-obsessed South Pasadena, Shiro's, once the only game in town, is fighting back by offering an excellent $35 four-course menu on Wednesdays. We wish the modern white setting was more charming, but the food and kind service more than compensate. ♥ 🍴

[Song] **383 S. Fair Oaks Ave., Pasadena, 626.793.5200. L & D daily. Thai. Beer & wine. AE, MC, V. $$ WHY** Romantic patio setting and an evocative, just-challenging-enough Thai menu. **WHAT** The glass-walled dining room is attractive, but the open-air patio—set off by 15-foot-tall steel panels laser-cut to suggest the patterns of Thai fabrics—is the ideal setting for consuming the street food-inspired dishes served at this sister restaurant to neighboring Saladang. Stand-outs include the crispy, addictive corn cakes, a salad of asparagus and chicken, and the fish balls with curry. **WHO** Date-night couples and post–mee krob Thai food enthusiasts looking for the kind of dishes you won't find everywhere else in town. ♥🍴○

[Southern Mini Town] 🏛 **833 W. Las Tunas Dr., San Gabriel, 626.289.6578. L & D daily. Chinese/Shanghai. No booze. MC, V. $ - $$ WHY** The spot-on cooking at this supremely nondescript place is something no food lover will want to miss. **WHAT** With small appetizer plates of Shaoxing wine-marinated blue crab, red-cooked Jia Xing duck and cool jade celery seasoned with sesame oil, plus a few orders of satisfying pastries and dumplings, you might be tempted to forgo entrées. Don't. The kitchen has honed the flavors of almost every dish: supremely rich deep-fried and red-cooked spare ribs; delicate gluten puffs in a soup lively with the contrasting textures of bow-tied fresh tofu sheet, glass noodles and torn napa cabbage; even simple al dente noodles dressed only with a modicum of scallion-infused oil. 📝🍴☺

[Supreme Dragon] **18406 Colima Rd., Rowland Heights, 626.810.0396. L & D daily. Chinese/dim sum. No booze. Cash only. $ WHY** Crusty-bottomed pan-fried pork bao with slightly fluffy coverings, the fresh scallion dumplings, the salted vegetables stir-fried with torn bean curd sheet, and more such little treasures. **WHAT** At Supreme Dragon, diners are given a long sushi bar-style list of about 80 northern and Shanghai-style pastries and small dishes. The restaurant's attempts at elegance—waterfall curtains, the golden and red placards in its two dining rooms—are beside the point. You're here to eat. The delicate bottle gourd squash makes an excellent balance for richer dishes such as braised duck with meaty black mushrooms and leeks, or

🍴 **VEGETARIAN** ☺ **KID FRIENDLY** ○ **PATIO DINING** � **DELIVERY** 🏛 **PRIVATE PARTY**

pork belly chunks braised with lightly pickled vegetables whose tang plays against the richness of the meat. 📖🦪☺

[Tasty Garden] 288 W. Valley Blvd., Alhambra, 626.300.8262, tastygarden.us. L & D daily to 1 a.m. (to 3 a.m. Fri.-Sat.). Chinese/Coffee shop. No booze. AE, MC, V. $ **WHY** Exceptional menu, cross-generational clientele. **WHAT** The fare at this lively, Hong Kong–style coffee shop is well made, fantastically tasty, mostly Chinese and definitely eclectic. Crowds come for the filet mignon with pepper and basil and (no kidding) the peanut butter pizza. **WHO** Seniors at tea time, clubbers in the wee hours. ☺ 📖

[Three Drunken Goats] 2256 Honolulu Ave., Montrose, 818.249.9950. L Tues.- Sun., D nightly. Spanish/wine bar. Beer & wine. AE, MC, V. $$ - $$$ **WHY** You'll be tempted to continue ordering tapas until you're full, but save room for the churros with chocolate dipping sauce, one of the best desserts ever invented. **WHAT** This Montrose hot spot (no, that's not an oxymoron) has a huge menu of delicious, light small bites (bacon-wrapped dates, croquettes, mushrooms of many kinds, grilled octopus, steamed clams, excellent stuffed peppers, small and complex salads) and larger grilled dishes (New York steak with blue-cheese butter), plus a fun selection of wines and live gypsy music some nights. The point is to order a bottle of wine or a carafe of sangria, then linger over a parade of interesting dishes in the warm, high-ceilinged, barn-like space. 🦪

[Tibet Nepal House] 36 E. Holly St., Old Pasadena, 626.585.0955, tibetnepalhouse.com. L & D Tues.-Sun., brunch Sat.-Sun. Nepalese. Beer & wine. AE, MC, V. $ - $$ **WHY** The buffet lunch is inexpensive and wonderful. **WHAT** The mountaineer/photographer/chef trained in Austria and brings a gourmet sensibility to Tibetan and Nepalese cuisine, which is reminiscent of both Chinese and Indian food but more subtly flavored. Karma Tenzing Bhotia's menu spans the Himalayas, from lowland curries and dals to highland yak, noodles and *momos* (dumplings). Try the savory, soup-like Tibetan butter tea. 📖🦪☺

[Tonny's] 843 E. Orange Grove Blvd., Pasadena, 626.797.0866. B, L & D daily. Mexican. No booze. MC, V. $ **WHY** Some of most delicious guacamole ever, chunky and fragrant with cilantro and limes. Homemade tortillas wrap *delicioso* burritos and seafood tacos, and the chile verde is heavenly. **WHAT** Warm and welcoming, this little family restaurant has an open kitchen, a tiny patio out back, about eight tables and very good home cooking. A small but sparkling gem in the heart of working-class Pasadena. 📖☺☼

[Vietnam Restaurant] 🏛 340 W. Las Tunas Dr., San Gabriel, 626.281.5577, vietnam-restaurant.com. L & D. Mon.-Wed. & Fri.-Sun. Vietnamese. No booze. MC, V. $ **WHY** The it spot of the moment for

---

🏛 ESSENTIALLY L.A. ☺LATE ♥ROMANTIC 📖VALUE 🔇QUIET 🌱SUSTAINABLE

pho, crisp spring rolls and a hugely portioned and delicious seven-course beef dinner. **WHAT** The result of a squabble in the family that owns the famed Golden Deli and Vietnam House led to two members of the family—including the former Vietnam House cook—splitting off to open this tidy little place. The result is yet another, even better Vietnamese café with all the standard dishes and a superb $13 seven-course beef dinner than can easily feed two. **WHO** Former Vietnam House groupies who followed the cook here. 🖅 ☺

[Xiang Wei Lou] **227 W. Valley Blvd., San Gabriel, 626.289.2276. L & D daily. Chinese/Hunan. Beer & wine. Cash only. $ WHY** Perhaps the best Hunanese food in the San Gabriel Valley. **WHAT** There's considerable talent behind the stoves at this plain but spiffy café next to the San Gabriel Hilton. The dishes showcase a multiplicity of chile types and styles: dried to an almost black-red or sun-bleached; whole or crushed into flakes; soft and almost sweet, yet blazing; and so forth. Try the cumin beef laced with dry and fresh red peppers; lamb riblets with a musky herbal heat; the broth with several varieties of fresh mush-rooms; and, to cool your palate, fresh cucumber cubes. **WHO** Spicy-food lovers who also appreciate the late (by Chinese-restaurant stan-dards) closing time of 11:30 p.m. ☺ 🖅

[Yang Chow] **3777 E. Colorado Blvd., East Pasadena, 626.432.6868, yangchow.com. L & D daily. Chinese/Sichuan. Beer & wine. AE, MC, V. $$ WHY** The slippery shrimp is twice-cooked, bathed in a subtly sweet, mildly hot sauce, and just about impossible to stop eating, unfortunately for your heart (it's a notoriously fatty and caloric dish). **WHAT** This branch of the Chinatown classic draws a huge and devoted clientele. The slippery shrimp is famous, and also good are the cashew chicken, fiery Sichuan won ton soup, pan-fried dumplings and dry-sautéed asparagus and green beans. Good service, too. **WHO** Families who come here once a week. 🍴 ☺ ✲

[Yujean Kang's] 🏠 **67 N. Raymond Ave., Old Pasadena, 626.585.0855, yujeankangs.com. L & D daily. Chinese/French. Full bar. AE, MC, V. $$$ WHY** Dishes like duck salad with black-bean sauce and Chinese "polenta" with shrimp, mushrooms and scallions, along with a wine list created by the oenophile chef to harmonize with his menu. **WHAT** The setting is sophisticated and so is the menu, reflecting a French chef's panache and a Chinese gourmand's sense of robust fla-vor. Don't miss the tea-smoked duck, won ton soup, crispy beef with sautéed vegetables and the stir-fried Blue Lake green beans. A great place for a business lunch in Old Pasadena. **WHO** A mature crowd, including lots of oenophiles. ♥ 🍴 🍸

[Yunnan Garden] **545 W. Las Tunas Dr., San Gabriel, 626.308.1896. L & D daily. Chinese. Beer. MC, V. $ WHY** To discover the flavors of China's Yunnan province. **WHAT** A brightly lit Chinese café like a thousand others in the area, with the brusque service that's the norm. But the culinary style is more uncommon: the robust, chile-laden food of the mountainous Yunnan province, which fills China's southwest corner. Try the crossing-the-bridge noodles, cumin lamb, and won tons in an addictive chile broth. 🗟

[Zeke's Smokehouse] 🏠 **2209 Honolulu Ave., Montrose, 818.957.7045, zekessmokehouse.com. L Mon.- Fri., D nightly, brunch Sat.-Sun. American/barbecue. Beer & wine. AE, MC, V. $$ - $$$ WHY** Sweet potato fries, pulled-pork sandwiches and Memphis-style baby-back ribs. **WHAT** A partnership between chefs Leonard Cohen (Maple Drive, 72 Market St.) and Michael Rosen (Reign) along with the Gelsinger family (Gelsinger's Meats) opened Zeke's in 2002. It's become a Montrose mainstay for its top-quality regional American barbecue and smokehouse cooking, as well as its charming retro-style interior. **WHO** Locals, families and 'cue fans from both valleys. ☺ ☼

EAST VALLEY

[Asanebo] 🏠 **11941 Ventura Blvd., Studio City, 818.760.3348. L Tues.-Fri., D Tues.-Sun. Japanese. Beer & wine. AE, MC, V. $$$$ - $$$$$ WHY** The omakase. **WHAT** Despite its unprepossessing location, Asanebo is a destination restaurant that serves top-quality sashimi, sushi and cooked specialties. It's expensive, so ask for the prices of specials if they aren't posted. Omakase starts at about $75 per person. **WHO** Loyal regulars, including some of L.A.'s top chefs, and visitors who want to eat at a Michelin one-star in a Valley strip mall.

[Bistro Provence] **345 N. Pass Ave., Burbank, 818.840.9050, bistroprovenceburbank.com. L Mon.-Fri., D Mon.-Sat. Californian/French. Beer & wine. AE, MC, V. $$ - $$$ WHY** For good-value French classics: endive salads, roast chicken with garlic fries, beef bourguignon, crème brûlée. **WHAT** Patina alum Miki Zivkovic has created a welcoming neighborhood restaurant in an unattractive strip mall next to a Starbucks. Inside it's romantic and warm, filled with regulars who've found a little bit of Paris in frumpy Burbank. **WHO** Studio workers and Toluca Lake residents in on the secret. ♥ 🗟

[Boneyard Bistro] **13539 Ventura Blvd., Sherman Oaks, 818.906.7427, boneyardbistro.com. D nightly, brunch Sat.-Sun. Barbecue/ American. Beer & wine. AE, MC, V. $$ - $$$ WHY** Pulled pork potstickers, barbecued tri-tip, grilled bone-in rib-eye and more than a hundred beers. **WHAT** Chef/owner Aaron Robins has successfully merged an upscale bistro with a barbecue joint, and the locals love it. Between the 'cue and the bistro sides of the menu, there's something to satisfy any palate; plus, the daily specials are usually excellent. Huge portions. **WHO** Big eaters from Sherman Oaks and environs.

🏠 ESSENTIALLY L.A. ☺ LATE ♥ ROMANTIC 🗟 VALUE 🍃 QUIET ☼ SUSTAINABLE

[Bua Siam] **12924 Sherman Way, North Hollywood, 818.765.8395. L & D daily. Thai. No booze. MC, V. $** **WHY** Consistently excellent cooking that doesn't pander to the sweet-craving American palate. Free delivery, too. **WHAT** It's not just the array of tapas-sized plates that draws us to this stylish boxcar-size spot. Although who can argue with $2.99 appetizers that include skewered meatballs, crunchy rice cakes with Thai chile, the Thai spaghetti called *knom jean* and southern fish curry? Regulars know to share entrée-size orders of mussel omelets or shatteringly crisp ground catfish on an incendiary green-papaya salad. Note that the blazingly spicy stir-fries are geared to Thai palates unless otherwise requested. **WHO** Lots of Thais, and non-Thais who like their cooking authentic.

[Ca' Del Sole] **4100 Cahuenga Blvd., Toluca Lake, 818.985.4669, cadelsole.com. L Mon.-Fri., D nightly, brunch Sun. Italian. Full bar. AE, MC, V. $$ - $$$** **WHY** Charm, consistently good rustic Italian cooking, and the chance that you might run into that producer who hasn't been returning your calls. **WHAT** Although it's full of showbiz people, Ca' Del Sole is not a scene—most people come here because they want to eat well and have a good conversation with their companions, whether on the walled Venetian patio or in the handsome, rambling interior. Try the octopus, the salumi, the baby artichokes with wild arugula and parmesan, and any of the house-made pastas. **WHO** At lunch it's a virtual commissary for folks from Warners, Universal, Disney and CBS Radford; at dinner, it's more filled with Toluca Lake locals having a date night.

[Caioti Pizza Café] 🏠 **4346 Tujunga Ave., Studio City, 818.761.3588, caiotipizzacafe.com. L & D daily, brunch Sat.-Sun. Pizzeria. BYOB. MC, V. $ - $$** **WHY** Superb salads (try the Humble Salad, a romaine wedge with bacon, goat cheese and roma tomatoes, or the "The" salad, said to induce labor in pregnant women) and Caioti's rightly famed individual pizza; don't forget to order some garlic rolls, too. **WHAT** Ed LaDou may have shuffled off this mortal coil, but the California pizza he invented (that's right, it was LaDou, not Puck) lives on in this casual, noisy café. Fun, affordable and delicious. **WHO** Valley families sharing salads and pizzas.

[Carnival] **4356 Woodman Ave., Sherman Oaks, 818.784.3469, carnivalrest.com. L & D daily. Lebanese/Middle Eastern. Beer & wine. AE, MC, V. $$** **WHY** Creamy hummus, fattouch salad with crispy pita chips, kebabs and grilled quail are all well prepared. Nightly specials run to such things as an unusual okra stew with lamb. **WHAT** With a huge menu of Lebanese specialties as well as takeout and catering, this comfy restaurant serving the San Fernando Valley's large Middle Eastern community will please both vegetarians and carnivores. Try the combination appetizer plate, which lets everyone taste a few salads.

🔖 VEGETARIAN ⊙ KID FRIENDLY ✿ PATIO DINING 🚚 DELIVERY 🎩 PRIVATE PARTY

[Cedar House Café] **4805 Whitsett Ave., Valley Village, 818.769.9994. L & D daily. Middle Eastern/Lebanese. Beer & wine. MC, V. $ - $$ WHY** Wonderful lentil soup, robustly garlicky hummus and kebabs of exceptional tenderness and flavor. **WHAT** Consistently delicious Lebanese food is the draw at this friendly neighborhood spot, known for its chicken and lamb kebabs, hummus, falafel and schwarma. Weekdays are relaxed, but weekend nights bring live music, so it gets loud. 📖 ☺ ✿

[Chadaka Thai] **310 N. San Fernando Blvd., Burbank, 818.848.8520. L & D daily. Thai. Full bar. AE, MC, V. $ - $$$ WHY** Full bar service (yes!) and tasty Thai make a great happy-hour combo. **WHAT** Amid the mega-chain restaurants at Burbank Media Center is a branch of Silver Lake's popular Rambutan Thai serving fresh, authentic Thai food in a gorgeous modern room overlooked by an illuminated Buddha above the bar. A great spot before or after a movie at the nearby cinemas. **WHO** Movie-goers and studio workers. ♥📖

[El Katracho] **14838 Burbank Blvd., Sherman Oaks, 818.780.7044, elkatrachorestaurant.com. B, L, D daily. Honduran. Beer & wine. MC, V. $ - $$ WHY** Well-prepared Honduran *baleadas* (fat quesadillas), marinated chicken and conch soup served by non-English speakers in a spotless and attractive storefront restaurant. **WHAT** Overmortgaged on your Van Nuys house? Then come to El Katracho for one of the $6 lunch specials, and you'll be fed for the day — and then some. Honduran cooking is rich and hearty (but not spicy), and here it's served in abundance: mountains of plantains, hillocks of very good rice, heaping bowls of not-so-great beans, big scoops of shredded-cabbage salad and big hunks o' chicken, pork or beef. Choose the subtly sweet marinated chicken over the dry fried chicken or, better yet, order the conch soup like the regulars do. 📖 ☺

[Katsu-Ya] **11680 Ventura Blvd., Studio City, 818.985.6976, katsu-yagroup.com. L Mon.-Fri., D nightly. Japanese. Beer & wine. AE, MC, V. $$$ - $$$$ WHY** Spicy tuna on crispy rice, seared spicy albacore sashimi, daily specials. **WHAT** The original Studio City location of the mini Katsu-Ya empire has gotten way too popular for many, but that doesn't deter hordes of sushi lovers from waiting in line for a table or a coveted seat at the sushi bar. Elaborate rolls and intricate presentations are a hallmark, but the fish is fresh and the vibe is hip and fun. **WHO** Stylish Valleyites, including plenty of show people, who don't mind the crowds or the noise level.

[Kiwami] 📖 **11920 Ventura Blvd., Studio City, 818.763.3910, katsu-yagroup.com. L Mon.-Sat., D nightly. Japanese/sushi. Beer & wine. AE, MC, V. $$$ - $$$$ WHY** At the time of this writing, über-sushi-chef Katsuya Uechi is not only in the house; he's preparing omakase in the small sushi bar at the back. **WHAT** After Katsu Michite closed Tama to open Katsu Sushi in Beverly Hills, Uechi took over the old space, notwithstanding the fact that he has the perennially popular Katsu-Ya just up the block. At Kiwami (which means "the ultimate" in Japanese), Uechi has created an elegant, sleek dining room where you can go high-end and savor superb omakase, or order à la carte and enjoy daily nigiri sushi and sashimi specials or classics such as miso-marinated black cod. To experience sushi prepared by Uechi himself, call well ahead of time to reserve seats in the back sushi bar. **WHO** Universal and CBS staffers on lunch break or after work, sushi hounds from all over, and Studio City families with sophisticated, chopsticks-wielding kids in tow.

[Krua Thai] 🛈 13130 Sherman Way, North Hollywood, 818.759.7998. L & D daily. Thai. No booze. MC, V. $ - $$ **WHY** Pad Thai, pan-fried noodle dishes, papaya salad with blue crab. **WHAT** A standout among the many excellent establishments in NoHo's "Thai Gulch," Krua serves robustly flavored dishes that can be dialed up or down in heat level. Don't miss its excellent version of pad thai as well as *pad kee mao*, flat noodles stir-fried with green chilies, mint leaves and pork. **WHO** Young people on a budget, Thai families. 🖼🍴☺

[La Cava] 13565 Ventura Blvd., Sherman Oaks, 818.981.1517, lacavashermanoaks.com. L Mon.-Sat., D nightly. Italian. Beer & wine. AE, MC, V. $$ - $$$ **WHY** Terrific, refined Italian fare without having to go over the hill. **WHAT** Florentine native and sometime actor Armando Pucci has created a delightful spot for fans of light, sophisticated Tuscan food. We are slaves to the chalkboard daily specials (the pappardelle with Dungeness crab and cherry tomatoes is sublime), but the regular menu has plenty of temptations, including thin-crust pizzas, fresh salads and excellent pastas (try the spaghetti with seafood in a light tomato sauce). The Italian desserts are house-made and authentic. **WHO** Young foodies to Valley retirees who wonder why eggplant parm isn't on the menu. ☼

[La Frite Café] 15013 Ventura Blvd., Sherman Oaks, 818.990.1791, lafritecafe.com. L & D daily, brunch Sat.-Sun. French. Full bar. AE, MC, V. $$ - $$$$ **WHY** Satisfying French bistro fare without having to go over the hill. **WHAT** Chef Gordon Ramsay's stem-to-stern redo of this Sherman Oaks mainstay (39 years!) resulted in a trimmer, more modern menu that focuses on what the kitchen does best: simple French bistro food and savory and sweet crêpes. Don't miss the onion soup, the mushroom-Brie crêpe, or the steak frites. Fans of the old La Frite can visit the Woodland Hills location, which retains the sprawling pre-Ramsay menu. **WHO** Locals and a smattering of ex-pat Parisians. 🍷

[Lotería Grill Studio City] 🛈 12050 Ventura Blvd., Studio City, 818.508.5300, loteriagrill.com. B, L & D daily. Mexican. Full bar. AE, MC, V. $$ - $$$ **WHY** The best Mexican food in the Valley—with margaritas,

🥬 **VEGETARIAN** ⊙ **KID FRIENDLY** ⌖ **PATIO DINING** 🚚 **DELIVERY** 🏠 **PRIVATE PARTY**

to boot. **WHAT** Chef Jimmy Shaw of the original Lotería Grill in the Farmers Market and its successful spinoff in Hollywood now rules the second floor of the strip mall at Ventura and Laurel Canyon. In an airy space decorated with blowups of vintage lotería cards, Shaw's cooks whip up all the Lotería favorites—tacos, tostadas, sopes and burritos with richly flavorful fillings like cochinita pibil, nopalitos and shrimp with spicy morita sauce—plus more substantial dishes, such as grilled skirt steak and chiles rellenos. The margaritas are killer. **WHO** Aficionados of real Mexico City cooking.

[Malbec] **10150 Riverside Dr., Toluca Lake, 818.762.4860, malbeccuisine.com. L & D daily. Argentinean. Beer & wine. AE, MC, V. $$ - $$$ WHY** Good, honest Argentinean cooking and wines at modest prices. **WHAT** This offshoot of the successful Pasadena original has the same affordable Argentinean wines, an equally nice staff, and the same menu of well-prepared classics: empanadas, *matambre* (rolled meat stuffed with vegetables and herbs), garlic fries, handmade pastas and such hearty entrées as grilled short ribs (great flavor but too chewy), skirt steak chimichurri (delicious) and grilled salmon. **WHO** Toluca Lake neighbors running into each other. 📝

[Mantee] **10962 Ventura Blvd., Studio City, 818.761.6565, manteecafe.com. L & D Tues.-Sun. Lebanese/Armenian. Beer & wine. AE, MC, V. $$ WHY** For mantee, of course (it's an Armenian specialty), along with many other Middle Eastern dishes. **WHAT** This little place serves all the usual suspects, and very well, too (fattoush salad, made with purslane, is terrific; garlicky labne toom is heavenly; lamb kebabs are tender and juicy). But don't miss the more unusual specialties, such as the toasted ravioli called *mantee*, served warm under a blanket of garlicky yogurt. Sweet and sour ground-beef kebabs with cherry sauce are another good pick. Weather permitting, the back patio is a fine spot, but be sure to reserve as tables go fast. ☼

[Maxmilian's] **11330 Weddington St., North Hollywood, 818.760.1300, maxiatnoho.com. L & D Tues.-Sun. Hungarian. Beer & wine. AE, MC, V. $$ - $$$$ WHY** For evolved, lighter-than-you-expect Austro-Hungarian cuisine. **WHAT** At this pretty and secluded NoHo spot, everyone seems to know chef Laszlo Bossanyi, who for 20 years built a following with his Hungarian comfort food at shuttered Hortobagy in Studio City. He smokes his own lower-fat *kolbász* (sausages), duck breast and salmon and makes such dishes as *loup de mer* (Mediterranean sea bass) in a delicate lobster ragout and the hefty Burgenländer platter for two, served tableside. **WHO** Patrons from the old-line Hungarian community, many who immigrated in the '50s, and those who yearn for a taste of crisp-skinned roast duck with spaetzle.

[Mistral] **13422 Ventura Blvd., Sherman Oaks, 818.981.6650, mistralrestaurant.net. L Mon.-Fri., Sun., D nightly. French. Full bar. AE,**

MC, V. $$$ - $$$$ **WHY** A reliably good and well-run French bistro with an elegant decor, a proper bowl of onion soup, excellent steak frites and a perfect chocolate soufflé. The steak tartare has a loyal following. **WHAT** Stick to the brasserie classics served in this wood-paneled, chandelier-lit French spot and you'll be as happy as everyone else who packs the place day and night: frisée lardon, steak tartare, steak frites covered in golden shallots and simple whitefish. Cracker-jack service. **WHO** French ex-pats and south-of-Ventura folks planning their next trip to France.

[Natas Pastries] **13317 Ventura Blvd., Sherman Oaks, 818.788.8050, nataspastries.com. B, L & D daily. Portuguese. Beer & wine. MC, V. $$ - $$$ WHY** For the chance to explore the rich flavors of authentic Portuguese cooking. **WHAT** Known for its traditional Portuguese pastries, Natas now has a full-on restaurant. You could be in Lisbon—the charming room, entirely lined in crisp blue-and-white tile, is one of the few places in town to sample dishes like *caldeirada*, a seafood stew, and *feijoada*, a sausage and bean stew served with rice. **WHO** Ex-pats and regulars who discovered this place via the famed bakery. ☺

[Pinot Bistro] 🏛 **12969 Ventura Blvd., Studio City, 818.990.0500, patinagroup.com. L Mon.-Fri., D nightly. Californian/French. Full bar. AE, MC, V. $$$ - $$$$ WHY** Belgian endive salad with Roquefort, whitefish fillet with brandade and a great roast chicken with frites, all served in a place right out of the 8th arrondissement. **WHAT** Pinot Bistro is the oldest and most reliable of Joachim Splichal's Patina spinoffs. Avant-garde when it opened, this handsome, artfully lit bistro has evolved into a neighborhood favorite that fits its upscale Sherman Oaks location to a T. A no-corkage-fee policy brings in the wine buffs. **WHO** An older, well-dressed crowd that appreciates good French food and professional service. ♥ 🍴 🏛

[Raphael] **11616 Ventura Blvd., Studio City, 818.505.3337, raphaelonventura.com. L Mon.-Fri., D nightly. French. Beer & wine. AE, MC, V. $$$ - $$$$ WHY** Because Studio City needs a civilized, elegant spot for lunch and dinner. **WHAT** Raphael is an intimate boîte with an eclectic yet traditional menu from chef Adam Horton, formerly of Saddle Peak Lodge. The interior, designed by Terry Raphael, is drop-dead gorgeous, with a comfortable lounge/bar and a warm dining room that has so many nooks, almost every table feels private. The globe-trotting menu (well-seasoned steak tartare, rich French onion soup, yellowfin tuna with crispy rice) offers something for everyone, from vegans to unabashed carnivores; don't miss the hand-cut French fries. A particularly good place for a quiet, scrumptious lunch. **WHO** Well-heeled Vals. ♥ 🍴

[Shiraz] **15472 Ventura Blvd., Sherman Oaks, 818.789.7788, shirazrestaurant.net. L & D daily. Persian/Middle Eastern. Beer & wine. AE,**

🌿 VEGETARIAN ◎ KID FRIENDLY ✿ PATIO DINING �DELIVERY 🏛 PRIVATE PARTY

MC, V. $ - $$ **WHY** The kebabs and Middle Eastern classics are good, but live a little and try some of the seasonal Persian specialties, like the chicken stewed with cherries. **WHAT** This fine old-timer is good for Persian classics; a specialty is fish pilaf, a traditional dish for the Iranian New Year. But most regulars return for the chicken kebabs, hummus, and robust stews served over basmati rice. Service is sometimes grumpy, and the setting is comfortable but nothing special, so the local delivery is popular. ☺🚗

[Skaf's Grill] **6008 Laurel Canyon Blvd., North Hollywood, 818.985.5701. L & D Mon.-Sat. Lebanese/Middle Eastern. No booze. AE, MC, V. $ WHY** Scrumptious, cheap Lebanese specialties, including a great cabbage salad, richly flavored hummus and excellent kebabs. **WHAT** Overlook the funky strip mall and cramped parking lot; Skaf's is a find if you enjoy Middle Eastern food but don't feel like spending a lot of dough. It has a slick new branch in Glendale, but the NoHo location is somehow more real. In addition to the kebabs, the daily specials can be good choices. **WHO** An eclectic crowd of budget-conscious diners. 📷🔖☺

[Smoke House] 🏛 **4420 W. Lakeside Dr., Burbank, 818.845.3731, smokehouse1946.com. L & D daily., brunch Sun. American. Full bar. AE, MC, V. $$$ - $$$$ WHY** Famous for the garlic bread, the Smoke House is best at old-school dinner-house fare like steak Sinatra, prime rib and shrimp Louie. A popular brunch buffet on weekends, early-bird specials and live entertainment in the lounge also draw fans. **WHAT** Judy Garland is no longer dining at the Smoke House, but the faux-Tudor restaurant looks nearly the same as it did in her day. Studio workers from Warner's and Disney, couples on dates and old-timers who have been eating here since opening day in 1946 love the vintage atmosphere, generous cocktails and retro menu. We usually stick to the cocktails. **WHO** Your dad—and maybe your grandpa, too. 💔🏛

[Sompun] **12051 Ventura Pl., Studio City, 818.762.7861. L & D Tues.-Sun. Thai. Beer & wine. MC, V. $ WHY** A long list of traditional noodle dishes infrequently seen outside Thai Town. **WHAT** In its hidden location, this simple spot has been surprising folks for more than 25 years with the quality of its food. Besides the excellent noodle dishes, you must try the swoon-worthy yet rarely seen "Indian"-style coconut curry and its northern cousin, *kao soi*. Also setting this place apart from the usual mom 'n pop Thai café are such dishes as the eastern-style sausage salad with chopped ginger and the flaky *roti* griddle bread that you dunk into rich curries. 📷🔖🚗

[Spark Woodfire Grill] **11801 Ventura Blvd., Studio City, 818.623.8883, sparkwoodfiregrill.com. L Mon.-Fri., D nightly. Italian/Californian. Full bar. AE, MC, V. $$ - $$$$ WHY** Fashionable cocktails, pretty salads and delicious pizzas and meat dishes cooked in the wood-burning oven. **WHAT** You name the trendy dish, this friendly Cal-Italian bistro serves it: burrata with tomatoes, grilled artichokes, individual pizzas, flat-iron steaks, retro-hip meatloaf, "smashed" potatoes, white chocolate bread pudding—what's not to like? Good bar and grill fare in a convenient Studio City location, at prices that are neither high nor low. 🏠

[Sushi House of Taka] **4627 Van Nuys Blvd., Sherman Oaks, 818.784.8777. L Mon.- Fri., D nightly. Japanese/sushi. Beer & wine. AE, MC, V. $$$ - $$$$ WHY** Generously sized, tasty pieces of sushi in a low-key setting. **WHAT** Don't be put off by the dated-looking interior of this restaurant around the corner from Ventura Boulevard. The sushi spots on Ventura may get more attention, but chef "Taka" Tanaka serves up impeccably fresh sushi and sashimi as well as such classics as tempura and teriyaki. Ordering off the specials board is the best approach. **WHO** Sushi fans from Sherman Oaks and Encino who would rather that their local find doesn't get discovered. 🖳🌣

[Sushi Nozawa] 🏠 **11288 Ventura Blvd., Studio City, 818.508.7017, sushinozawa.com. L & D Mon.-Fri. Japanese/sushi. Beer & wine. MC, V. $$$$ - $$$$$ WHY** A limited selection of impeccably fresh sushi prepared with warm rice. **WHAT** Kazunori Nozawa is one of the chefs who put Studio City's Sushi Row on L.A.'s culinary map, thanks to his rigid standards for seafood—not to mention for customer behavior. You either tolerate his "my way or the highway" approach or you're offended by it, but many who understand the subtleties of traditional sushi service are big fans of Nozawa's omakase. **WHO** Sushi purists and out-of-towners curious about "the Sushi Nazi."

[Sushi Yuzu] **10118 Riverside Dr., Toluca Lake, 818.763.8355. L Mon.- Fri., D nightly. Japanese/sushi. Beer & wine. AE, MC, V. $$ - $$$ WHY** To savor impeccably fresh sushi and terrific rolls. **WHAT** A sophisticated hideaway in upscale Toluca Lake, Sushi Yuzu boasts a loyal following of diners who appreciate top-quality seafood and creative flavor combinations. The specials list is a treasure-trove of temptations, from cold and hot appetizers, to nigiri sushi made with warm rice, to exquisitely fashioned hand rolls and richly flavored cut rolls. Parking is a challenge, particularly at lunch, but it's well worth a walk. **WHO** Studio staffers, real estate brokers, sushi mavens.

[Swan Restaurant] **12728 Sherman Way, North Hollywood, 818.764.1892, swanthaifood.com. L & D daily. Thai. No booze. MC, V. $ WHY** Unusual dishes like acacia omelet curry and a standout Crying Tiger beef with a complex dipping sauce. **WHAT** Despite the modest interior, there's some serious Thai cooking going on here. Ask one of the very kind servers for the special small-plates menu. 🖳🍷🌣�Delivery

---

🥬 VEGETARIAN ⊙ KID FRIENDLY ☼ PATIO DINING 🚚 DELIVERY 🏠 PRIVATE PARTY

WEST VALLEY

[Adagio] 22841 Ventura Blvd., Woodland Hills, 818.225.0533. D Tues.-Sun. Italian. Full bar. AE, MC, V. $$$ **WHY** Upscale Italian food and service of a higher caliber than you'd expect from such a modest-looking place, at prices that are more than fair. **WHAT** A real find in the west Valley, Adagio is all about comfort: a cozy but not too fancy setting, solicitous but not too formal service, and well-prepared Italian food that makes everyone happy: tableside Caesars, excellent soups, rich osso buco and a large roster of daily specials. **WHO** West Valley boomers taking their parents out for a nice dinner. 🗃 🍸 ☺

[Alcazar] 17239 Ventura Blvd., Encino, 818.789.0991, al-cazar.com. L & D daily. Lebanese/Middle Eastern. Full bar. AE, MC, V. $ - $$$ **WHY** Chef's hummus, spicy muhammara, chicken livers with pomegranate juice, grilled kebabs. **WHAT** This spacious restaurant with a covered outdoor dining area for hookah smoking serves terrific Lebanese specialties, ranging from the familiar (hummus, kebabs) to the exotic (quail, frogs' legs, lamb tongue, beef brains). The vegetarian plate is a great option for sharing, and a side dish of toasted bulgur (*firik*) is a delicious complement to the kebabs. Come on a Friday or Saturday evening for live music. Another location in Westwood. **WHO** The Lebanese diaspora, and a lot of non-Lebanese folks who think this is the best Middle Eastern restaurant around. ☺ ☼

[Alexis Greek Restaurant] 9034 Tampa Ave., Northridge, 818.349.9689, alexisgreek.com. L Mon.-Sat., D nightly. Greek/Portuguese. Beer & wine. MC, V. $$ **WHY** The best of both coasts: Portuguese dishes alongside classic Greek fare. **WHAT** Alexis Kavvadias's 37-year-old restaurant evolved when his Portuguese-born wife, Fatima, came on board. The candlelit dining room is more elegant, and the wine list and menu more diverse. Greek country-style specialties like braised lamb with artichoke hearts in lemon sauce already made it a standout. Now there's Portuguese broiled chicken with peppery *piri piri* sauce, a fabulous *coelho estufado* (braised rabbit) and a selection of international pastries. **WHO** West Valley residents glad to have authentic Greek in a white tablecloth setting, and, of course, Portuguese food lovers. ♥🗃

[Bistro Orient] 21799 Ventura Blvd., Woodland Hills, 818.456.4564, orientla.com. L Mon.-Sat., D nightly. Asian. Beer & wine. MC, V. $$ **WHY** For top-quality Vietnamese and Thai cooking. **WHAT** Owner-chef Dan Nguyen, who seems omnipresent in this small, stylish café in Warner Center Shopping Plaza, has created a gem offering Vietnamese and Thai specialties, including pad thai, sates, salads, curries and stir-fries. Don't miss the pho and other noodle soups, the succulent, porky baby-back riblets with sate sauce, and the caramelized sea bass stir-fried with mushrooms, green onions and dill. Nothing is spicy-hot (this is the West Valley, after all), but porcelain condiment trays dispense fiery add-ons. **WHO** Woodland Hills foodies. 🍴☺☼

[Bleecker Street] **5442 Yolanda Ave., Tarzana, 818.996.3008, the-bleeckerstreet.com. L Tues.- Fri, D Tues.- Sun. Modern American. Full bar. AE, MC, V. $$ WHY** Because there's nothing like it in Tarzana: an up-scale but casual spot serving the kind of food we like to eat. **WHAT** A couple of smart restaurateurs (they own 22 places around the country) opened Bleecker Street in 2009, in affluent but restaurant-challenged Tarzana, and it took off like a rocket. The two-story space doesn't resemble the Greenwich Village restaurants it's supposed to evoke, but no matter. Get a thin-crust pizza served on a board (gorgonzola, fig jam and onion is a winner) and one of the good salads (but not the oily, chewy kale Caesar); or indulge in a New York strip with excellent horseradish mashed potatoes. About 50 wines by the glass are served from an argon-based preservation system. **WHO** A grown-up crowd. 🦪

[Brandywine] **22757 Ventura Blvd., Woodland Hills, 818.225.9114. L Tues.-Fri., D Mon.-Sat. French/Modern American. Beer & wine. AE, MC, V. $$$$ - $$$$$ WHY** Personal service and cooking in an intimate, romantic, special-occasion setting. **WHAT** In a twist on the old French standard, at Brandywine the wife does the cooking and the husband runs the front, and it's clearly a harmonious relationship. This tiny place is romantic as all get-out, and chef Peggy McWilliams makes the kind of food you want when you're celebrating or seducing: caviar, tableside Caesars, rack of lamb, Muscovy duck, even chateaubriand for two. **WHO** Couples who want to cozy up in one of the booths. ♥ 🍷

[Brent's Delicatessen] 🏛 **19565 Parthenia St., Northridge, 818.886.5679, brentsdeli.com. B, L & D daily. Deli. No booze. AE, MC, V. $ - $$ WHY** Whitefish salad, tender corned beef on rye, silken cheesecake. **WHAT** Smoked-fish and corned-beef addicts from such deli-starved places as Pasadena and Burbank think nothing of driving 40 minutes to eat at Brent's. This is the real thing, with the full range of deli essentials, from hand-sliced lox and kreplach soup to brisket dips and a famed Cobb salad, all served in a basic coffee-shop setting. **WHO** A constant crush of West Valleyites, from young families to seniors who've been eating pastrami here for 40 years. 🖼🍴☕

[Hummus Bar & Grill] **18743 Ventura Blvd. , Tarzana, 818.344.6606, hummusbargrill.com. L & D daily. Israeli/Middle Eastern. No booze. AE, MC, V. $$ - $$$ WHY** The velvety hummus, of course, as well as a toothsome array of all-you-can-eat housemade salads and side dishes for just $6 per person with a main-course order. **WHAT** Conversations, many in Hebrew, fill the air in this popular casual-dining restaurant, along with a near-constant slapping sound of fresh dough being formed into *laffa*, a puffed Iraqi bread that is brought hot to every table. Skewered beef, chicken and lamb are popular entrées, but vegetarians can have a field day with the piquant salads, the hummus combos (it's served with chickpeas, pine nuts, or marinated mushrooms) and such classics as falafel with tahini. **WHO** The Israeli

---

🦪 VEGETARIAN ⊙ KID FRIENDLY ⊙ PATIO DINING �MDELIVERY 🎁 PRIVATE PARTY

diaspora and West Valleyites of all ethnic backgrounds who simply like terrific, freshly prepared Middle Eastern food. ☺ 🖼

[Itzik Hagadol Grill] **17201 Ventura Blvd. , Encino, 818.784.4080, itzikhagadol.com. L & D daily. Israeli/Middle Eastern. Beer & wine. AE, MC, V. $$ - $$$ WHY** For the dazzlingly colorful appetizer of 20 Israeli salads, the homemade flatbread and the array of grilled things on skewers. **WHAT** Come hungry to this upscale *shipudia* (Israeli skewer house), because regardless of your intentions, you'll eat too much. Pretty much every table orders the signature appetizer of 20 salads (carrots, eggplant, tabbouleh, mushrooms, etc.), and whichever ones you finish, the nice waiters will refill, no charge. Warm flatbread will magically appear on the table as fast as you eat it. And then there are the mesquite-grilled skewers: sizzling baby chicken thighs, chicken livers, filet of beef, foie gras and, yes, turkey testicles. It's not cheap, but it's good and it's great fun, especially for special occasions. **WHO** People who've been to the parent restaurant in Tel Aviv. 🖼 ☺

[Koko's Middle Eastern Restaurant] **16935 Vanowen St., Van Nuys, 818.708.1877. L & D Tues.-Sun. Armenian/Middle Eastern. No booze. AE, MC, V. $ - $$$ WHY** Mezze good enough—and generous enough—to make an entire meal. **WHAT** The ginormous bowl of pickled vegetables and tower of pita that show up as soon as you sit down sets the tone for the staggeringly generous portion sizes that are to come. Arrive hungry, or go with a group and share. *Muhamara* (crushed walnut dip with pomegranate juice), smoky eggplant dip, hummus and sliced lamb tongue in a lemon marinade are good choices from the appetizer list; a fine share-worthy entrée is *arayes-maria*, a garlicky round of ground lamb and beef laced with pine nuts and served in pita. ☺

[Lum-Ka-Naad] **8910 Reseda Blvd., Northridge, 818.882.3028, lumkanaad.com. L & D daily. Thai. No booze. MC, V. $ - $$ WHY** Rewarding Thai dishes not often seen outside of Thai Town, served in a warm little Northridge storefront. **WHAT** The brash tart heat of the south and the warm mellow flavors of the north come together in this rustically styled dining room, where the restaurant's forward-thinking owners aim to spread the word about "true" Thai flavors. The food is meticulously prepared—*laap plaa duk* (crispy catfish salad) and *laap kua* (ground pork salad), for example—and often comes with the restaurant's signature platters of palate-cooling fresh vegetables. 🖼

[Mercado Buenos Aires] **7540 Sepulveda Blvd., Van Nuys, 818.786.0522. L & D daily. Argentinean. Beer & wine. AE, MC, V. $ - $$ WHY** Excellent and authentic Argentinean classics: empanadas, milanesa, white fish, huge platters of sizzling meat, mashed potatoes and bread pudding, all at more than reasonable prices. **WHAT** At this quirky café in the middle of a deli and meat market, patrons cheer their soccer team on TV or simply kibitz while munching on sand-wiches slathered with herby chimichurri or on a grilled steak from the meat department, where every cut for a good parillada is sold. After your lunch or dinner, you can pick up pastries, tortas, cold cuts and upscale Latin American groceries from the market. **WHO** Who knew there were so many Argentineans in the Valley? 🖼️ ☺

[Puro Sabor Peruvian Food] 🏛️ **6366 Van Nuys Blvd., Van Nuys, 818.908.0818. B, L & D daily. Peruvian. BYOB. MC, V. $ - $$ WHY** Pure, unadulterated Peruvian flavors (*puro sabor* means "pure flavor") in a sweet Valley spot with modest prices. **WHAT** This isn't the most scenic neighborhood in Van Nuys, but inside is a cheerful, spotless café that showcases the accomplished cooking of chef Juana Paz, a bank teller from Peru who succeeded in achieving her twin dreams of moving to the United States and having her own restaurant. Everything she makes is wonderful: sparkling, well-balanced ceviches; a superb *parihuela*, the South American answer to bouillabaisse; *seco de chivo*, a rich, long-simmered kid stew; lumberjack-size Peruvian breakfasts on weekends; and, for dessert, heavenly *picarones*, tempura-light pumpkin doughnuts. 🖼️

[Rincon Taurino] **8708 Van Nuys Blvd., Panorama City, 818.892.7444. B, L & D daily (to 3 a.m. Sat.-Sun.). Mexican. No booze. Cash only. $ WHY** Tender al pastor with a crunchy glaze, pit-barbecued lamb and chicken on weekends, and tender but lean *pierna de cerdo* (pork leg), served in burritos or tortas. **WHAT** First-timers come for the excellent tacos and burritos, then return for the Saturday and Sunday *barbacoa*, whole pit-roasted lamb, served in two courses: lamb soup, followed by the roasted lamb with rice, beans and guacamole. **WHO** North Valley carnivores—and even a few vegetarians, who come for the fine vegetarian burrito. ☺ 🖼️🥡☺

[Saddle Peak Lodge] 🏛️ **419 Cold Canyon Rd., Calabasas, 818.222.3888, saddlepeaklodge.com. D Wed.-Sun., brunch Sun. Modern American. Full bar. AE, MC, V. $$$$ - $$$$$ WHY** The country-rustic, ultra-atmospheric setting, not to mention the seared foie gras, elk tenderloin and a wine list bulging with trophy cabs. **WHAT** Decorated like a rustic hunting lodge and set in the spectacular mountains that divide Malibu from the Valley, Saddle Peak is that rarest of birds: a special-occasion restaurant that has remained special for years, despite several changes of chef. Expect a menu heavy on exotic meats and poultry (quail, venison, elk), excellent and attentive service and, at the end of the evening, a whacking big bill. **WHO** Well-heeled, well-dressed Angelenos who may have driven quite a distance to get here, and they're typically celebrating something. ❤️ 🍴 ☺ ☼ 🏛️

[Sako's Mediterranean Cuisine] **6736 Corbin Ave., Reseda, 818.342.8710, sakosmediterraneancuisine.com. L Sat.-Sun., D Wed.-Sun.**

🍴 **VEGETARIAN** ☺ **KID FRIENDLY** ☼ **PATIO DINING** 🚗 **DELIVERY** 🏛️ **PRIVATE PARTY**

Turkish/Armenian. No booze. MC, V. $ - $$ WHY *Iskender kebab*, an astonishingly tasty dish of seasoned ground beef cooked on a rotisserie then sliced very thin and served in a heap with a splash of light, fresh tomato sauce, grilled pita and yogurt swirled with brown butter. **WHAT** You have to really look to find this place, which is hidden behind a Del Taco and the Venetian Palace Gourmet Hall, but it's worth the hunt. In the cheerful, simple dining room you'll sample the delicious food of Istanbul: kebabs, surprisingly delicious fried eggplant, tripe soup and a beautiful *borek*, flaky tubes of phyllo filled with seasoned feta. Try the candied apple for dessert. **WHO** Homesick Turks and West Valleyites grateful for the good, inexpensive food. 🍸☺

[Sol y Luna] 19601 Ventura Blvd., Tarzana, 818.343.8488, solylunarestaurant.com. L Mon.-Fri., D nightly. Mexican. Full bar. AE, MC, V. $$ **WHY** Cal-Mexican food that's a notch above most; try the fresh tableside guac, housemade sopes and tamales, and luscious (if mild) chile verde. **WHAT** The family that owns the funkier Las Fuentes has done a fine job providing the West Valley with a good all-around full-bar Mexican restaurant. It's colorful and just kitschy enough, the food is better than it needs to be (places like this that serve margaritas seem to be packed no matter what refried gloop they serve), and the cadillac margaritas are excellent (but avoid the fruity ones). Cons: No reservations, so there's often a wait for dinner, and lots of noise when it's full. **WHO** Local working folks at lunch, and cheerful groups of families and friends at night. 🍸☺

[Springbok Bar & Grill] 16153 Victory Blvd., Van Nuys, 818.988.9786, thespringbok.com. L & D daily. South African. Full bar. AE, MC, V. $ - $$$ **WHY** Well-executed versions of South Africa's culinary hits: curries, chile sauces, meaty barbecues, a subtly spicy Naidoo's Durban curry, and tasty kebabs called *sosaties*. **WHAT** Because this is L.A.'s only South African restaurant, you might envision a modest, family-owned spot where you could sample a few of those wonderful South African wines and explore a delicious multicultural cuisine with European, Malaysian, East Indian and African elements. A cuisine, it would seem, perfectly suited to L.A. tastes. At first, the fantasy is crushed by the sports bar setting. But chef Trevor Netmann is turning out the real thing in a sea of flat-screen TVs and rugby matches. **WHO** South African ex-pats, rugby fans and curious diners. ☺🍸

[Sushi Ichiban Kan] 19723 Ventura Blvd., Woodland Hills, 818.883.8288, sushiichiban-kan.com. L Mon.-Fri., D nightly. Sushi/Japanese. Full bar. AE, MC, V. $$ - $$$ **WHY** Yes, Virginia, there is good sushi in the West Valley. **WHAT** Located in affluent, restaurant-hungry Woodland Hills, this place has a menu rich with cooked Japanese specialties such as tempura, teriyaki and grilled seafood, as well as sushi, sashimi and a variety of creative cut rolls. Regulars rave about the lunch combo specials, but at lunch or dinner the kitchen's real talent is behind the sushi counter. Service is warm and deferential; after a meal, you'll be ushered out with a flurry of bows from every staffer you pass. **WHO** A cross-section of sushi-loving West Valleyites. ♥ 🍸

[Sushi Iki] 18663 Ventura Blvd., Tarzana, 818.343.3470, sushiiki.com. L Tues.-Fri., D Tues.-Sun. Japanese/Sushi. Beer & wine. AE, MC, V. $$$$ - $$$$$ **WHY** Spectacular, if pricey, sushi. **WHAT** In addition to the familiar sushi and sashimi offerings, chef "Crazy Eddie" Okamoto offers exotic and unusual seafood items imported from around the world. If you're not on a budget, this is a great west Valley sushi option. ♥ 🍸

[Swiss Chef At San Remo] 13727 Victory Blvd., Valley Glen, 818.904.1500, swisschefusa.com. L Fri., D Wed.- Sun. Swiss/German. Full bar. AE, MC, V. $$ - $$$$ **WHY** To travel back in time in the heart of the Valley. **WHAT** Swiss-trained chef Ueli Huegli has transformed a tired Italian restaurant, with a menu pulled largely from the late, lamented Matterhorn Chef, where he used to cook. The extensive menu includes Italian pastas (handmade gnocchi is a specialty) as well as hearty Swiss-German dishes, such as sauerbraten, fondue, schnitzels and wursts. We wish the raclette was made with more flavorful cheese, and that the wienerschnitzel was tastier. But the Berner plate, a groaning board of grilled sausages, smoked pork and pork belly, is an indulgent treat, and a hefty portion of osso buco is rich and satisfying. A few items are pricey—the warm, oversized Bavarian pretzel is terrific but costs $8. **WHO** Older folk reminiscing about the good old days.

[Top Thai Cuisine] 7333 Reseda Blvd., Reseda, 818.705.8902. L & D Tues.- Sun. Thai. Beer & wine. AE, MC, V. $ - $$ **WHY** Superb northern Thai food in an unlikely Reseda location—it's a blessing for Northridge and Reseda locals and is worth a trip for Thai-food aficionados from farther away. **WHAT** It may be on a less-than-hip stretch of Reseda Boulevard, but the dining room is handsome and the china elegant. Proceed directly to the back page of the menu for the northern specialties—proprietress Noi Sriyana will be happy to make recommendations. Don't miss the *muu ping*, garlic-infused strips of pork; *khao sawy* noodle curry; or *sai ua* pork sausage. 🍸

[Uerukamu] 19596 Ventura Blvd., Tarzana, 818.609.0993. D Mon.- Sat. Japanese. Beer & wine. AE, MC, V. $$ - $$$ **WHY** Excellent range of sakes and very good food to accompany your sake. **WHAT** The menu at this izakaya and sake bar in a mini-mall offers carefully made classical dishes such as *chawan mushi* (steamed egg soup), fried eggplant with a miso glaze and pork chunks braised in sukiyaki sauce, as well as some good sushi standards. The extensive sake selection includes several flights and monthly sake deals. 🍸

[Woodlands] 9840 Topanga Canyon Blvd., Chatsworth, 818.998.3031, woodlandsinla.com. L & D Tues.- Sun. Indian/vegetarian. Beer & wine. AE,

MC, V. $ - $$ **WHY** "Dosa Night" (Wednesday), when you can pick a dosa and gorge yourself at the sumptuous buffet—all for $10. **WHAT** Who needs meat when you can feast on south Indian vegetarian fare that's this scrumptious? Go-to dishes include tamarind and lemon rice, coconut chutney and the amazing *chana batura*—fried bread that's as crisp as an eggshell and as big as a volleyball. **WHO** South Indians and vegetarians making a pilgrimage.

WESTSIDE: CENTRAL

[A-Frame] **12565 Washington Blvd., Culver City, 310.398.7700, aframela.com. L Sat.-Sun., D nightly. Asian/American. Full bar. AE, MC, V. $$ - $$$$ WHY** Asian, American, Latin and whatever-else-Roy-Choi-feels-like-cooking dishes intermingle in perfect harmony at this unfussy neighborhood restaurant that's something of an indoor picnic. **WHAT** Whether it's the crisp Beer Can Chicken or the cheekily named Knuckle Sandwich (a massive bowl of broth bobbing with oxtail, tendon and other unloved meaty bits), the man who invented the Kogi taco proves he's no one-hit-wonder. The house-made bread—a lightly sweet, five-grain pan de sal studded with sesame seeds—is a must. So are the "churros," thick rectangles of deep-fried, cinnamon-coated pound cake served with vanilla ice cream in a cup of chocolate-malt dipping sauce. **WHO** Taco-truck junkies looking for a more grown-up fix, meat lovers, architecture fans who enjoy seeing an old IHOP put to good use.

[Annapurna Cuisine] **10200 Venice Blvd., Culver City, 310.204.5500, annapurnacuisine.com. L & D daily. Indian/vegetarian. Beer & wine. AE, MC, V. $ - $$ WHY** Dosas and southern-style curries in a tech-savvy setting complete with Bollywood offerings on plasma screens. **WHAT** Annapurna showcases classic southern Indian cooking in an urbane setting (complete with WiFi). Try the ultra-thin paper dosa or a curry accompanied by pickles, chutneys and sambars.

[Bouchon Beverly Hills] 🔒 **235 Cañon Dr., Beverly Hills, 310.271.9910, bouchonbistro.com. L Mon.- Fri., D daily, brunch Sat.-Sun. French. Full bar. AE, MC, V. $$$$ - $$$$$ WHY** For a fantasy French bistro experience when your ship has come in. **WHAT** Chef Thomas Keller, he of the French Laundry, Per Se and Ad Hoc, has at last come to Los Angeles. It's supposed to be a branch of the original Bouchon in Yountville, but this is pure Beverly Hills, large and lavish and expensive. If your pockets are deep, it's well worth going for the bistro decor, the people-watching and, most of all, Keller's simply perfect French bistro fare: frisée lardons salad, oysters, onion soup, steamed mussels, gigot d'agneau and what is likely to be the best roast chicken of your life. The desserts are textbook but a little dull (crème caramel, lemon tart, île flottante), and the waiters are attentive, if sometimes too chatty. For a more economical way to soak up the vibe and taste

the food, hit the movie-set-handsome downstairs bar.
WHO The powerful, the face-lifted and the powerful, with a good sprinkling of Thomas Keller acolytes. ♥ ♫ ⌂

[Café Bella Roma S.P.Q.R.] **1513 S. Robertson Blvd., Pico-Robertson, 310.277.7662, bellaromaspqr.com. B, L & D Tues.-Sun. Italian. BYOB. AE, MC, V. $$ WHY** The sort of friendly, affordable, garlic-scented trattoria that every neighborhood deserves and this one finally got.
WHAT A *mamma-and-pappa* spot with more tables on the sidewalk than inside, Bella Roma is a modest Italian café with a better kitchen than you might expect. Don't be in a big hurry, because the food's made from scratch: seasonal soups, house-made gnocchi, tagliatelle frutti di mare, tasty small pizzas and late-breakfast (it doesn't open until 10 a.m.) frittatas. Pass on dessert, but do have a good espresso.
WHO Pico-Robertson neighbors who can walk here. 📷🥄☺ ✿

[Chego] **3300 Overland Ave., Palms, 310.287.0337, eatchego.com. D Tues.-Sat. Korean/Mexican. No booze. AE, MC, V. $ WHY** Kogi goes stationary. **WHAT** The thing to get at this simple little café is the rice-bowl version of owner Roy Choi's infamous short rib and spicy pork tacos, though the grains are somehow not as captivating as the Kogi Truck tortillas. But at these bargain prices, it's still a fun-to-taste game. The prime rib bowl, double-spiced with horseradish and serranos, stands on its own, but the chicken with sour cream and Chinese broccoli is less compelling. Take one or two of the interesting desserts, like the Sriracha chocolate candy bar, to dissect at home. **WHO** The young, younger and hippest. 📷

[Craft] ⌂ **10100 Constellation Blvd., Century City, 310.279.4180, craftrestaurant.com. L Mon.-Fri., D Mon.-Sat. Steakhouse/American. Full bar. AE, MC, V. $$$$ - $$$$$ WHY** Servers who make you feel like Trump, special-occasion food (veal sweetbreads with kumquats, rabbit saddle with wild cherries) and a Wall Street atmosphere for those times when laid back L.A. just won't do. **WHAT** Part of Tom Colicchio's New York–based mini-empire, this elegant place has a design-your-own menu where everything is à la carte — at upscale steakhouse prices (think $15 for a side of forest mushrooms, although to be fair, dishes are larger to share). But if you have deep pockets, it's worth it. If your stocks just flopped, hit the adjacent Craftbar for superb cured meats and cheeses at half the price of the dining-room dishes.
WHO Power suits and handsome families with adult kids celebrating birthdays, big-boy style.

[Culina] **Four Seasons Hotel, 300 S. Doheny Dr., Beverly Hills, 310.860.4000, culinarestaurant.com. L & D daily, brunch Sun. Italian. Full bar. AE, MC, V. $$$ - $$$$$ WHY** To bask in luxurious five-star service, eavesdrop on a few Industry conversations and partake of a sophisticated modern Italian menu. **WHAT** The wrap-around patio,

---

🥄 **VEGETARIAN** ☺ **KID FRIENDLY** ✿ **PATIO DINING** 🚗 **DELIVERY** ⌂ **PRIVATE PARTY**

the long, undulating crudo bar (pricey), the wall of chic aperitivi—all add Euro-cache to this decidedly upmarket Italian dining room, where the kitchen makes pasta twice daily and where the $12 *picoli piatti* combination—your choice of a salumi, a cheese and a vegetable appetizer—is a very a good deal. Conservative diners may choose pizza, lasagne served in its own baking dish, or *polpette*, meatballs fashioned from Wagyu beef. **WHO** Beverly Hills doyens and doyennes and well-funded hotel guests. ♥ 🍸 ☼

[Cut] 🏛 **Beverly Wilshire Hotel, 9500 Wilshire Blvd., Beverly Hills, 310.276.8500, fourseasons.com/beverlywilshire. D Mon.-Sat. Steakhouse. Full bar. AE, MC, V. $$$$$ WHY** Bone-marrow flan with parsley salad, dry-aged prime rib-eye steak and possibly the best people-watching in Beverly Hills. **WHAT** With its sleek Richard Meier–designed interior and menu showcasing the finest beefsteaks and seafood from all over the world, Wolfgang Puck's Cut has been a runaway success since its 2006 opening. If you're on an expense account or have money to burn, get a reservation and settle in for exceptional service, expertly selected wines and a superb meal. **WHO** Celebrities galore, young turks from the studios, Maybach drivers. ♥ 🍸

[Fogo de Chão] **133 N. La Cienega Blvd., Beverly Hills, 310.289.7755, fogodechao.com. L Mon.-Fri., D nightly. Brazilian. Full bar. AE, MC, V. $$$$ - $$$$$ WHY** When you're starving, celebrating and have $55 to blow on a single dinner, not counting drinks, tax and tip (or dessert, but you won't have room for it anyway). **WHAT** Of Southern California's several churrascarias, none has been more successful than this grand temple of meat, where spits of lamb, beef, pork and chicken turn day and night on a massive, mesquite-fed rotisserie grill. It costs a bundle but is worth it for a splurge, thanks to the most spectacular salad bar in L.A. and the quality of the meat, carved tableside by swashbuckling gauchos. **WHO** Lots of upscale family groups celebrating birthdays and graduations with vast quantities of gorgeous meat. 🍸 ☺

[Ford's Filling Station] **9531 Culver Blvd., Culver City, 310.202.1470, fordsfillingstation.net. L & D daily. Modern American. Full bar. AE, MC, V. $$ - $$$$ WHY** For a robust service and modern comfort food: platters of cured meats, fried Ipswich clams, pizza-like flatbreads, oxtail soup and a hearty pub burger, all accompanied by boutique beers (it considers itself a gastropub) and chic wines. **WHAT** Emblematic of the new Culver City, this is one of the hottest of a dozen hot restaurants that are drawing Angelenos to the town that was once L.A.'s sleepiest secret. Owner/chef Ben Ford has capitalized on both his celebrity name (he's Harrison's son) and his talent for making food that people want to eat now. It's jam-packed, screamingly loud, a little overpriced and undeniably fun. **WHO** People who wouldn't have been caught dead in Culver City a decade ago. ☼

🏛 ESSENTIALLY L.A. ☼ LATE ♥ ROMANTIC 💲 VALUE 🍸 QUIET ☘ SUSTAINABLE

[Fraiche] **9411 Culver Blvd., Culver City, 310.839.6800, fraicherestaurantla.com. L & D daily, brunch Sun. French/Italian. Full bar. AE, MC, V. $$$ WHY** It's got it all: indoor-outdoor dining in hip Culver City, a fun vibe, a great happy hour and excellent dishes made with such au courant things as burrata, Kurobuta pork and shaved goat cheese. **WHAT** What was a trendy Culver City newcomer not so long ago has now eased into a comfortable adulthood, with pro service and appealing menus for lunch, brunch, dinner, happy hour and late night. Chef Ben Bailly knows what he's doing, whether it's a simple turkey burger or a sophisticated crab risotto with corn, mint and preserved lemon oil. **WHO** Good-looking studio folks. ☺ 📷 ✧

[The Grill on the Alley] 🔖 **9560 Dayton Way, Beverly Hills, 310.276.0615, thegrill.com. L Mon.-Sat., D nightly. American. Full bar. AE, MC, V. $$$ - $$$$ WHY** The Cobb and Caesar salads, and the chance to sit in the same room with the people who greenlit the movie your kids saw last weekend. **WHAT** This clubby institution offers an old-school menu (shrimp cocktail, chicken pot pie, meatloaf) to its power-lunching Hollywood faithful. Even though some of the lunch-hour heat has migrated to Century City, along with many of the town's talent agents, the Grill is still a draw, and its table assignments are a time-honored barometer of mogul status. **WHO** Everybody who's anybody in Hollywood and (way) beyond, including a certain moon-walking astronaut. 📷

[Haifa] **8717 W. Pico Blvd., Pico-Robertson, 310.888.7700, haifala.com. L Sun.- Fri., D Sun.- Thurs. Israeli/Middle Eastern. No booze. AE, MC, V. $ - $$ WHY** For kosher, Israeli-style Middle Eastern cooking that's fresher, lighter and more flavorful than most. **WHAT** This storefront looks cheesy from the outside, but inside is a cheerful café with yellow walls, vintage French posters and granite café tables. Its Middle Eastern cooking is a bit different from the Lebanese norm: easier on the oil and garlic, with less of an emphasis on sour/tart flavors. The salads are standouts, from the cumin-infused carrots to the crisp, light Israeli salad, a tangy dice of cucumber, tomato and onion. Kebabs are tender, the chicken dishes have lots of flavor, the falafel is exceptionally crisp, and the rich hummus is as addictive as the fresh pita. Service is brusque but good. **WHO** Middle-aged businessmen talking on cell phones, locals who kep kosher, and falafel-and-hummus junkies from all over. 📷

[Industry Café & Jazz] **6039 Washington Blvd., Culver City, 310.202.6633, industrycafeandjazz.com. L & D daily. Ethiopian. Beer & wine. AE, MC, V. $ - $$ WHY** Friendly Ethiopian food and even friendlier live jazz—with no cover charge. **WHAT** This simple little spot is fun for a change-of-pace dinner: tasty Ethiopian food, with some American soul food for good measure, paired with jazz on weekends and Wednesdays and comedy on Thursdays. ☺ 📷

🌿 **VEGETARIAN** ☺ **KID FRIENDLY** ✧ **PATIO DINING** �</> **DELIVERY** 🏛 **PRIVATE PARTY**

[The Ivy] 113 N. Robertson Blvd., Beverly Hills, 310.274.8303. L & D daily. Modern American. Full bar. AE, MC, V. $$$$$ **WHY** To channel Danny DeVito in *Get Shorty*. **WHAT** There's a white picket fence to keep the looky-loos out and the celebrities in, and the remarkable thing is how well it works. Movie and music stars really do come here, as do the agents, managers and publicists who feed off of them, and they're all delighted to pay $30 for a burger or a bowl of spaghetti. The surprise is that the hearty regional American food (especially the corn chowder, crab cakes and desserts) is actually good. It's nowhere near worth the money, of course, but can you put a price on sitting next to Mandy Moore or Conan O'Brien? **WHO** The famous, semi-famous and wanna-be-near-the-famous. ☼

[Koutoubia] 2116 Westwood Blvd., Westwood, 310.475.0729, koutoubiarestaurant.com. D Tues.-Sun. Moroccan. Full bar. AE, MC, V. $$$ **WHY** For L.A.'s best full-experience (ritual hand washing, sitting on pillows, belly dancing on weekends) Moroccan restaurant. **WHAT** Longtime Koutoubia owner Michel Ohayon is one of L.A.'s most legendary hosts. More often than not, it will be him who washes your hands with rosewater and him who checks on you a half-dozen times during your dinner. His careful attention has kept this place at the top of the heap, with delicious traditional Moroccan food (tagines, couscous, b'stilla) and an enveloping and romantic atmosphere and experience. **WHO** Celebrators, romantics and b'stilla junkies. ♥☼🐦

[Lawry's the Prime Rib] 100 N. La Cienega Blvd., Beverly Hills, 310.652.2827, lawrysonline.com. D nightly. American. Full bar. AE, MC, V. $$$$ - $$$$$ **WHY** Luscious prime rib and a theatrical sense of "going out." **WHAT** It's kinda like the Disneyland of restaurants. Lawry's has characters (waitresses in uniforms and perky caps and imposing carving men in stiff toques), adventures (salad tossed tableside in a huge spinning bowl, prime rib carved from a silver cart) and tons of Japanese tourists. But don't let the kitschy show have you thinking this place isn't good—it's great. **WHO** Three-generation families celebrating occasions, couples on special dates and lots of happy Japanese business people and travelers. ☼

[Le Saint Amour] 9725 Culver Blvd., Culver City, 310.842.8155, lesaintamour.com. L Mon.- Fri., D nightly. French. Beer & wine. AE, MC, V. $$ - $$$ **WHY** A meal at this reasonably priced, entirely charming bistro is way cheaper than a ticket to France—with a wait staff that's as professional as in Paris, but so much nicer. **WHAT** This fantastic and blessedly affordable (and quiet) French bistro is the creation of charcuterie maker Bruno Commereuc (whose pâté and head cheese are also available a few doors down at Fraîche). It's got it all: a tree-shaded sidewalk patio, romantic bistro interior, easy-drinking French wines, and bistro classics designed by consulting chef Walter Manzke: onion soup, salade de choux aux lardons, moules frites, duck confit salad, roast Jidori chicken, pot de crème—simple comfort food of the highest order. **WHO** Francophiles and well-dressed, grown-up couples and groups of friends. ♥ 🗺 ☼

[Lukshon] 🍴 3239 Helms Ave., Culver City, 310.202.6808, lukshon. com. D Mon.-Sat. Asian. Full bar. AE, MC, V. $$$ - $$$$ **WHY** Southeast Asian flavors refracted through the refined lens of Sang Yoon. **WHAT** Yoon's follow-up to the gastropub scrum that is Father's Office, this well-oiled restaurant is beautiful and sleek, worthy of a case study in modern design. The menu, like at so many of the city's new places, is intent on obliterating the concept of a three-course dinner with a series of small, shareable plates. There are Vietnamese flavors (wonderful baby squid stuffed taut with pork sausage atop a pool of rau ram pesto) as well as Indonesian ones (beef short rib rendang that collapses into a coconut curry). Dan dan noodles pack enough stinging Sichuan heat to numb your mouth for a week, while the excellent chicory-coffee pork ribs will immediately wipe any upcoming barbecue pilgrimages from your calendar. Cocktails are cut with calamansi juice and Fujianese black tea, and dessert—typically a trio of miniaturized sweets—is on the house. **WHO** Food fetishists and westside diners of all stripes. ☼

[Mako] 225 S. Beverly Dr., Beverly Hills, 310.288.8338, makorestaurant. com. L Tues.-Fri., D Tues.-Sat. Asian. Full bar. AE, MC, V. $$ - $$$ **WHY** Everything on the menu is tempting, from sizzling soft-shell crab with ginger dressing and grilled sweet Japanese prawns to Beijing Duck and Kobe meatballs. **WHAT** The former chef of Wolfgang Puck's Chinois runs this tranquil, softly lit Asian small-plates spot with an open kitchen (sit at the counter and watch the cooks) and carefully nuanced dishes with an accent on seafood. A good date-night spot. ♥ 🗺 🎵

[Mastro's Steakhouse] 246 N. Cañon Dr., Beverly Hills, 310.888.8782, mastrosrestaurants.com. D nightly. Steakhouse. Full bar. AE, MC, V. $$$$$ **WHY** The Beverly Hills comedy writ large, with really good steaks to boot. **WHAT** It's loud, it's showy, the bar's a scene, the prices are high, and everyone is having a blast at Mastro's, which has held firm as one of Beverly Hills's "it" spots for several years now. What's kept it so popular is not just the scene, which is considerable, but the fact that the prime steaks, as well as the cocktails, onion rings, potatoes and spinach, are skillfully cooked and massively portioned. **WHO** Movie stars, plastic-surgery victims, anniversary celebrants from Van Nuys. 🏚

[Matsuhisa] 🍴 129 N. La Cienega Blvd., Beverly Hills, 310.659.9639, nobumatsuhisa.com. L Mon.-Fri., D nightly. Japanese. Beer & wine. AE, MC, V. $$$ - $$$$ **WHY** For Nobu Matsuhisa's Peruvian-influenced Japanese cuisine, which came to fame here and later swept the food world. **WHAT** The Nobu craze started here, in a restaurant far simpler than its

🌿 VEGETARIAN ⊙ KID FRIENDLY ☼ PATIO DINING 🚗 DELIVERY 🏚 PRIVATE PARTY overwrought Beverly Hills neighbors, and while the Nobus in Malibu, New York, Aspen and beyond may be a bigger deal these days, we still prefer the parent. The famed dishes—black cod with miso, mussels in spicy garlic sauce, shrimp with caviar, the range of rolls and sushi— are pretty much the same, but somehow they seem better and, well, more real here. **WHO** The scene people have long since moved on, but the loyal fans remain. ♥ 🔊

[Mayura] 10406 Venice Blvd., Culver City, 310.559.9644, mayura-indi- an-restaurant.com. L & D Tues.-Sun. Indian. Beer. MC, V. $ - $$
WHY Good-value Indian cooking in an area that appreciates it, with free delivery to boot. **WHAT** Bright and busy, this affordable café has an extensive vegetarian menu, prepared in a separate kitchen, but car- nivores are not neglected—the tandoor chicken is savory, and the tikka masala is satisfying. Be warned that the hot dishes are seriously hot, and the garlic naan is impossible to stop eating. **WHO** Cheerful family groups and posses of scruffy twentysomethings. 📷🔊☺🚗

[Mezze] 401 N. La Cienega Blvd., Beverly Hills, 310.657.4103, mezzela. com. L Mon.-Fri., D Mon.-Sat. Middle Eastern. Full bar. AE, MC, V. $$ - $$$
WHY To break the hummus-and-kebab stalemate of most L.A. Middle Eastern places, in a handsome, hardwood-floor bistro setting. Also for the late-night menu, which includes half-price wines. **WHAT** A farmers'-market sensibility permeates the small and large plates made by Craft alum Micah Wexler: pizza-like flatbreads topped with trendy produce, veal *mantee* (baby tortellini), quail in consommé flanked by tiny stuffed kebbeh balls, and a sublime lamb and burnt-onion risotto. Okay, there *is* schwarma, but that's not what you came here for. **WHO** A buzzy, linked-in crowd that doesn't mind paying Beverly Hills prices for average wines and good food. ☺ ☼🔊

[Napa Valley Grille] 1100 Glendon Ave., Westwood, 310.824.3322, napavalleygrille.com. L & D daily. Californian. Full bar. AE, MC, V. $$$$ - $$$$$ **WHY** The creative sandwiches and burgers, including the "Coastal Oregon sushi-quality smoked albacore tuna melt," the grilled ahi tuna burger and the Niman Ranch cheeseburger. **WHAT** A burnished take on wine-country rusticity, the Napa Valley Grille is a good option for a business lunch or dinner before the curtain goes up at the Geffen. It serves good salads, grilled fish, pastas and a nice selection of cheeses accompanied by raisin-pecan bread, along with a wine list that draws prominently—but not exclusively—on bottles from its namesake county. **WHO** Well-dressed folks headed to or from the Geffen Theatre. 🔊🔊☼🏮

[Obikà] Westfield Century City, 10250 Santa Monica Blvd., Century City, 310.556.2452, obikala.com. L & D daily. Italian. Beer & wine. AE, MC, V. $$ - $$$ **WHY** Without booking a trip to Rome, you can taste

farmstead mozzarella di bufala from cheese makers working in the
DOP (Denomination of Protected Origin). The cheese, sourced from
Agro Pontina (where the bufala roam) and Paestum (south of Naples)
is flown to L.A. three times weekly. **WHAT** Based on the sushi bar
concept, Obikà sprang to life in Rome and now has branches in 14 cities, including Tokyo and London. As with sushi, the servers construct
your meal from ingredients displayed at the bar. Smoked mozzarella,
creamy burrata, and fresh ricotta are rolled with various salumi, made
part of a salad or worked into a pasta dish. You'll also find excellent
cured meats: bresaola, speck, prosciutti and pistachio-studded mortadella. Carefully selected regional wines and ricotta-based desserts
round out the spectacular menu. ☼

[Pampas Grill] **3857 Overland Ave., Culver City, 310.836.0080,
pampas-grill.com. L & D daily. Brazilian. Beer & wine. AE, MC, V. $$**
WHY For affordable, casual Brazilian barbecue. **WHAT** This offshoot
of the Farmers Market original is built around a large buffet laden with
all the Brazilian churrascaria standards: barbecued meats, garlic rice,
black beans, plantains, salads, roasted vegetables, fried yucca and that
dreamy cheese bread. It's sold by weight, so go easy on the meats for
the best value—and your cardiologist will thank you. 🖼☺☼

[Picca] 🏷 **9575 Pico Blvd., West L.A., 310.277.0133, piccaperu.com.
D Mon.-Sat. Peruvian. Full bar. AE, MC, V. $$ - $$$ WHY** Innovative
creations from Ricardo Zarate, *Food & Wine's* best New Los Angeles
chef, 2011. **WHAT** The new descendant of Zarate's ultra-modest Mo-
Chica is a trend-setting cantina whose robata bar items look Japanese
but taste Peruvian (skewered grilled scallops painted with aji amarillo
pepper) and whose ceviche bar garnishes flash-marinated fish and
sashimi-like tiradito with rocoto chile, choclo and other Peruvian in-
gredients. Small plates also show off his flair for layering culinary cul-
tures in unimagined ways, as well as his sushi-chef experience earned
at such high-end spots as Zuma in London. Seasonal craft cocktails
based on Peruvian pisco and other Latin ingredients complement the
fare. It's a leap forward for Latin American cuisine. **WHO** Enraptured
food lovers who are thrilled to find Zarate in a real restaurant. 🖼🎋

[Polo Lounge] **Beverly Hills Hotel, 9641 Sunset Blvd., Beverly Hills,
310.276.2251, beverlyhillshotel.com. B, L & D daily. American. Full bar.
AE, MC, V. $$$$ - $$$$$ WHY** For a slice of old Hollywood, with a
gentlemen's club-style lounge, a pretty garden dining room and lovely
tables under the overhanging oak trees on the patio. **WHAT** Food isn't
the main attraction at this fabled spot, although the eggs Benedict at
brunch are one of the city's best versions, and the ladies who lunch
enjoy the Molly salad. Mostly you come for the atmosphere and
history—and perhaps one of the sturdy drinks served in the lounge.
WHO Beverly Hills dowagers, industry players of all ages. ♥ 🍸 ☼

🍃 **VEGETARIAN** ☺ **KID FRIENDLY** ☼ **PATIO DINING** �"delivery" **DELIVERY** 🎋 **PRIVATE PARTY**

[Red Medicine] **8400 Wilshire Blvd., Beverly Hills, 323.651.5500, redmedicinela.com. L & D daily. Vietnamese/Asian. Full bar. AE, MC, V. $$$ WHY** Vietnamese fusion restaurants have exploded in recent years, but Red Medicine is no ordinary pho-taco joint. **WHAT** Jordan Kahn's painterly riffs on Vietnamese flavors are under the radar—he's doing some of the city's most creative cooking right now. The chic, industrial polished-concrete space makes a neutral backdrop for eye-popping compositions. Unusual ingredients—rose marmalade, smoked Chinese dates, lily bulbs—elevate Vietnamese-style chicken dumplings, soft-shell crab, lamb belly or duck, or vegetables like a green papaya salad or a giant nest of fried sweet potatoes to wrap in lettuce and herbs. Zingy cocktails incorporate such things as pickled peaches, while Asian-inflected dessert collages dance on the edge of savory. At lunch, a simpler menu includes an impossibly rich pork belly-pâté banh mi sandwich, bun noodles or Vietnamese chicken salad. **WHO** Scenery-matching grey-clad grown-up fashionistas with statement eyeglasses; Beverly Hills businessmen. ☺ 📵

[Samosa House East] **11510 W. Washington Blvd., Culver City, 310.398.6766, samosahouse.net. L & D daily. Indian. No booze. MC, V. $ - $$ WHY** To sup on Indian cooking so good you'll forget you're eating vegetarian. **WHAT** In a former Winchell's, owners of the original Samosa House dish up their contemporary take on India's vegetarian cuisine, often eschewing butter-based ghee for olive oil and replacing yogurt with ground nuts in some creamy sauces. The Mumbai-style street foods, such as *bhel puri*, a crunchy, chutney-doused, salad-like snack, and the namesake veggie-filled dough triangles, join a rotating selection of curries, dals and kormas. It's all delicious. **WHO** Joyful westside vegetarians, thrilled with the variety of flavors minus the trip to Little India. 📵

[Scarpetta] **Montage Beverly Hills, 225 N. Canon Dr., Beverly Hills, 310.860.7970, montagebeverlyhills.com. L & D daily. Italian. Full bar. AE, MC, V. $$$$ - $$$$$ WHY** The pampering, the prestige and the people-watching. Also the spaghetti with tomato and basil, which is as good as its $24 price tag would suggest. **WHAT** Scott Conant's unfussy Mediterranean fare appeals both to the conservative older crowd and the moneyed young bucks who frequent this deluxe hotel restaurant. The kitchen shines at pasta, and although you have to ask for it, there's an entire vegetarian menu. Foodies take note: The chefs welcome visitors to the spectacular kitchen, so ask your waiter to take you back there. 🎵 📵 🏛

[Shaherzad Restaurant] **1422 Westwood Blvd., Westwood, 310.470.3242. L & D daily. Persian/Middle Eastern. Beer & wine. AE, MC, V. $$ - $$$ WHY** A fun and affordable choice for Westwood Village dining. Just don't fill up on that amazing bread. **WHAT** The only restaurant around that serves you hot flatbread straight from the tandoor-style oven, Shaherzad is a good place for kebabs, fluffy Persian rice, beef barg and traditional stews. **WHO** Middle Eastern UCLA students and Iranian ladies who lunch. ☺

[The Six] **10668 W. Pico Blvd., West L.A., 310.837.6662, thesixrestaurant.com. L & D daily. Modern American/vegetarian. Beer & wine. AE, MC, V. $$$ WHY** With its chill vibe and entertaining concept—six choices in each category (appetizers, sides, entrées), six brews on tap and six wines by the glass—the Six fills a gaping need in the Overland-Pico neighborhood, where the mall overwhelms sidewalk life. **WHAT** This café-pub is a relaxed but confident departure for owners Will Karges and Jake King, who've tended toward trendy lounge-spaces. Although focused, the menu also has something for every mood: thin-crust pizzas and small plates; hearty-homey entrées (steak frites, potato-chip-crusted salmon); lots of market veggies; and such kid-friendly picks as turkey sloppy-joe sliders. Or just order all three kinds of fries—air-baked, twice-fried and sweet potato—to enjoy with your beer. **WHO** Pedestrians from Cheviot Hills and a smattering of mall shoppers savvy enough to find their way here. ☺🍴

[Sotto] **9575 W. Pico Blvd., West L.A., 310.277.0210, sottorestaurant. com. L Tues.-Fri., D Tues.-Sun. Italian. Full bar. MC, V. $$ - $$$$ WHY** Chefs Steve Samson and Zack Pollack, formerly of David Myer's Pizza Ortica in Costa Mesa, bring their love for lardo, guanciale and pancetta to West L.A. **WHAT** In the ground floor of the old Test Kitchen space, this mostly Southern Italian restaurant sports a menu of house-cured meats, hand-made pastas and pizzas fired in a $15,000 hand-built Neapolitan oven. The ingredients—whether it's the bottarga served with the squid ink fusilli lunghi or a simple burrata—are all top-notch. The *pittule pugliese*, appetizer doughnuts drizzled with a sweet wine reduction and served with superb ricotta, are a must. **WHO** Italian food fanatics, Test Kitchen denizens and hip couples queuing up at the bar for Julian Cox's grappa, sambucca and Campari cocktails. ♥ ☼

[Spago] 🏛 **176 N. Cañon Dr., Beverly Hills, 310.385.0880, wolfgangpuck.com. L Mon.-Sat., D nightly. Modern American/Californian. Full bar. AE, MC, V. $$$$$ WHY** To worship at the shrine of California cuisine. **WHAT** Wolfgang Puck still works the room from time to time, when he's not off overseeing his global empire, but this is really Lee Hefter's kingdom, and it's a magical kingdom indeed. Hefter-Puck (with chef de cuisine Tetsu Yahagi) have kept the standards at peak level for years, and the cooking today is every bit as exciting, beautiful and delicious as it was a decade ago. And Sherry Yard's desserts are fantastic. The über–Beverly Hills setting and service do the kitchen justice. Worth the considerable splurge, especially if you're entertaining out-of-towners. **WHO** International hot shots, movie stars and serious eaters. ♥🍴☼🏛

🍴 **VEGETARIAN** ☺ **KID FRIENDLY** ☼ **PATIO DINING** 🚗 **DELIVERY** 🏛 **PRIVATE PARTY**

[Sunnin] 1776 Westwod Blvd., Westwood, 310.475.3358, sunnin.com. L & D daily. Lebanese. Beer & wine. AE, MC, V. $ - $$ **WHY** For earthy Lebanese classics with an edge of sophistication, served all day long. **WHAT** Some may remember owner Em Tony's handiwork from the luxe Al Amir opposite LACMA, where she cooked in the '80s. Now she reigns over a sparkling open kitchen in a big, buzzing space, where you can often watch her turning out pristine *kibbeh* (beef-stuffed wheat ovals), *moujadrah* (caramelized onion–topped lentil pilaf) or a layered moussaka. It's likely the best Lebanese on the westside. **WHO** Persians from the neighborhood who want a change of pace, UCLA profs and students, and a huge following of regulars. 🗺️

[Sushi Zo] 9824 National Blvd., Palms, 310.842.3977. L Mon.-Fri., D Mon.-Sat. Japanese/Sushi. Beer & wine. AE, MC, V. $$$$ - $$$$$ **WHY** Rich ankimo liver, blow-torched butterfish, blue crab hand roll, luscious toro—it's best to just sit back and let it roll out. Beer and specially selected sakes are available. **WHAT** This austere spot is many people's favorite L.A. sushi bar; there's no scene, fancy rolls or cellphone use allowed, just the freshest fish, simply presented. Reserve ahead, sit at the granite-topped bar and order *omakase*, or chef's choice, for the full experience. **WHO** Serious sushi lovers. 🔈

[Tara's Himalayan] 10855 Venice Blvd., Palms, 310.836.9696. L & D daily. Himalayan/Nepalese. Beer & wine. Cash only. $$ **WHY** If only to give the yak dishes a try. **WHAT** Owner Tara Gurund Black traded her classical Nepalese dance career to helm this modest place, which turns out Indo-Chinese food from that mountainous region. The chicken-filled *momos* resemble Chinese pot stickers and taste vaguely Indian. There are lots of Indianesque vegetable and meat dishes, like pokhareli chicken sautéed with ground coriander and mango powder then sprinkled with fresh cilantro—a lighter, brighter take on Indian spicing. And yes, she serves Colorado-raised yak, in both a noodle-vegetable soup and a slow-cooked stew called "chili." **WHO** Lonely Planet travel guide readers and curious food lovers with few coins to spend on dinner. 🗺️🔋

[Tender Greens] 9523 Culver Blvd., Culver City, 310.842.8300, tendergreensfood.com. L & D daily. Modern American/vegetarian. Beer & wine. AE, MC, V. $ - $$ **WHY** Have-it-your-way salads and healthy entrées at low prices, given the mostly organic and local produce. **WHAT** Long lines snake out the door of this pioneering invent-your-own salad spot with a buzzing patio. Diners wait at the counter while their salads are tossed from fresh vegetables and meats, then choose beer, wine, lemonade and cupcakes to go with the salads or entrees. **WHO** Families with active children, retirees and everyone else. 🗺️🔋🔈☺⚙

[Torafuku] **10914 W. Pico Blvd., Century City, 310.470.0014, torafuku-usa.com. L Mon.-Sat., D nightly. Japanese. Beer & wine. AE, MC, V. $$ - $$$ WHY** Very good, close-to-the-earth country-style meals you might expect at a *ryokan*, or Japanese country inn. **WHAT** Locavores will love the ingredients—organic vegetables, local free-range chicken and eggs, Santa Barbara prawns, grass-fed beef—that chef Tetsuya Harikawa sources for his simply cooked meals. For rice connoisseurs, the star of the show is the early-crop rice cooked in 500-pound ceramic kamado pots that give it a toasty flavor.

[Totoraku Teriyaki House] **10610 W. Pico Blvd., Century City, 310.838.9881. By reservation only. Japanese. BYOB (no corkage). AE, MC, V. $$$$$ WHY** To pole-vault into the league of the coolest foodies in town. **WHAT** One might assume from the "Pico Teriyaki House" sign outside that this might be a divey neighborhood spot for a cheap plate of chicken teriyaki and shrimp tempura. And one would be very, very wrong. This is L.A.'s great "secret" restaurant, where you can only get a reservation through a personal connection to chef Oyama, and you'd better bring him a serious bottle of wine if you hope to return. In return for your considerable trouble, and upwards of $200 of your money, you'll get a many-course beef-based meal that you may never forget. **WHO** Chefs and people who know people. 🍷

[Tuk Tuk] **8875 W. Pico Blvd., Pico-Robertson, 310.860.1872, tuktukla. com. L & D daily. Thai. Beer & wine. AE, MC, V. $ - $$ WHY** Beef salad makes a light summer supper, and curries are also satisfying. **WHAT** One of the best Thai options on the westside, with clean, updated versions of favorite Thai dishes, served in a pleasant Asian décor. 🍷🥢☺

[Urasawa] 🔖 **218 N. Rodeo Dr., Beverly Hills, 310.247.8939. D nightly. Japanese/sushi. Full bar. AE, MC, V. $$$$$ WHY** For an omakase meal of astonishing complexity, diversity and luxury. **WHAT** If you have to ask how much it costs, you can't afford it—so we can't afford it. L.A.'s most expensive sushi restaurant (and that's really saying something) requires an outlay of what would be a month's rent in some parts of the country. But if you're serious about sushi and are ready to put yourself in the hands of a master, Hiroyuki Urasawa will present you with 30-plus tiny dishes that will amaze you. **WHO** Not everyone who dines here is rich—some save for months and consider the effort worth it. 🍷

[Versailles] 🔖 **10319 Venice Blvd., Culver City, 310.558.3168, versaillescuban.com. L & D daily. Cuban. Beer & wine. AE, MC, V. $ - $$ WHY** Succulent roast pork and Cuban-style roast chicken, and (when it's available) amazing oxtail, too. **WHAT** A no-frills, inexpensive L.A. landmark beloved for its garlicky marinated roast chicken, juicy, salty Cuban roast pork, plantains, black beans and rice. Branches on south La Cienega and in Encino and Manhattan Beach. 🛵

🌿 **VEGETARIAN** ◎ **KID FRIENDLY** ☼ **PATIO DINING** 🚗 **DELIVERY** 🎉 **PRIVATE PARTY**

[WakaSan] **1929 Westwood Blvd., Westwood, 310.446.5241. L Wed.-Sun, D Mon. & Wed.- Sun. Japanese. Beer & wine. MC, V. $$$** **WHY** A great-value $35 omakase meal, usually 11 or 12 carefully made courses. A real find. **WHAT** At this rustic charmer in a Westwood strip mall, a delicious multi-course *omakase* (chef's choice) menu of home-style dishes is the only option—but no one is complaining. It's a great deal for a complex and interesting meal. **WHO** UCLA professors and Japanese-food lovers seeking an affordable splurge. ☺ 🗽

[Wolfgang's Steakhouse] 🏛 **445 N. Cañon Dr., Beverly Hills, 310.385.0640, wolfgangssteakhouse.net. L Mon.-Sat., D nightly. Steakhouse. Full bar. AE, MC, V. $$$$ - $$$$$ WHY** You can't underestimate the amusement factor of seeing emaciated, middle-aged Beverly Hills social X-rays being presented with massive, glistening porterhouses. **WHAT** Wolfgang Zwiener learned a lot of things in his decades as headwaiter at Peter Luger in New York, especially the importance of good service in an expensive steakhouse. So he has this handsome outpost of his growing chain running like a Swiss train station. Everyone gets the massive porterhouse for two (or an even more massive one for four), and it's a gorgeous piece of meat, tasting of its age (in a good way) and unadorned with sauces or fripperies. It's worth going easy on the steak (which takes home well) and the excellent onion rings and spinach to save room for the purist's cheesecake. **WHO** A parade of beautiful-but-not-young people who are old enough to appreciate the impeccable service, not to mention to be able to afford the place. ☼ 🗽

WEST OF THE 405

[26 Beach Café] **3100 Washington Blvd., Venice, 310.823.7526, 26beach.com. L & D daily, brunch Sat.-Sun. Californian/American. Full bar. AE, MC, V. $$ - $$$$ WHY** The King Kobe burger, the housemade buns, and the casual vibe. **WHAT** So what if it's not really at the beach? The food is good, the prices are reasonable. and the setting is flea-market cute, complete with a fetching covered garden. Follow the regulars' lead and go with the burgers, which come in variations including salmon, turkey and veggie, or one of the entrée salads, such as the ginger-infused salmon with asparagus, mushrooms, greens and soy dressing. Breakfast is also a winner; try the famed french toast. **WHO** Loyal locals who need a weekly burger or salad fix. 🗽🍸☼

[Antica Pizzeria] **location changing (Marina del Rey area), anticapizzeria.net. L & D daily. Pizzeria/Italian. Beer & wine. AE, MC, V. $$ WHY** The perfect and characteristic char on the bottom crust of each exquisitely baked pizza. The margherita is simple, sauceless and spectacular. **WHAT** Alas, Antica lost its lease just as we went to press, but we are keeping it in the book because we have faith that it will have a new home by the time you read this. Chef and Naples native Peppe Miele was the first U.S. resident accepted into the Associazione Verace

Pizza Napoletana, and he follows its strict rules on baking methods (wood-burning ovens) and dough (just flour, natural yeast and water). The result: small pizzas that taste utterly fantastico. **WHO** True believers who know how it's done back in the old country (and we don't mean New York). 🥡 ☺ 🚚

[Aunt Kizzy's Back Porch] 523 Washington Blvd., 2nd Fl., Marina del Rey, 310.578.1005. L & D daily, brunch Sun. Southern/Soul Food. No booze. AE, MC, V. $ - $$$ **WHY** The only place by the beach for traditional, down-home soul food. **WHAT** Aunt Kizzy's offers a comforting menu of smothered pork chops, fried chicken, meatloaf and jambalaya, all generously served with the requisite okra, corn, red beans and collard greens. Best bets: mac 'n cheese, corn muffins, braised oxtails, fried catfish and peach cobbler pie. **WHO** Dressed-for-church Sunday brunchers and birthday partiers (the whole place regularly breaks out in singing Stevie Wonder's *Happy Birthday*). ☺

[Axe] 1009 Abbot Kinney Blvd., Venice, 310.664.9787, axerestaurant. com. L & D Wed.-Sun., brunch Sat.-Sun. Modern American. Beer & wine. AE, MC, V. $$$ **WHY** That Abbot Kinney esprit, plus a chance to feel virtuous and catered-to at the very same meal. **WHAT** From the sidewalk, Axe (pronounced "ah-shay") looks so understated as to be practically unmarked, but that hasn't stopped the hordes from discovering its green-friendly menu and tastefully minimalist vibe. The entrées, like the porterhouse pork chop with a cider reduction, tend to be overpriced, heavy on the organic hype and light on flavor. Stick with the small plates such as shaved baby artichokes in lemon dressing or soy-braised short ribs with chestnuts. **WHO** Venice habitués too cool to make a scene over spotting celebs like Orlando Bloom at lunch; stroller moms catching up over organic salads. 🚚🥡 ☼

[Bar Hayama] 1803 Sawtelle Blvd., West L.A., 310.235.2000, bar-hayama.com. L Mon.-Fri., D nightly. Japanese. Beer & wine. AE, MC, V. $$$ - $$$$ **WHY** To sip sake and nibble on gorgeous small plates and sushi on the patio, next to the romantic fire pit. **WHAT** The current star of the Sawtelle Japanese scene, Hayama is winner for its bamboo-lined patio, its two sake bars and the excellent small-plates-and-sushi food of Toshi Sugiura: scallop sashimi, grilled yellowtail collar, soft-shell crab salad, agedashi tofu and more. ♥🥡 ☼

[Beachcomber Café] Malibu Pier, 23000 Pacific Coast Hwy., Malibu, 310.456.9800, thebeachcombercafe.com. L daily, D Wed.-Sun. American. Full bar. AE, MC, V. $$ - $$$$ **WHY** Because it's on the Malibu Pier and the food doesn't suck. **WHAT** The folks behind the restored 1940s Beachcomber at Crystal Cove run this place on Malibu Pier, and the look is identical to its parent: green leather booths, warm wood paneling and plenty of windows to bring in the Pacific. There's a large bar, a row of outdoor tables with dreamy views of the Santa Monica Bay,

🥡 VEGETARIAN ☺ KID FRIENDLY ☼ PATIO DINING 🚚 DELIVERY 🏛 PRIVATE PARTY

and a dining room with more views. The cooking is a little better than it needs to be, given the location: breakfast scrambles; albacore tuna melts and burgers for lunch; and for dinner, festive cocktails, grilled seafood and meat (choose those over the heavy seafood pot pie) and big, sugary desserts. **WHO** Rich surfers, date-nighters, tourists and Malibu families celebrating birthdays. ♥ 🍸 ☺ ✿ 🏚

[Beechwood] 822 W. Washington Blvd., Venice, 310.448.8884, beechwoodrestaurant.com. D nightly, bar menu nightly. Modern American. Full bar. AE, MC, V. $$ - $$$ **WHY** Killer french fries and sweet potato fries, a suave croque madame, interesting fish and steak entrées, and desserts as comfy as grandma's lap. **WHAT** Located where way-cool Abbot Kinney meets the more prosaic Washington, Beechwood is rich in Venice style but free of hipster attitude—and its bar menu is one of the best values in the 'hood. The midcentury-modern building houses a booth-lined dining room, a spacious lounge, and a terrific bar patio warmed by a big fire pit. No matter where you eat, it's all good, stylish and reasonably priced. **WHO** Handsome young folks in the bar, with date-night boomers in the quieter dining room. ☺ 🍸 🦞 ✿

[Border Grill] 🏛 1445 4th St., Santa Monica, 310.451.1655, bordergrill.com. L & D daily, brunch Sat.-Sun. Mexican. Full bar. AE, MC, V. $$ - $$$$ **WHY** Designer margaritas and superb appetizers from California-cuisine pioneers. **WHAT** Chef/owners Susan Feniger and Mary Sue Milliken are foodie rock stars whose first, shoebox-size restaurant City morphed into the original Border Grill. Today, TV's "Two Hot Tamales" have an empire that includes two other Border Grills (Downtown and Vegas) and Feniger's Street. This is where Santa Monica meets for happy hour: margaritas, mojitos, aged tequilas and wonderful appetizers: shrimp ceviche, wild-mushroom quesadillas, chicken panuchos and great guacamole. The main courses are less rewarding (and more expensive) so the savvy stick to appetizers and drinks. The setting matches the food: vibrantly colorful and powerfully noisy. **WHO** Santa Monica's happy (hour) people; out-of-town admirers of the Two Hot Tamales. 🦞

[Café Brasil] 11736 W. Washington Blvd., Mar Vista, 310.391.1216, cafe-brasil.com. B, L & D daily. Brazilian. Beer & wine. AE, MC, V. $ - $$ **WHY** Tasty, inexpensive Brazilian sandwiches, grilled meats, collard greens, black beans and *feijoada*, the famed pork stew. **WHAT** It's a simple order-at-the-counter, paper-napkin café but an exceptionally charming and colorful one, with a greenery-lined sidewalk terrace and an intensely colorful dining room. There's beer and wine, but don't neglect the fresh mango juice or the excellent coffee. 🦞 ☺ ✿

[Café del Rey] 4451 Admiralty Way, Marina del Rey, 310.823.6395, cafedelreymarina.com. L Mon.-Sat., D nightly. Californian. Full bar. AE, MC, V. $$$ - $$$$$ **WHY** The view and the weekend prix-fixe brunch.

WHAT In a modern space overlooking bobbing boats, the dinner crowd sips cocktails and dines on oysters, sushi, black spaghetti with seafood, and Alaskan halibut with braised fennel and baby artichokes. The cooking's appealing and consistent, though not quite worth the steep dinnertime tab. Lunch or brunch is a better option, and the bar is a good spot for a nightcap. Welcoming service. **WHO** Boat owners, business folk, Marina residents, all sporting judicious tans. ♥ ☼

[Capo] **1810 Ocean Ave., Santa Monica, 310.394.5550, caporestaurant.com. D Tues.-Sat. Italian. Full bar. AE, MC, V. $$$$ - $$$$$**
WHY A Bruce Marder gem worth finding amid the posh Ocean Avenue hotels. **WHAT** The luxuriously simple, farm-fresh fare served in this tiny, romantic Italian restaurant is worth a special-occasion splurge. Meats are a specialty, so resist the handmade pastas and dive into the steaks and chops, grilled in the wood-burning fireplace in the corner of the dining room. The service and wine list are both excellent, as well they should be at these prices. ♥ 🍸

[Catch] **Hotel Casa del Mar, 1910 Ocean Way, Santa Monica, 310.581.7714, hotelcasadelmar.com. B, L & D daily. Seafood/sushi. Full bar. AE, MC, V. $$$ - $$$$$ WHY** This carefully constructed Cal-Mediterranean seafood menu is worth the splurge, especially when you consider the setting. **WHAT** High ceilings, crisp white walls and floor-to-ceiling windows frame the dazzling view at this privileged outpost of elegant, yet unshowoffy, cuisine. A chef change led to a menu change as well, so the Asian influences gave way to ones from the Mediterranean—so now you see lemon confit, fresh pastas, lentils, fennel and even steaks and sides of garlic spinach and thyme-roasted fingerlings. It's more generic upscale-hotel, but it satisfies, and when you add the setting, it satisfies a hell of a lot. **WHO** Beautiful people with big bank accounts, sipping $15 pre-dinner cocktails in the adjacent lounge. ♥ 🍸

[Chalet Edelweiss] **8740 Sepulveda Blvd., Westchester, 210.645.8740, chaletedelweiss.us. L & D daily. Swiss/German. Beer & wine. AE, MC, V. $$ WHY** Because L.A. is very short on Swiss restaurants— this is about it. **WHAT** This is not destination dining, but it's good to know about if you're in the Westchester/LAX area and have a hankering for a whole lotta cheese and some accordian music. Try the raclette, the fondue, the schnitzels with good spaetzle, and the gut-busting Swiss mac 'n cheese, but skip dessert. That way you might be able to manage another Bitburger Pils, which they have on tap. **WHO** Westchester families and birthday celebrants. 🗐 ☺

[Chaya Venice] **110 Navy St., Venice, 310.396.1179, thechaya.com. L Mon.-Fri., D nightly. Asian/Californian. Full bar. AE, MC, V. $$$ - $$$$ WHY** Lobster enchiladas, and one of the best happy hours in town. **WHAT** Chaya Venice's once-pioneering East-meets-West cuisine is now found all over L.A., but it's good to revisit the source for good sushi, seaweed salads, pastas and such French-Japanese hybrids as miso-marinated sea bass with a wasabi-tamarind beurre blanc. **WHO** Venice artists and musicians, when they can afford it, and Hollywood moguls, who can always afford it.

[Chez Jay] **1657 Ocean Ave., Santa Monica, 310.395.1741, chezjays. com. B Sat.-Sun., L Mon.-Fri., D nightly. American. Full bar. AE, MC, V. $ - $$$ WHY** Jay Fiondella has passed on, but his eponymous beach shack remains an oasis in a sea of gentrification, complete with a peanut-shell "carpet." **WHAT** This tiny shack festooned with Christmas lights is the only unchanged element amid the upscale hotels and overpriced restaurants that now dominate this strip of Ocean Avenue. Chez Jay still packs 'em nightly with old-school food that'll fill you up just fine. It's also an inviting place to hit for a drink after dinner, when the red leatherette booths start to empty out. **WHO** Locals and tourists who can't resist the midcentury appeal and celebrity-dive cachet (Warren Beatty and Sean Penn were regulars for years).

[Chinois on Main] **2709 Main St., Santa Monica, 310.392.9025, wolfgangpuck.com. L Wed.-Fri., D nightly. Asian. Full bar. AE, MC, V. $$$$ - $$$$$ WHY** It's a delicious '80s-era time warp—noisy, pricey and crowded—with desserts worth sticking around for, like the dim sum dessert box and the crème brûlée trio. **WHAT** It's been a quarter-century since Wolfgang Puck opened Chinois on Main, and not much has changed—which, oddly enough, turns out to be a good thing. It all works: that hot-pink-and-turquoise décor, those Cal-Asian dishes that started the craze, and such deserving menu staples as Shanghai lobster in ginger-curry sauce with the paper-thin, crispy fried spinach that so mysteriously dissolves on your tongue.

[Divino] **11714 Barrington Ct., Brentwood, 310.472.0886. L & D daily. Italian. Beer & wine. AE, MC, V. $$ - $$$ WHY** Personal service, carefully cooked pastas and charm galore in a hidden Brentwood location. **WHAT** Italian trattorie are as plentiful in Brentwood as Guatemalan nannies, and most of them are good. This is one of the least known—and one of the best. The high-ceilinged space is decorated with old black-and-white family photos of brother/owners Davor and Goran Milic, who hail from the Yugoslav side of the Adriatic, where the cooking is comparable to the Italian side. Seafood is a specialty (wonderful basil-bathed orecchiette with branzino), as are crisp pizzas, lemony salads, light gnocchi porcini and good gelati. **WHO** Down-to-earth Brentwood locals who are in on the secret.

[Drago Ristorante] **2628 Wilshire Blvd., Santa Monica, 310.828.1585, celestinodrago.com. L Mon.-Fri., D nightly. Italian. Full bar. AE, MC, V. $$$ - $$$$$ WHY** Simple, handmade and delicious trattoria fare, and fellow diners who remember what it means to dress for dinner. **WHAT** This showpiece of Celestino Drago's mini-empire offers

ESSENTIALLY L.A. **LATE** **ROMANTIC** **VALUE** **QUIET** **SUSTAINABLE**

hearty regional cooking in an elegant setting. But all pretense vanishes when Celestino strolls from table to table, grinning and chatting as customers dine on dishes such as handmade pumpkin tortelloni in sage cream and fettuccine with pheasant-morel sauce. Things like veal chops and fresh fish can get pricey, but we're happy to pay $16 for the venison ragú with fresh cavatelli. The wine-by-the-glass route makes more sense than the inflated wine list **WHO** Dolled-up habituées and special-occasion diners, with no shortage of baubles on display. ♥🍸

[Echigo] **12217 Santa Monica Blvd., West L.A., 310.820.9787. L Mon.-Fri., D Mon.-Sat. Sushi/Japanese. Beer & wine. AE, MC, V. $$ - $$$ WHY** Because sushi masters are judged by their rice. **WHAT** "No cooked stuff" warns a hand-scribbled notice at this no-frills Tokyo-style sushi restaurant in a generic West L.A. strip mall. They're not kidding—there's no edamame, no California rolls, no attitude. Just Hitoshi Kataoka's glistening, warm sushi rice topped with supremely fresh fish, plus a simple miso soup and a seaweed salad. "Trust me" proclaims the daily catch chalkboard—it's *omakase* (chef's choice) only at the sushi counter, although tables can be à la carte or omakase. Lunchtime brings a great bargain: a $14 "sushi lunch set," with five pieces and a blue crab hand roll. **WHO** Westside sushi buffs who want everything from ankimo to uni at a more reasonable price than some of the better-known competition. 🍴

[El Texate] **316 Pico Blvd., Santa Monica, 310.399.1115, eltexate.com. B, L & D daily. Mexican/Oaxacan. Full bar. MC, V. $ WHY** Cheap and tasty moles, goat tacos, and chicken soup with rice and avocado. **WHAT** To understand why Southern California is such a great place to live, head to El Texate in Santa Monica. Here you are, just a few blocks from the Pacific, eating a Oaxacan meal for less than $12, and it tastes equally good whether you live in a $5 million north-of-Montana chateau or a rent-controlled south-of-Pico shack. The soccer-watching bar makes a decent margarita on the rocks. **WHO** Ocean Park locals, and not too many of them—the shabby-but-shady patio and intensely colorful dining room are typically empty. 🍴☺☼

[Fig] **Fairmont Miramar, 101 Wilshire Blvd., Santa Monica, 310.319.3111, figsantamonica.com. B daily, L Mon.-Sat., D Tues.-Sat., brunch Sun. Modern American/French. Full bar. AE, MC, V. $$$ - $$$$ WHY** Because if beef tongue is the must-have dish, when tarte flambé and amazing sweetbreads with mushroom fricassée are also on the menu, chef Ray Garcia must be on to something. **WHAT** If you didn't have to walk past the spa, you'd never guess this is the Fairmont Miramar's bistro. The food is top-notch, the atmosphere laid-back, and the wine and beer selection actually interesting and fairly priced—hardly your typical hotel restaurant. Only the desserts are uninteresting. Try to find time for the bacon-centric Sunday brunch—yes, there's even a bacon bloody mary. **WHO** Well-heeled locals spreading arugula butter

---

🥬 VEGETARIAN ⊙ KID FRIENDLY ✿ PATIO DINING 🚗 DELIVERY 🏛 PRIVATE PARTY

on warm baguettes at the bar and chatty hotel guests tossing back fig mojitos on the patio. ♥ 🍸 🍴 ☼ 🏛

[Furaibo] **2068 Sawtelle Blvd., West L.A., 310.444.1432. L Mon.- Fri., D nightly. Japanese. Beer & wine. MC, V. $$ - $$$ WHY** Small, tapas-like plates of fried chicken wings, calamari, grilled tofu, various yakitoris and other things that go down very well indeed with pitchers of cold beer. **WHAT** This izakaya place specializes in *tebasaki*, Japanese-style fried chicken wings. They head an enormous a la carte menu that includes about 30 varieties of grilled fish, dozens of vegetable dishes and kushiyaki. **WHO** This noisy, lively place is a favorite haunt of Japanese university students and young professionals. ☺ 🍸

[Gaby's Mediterranean] **20 Washington Blvd., Marina del Rey, 310.821.9721, gabysexpress.com. L & D daily. Mediterranean. No booze. AE, MC, V. $ - $$ WHY** Savory stuff, served outdoors by the beach at low prices. **WHAT** The small inside room is rather grim, with too-loud music, but out on the sidewalk, with a constant parade of people headed for the sand and nearby Venice Pier, this seems like a perfect beach café. Fat, soft pita bread, smooth hummus, fresh tabbouleh and long-roasted chicken make a fine lunch on a sunny, salt-air day, and the pita wraps are excellent, so it's easy to forgive any kitchen haphaz-ardness—or that too-tart dressing on the green salads. Another branch is in a parking-lot tent in Palms. **WHO** Flip-flop people. 🍸 ☺ ☼

[The Galley] **2442 Main St., Santa Monica, 310.452.1934, thegalleyrestaurant.net. L Sun., D nightly. American/steakhouse. Full bar. AE, MC, V. $$ - $$$$$ WHY** A crooner's jukebox, a nostalgia-inducing menu and lighting dim enough to make you fall in love with the person across from you—and with this old-school steakhouse—all over again. **WHAT** Santa Monica's oldest restaurant/bar has been a local treasure since it opened in 1934. Regulars love the martinis with mermaid toothpicks, along with the steaks, littleneck clams and signa-ture salads with the "secret-recipe" dressing (tastes like a tangy Green Goddess to us). The nautical décor is one of its many old-fashioned charms. ♥ 🍸

[Gjelina] 🔒 **1429 Abbot Kinney Blvd., Venice, 310.450.1429, gjelina. com. L Mon.-Fri., D nightly, brunch Sat.-Sun. Modern American. Beer & wine. AE, MC, V. $$ - $$$ WHY** The kitchen knows when to take a fish off the grill and how to bring out the best in each dish—without overcomplicating it. The setting and the food combine to make this the perfect California restaurant. **WHAT** This lively (i.e. noisy) Abbot Kinney hot spot has a '70s open-air Big Sur vibe but a decidedly more modern menu and a seriously skilled kitchen. Try the plump steamed mussels in a pungent fat-free broth, served with a hunk of grilled sour-dough; the delicious thin-crust pizzas; the extraordinary roast Jidori chicken; any of the vegetable dishes; and the incredible butterscotch budino with sea-salted caramel. **WHO** A constant crowd of Venice cool people—make reservations well in advance for weekends, especially if you want to sit on the quieter back patio. 🐚 ☼

[Hal's Bar & Grill] **1349 Abbot Kinney Blvd., Venice, 310.396.3105, halsbarandgrill.com. L & D daily. Californian. Full bar. AE, MC, V. $$ - $$$$** **WHY** No cover, no drink minimum, no kidding. **WHAT** Listening to jazz and sipping martinis at this stylish neighborhood restaurant on a Sunday night—when the rest of the world is nodding off during *60 Minutes*—is deliciously fun and indulgent. Grab a seat at the bar to hear such accomplished musicians as blues guitarist Phil Upchurch and sax player Cal Bennett, and enjoy one of the very good salads, burgers or modern American main courses. **WHO** Venice artists, musicians and the occasional celebrity.

[Hama Sushi] **213 Windward Ave., Venice, 310.396.8783, hamasushi.com. D nightly. Japanese/Sushi. Full bar. AE, MC, V. $$ - $$$$** **WHY** Inventive sushi rolls and exuberant chefs. (If you stay until closing, you'll get to hear them belt out *Hotel California*, perhaps accompanied by a few well-served patrons.) **WHAT** One of the nation's first sushi restaurants, Hama has been hot since 1979, combining a flip-flops-friendly atmosphere with fresh, carefully prepared sushi, sashimi and cooked Japanese classics such as spicy tuna shiso, seaweed salad, and grilled yellowtail collar with ponzu. With its surf videos and free-flowing Asahi and sake, this is a must-visit in Venice. ☼

[Hostaria del Piccolo] **606 Broadway, Santa Monica, 310.393.6633, hostariadelpiccolo.com. L & D daily, brunch Sun. Italian. Full bar. AE, MC, V. $$ - $$$ WHY** Because you can snack on squid-ink tagliolini and romanesco pizza at 3:30 in the afternoon. **WHAT** This casual spinoff of Piccolo in Venice may be a lot less expensive, but it has the same authentic culinary bent—think veal tongue in tuna sauce and baccalà-filled ravioli. An upmarket pizza list of sauced and unsauced varieties includes toppings of roasted butternut squash and tuna crudo. There's a gluten-free crust, too. Choose the vibrant, noisy dining room or the cool leafy patio to enjoy your meal. **WHO** Young and not so young professionals. ☺ ☼

[Il Grano] **11359 Santa Monica Blvd., West L.A., 310.477.7886, il-grano.com. L Mon.-Fri., D Mon.-Sat. Italian. Full bar. AE, MC, V. $$$ - $$$$** **WHY** High-quality fresh fish, Italian style; try the crudos, the squid-ink pasta with sea urchin and the salt-baked sea bass. The three-course business lunch is a good value. **WHAT** Sal Marino grew up in the restaurant business (at Marino's), and now, in his own modern, elegant place, he's exploring his own culinary passions: ultra-fresh seafood and handmade pastas. His early days were uneven, but Il Grano has matured into a fine and sophisticated ristorante with delicious, celebratory cooking. The tasting menus (including a vegetarian one) are

---

🍃 VEGETARIAN ⊙ KID FRIENDLY ☼ PATIO DINING 🚗 DELIVERY 🎩 PRIVATE PARTY

worth trying. Serious wine list, too. **WHO** Chic, modern westsiders in a chic, modern space. ♥ 🌙 ⚲🏛

[Inn of the Seventh Ray] 🏛 **128 Old Topanga Canyon Rd., Topanga, 310.455.1311, innoftheseventhray.com. L Mon.-Sat., D nightly, brunch Sun. Vegetarian/Modern American. Beer & wine. AE, MC, V. $$ - $$$$ WHY** As they say, "partake of the angelic vibrations of the violet ray," baby. The food's great. **WHAT** Although it's tempting to make fun of this '70s-era hippie landmark, the food is no joke. The diverse menu features raw food dishes like a summer-squash lasagne, vegetarian choices such as agave-glazed vegan duck and carnivore-pleasers such as naturally raised filet mignon with a mirepoix of asparagus. The Sunday brunch, while not cheap, is peaceful and lovely. **WHO** Wedding parties drawn to its gardens, terraces, gazebos and fountains, plus a wide array of raw-food enthusiasts, vegetarians and even the occasional carnivore. ♥ 🌙 🌀⚲☺ ✿🏛

[Javan] **11500 Santa Monica Blvd., Brentwood, 310.207.5555, javanrestaurant.com. L & D daily (to midnight Fri.-Sat.). Persian/Middle Eastern. Full bar. AE, MC, V. $$ - $$$ WHY** Tasty kebabs, delectable little grilled lamb chops, saffron rice and other Persian dishes. Local delivery, too. **WHAT** The leading Iranian restaurant on Santa Monica Boulevard, with excellent kebabs and a particularly suave-looking bar. Pass on the salads in favor of the kebabs, lamb chops and delicious lentil-based *ashjoe* soup. 🌙🚗

[JiRaffe] **502 Santa Monica Blvd., Santa Monica, 310.917.6671, jirafferestaurant.com. D Mon.- Sat. Californian/French. Full bar. AE, MC, V. $$$$ - $$$$$ WHY** The seafood's usually outstanding, including almond-crusted rainbow trout and pepper-crusted ahi with green-tea soba noodles. **WHAT** JiRaffe epitomizes the California bistro, with its elegant chandeliers hung above cozy tables, first-rate service and the creative market-based California-French cuisine of surfer-chef Raphael Lunetta. Bargain hunters, take note of Lunetta's fantastic three-course Monday-night dinner, a bistro-style menu for $38: perhaps duck confit with haricots vert, pan-roasted Alaskan halibut with a spaghetti of zucchini, and a lemon bar with crème fraîche ice cream. **WHO** Santa Monica creative types, businesspeople and politicians, often celebrating an achievement. ♥🌀🏛

[Joe's] 🏛 **1023 Abbot Kinney Blvd., Venice, 310.399.5811, joesrestaurant.com. L Tues.-Fri., D Tues.-Sun., brunch Sat.-Sun. Modern American. Full bar. AE, MC, V. $$ - $$$$ WHY** Not that you'd regret shelling out for dinner, but the best deal in town is lunch at Joe's, where for $19 you get a superb three-course meal—perhaps parsnip-fennel soup, shrimp risotto-sofrito and chocolate crunch cake. Great brunch, too. **WHAT** Before Abbot Kinney was the coolest place in L.A., Joe Miller gambled and opened a tiny restaurant there. His first-rate cooking and the warmth of the handsome little place paid off; he expanded into a neighboring space and watched the neighborhood gentrify around him. This still-young chef now ranks as a Venice old-timer, respected for the excellence of his food, which is served with skill in this clean-lined, California-elegant bistro. **WHO** Very attractive middle-aged surfers, clothing designers and software developers. ♥

[Josie] 2424 Pico Blvd., Santa Monica, 310.581.9888, josierestaurant.com. D nightly. Modern American/Californian. Full bar. AE, MC, V. $$$$ **WHY** Thoughtful, creative dishes made from seasonal ingredients—perhaps a pluot and burrata salad followed by a whole boneless trout cooked "campfire" style (fabulous) or a buffalo burger with truffle fries, and concluding with a Meyer lemon cheesecake with roasted blueberries. **WHAT** Josie Le Balch grew up in an L.A. restaurant, and now she has become one of the city's best chefs. Her place is mature and serious about its food, yet it's unpretentious in an east Santa Monica kind of way. When you need to eat really well but don't want an overblown scene, come here. Confident and competent service. **WHO** Intelligent food lovers, often celebrating an occasion. ♥ ◔

[Katsuya Brentwood] 11777 San Vicente Blvd., Brentwood, 310.207.8744, sbe.com/katsuya. L & D daily. Japanese. Full bar. AE, MC, V. $$$ - $$$$$ **WHY** Who knew Brentwood could be this happening? **WHAT** This upscale, always-packed, almost manic place is very *Lost in Translation*—lots of neon, purple and white leather, all of it created by famed French designer Philippe Starck. The menu, from sushi chef Katsuya Uechi, includes a variety of hot and cold items, including scallops with kiwi in yuzu vinaigrette, baked black cod and very good sushi rolls. The robata bar turns out delectable skewers of grilled shrimp, chicken meatballs, vegetables and steak. **WHO** Brentwood's beautiful people.

[La Cachette Bistro] 1733 Ocean Ave., Santa Monica, 310.434.9509, lacachettebistro.com. L Tues.-Fri., D Tues.-Sun. French/Californian. Full bar. AE, MC, V. $$$ **WHY** A prime location on Ocean near the hotels, serving a market-based menu of sophisticated Cal-French bistro dishes and stylish mixologist-designed cocktails. **WHAT** Accomplished French chef Jean François Meteigner left his posh Century City dining room for this more informal beach-adjacent spot with a large patio, comfortable bar and handsome bistro décor. His cooking is also a little more informal (and affordable) than at the old place, with an extensive roster of French tapas (house-smoked trout, homemade pâté, foie gras with polenta brûlée), nightly classic bistro specials, and excellent happy-hour cocktails for $8. **WHO** A grown-up crowd, doing business at lunch and relaxing at dinnertime. ◔ ☼ ⌂

◆ VEGETARIAN ◔ KID FRIENDLY ☼ PATIO DINING ◚ DELIVERY ⌂ PRIVATE PARTY

[Lares] **2909 Pico Blvd., Santa Monica, 310.829.4559, lares-restaurant. com. B, L & D daily. Mexican. Full bar. AE, MC, V. $ - $$ WHY** Chiles rellenos, lengua en mole and good margaritas, all at low prices. **WHAT** Manny Lares seems to be the main man at this family restaurant, but then there's his brother, his two sisters, his niece.... "We all cook, we all wash dishes, we all go to the bank," he says. Downstairs is a quiet room for eating enchiladas in peace, but the place to be is upstairs, where the flamenco guitarist entertains the diners, many of whom return weekly for the hearty southern Mexican classics. **WHO** Rent-controlled south Santa Monicans. 🗊 😊

[Le Petit Café] **2842 Colorado Ave., Santa Monica, 310.829.6792, lepetitcafebonjour.com. L Mon.-Fri., D Mon.-Sat. French. Beer & wine. AE, MC, V. $$ - $$$$ WHY** Honest fare at great prices: *pourquoi pas*? **WHAT** So many restaurants claim to be a neighborhood bistro these days, but it's a shock to actually find one. Le Petit Café is the real deal, with chalkboard-toting waiters, tiny bistro tables topped with Provençal linens and fine, straightforward bistro food at surprisingly good prices. **WHO** By day, a business crowd from nearby studios; in the evening, locals take over, with couples sharing *escargots* and friends lingering long after their *steak au poivre* has been cleared. 🗊

[Lilly's French Café] **1031 Abbot Kinney Blvd., Venice, 310.314.0004, lillysfrenchcafe.com. L Mon.-Sat., D nightly, brunch Sun. French. Beer & wine. AE, MC, V. $$ - $$$$ WHY** French bistro food at reasonable prices—especially the $12 brunch specials—in a convivial setting. **WHAT** In a charming old house in the heart of Abbot Kinney lies a French café that combines Venice style with traditional bistro cooking. Terrine de canard, salade frisée aux lardons, moules frites, entrecôte grillée, soufflé au chocolat chaud—it's all here, just like at your favorite Parisian bistro. ♥🗊☼

[The Lobster] **1602 Ocean Ave., Santa Monica, 310.458.9294, thelobster.com. L & D daily. Seafood. Full bar. AE, MC, V. $$$ - $$$$$ WHY** Cosmopolitan cooking without pretension, with a beach-friendly location that can't be beat. **WHAT** It has every right to be a tourist trap, but this pierside seafood restaurant is anything but. Always packed and always noisy, the modern concrete-and-glass space gives diners stellar views of the sea, sky and Ferris wheel—along with a daily-changing menu of fine (and pricey) seafood. You might find fat scallops seared and served with a simple trio of sides (grilled tomatoes, spinach and grilled asparagus) or black bass with sesame seeds, grilled shiitake mushrooms and a ginger-wasabi sauce. Don't even think of coming without a reservation.

[Locanda Portofino] **1110 Montana Ave., Santa Monica, 310.394.2070, locandaportofino.com. L Mon.-Sat., D nightly. Italian. Beer**

& wine. AE, MC, V. $$$ - $$$$ **WHY** Despite its strip-mall location, this is the kind of intimate, authentic trattoria you dream of finding in your own backyard. **WHAT** You arrive to seductive, garlicky odors wafting through the door and the attentions of cute, heavily accented Italian waiters—and food that lives up the anticipatory promise, from the hearty pasta arrabbiata to a hand-cut grilled swordfish of a quality that's hard to find these days. The risotti and pasta are appealing and the filet mignon is superb. It's a little place, so reservations are recommended. **WHO** North of Montana locals, including famous folks who just want (and get) a nice, quiet dinner. ♥ ☼

[Mélisse] 🔒 1104 Wilshire Blvd., Santa Monica, 310.395.0881, melisse. com. D Tues.-Sat. French/Modern American. Full bar. AE, MC, V. $$$$$ **WHY** The seasonally inspired and hard-to-resist four-course tasting menu; at $105 without wine, it's a serious indulgence, but one you're not likely to forget. Believe it or not, it's worth the extra $30 for the roast chicken, which is not like any roast chicken you've ever had. Beautiful vegetarian tasting menu, too. **WHAT** Mélisse is luxuriously French, with just a bit of California flair and a farmers' market sensibility. Josiah Citrin has created a romantic, dimly lit space, with formal tables set with French cutlery, an occasionally haughty wait staff and, yes, an actual cheese cart brimming with oozing, stinking delicacies. The dry-aged côte de boeuf (for two) with potato-leek torte, wild mushrooms and braised lettuce deserves its status as a menu classic. **WHO** Food- and romance-lovers willing to invest in a memorable meal. ♥ 🍷 🌣 📵 🏠

[M Street Ktichen] 2000 N. Main St., Santa Monica, 310.396.9145, mstreetkitchen.com. B, L & D daily. American. Full bar. AE, MC, V. $$ - $$$ **WHY** A crisp margarita on the sidewalk patio is a beautiful thing. **WHAT** The former La Grande Orange is now M Street Kitchen, part of the huge Lettuce Entertain You restaurant chain, which makes us disinclined to like the place. That said, it's worth knowing about for its sidewalk tables, breakfast sandwiches, brussels sprouts salad (an LGO carryover), happy hour and burgers. Prices are modest given the high-rent neighborhood. **WHO** A diverse crowd of 20something cocktail kids, tousled young families and date-night boomers. 🚚 ☺ ☼

[Michael's] 1147 3rd St., Santa Monica, 310.451.0843, michaelssantamonica.com. L Mon.-Fri., D Mon.-Sat. Californian. Full bar. AE, MC, V. $$$ - $$$$$ **WHY** Its patio, its still-amazing art collection and its new front-of-the-house cocktail lounge. **WHAT** Michael McCarty opened his namesake restaurant back in 1979 and was hugely influential in defining what was dubbed California cuisine and went on to become modern American cooking. His kitchen helped make goat cheese, arugula and caramelized onions a wildly popular culinary

🥬 VEGETARIAN ⊙ KID FRIENDLY ☼ PATIO DINING 🚚 DELIVERY 🏠 PRIVATE PARTY

trinity, and he took California wines seriously long before many others. After a long period of stagnation, the place has new life with its lounge, where ultra-stylish cocktails are made from ingredients grown in the rooftop garden and beautiful people nosh on oysters, truffle-thyme frites and tuna poke. Lunch in the garden still delivers the California dream. **WHO** Artists, writers, actors and tourists who can afford it. ♥ 🍸 🐾 ☼

[Monte Alban] **11927 Santa Monica Blvd., West L.A., 310.444.7736, restaurantemontealban.com. B, L & D daily. Mexican/Oaxacan. Beer & wine. AE, MC, V. $ WHY** The many moles—black, yellow, green, red, colorado—served in tamales, with chicken, in all sorts of dishes. Good huevos for breakfast, too. **WHAT** A fine and most affordable Oaxacan café known for its moles and its breakfast (good cinnamon-infused coffee). Try the mole negro tamale and the huitlachoche and *frijoladas*, a wonderful mix of beans, chicken and mole. 📷 ☺

[Musha] 🏠 **424 Wilshire Blvd., Santa Monica, 310.576.6330, musha.us. D nightly. Japanese/Californian. Beer & wine. AE, MC, V. $$ - $$$ WHY** Fatty pork belly (you know you want it), kim chee udon, tuna poke, seafood-filled baguette au gratin ... amazing and delicious dishes that typify the best of modern Japanese-L.A. fusion cooking. **WHAT** It's crowded and the waitresses are harried, so you might expect trouble—except Musha diners always seem relaxed and happy. Perhaps it's the slow-cooked pork belly. Or the moderate prices. Or the sake. Or the communal table that inspires new friendships. Whatever the reason, this modern small-plates Cal-Japanese bistro is lots of fun, and the food is terrific. ☺ 📷

[Nanbankan] **11330 Santa Monica Blvd., West L.A., 310.478.1591. D nightly. Japanese. Beer & wine. MC, V. $$ - $$$ WHY** Trust your waiter and order the specials he recommends, perhaps corn, Australian lamb, mixed mushrooms, burdock rolled in pork, *yaki onigiri* (rice ball) and *ninniku no me* (garlic sprouts sautéed with mushrooms and scallops). Just make sure you get some of the amazing chicken wings. **WHAT** For three decades Nanbankan has been L.A.'s yakitori destination, long before everyone was rushing to the latest izakaya (small plates) hot spot. The aroma of grilling meat, chicken and vegetables fills the modest room, where small groups of friends (seating is tight) share orders of wonderful things on skewers. If you haven't been in years, go back—you won't be sorry.

[Nobu] **Malibu Country Mart, 3835 Cross Creek Rd., Malibu, 310.317.9140, nobumatsuhisa.com. D nightly. Japanese/sushi. Full bar. AE, MC, V. $$$ - $$$$ WHY** Celeb spotting, perfectly fine food and a chance to make like one of the Malibu locals who've adopted Nobu as their neighborhood canteen (baseball cap, flip flops and iPhone optional). **WHAT** It's Disneyland Malibu here: a perfectly orchestrated miniature version of clichéd Malibu life, complete with omnipresent celebrities (think Cindy Crawford, David Duchovny, Courtney Cox, Kelsey Grammer...), hilarious cosmetic-surgery chatter in the restrooms and good though largely unexciting food: delectable black cod in miso, basic sushi, tasty but soggy rock-shrimp tempura, yellowtail sashimi with jalapeño. **WHO** The famous, the fabulous, the families with kids—sometimes all at the same table.

[Noma Sushi] **2031 Wilshire Blvd., Santa Monica, 310.453.4848. L & D daily. Japanese/Sushi. Beer & wine. AE, MC, V. $$ WHY** High-quality sushi and regional specialties served in an intimate setting. **WHAT** Step inside this curbside sushi joint on a Friday night and you'll be transported to a bustling Manhattan hot spot with its shotgun interior, cozy booths and frantically busy staff delivering quality sushi with a few unexpected surprises (think black pig sausage from your waiter's hometown, with a side of ballpark mustard). **WHO** Anyone who loves a booth: couples, families with neighborhood kids in tow, and friends meeting after work. 🍴🙂

[Nook Bistro] **11628 Santa Monica Blvd., West L.A., 310.207.5160, nookbistro.com. L Mon.-Fri., D Mon.-Sat. Modern American. Beer & wine. AE, MC, V. $$ - $$$ WHY** Farmers' market–fresh comfort food like shrimp and grits (the house special), shiitake-and-Gruyère bread pudding, and pear crumble. Extras include a big communal table, a modest $10 corkage and no corkage on Mondays. **WHAT** Nook Bistro is indeed a nook, a tiny spot hidden in the back corner of a little strip mall with not enough parking. It's hard to spot, but that hasn't stopped it from becoming very popular, thanks to its excellent prices and simple, well-prepared dishes. It's the kind of place a chef would open for other chefs, and the loyal locals are the beneficiaries. **WHO** Regulars who know to make a reservation and come before 8 p.m.—after that the wait can be brutal. 🍴🌱🚗🙂

[Orris] 🏛 **2006 Sawtelle Blvd., West L.A., 310.268.2212, orrisrestaurant. com. D Tues.-Sun. French/Asian. Beer & wine. AE, MC, V. $$ - $$$ WHY** Such exquisite French-influenced small plates as shrimp-mousse-filled ravioli with shiitake sauce, grilled hearts of romaine salad, filet mignon with Roquefort butter and foie gras with Japanese eggplant. **WHAT** After running Franco-Japanese restaurant Shiro for many years, chef Hideo Yamashiro flipped the name and opened the smaller and more casual Orris on Sawtelle's Japanese restaurant row. Reservations aren't accepted for the spare, modern eatery, but there is seating at the chic granite bar and on the patio. Yamashiro pairs his food with premium sakes and good wines. 🍴☼

[Osteria Latini] **11712 San Vicente Blvd., Brentwood, 310.826.9222, osterialatini.com. L Mon.-Fri., D nightly. Italian. Beer & wine. AE, MC, V. $$ - $$$$ WHY** There are lots of Italian eateries in Brentwood; this

---

🌿 **VEGETARIAN** ⊙ **KID FRIENDLY** ☼ **PATIO DINING** 🚗 **DELIVERY** 🏛 **PRIVATE PARTY**

one stands out because it's friendly, homey and has reasonable prices. **WHAT** Trieste native Paolo Pasio has the warmth required of a good trattoria owner, and his dining room is inviting and often crowded. His kitchen turns out very fine Italian comfort food: beet salad, burrata with red and yellow tomatoes, buttery whole roasted branzino, delicious lobster risotto, excellent pastas. Our only complaints: weak desserts and the recitation of far too many daily specials to remember.

[Paco's Tacos] **4141 Centinela Ave., West L.A., 310.391.9616, pacoscantina.com. L & D daily. Mexican. Full bar. AE, MC, V. $ - $$ WHY** Cal-Mex cuisine at its gut-busting best, plus an excellent cadillac margarita and low prices. **WHAT** If you grew up in Southern California, this is the kind of restaurant you dreamt of when you went away to college. It boasts every Mexican-restaurant cliché: hokey paintings, a logo with a sombrero-sporting hombre, rustic ranchero-style leather chairs and a costumed señora making tortillas on a griddle. (Plus walls crammed with antlers, armor and St. Patrick's Day decorations.) There's often a wait, but the food's worth it: juicy carne asada, a huge tostada and gooey enchiladas. 🖼️ ☺

[Pecorino] **11604 San Vicente Blvd., Brentwood, 310.571.3800, pecorinorestaurant.com. L Mon.-Fri., D nightly. Italian. Beer & wine. AE, MC, V. $$$ WHY** Basic pastas like *cacio e pepe* (spaghetti with pecorino, parmesan and pepper) that are so satisfying you'll wonder what else they're sneaking into the bowl. **WHAT** Step inside Pecorino, and you'll be greeted by a gush of warmth—brick walls, cozy bistro tables, rustic chandeliers—and exuberant host Mario Sabatini. As he hops around the dining room, his twin brother Raffaele is in the kitchen cooking up dishes from their hometown of Abruzzo and beyond. The food's good—even the amaretto-soaked tiramisu (really). No reservations, so come early or you'll have to wait.

[Piccolo] 🔒 **5 Dudley Ave., Venice, 310.314.3222, piccolovenice.com. D nightly. Italian. Beer & wine. AE, MC, V. $$$ - $$$$$ WHY** Seductive charm, a setting right out of Venice, Italy, and superb Italian food make it ideal for a memorable date or celebration. Just be prepared to pay for the experience. **WHAT** This beachside trattoria is so warm and intimate that you'll feel like you've been invited to a friend's house for dinner—a friend who is passionate about Italian food and wine and can cook like nobody's business: homemade tagliolini with venison ragú, stuffed rabbit with polenta, scallops with black truffles, flourless chocolate cake. The monthly *centro al contrario* (reversal) dinner is great fun—you choose your wines, and the chef makes your meal accordingly. **WHO** Moneyed Venice artists and entrepreneurs. ♥ ☼ 🏠

[Pizzicotto] 🔒 **11758 San Vicente Blvd., Brentwood, 310.442.7188. L Mon.-Sat., D nightly. Italian. Beer & wine. AE, MC, V. $ - $$$ WHY** The irresistible *pesce cuocopazzo*—fresh whitefish with a horseradish-pistachio crust and sauce of white wine, garlic, lemon and fresh tomatoes. **WHAT** There's always a crowd at this Brentwood trattoria, perhaps the best of the large Italian bunch in the neighborhood—so don't even think of coming without a reservation. The ceilings are high (and so are the noise levels) and everybody looks happy tucking into bruschetta, panini, crisp-crusted pizzas and risotto with wild mushrooms.

[Raku] 11678 W. Olympic Blvd., West L.A., 310.478.3090. D Wed.-Mon. (to 1:30 a.m. Fri.-Sun.). Japanese/Korean. BYOB (no corkage). AE, MC, V. $$ - $$$ **WHY** With a long, elegant dining counter, a lengthy menu of homey dishes and late hours, this simple strip-mall spot is a boon for night-owl industry types working in West L.A.'s studios and creative offices. **WHAT** A motherly woman behind the stoves of the open kitchen at this Japanese-Korean café turns out tamago with free-range eggs, braised black pork chunks, simmered fiddlehead fern tops and for the brave, home-style pickled squid guts to perk up your rice. ☺

[Real Food Daily] 514 Santa Monica Blvd., Santa Monica, 310.451.7544, realfood.com. L & D daily, brunch Sun. Vegan/American. No booze. AE, MC, V. $$ **WHY** The Ciao Bella—roasted veggies with pesto on hemp bread. **WHAT** Chef/owner Ann Gentry serves enticing meat-free and dairy-free fare in her casual café. The faux Reuben and mock club try too hard to mimic their meat counterparts, so try instead the seasonal vegetables in a wasabi vinaigrette, the Yin Yang veggie salad with peanut-sesame dressing and the chunky miso soup. **WHO** Westside vegans, vegetarians and plain old vegetable lovers. ✿✎☺🚗

[Rustic Canyon] 🍴 1119 Wilshire Blvd., Santa Monica, 310.393.7050, rusticcanyonwinebar.com. D nightly. Modern American/ wine bar. Beer & wine. AE, MC, V. $$$ - $$$$ **WHY** The burger—made with Meyer beef, Niman Ranch bacon, wild greens, a brioche bun and either Point Reyes blue cheese or sharp Tillamook cheddar—may be even better than the one at Father's Office On Mondays, the chef experiments and makes more creative burgers that he pairs with craft beers. **WHAT** We wish all neighborhood restaurants were this fine. The market-inspired menu served in this high-ceilinged, candlelit dining room changes monthly; there are always a couple of gossamer-light pastas and a stronger Italian bent overall, reflecting chef Evan Funke's time in Emilia-Romagna. Not to worry, though—the pan-roasted Jidori chicken with caramelized baby onions is always offered, and it's amazing. Don't miss the desserts from sister café Huckleberry: salted chocolate-caramel tart, plum and grape crostata, and perhaps the best chocolate chip cookie in town. Expect pricey, small-producer varieties on the wine list, really interesting beers (there's a beer sommelier) and a serious commitment to organic and sustainable products. **WHO** An after-work wine-sipping crowd at the bar and a food-focused crowd (including some off-duty chefs) at the tables. ✿

✎ VEGETARIAN ☺ KID FRIENDLY ✿ PATIO DINING 🚗 DELIVERY 🎩 PRIVATE PARTY

[SaSaYa] 11613 Santa Monica Blvd., West L.A., 310.477.4404, izakaya-sasaya.com. D Mon.-Sat. Japanese. Beer & wine. MC, V. $$ - $$$ **WHY** Excellent izakaya is paired with a vast collection of sakes and shochus. Good weeknight happy hour, too. **WHAT** In a rustic, wood-paneled space that looks like a Japanese country inn, customers share tips at the massive communal table. Signs in calligraphy describe special sakes and seasonal dishes that are simple yet perfectly cooked.

[Sauce on Hampton] 259 Hampton Dr., Venice, 310.399.5400, sauceonhampton.com. B, L & D daily. American. BYOB. MC, V. $ **WHY** Shiraz frittata, a scramble with grilled onions, tomatoes and turmeric; luscious breakfast sandwiches; the chopped baby spinach salad; and a turkey burger that is juicier and more flavorful than most, topped with baby spinach, sliced tomato, red onion, applewood-smoked bacon and cheddar. **WHAT** A teeny café with teeny tables, this spot is the product of gregarious chef/owner Sassan (Sass) Rostamian, once the lunch chef at Rustic Canyon. It perfectly suits the neighborhood: It's a breakfast place that doesn't open until 10 and a dinner place for burger lovers, and everything is organic and carefully prepared, with most dishes costing less than $11.**WHO** The sort of Venice folks who have breakfast at 11:30—on weekdays.

[Savory] 29169 Heathercliff Rd., Malibu, 310.589.8997, savorymalibu. com. D nightly (limited menu Mon.). American. Beer & wine. AE, MC, V. $$$ **WHY** Because Malibu has long needed a sophisticated, ingredient-driven dinner house. **WHAT** Chef Paul Shoemaker, who's cooked at Bastide and the Water Grill, refines American comfort foods (smoky clam chowder, Jidori chicken pot pie, house-baked breads) with a seasonal menu based on produce that's often sourced from nearby farms. His straightforward preparations elevate but don't overwhelm the food's fresh essences. A smart, simple bar and subtle beach-resort décor suits the J Brand jeans set, who occasionally spring for a $2,000 Bordeaux. **WHO** A well-mannered crowd who wouldn't dream of asking the Oscar nominee at the next table for an autograph.

[Tasting Kitchen] 1633 Abbot Kinney Blvd., Venice, 310.392.6644, thetastingkitchen.com. D nightly, brunch Sat.-Sun. Modern American. Full bar. AE, MC, V. $$$ - $$$$ **WHY** An elegant Lucques-meets-Portland gem with an ever-changing selection of inspired, intensely flavored but not at all fussy creations, ranging from delicate market greens tossed with walnut anchoïade to roast branzino with chanterelles. The $50 set menu has got to be one of the best fine-dining deals in town. **WHAT** A crew of former ClarkLewis folks create not only great food but an infectious enthusiasm that fills this buzzing dining room. Casey Lane works the stoves, while young manager and resident Italian wine buff Maxwell Leer chats up guests about the unfiltered Prosecco and Sagrantino (an indigenous grape from Umbria that is grown in limited quantities). The beer, wine and cocktail list may contain only two dozen options, but somehow here it feels complete. The hand-scrawled menu is a bit precious and hard to decipher, but it's worth the effort. Don't skip the fantastic desserts, such as a pecan derby pie, by pastry chef Joey Messina. **WHO** Married couples out for a special night and young singles gathered around the bar. ☞

[Tavern Brentwood] 🏠 **11648 San Vicente Blvd., Brentwood, 310.806.6464, tavernla.com. B Mon.-Fri., L & D daily, brunch Sat.-Sun. Modern American. Full bar. AE, MC, V. $$$$ WHY** Except for low prices, this place has everything that's missing from Suzanne Goin and Caroline Styne's other restaurants with similar farmers'-market-friendly Cal-French cuisine: breakfast, brunch, kids' menus, cocktail bar, even a takeout counter. **WHAT** This glammed-up addition to the Lucques/AOC family is light-filled by day and romantic by night, with a takeout-friendly café as a bonus. (You'd never guess this used to be a Hamburger Hamlet.) The food's excellent, if affordable only to 90049 residents. We also love the clever kid's menu ("no parsley" pasta with butter and parmesan), the great but overpriced bar ($14 vodka gimlets?) and, finally, bread worthy of Goin's food, made by in-house baker Nathan Dakdouk, who is sure to be christened L.A.'s next sourdough king. **WHO** Goin worshippers with deep pockets in the dining room; locals picking up prepared salads, multigrain cherry-cashew bread and cookies from the takeout "larder." ☺

[Tlapazola Grill] 🏠 **636 Venice Blvd., Venice, 310.822.7561, tlapazolagrill.com. L Mon.-Sat., D nightly. Mexican/Oaxacan. Full bar. AE, MC, V. $$ - $$$ WHY** Lobster chile relleno with tamarindo-hoisin sauce, grilled salmon with mole pipian and a spinach-garlic quesadilla, and grilled half-chicken with two moles. **WHAT** This nouvelle Oaxacan café serves very good, modestly priced southern Mexican dishes in a colorful dining room or out on a quiet walled patio. Note that while it shares a name with the (also good) Tlapazola in West L.A., they are run by different family members. **WHO** A loyal crowd that's sick of the typical beach-town melted-cheese Mexican food. ☞ 🦷 ☼

[Tlapazola Grill] 🏠 **11676 Gateway Blvd., West L.A., 310.477.1577, tlapazola.com. L Tues.-Sun., D nightly. Mexican/Oaxacan. Full bar. AE, MC, V. $$ WHY** Inventive and rewarding modern Oaxacan food and solid margaritas. **WHAT** The two Cruz brothers started this sweet place, but their business partnership split, and each brother has his own Tlapazola. This one is more gracious than its strip-mall setting would suggest, serving a hybrid cuisine that combines Oaxacan staples (awesome mole negro) with Mexican classics (pass on the barbacoa in favor of any pork specials) with a California approach to fresh vegetables, seafood, sauces and presentation. Kind people, moderate prices and great margaritas make it a westside winner. ☞

🍃 **VEGETARIAN** ⊙ **KID FRIENDLY** ☼ **PATIO DINING** 🚗 **DELIVERY** 🏛 **PRIVATE PARTY**

[Typhoon] 🏛 **3221 Donald Douglas Loop S., Santa Monica, 310.390.6565, typhoon.biz. L Mon.-Fri., D nightly, brunch Sun. Asian. Full bar. AE, MC, V. $$ - $$$ WHY** Pan-Asian delicacies, with an unforgettable side serving of small planes taking off over the Pacific at sunset. **WHAT** This place is just plain fun. With a window-lined dining room overlooking retro Santa Monica Airport, a chic Asian décor with aeronautical touches, a good bar and a fairly priced menu of dishes from Singapore, Korea, China, Thailand, Vietnam, the Philippines and Burma, Typhoon can't go wrong. Thrill seekers try the deep-fried white sea worms or Singapore-style scorpions; everyone else shares sui mai, Vietnamese egg rolls, Korean-style short ribs and Thai river prawns with a cilantro-garlic-peanut paste. Great jazz on Tuesday nights. **WHO** Adventurers, aviation enthusiasts and savvy hosts with hard-to-wow out-of-town guests. ♥ ☺

[Valentino] **3115 Pico Blvd., Santa Monica, 310.829.4313, valentinorestaurant.com. L Fri., D Mon.-Sat. Italian. Full bar. AE, MC, V. $$$$$ WHY** For the newish Vin Bar, a more casual and affordable spot situated rather awkwardly within the restaurant. **WHAT** This groundbreaking Italian restaurant has impeccable silver and service, the atmosphere exudes self-satisfied wealth, and the kitchen is accomplished, turning out such delicacies as truffle-topped risotto, agnolotti with braised Sonoma lamb, and a garlic-rubbed veal chop on wilted wild greens. But at well over $100 a head for dinner with wine (much more if you go nuts with the amazing wine list), we don't find it always worth the investment. But we love the Vin Bar, which has sleek small plates, a fantastic salumi platter, and rarely seen wine gems served by the glass. **WHO** Serious wine lovers and mature romantics with cash to burn. ♥ 🍷 🏛

[Vincenti] 🏛 **11930 San Vicente Blvd., Brentwood, 310.207.0127, vincentiristorante.com. L Fri., D Mon.-Sat. Italian. Full bar. AE, MC, V. $$$$ - $$$$$ WHY** Owner Maureen Vincenti's contagious laugh and doting attention to each guest, plus the house-made porchetta, spit-roasted until it's a perfectly charred, juicy hunk of pure pork bliss. **WHAT** Step inside the elegant dining room, with its marble counters and slick leather banquettes, and it's clear this isn't your average homespun trattoria. Chef Nicola Mastronardi turns out gutsy cuisine, such as osso buco tortelloni with wild mushroom sauce and sliced steak with herb ravioli, endive and green peppercorn sauce. For dessert, try one of pastry chef Willy Sifuentes's creations: a delicious twist on tiramisu, served in a martini glass, or the light, heavenly lemon ricotta cake. This kind of dining experience doesn't come cheap, but Vincenti is one Italian that's worth the price. **WHO** Well-heeled, well-dressed westsiders. ♥ 🍷 🏛

🏛 ESSENTIALLY L.A. ☺ LATE ♥ ROMANTIC 🎫 VALUE 🍷 QUIET ☘ SUSTAINABLE

[Wabi-Sabi] **1637 Abbot Kinney Blvd., Venice, 310.314.2229,
wabisabisushi.com. D nightly. Japanese/Asian. Beer & wine. AE, MC, V. $$$**
WHY Crunchy shrimp rolls, Thai snapper over summer beans, lovely
sushi and sashimi. **WHAT** One of the better restaurants on a restaurant-
choked street, Wabi-Sabi is stylish yet relaxed, with consistently good
sushi and Asian-fusion dishes. **WHO** Neighborhood locals—which
means very attractive creative types who can afford a $1 million Ven-
ice cottage and chic sushi cafés like this one. ☼

[Warszawa] **1414 Lincoln Blvd., Santa Monica, 310.393.8831,
warszawarestaurant.com. D Tues.-Sun. Polish. Full bar. AE, MC, V. $$ - $$$**
WHY In winter, sustaining pierogis, stroganoff and heavenly hot dried
plums wrapped in bacon; in summer, a table on the pretty patio and
a bowl of the best cold borscht you've ever had, at least in South-
ern California. **WHAT** L.A.'s longstanding center of Polish culinary
life continues to thrive in this charming cottage on not-so-charming
Lincoln. The rich food—pierogis, roast duckling with apples, hunter's
stew, potato pancakes—is consistently good. **WHO** Eastern European
ex-pats and romance seekers. ♥ ⑨ ☼ 🏛

[Whist] **Viceroy, 1819 Ocean Ave., Santa Monica, 800.670.6185,
viceroysantamonica.com. B, L & D daily, brunch Sat.-Sun. Modern
American/Mediterranean. Full bar. AE, MC, V. $$$$ - $$$$$ WHY** An
only-in-L.A. combo: creative Cal-Mediterranean dishes meet Justin
Timberlake–worthy poolside dining. **WHAT** Mega-style meets better-
than-the-norm hotel dining at this too-hip-for-most beach hotel. You
can dine out on the green patio, in your own private tent or in the glam
dining room; while it's more romantic at night, it's pricier, too, so we
like coming at lunchtime for a grilled short rib and cheddar sandwich
or Cobb salad. **WHO** International hotel guests with fat wallets, fash-
ionistas lounging in the bar, and locals coming for the Sunday brunch
or the bargain prix-fixe Sunday family dinner. ♥ ☼ 🏛

[Wilshire] 🏛 **2454 Wilshire Blvd., Santa Monica, 310.586.1707,
wilshirerestaurant.com. L Mon.-Fri., D Mon.-Sat. Modern American/
steakhouse. Full bar. AE, MC, V. $$$$ - $$$$$ WHY** With its California-
dream patio and organic, market food, this place is bucking to be the
Michael's for the new millennium. It's not that, but we appreciate the
effort. **WHAT** Wilshire has a too-cool country-club vibe, complete
with leather club chairs and a cover-charge scene at the bar after 9:30,
but it's not just the latest hot spot to jump on the organic, sustain-
able bandwagon. The kitchen turns out very good (if pricey) farmers'
market–inspired dishes like sweet corn ravioli with creamed morels,
and whole Thai-style fried snapper with soba noodles. Save room
for the updated comfort-food desserts, like the sticky toffee pudding.
WHO A moneyed crowd that's as beautiful as the enclosed patio, with
its fireplace and burbling fountains. ♥♻☼🏛

🌿**VEGETARIAN** ◎ **KID FRIENDLY** ☼**PATIO DINING** 🚗 **DELIVERY** 🏛 **PRIVATE PARTY**

SOUTH BAY TO SOUTH L.A.

[Aimee's] 800 S. Pacific Coast Hwy., Redondo Beach, 310.316.1081, aimeesbistro.com. D Tues.-Sun. French. Full bar. AE, MC, V. $$ - $$$
WHY The warmth of owner Aimee Mizrahi, the heartwarming French bistro cooking and the modest prices. **WHAT** Homey beyond its strip-mall setting, Aimee's is beloved by locals for its great service and fine food: bouillabaisse, scallops with foie gras, coq au vin and crème brûlée. Tables are tightly packed, so don't plan on gossiping much. 🗫

[Aki Sushi] 665 Redondo Ave., Long Beach, 562.439.4025. D Mon.-Sat. Japanese/sushi. Beer & wine. AE, MC, V. $$$ **WHY** To sit at the sushi bar and let Aki make you some very good things. **WHAT** Chef Aki developed a following years ago at Sushi of Naples, and his fans followed him to a couple more locations. Now he's well settled here (and don't confuse this with the other Aki on 7th). His fish is carefully selected, his skill level is high, and his prices are fair. **WHO** Loyal regulars.

[At Last Café] 204 Orange Ave., Long Beach, 562.437.4837, jmchefcatering.com. L & D Tues.-Sat. American. BYOB. AE, MC, V. $ - $$
WHY Simple Americana with refined flair. **WHAT** At Last may be tiny, but it has quickly become one of the most popular neighborhood spots in a city full of them. Behind its success is American cooking that capably twists the classics. At lunch, expect good sandwiches head-lined by a charred burger and a vegetarian option stuffed with grilled zucchini, eggplant, peppers, lettuce and olives. Dinner brings on the acclaimed brick chicken, which is flattened (yes, with a brick) and cooked to a crisp, as well as pot roast, lamb shoulder and a supremely creamy mac 'n cheese. **WHO** A diverse chunk of Long Beach looking for gourmet on the cheap and happy to bring their own wine. 🗫🗐☺

[Azuma Izakaya] 16123 S. Western Ave., Gardena, 310.532.8623. L Mon.-Fri., D nightly. Japanese. Beer & wine. MC, V. $$ **WHY** Bargain izakaya dishes served in a casual, fun setting: udon, fresh mussels, fried chicken, miso black cod and much, much more. **WHAT** Three grill chefs send out excellent food until midnight from a menu with at least 100 items. Sake drums and beer kegs stacked in a corner decorate the tiny dining room, which has the feel of a '40s-era coffee shop and is usually packed. ☺ 🗫

[Beachwood BBQ & Brewing] 210 E. Third St., 562.436.4020, beachwoodbbq.com. L & D daily. American/Barbecue. Beer & wine. AE, MC, V. $$ **WHY** Seal Beach's legendary smokehouse and beer bar has finally crossed county lines. **WHAT** Many consider Beachwood to be the region's top beer bar, a place where the craft movement gained legs and hopheads were born. Now there's even more Beachwood to go around with its new downtown Long Beach location. The menu remains the same—cold-smoked albacore, thoroughly tender chicken, wild game pies, beer-braised beef dips—though the space is far larger, full of smartly styled mid-century Americana. There are two dozen rotating taps (viewable, of course, via the online HopCam), but this location is also brewing its own—eight or so craft brews and occasional specials. **WHO** Beachwood loyalists, knowledgeable hopheads and barbecue-loving families. ☺ ☺

[Benley] 🏛 8191 E. Wardlow Rd., Long Beach, 562.596.8130. L Tues.-Sat., D Mon.-Sat. Vietnamese. Beer & wine. AE, MC, V. $ - $$
WHY Upscaled Vietnamese cuisine with an eye for authenticity. **WHAT** Stashed in a strip mall that butts up against the Orange County border, Benley is one of Long Beach's most consistent restaurants. That's because it has a very clear handle on the kitchen, which turns out refined and thoughtful Vietnamese cuisine: great bowls of pho and expert renditions of bun cha that are highlighted by fantastically crisp sheets of pork. The pan-seared salmon and chicken curry are worthy, too, though you'll want to save room for the warm cassava cake with vanilla crème anglaise. **WHO** Middle-aged east Long Beachers and young couples bonding over spring rolls. 🦪

[Bento Asian Kitchen] 1000 Torrance Blvd., Redondo Beach, 310.792.5185, bentoasiankitchen.com. L & D Mon.-Sat. Japanese. No booze. AE, MC, V. $ - $$ **WHY** A lengthy menu of carefully prepared boxed lunches from a sparkling kitchen. **WHAT** When you don't want to pony up big bucks for the omakase at your favorite sushi bar, this place is a bargain alternative. They offer great variety: 20 options of made-to-order bento, including many sushi roll combinations. **WHO** Harried parents and sushi lovers on a budget. 📷 ☺

[Can Coon] 9887 Alondro Blvd., Bellflower, 562.925.0993. L & D Tues.-Sun. Thai. No booze. Cash only. $ **WHY** Any one of the blistering salads, seasoned with *pak pai*, a Thai herb that tastes like cilantro raised to the 10th power. **WHAT** Although its setting is beyond nondescript, the flavors at this six-table Isaan-style place leap from the plate. The fermented sour rice sausage and shrimp laap (larp kroong on the menu) are some of the best in town. 📷 🍴

[Chaba Thai Bay Grill] 🏛 525 S. Pacific Coast Hwy., Redondo Beach, 310.540.8441, chabarestaurant.com. L & D daily. Thai. Full bar. AE, MC, V. $ - $$$ **WHY** Sumptuous New Thai cookery and a full bar. **WHAT** For the best of new-generation Thai cooking, this handsome bistro is the place. The dishes blend Thai ingredients and techniques with a presentation style that's almost French in its elegance. The fusion is particularly true of the daily specials, which can run from braised lamb in panang curry on a bed of steamed cabbage to filet mignon with shiitake-green peppercorn sauce and galangal rice. ☼ 🚗

🦪 VEGETARIAN ☺ KID FRIENDLY ☼ PATIO DINING 🚗 DELIVERY 🎩 PRIVATE PARTY

[Dal Rae] 🏛 9023 E. Washington Blvd., Pico Rivera, 562.949.2444, dalrae.com. L Mon.-Fri., D nightly. Continental/American. Full bar. AE, MC, V. $$$ - $$$$$ **WHY** When nothing will do but oysters Rockefeller, prime rib and a one-man band in a tux singing Bruce Springsteen's *Pink Cadillac*. **WHAT** This landmark was founded in 1958, and inside, it remains 1958. The lobster is still being Thermidored, the bananas still flambéed, and the spinach salad still wilted. "Ah," you might be thinking, "that sounds like a depressing, off-the-Vegas-strip hangout for fourth-rate goombas and washed-up Peggy Lee wannabes." But you would be wrong. The sons of the founder have kept the Dal Rae fresh and first-rate. The booths are high-backed, the cocktails are stiff, and the Caesar is prepared tableside. A little bit of high-fat, high-calorie heaven. **WHO** A cross-section of folks from Pico-Rivera, Downey and Whittier, from families out to celebrate Grandma's 85th birthday to young couples splurging on a special date. ♥ 🍸 ☺ 🏛

[Darren's Restaurant & Bar] 1141 Manhattan Ave., Manhattan Beach, 310.802.1973, darrensrestaurant.com. D Mon.-Sat. Modern American. Full bar. AE, MC, V. $$$ - $$$$ **WHY** Inventive, flavorful, beach-friendly Cal-Asian fusion cooking is served in a ten-table boîte overseen by the friendly owner/chef, who doubles as sommelier and keeps a close watch over the dining room. Great happy-hour menu at the tiny bar. **WHAT** Local boy Darren Weiss, perhaps L.A.'s only deaf owner/chef, spent his formative years cooking in swank Hawaiian restaurants, so it makes sense that he loves to blend sweet and spicy, as with the lobster chowder, which marries a coconut-milk broth with a spicy undercurrent. Most of the time his mélanges work beautifully. Desserts are a weak spot. Excellent service, expensive wines, well-made cocktails. **WHO** Middle-aged moms/triathletes celebrating a birthday, Tommy Bahama couples, small groups of twentysomething friends who can afford good food and wine. ♥ 🍸 ☼

[The Depot] 1250 Cabrillo Ave., Torrance, 310.787.7501, depotrestaurant.com. L & D Mon.-Sat. Californian. Beer & wine. AE, MC, V. $$$ - $$$$ **WHY** For a good business lunch or a lively dinner with friends. **WHAT** Chef Michael Shafer is one of the culinary leaders in the South Bay, and his Depot is one of the best destinations in the area for martinis, steaks and Asian-influenced California cuisine. **WHO** The Torrance A-list of business leaders, politicians and social sorts. 🏛

[Derrick's Jamaican] 6806 La Tijera Blvd., Ladera Heights, 310.641.7572, derricksjamaican.com. L & D daily. Jamaican. Beer & wine. MC, V. $$ - $$$ **WHY** For Caribbean specialties that are a cut above the usual hole-in-the-wall fare. **WHAT** Yes, Derrick's offers the traditional beef patties, oxtail and a mean jerk pork. But at this stylishly decorated spot there's more emphasis on seafood, lean chicken and fresh veggies: marinated grilled shrimp flamed with barrel-aged Jamaican rum, spice-infused grilled rainbow trout fillet and marinated halibut steak in a pool of gingery sauce flecked with tiny mango cubes. Another location on Hoover near USC. **WHO** A Jamaican community that dresses up for the weekend breakfasts of ackee, salt fish and calaloo.

[Eatalian Café] 🏠 15500 S. Broadway St., Gardena, 310.532.8880, eataliancafe.com. B, L & D daily. Italian. No booze. MC, V. $ **WHY** A former textile factory transformed into a warehouse of authentic Italian cooking. **WHAT** Owner Antonio Pellini originally intended for Eatalian to be just a production facility for cheeses, gelati and baked goods. But the airy, industrial space is so big that a dining room was an easy addition. The restaurant veteran (he ran five restaurants in northern Italy) does it all: seriously thin brick-oven pizzas, wonderful fresh pastas, just-baked breads and pastries and rich gelati and sorbetti. Try the *capricciosa* (prosciutto, mushrooms and tender crumbles of sausage) and grilled vegetable pizzas or the gnocchi, dream-like clouds of potato in a garlic-heavy pesto. Sample the two dozen flavors of gelato and sorbetto (supremely creamy hazelnut, powerfully pure strawberry) before settling on a bready gelato sandwich, a few scoops packed within a *focaccina*, a faintly sweet, whipped cream-enriched roll studded with golden raisins. **WHO** Municipal officials, company executives and Italophiles. 🖼️ ☺

[El Pollo Inka] 15400 Hawthorne Blvd., Lawndale, 310.676.6665, elpolloinka.com. L & D daily. Peruvian. Beer & wine. AE, MC, V. $ **WHY** Fantastic roast chicken or the traditional saltado de pollo. Add the famed cilantro sauce and an order of plantains and you'll be in heaven. **WHAT** The name may imply a competitor to El Pollo Loco, but this is actually a very sweet little sit-down restaurant with seductive and inexpensive Peruvian food, most notably the juicy, wood-smoked pollo a la brasa and the saltado de pollo, a stir-fry of chicken with onions and tomatoes, served with a double-carb whammy of potatoes and rice. **WHO** Families attacking orders of roast chicken. 🖼️ ☺

[El Puerto Escondido] 915 Arbor Vitae St., Inglewood, 310.670.1014; 4182 W. El Segundo Blvd., Hawthorne, 310.978.9609; elpuertoesc.com. B, L & D 24 hours daily. Mexican/seafood. Beer & wine. MC, V. $ - $$ **WHY** Ultra-fresh Mexican-style seafood, including Happy Oysters, freshly shucked and topped with a vibrant chopped shrimp cocktail, and *caldo de siete mares*, a light, fresh soup generously stocked with Alaskan crab legs, mussels and shrimp—served 24 hours a day, a stone's throw from LAX! **WHAT** There are now three branches of this beloved restaurant, which serves the seafood dishes of Mexico's Pacific Coast beach towns, but this is the original and the only one open 24 hours a day. Stick with the same dishes you'd order in Los Cabos—camarones al mojo de ajo, ceviches, shrimp cocktails, whole fried fish, even cold Coronas in a bucket—and you'll be as happy as the regulars. **WHO** LAX workers, surfers pining for Mexico's beaches, and construction workers. ☺ 🖼️

🌿 **VEGETARIAN** ☺ **KID FRIENDLY** 🌸 **PATIO DINING** 🚚 **DELIVERY** 🎩 **PRIVATE PARTY**

[Enrique's] 🔒 6210 E. Pacific Coast Hwy., Long Beach, 562.498.3622. L & D daily. Mexican. Beer & wine. MC, V. $ - $$ **WHY** Absolutely superb Mexican food: a huge, tender pork shank with tomatillo sauce, addictive potato taquitos, grilled shrimp and achiote-infused chicken, rice so good it makes Mexican-Americans weep in memory of their grandmothers, and heavenly chocolate bread pudding. **WHAT** Enrique Perez can make a burrito if that's what you really want, but you're better off letting this Guadalajara native show you his real stuff, perhaps the roasted peppers filled with cheese and potatoes and served with guac and a tomato-onion pico de gallo. Between the ranchera music, the low prices and the outstanding food, this place give its regulars lots of reasons to be happy. **WHO** A great Long Beach cross-section, minus the party-hearty margarita crowd (beer and wine only): upscale couples, working-class families, golfers from the neighboring course, college students, other restaurateurs. 🖼️ ☺

[Fora] 5730 E. 2nd St., Long Beach, 562.856.9494, fora-naples.com. D Tues.-Sun. Modern American. Full bar. AE, MC, V. $$$ - $$$$ **WHY** A charming little place whose modern bistro cooking is best showcased in the four- or five-course tasting menus paired with a wine flight ($57 and $66, respectively). **WHAT** An intimate spot on intimate Naples Island, Fora has an appealing, not-too-overpriced menu of modern classics: lobster martini, roasted tomato soup, seared sushi-grade tuna and, most surprisingly and deliciously of all, beef strognanoff. Good cheeses and even better soufflés. **WHO** Beach dwellers looking for a little romance, a good glass of wine and the delicious ahi tower. ♥ 🍷 🦞

[Fuego] Hotel Maya, 700 Queensway Dr., Long Beach, 562.481.3910, fuegolongbeach.com. B,L & D daily. Mexican. Full bar. AE, MC, V. $$$ **WHY** Upscale Mexican cuisine with a beautiful Long Beach view. **WHAT** A centerpiece of the redesigned and rebranded Hotel Maya, Fuego delivers a Mexican menu focused on coastal cooking. That translates to dishes like citric ceviches of shrimp and lobster scooped up with plantain chips, Yucatán-style pork two ways (presented as an achiote-glazed fillet and a pibil-stuffed tamale) and pepita-crusted wild salmon. The bar is also one of Long Beach's best, stocked with an impressive supply of tequila as well as inventive, well-crafted cocktails. **WHO** Travelers on the way to the Queen Mary and locals lingering over an oceanfront brunch. ♥ ☼

[Gaja] 2383 Lomita Blvd., Lomita, 310.534.0153, gajamoc.com. L Tues.-Sat., D Tues.-Sun. Japanese. Beer & wine. MC, V. $ - $$ **WHY** The South Bay's preeminent specialist in *okonomiyaki*, a Japanese pub dish that straddles the line between savory pancake and omelet. **WHAT** There's more to Gaja's menu than just okonomiyaki, but all the izakaya-style small plates combined can't topple the popularity of its various permutations of the pancake-like dish. You can cook for yourself on tabletop griddles or let the kitchen handle the duties, which is a smart choice given okonomiyaki's potential complexity. The base batter is a hearty mix of shredded cabbage, grated mountain yam, pickled ginger, onion, egg and a bit of flour. Inside might be any number of mix-ins, options like beef and scallops, mochi and cheese, pork and kim chee, or an umami-rich blend of mushrooms. It's Japanese bar food at its most customizable and communal. ☺

[George's Greek Café] 🏠 135 Pine Ave., Long Beach, 562.437.1184, georgesgreekcafe.com. L & D daily. Greek. Beer & wine. AE, MC, V. $ - $$$ **WHY** Dolmathes, saganaki, taramosalata, gyros, grilled lamb chops—and bonhomie. **WHAT** George Loizides greets customers like family at this Pine Avenue institution serving hearty Greek specialties at reasonable prices. (Long Beach once had a vibrant Greek community, and this place carries on the tradition.) It's a great place to go with a group and share the array of dips and appetizer combinations as well as the fun of saganaki, cheese flamed with brandy. Opa! **WHO** Birthday partiers and families. 🎁☺

[Golden Triangle] 🏠 7011 Greenleaf Ave., Whittier, 562.945.6778. L & D daily. Burmese. Beer & wine. MC, V. $ **WHY** A longtime leader of Burmese cuisine in L.A. **WHAT** Golden Triangle has for decades been an uptown Whittier stalwart, its Burmese food reason enough to trek to Greenleaf Avenue. And even this long into its existence, enough can't be said of the spritely ginger salad, earthy tea leaf salad, goat curry with coconut rice and *panthe kauekswe*, a comforting dish of soft, curried noodles. Plus, there's durian ice cream. **WHO** Uptown neighbors, Whittier College kids and Burmese traditionalists. 🎁🍴

[The Green Temple] 1700 S. Catalina Ave., Redondo Beach, 310.944.4525, greentemple.net. B Sun., L & D Tues.-Sun. Vegetarian/ Californian. No booze. MC, V. $$ **WHY** Vegetarian and vegan meals in a bucolic garden setting. **WHAT** The board of changing daily specials at this serene, Buddha-filled indoor-outdoor eatery may offer sweet white corn chowder or a nut-strewn salad. House dressings include balsamic-virgin olive oil vinaigrette and sesame-tamari-lemon. And the delicious house favorites, enchiladas and the kamut spaghetti with a rich tofu cream sauce, keep the clientele loyal. 🍃🎁🍴☺☼

[Iccho] 25310 Crenshaw Blvd., Torrance, 310.325.7273. D nightly (to 2 a.m.). Japanese. Beer & wine. MC, V. $$ **WHY** Pitchers of Japanese beer, bottles of sake and fun small dishes, from the udon-and-yakitori standards to such novelties as fried kim chee with pork and caterpillar sushi rolls. **WHAT** In the shopping-intensive locale of Rolling Hills Plaza, this family-style izakaya comforts everyone with an enormously long menu that ranges from the basic to the inventive, and it's all served until 2 a.m. ☺🎁

🍃 **VEGETARIAN** ☺ **KID FRIENDLY** ☼ **PATIO DINING** � **DELIVERY** 🎁 **PRIVATE PARTY**

[Izakaya Yuzen Kan] 2755 Pacific Coast Hwy., Torrance, 310.530.7888, izakayakan.com. D nightly. Japanese. Beer & wine. AE, MC, V. $$ - $$$ **WHY** Intelligent and sometimes almost whimsical dishes like ground chicken with a light miso glaze in lettuce wraps, as well as exquisitely fresh, flown-in-from-Japan sashimi. **WHAT** This modern izakaya hidden in a shopping center has an airy open kitchen and sleek lines that give it a quiet dignity. Ultra-fine as well as more modest sakes (ask for the bound notebook that holds the labels) have been smartly selected to pair with the modern Japanese fare. **WHO** Izakaya diners more interested in the quality of the food than a noisy scene.

[Japonica] 1304 1/2 S. Pacific Coast Hwy., Redondo Beach, 310.316.9477, japonicadining.com. D nightly. Japanese. Beer & wine. AE, MC, V. $ - $$ **WHY** Sake, romance, careful service and excellent izakaya. **WHAT** Curtained booths allude to the tatami rooms of the past at this sleek South Bay looker serving great food and an extensive sake list that includes several flights. Every dish, including crunchy fried baby Spanish mackerel, fresh salmon roe omelet and seared albacore with spicy sauce, confirms the kitchen's skill. ♥ 🍵

[Jay Bharat] 18701 Pioneer Blvd., Artesia, 562.924.3310, jaybharat. com. L & D Tues.-Sun. Indian. No booze. MC, V. $ **WHY** Inexpensive and excellent Gujarati food. **WHAT** One of Little India's top chat shops, Jay Bharat is a standard-bearer on Pioneer Boulevard. And though you can eat well sampling the sweets and snacks, don't ignore the precise Gujarati cooking. Everything is vegetarian—appetizers like the potato-patty slider *pav vada* and the *pettis*, a six-piece plate of fried coconut, potato, raisin and nut fritters, are fine starters. But it's ultimately the thalis that are the draw. Try the Gujarati or Kathiyawadi ten- to twelve-item combos (think curries, pickles, flatbreads, soups and the like), which present a range of regional tastes. **WHO** Lunching locals and vegetarians from all around L.A. 📷🍃

[Johnny Reb's] 4663 Long Beach Blvd., Long Beach, 562.423.7327, johnnyrebs.com. B, L & D daily. Southern/American. Beer & wine. AE, MC, V. $$ **WHY** Fried pickles, fried green tomatoes, fried chicken and, if you're trying to go easy on the fried foods, pulled pork and mac 'n cheese. It's a theme restaurant, but a good one. **WHAT** Southern-food buffs (and really, does anyone not love fried chicken and cornbread?) wept when Johnny Reb's burned down a couple of years ago, but it's back and thriving. Choose the chicken, catfish or pulled pork over the baby-back ribs (this is more a Southern restaurant than a rib joint) and explore the interesting sides, which include black-eyed peas and Brunswick stew. **WHO** Big eaters. 📷☺

[Katsu] 302 Rosecrans Ave., Manhattan Beach, 310.546.3761, katsu-sushi.com. L Mon.-Fri., D nightly. Japanese. Beer & wine. AE, MC, V. $ - $$ **WHY** Superb lunchtime sushi bento boxes ($12.95) and excellent happy-hour deals. **WHAT** A pleasant and modest sushi bar, Katsu bears no relation to the über-trendy Katsu-ya chain. Very good, reasonably priced sashimi, sushi, spicy tuna and tempura are served in a modest lime-green dining room just a roll's throw from the ocean. **WHO** Locals who come here weekly. 🍴☺

[The Kettle] 1138 Highland Ave., Manhattan Beach, 310.545.8511, thekettle.net. Daily 24 hours. American. Beer & wine. AE, MC, V. $ - $$$
WHY A 24/7 godsend for insomniacs, students and night-shifters.
WHAT The food's fine, but the real value of this '70s-woodsy coffee shop is that it's open 24 hours a day, a rarity for a large, full-service restaurant anywhere in L.A., let alone a beach town. Regulars get the muffins, crab cake Benedict, burgers and egg dishes. **WHO** It all depends on the hour: seniors for early breakfast and dinner, families and beach-goers during the day and a sometimes rowdy post-party crowd late at night (which is when the bouncer shows up). ☺ 🍴☺☼

[Khun Lek Kitchen] 9208 Alondra Blvd., Bellflower, 562.804.6602.
L & D Mon.-Tues. & Thurs.-Sun. Thai. BYOB. MC, V. $ - $$ **WHY** For the specials menu, listed on a handwritten daily menu. **WHAT** Crisp white tablecloths, contemporary art and a mirrored karaoke room mark this as a restaurant with aspirations, and the light, clean food lives up to the look. Check the menu and daily specials board for such Isaan favorites as raw shrimp laap or catfish salad.

[Komatsu Tempura Bar] 🏠 1644 W. Carson St., Torrance, 310.787.0787. L Mon.-Fri., D Mon- Fri. Japanese. Beer & wine. MC, V. $$ - $$$ **WHY** For exquisitely made tempura and high-caliber izakaya-style little dishes. **WHAT** If there were a Tempura Olympics, chef Hiroshi Komatsu would surely get the gold. He plucks your tempura from his proprietary blend of scalding oil and serves the lacy, crackle-crusted fish and vegetables one piece at a time so they never cool and wilt. He also comes up with such novelties as tempura chestnuts stuffed with umeboshi plums. **WHO** Discriminating tradition-loving Japanese and anyone wanting to graduate from mundane fried chicken.

[La Casita Mexicana] 🏠 4030 E. Gage Ave., Bell, 323.773.1898, casitamex.com. B, L & D daily. Mexican. No booze. AE, MC, V. $$
WHY Food just like Grandma's—if Grandma happened to be a meticulous Mexican village cook committed to using locally grown ingredients. Try to come on Wednesdays, which are pozole days.
WHAT Spanish-language media cooking stars Jaime Martin del Campo and Ramiro Arvizu have created a place that draws fans from all over the L.A. basin. Absolutely everything—from table salsas to *refrescos* (juice drinks) and *raspados* (snow cones)—is made from scratch. Unfamiliar veggies like huauzontle and romerito may adorn the Lenten menu, although most dishes will be familiar. But even the enchiladas and moles have a particular flair. Remarkable Mexican home cooking

🍃 VEGETARIAN ☺ KID FRIENDLY ☼ PATIO DINING 🚚 DELIVERY 🎩 PRIVATE PARTY

that's worth a drive. **WHO** Devotees who drive long distances for a special meal here. 🗺️ ⊙ ☼

[La Concha] **2612 E. Anaheim St., Long Beach, 562.438.9499. L & D daily. Mexican. Beer. MC, V. $ WHY** Hunger-killing tortas ahogadas. **WHAT** An unassuming place crammed into a corner strip mall that often goes unnoticed on this busy block, this place covers all the expected Mexican bases— but the real reason to visit is the Guadala-jaran specialties. La Concha's torta ahogada is the best around: slabs of crusty bread stuffed with crisp pork and drowned in a manageably spicy chile de árbol sauce. If you're not up for the torta, try a plate of diced pork tossed with strips of cactus or a stout bowl of carne en su jugo instead. **WHO** Local heat seekers and Chivas fans cheering on every goal. 🗺️

[La Huasteca] **3150 E. Imperial Hwy., Lynwood, 310.537.8800, lahuasteca.com. L & D daily. Mexican. Full bar. AE, MC, V. $$ WHY** A newly revamped menu inspired by pre-Columbian Mexican cooking. **WHAT** La Huasteca has long been Plaza Mexico's grand stage: sylvan murals, wrought-iron chandeliers, a fully stocked bar. But with a reinvigoration by chef Rocio Camacho (formerly of Moles la Tia), it is charting a new course, one that celebrates ingredients and techniques native to Mexico. This means sublime squash-blossom empanadas, a cactus salad splashed with a tart cactus vinaigrette, and *caldo de pie-dra*, a "stone soup" in which a white-hot rock speeds cooking. Many of Camacho's moles made the move here, including her pistachio and coffee versions, but you should choose the *mole de los dioses*, a rich, dark-as-tar mole fortified with huitlacoche. **WHO** Families from across the Gateway Cities. ☺

[La Parolaccia] **2945 E. Broadway, Long Beach, 562.438.1235, laparolacciausa.com. L Sun., D nightly. Italian. Beer & wine. AE, MC, V. $$ WHY** Charming plates of Italian classics. **WHAT** Though it's not completely unique to Long Beach (there's a Claremont branch), La Pa-rolaccia is as entrenched in local stomachs as any of the city's famous greasy spoons. The reason is clear: Its osteria-style cooking stands well above the nearby red-sauce joints. Consider trying the fluffy gnocchi, rich risotto, penne Cinque Terre (with goat cheese, pesto and sun-dried tomatoes) and great, simple pizzas from the wood-burning oven. **WHO** Bluff Heights residents in need of a glass of wine and a plate of pasta. 🖋️

[Magic Wok] **11869 Artesia Blvd., Artesia, 562.865.7340. L & D Tues.-Sun. Filipino. No booze. MC, V. $ WHY** No-frills Filipino home cooking. **WHAT** Magic Wok prepares pork at its most glorious. Order the crispy *pata*, a bone-in leg of pork brined and fried until its skin is a crisp mahogany and its meat falls away simply because of gravity. *Sisig*, cubes of fatty, crunchy fried pork tossed with bits of ginger, scallions, peppers and a touch of citrus, offers a bit more nuance. There are non-pork options—tart tamarind soups, thin strips of steak lacquered with soy sauce, chicken adobo, light noodle stir-fries—but it's best to follow the regulars' lead and go whole hog. **WHO** Generations of Filipino families. 🖐

[Mar'sel] **Terranea Resort, 6610 Palos Verdes Dr. South, Palos Verdes, 310.265.2836, terranea.com. D Wed.-Sat. Modern American. Full bar. AE, MC, V. $$$$ - $$$$$ WHY** Carefully constructed Cal-Med cooking in a gorgeous coastal setting. **WHAT** The sprawling, luxurious resort on the site of the former Marineland is trying very hard with its seven restaurants to rise above the hotel norm, especially in this flagship dining room. Talented young chef Michael Fiorelli uses produce from the garden right outside his door to make such things as roasted young beets with dried cranberries, hazelnuts, goat cheese, asparagus and orange vinaigrette. Whether they're local or from halfway around the world (Dover sole, wild Alaskan halibut, Spanish octopus), the ingredients are superb, and the prices reflect the quality. So does the setting: a warm, wood-paneled dining room and a stunning oceanview terrace. **WHO** More locals than the typical fancy hotel dining room gets, in part because Palos Verdes has so few good restaurants. ♥ 🖐 ☼

[Michael's Ristorante] **5620 E. 2nd St., Long Beach, 562.439.7080, michaelsonnaples.com. D nightly. Italian. Full bar. AE, MC, V. $$$ - $$$$ WHY** Sophisticated Italian cooking, including light yet flavorful lasagne, various homemade pastas and gorgeous branzino with olives and capers, best enjoyed on the rooftop terrace on a warm summer evening. **WHAT** Naples' most sophisticated restaurant is its newest: this handsome, modern Italian with comfortable booths downstairs and a fab upstairs terrace with a heated dining area and fireplace-warmed hanging-out area. The service is young and inexperienced, but the cooking is assured and delicious, and the wine list is worthy. Good-value happy hour, too. **WHO** Well-heeled couples and effervescent gaggles of friends sharing bottles of wine. ♥ 🖐 🍴 ☼

[Mumbai Ki Galliyon Se] **17705 Pioneer Blvd., Artesia, 562.860.6699. L & D Tues.-Sun. Indian. No booze. MC, V. $ WHY** An unrivaled menu of Mumbai street food. **WHAT** Mumbai Ki Galliyon Se (literally "from the streets of Mumbai") specializes in the street food of India's largest city, a cosmopolitan menu of vegetarian curries, fritters, sandwiches and snacks. These are dishes you won't find just anywhere: fried tapioca pearl patties, bowls of pulses and sprouted mung beans in rich, complex gravies, and fabulous potato-based sliders studded with pomegranate seeds, grapes, peanuts and onions. Spice happens here, so beat the heat with a cup of *piyush*, a drink of homemade yogurt infused with saffron, cardamom, pistachios and almonds. **WHO** Mumbaikars from all around L.A. and Little India regulars looking for something different. 🖐🍴

🍴**VEGETARIAN** ☺**KID FRIENDLY** ☼**PATIO DINING** 🚗**DELIVERY** 🏛**PRIVATE PARTY**

[Musha] 🏛 1725 Carson St., Torrance, 310.787.7344, musha.us. D nightly. Japanese/Californian. Beer & wine. AE, MC, V. $$ **WHY** Fatty pork belly (you know you want it), kim chee udon topped with butter and caviar, tuna poke, seafood-filled baguette au gratin... amazing and delicious dishes that typify the best of Japanese-L.A. fusion cooking. **WHAT** The loud, chaotic (and fun) Torrance branch is a contrast to the more sedate (and fun) Santa Monica location of this anything-goes pub, where European ingredients and concepts (roasted garlic, dips and crackers) are incorporated into Japanese pub fare. ☺ 📝

[Mutiara Food & Market] 225 S. La Brea Ave., Inglewood, 310.419.7221. L & D Tues.-Sun. Burmese/Malaysian. No booze. MC, V. $ **WHY** An LAX-adjacent taste of Burmese and Malaysian cuisines. **WHAT** Owner Myo Aung honed his simple, satisfying Burmese cooking at Jasmine Market, and here, he's added a number of Malaysian specialties. It's all halal, with standouts like the crêpe-esque murtabak loaded with ground chicken, finely spiced lamb biryani and *daging lembu*, a Malaysian stew of beef, black pepper, cilantro and green onion. Weekends bring the Burmese specials; try the catfish chowder (*moh hin gha*) and coconut-broth noodle soup (*ohn no khauk swe*). From the market, make sure to pick up a buttery cardamom cookies, imported spices and other halal pantry essentials. **WHO** Burmese and Malaysian ex-pats. 📝

[New Orleans Cajun Café] 140 Pier Ave., Hermosa Beach, 310.372.8970, neworleanshermosa.com. L & D Mon. & Thurs.-Sun. Cajun/ Southern. Beer & wine. MC, V. $$ - $$$ **WHY** A New Orleans native, the owner/chef knows how to cook Cajun-Creole food to perfection. Sit at the counter to enjoy some easygoing repartee while the cooks make mounds of red beans and rice, jumping jambalaya and hush puppies. **WHAT** This busy, narrow, corner café reminiscent of Louisiana's shotgun houses serves the finest catfish you'll eat, because the chef flies the seafood and sausages in from New Orleans. Just-right spices sizzle but don't scorch the palate, and the sock-it-to-me desserts provide a Southern sugar rush. **WHO** Anyone aching for a real Creole meal and singles out for a date. 🌙 💌

[Open Sesame] 5215 E. 2nd St., Long Beach, 562.621.1698, opensesamegrill.com. L & D daily. Lebanese/Middle Eastern. Beer & wine. AE, MC, V. $ - $$ **WHY** For one of the most convivial, food-celebrating places in Belmont Shore, with happy groups sharing *fattoush* (a chopped salad), schwarma, crisp-soft fried potatoes, vegetarian platters, Belmont Brewing beers on tap and, of course, baklava. But whatever you order, just make sure you include some of those potatoes. **WHAT** Ali Kobeissi's Lebanese bistro is so popular that he took over the lease for a failed restaurant a few doors down, and now that Open Sesame is every bit as crowded as its parent; expect to wait at least a half-hour at either place. The original is well designed, with comfortable booths and a noise level that's manageable even at peak times, and the service is prompt and cordial. 🖼🦪☺☼

[Otafuku] 🏠 **16525 S. Western Ave., Gardena, 310.532.9348. L & D Mon.-Sat. Japanese. Beer & wine. AE, MC, V. $ - $$ WHY** The best soba noodles in the South Bay. Great izakaya, too. **WHAT** Noodles made by hand in small batches are the draw at this dinky, hard-to-find noodle and izakaya spot (hint: enter from the back parking lot). While it makes fine eel tempura, grilled steak and wild mushrooms over rice, the reason to drive out of your way for a meal here is the absolutely superb soba noodles, either cold with a dipping sauce with green onions and wasabi or hot in a delicious soup. Since you're there, make sure to try the Otafuku fried chicken, too. 🖼☺

[Oumi Sasaya] **2383 Lomita Blvd., Ste. 101, Lomita, 310.530.4661, oumisasaya.com. L & D Tues.-Sun. Japanese. Beer & wine. MC, V. $ - $$ WHY** A simple, elegant noodle house where udon reigns. **WHAT** Udon is the neglected noodle in the Japanese canon, often overlooked in favor of ramen and even soba. But here it's the sole focus. Oumi Sasaya imports its wheat flour and makes its noodles daily, a difference you can taste in the sesame chicken tempura udon, a tangle of chubby, silken noodles topped with cucumber, cabbage, seaweed, roasted bell pepper and chicken tempura. There's traditional *kitsune* udon (a delicate soup blanketed with sheets of sweetened fried tofu) and a nice bowl of curry udon crowded with shrimp and mochi tempura. For dinner, try the udon-*suki*, a communal hot pot of seafood, meat, vegetables and noodles. **WHO** Udon addicts and Japanese-American families. 🍴

[Pann's] 🏠 **6710 La Tijera Blvd., Inglewood, 323.776.3770, panns. com. B, L & D daily. Coffee shop/American. Beer & wine. AE, MC, V. $ - $$$ WHY** An L.A. classic for its '50s roots and Googie architecture alone—but when you add the waffles, patty melt, fried chicken and incredible biscuits... well, it's a downright treasure. **WHAT** George and Rena Panagopoulos opened this Jetsons-style restaurant in 1958, and the family still runs it today. They've kept the place in tip-top condition, and the food is exactly what you would hope for in such a place: good egg dishes, country-fried steak, patty melts, shakes, and perhaps the best fried chicken and biscuits in town. The burgers, however, are surprisingly blah, and everyone knows that the vegetables are best left uneaten. **WHO** Seniors, college students, travelers coming and going from LAX, and pretty much every sort of Angeleno. 🖼☺

[Petros] **451 Manhattan Beach Blvd., Manhattan Beach, 310.545.4100, petrosrestaurant.com. L & D daily. Greek. Full bar. AE, MC, V. $$$ - $$$$ WHY** The exuberant Greek flavors go down well so close to the ocean. **WHAT** Don't expect plate-smashing hokum at this modern Greek bistro, just very good food: feta bruschetta, grilled octopus, shrimp saganaki with tomato, basil and feta, grilled pita with a dip of olives and sun-dried tomatoes, lovely fresh-fish entrées, a hearty lamb pasta and terrific cheeses. The setting is cool and whitewashed, with an awning-shaded patio that's great for lunch, and the Greek music in the background doesn't interfere with conversation. ☺ ☼

[Pho Pioneer] 17701 Pioneer Blvd., Artesia, 562.809.9250. L & D daily. Vietnamese. No booze. MC, V. $ **WHY** The Pioneer rice special, a combination of crispy minced shrimp cake, slabs of grilled marinated pork, delicate steamed egg loaf and a salad garnish, has customers returning again and again. **WHAT** The small city of Artesia may be famed for Little India, in which this Vietnamese place sits, but in fact it's as multinational as Coca-Cola—so Pho Pioneer has thrived here. Its phos include a seafood version, a shrimp version, a vegetarian version and one with chicken breast strips—one for every taste. And to keep pace with trends, it offers traditional Vietnamese smoothies with boba tapioca pearls. **WHO** Indian-American families checking out the pho scene. 🗫🍴☺

[Rajdhani] 🏛 18525 Pioneer Blvd., Artesia, 562.402.9102. L & D Tues.-Sun. Indian. No booze. MC, V. $$ **WHY** Wonderful dinner theater in the form of a bottomless Gujarati thali. **WHAT** Of the many buffets scattered throughout Little India—where idle curries sometimes congeal under heat lamps—none approach the exacting elegance of Rajdhani. Here, all-you-can-eat meals aren't ladled from steam tables but delivered by a cast of waiters armed with the components of a first-rate vegetarian thali. No two meals are exactly alike; however, there will probably be *dal* (lentils simmered into spicy submission), *khadi* (soupy, spiced yogurt) and maybe *khandvi* (springy gram-flour rolls covered in cilantro, shaved coconut and coriander seeds). There will always be crisp, pliable *chapati* (flatbread) and a vegetable curry, perhaps spears of tender okra or soft-as-jam eggplant. Eventually, there will be *gulab jamun*, fresh little donuts swimming in sweet cardamom and saffron syrup. **WHO** Discerning Little India locals and well-traveled vegetarians. 🍴

[Ramen California] 24231 Crenshaw Blvd., Torrance, 310.530.2749. L & D Tues.-Sat. Japanese/modern American. Beer & wine. AE, MC, V. $ - $$ **WHY** A new, radical wave of ramen that fuses Japanese tradition with Californian innovation. **WHAT** Ramen California sprang from the mind of Shigetoshi Nakamura, a Japanese ramen prodigy who has taken on the task of reinventing the noodle soup. Indeed, diners should be advised to abandon all previous ramen knowledge—Nakamura's noodle soups are all about fresh, market-driven produce. In the signature California ramen, more than 30 vegetables bob through the powerful and clean chicken broth. The heirloom tomato ramen is a study in fresh flavor, while the wildly inventive Reggiano-tofu ramen is all about experimentation. There's a rotating selection of small plates, too, including excellent bao-like bread crusted with rosemary and sea salt and consistently good carpaccios. **WHO** Ramen lovers willing to set aside their purist tendencies. 🌀🥢

[Renu Nakorn] 🏠 13019 E. Rosecrans Ave., Norwalk, 562.921.2124. **L & D daily. Thai. Beer & wine. MC, V. $$ WHY** Robustly seasoned and beautiful food: jackfruit curry with pork, *khao soi* curry with noodles and chicken, an incendiary papaya salad, lemongrass-infused Isaan sausages and much, much more. **WHAT** Anxious fans can breathe easy—the destination Isaan-style Thai restaurant is back after a major (and much-needed) remodel, and it's still worth the drive to Norwalk. The basics—pad Thai, panang curry, satay—are excellent, but it's the northern Isaan dishes that are worth the trip. The dining room is pleasant now, and the service is good. **WHO** Serious Thai food fans. 📷

[Restaurant Christine] 🏠 24530 Hawthorne Blvd., Torrance, **310.373.1952, restaurantchristine.com. L Mon.-Fri., D Mon.-Sat. Mediterranean/Asian. Beer & wine. AE, MC, V. $$$ - $$$$ WHY** The avocado tower, lobster salad and the tasting menu. **WHAT** Christine Brown combines flavors of the Mediterranean and the Pacific Rim in this color-washed bistro, and the results are generally successful. The "greens and grazing plates" are typically big enough to share as a starter; half the room seems to get the avocado tower, with napa cabbage, mango and sesame. For an entrée, depending on your global mood, you can go Italian (cioppino) or Asian (sesame-glazed salmon). 🌀🏠

[Riviera Mexican Grill] 1615 S. Pacific Coast Hwy., Redondo **Beach, 310.540.2501. L daily, D nightly, brunch Sun. Mexican. Full bar. AE, MC, V. $ - $$ WHY** Great margaritas, grilled fish tacos and a chill surf-town atmosphere. **WHAT** An active member of the local ocean community, Riviera sponsors an annual paddle contest and keeps the prices low so hard-surfing regulars stay properly fueled. The Cal-Mex food is simple and satisfying, and the cadillac margaritas really are the best in Redondo. **WHO** Old and young surfers, blond families and Rainbow-shod friends sharing a pitcher of margaritas. 📷☺🌀

[Royal Kabob] 5245 W. Rosecrans Ave., Hawthorne, 310.297.6870, **kabobtogo.com. L & D daily. Indian/Pakistani. No booze. MC, V. $$ WHY** For meticulously cooked tandoori specialties. **WHAT** It's not until you take the first bite of flavor-packed free-range tandoori chicken that the virtues of this small, stylish restaurant emerge. Co-owner Tariq Amin, a graduate of École Hôtelière de Lausanne in Switzerland, knows how to cook and source superior stuff—his halal birds, for instance, come from Pitman Farms in Sanger. An inspired citrus marinade deftly banishes any gaminess of both goat and New Zealand French double lamb racks. His hip, Pakistani-inspired creations (like the tandoori chicken salad with balsamic dressing and mint-pomegranate chutney) up the creative ante. **WHO** Carnivores thrilled to find something different on the barbie.

🌿 VEGETARIAN ⊙ KID FRIENDLY 🌀 PATIO DINING �m DELIVERY 🏠 PRIVATE PARTY

[Siem Reap] **1810 E. Anaheim St., Long Beach, 562.591.7414. L & D daily. Cambodian. Full bar. MC, V. $ - $$ WHY** A decades-old centerpiece of Long Beach's Cambodia Town. **WHAT** A lot of heat courses through Siem Reap. Sometimes it's a subtle, slow burn, other times it's a fully loaded assault. Although the menu is large enough to accommodate a few Thai and Chinese offerings, the Cambodian classics are what keep this place relevant after so many years. Beef *loc lac* (bits of beef on a mound of rice with tomato, cucumber, green eggplant, a fried egg and herbed lemon sauce) is an easy entry point, though you should also consider more curious options like *amok*, a powerfully spicy fish curry steamed and formed into patties. The menu can be a bit daunting, but don't hesitate to ask for help. And make sure to grab a taro shake to cool off—you'll need it. **WHO** Cambodian locals and first-time diners exploring Khmer cuisine. 🦐

[Starling Diner] **4114 E. 3rd. St., Long Beach, 562.433.2041, starlingdiner.com. B & L Tues.- Sun. American. Beer & wine. AE, MC, V. $$ WHY** Neighborhood charm with gourmet soul. **WHAT** Surrounded by a quaint neighborhood of historic homes and breezy apartments, this bright, quirky café has become a hub of local life. (Come in alone and you can sit at a long communal table with soon-to-be friends.) For breakfast, try the mascarpone-stuffed French toast or the sweet and creamy polenta with seasonal berries and cream. At lunch and dinner, the menu is all about sandwiches and pizzettes, well-conceived cheesy flatbreads that keep the neighbors coming back. **WHO** Early risers, hungry friends and dog-walking diners. 🦐☺

[Tin Roof Bistro] **3500 Sepulveda Blvd., Manhattan Beach, 310.546.6180, tinroofbistro.com. L & D daily. Modern American. Full bar. AE, MC, V. $$ - $$$ WHY** Excellent and affordable cocktails and wine by the glass, a killer burger and farmers' market produce. **WHAT** Mike Simms has hit a home run with this indoor-outdoor bistro that rises above its shopping-mall setting. Skip the undercooked pizzas and too-small crab cakes in favor of the terrific curry spinach dip, caramelized brussels sprouts, thick burgers, salads, roast chicken, fresh fish, shoe-string fries and homey desserts (strawberry icebox pie, lemon soufflé cake). **WHO** Shaggy old surf hippies, golf-shirt-wearing business folk and blond families. 🗺🦐☺○

[Toko Rame] **17155 Bellflower Blvd., Bellflower, 562.920.8002. L & D Tues.-Sun. Indonesian. No booze. MC, V. $ WHY** A long-standing source of Indonesian excellence. **WHAT** The decades-old, family-run Toko Rame touches on what seems like every Indonesian entrée, from lightly charred satay and dishes constructed around the glutinous rice cake known as *lontong* to carefully executed curries and combination plates like *nasi bungkus*. There are more than 100 options (because Toko Rame adheres to halal standards, the only thing you won't find is pork), giving you many reasons for a return trip. **WHO** Indonesian families and hungry drivers pulling in off the 91. 🖼🔖

[Torihei] **1757 W. Carson St., Torrance, 310.781.9407. D nightly. Japanese. Beer & wine. AE, MC, V. $ - $$ WHY** A near-perfect pairing of yakitori and oden. **WHAT** Torihei splits its kitchen equally between yakitori and oden, a relatively rare but harmonious coupling. The yakitori is made from tender, flavorful Jidori chicken. *Oden* is the more unusual of the specialties, a homey dish that's typically prepared as a one-pot stew. Here, however, items are parceled out and presented à la carte. The fresh fish cake is essential, a pillowy triangle that's even airier than a marshmallow. But the ultimate oden item is the soft-boiled egg set afloat in a shallow pool of dashi and topped with little piles of brilliant orange cod roe. Like so many of Torihei's dishes, it's an ode to simple, precise flavor. **WHO** Torrance businessmen fresh off work and young couples sharing skewers. ☺

[Udupi Palace] **18635 Pioneer Blvd., Artesia, 562.860.1950, udupipalace.net. L & D Tues.-Sun. Indian. No booze. MC, V. $ WHY** The dosa are among the biggest—and lightest—in Little India. **WHAT** Maybe you can't spell it, but you should definitely order the *kancheepuram idli*. The ginger-and-cashew dumplings are a specialty at this restaurant, which is named for a temple city in India's Karnataka state. Also check out the kadi fritters in coconut curry and the "tomato omelet," actually a pizza-like uttappam made with chickpea flour. 🖼🔖☺

[Woodlands] **11833 Artesia Blvd., Artesia, 562.860.6500, woodlandsartesia.com. L & D Tues.-Sun. Indian/vegetarian. Full bar. MC, V. $ - $$ WHY** Go on Dosa Nights (Wednesday and Friday), when you can pick a dosa and gorge yourself at the sumptuous buffet—all for $10. **WHAT** Who needs meat when you can feast on south Indian vegetarian fare that's this scrumptious? Go-to dishes include tamarind and lemon rice, coconut chutney and the amazing *chana batura*—fried bread that's as crisp as an eggshell and as big as a volleyball. 🖼🔖☺

[Yuzu Torrance] **1231 Cabrillo Ave., Torrance, 310.533.9898. L Mon.-Fri., D Mon.-Sat. Japanese. Beer & wine. AE, MC, V. $$$ - $$$$ WHY** It brings the spirit of *washoku*—the revival of traditional Japanese flavors and methods updated with today's artisanal ingredients—from Japan to California. **WHAT** The two bars, a wine bar, an open robata-style kitchen, tatami rooms and outdoor seating add up to a luxe, sexy environment to indulge in some elegant and traditional Japanese fare: sashimi from the Tsukiji market, honey-marinated Kurobuta pork, skewered Kobe beef balls, tempura-fried sweet potato and more. **WHO** Always full with an upscale crowd, including many Japanese; make reservations a few days in advance. ♥ ☼ 🏠

🔖 VEGETARIAN ☺ KID FRIENDLY ☼ PATIO DINING 🚙 DELIVERY 🏠 PRIVATE PARTY

Drink + Eat

Sometimes the sustenance you seek is as much about the liquids as the solids. But that's not to say you want to drink your dinner. Los Angeles is enjoying a boom in places that celebrate the art of the cocktail, the brew and/or the grape, and many of them serve good food, too. Here are our favorite wine bars, pubs and cocktail lounges.

[ESSENTIALLY L.A.]

Bar Marmont, West Hollywood (PAGE 180)

Cat & Fiddle, Hollywood (PAGE 180)

Cole's, Downtown (PAGE 185)

Craftbar, Century City (PAGE 193)

The Edison, Downtown (PAGE 186)

Father's Office, Culver City & Santa Monica (PAGES 194 & 196)

The Golden State, Fairfax (PAGE 180)

La Descarga, Hollywood (PAGE 181)

Lazy Ox Canteen, Little Tokyo/Arts District (PAGE 187)

Lou, Hollywood (PAGE 187)

Musso & Frank Grill, Hollywood (PAGE 181)

Nelson's, Rancho Palos Verdes (PAGE 201)

The Varnish, Downtown (PAGE 188)

Vertical Wine Bistro, Pasadena (PAGE 175)

Ye Olde King's Head, Santa Monica (PAGE 199)

The York, Highland Park (PAGE 188)

⌂ ESSENTIALLY L.A. ☺ LATE ♥ ROMANTIC ⑤ VALUE ♪ QUIET ♻ SUSTAINABLE

CONVIVIAL WINE-SHOP TASTINGS

55 Degrees, Atwater (PAGE 368)
Colorado Wine Co., Eagle Rock (PAGE 368)
Mission Wines, South Pasadena (PAGE 370)
Off the Vine, San Pedro (PAGE 371)
Red Carpet, Glendale (PAGE 371)
Silverlake Wine, Silver Lake (PAGE 372)

RESTAURANT BARS OF NOTE

Beachwood BBQ & Brewing, Long Beach (PAGE 162)
Beechwood, Venice (PAGE 144)
Bouchon, Beverly Hills (PAGE 130)
Chaya, Downtown (PAGE 80)
Chaya Venice, Venice (PAGE 145)
Chez Jay, Santa Monica (PAGE 146)
The Depot, Torrance (PAGE 164)
The Foundry, Melrose (PAGE 59)
The Grill on the Alley, Beverly Hills (PAGE 133)
Hal's Bar & Grill, Venice (PAGE 149)
La Grande Orange, Pasadena (PAGE 105)
Lucques, Melrose (PAGE 64)
Luna Park, Miracle Mile (PAGE 64)
Mas Malo, Downtown (PAGE 87)
Mike & Anne's, South Pasadena (PAGE 107)
Mohawk Bend, Echo Park (PAGE 88)
Noé Restaurant & Bar, Downtown (PAGE 89)
Pete's Café & Bar, Downtown (PAGE 90)
Playa, Beverly/Third (PAGE 69)
Public Kitchen & Bar, Hollywood (PAGE 70)
Rivera, South Park/Fashion District (PAGE 91)
Rustic Canyon, Santa Monica (PAGE 157)
Smoke House, Burbank (PAGE 122)
Tin Roof Bistro, Manhattan Beach (PAGE 176)
Tower Bar, West Hollywood (PAGE 75)
Typhoon, Santa Monica (PAGE 160)
Wilshire, Santa Monica (PAGE 161)
Yxta Cocina, Downtown (PAGE 95)

🌿 VEGETARIAN ☺ KID FRIENDLY ☼ PATIO DINING 🚐 DELIVERY 🏠 PRIVATE PARTY

CENTRAL CITY

[Bar Covell] **4628 Hollywood Blvd., Los Feliz, 323.660.4400, barcovell. com. D nightly. Wine bar. Beer & wine. MC, V. $ - $$ WHY** The owners, alums of nearby Café Stella and Silver Lake Wine, know exactly what the neighborhood wants: zero pretension and decent value. **WHAT** This Los Feliz wine and beer bar has a rustic-industrial feel, with a weathered wood bar and comfy bar stools. A carefully curated wine list offers some 40 well-priced varieties at a time, as well as an excellent list of craft beers. A light menu includes cheese and charcuterie plates and light bites from Heirloom LA catering. 🗟

[Bar Marmont] 🏛 **Chateau Marmont, 8221 W. Sunset Blvd., West Hollywood, 323.650.0575, chateaumarmont.com. D nightly. Modern American. Full bar. AE, MC, V. $$$ - $$$$ WHY** For the eternal Hollywood scene. **WHAT** You're probably not cool enough to come here—we're certainly not—but you might want to come anyway, just to check out the never-ending scene, have an overpriced cocktail and taste the rustic food (oxtail bruschetta, burger with bacon, avocado and onion rings, roasted halibut with garlic sauce), which is much better than it needs to be, given that nobody comes here just to eat. **WHO** People who are younger, richer, better looking and more gregarious than you—or at least appear to be in the moment. ☺ 🏛

[Cat & Fiddle] 🏛 **6530 W. Sunset Blvd., Hollywood, 323.468.3800, thecatandfiddle.com. L & D daily to 2 a.m. Pub/English. Full bar. AE, MC, V. $ - $$ WHY** English-pub warmth mixed with California style, with excellent house-made bangers, crisp pasties, decadent Scotch eggs and a sherry trifle with fresh sweet cream. **WHAT** Founded in 1982 by the late British rocker Kim Gardner and his wife, Paula, a fashion retailer, this landmark Sunset pub has been a music- and movie-industry hangout since the beginning. Outside is a courtyard with a friendly vibe and a real California feeling; inside the 1920s Mission Revival building is a cozy fireside seat and a dart room. **WHO** An after-work crowd of creative types from studios and music-biz offices nearby. ☺ ☼

[The Golden State] 🏛 **426 N. Fairfax Ave., Fairfax District, 323.782.8331, thegoldenstatecafe.com. L & D Tues.-Sun. American/pub. Beer & wine. AE, MC, V. $ WHY** Locally sourced foods meet excellent beers at this casual café. **WHAT** A minimalist ode to the joy of pairing craft brews—mostly from the Golden State (that's California for you newcomers)—with food from the state's purveyors, including Scoops' unexpected ice cream flavors (including beer- and wine-inspired tastes), Let's Be Frank dogs and sausages, and naturally raised beef. Don't miss the crunchy fish 'n chips and zingy jalapeño coleslaw. Ask knowledgeable owner Jason Bernstein to help select the perfect beer for the food. **WHO** Daytime families, nighttime club-goers and sports fans (there's a TV for the big games). 🗟

🏛 ESSENTIALLY L.A. ☺ LATE ♥ ROMANTIC 🗟 VALUE 🔇 QUIET ♻ SUSTAINABLE

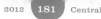

[La Descarga] 🔒 1159 N. Western Ave., Hollywood, 323.466.1324, ladescargala.com. Tues.-Sat. until 2 a.m. Cuban. Full bar. MC, V. $$ - $$$$
WHY The hottest bar of the last few years, it takes speakeasy chic to new heights. **WHAT** It's hard to believe such a classy joint hides behind such a grimy exterior. That's the idea. This dim bar, perfumed with the scent of cigars, is a paean to bartender Pablo Moix's sweet and fancy rum cocktails. Floor shows, featuring flapper-ish burlesque dancers and hot-to-trot jazz bands, make it seem like Hollywood's idea of an underground Havana nightclub. Dress to impress, and on weekends, make a reservation. (At a bar? Yes, really.) **WHO** Cocktail hipsters, upscale party people, the occasional celeb and Silver Lake hipsters slumming west of Hyperion. ☺

[Little Spain] Farmers Market, 6333 W. 3rd St. #120, Fairfax District, 323.634.0633, littlespainla.com. B, L & D daily. Spanish. Beer & wine. AE, MC, V. $ - $$ **WHY** Tapas, sangria and paella make a lively addition to Farmers Market. **WHAT** A long wine bar and a few tables update the old Kokomo stall, where Spanish wines are reasonably priced, and pitchers of fruity sangria are fun to share on warm evenings. Tapas include *pa amb tomaquet* (tomato-smeared toast with charcuterie, cheese or vegetables), calamari, chicken and ham croquetas and addictive mini chorizo sausages. Five types of paella make a heartier meal, and beers and foodstuffs round out the Iberian bounty. **WHO** Tourists from all over the world, and workers from CBS and the Writers Guild. ☼

[Lou] 🔒 724 Vine St., Hollywood, 323.962.6369, louonvine.com. D Mon.-Sat. Wine bar/Mediterranean. Beer & wine. MC, V. $$ - $$$
WHY Terrific, reasonably priced wines by the glass, a dreamy cheese and charcuterie platter, and the famed pig candy (thick bacon caramelized with brown sugar). **WHAT** The perfect neighborhood bistro, Lou is a dark and fetching spot hidden next to a laundromat in a crummy strip mall. Stop in for a quick glass of biodynamic Coteaux du Languedoc and a bit of cheese, or settle in with friends for a relaxed dinner. Trust their advice on wine, make sure to try some cheese, and come on Mondays for the fantastic three-course, five-wine French-bistro supper. **WHO** Savvy baby boomers from Hancock Park and not-insufferably-hip GenXers from Hollywood. ♥ 🗐

[Musso & Frank Grill] 🔒 6667 Hollywood Blvd., Hollywood, 323.467.7788. B, L & D Tues.-Sat. American. Full bar. AE, MC, V. $$$
WHY Martinis, atmosphere, flannel cakes, atmosphere, chicken pot pie and atmosphere. **WHAT** God knows it isn't the cooking that makes this place an essential L.A. restaurant—it's the rich blend of traditional architecture and Hollywood history, faded smoke and legendary lies, all aged to an irresistible patina. (Okay, the cocktails are part of the draw, too.) Don't eat the vegetables or try to chat up the old-school waiters, but do linger at the bar as long as possible. **WHO** Crusty old showbiz men, young bucks. 🍸

🥬 **VEGETARIAN** ☺ **KID FRIENDLY** ☼ **PATIO DINING** � **DELIVERY** 🏛 **PRIVATE PARTY**

[Ray's & Stark Bar] LACMA, 5905 Wilshire Blvd., Miracle Mile, 323.857.6180, lacma.org. L & D Thurs.-Tues. Mediterranean. Full bar. AE, MC, V. $$$ - $$$$ **WHY** The Los Angeles County Museum of Art finally gets the high-style bar and restaurant it deserves. **WHAT** With bright red Saarinen chairs and a display of colorful teacups from the museum's collection, the bright, airy restaurant complements the recently added Renzo Piano–designed pavilion opposite. On chef Kris Morningstar's menu, flavorful fare like wild mushrooms, black vinegar and artichoke chips enliven basic proteins like hangar steak and arctic char. The best part? Each table gets a loaf of fresh-baked sourdough bread. Outside, creative cocktails are served at Stark's Bar, along with adventurous bar bites—think head cheese and beef tendon alongside flatbreads with tasty toppings. **WHO** Monied museum docents and donors, camera-toting tourists. 🍸 ☼

[Rockwell, VT] 1714 N. Vermont Ave., Los Feliz, 323.669.1550, rockwellvt.com. D nightly, brunch Sat.-Sun. American. Full bar. AE, MC, V. $$ **WHY** A fabulous outdoor space, a good happy hour and flatbread pizzas to share with friends. **WHAT** This cousin to Vermont is a two-level, mostly outdoor space built around an artfully lit coral tree. The vibe varies greatly depending on when you come—weekend brunch is peaceful, early weeknights are rich with candlelit romance, and from Wednesday through Saturday nights, the music gets louder and the crowd gets younger. Very good cocktails are a reasonable $9; some object to the shatter-proof acrylic glasses, but we think they're a wise move. The smart and affordable wines, however, are served in proper glasses. As for the food, it's friendly-as-a-puppy bar chow: Kobe beef sliders, flatbreads and salads with such de rigueur ingredients as beets and burrata. **WHO** A few quiet conversationalists for happy hour and a more convivial and celebratory crowd in the later hours. ♥ 🍸 ☼

[Surly Goat] 7929 Santa Monica Blvd., West Hollywood, 323.650.4628, surlygoat.com. D nightly. Pub. Full bar. MC, V. $ **WHY** A low-key West Hollywood tavern for discerning beer enthusiasts. **WHAT** Ryan Sweeney opened the Surly Goat after making a splash in the local beer community with his first bar, the Verdugo. His new place has an impressive array of more than two dozen taps and a rotating brew on cask. Rare and fascinating beers are the norm, from the Bruery's locally made Marron Acidifie (sour chestnut) to a few choice Belgian ales, with the focus on the west coast. Happy hour until 8 p.m. with $4 drafts makes it a good after-work stop—later in the evening it fills up with Hollywood partiers and rotating DJs. There's no kitchen, but regulars order in from Baby Blues BBQ next door. **WHO** Diehard beer aficionados and young drinkers looking for a more casual alternative to the Hollywood club scene. 🍸

[Tar Pit] 609 N. La Brea Ave., Hollywood, 323.965.1300, tarpitcocktails.com. D nightly. Modern American. Full bar. AE, MC, V. $$ - $$$

🏛 ESSENTIALLY L.A. ☾ LATE ♥ ROMANTIC 🍸 VALUE 🍷 QUIET ☼ SUSTAINABLE

WHY Art deco elegance reminiscent of old Hollywood, with superb cocktails and Mark Peel's take on bar food. Great happy hour, too. **WHAT** More luxe than the address would suggest, this cocktail lounge by Campanile's Mark Peel is as retro as they come, from the steak Diane to the high-backed white leather banquettes. Don't wuss out and have a cosmo—instead, try one of Tar Pit's creations (all $12), like the Jamaican Firefly (rum, house-made ginger beer, lime juice) or the Lil Gig (tequila, yellow chartreuse, Thai basil). We're less impressed with the restaurant food than the smaller bar snacks, and we wish it wasn't so noisy at peak times, but the cocktails and setting are worth the trip. **WHO** A crowd as well-dressed as the setting. ☺ ♥

[The Village Idiot] **7383 Melrose Ave., Melrose, 323.655.3331, villageidiotla.com. L & D daily. Pub/American. Full bar. AE, MC, V. $ - $$ WHY** A fairly deep and thoughtful tap-beer selection, excellent fish 'n chips and spinach pie, and a pretty normal crowd for Melrose, especially midweek. **WHAT** The crush is too much for us on weekend nights, but otherwise we're happy to stop into this brick-walled pub for a Guinness and a steak sandwich or some fish 'n chips. The wine selection isn't nearly as good as the beer, but sometimes there's a good buy by the bottle. **WHO** Beer boys and girls seeking Boddingtons or Craftsman beers, something good to eat, and a jovial time. ☺ ☺

EASTSIDE

[Allston Yacht Club] **1320 Echo Park Ave., Echo Park, 213.481.0454, allstonyachtclub.com. D Tues.-Sat. Wine bar/modern American. Full bar. AE, MC, V. $$ - $$$ WHY** A smart, international wine list, tasty small plates and good-value specials. **WHAT** A sign if there ever was one of Echo Park's gentrification, Allston is a small, dark, clubby place with very good wines, a full bar, tasty small-plate dishes and a couple of very nice owners who are longtime Silver Lake/Echo Park residents—but who originally hailed from Boston, hence the eccentric name. Check the website for frequent happy-hour and special-night bargains. **WHO** Echo Park Town Council folks, locals from the hills above and adventurers from Silver Lake and Downtown. 🖼 ⑨

[Angel City Brewery] **216 S. Alameda St., Little Tokyo/Arts District, 213.622.1261, angelcitybrewing.com. D Thurs.-Sun. American. Beer & wine. MC, V. $ WHY** Tasty beers made right in Downtown L.A. in a vast, vintage warehouse. **WHAT** The warehouse is still being renovated at this writing, but the beer garden/sampling room is taking shape with tastings of several of Angel City's brews, local art on the walls, and food trucks in the parking lot. Close to the Gold Line station and near Little Tokyo restaurants, Angel City is a worthy stop on a Downtown beer crawl. Brews tend to be on the lighter side, like the signature Angel City amber ale, Charlie Parker lager or Lester Young Porkpie Hat dark lager.

🍃 VEGETARIAN ☺ KID FRIENDLY ☼ PATIO DINING 🚗 DELIVERY 🎉 PRIVATE PARTY

[Bacaro] **2308 S. Union Ave., USC, 213.748.7205, bacarola.com. Nightly from 5 p.m. Wine bar/Italian. Beer & wine. AE, MC, V. $ WHY** Because you're bored with most wine-bar offerings and tired of paying through the nose for a glass of wine. **WHAT** On a funky block between Pico-Union and USC is a tiny haven for wine lovers, where the wines of the day are artfully written on the blackboard walls. The kitchen turns out Venetian-style *cichetti* (small bites), including bruschetta, crostini and such heartier dishes as a deconstructed BLT made with Niman Ranch bacon; almost all the dishes are a mere $7. Bacaro is one of those spots you wish would open within walking distance of your house, a place where enthusiasm for esoteric Italian bottlings is matched by a menu of unfussy, simply delicious snacks. **WHO** Oenophiles with more taste than dough from USC and West Adams. 🗳 🍸

[Barbrix] **2442 Hyperion Ave., Silver Lake, 323.662.2442, barbrix. com. Nightly from 6 p.m. Wine bar/Mediterranean. Beer & wine. AE, MC, V. $ - $$ WHY** A bohemian-chic indoor/outdoor wine bar with spot-on Mediterranean-inspired small plates. **WHAT** Interesting, well-priced wines from California to Croatia are the centerpiece of this house-turned-festive wine bar. The food's just as good, from cheese and charcuterie samplers to flavorful farmers' market vegetable salads and meaty plates of pork belly, Moroccan-style lamb chops and wild boar sausage. If you hope to hold a conversation, reserve a table on the quieter off-the-street patio—inside, it's lively but deafening. **WHO** The hippest people in Silver Lake, which is saying something. ☺ ♥ ☼

[BottleRock] **1050 Flower St., South Park/Fashion District, 213.747.1100, bottlerock.net. L Mon.-Sat., D daily. Wine bar/modern American. Beer & wine. AE, MC, V. $$ WHY** To taste oddball whites, rare reds and exotic microbrews and banter about same with BottleRock's urbane, wine-savvy GM George Skorka, former sommelier at an impressive list of high-end eateries. **WHAT** On the ground floor of the Metropolitan Lofts building, in starkly modern rooms lined with hundreds of intriguing bottles, this branch of the Culver City original may be Downtown's most intelligent wine-and-food destination. The open kitchen turns out tempting, wine-friendly treats during rush hour (4 to 6:30 p.m.) and an extensive menu of cheeses, charcuterie and small plates (green curry mussels, pork-belly risotto, agnolotti with bacon and dates). The 900-plus wines and beers are all available for retail sale, a boon for nearby loft dwellers. **WHO** A crowd as sophisticated and eclectic as the wine list. ☺ 🍸

[Caña Rum Bar] **714 W. Olympic Blvd., South Park/Fashion District, 213.745.7090, canarumbar.la. Tues.-Sun. to 2 a.m. Full bar. MC, V. $$ - $$$ WHY** Some of L.A.'s most original and inspired cocktails in an atmosphere that oozes discreet charm. **WHAT** The mellow ambience belies the rigorous attention to detail bestowed on every cocktail by Allan Katz and his crew. The location doesn't make it easy to find (you have to walk through the Doheny's parking lot), but once inside you can actually relax and hear yourself talk. Note: It's technically a club requiring a $20 annual membership fee, but they often waive that during happy hour. **WHO** Cocktail aficionados, LA Live refugees who know where to hole up before (or after) a concert, SoDo (south Downtown) hipsters. ☺ ♥ 🍸 ☼

[City Sip] 2150 W. Sunset Blvd., Echo Park, 213.483.9463, citysipla. com. D Tues.-Sun. Wine bar/Mediterranean. Wine. MC, V. $ - $$ **WHY** "Wine for the people" (or so says its slogan), in working-people's Echo Park, with affordable tastings, charcuterie and small plates, as well as fun wine classes. **WHAT** A groovy wine bar for an increasingly groovy neighborhood, City Sip is part wine bar and part school. Six nights a week, owner Nicole Daddio pours wine (for as little as $3 during the midweek happy hour) and serves charcuterie (Spanish chorizo, prosciutto with figs, speck with sauerkraut), cheeses, panini and a salad or two. The two-hour, $50 wine classes are unpretentious and worthwhile. 🗭

[Cole's] 118 E. 6th St., Downtown, 213.622.4090, colesfrenchdip.com. L & D daily. American. Full bar. AE, MC, V. $$ **WHY** Classic cocktails and sandwiches in an old-timey setting in the heart of Downtown. And the speakeasy-like Varnish Bar in the back is one of the coolest watering holes in L.A. **WHAT** Vintage L.A. meets the modern cocktail culture at this renovated landmark. It's appropriate that for a tavern that claims to be the city's oldest public house, the featured (and very well-made) cocktails are longtime favorites like Manhattans and Sazeracs. And the dips—beef, turkey, lamb or pastrami—and their accompaniments (cole slaw, fries, mac 'n cheese) hit the spot.

[Corkbar] 403 W. 12th St., South Park/Fashion District, 213.746.0050, corkbar.com. L & D daily. Wine bar/modern American. Beer & wine. AE, MC, V. $$ **WHY** Wholly addictive *gougères* (cheddar pastry puffs), excellent if somewhat pricey California wines by the glass, easy street parking and a location within walking distance of Staples Center and LA Live. **WHAT** Corkbar distinguishes itself from the 7,000 other places to get a drink Downtown by its smart roster of California wines, its wine-loving staff and its menu: salads, shrimp risotto, a burger and the usual cheese and charcuterie. The modern space is relaxed and blessedly quiet. **WHO** South Park residents and a quietly hip pre- and post-Club Nokia crowd. 🍸 🕔

[Eagle Rock Brewery] 3056 Roswell St., Glassell Park, 323.257.7866, eaglerockbrewery.com. Wed.-Sat. from 4 p.m., Sun. from noon. Pub. Beer & wine. Cash only. $ **WHY** A place to taste made-in-L.A. beer right at the source. **WHAT** Actually in adjacent Glassell Park, Eagle Rock Brewery is a friendly spot to quaff the brews that are pioneers in L.A.'s craft-beer scene. Manifesto Eagle Rock Wit (wheat

🍃VEGETARIAN ☺KID FRIENDLY ☼PATIO DINING ⊜DELIVERY 🏠PRIVATE PARTY beer), Solidarity black mild (a dark beer with a light taste) and Revolution XPA pale ale are just a few of the beers made by father-and-son brewmasters Steve and Jeremy Raub. Food trucks and taco tables cook up beer-friendly snacks in the parking lot, and the brewery holds beer education sessions and supplies dozens of L.A. bars and restaurants. **WHO** Eastside bohos and citywide beer geeks.

[The Edison] 108 W. 2nd St., Downtown, 213.613.0000, edisondowntown.com. Wed.-Fri. from 5 p.m., Sat. from 8 p.m. American. Full bar. AE, MC, V. $ - $$ **WHY** To take a glamorous step back in time—and for the double-take the first time you spot the Absinthe Fairy. **WHAT** This nostalgic cocktail bar reignites 1920s elegance and romance in an unbelievable multi-level space that was L.A.'s first private power plant. Each night brings new revelries, from live music to burlesque, but it's enough of a show just to wander through the endless nooks and crannies decorated with antiques, leather wing chairs, tufted velvet and old power-plant equipment. Mixologists from all over the country visit here, so the cocktail list changes often, but absinthe is always a crowd favorite, sold by an ethereal winged woman pushing a glowing green cart. To soak up the liquor, try the sweet potato Tesla fries, the grilled cheese with tomato soup, or a couple of Auntie Em's cupcakes. The foolish few who show up in T-shirts or flip flops are turned away by a beautiful blonde wearing seemingly nothing but beads. **WHO** The hippest of the hip (often dressed to the nines) and rockabilly types on Friday and Saturday, and a surprisingly diverse after-work crowd on Wednesday and Thursday.

[Golden Gopher] 417 W. 8th St., Downtown, 213.614.8001, goldengopher.la. Nightly to 2 a.m. American. Full bar. AE, MC, V. $ - $$ **WHY** One of the first spruced-up bars of Downtown's renaissance. Kogi fans take note that the taco truck sometimes parks outside. **WHAT** The funky name and neon sign date from the original bar, but this modern version is a sleek stop on the Downtown bar circuit, with an outdoor smoking area complete with couches. Also left over from the previous century: It's one of the city's few bars where it's legal to buy a bottle to take home. **WHO** An after-work cocktail crowd gives way to seriously partying young folks later in the evening.

[Lazy Ox Canteen] 241 S. San Pedro St., Little Tokyo/Arts District, 213.626.5299, lazyoxcanteen.com. L & D daily. Pub/modern American. Beer & wine. MC, V. $$$ **WHY** To pretend you're in Barcelona, or the East Village, or maybe Berkeley, if only for an evening. **WHAT** On the edge of Little Tokyo, in a no-frills, noisy modern pub, chef Josef Centeno turns out food that will make you think you're not in L.A. anymore. Every night brings a different main course served for two— perhaps leg of lamb with side dishes for just $29. Centeno's food is what fusion cooking should be: vibrant, complementary flavors in exciting combinations. Don't miss the batter-dipped fried anchovies

ESSENTIALLY L.A. LATE ♥ROMANTIC VALUE QUIET SUSTAINABLE

drizzled with saffron honey, the buttermilk-fried chicken (eat your heart out, Paula Deen) and the hand-torn egg pasta with a sunnyside-up egg. This is no place for timid eaters—the menu is gleefully larded with lamb cheeks, veal tongue, pig's ears and other esoterica. The eclectic wine list has tons of choices under $35, and the globe-trotting beer list omits anything bland. **WHO** A throng of Downtown denizens who appear to lead far more interesting lives than you do. ☺ ♪ ☺ ☼

[Mignon] **128 E. 6th St., Downtown, 213.489.0131, mignonla.com. Nightly from 5 p.m. Wine bar. Beer & wine. AE, MC, V. $ WHY** A wee spot with affordable wines, cheeses and charcuterie—just the place to transition from the work day to the evening. **WHAT** The smart folks behind one of our favorite wine bars, Bacaro, run this 600-square-foot spot in the heart of Downtown. Where Bacaro's focus is Italian, here it's French, with affordable French, Croatian and Spanish wines by the glass and, to eat, quality cheeses, olives, dried farmers' market fruit, nuts and charcuterie. Seats are few, so quit work early. ☕ ☼

[Perch] **448 S. Hill St., Downtown, 213.802.1770, perchla.com. D nightly. French. Full bar. AE, MC, V. $$$ WHY** Because you need a rooftop bar Downtown that *isn't* overpriced and played out (like The Standard). **WHAT** This multi-story bar and restaurant boasts wraparound patios with gorgeous views of Pershing Square on one side and Bunker Hill on the other. The décor is art deco, the food is French (coq au vin, onion soup), and the vibe is mellow—but you should dress upscale casual. **WHO** People trying to impress a date, a client or an out-of-town relative, and well-off Downtown hipsters and business types. ☺ ♥ ☼

[Redwood Bar & Grill] **316 W. 2nd St., Downtown, 213.680.2600, theredwoodbar.com. L Mon.-Fri. & Sun., D nightly. Pub/American. Full bar. AE, MC, V. $ - $$ WHY** Solid pub grub, stiff drinks and good tunes. **WHAT** Ink-stained *L.A. Times* staffers used to hang out here when it was a true dive bar, but the pirate-theme update retains a certain divey feel. Fish 'n chips, crunchy cole slaw and hefty burgers go down well with ale or cocktails, which in turn are well suited to the often-worthwhile live music that happens most nights. **WHO** Downtown office workers during the day; music-loving younger folk at night. ☺

[Swill Automatic] **1820 Industrial St., Downtown, 213.239.9088, swillautomatic.com. D nightly (to 1:30 a.m. Thurs.-Sat.), brunch Sat.-Sun. Wine bar. Beer & wine. AE, MC, V. $ - $$ WHY** All the fun of wine tasting without the pretension. **WHAT** With its self-service Enomatic machines, high communal tables and chill vibe, Swill is a swell place to try lots of the 70 wines (in pours as small as one ounce) and share a global sampling of small plates: banh mi sliders, Moroccan meatballs, garlic shrimp, prosciutto-wrapped asparagus. We also like the tasty, inexpensive weekend brunch. **WHO** Young Downtowners and folks who couldn't get in to neighboring Church & State. ☺ ☕ ♪ ☼

VEGETARIAN ☺ KID FRIENDLY ☼ PATIO DINING ⊜ DELIVERY 🏠 PRIVATE PARTY

[The Varnish] 🔒 **Inside Cole's, 118 E. 6th St., Downtown, 213.622.9999, thevarnishbar.com. Nightly until 2 a.m. American. Full bar. AE, MC, V. $$ WHY** The closest L.A. has to a speakeasy, with a discreetly marked door in the back of Cole's and exquisitely crafted cocktails. **WHAT** 1920s-style barmen, a jazz soundtrack and fresh fruit juices make the Varnish old-school — yet it's current on the latest in mixology. **WHO** The Downtown bar-crawling crowd is youngish, but high-end cocktails keep out drinkers looking for cheap well drinks and a loud party scene.

[Verdugo] **3408 Verdugo Rd., Glassell Park, 323.257.3408, verdugobar. com. Mon.-Sat. from 6 p.m., Sun. from 3 p.m. Pub/American. Full bar. AE, MC, V. $$ WHY** Well-selected beers from small breweries in a location that's a bit hard to find, but worth the search. **WHAT** Choose from two rooms and a beer garden with picnic tables for sampling rare Belgian and California craft brews at this hidden hot spot. There's a full bar, wine and special cask-beer nights, but no food — ah, but you can find plenty of taco trucks and street vendors nearby. **WHO** Craft-brew geeks from Eagle Rock, Highland Park and Silver Lake. ☺ ♻

[Wurstküche] **800 E. 3rd St., Little Tokyo/Arts District, 213.687.4444, wurstkucherestaurant.com. L & D daily; open late Thurs.-Sat. German. Beer & wine. AE, MC, V. $ WHY** The perfect blend of juicy sausage, soft bun and sweet-savory onions and peppers — just the thing to eat with a pint or two. **WHAT** This industrial-hip beer garden keeps it simple: You got your beer, your sausage and your fries. What more could you possibly need? Ranging from the classic (brats, kielbasa) to the Californian (several vegetarians) to the adventurous (rattlesnake-rabbit-jalapeño), the sausages are grilled, tucked in a compact bun and topped with grilled onions, sweet peppers and/or sauerkraut. There are mustards galore, and even more dipping sauces to try with the thick but crisp Belgian fries. To drink are Belgian and German draft beers and cool bottled sodas. **WHO** By day, a youngish crowd of creative types; by night, an even younger crowd of Downtown bar-hoppers. ☺ ♪

[The York] 🔒 **5018 York Blvd., Highland Park, 323.255.9675, theyorkonyork.com. D nightly, brunch Sat.-Sun. Pub/American. Full bar. AE, MC, V. $ - $$ WHY** Local microbrews, good wine by the glass and tasty, affordable modern pub chow. Try the quick-fried garbanzo beans, the soups, the shrimp bruschetta and the fish 'n chips. **WHAT** A high-ceilinged old brick building in gentrifying Highland Park is home to this simple but stylish pub, a pioneer in L.A.'s gastropub movement. Order your homemade soup, Caesar salad, Cuban pulled-pork sandwich, very good burger or cheese platter from the bartender, and someone will deliver the food (and drink) to your table. We wish it was as uncrowded as in the early days, but we're happy for the York's success. **WHO** The hip and savvy of Highland Park and Eagle Rock, along with slummers from Pasadena and Los Feliz. ☺ 📧 ♪

🔒 **ESSENTIALLY L.A.** ☺ **LATE** ♥ **ROMANTIC** 📧 **VALUE** 🔔 **QUIET** ♻ **SUSTAINABLE**

SAN GABRIEL VALLEY

[1886 Bar] The Raymond, 1250 S. Fair Oaks Ave., Pasadena, 626.441.3136, theraymond.com. Closed Mon. American. Full bar. AE, MC, V. $$ **WHY** Downtown-style cocktail chic in a formerly frumpy landmark restaurant. **WHAT** It was a stroke of genius for the owners of the Raymond, a pricey restaurant in a circa-1886 cottage, to turn space over to cocktail guru Aidan Demarest (of Edison and Seven Grand fame). The drinks are terrific, the cozy interior has a real speakeasy feel, and the new candlelit patio is pure romance. Just-fine bar food and good but not-too-loud music. **WHO** Who knew Pasadena could attract such hipsters? And that said hipsters would be willing to share a bar with gray-haired Caltech professors and well-groomed Pasadena moms? ♥ ☼

[Lucky Baldwins] 17 S. Raymond Ave., Old Pasadena, 626.795.0652, luckybaldwins.com. B, L & D daily. Pub/English. Beer & wine. AE, MC, V. $ - $$ **WHY** 63 beers on tap, including some wonderful Belgians, along with such reliable pub standards as pasties and a tasty chicken curry. **WHAT** Co-owner David Farnsworth is from the north of England, and with partner Peggy Simonian he's created an authentically English pub in a brick-walled Old Town space, with nooks, crannies and a lovely patio on the pedestrian alley in back. Aficionados come from far away for such annual events as the Belgian beer festival in February and Oktoberfest, when German beers are front and center. **WHO** Caltech students, professors and others who prefer earnest conversation over a good pint to a raucous bar scene. 🍺 ☼

[Lucky Baldwins Delirium Pub & Café] 21 Kersting Court, Sierra Madre, 626.355.1140, luckybaldwins.com. B, L & D daily. Pub/English. Beer & wine. AE, MC, V. $ - $$ **WHY** For 46 beers on tap, with great choices from Ireland, England and Belgium, and solid English fare, including a good chicken curry. **WHAT** A pleasantly old-school pub (pressed tin ceilings, polished wooden floors, walled patio) that perfectly suits its old-fashioned setting in Sierra Madre's village center. In the back is a tiny but richly rewarding package shop with a few British foodstuffs and hard-to-get beers. **WHO** Patagonia-clad locals taking a break from restoring their Craftsman cottages and hiking the Mt. Wilson Trail. 🖼 🍺 ☼

[Noir Food & Wine] 40 N. Mentor Ave., Pasadena, 626.795.7199, noirfoodandwine.com. L Tues.-Fri., D nightly. Wine bar/modern American. Beer & wine. AE, MC, V. $$ - $$$ **WHY** For the great wine list, with lots of worthy choices for less than $10 a glass; the well-conceived and fairly priced small-plates menu; and the gregarious charm of Chef Beltran, who spends a lot of time checking on diners. **WHAT** After years of bouncing around various restaurants, success has come to chef Claud Beltran and wine expert Mike Farwell, owners of this wine bar/bistro. There's a handful of tables in the chocolate-box of a dining room, modeled on Farwell's beloved Willi's Wine Bar in

Drink + Eat

Paris, a compact new bar counter for a dozen, and more seating on the heated, candlelit outdoor passageway and walled patio. You can have just a glass of wine and a cheese plate, or live it up with a good bottle and several small dishes (try the burger, the haricots verts with garlic, shallots and mint, and whatever fresh fish is offered). **WHO** Boston Court theater-goers, Caltechers and an appealing mix of young and mature Pasadenans. ♥

[The Tap Room] Langham Huntington Hotel, 1401 S. Oak Knoll Ave., Pasadena, 626.568.3900, pasadena.langhamhotels.com. Mon.-Thurs. to 1 a.m., Fri.-Sat. to 2 a.m., Sun. to midnight. American. Full bar. AE, MC, V. $$$$ - $$$$$ **WHY** When you need to celebrate or seduce. **WHAT** Our new favorite place to celebrate an occasion, the Langham's remodeled bar is a thing of beauty, from the old-money, living room–style interior to the fabulous heated terrace overlooking the grounds. The cocktails and the bar chow (lobster corn dogs, Kobe beef sliders) are as superb as the bill is high. But it's cheaper, and lots more fun, to eat and drink here than at the Royce, the hotel's ambitious dining room.**WHO** New-era prepsters from the best Pasadena families. ☺ ♥ 🍸 ✿

[Vertical Wine Bistro] 🏛 70 N. Raymond Avd., Old Pasadena, 626.795.3999, verticalwinebistro.com. D Tues.-Sun. Wine bar/modern American. Full bar. AE, MC, V. $$$ - $$$$ **WHY** About 100 wines by the glass, with lots of flight options, and LQ's food to accompany those wines. **WHAT** A-list movie producer and Pasadenan Gale Anne Hurd brings a little Hollywood zing to non-showy Pasadena with her wine-focused restaurant—although the look is actually more New York sleek than Hollywood glitz, and it suits Pasadena well. So does the menu from acclaimed chef Laurent Quenioux; we particularly love the charcuterie, flatbread pizzas, great burgers and family-style Sunday suppers. The vast wine-by-the-glass selection has elite choices, of course, but also a few tasty $10-or-less glasses for the cheapskates among us, and the happy hour is a relative bargain. **WHO** A handsome crowd of professionals and eastside entertainment-industry folks. ♥

[Wine Detective] The Commons, 146 S. Lake Ave., Pasadena, 626.792.9936, winedetective.com. L & D daily. Wine bar. Wine. AE, MC, V. $$ - $$$ **WHY** A comfortable place to sit, sip, nosh and talk, with two lounge-y seating areas, a wooden communal table, and room to stand and chat around the gleaming tasting machines. **WHAT** Part retail store, part wine bar and part high-tech tasting center, this quiet little spot was created by two wine-loving couples who invested in state-of-the-art Enomatic machines, which make tasting a fun, self-serve game. Pours can be as small as one ounce and as large as you like, and prices are in the $2 to $5 an ounce range. To eat are a good assortment of cheeses, charcuterie and *pintxos*, small, open-face Basque sandwiches (try the Serrano ham, Manchego cheese and oven-roasted tomatoes). **WHO** Friends meeting after work to taste and talk. 🍸

🏛 ESSENTIALLY L.A. ☺LATE ♥ROMANTIC 📷 VALUE 🍸 QUIET ✿ SUSTAINABLE

EAST VALLEY

[8 1/2 Taverna] 11334 Moorpark St., Studio City, 818.308.1100, 8andahalf.com. L & D daily. Italian/pizzeria. Beer & wine. AE, MC, V. $$ **WHY** Proper pizzas made by a Naples native and tasty, reasonably priced wines and beers to wash them down with. **WHAT** This handsome hangout gives locals a great alternative to oft-crowded Laurel Tavern. The kitchen turns out very good steamed mussels, thin-crust, Neapolitan-style pizzas, arugula salads and burgers; to drink are lesser-known Italian wines and a great beer selection, including several Allagash varieties on tap. Seating is comfortable, the TVs are tuned to the most popular game of the moment, and there's patio dining (and drinking) for outdoorsy types. **WHO** Assistant directors, PAs, post-production workers, writers and other Tujunga Village locals. ☉ ♪ ☼

[Blue Dog Beer Tavern] 4524 Saugus Ave., Sherman Oaks, 818.990.2583, bluedogbeertavern.com. L & D daily. American. Beer & wine. MC, V. $ - $$ **WHY** Relaxed neighborhood bar with an uncommonly good beer selection and premium burgers. **WHAT** If you've ever wished your favorite craft beer bar served decent food, you're finally home. The burgers are large and messy, made with high-quality stuff, and they're a buck or two cheaper than they'd be at most self-proclaimed gastropubs. Can't decide between a pilsner and a Belgian strong ale? Choose a $12 flight of four beers from any of their eight taps. Another three dozen bottles and cans round out the impressive beer menu. Any place that has Unibroue's Blanche de Chambly on tap knows a thing or two about beer. **WHO** Beer fiends, burger hounds, cubicle dwellers splurging on lunch, thirty- and fortysomethings relaxing and chatting, and twentysomethings whooping it up and flirting. ☼

[The Federal Bar] 5303 Lankershim Blvd., North Hollywood, 818.980.2555, thefederalbar.com. L & D daily. Pub. Full bar. MC, V. $$ - $$$ **WHY** Great crowd, tunes, drinks and brews, although the food could use a little improvement. **WHAT** Music venue operator Knitting Factory Entertainment took over an old bank building (recently another restaurant) to open this gastropub, which has upscale pub fare and plenty of microbrews and wines to wash it all down. Burgers are a good bet, particularly the Greco lamb burger with feta and tzatziki. Live music in the upstairs lounge many nights. **WHO** NoHo hipsters and studio workers kicking back. ♪ 🏠

[Laurel Tavern] 11938 Ventura Blvd., Studio City, 818.506.0777, laureltavern.net. L & D daily. Pub/American. Beer & wine. AE, MC, V. $ - $$ **WHY** A well-edited lineup of scrumptious bar food, including skewered chunks of pork belly so succulent they'll make you weak in the knees. **WHAT** The Valley's coolest gastropub is a long room with exposed brick walls and French doors opening onto the busy boulevard. Some of the nicest barkeeps in town make sure patrons are well lubricated with an ambitious all-California draft beer list and unpretentious

🌿 VEGETARIAN ☉ KID FRIENDLY ☼ PATIO DINING 🚗 DELIVERY 🏠 PRIVATE PARTY

wines by the glass (almost all under $10) or bottle. The limited menu is heavy on terrific burgers; the arugula salad is top-notch; and you can make a meal out of the steamed Penn Cove mussels. **WHO** Industry folk unwinding after a long day behind the cameras and neighbors who have adopted this as their local pub. ☺ 🗟

[The Local Peasant] 14058 Ventura Blvd., Sherman Oaks, 818.501.0234, thelocalpeasant.com. D nightly, brunch Sat.-Sun. Full bar. MC, V. $$ **WHY** Terrific small-plates fare and upscale nibbles to go with cocktails, wine and microbrews. **WHAT** The peasants of Sherman Oaks and environs quickly made themselves at home here, where well-made cocktails, a lengthy list of craft beers and hand-picked bottlings from nearby wineries help fuel the buzz. The house wines are a great deal, served in adorable eight-ounce carafes for just $8. We can't resist the crisp potato chips sprayed with malt vinegar or the deviled eggs with bacon, but there are plenty of lighter, healthier items on the menu, including the grilled peach salad with fennel and the red snapper ceviche. Be prepared: When the Peasant gets busy (most nights), the noise level is excruciating. **WHO** Locals relaxing after a day at the office or on the set, and gastropub pilgrims making the rounds.

[Tony's Darts Away] 1710 W. Magnolia Blvd., Burbank, 818.253.1710, tonysda.com. L & D daily until 2 a.m. (1 a.m. on Sun.). American. Beer & wine. AE, MC, V. $ **WHY** Because darts, vegan sausages and beer go well together. Even in Burbank. **WHAT** A neighborhood pub with more than 40 draft beers, Tony's has a no-bottle policy — all beers, wines and sodas are served on draft. The multi-animal/ no-animal sausage menu comes with the de rigueur selection of über toppings, and a nice chili comes "sin carne" for vegetarians. A few good salads, sweet potato fries and house-made potato chips round out the menu. Oh, and did we mention darts? **WHO** Eco-beer geeks and studio refugees who don't feel the need to be seen in Hollywood or Downtown. ☺ 🗟 ♻ ♪

WEST VALLEY

[Ireland's 32] 13721 Burbank Blvd., Van Nuys, 818.785.4031, irelands32pub.com. L & D daily. Pub/Irish. Full bar. AE, MC, V. $ - $$ **WHY** A friendly Irish pub in the heart of the Valley, with good beer (Guinness, Harp, Bass, Smithwick's), well-made burgers and crisp fish 'n chips. **WHAT** It's a bit gloomy at first, but once your eyes adjust you'll find a handsome room, friendly locals and fresh beer. If the bar's too crowded, grab a table by the dance floor. Hungry? Check out the board list, then mosey over to the kitchen and tell the cook what you'd like, and a good meal will appear a few minutes later. **WHO** Couples watching football or meeting friends for a pint and some fish 'n chips. 🗟

🔒 ESSENTIALLY L.A. ☺ LATE ♥ ROMANTIC 🗟 VALUE 🕯 QUIET ♻ SUSTAINABLE

[Pickwick's Pub] 21010 Ventura Blvd., Woodland Hills, 818.340.9673, pickwickspub.org. L & D daily. Pub/English. Full bar. AE, MC, V. $ - $$ **WHY** Fourteen draft beers (stouts, lagers, ales and ciders) at modest prices, live music and a fun trivia night. **WHAT** A proper English pub with a proper English barkeep and, to eat, Cal-Val standards (salads, barbecued chicken breast) and pub classics (juicy, salty onion rings and comforting mashed spuds and peas). The pretty, open-layout room is equally comfortable for dining or just getting together for drinks. Note that in football season, it's a Packers hangout. **WHO** Friendly and loyal West Valley regulars, mostly young, including some very good darts players. 🖼 🎵

WESTSIDE: CENTRAL

[Alibi Room] 12236 Washington Blvd., Culver City, 310.390.9300, alibiroomla.com. D Mon.-Sat. to midnight (bar to 2 a.m.). American/Korean. Beer & wine. AE, MC, V. $ **WHY** To eat Kogi's tacos and other good things without having to stand in a 90-minute line at the truck—plus you can have a Duvel Golden Ale or Los Carlos Malbec with your kim chee sesame quesadilla. **WHAT** We loved this chill neighborhood pub before Kogi took over the kitchen, and now we love it more, although now too many other people do, too. Come early (it opens at 5:30) if you want to snag some of the comfy, low-slung seating, and go wild sampling the Korean tacos, Korean spiced fries, and tofu and citrus salad. To drink are good-value wines by the glass, bottled beers and a handful of hip draft brews. **WHO** Twentysomething studio toilers meeting after work, with some middle-aged Culver City locals for good measure. 😊 🖼 🎵

[BottleRock] 3847 Main St., Culver City, 310.836.WINE, bottlerock. net. L Tues.-Sat., D nightly. Wine bar/modern American. Beer & wine. AE, MC, V. $ - $$ **WHY** Plenty of wine by the glass and good bar snacks (fried Marcona almonds, charcuterie and cheese), plus (surprisingly, for a wine bar) a terrific beer menu. **WHAT** This hybrid wine bar/ wine shop sits on the cusp of trendy, but fortunately it stays just this side of cozy. A good stop for a pick-me-up and a snack. **WHO** Folks waiting for their reservation at Fraîche and post-movie sippers.

[Craftbar] 🏠 10100 Constellation Blvd., Century City, 310.279.4180, craftrestaurant.com. D Mon.-Sat. Modern American. Full bar. AE, MC, V. $$ **WHY** An affordable version of Tom Colicchio's terrific (and adjacent) Craft restaurant, a sleek brother to the New York original. **WHAT** Everything on the menu in the front lounge and patio at Craft is $5 to $12 and just as interesting: seafood pie, flatbread with goat cheese and cherry tomatoes, short-rib raviolis. **WHO** Junior ICM agents reveling in their potential while their bosses seal the deal over $50 steaks inside. ♥ 🖼 ☼

🌿 VEGETARIAN ⊙ KID FRIENDLY ☼ PATIO DINING � DELIVERY 🏠 PRIVATE PARTY

[Father's Office] 🔒 3229 Helms Ave., Culver City, 310.736.2224, fathersoffice.com. L Fri.-Sun., D nightly. Pub/American. Full bar. AE, MC, V. **$$** **WHY** The justly famed medium-rare burger topped with caramelized onions, smoked applewood bacon and blue cheese is worth the wait, the price and the fat grams. Only you can decide if it's worth the hype. **WHAT** The square footage is greatly improved from the Santa Monica original, with lots of patio seating, but don't think you still won't have to stand in line to enjoy one of Sang Yoon's famous burgers, some sweet potato fries and a small-producer tap beer or two. No substitutions on the famous burger, no kids (21 and over only). Take heart that the line moves quickly. **WHO** Youngish men who take their beer and burgers very seriously. ◔ ☼

[Nic's Martini Lounge] 453 N. Cañon Dr., Beverly Hills, 310.550.5707, nicsbeverlyhills.com. D Mon.-Sat. American. Full bar. AE, MC, V. $$ - $$$$ **WHY** Dress-up fun in the heart of Beverly Hills, with a piano bar, often-good jazz and a walk-in vodka freezer that brings out the Russian in everyone. **WHAT** Larry Nicola was well ahead of the cocktail craze—he decamped from Silver Lake years ago to open this swank (and only slightly tongue-in-cheek) Beverly Hills boîte. Come for a martini, come for a meal, come for some jazz—but note that the scene gets louder and more intense after 9 p.m. on weekends. **WHO** Suave youngsters and hip middle-agesters who value a well-made cocktail, a proper platter of oysters and a good piano player. Some are famous, but Larry keeps 'em on the down low. ◔ ♥ ☼

[Rush Street] 9546 Washington Blvd., Culver City, 310.837.9546, rushstreetculvercity.com. L & D daily, brunch Sat.-Sun. Pub/modern American. Full bar. AE, MC, V. $$ - $$$ **WHY** Food that's much, much better than it has to be, given that it's a tribute to Chicago's Rush Street, a strip known for its bar scene, not fine dining. Order the truffle asiago fries while you peruse the menu. Good happy hour, too. **WHAT** In an enormous, barn-like room in the heart of Culver City, Rush Street serves snazzy cocktails and an eclectic array of dishes, from terrific sandwiches and salads at lunch to an even more varied assortment at dinner: lobster and shrimp egg rolls, falafel sliders, a spinach, shiitake and gorgonzola pizza. At a recent lunch we had the best tortilla soup we've ever eaten, followed by a tangy Asian shrimp salad topped with a half-dozen enormous, impeccably fresh shrimp impaled on lemongrass skewers. There's some real talent in Rush Street's kitchen, but the word is out—the crowds can be considerable. **WHO** Sony Studios foodies and lots of young, sideburned guys in ironic hats. ◔ 📷 🍸

[Sublime Food Lounge] 8631 Washington Blvd., Culver City, 310.287.2093, sublimefoodlounge.com. L & D Tues.-Sat. American. Full bar. MC, V. $ - $$$ **WHY** A loungey little restaurant that's upscale enough to impress a date but casual enough to pop into with friends. **WHAT** The ambience is intimate and friendly. Happy hour is the best time to come: $2 off all wines by the glass and half-off crisp flatbreads, like the one topped with burrata, cippolini onions and guanciale. The menu is modern global comfort food, a mix of small and large plates. Make a beeline for the mac 'n cheese, baked with generous doses of lobster and bacon. **WHO** Young movers and shakers, and locals seeking an improved happy hour. 📖 ☼

[Westside Tavern] **Westside Pavilion, 10850 W. Pico Blvd., Rancho Park, 310.470.1539, westsidetavernla.com. L & D daily. American. Full bar. AE, MC, V. $$ - $$$$ WHY** For a post-movie bite that doesn't involve a food court or corporate chain restaurant. **WHAT** The pub grub from former Whist chef Warren Schwartz—ale-battered fish with tarragon-dill tartar sauce, asparagus salad with burrata—is leaps and bounds above the average mall fare, so we're grateful for this Westside Pavilion hangout. Great craft beer list; tempting but overpriced cocktails for such a casual joint. **WHO** Friends and families sporting butter popcorn lip gloss and Nordstrom shopping bags.

[X-Bar] **Hyatt Regency Century Plaza, 2025 Avenue of the Stars, Century City, 310.551.3332, xbarla.com. D Mon.-Sat. until 2 a.m. Modern American. Full bar. AE, MC, V. $$ - $$$ WHY** Because mall shopping requires constant refueling with mocha-espresso martinis and chile-lime crab cakes. **WHAT** Cocktails with cheesy names like the astrology-inspired Leo and Scorpio (which arrive tableside in the appropriate birthstone color) are actually pretty good, if overpriced and on the sweet side. Garlic fries with chipotle aioli will come to the rescue to temper the sweetness. A pleasant spot for a Century City drinks-and-hors d'oeuvres rendezvous. **WHO** Shoppers and CAA agents who have discovered this gorgeous open-air outdoor patio, as well as out-of-towners convinced that all L.A. bars are required to have the same slick designer with a penchant for white-on-white. ☺ ♥ ☼

WEST OF THE 405

[Bar Pintxo] **109 Santa Monica Blvd., Santa Monica, 310.458.2012, barpintxo.com. L Sat.-Sun., D nightly. Wine bar/Spanish. Beer & wine. AE, MC, V. $ - $$ WHY** Quick, authentic and California-inspired tapas, including jamón serrano, served until midnight. **WHAT** This New York shotgun-style bar has tapas lined up behind a counter up front, a side-walk "counter" and a half dozen bar tables in back for a delicious—though pricey—snack and glass of vino. **WHO** Fans of chef/owner Joe Miller who don't want the commitment of a full meal at Joe's; couples out for a glass of wine and a light bite after a movie in an area dominated by louder pubs and bars. ☺ ☼

[Bar Toscana] **11633 San Vicente Blvd., Brentwood, 310.820.2448, toscanabrentwood.com. Nightly. Italian. Full bar. MC, V. $ - $$$ WHY** Because people need somewhere to drink in Brentwood. **WHAT** Situated

---

🍃 VEGETARIAN ☺ KID FRIENDLY ☼ PATIO DINING 🚗 DELIVERY 🏛 PRIVATE PARTY next to longstanding Italian restaurant Toscana, this swank, nominally Italian bar goes heavy on the Amaro, Cynar, Campari and Fernet. The cocktails are a few bucks more expensive than they deserve to be, but the décor is pretty and clever. Suitable for a happy-hour cocktail, especially if you have an expense account. **WHO** Well-off folks who live or work within a two-mile radius, including women who carry handbags that cost more than a normal person's rent. ♥

[Copa D'Oro] **217 Broadway, Santa Monica, 310.576.3030, copadoro. com. Nightly from 5:30 p.m. American. Full bar. AE, MC, V. $$** **WHY** For cocktails you won't find at the corner bar. **WHAT** Cocktail guru Vincenzo Marianella's Promenade-adjacent lounge feels like a cozy Manhattan bar, thanks to its weathered brick walls, French-mod leather wingbacks, well-coiffed bartenders and big-city prices. If you want to spend $12 for a gin and tonic here, that's your business, but the smart money's on such concoctions as the Smoke of Scotland (two Scotches, dry vermouth and elderflower liqueur) and the Emerald (gin, elderflower liqueur, lemon juice, black grapes and sage). Add very good paninis and shareable dips, and you've got a well-balanced meal, at least in some circles. **WHO** The young and the restless. ☺

[Daily Pint] **2310 Pico Blvd., Santa Monica, 310.450.7631, thedailypint.net. Mon.- Fri. from 2 p.m., Sat. & Sun from 11 a.m. Pub. Full bar. AE, MC, V. $$ WHY** At least two cask-conditioned "real" ale firkins always on tap and what has to be the largest Scotch collection in California. **WHAT** This dark, tattered bar hardly looks like much—until you discover its hundreds of interesting beers and whiskeys. The cask ales, typically from San Diego breweries, vary weekly, and the fantastic house-made potato chips go down just as easy. **WHO** Regulars who look as tired as the barstools, home brewers after a club meeting, and college students pretending that they always spring for good beer. ☺

[Father's Office] 🏠 **1018 Montana Ave., Santa Monica, 310.736.2224, fathersoffice.com. L Sat.-Sun., D nightly. Pub/American. Beer & wine. AE, MC, V. $$ WHY** A chance to decide for yourself whether this is the best burger in America. **WHAT** When Sang Yoon, formerly chef at Michael's, said goodbye to haute cuisine to open a pub, he set about creating a world-class hamburger. It's a rare, dry-aged beef patty topped with Maytag blue cheese, smoked applewood bacon and caramelized onions—and don't even think about asking for substitutions. The dark, shotgun bar has only a few bistro tables, and even with the larger branch in Culver City, the line's often out the door. The ever-changing selection of seasonal boutique beers is worth waiting for, but the over-21 rule is strictly enforced, so leave the kids at home. **WHO** Beer and burger aficionados.

[Finn McCool's] **2702 Main St., Santa Monica, 310.452.1734, finnm-ccoolsirishpub.com. L & D daily. Pub/Irish. Full bar. AE, MC, V. $$**

WHY For a fantastic old carved wooden bar from Ireland, Guinness, good Irish appetizers (try the mini Yorkshire puddings) and, on Sunday afternoon, musicians playing Irish tunes around an old wooden table, just like in Galway. **WHAT** The bar gets boisterous late on weekend nights, but at other times this handsome, high-ceilinged pub from L.A.'s best-known Irish chef, Gerri Gilliland, is a surprisingly sweet spot. The extensive menu is tempting, but we'd advise passing on the dinner entrées in favor of the much better appetizers, snacks and desserts. They move a lot of Guinness here, and the deft bartenders are fun to watch. **WHO** Families for weekend lunches; mates meeting for a few pints and a meal in the evening. ☺ ☺

[Hotel Shangri-La] **1301 Ocean Ave., Santa Monica, 310.394.2791, shangrila-hotel.com. B, L & D daily. American. Full bar. AE, MC, V. $$ - $$$$ WHY** Classic cocktails in goblets and vintage ship's-deck views of palm trees and the Pacific. **WHAT** This streamline moderne boutique hotel was redone to within an inch of its 1939 glamour, yet it retains its quiet, hideaway feel. The cocktail menu reflects the era—old fashioneds, Singapore slings—while the food is contemporary and local: goat cheese–stuffed dates with smoked almond pesto, short rib or lobster sliders, grilled flatbreads topped with ingredients from the farmers' market, right outside the door. Take advantage of the weeknight happy hour ($5 wines, 30% off well drinks) in one of four chic spaces, including a rooftop patio that really does feel like a ship's deck. **WHO** Men in jeans, women in stilettos and anyone with a yen to be Nick or Nora Charles. ♥ ☼

[Library Alehouse] **2911 Main St., Santa Monica, 310.314.4855, libraryalehouse.com. L & D daily until 11 p.m. Pub/American. Beer & wine. AE, MC, V. $$ WHY** For dozens of beers on tap, mainly Californian, Belgian and German brews, which you can try in four-ounce, five-shot sample flights. **WHAT** This aptly named bar has a polished professor vibe with better-than-average bar food: chipotle shrimp quesadillas, a solid build-your-own beef, turkey, veggie or salmon burger, and salmon fish 'n chips that tastes healthier than its cod cousin. The outdoor patio is quite appealing, but you'll get better service if you can snag a seat at the bar. **WHO** Beer-loving regulars at the bar and Santa Monica families on the outdoor patio. ☺ ♪ ☼

[On the Waterfront Café] **205 Ocean Front Walk, Venice, 310.392.0322, waterfrontcafe.com. L & D daily, brunch Sat.-Sun. German/ American. Beer & wine. AE, MC, V. $ - $$ WHY** Good German brats, fat pretzels and German beer on tap, including a hefeweizen that goes down very well on a sunny beach afternoon while the Boardwalk parade flows by. **WHAT** A refreshing break from the generic sidewalk cafés that line the Boardwalk, this German beer garden has decent food and convivial picnic-table seating. Fun for a weekend lunch or weekday sunset happy hour. **WHO** An amusing mix of scruffy local

---

🍃 VEGETARIAN ☺ KID FRIENDLY ☼ PATIO DINING � DELIVERY 🎩 PRIVATE PARTY

regulars and tourists, all of whom seem happy all the time; sometimes after a few Erdingers on tap they can get *really* happy. ▦ ☼

[Primitivo Wine Bistro] **1025 Abbot Kinney Blvd., Venice, 310.396.5353, primitivowinebistro.com. D nightly. Wine bar/Mediterranean. Beer & wine. AE, MC, V. $$ - $$$ WHY** For wine-friendly and delicious small dishes, such as paella, asparagus risotto with lemon and parmesan, and roasted salmon with couscous, plus satisfying true tapas like marinated olives and cured meats. **WHAT** Is it a set design or tapas bar? You be the judge. But first you'll have to land one of the small wooden tables in the high-ceilinged space that's filled with columns, old stained-glass church windows and acres of linen drapes. The by-the-glass collection of wines is extensive, if rather costly. **WHO** Lots of beautiful Venice folk. ♥

[Steingarten] **10543 W. Pico Blvd., West L.A., 310.441.0441, steingartenla.com. L & D daily (to 1 a.m. Thurs.-Sat.). German/pub. Full bar. MC, V. $$ WHY** Your friendly, neighborhood German beer hall, now with a stellar beer list and an array of snazzy sausages. **WHAT** Every neighborhood should have a place like this. Large, friendly and unpretentious, it's equally comfortable for highbrow beer geeks and families with young children. In warm weather, the patio is the perfect spot for a warm pretzel, a cone of crisp fries and a spicy Hungarian sausage (or maybe a platter of bock, brat and duck-and-bacon wurst), all of which should be accompanied by a rare Trappist ale or a hearty imperial stout. **WHO** Craft beer addicts, westsiders desperate for a good happy hour, neighborhood families, Fox execs and cubicle workers sneaking a lunchtime beer. ☉ ☺ ☼

[Venice Beach Wines] **529 Rose Ave., Venice, 310.606.2529, venicebeachwines.com. L & D daily. Wine bar/Italian. Beer & wine. AE, MC, V. $ WHY** A lovely covered sidewalk patio, worthy wines to drink here or take home, and mighty fine panini. **WHAT** Part wine shop and part outdoor café, this place was cleverly designed to keep the indoors temperature-controlled for the wine while having that indoor-outdoor flow so essential to Venice living. The wine-by-the-glass list is relatively short but deeply appealing: an international collection of lesser-known choices at fair prices, including some for under $10. To accompany your Portuguese Vale de Torre are cheeses, charcuterie, salads and panini, all of which are good enough to attract lunchtime folks who are drinking Pellegrino instead of Pinot. **WHO** Mostly locals who can walk here for a drink and a panini. ♪ ☼

[Waterloo & City] **12517 Washington Blvd., Mar Vista, 310.391.4222, waterlooandcity.com. D nightly. Modern American. Full bar. AE, MC, V. $$ - $$$ WHY** Tasty cocktails, a comfortable bar and a menu with something for everyone. **WHAT** The name is a tribute to owner/chef Brendan Collins's home country, England, but his cooking is not English—his training is French, and his experience includes a long stint at Mélisse. Now, in the 1960s building that long housed the Crest family restaurant, he's created a relaxed pub, where you can nurse a beer at the bar, sample from the good list of $10 cocktails and share a crisp-crusted pizza with a friend, or have a full-fledged dinner or weekend brunch. Good food, creative drinks, reasonable prices and free parking have made it a hit. **WHO** An amusing mix, from young hipsters at the communal table, to middle-aged businesspeople checking each other out, to senior couples having a date night. ☉ ♪ ☼

[The Yard] 119 Broadway, Santa Monica, 310.395.6037, theyardsm. com. D nightly, brunch Sat.-Sun. Pub/American. Full bar. AE, MC, V. $$ - $$$ **WHY** Funky wine bar meets art gallery space, with a laid-back neighborhood pub vibe and a terrific happy-hour menu. **WHAT** The vibe is great, with rotating art on the walls, a lounge-type atmosphere and a friendly staff. We're happy to report that the once-dismal beer list has improved, and we still like the classic cocktails (margaritas, cosmos). The food is better than the average bar fare: pulled-pork sandwiches, grilled farmers' market corn, cheeses from Andrew Steiner. Savvy snackers come between 5 and 7 for the happy hour—everything tastes better at $5 to $6 a pop. **WHO** Young and artsy. ☉ ⌨

[Ye Olde King's Head] 🏛 116 Santa Monica Blvd., Santa Monica, 310.451.1402, yeoldekingshead.com. B, L & D daily. Pub/English. Full bar. AE, MC, V. $$ - $$$ **WHY** Fresh beer, tasty English pub fare and a gregarious and interesting crowd. **WHAT** L.A.'s best-known pub has grown over the decades, now boasting two pub rooms and a dining room stretching between the Promenade and the shore. It's touristy as hell, but it's saved by the quality of food and the 20-some beers on tap. Try the sausage rolls, vegetable samosa, fish 'n chips or shepherd's pie. **WHO** College students and tourists (including visitors from England) in the busier pub side, quieter conversationalists in the "snug," and fish-'n-chips-eating families in the dining room. ☉ ☺

SOUTH BAY TO SOUTH L.A.

[4th Street Vine] 2142 E. 4th St., Long Beach, 562.343.5463, 4thstreetvine.com. Mon.-Fri. from 5 p.m., Sat.-Sun. from 2 p.m. Wine bar. Beer & wine. AE, MC, V. $ - $$ **WHY** Generous pours of good, modestly priced wines in a very cool Retro Row shop, with $3 glasses on Thursdays and often-terrific live music. **WHAT** Almost every afternoon and evening, bartender Evan mans the small, living-room-like wine bar in back of the store, and regulars stop in to ask him what he's pouring and to hear what he's playing on the stereo. For just $12, he'll pour you a taste of four wines and give you a smart, succinct explanation of each. **WHO** Pre-dinner wine sippers and people coming out of the Art Theater across the street, looking for a place to sip and talk. ⌨ 🏛

🌿 VEGETARIAN ☉ KID FRIENDLY ☼ PATIO DINING 🚙 DELIVERY 🏛 PRIVATE PARTY

[Bottle Room] **6741 Greenleaf Ave., Whittier, 562.696.8000, thebottleroombar.com. L & D daily. American/pub. Beer & wine. AE, MC, V. $$ WHY** A smart selection of beer and wine and a very good burger. **WHAT** The Bottle Room is a gastropub in the truest sense, a casual place where classics are tweaked and craft beers and small-batch wines flow. The restaurant's signature burger follows the Father's Office mold with sweet onion relish, arugula and blue and Swiss cheeses. In the right season, there might be a nice heirloom tomato salad with barbecued prawns or baby beets topped with crumbles of feta and golden raisins. There are strong flatbreads and sandwiches, too, but ultimately it all falls back on the burger. **WHO** Whittier locals just off work and neighbors in for a leisurely drink. ☺

[Congregation Ale House] **201 E. Broadway Ave., Long Beach, 562.432.2337, congregationalehouse.com. L & D daily. American/pub. Beer & wine. AE, MC, V. $$ WHY** Lively suds and modernized pub grub. **WHAT** Congregation may take its religious shtick too far — stained glass windows, Catholic school uniforms, Monday "mass" — but it's one of Long Beach's essential beer bars, with a commendable list of Belgian and craft brews. The menu presents done-up pub classics like a pork and goat cheese sausage sandwich, grilled rib-eye burger and a fresh pretzel with Chimay cheese. Just leave room for more beer. **WHO** Beer-swillers from all over Long Beach. ☺

[Friends of the Vine] **221 Ave. Del Norte, Redondo Beach, 310.792.5940, friendsofthevine.net. D Tues.-Sat. Wine bar. Beer & wine. AE, MC, V. $ - $$ WHY** A friendly, neighborly spot to sample from a large list of wines. **WHAT** In the late afternoon, this rambling, somewhat cluttered wine shop turns into a lively wine bar, and it almost feels like a party in a friend's house. Owners Fred and Tracy play their favorite CDs and pour wine by the glass or the flight, or you can buy a bottle, pay a modest corkage, and drink it here. Accompaniments include a generous cheese plate, charcuterie and a few other snacks. **WHO** PV and south Redondo locals meeting friends for a drink and a cheese plate before moving elsewhere for dinner.

[Hudson House Bar] **514 N. Pacific Coast Hwy., Redondo Beach, 310.798.9183, hudsonhousebar.com. D nightly, L Sat.-Sun. Pub/American. Full bar. Cash only. $ - $$ WHY** A gastropub without inflated prices and a good happy hour weekdays from 5 to 7 p.m. **WHAT** We come here for the sharable bar bites, especially the crispy beer-batter-fried cauliflower and $4 buckets of the same fantastic sweet potato and French fries served at Beechwood (same chef/owners), as well as heartier fare like the chicken meatball sandwich with a spicy kick. If there's a fault, it's been inconsistency on repeat visits. But with more than 50 beers and such great food prices, it's hard to complain. Don't skip the house-made ice cream sandwiches. **WHO** Neighborhood folks stopping by for a low-key beer and a nosh. ☺ 📷

[Manhattan Beach Post] 1142 Manhattan Ave., Manhattan Beach, 310.545.5405, eatmbpost.com. D nightly. Modern American. Full bar. AE, MC, V. $$$ **WHY** A parade of cocktail-friendly small plates with a beach breeze. **WHAT** David LeFevre's first project since his departure from the Water Grill, this so-called "social house" is in the oceanfront spot once occupied by the Post Office. Not everything wows or works, but there are some very good dishes. The bacon-cheddar buttermilk biscuits are an essential, served with maple butter as light as whipped cream. Yellow cauliflower is roasted with sultanas, mint, pine nuts and caper berries, while perfect thick-cut fries are as wide as two-by-fours. An Asian influence guides the Vietnamese-style caramel pork jowl, rich and sweet and cut nicely by a papaya salad. Cocktails tweak the classics, like the Manhattan Avenue: Sazerac rye, vanilla, caramel and bacon. **WHO** Beach bodies and South Bay socializers.

[Nelson's] 🏛 Terranea Resort, 6610 Palos Verdes Dr. South, Palos Verdes, 310.265.2836, terranea.com. L & D daily. American. Full bar. AE, MC, V. $$ - $$$ **WHY** Solid pub fare and a good bar with reasonable prices, given the oh-wow setting. **WHAT** You can hardly do better at sunset than to score an outdoor picnic table, with or without your dog, at this casual café-bar on what appears to be the westernmost tip of the United States. Named for the fictional Mike Nelson of *Sea Hunt* fame (it was filmed on the coves below), Nelson's is an unpretentious place in a fancy resort, with a respectable clam chowder, a lush pulled-pork sandwich, a great kids' menu and a swell bar. Inside are TVs for sports and windows for views; outside are teak tables, fire pits and more ocean than you can imagine. **WHO** Hotel guests and PV locals. ☺ ✿

[The Pike] 1836 E. 4th St., Long Beach, 562.437.4453, pikelongbeach. com. L & D daily, B Sat.-Sun. American. Full bar. AE, MC, V. $ - $$ **WHY** A plate of retro charm and a side of rock 'n roll. **WHAT** A key in the rise of Retro Row—the vintage-loving stretch of 4th Street famous for its pin-up poses and deadstock designs—the Pike is owned by former Social Distortion drummer Chris Reece. It's themed around the icons of lost Long Beach—namely the long-gone Pike amusement park. When DJs aren't spinning everything from Lee Hazlewood to Os Mutantes, it becomes more of a restaurant, with quality sandwiches, burgers, pastas and seafood. Fish 'n chips is the essential dish, a basket of golden, beer-battered sole that's perfect with a draft ale. **WHO** A well-inked crowd hungry for simple cocktails—lobster and otherwise. ☺ ♪

[Simmzy's] 229 Manhattan Beach Blvd., Manhattan Beach, 310.546.1201, simmzys.com. L & D daily. Pub/American. Beer & wine. AE, MC, V. $ - $$ **WHY** An open-air beach bar with good food and drink. **WHAT** Not much more than a single room opening onto a street patio, this tiny gastropub has two dozen really good rotating tap beers, gobs of wine by the glass and an Angus burger with sweet smoked onions, cheddar, and garlic aioli that rocks. Don't skip the fries. ✿

Breakfast + Lunch

Fancy restaurants are all well and good, but nothing makes most of us happier than a simple café that specializes in breakfast. Except perhaps a place that makes a really great lunchtime salad, panini or pastrami on rye.

[ESSENTIALLY L.A.]

Auntie Em's Kitchen, Eagle Rock (PAGE 208)
BLD, Beverly/Third (PAGE 204)
Coast, Shutters Hotel, Santa Monica (PAGE 222)
Euro Pane, Pasadena (PAGE 213)
Figtree's Café, Venice (PAGE 223)
Fisherman's Outlet, Downtown (PAGE 209)
Homegirl Café, Chinatown (PAGE 210)
Huckleberry, Santa Monica (PAGE 223)
Hugo's, West Hollywood (PAGE 206)
John O'Groats, Rancho Park (PAGE 220)
Jongewaard's Bake N Broil, Long Beach (PAGE 226)
Julienne, San Marino (PAGE 214)
Langer's Deli, Downtown (PAGE 211)
Marmalade Café, Malibu (PAGE 224)
Mi India Bonita, East L.A. (PAGE 211)
Momed, Beverly Hills (PAGE 221)
Nickel Diner, Downtown (PAGE 212)
North End Caffé, Manhattan Beach (PAGE 227)
Olive & Thyme, Toluca Lake (PAGE 218)
Pie 'n' Burger, Pasadena (PAGE 310)
Studio Café Magazzino, Toluca Lake (PAGE 218)

🏛 ESSENTIALLY L.A. ☺ LATE ♥ ROMANTIC 💲 VALUE 🌙 QUIET ♻ SUSTAINABLE

THE FOLLOWING RESTAURANTS ARE PARTICULARLY
KNOWN FOR BREAKFAST OR BRUNCH:

26 Beach Café, Venice (PAGE 142)

Beachcomber Café, Malibu (PAGE 143)

Bottega Louie, Downtown (PAGE 78)

Brent's Delicatessen, Northridge (PAGE 125)

Café del Rey (brunch), Marina del Rey (PAGE 144)

Campanile (brunch), Miracle Mile (PAGE 54)

Canelé (brunch), Atwater (PAGE 79)

Cliff's Edge (brunch), Silver Lake (PAGE 81)

Delphine, Hollywood (PAGE 57)

Gjelina (brunch), Venice (PAGE 148)

Jar (brunch), Beverly/Third (PAGE 61)

Joe's (brunch), Venice (PAGE 150)

Johnny Reb's, Long Beach (PAGE 168)

The Kettle, Manhattan Beach (PAGE 169)

La Grande Orange, Santa Monica (PAGE 152)

Lamill, Silver Lake (PAGE 86)

La Parrilla, Westlake & Silver Lake (PAGE 86)

Little Dom's, Los Feliz (PAGE 64)

Lotería Grill, Hollywood & Studio City (PAGES 64 & 119)

Mas Malo (brunch), Downtown (PAGE 87)

Pacific Dining Car, Downtown (PAGE 89)

Pann's, Inglewood (PAGE 173)

Petrossian (brunch), West Hollywood (PAGE 68)

Roscoe's House of Chicken & Waffles, Hollywood (PAGE 71)

Rush Street (brunch), Culver City (PAGE 194)

THESE DIM SUM/DUMPLING/NOODLE PLACES ARE
ALSO GREAT FOR LUNCH OR BRUNCH:

888 Seafood, Rowland Heights (PAGE 95)

Din Tai Fung, Arcadia (PAGE 100)

Dumpling House, Arcadia (PAGE 264)

Elite, Monterey Park (PAGE 101)

Empress Pavilion, Chinatown (PAGE 83)

Lunasia, Alhambra (PAGE 105)

Mandarin Noodle House, Monterey Park (PAGE 106)

Ocean Star Seafood, Monterey Park (PAGE 108)

Sea Harbour, Rosemead (PAGE 112)

Supreme Dragon, Rowland Heights (PAGE 113)

VEGETARIAN KID FRIENDLY PATIO DINING DELIVERY PRIVATE PARTY

CENTRAL CITY

[Alcove Café & Bakery] **1929 Hillhurst Ave., Los Feliz, 323.644.0100, alcovecafe.com. B, L & D daily. American. Beer & wine. AE, $$ WHY** Custardy omelets, as well as very good baked goods and a terribly charming patio. **WHAT** Lunch and dinner dishes can be uneven, but you can't go wrong with breakfast and desserts at this order-at-the-counter café with a rambling, greenery-lined front patio and a famed desk inside in which people leave little notes—a neighborhood literary happening in progress. **WHO** Musicians, costume designers, blind-daters and Los Feliz women sporting subtle tattoos and Kingsley-clad preschoolers. ☺ ♥ ▦ ✿ ✎ ☺ ✿

[Black Cat Bakery & Café] **519 S. Fairfax Ave., Fairfax District, 323.932.1500, blackcatla.com. B & L daily. American. No booze. AE, MC, V. $ - $$ WHY** Creative breakfasts, lunches and even occasional dinners, paired with Homeboy breads. **WHAT** More than a bakery, Fairfax's Black Cat has a freshened-up vintage café look and an evolving menu with unusual selections like the terrific farro bibimbap deeply flavored with shiitake mushrooms, burrata and a fried egg, pig trotter eggs Benedict, multigrain pancakes and flavorful Thai shrimp salad. Lots of sidewalk tables and all-day breakfast menu made the café instantly popular on weekends. **WHO** Screenwriters, office workers, LACMA-goers, families on weekends. ☺ ✿

[BLD] 🏛 **7450 Beverly Blvd., Beverly/Third, 323.930.9744, bldrestaurant. com. B, L & D daily. American. Beer & wine. AE, MC, V. $$ - $$$ WHY** Fried-egg sandwich (made with gruyère, sourdough and thick-cut Nueske bacon), frittata with bacon-wrapped asparagus, big salads, good burgers, great cheese platter, gingerbread pudding with vanilla ice cream, and more such modern classics. **WHAT** An upscale coffee shop for the goat-cheese-and-mizzuna crowd, BLD is run by star chefs Neal and Amy Fraser, who are soon to open a fancy spot in the old St. Vibiana's Cathedral. Short for "Breakfast, Lunch and Dinner," BLD turns out everything from ricotta-blueberry pancakes to house-cured salmon salads. It's hip but not too trendy, busy but not too noisy, upscale but not overpriced. Expect a long wait for weekend brunch. **WHO** Miracle Mile office workers, low-key industry types, Hancock Park moms out for lunch. ▧ ☺

[Bloom Café] **5544 W. Pico Blvd., Mid-City, 323.934.6900, bloomcafe. com. B, L & D daily. Modern American. BYOB (no corkage). AE, MC, V. $ - $$ WHY** Organic eggs are used in breakfast dishes like poached eggs with goat cheese and smoked bacon. There are plenty of vegetarian choices, and lunches include grass-fed beef burgers and free-range chicken and apple salad. **WHAT** This zippy, modern café on an up-and-coming stretch of Pico draws neighborhood faithfuls for breakfasts with a healthy touch. An adjacent pizzeria turns out creative pies at dinner. Delivery in the area. ▦ ✿ ▧ ☺ 🚗

[Bricks & Scones] 403 N. Larchmont Blvd., Hancock Park, 323.463.0811, bricksandscones.com. B, L & D daily. American. No booze. AE, MC, V. $ **WHY** House-baked pastries, good sandwiches, Intelligentsia coffee, Lupicia teas and tomb-like quiet for working. **WHAT** With a no-talking upstairs study area and a quiet downstairs lounge, plus a leafy patio with plenty of shade umbrellas and no restriction on chatting, Bricks & Scones appeals to serious students and screenwriters as well as ladies who lunch and have afternoon tea. We aren't partial to the heavy, salty scones that everyone seems to adore, but the muffins and sandwiches are quite good (try the mango curried chicken salad sandwich). **WHO** Laptop-toters and people fresh from yoga. 🌿🥪☼

[Du-par's] Farmers Market, 6333 W. 3rd St., Fairfax District, 323.933.8446, du-pars.com. B, L & D 24 hours daily. American. No booze. AE, MC, V. $ - $$ **WHY** Nostalgic charm for natives, and decent coffee-shop fare at 3 a.m. **WHAT** L.A.'s original Du-par's still has the red Naugahyde booths but is brighter and prettier after an overhaul a few years back. Seen-it-all waitresses in gingham-trimmed uniforms and tiny white caps deliver huge (if overcooked) omelets, good (if not as good as in our childhoods) french toast, lovely pancakes and steaming pot pies. Outside is a patio that looks like a French sidewalk café; would that the lukewarm coffee was as good as in France. Oh well, the cooking is satisfying — and Du-par's is open 24/7. **WHO** Seniors, high-school kids, screenwriters on a budget. ☺ 🚚☺☼

[Ed's Coffee Shop] 460 N. Robertson Blvd., West Hollywood, 310.659.8625. B & L Mon.-Sat. American. No booze. MC, V. $ **WHY** First-rate short-order cooking served in a lunch-counter diner that's older than anyone admits to being in WeHo. **WHAT** With its black-and-white linoleum floor and retro feel, this coffee shop seems more suited to the Midwest than West Hollywood. But it's beloved by locals for that old-time atmosphere (and service), as well as the up-dated diner fare: great huevos rancheros, omelets, blueberry pancakes, fresh-spinach quesadillas and tuna melts. **WHO** Some of L.A.'s best chefs, who just want a good plate of eggs and turkey sausage. 🚚🥪☼

[Food + Lab] 7253 Santa Monica Blvd., West Hollywood, 323.851.7120, foodlabcatering.com. B, L & D daily. American/Austrian. No booze. AE, MC, V. $ - $$ **WHY** Fantastic sandwiches, excellent espresso, lovely patios both front and back, and all sorts of good food to take home and pretend you made. **WHAT** Nino Linsmayer and his chef mom, Esther, have a devout following for their sandwiches (Austrian meatloaf, prosciutto with ricotta and honey, veggie-pesto), salads, soups and breakfast dishes, made with organic ingredients. They're Austrian, which explains the Viennese coffee and strudels. Success has brought a new location in Silver Lake. **WHO** Mostly neighborhood locals, including people who actually walk here. 🌿🥪☼

+ Lunch

🥪 **VEGETARIAN** ☺ **KID FRIENDLY** ☼ **PATIO DINING** 🚚 **DELIVERY** 🍴 **PRIVATE PARTY**

[Grub] 911 N. Seward St., Hollywood, 323.461.3663, grub-la.com. B Sat.-Sun., L & D daily. American. No booze. MC, V. $ - $$ **WHY** If you work in Hollywood, this is a fine spot for lunch. **WHAT** Lunch—or weekend breakfast—at a table in the walled patio behind this long, narrow bungalow is a fine thing indeed, and it's almost as nice sitting inside. Chef Betty Fraser had her Hollywood moment on *Top Chef*, and now she's back to making tasty Peruvian saltado, rosemary-steak salad, a hearty beet salad and her beloved "After School Special," a grilled-cheese sandwich with a cup of tomato soup. **WHO** Below-the-line folks from places like Glen Glenn and LaserPacific.

[Hugo's] 8401 Santa Monica Blvd., West Hollywood, 323.654.3993, hugosrestaurant.com. B, L & D daily, brunch Sat.-Sun. Californian. Full bar. AE, MC, V. $$ **WHY** Pasta Mama and Pasta Papa, two of the most addictive pasta-egg scrambles imaginable. **WHAT** Hugo's serves dinner, and it's a good dinner, but what brings the many regulars back are the breakfasts and brunches. Organic, generally lowfat ingredients are turned into terrific scrambles, pancakes, vegan breads and, for true brunch sybarites, a tasty but potent cocktail called the Mangorita. Lunchtime brings things like hummus wraps, mac 'n cheese and turkey burgers. A modern L.A. classic with consistently good food. **WHO** An exceptionally handsome crowd, including lots of once-a-week regulars and some famous faces.

[The Mercantile] 6600 W. Sunset Blvd., Hollywood, 323.962.8202, themercantilela.com. L & D daily, brunch Sat.-Sun. French. Beer & wine. AE, MC, V. $$ **WHY** French charm and very good café cuisine. **WHAT** Yes, it's owned by serial restaurateur George Abou-Daoud, but nonetheless we love this order-at-the-counter café, wine bar and gourmet market (its adjacent dinner restaurant, the District, ain't bad either). High ceilings, vintage fixtures, sidewalk tables and nice people make the experience enjoyable, and the kitchen turns out wonderful sandwiches (try the crispy pork belly with napa cabbage, jalapeño, carrots, cilantro and a spicy-sweet sauce), perfect French salads and lovely tarts and macarons. **WHO** Studio folks and creative types who can afford a $13 sandwich.

[Milk] 7290 Beverly Blvd., Beverly/Third, 323.939.6455, themilkshop. com. B, L & D daily. American. No booze. MC, V. $ **WHY** The *media noche* Cuban sandwich is great, and there's also an unusual soba shrimp salad, burgers and a kids' menu, so the critters can get something solid before they start in on the ice cream. **WHAT** It's not all about desserts at this stylish bakery and café—eat a proper sandwich and *then* try an ice cream creation, or pick up lunch to take back to the office. **WHO** Hip Hancock Park families and Miracle Mile office workers.

[Nite Moon Café] Golden Bridge Yoga Center, 1357 N. Highland Ave., Hollywood, 323.988.4052, goldenbridgeyoga.com. B & L daily, D

Mon.-Thurs. Vegetarian. No booze. AE, MC, V. $ **WHY** The terrific vegan BLT could make a person forsake meat, while the salad bar offers out-of-the-ordinary choices such as roasted cauliflower. The truly virtuous can order mung beans and rice. Hot tip: Magical chocolates sold in the herb shop are said to improve skin tone and overall health. **WHAT** It's actually possible to find inner peace while eating a vegan brownie at this café inside the cavernous Golden Bridge Yoga Center. Order cafeteria-style and then sit at long communal tables to enjoy your tasty vegetarian fare. **WHO** Pregnant ladies ravenous after prenatal yoga class, turbaned Sikhs, hungry yogis glowing from within. 🖼🌀🦪☺

[Olio Pizzeria] **8075 W. 3rd St., Beverly/Third, 323.930.9490, pizzeriaolio.com. L & D daily, brunch Sat.-Sun. Pizzeria/Italian. No booze. AE, MC, V. $ - $$ WHY** Pizzas as good as Mozza's, only less expensive and with less hoopla surrounding them. **WHAT** Bradford Kent is an obsessive fellow, prone to toss out dough that he feels isn't just right, and refusing to serve a pizza that is the slightest bit overcooked. Given the tendency toward overly blackened crusts these days, that alone endears him to us. Everything in this simple corner café is touched by the wood oven, from the superb Naples-style pizzas (try the Margherita Plus with burrata) to the addictive breakfast bialys with the roasted shishito peppers. When they get their wine license and add sidewalk tables, it'll be even better. **WHO** Neighbors stopping in for a bialy or pizza to take our or a quiet meal at the café. 🖼🌀🦪☺

[Shaky Alibi] **7401 Beverly Blvd., Beverly/Third, 323.938-5282, shaky-alibi.com . B & L daily, D Fri.-Sat. Belgian. No booze. AE, MC, V. $ WHY** To indulge in the crunchy, sweet, chewy waffles that put Liège, Belgium on the snack-food map. **WHAT** Forget what you think you know about waffles. These are Liège waffles, which are crisp, fat, irregularly edged confections made with yeast dough containing chunky pearl sugar, which caramelizes in the heat of the waffle iron. The savory waffles make crisp sandwiches with sliced meats and cheese; the sweet ones are vehicles for all sorts of indulgent toppings. Try them with *speculoos*, a Belgian spread made from pulverized graham crackers. **WHO** Neighbors and families with lucky, spoiled children. 🦪☺☼

[Simplethings Sandwich & Pie Shop] **8310 W. 3rd St., Beverly/Third, 323.592.3390, simplethingsrestaurant.com. B Sat.-Sun., L & D daily. American. No booze. AE, MC, V. $ - $$ WHY** Mini pies, medium pies, maxi pies.... **WHAT** A sunny yellow-and-white-striped color scheme complements a case full of pies at this perky café with plenty of room for sit-down diners. Salads, sandwiches (pulled barbecue chicken on pretzel bread), main dish pot pies (chicken curry) and side dishes (roasted brussels sprouts) are more than just excuses on the way to dessert. Cutie pies, at $2.50, are just right for one person, while a simple pie ($5.50) can be shared by two or three. Check the pie schedule to find out which days flavors like peanut butter chocolate, key

🦪 VEGETARIAN ☺ KID FRIENDLY ☼ PATIO DINING 🚐 DELIVERY 🎩 PRIVATE PARTY

lime, blueberry, apple and salted caramel are offered. Our only wish? More fruit flavors. **WHO** Who doesn't love pie? ☺ ☼

[Square One] 4854 Fountain Ave., East Hollywood, 323.661.1109, squareonedining.com. B & L daily. American. No booze. AE, MC, V. $ - $$ **WHY** It's hard to decide between farm-fresh egg dishes with chorizo, eggs Benedict with smoked salmon, banana-caramel french toast and creative lunchtime sandwiches and salads, so you'll have to return often—as we do—to try them all. **WHAT** This sunny diner with a large walled patio cooks up some of the best breakfasts on the eastside, using top-quality ingredients and farmers' market produce. A great spot that is blessedly quiet during the week. **WHO** Los Feliz locals, including families with really cute babies. ♪ ▨ ☺ ☼

[Tender Greens Hollywood] 6290 Sunset Blvd., Hollywood, 323.382.0380, tendergreensfood.com. L & D daily. American. Beer & wine. AE, MC, V. $$ **WHY** Big salads of local provenance, and a sunny patio on which to enjoy them. **WHAT** This always-busy outpost of the upscale cafeteria is notable for its 1,200-square-foot patio in back, as well as its salads (grilled chicken Cobb; prawns with chorizo, lima beans, arugula, butter lettuce and lemon vinaigrette) and sandwiches. Most of the produce comes from Southern California farms, most of it is organic, and the meat, poultry and seafood are raised/caught sustainably. Given all that, the prices are reasonable—although the salads are sometimes mysteriously bland. **WHO** ArcLight moviegoers, Hollywood moms and PAs picking up lunch for the writers' room. ☼ ▨ ☼

[The Trails] 2333 Fern Dell Dr., Los Feliz, 323.871.2102, thetrailslosfeliz.com. B & L Tues.-Sun. American/Vegetarian. No booze. Cash only. $ **WHY** Fresh, simple café fare is served at picnic tables under the pine trees in Fern Dell, making it paradise for people (and their dogs) returning from a long hike. Good vegetarian choices. **WHAT** Had a long hike or a hard day cutting your student film at neighboring AFI? Then head to Trails to refuel with a tasty avocado sandwich and a fresh lemonade or, even better, a piece of apple pie with Fosselman's ice cream. A little bit of country in the heart of the city. **WHO** Hikers, dogs, kids, AFI folks and dessert lovers. ♪ ▨ ☺ ☼

EASTSIDE

[Auntie Em's Kitchen] 🏛 4616 Eagle Rock Blvd., Eagle Rock, 323.255.0800, auntieemskitchen.com. B & L daily, early D Mon.-Fri. Modern American. No booze. AE, MC, V. $ - $$ **WHY** Open-faced breakfast sandwiches, the grilled steak salad and spectacular cupcakes, scones and brownies. **WHAT** This funky and fetching retro-American roadhouse features delicious modern-diner cooking. For breakfast, try an open-faced egg sandwich topped with bacon, Cajun turkey sausage or portobello mushroom and roasted red peppers. For lunch, the tuna salad sandwich and the grilled-steak salad are standouts. The home-made baked goods are all fab, especially the huge chocolate cupcakes. **WHO** Eagle Rock hipsters, from Oxy professors to tattooed Highland Park performance artists. 🛍️☺️☼

[Blue Star] **2200 15th St., Vernon, 213.627.2022, bluestarrocksdtla. com. B & L Mon.-Sat. Modern American. Beer & wine. AE, MC, V. $ - $$ WHY** A great tuna sandwich, fresh salads, a huge enclosed patio, a swell jukebox and a relaxed, hang-out-as-long-as-you-like vibe. **WHAT** Surely the coolest secret spot Downtown, Blue Star sits on the edge of the scrap-metal yards off Alvarado in Vernon—in other words, the last neighborhood you'd expect to find a modern diner serving caprese sandwiches and ahi niçoise salads. It's not open for dinner, which makes it a great place for evening private parties. **WHO** A diverse mix of rag traders (from Guess and other local fashion companies), produce-warehousers, art-lofters and adventurers from further north in Downtown. 📖🛍️☼🏛️

[Café Tropical] **2900 W. Sunset Blvd., Silver Lake, 323.661.8391. B, L & D daily. Cuban/Mexican. No booze. MC, V. $ WHY** Café con leche, fresh-squeezed fruit juices, guava cheese pastry and a hearty Cuban sandwich. **WHAT** Catch a vestige of Silver Lake before it was completely gentrified at this funky Cuban café, which was once filled with actual cigar-smoking refugees. **WHO** A regular and longstanding crowd of bohemians. ☺️☼

[Coffee Table Bistro] **1958 Colorado Blvd., Eagle Rock, 323.255.2200, coffeetablebistro.com. B, L & D daily. American. Beer & wine. AE, MC, V. $ - $$ WHY** Breakfast burritos are a favorite, and the wide selection of Sweet Lady Jane cakes makes a good accompaniment to coffee drinks. **WHAT** Chat or work in this Eagle Rock offshoot of the original Silver Lake screenwriter's paradise. Thanks to the liquor license and adjacent bar and lounge, it's easy to move from coffee to evening entertainment. **WHO** Eagle Rock artists, writers, entrepreneurs and families. 📖☺️

[Fisherman's Outlet] 🏛️ **529 S. Central Ave., Downtown, 213.627.7231, fishermansoutlet.net. B & L Mon.-Sat. Seafood/American. Beer & wine. Cash only. $ - $$ WHY** Very fresh char-broiled fish (yellowfin, mahi mahi, catfish, swordfish) that is not overcooked like it usually is at these kinds of places, served with rice or perfect fries. **WHAT** Don't be put off by the paper plates, concrete picnic tables or crowds—this seafood-market and café has fish better than at many a fancy restaurant. We prefer the char-broiled choices over the fried, which are more generic; the lobster is worth the splurge. Some, though, swear by the fried scallops and sand dabs. **WHO** Working men and families who have been coming here for generations. 📖☺️☼

+ Lunch

🛍️ **VEGETARIAN** ☺️ **KID FRIENDLY** ☼ **PATIO DINING** 🚗 **DELIVERY** 🏛️ **PRIVATE PARTY**

[Food + Lab] **3206 W. Sunset Blvd., Silver Lake, 323.661.2666, foodlabcatering.com. B & L daily. American/Austrian. No booze. AE, MC, V. $ - $$ WHY** European-inspired salads, sandwiches and pastries hit the right spot for Silver Lake. **WHAT** This is the third outpost of Food + Lab in L.A., and diners are digging the imaginative sandwiches and breakfast dishes with subtle references to the owners' native Vienna. At breakfast, try coffee with whipped cream and Belgian waffles, muesli cereal with fruit, or organic eggs with Austrian speck ham. Sandwich winners include prosciutto and fig with ricotta on raisin bread or organic chicken weinerschnitzel with lingonberry chutney. It's open until 8 p.m. for last-minute takeout dinner items.

[Four Café] **2122 1/2 Colorado Blvd., Eagle Rock, 323.550.1988, fourcafe.net. B Sat.-Sun., L & D daily. Modern American. BYOB. MC, V. $ - $$ WHY** Tasty, fairly priced salads, soups, sandwiches and desserts made from vibrantly fresh, organic ingredients, almost all of which come from local producers. Add a great kids' menu and the ability to BYOB, and Eagle Rock's got a hit. **WHAT** Four is a venture of considerable passion by chef Michelle Wilton and her artist husband, Corey Wilton. Michelle's experience at Patina and Sona gave her a grounding in classic cooking and sophisticated presentation, which she's incorporated into a seasonal menu focused on stylishly casual dishes for less than $12. Try any of the robustly flavorful soups (perhaps spicy red lentil), the breakfast egg dishes, the baby spinach salad with crispy pancetta and figs, and the oven-roasted tomato panini. **WHO** Solo diners at the long counter against one wall and families and creative-industry types at the small tables. 📖 ☺

[Homegirl Café] 🏛 **130 W. Bruno St., Chinatown, 213.617.0380, homegirlcafe.org. B & L Mon.-Fri., brunch Sat. Mexican/Californian. No booze. MC, V. $ WHY** Modern Mexican fare with lots of vegetarian choices (tofu chorizo, anyone?)—and eating here supports a fantastic nonprofit. **WHAT** This café/bakery teaches young women who would otherwise be drawn into gang life the restaurant business. It's a bright space with art-for-sale and an open kitchen, which turns out tasty, healthful salads, tacos and breakfast dishes, all at low prices. Tip well! **WHO** City Hall workers, business folks and pierced punks. 📖 ♻ 📖 ☺

[Kim Chuy] **727 N. Broadway, Chinatown, 213.687.7215, kimchuy. com. B, L & D daily. Chinese. No booze. AE, MC, V. $ - $$ WHY** For Chiu Chow noodles and nothing but: egg noodles with sliced pork; beef noodle soup; chow mein with beef, Chinese broccoli and oyster sauce; or, for special occasions, Pork Variety (aka intestines) noodle soup. **WHAT** Richly flavored, sustaining noodle soups and fried noodle and rice dishes from the Chaoshan region of southeastern China are the focus at this plain little Chinatown café. Start your morning with a bowl of egg-noodle soup, and move on at lunchtime to the heartier beef chow mein. 📖 ☺

[La Caridad] **2137 W. Temple St., Westlake, 213.484.0099. B, L & D daily. Cuban. No booze. Cash only. $ WHY** The *media noches* (Cuban sandwiches made on eggy bread that's just a little sweet) just might be the best in the city. **WHAT** This Filipinotown hole-in-the-wall features a Formica countertop and an ancient iron stove where sandwich magic is regularly performed: The classic cubano sandwich is composed of fresh-roasted pork piled on enormous slices of bread with the requisite ham, cheese and pickles. You'll also find fresh squeezed carrot and orange juices and good Cuban coffee from the espresso machine.

[Langer's Deli] **704 S. Alvarado St., Westlake, 213.483.8050, langersdeli.com. B & L Mon.-Sat. Deli. Beer & wine. MC, V. $ - $$ WHY** The best pastrami on rye in Southern California; very good corned beef, too. **WHAT** Langer's is so beloved that the city named the intersection of 7th and Alvarado Langer's Square—and Metrolink put a subway stop right across the street. The subway furthers the happy feeling of a proper New York deli, from the vinyl booths to the chewy rye bread to the dames who serve the chow. But this is no New York pretender—it's an L.A. classic. **WHO** Downtown's Brooks Brothers crowd meets Mid-City seniors and blue-collar folks... a great mix.

[Local] **2943 W. Sunset Blvd., Silver Lake, 323.662.4740, silverlakelocal. com. B & L daily, D Tues.-Sun. Modern American. No booze. AE, MC, V. $ - $$ WHY** A good and indulgent breakfast served until the afternoon—but as befits Silver Lake, not served until 9 a.m. **WHAT** Local does justice to its name—the ingredients are local, the diners all know each other, and the staff is incredibly friendly. For breakfast, try the brioche french toast lathered in butter and powdered sugar; for lunch, consider the curried chicken salad sandwich with fantastic spicy fries. Or opt for the salad bar, complete with every vegetable imaginable and many organic and/or vegan dressings. It may seem pricey, but the portions are huge, so if you share, it's reasonable. **WHO** Every breed of Silver Lake indie kid and an extraordinary number of hungry pregnant women trying to eat healthfully.

[Mi India Bonita] **4731 E. Olympic Blvd., East L.A., 323.267.8505. B & L daily. Mexican. No booze. MC, V. $ WHY** Huevos rancheros, huevos oaxaqueños, tender barbacoa, weekend pozole and everyday albondigas soup, just like you wish your grandmother made. **WHAT** Substantial breakfasts and meaty, nourishing soups are the specialty at this hole-in-the-wall café, where fans get weepy over the quality of the fluffy albondigas, pozole, *cocido de res* (beef) and menudo. Worth a trip.

[Millie's] **3524 W. Sunset Blvd., Silver Lake, 323.664.0404, milliescafe. net. B & L daily. American. No booze. MC, V. $ - $$ WHY** Famous for the Devil's Mess egg dish, but also good for biscuits, gravy and healthier alternatives like spinach, pine nuts and eggs. Try the chipotle grilled

---

VEGETARIAN ◦ KID FRIENDLY ◦ PATIO DINING ◦ DELIVERY ◦ PRIVATE PARTY

cheese at lunch. **WHAT** The tiny Silver Lake diner has been sort of a punk rock commissary for some 25 years and was a real diner for 40 years before that. The history that griddle has seen.... Sit at the counter to kibitz with the colorful fry cooks, or try the small adjacent dining room or sidewalk seating with a bit more breathing room. Note the strict no-cell-phone policy. **WHO** The half of Silver Lake that gets up at noon on weekend mornings and the half that seems to never go to work on weekdays. 🍴🐌☼

[My Taco] 6300 York Blvd., Highland Park, 323.256.2698, my-taco.com. B, L & D daily. Mexican. No booze. MC, V. **$** **WHY** Gut-pleasing Mexican breakfast dishes served all day. Good carne asada, too. **WHAT** Come here for a $5.50 breakfast of huevos rancheros or chorizo and eggs and you won't need lunch. The chilequiles are like nachos that have gone to heaven and, as their reward, got covered in eggs and cheese. If you come for lunch or dinner, try the goat tacos, the barbacoa plate or, if you are a 17-year-old boy who burns calories like a jet burns fuel, the carne asada fries with guacamole. 🍴

[Nickel Diner] 🗄 524 S. Main St., Downtown, 213.623.8301, nickeldiner.com. B & L Tues.-Sun., D Tues.-Sat. American. No booze. AE, MC, V. **$** **WHY** Bacon maple doughnuts. **WHAT** This retro diner at Main and 5th (5th being called "the Nickel" by the tougher locals in this hardscrabble neighborhood) has won local fame for bringing L.A. the bacon doughnut. But that's not the only thing worth eating here. Come for any of the very good breakfast dishes, like the egg scramble with bacon, goat cheese, garlic and spinach, or a lunchtime sandwich or salad, or skip all that and go straight for the chocolate peanut-butter potato-chip layer cake. **WHO** Not nearly as many annoying hipsters as you might think—instead, it's a good cross-section of Downtown residents, workers and explorers. 🍴

[Shekarchi Downtown] 914 S. Hill St., South Park/Fashion District, 213.892.8535, shekarchirestaurant.com. L Mon.-Fri. Middle Eastern/Persian. No booze. AE, MC, V. **$** **WHY** Excellent kebabs (try the *koubideh*, a ground-beef blend), particularly good rice and refreshing yogurt drinks. And they deliver! **WHAT** This very good Iranian lunch place in an historic part of Downtown has a far more fashionable décor than you'd suspect from the outside. It's open on weekdays only and is packed at prime lunch time, so don't be in a big rush. 🍴🚗

[Starry Kitchen] 350 S. Grand Ave., Downtown, 213.617.3474, starrykitchen.com. L Mon.-Fri., D Thurs.-Fri. Asian/Vietnamese. No booze. AE, MC, V. **$** **WHY** Starry Kitchen spices up the Downtown lunch scene with a modern, irreverent approach to Vietnamese-influenced cooking. **WHAT** California Plaza is a little less corporate with the success of freewheeling Starry Kitchen, which started as an underground restaurant in the owner's apartment. You pick a protein (free-range lemongrass chicken, the famed crispy tofu balls, spicy pork belly) and a "vessel" (banh mi sandwich, wrap, salad or rice/veggies), and there's your meal. They serve dinner two nights a week, unless something comes up, so check first. 🖼🥢

SAN GABRIEL VALLEY

[Cham Korean Bistro] 851 Cordova Ave., Pasadena, 626.792.2474, chamkoreanbistro.com. L & D Mon.-Sat. Korean. Beer & wine. AE, MC, V. $ - $$ **WHY** Vibrant classic and modern Korean cooking made with love by do-gooders. **WHAT** Kimmy Song, founder and CEO of !It Jeans in Vernon, wanted to use her success to give back, and because she loves food, she decided to do it by opening a restaurant. The result is a light-filled café manned by incredibly nice people who serve flavorful salads, bibim bap, lettuce wraps and tofu pocket sandwiches to a grateful crowd that's sick of the chain lunch joints in the area (it's just off of Lake). A goodly amount of the profits go to help villages in developing countries, but the food's tasty enough that you don't even need to know that to want to eat here regularly. **WHO** Young Lake Avenue office workers and Pasadena loft-dwellers. 🥢☺

[Dish] 734 Foothill Blvd., La Canada, 818.790.5355, dishbreakfast-lunchanddinner.com. B, L & D daily. American. Full bar. AE, MC, V. $ - $$ **WHY** No-frills home cooking, only you don't have to do the dishes. **WHAT** A handy spot for an all-American breakfast: cornmeal johnny-cakes, applewood-smoked bacon and the usual egg dishes. Lunch brings simple sandwiches, soups and salads. The Americana theme extends to the décor and the Awesome Dish Root Beer Float on the kids' menu. **WHO** Families with kids and empty-nester couples. 🖼🍴☺

[Euro Pane] 🏛 345 E. Colorado Blvd., Pasadena, 626.844.8804. B & L daily. American/French. No booze. MC, V. $ **WHY** Breakfast croissants that are the best for many miles, and fab lunchtime sandwiches: egg salad, chicken salad and an amazing BLAT (bacon, lettuce, avocado and tomato). Excellent coffee, too. **WHAT** Sumi Chang's extraordinary bakeries are also swell places for breakfast and lunch, especially this newer location, with its huge pecan communal table and large patio; the original location (950 E. Colorado Blvd., 626.577.1828) is more utilitarian. The new place has a larger selection of baked goods, including more whole wheat breads, but it also has many of the same dishes as the original, including the legendary egg salad sandwich. **WHO** Pasadena's intelligentsia read their *New Yorkers* at café tables over pains aux chocolats or lunchtime sandwiches. 🥢☼

[Fiore Market Café] 1000 Fremont Ave., South Pasadena, 626.441.2280, fioremarketcafe.com. L & D Mon.-Sat. American. No booze. MC, V. $ **WHY** Piccolo cappuccinos and two sandwiches: short rib or roast chicken with burrata and pesto. **WHAT** Just the right sort of new-millenium small-town café, this husband-and-wife operation has outdoor-only seating on vintage garden furniture, salads made from South Pas Farmers' Market produce, coffee from Cafecito Organico, and dreamy sandwiches made on house-baked bread. Great soups and vegetarian options, too. **WHO** Cool moms, South Pas High kids, and relaxed business folks. ⚙🔖☺ ☼

[Green Street Restaurant] 146 S. Shoppers Lane, Pasadena, 626.577.7170, greenstreetrestaurant.com. B, L & D daily. American. Full bar. AE, MC, V. $$ - $$$ **WHY** Ordering the Dianne salad marks you as a true Pasadenan. **WHAT** This institution does a brisk business in Cal-American cuisine. There's a popular outdoor patio and a modern-coffee-shop interior, but wherever you choose to sit, the go-to dish is the Dianne salad, its ginormous take on Chinese chicken salad (for a more reasonable serving, get the "dinner" size, not the full). It's impossible to stop eating, as thousands of Pasadenans before you have discovered. **WHO** Pasadena moms and their moms. 𝕯 ☺ ☼ 🚗

[Huge Tree Pastry] 423 N. Atlantic Blvd., #105, Monterey Park, 626.458.8689 . B & L daily. Taiwanese. No booze. Cash only. $ **WHY** For excellent Taiwanese breakfasts and snack foods. **WHAT** For a couple of decades, Yi Mei Bakery was the place to go for morning bowls of soy milk, Chinese crullers and savory buns. Now they've opened a real restaurant serving the same great stuff—and more. Of course the breakfast pastries—red bean buns, sweet sesame cake, green onion pancakes—are made throughout the day. They've added such light meals as savory oyster pancakes, divine smoked chicken legs, yummy rice plates and noodle soups with every pork innard you can think of. **WHO** Taiwanese (natch) and lovers of savory Chinese pastries. 📷☺

[Julienne] 🏠 2649 Mission St., San Marino, 626.441.2299, juliennetogo.com. B & L Mon.-Sat. Modern American. Beer & wine. AE, MC, V. $ - $$$ **WHY** Signature rosemary bread for toast and sandwiches, not one but two great bacon offerings (applewood smoked and candied) on the breakfast menu and killer chocolate-mint brownies in the dessert case. Plus fantastic takeout baskets for the plane or the Hollywood Bowl. **WHAT** Breakfast or lunch on the shaded sidewalk terrace fronting this impossibly charming café and gourmet-to-go store is a fine treat, and well worth the wait if you come at peak hours. Lunch standouts include the lamb sandwich with caramelized onions and the chopped salad with grilled chicken, roasted vegetables and pesto. At breakfast, try the wonderful salmon hash or a perfectly cooked omelet. **WHO** San Marino ladies-who-lunch, families with out-of-town guests and folks on the bridal/baby-shower circuit. ♥ 𝕯 ☼

[Le Pain Quotidien] 88 W. Colorado Blvd., Old Pasadena, 626.396.0814, lepainquotidien.com. B, L & early D daily. Modern American/French. Beer & wine. AE, MC, V. $ - $$ **WHY** Our favorite breakfast in Pasadena: flawless omelets (try the pesto-parmesan), fresh fruit with yogurt, fresh juices and pains aux chocolat. **WHAT** Yes, we generally eschew chains, but these Belgian-based cafés offer a level of quality that's almost never seen on a large scale. Flavorful, often organic ingredients go into the delicious open-face sandwiches, quiches, salads, soups and sweets. The bread, *naturellement*, is substantial and flavorful. And even with the prime Old Town location, we can always snag a good table. **WHO** The Patagonia-and-Prius crowd, some toting the cutest babies in town. 🌱🚗☺✿

[Market on Holly] 57 E. Holly St., Old Pasadena, 626.844.8811, themarketonholly.com. B & L Mon.-Sat. American. Beer & wine. AE, MC, V. $ - $$ **WHY** Beautiful salads, Stumptown coffee and the best chocolate-chip cookie in town. **WHAT** A little bit of San Francisco in Old Pasadena, the Market on Holly is the creation of two longtime locals, a caterer and a food-loving composer. There's a small market (pastas, oils, local organic milk), a swell coffee bar with fabulous baked goods, a cheese counter, a deli case, large communal tables inside and small sidewalk tables outside, where regulars come back at least weekly for the breakfast sandwich, roast pork shoulder sandwich, and the lime-cilantro or baby spinach salads. It may be serving dinner and Sunday brunch by the time you read this. **WHO** Locals grateful for a quality place owned by other locals in chain-packed Old Town. 🌱☺✿

[Marston's] 151 E. Walnut St., Pasadena, 626.796.2459, marstonsrestaurant.com. B & L daily, D Wed.-Sat. American. Beer & wine. AE, MC, V. $ - $$$ **WHY** The legendary cornflake-coated french toast. **WHAT** The breakfasts are excellent, as are the lunch salads, but insanely long weekend waits for a table are an unfortunate fact of life at this vintage Pasadena bungalow. Come on a Tuesday to more easily snag a front-porch table to eat your generous omelet in peace. ♥☺✿

[Nicole's Gourmet Foods] 921 Meridian Ave., South Pasadena, 626.403.5751, nicolesgourmetfoods.com. B & L daily, D Thurs. French. Beer & wine. AE, MC, V. $ **WHY** An excellent, well-edited selection of cheese and wine. **WHAT** Nicole Grandjean has created a little corner of Paris by the Mission Gold Line station. Order at the counter, grab a table on the flower-lined sidewalk patio and enjoy a delicious baguette sandwich, salad or quiche. Don't leave without stocking up on cheese, pâté and one of the frozen delicacies. **WHO** Eclectic mix of commuting locals, serious Francophiles and foodie chefs. ✿

[Pie 'n' Burger] 🏠 913 E. California Blvd., Pasadena, 626.795.1123, pienburger.com. B, L & D daily. American. No booze. Cash only. $ **WHY** Cheeseburgers and banana cream pie. **WHAT** This no-frills diner with a long counter and even longer lines serves fantastic burgers, very good short-order breakfasts and house-made pies that are famous enough to draw folks from around Southern California. In fact, just

Breakfast + Lunch

🌱 VEGETARIAN ☺ KID FRIENDLY ✿ PATIO DINING 🚐 DELIVERY 🎩 PRIVATE PARTY about every food group on the wall-mounted menu has its passionate devotees, including the toast and the bacon. Thanks to its new truck, you can have pies 'n burgers all over town. **WHO** Caltech students and profs, older couples, paperback-toting singles. 🖼️☺

[The Terrace] Langham Huntington Hotel, 1401 S. Oak Knoll Ave., Pasadena, 626.585.6218, pasadena.langhamhotels.com. B, L & D daily. Modern American. Full bar. AE, MC, V. $$ - $$$$ **WHY** A chance to live the California dream without actually checking in. **WHAT** Ah, the good life: lunch at an umbrella-shaded table overlooking the pool of this grande dame hotel, iced tea or Chardonnay in hand. Order a flawless chicken Caesar, a gorgeous Cobb or a rich turkey pesto panini and watch the world's troubles drift away. **WHO** Ladies who lunch, business folk and lucky hotel guests with time to linger poolside. ♥ 🌙 ⚪ ☼

EAST VALLEY

[Aroma Café] 4360 Tujunga Ave., Studio City, 818.508.0677, aromacoffeeandtea.com. B, L & D daily. American. No booze. MC, V. $ - $$ **WHY** Good breakfasts served until 2:30 p.m., with huge salads and chic sandwiches for those who don't want breakfast. **WHAT** Owned by the same folks behind Alcove in Los Feliz, this café/coffeehouse/bookstore is in a fetching old cottage with an enclosed brick patio. The menu is extensive; try a breakfast burrito, the scrambled eggs atop spinach puff pastry, or a vegetarian scramble. Partial table service (order at the counter) can be spotty and a little full of attitude, and you'll have to wait at peak times, but the food and setting are usually worth it. **WHO** Studio City beautiful people. ♥⚪☼

[Art's Delicatessen] 12224 Ventura Blvd., Studio City, 818.762.1221, artsdeli.com. B, L & D daily. Deli. Beer & wine. AE, MC, V. $ - $$ **WHY** When you don't have time to drive to Brent's and you've gotta have deli. **WHAT** We're not as fond of Art's as its diehard fans, but neither will we turn down its corned beef on rye. An all-around traditional deli: vinyl booths, Formica tables, smoked fish, deli sandwiches and always-amusing people-watching. **WHO** Seniors, TV writers and studio folks, many of whom have been coming here for 30 years. ☺🚗

[Du-par's] 12036 Ventura Blvd., Studio City, 818.766.4437, du-pars.com. B, L & D 24 hours daily. American. No booze. AE, MC, V. $ - $$ **WHY** For classic breakfasts, including custardy french toast, corned beef hash with poached eggs and a short stack of pancakes, served 24 hours a day. **WHAT** The Studio City branch of the L.A. Farmers Market icon is a Valley favorite for hearty breakfasts served by staffers who know regulars by name. Du-par's bacon is crisp and flavorful, and the eggs are cooked to order, even if the place doesn't serve such newfangled coffee drinks as cappuccino. If you like thinner pancakes, jut ask; sometimes if the batter has been sitting too long they come out too thick. **WHO** Folks from the 'hood, including a smattering of celebs trying to avoid attention before they've had their coffee. ☺ ☺

[Good Neighbor] 3701 Cahuenga Blvd., Studio City, 818.761.4627. B & L daily. American. Beer & wine. MC, V. $ **WHY** Breakfast, and a good one at that, served all day, along with good American coffee and personal service. **WHAT** The parking stinks, but that keeps the crowds at bay, so the wait's not too bad for a table in this fine mom 'n pop diner in the Cahuenga Pass. Generous omelets, a delish pancake sandwich and surprisingly good vegetarian options. Lunchtime sandwiches are perfectly fine. **WHO** Below-the-line working folk from the local studios, some of whom have been coming here for decades. ▦ ◱ ☺

[Hugo's] 12851 Riverside Dr., Studio City, 818.761.8985, hugosrestaurant.com. B, L & D daily. Californian. Full bar. AE, MC, V. $$ **WHY** Pasta Mama and Pasta Papa, two powerfully addictive pasta-egg scrambles. **WHAT** Hugo's serves dinner, and it's a good dinner, but what brings the regulars back are the breakfasts and brunches. Organic, hormone-free, processed-sugar-free ingredients are turned into terrific scrambles, pancakes, vegan breads and, for true brunch sybarites, a tasty and potent cocktail called the Mangorita. Lunchtime brings things like hummus wraps, mac 'n cheese and turkey burgers. A modern L.A. classic with consistently delicious food. **WHO** Hip and healthy Valley families, studio people and some famous faces. ♨ ◱ ☺

[Jinky's Café] 14120 Ventura Blvd., Sherman Oaks, 818.981.2250, jinkys.com. B, L & D daily. American. No booze. AE, MC, V. $ - $$ **WHY** Santa Fe egg scramble, pumpkin pancakes, french toast coated in honey nut cornflakes and, at lunch, good quesadillas and a Chinese chicken salad. **WHAT** Not everything is good at this health-conscious, fairly pricey café, but many of the breakfast dishes are, which is why it's so hard to find parking on weekend mornings and the wait for a table can be interminable. Come instead on a weekday for the famous french toast or some very good pancakes. **WHO** A huge throng on weekend mornings—come early or on a weekday. ◱ ☺ ☼

[Moore's Delicatessen] 271 E. Orange Grove Ave., Burbank, 818.478.1251, mooresdeli.com. B & L daily. Deli. Beer & wine. AE, MC, V. $ **WHY** Our new favorite chicken soup in town, plus quality, classic deli fare and tasty, affordable wines and beers. **WHAT** Robert Moore serves straightforward deli fare in a concrete-floored, order-at-the-counter, diner-style spot. We're not crazy about the corned-beef sandwiches, but we love the poached eggs on toast, hearty chicken soup, veggie salad and peel-and-eat shrimp. Extras include a mini-farmers' market of fresh produce, Little Flower candies, and meat and cheeses to take home. Check out the walls in the back room, which have been illustrated by artists from local animation studios. **WHO** Creative types from the Cartoon Network and Nickelodeon mingle. ◱ ☺

+ Lunch

◱ VEGETARIAN ☺ KID FRIENDLY ☼ PATIO DINING ⊖ DELIVERY ⌂ PRIVATE PARTY

[Olive & Thyme] 4013 Riverside Dr., Toluca Lake, 818.557.1560, oliveandthyme.com. B, L & D Mon.-Fri. Modern American. Beer & wine. AE, MC, V. **$$** **WHY** Café fare of a quality never before seen in the Valley, at prices that are more Brentwood than Burbank. **WHAT** This spacious new place from neighbors and restaurant investors Melina and Christian Davies satisfies all cravings, offering Intelligentsia coffee, breakfast pastries and desserts from Valerie Confections (the salted caramel croissant is flaky bliss; the white chocolate coconut cake makes us weak in the knees), salads and sandwiches for lunch and early dinner (superb curried chicken salad, a succulent braised short-rib sandwich with horseradish crème fraîche), a well-curated array of cheeses and artisanal foodstuffs, and a wine bar with savvy selections from Matthew Kaner of Silverlake Wine. We're besotted. At lunch it's packed; arrive early to snag a table. ☼

[Paty's] 10001 Riverside Dr., Toluca Lake, 818.761.0041, patysrestaurant.com. B, L & D daily. American. Beer & wine. AE, MC, V. **$ - $$** **WHY** Breakfast is served all day, either on the patio or inside among the photos of celebrities, some of whom actually come here. **WHAT** A good vintage coffee shop, no more and no less. You can hang out on the patio or in a booth with a screenplay and some scrambled eggs, or treat your kids to a shake. Service can be slow, but what's your rush? **WHO** Toluca Lake grandmas, TV actors, teens and office workers. 📷 🍸 ☺ ☼

[Studio Café Magazzino] 109 N. Pass Ave., Toluca Lake, 818.953.7220, cafemagazzino.com. B & L Mon.-Fri. American. No booze. AE, MC, V. **$** **WHY** Excellent soups, a killer tuna sandwich, good vegetarian options, peach iced tea and very nice people—in short, the perfect little lunch café. **WHAT** A charming café within spitting distance of Warner Bros., this treasure is packed at lunch but quieter for breakfast. Let Rose take your order at the counter and hope you can snag one of the few tables inside or outside. Rose's kitchen makes delicious daily soups (including a fabulous split pea) and generous sandwiches and salads. After the lunch rush, you can linger over an espresso and dessert. **WHO** A steady stream of studio people. 📷 🥢 ☼

[Sweet Butter Kitchen] 13824 Ventura Blvd., Sherman Oaks, 818.788.2832, sweetbutterkitchen.com. B & L daily. American. No booze. AE, MC, V. **$ - $$** **WHY** To hobnob with Sherman Oaks neighbors. **WHAT** Veteran caterer Leslie Danelian debuted her coffeehouse/café/ market in 2010 and it quickly became *the* spot to meet in the mid-Valley. Except for a few tables in the covered courtyard, seating is outdoors, but on days when the weather cooperates this is one of the best places around to enjoy fresh pastries, cooked-to-order breakfasts (Nueske bacon!), luncheon salads and gourmet sandwiches. Temptations abound, so you'll see many patrons with good intentions ordering salads followed by salted caramel chocolate brownies. 🥢 ☺ ☼

🏛 ESSENTIALLY L.A. ☺ LATE ♥ ROMANTIC 📷 VALUE 🍸 QUIET ☼ SUSTAINABLE

WEST VALLEY

[More Than Waffles] 17200 Ventura Blvd., Encino, 818.789.5937, morethanwaffles.com. B & L daily. American. No booze. MC, V. $ - $$ **WHY** Waffles. Okay, maybe pancakes, too. **WHAT** This strip-mall café is quite the place to be on weekend mornings, when a musician plays on the patio and dogs and kids are everywhere. Even though the name implies otherwise, waffles are the thing to get. ☺ ☼

[Nat's Early Bite] 14115 Burbank Blvd., Van Nuys, 818.781.3040, natsearlybite.com. B & L daily. American. No booze. MC, V. $ **WHY** For a satisfying breakfast (delicious scrambles and omelets, carrot muffins, truly crisp hash browns) and a well-made cup of coffee. **WHAT** Pass on lunch and dinner, but don't miss the chance for breakfast at this honest, old-school diner. There's a wait on weekends, but it's worth it. **WHO** Regular Van Nuys diner folks—it's not a hipster scene. 📷📶☺

[Vinh Loi Tofu] 18625 Sherman Way, Reseda, 818.996.9779, vinhloitofu.com. B, L & D daily. Vietnamese. No booze. MC, V. $ **WHY** Fresh, tasty Vietnamese fare, all vegetarian and most of it vegan, with many dishes featuring quality tofu made in the adjacent factory. **WHAT** In a dining room barely bigger than a lunch truck, Kevin Tran mans the counter and chats with regulars at his café next to his tofu factory. Try any of the vegan soups, the spring rolls, the soya shrimp, the fake meat dishes, the carrot cake... they're all delicious. **WHO** A steady stream of regulars, as diverse as they come: Asian chefs, vegan moms with toddlers in tow, bikers, women in hijabs. 📷⚙📶☺

WESTSIDE: CENTRAL

[Al Gelato] 806 S. Robertson Blvd., Beverly Hills, 310.659.8069. Daily. Italian/Ice cream. No booze. Cash only. $ - $$ **WHY** For red sauce-dishes like rigatoni, as well as pizza, prosciutto or meatball sandwiches and salads. The tuna sandwich and the chili have many admirers. **WHAT** Gelati (or the amazing coffee granita) are the endings, but the meals start with hearty pastas, soups and sandwiches. Behind the tempting, extensive gelato counter is a casual, no-frills dining room with table service. Good for a low-key Beverly Hills lunch. ☺

[Bluebird Café] 8572 National Blvd., Culver City, 310.841.0939, bluebirdcafela.com. B & L Mon.-Fri. American. Beer & wine. AE, MC, V. $ **WHY** Excellent cupcakes and reliable lunch fare: pressed chicken-and-cheddar or prosciutto-mozzarella sandwiches, a delish turkey Reuben and parsley-flecked fries. **WHAT** A cheerful, simple neighborhood café with a pleasant enclosed patio and justly famed cupcakes. Breakfast is usually pretty quiet during the week. It's not cheap, but this isn't a cheap neighborhood anymore. **WHO** Culver City studio and creative types, who try to score tables on the patio for lunch. 📶☺☼

📶 VEGETARIAN ☺ KID FRIENDLY ☼ PATIO DINING �'DELIVERY 🏛 PRIVATE PARTY

[Cabbage Patch] **214 S. Beverly Dr., Beverly Hills, 310.550.8655, cabbagepatchbh.com. L & D Mon.-Sat. Modern American. No booze. AE, MC, V. $ - $$ WHY** Beautiful salads, bowls and sandwiches made from ingredients as fresh, locally sourced and organic as possible, served in a bright, cheerful café. **WHAT** Handsome young owner Samir Mohajer has brought the same devotion to high-quality ingredients seen at his old home, Rustic Canyon, to this casual, order-at-the-counter café. Salads are generous and perfectly balanced; try the one made with baby greens, free-range Jidori chicken, applewood-smoked bacon, brioche croutons and a Champagne vinaigrette. Bowls are generous and gorgeous, and sandwiches hold things like Niman Ranch ground beef, wild arugula, shaved parmesan and eggplant caponata. **WHO** Beverly Hills locals who value quality food over a scene. ♻

[The Farm of Beverly Hills] **439 N. Beverly Dr., Beverly Hills, 310.273.5578, thefarmofbeverlyhills.com. B, L & D daily. American. Beer & wine. AE, MC, V. $$ - $$$ WHY** The breakfasts, weekend brunch and brownies. **WHAT** This original of the three-branch mini-chain serves three meals a day, plus weekend brunch, but we like it best for breakfast: good coffee, chocolate croissants, frittatas built to order, brisket omelets and homemade granola. Lunch brings excellent club sandwiches and good salads and cheeseburgers, but the Farm's real claim to fame is its dense, fudgy brownies, which they sell at all three branches and online. Be prepared to wait, and have patience with the service. Other locations at the Grove and at L.A. Live. **WHO** Beverly Hills tourists and locals alike, including lots of pretty people. 🛍 ☺ ♻

[Fountain Coffee Room] **Beverly Hills Hotel, 9641 Sunset Blvd., Beverly Hills, 310.276.2251, thebeverlyhillshotel.com. B, L & D daily. American. No booze. AE, MC, V. $$ - $$$ WHY** To treat a special kid or grandkid to waffles or a big ol' ice cream sundae, but only if your wallet isn't easily offended. **WHAT** Dripping with old Beverly Hills panache, this 20-seat 1949 diner counter is overpriced, of course, but you're paying for the setting, and it's a great one. Splurge on the caviar and sour cream omelet if you must, but you'll be just as happy with pancakes and good coffee. A real milkshake makes a heavenly afternoon indulgence. **WHO** Big spenders having a treat. ☺

[John O'Groats] 🏛 **10516 Pico Blvd., Rancho Park, 310.204.0692, ogroatsrestaurant.com. B & L daily. American. No booze. AE, MC, V. $ - $$ WHY** Corned beef hash, biscuits, thick-cut bacon and pumpkin or fresh-fruit-topped pancakes. **WHAT** Fans line up every weekend morning (and sometimes on weekdays) for a spot at a table or the counter in this rustic-charming diner named for a village in Scotland. The food isn't authentically Scotch (a good thing, perhaps), but the breakfasts are hearty and totally delicious. **WHO** Stroller-pushing families and couples with their newspapers to read over breakfast. ☺

[L'Epicerie Market] **9900 Culver Blvd., Culver City, 310.815.1600, lepiceriemarket.com. B, L & D daily. French/Californian. Beer & wine. AE, MC, V. $$ - $$$ WHY** A French-accented restaurant, wine bar and deli that's good for brunch, lunch, tapas or drinks. **WHAT** Chef Thierry Perez chose a large industrial space for his latest Culver City venture, which combines a wine shop, gourmet-to-go and a full-service menu offering everything from crêpes to polenta with veal brains. The tapas happy hour runs from 5-9 p.m., with small plates for just $3. **WHO** Parents and writers munching on fresh croissants and coffee in the a.m.; p.m. couples and singles sampling the wine selection.

[Momed] 🛆 **223 S. Beverly Dr., Beverly Hills, 310.270.4444, atmomed. com. B, L & D daily. Mediterranean/Middle Eastern. Beer & wine. AE, MC, V. $ - $$ WHY** Vividly colorful modern Mediterranean dishes made from organic, often local ingredients, served on a sunny Beverly Hills sidewalk patio. **WHAT** South Beverly is full of good places to eat, but few give the value that this order-at-the-counter café does. We dream of the rich duck confit schwarma wrapped in a warm pita with oven-dried tomatoes, fig confit and garlic spread, and the seafood salad is a thing of beauty. Also worth trying is the Turkish flatbread, a cousin of the Armenian lahamajune. Really nice people, modest prices, and good wine by the glass. **WHO** South Beverly habitués: entertainment attorneys, party planners, shoppers. 🕸🔖⊙ ✿🚙

WEST OF THE 405

[3 Square Café & Bakery] **1121 Abbot Kinney Blvd., Venice, 310.399.6504, rockenwagner.com. B, L & D daily. American/German. Beer & wine. AE, MC, V. $$ WHY** Pretzel bread, the pretzel burger, avocado fries and outdoor seating on Abbot Kinney. **WHAT** Hans Röckenwagner has found steady success with this elegantly simple café and bakery. His German heritage is evident in the brats and the famed pretzel bread, and all the food is excellent, if on the pricey side. Still, this is Abbot Kinney, and you pay for such prime real estate. **WHO** Venice beautiful people enjoying a quiet breakfast or lunch. 🍃🔖✿

[Back on the Beach Café] **445 Pacific Coast Hwy., Santa Monica, 310.393.8282, backonthebeachcafe.com. B & L daily, D Fri.-Sun. American. Beer & wine. AE, MC, V. $ - $$$ WHY** Tables on the sand, smack in the middle of Santa Monica Beach. **WHAT** This longtime on-the-sand café is now part of the public Annenberg Beach Club next door. The straightforward fare is pretty much the same—nothing amazing, but that omelet, breakfast quesadilla or burger tastes so much better when the sun is sparkling on the Pacific and you've just had a ride on the bike path. A fun and affordable place to bring out-of-town guests on a sunny day. **WHO** Volleyball players, families with little kids, bike-path cruisers. 🕸⊙✿🏛

🍃 **VEGETARIAN** ⊙ **KID FRIENDLY** ✿ **PATIO DINING** 🚙 **DELIVERY** 🏛 **PRIVATE PARTY**

[The Bookmark Café] Santa Monica Main Library, 601 Santa Monica Blvd., Santa Monica, 310.587.2665. B Mon.-Sat., L daily, D Mon.-Thurs. American. No booze. AE, MC, V. $ **WHY** It's the best secret café in Santa Monica. **WHAT** You don't have to keep this quiet: The café in Santa Monica's fabulous Main Library offers good, made-to-order food including turkey burgers, panini, wraps and an amazing range of salads (chef's, Cobb, Caesar, Greek, apple-walnut). You can eat in a large, sunny courtyard, and savor the fact that almost everything on the menu costs less than $8. Breakfast brings omelets, pancakes and good coffee. **WHO** Quiet, studious types. 🖙 🍴 🥄 ☺ ☼

[Bread & Porridge] 2315 Wilshire Blvd., Santa Monica, 310.453.4941, breadandporridge.com. B, L & D daily. American. Beer & wine. AE, MC, V. $ - $$ **WHY** Omelets made with interesting sausages; goat cheese salad; tender brisket. **WHAT** High wooden booths, chalkboard menus and retro tile make for a setting of Rockwellian charm, just the place to wallow in the comfort of eggs, sausages, pancakes, fashionable salads and hearty entrées. Locals come for an early supper with a glass of good wine. Quality ingredients at fair prices. **WHO** Folks who shop the Santa Monica Farmers' Market and hip nursing moms coming from the Pump Station on the block. 🖙 🥄 ☺

[Café Vida] 15317 Antioch St., Pacific Palisades, 310.573.1335, cafe-vida.net. B, L & D daily. American/Mexican. BYOB. AE, MC, V. $$ **WHY** A chance to eat healthy food in the Palisades, plus no corkage fee. **WHAT** This is the place that triggered a local epiphany: "Healthy" food can actually taste good! Winning dishes include a delicious egg-white frittata with sausage and roasted vegetables. Get there before 11:30 for brunch or lunch and before 6 p.m. for dinner, or you'll wait, wait, wait. **WHO** Huevos rancheros–lovin' locals. 🥄 ☺ ☼

[Coast] 🏛 Shutters on the Beach, 1 Pico Blvd., Santa Monica, 310.587.1707, coastsantamonica.com. B & D daily, L Mon.-Fri., brunch Sat.-Sun. American. Full bar. AE, MC, V. $$ - $$$$ **WHY** Luxe breakfast and lunch on the beach. **WHAT** Is $17 too much to pay for bacon 'n eggs? Not with a setting like this—a white-washed California dream of a café at sand level in the beachfront Shutters hotel, with windows open to the ocean air and the cyclists a few feet away on the bike path. Go ahead, splurge on that mimosa—surely you deserve it. Fortunately, it's not just about the setting. The food is solid (particular snaps for the thick bacon and the lemon-ricotta pancakes) and the service is sharp. **WHO** Shiny happy people. ☺ ☼

[Cora's Coffee Shoppe] 1802 Ocean Ave., Santa Monica, 310.451.9562, corascoffee.com. B & L Tues.-Sun. Modern American. Beer & wine. MC, V. $ - $$ **WHY** Surprise: Aging starlet gets a good facelift and comes out of it lovelier than ever. **WHAT** High-end restaurateur Bruce Marder runs this miniature and adorable restored diner, where a funky-chic bougainvillea-shaded patio is furnished with marble tables and bistro chairs. It's a lovely place to linger over a burrata caprese omelet or organic rotisserie chicken. You may linger longer than you'd intended (service can be spotty) and pay more than you'd like, but nothing out of line for an outdoor café with really good food a block from the beach. **WHO** Everyone looks like a movie star trying not to be noticed, wearing jeans and no makeup. ♥ 🌴 ❧ ☼

[FarmShop] **Brentwood Country Mart, 225 26th St., #25, Santa Monica, 310.566.2400, farmshopla.com. B & L daily, brunch Sat.-Sun. American. Beer & wine pending. AE, MC, V. $$ WHY** Yountville foodie elegance in Brentwood. **WHAT** Freshness is a fetish here, whether it's braised sunchokes or perfectly cut shoestring fries from Weiser Farms potatoes. Jeffrey Cerciello, former culinary director of Thomas Keller's casual dining division, has created an upscale larder featuring dishes (salmon rillettes, poached chicken salad) made with the best local produce alongside top-notch charcuterie, cheese and baked goods. Family-style dinner should be on offer by the time you read this, if they've secured a wine license. **WHO** Westside trophy wives, hot yoga moms, people who look like they stepped out of *Dwell* magazine, and movie stars acting like regular folk. ❧🌴☺☼

[Figtree's Café] 🏠 **429 Oceanfront Walk, Venice, 310.392.4937, figtreescafe.com. B, L & D daily. American. Beer & wine. AE, MC, V. $ - $$ WHY** Sunny-side-up tables overlooking the Venice Boardwalk and the beach. **WHAT** Of the parade of tourist-bait sidewalk cafés on the Boardwalk, this has been our favorite since the '70s, when sandwiches with avocado and sprouts were considered exotic. Today we like the egg scrambles, turkey burgers and big salads. **WHO** Aged hippies and a new generation of tastefully tattooed young parents. ❧🌴☺☼

[French Market Café] **2321 Abbot Kinney Blvd., Venice, 310.577.9775, frenchmarket-cafe.com. B & L daily, D Tues.-Sun. French. Beer & wine. AE, MC, V. $ - $ WHY** You wish you were in Paris. **WHAT** This indoor/outdoor café and market on south Abbot Kinney has catered to homesick ex-pats since 1993. You may be the only English speaker in line waiting to order French comfort food: omelets with a green salad; *le cheval* (fried egg atop ham and melted Swiss on a toasted baguette); salade niçoise (with Michel Blanchet smoked trout); and traditional boeuf bourguignon and blanquette de poulet. Shelves and cases hold frozen entrées, wines, stinky cheeses, canned escargots, pâtés, French magazines and such sweets as calissons from Aix-en-Provence. **WHO** Both chic and tracksuit-clad French folks. ☼

[Huckleberry Bakery & Café] 🏠 **1014 Wilshire Blvd., Santa Monica, 310.451.2311, huckleberrycafe.com. B & L Tues.-Sun., early D Tues.-Fri. American. No booze. AE, MC, V. $ - $$ WHY** Really fantastic café food: sandwiches on fresh bread, homemade soups, a perfect chopped salad, wonderful desserts. **WHAT** The bakery and café from the husband-and-wife chefs at Rustic Canyon, Josh Loeb and Zoe Nathan, is a place of deafening noise and recession-resistant crowds, who line up at breakfast and lunch to order pricey ciabatta sandwiches filled with burrata, marinated peppers and prosciutto; irresistibly aromatic rotisserie Jidori chicken; salads of flawless ingredients; and the best cookies we've had in ages. **WHO** Impeccably manicured westside women who don't bat an eye at $8 tarts. 🔖 ☺

[Izzy's Deli] **1433 Wilshire Blvd., Santa Monica, 310.394.1131, izzysdeli.com. B, L & D 24 hours daily. Deli. Beer & wine. AE, MC, V. $$** **WHY** Honest food served 24 hours a day—and valet parking is free during the day! **WHAT** An essential place to know about if you find yourself hungry on the westside at 3 a.m. Even at the more conventional dining hours, Izzy's serves reliable matzo ball soup, pastrami sandwiches, bagels 'n lox, brisket and all the deli classics. **WHO** A wonderful cross-section of old and young Santa Monica. ☺ 🗺 ☺

[Le Pain Quotidien] **316 Santa Monica Blvd., Santa Monica, 310.393.6800; 11702 Barrington Ave., Brentwood, 310.476.0969; pain-quotidien.com. B, L & early D daily. Modern American/French. Beer & wine. AE, MC, V. $ - $$** **WHY** Great chicken curry and egg salad open-face sandwiches; good lemon tarts; a communal table with loaves of bread serving as idiosyncratic napkin holders; excellent vegan and vegetarian options. **WHAT** These Belgian-based cafés offer a level of quality that's almost never seen in chains. Fresh, flavorful, often organic ingredients go into the delicious open-face sandwiches, quiches, salads, soups and sweets. The bread, *naturellement*, is substantial and flavorful. **WHO** Beautiful people. 🏛🔖☺ ✿

[Marmalade Café] 🏛 **3894 Cross Creek Rd., Malibu, 310.317.4242, marmaladecafe.com. B, L & D daily. Californian. Beer & wine. AE, MC, V. $$** **WHY** Though not on the water, this is one of the best beach-town cafés around—and a perfect lunch stop if you're driving up the coast. **WHAT** This branch of the Marmalade restaurant/caterer mini-chain serves wine and has an actual dining room, unlike the Santa Monica flagship. The draw is very good food in a casual, indoor/outdoor setting and a chance to rub shoulders with Malibu people in their native habitat. **WHO** Beautiful people—*really* beautiful people. ✿

[Panini Garden] **2715 Main St., Santa Monica, 310.399.9939, paninigarden.com. B, L & D daily. Italian. No booze. AE, MC, V. $ - $$** **WHY** A little bit of heaven right on bustling Main Street. Delicious panini, a nice breakfast and lovely sweet crêpes. **WHAT** This modest café is a sleeper find on Main Street—a welcome alternative to the many overpriced and/or touristy eateries. Take your crisp, absolutely delicious panini to the hidden rear garden, where umbrellas shade the tables, lavender lines the walk and a fountain burbles. There are also lots of good salads with organic fixings. 🍽 🍷 🥡 ☺ ♨

[Patrick's Roadhouse] 106 Entrada Dr., Santa Monica, 310.459.4544, patricksroadhouse.info. B & L daily. American. No booze. MC, V. **$ WHY** A hearty breakfast in vintage beach-bum splendor. **WHAT** What looks like an Irish pub thanks to the jolly green paint job is actually a booze-free greasy spoon that's been greeting PCH passersby since 1974. It's a breakfast dive complete with flea-market antiques, worn wood tables and a hodgepodge of photos (including of former patron Arnold Schwarzenegger, although maybe they're taking those down now). Go for the pancakes, omelets and scrambles. **WHO** Surfers, body builders, newspaper-toting locals. ☺

[Thyme Café & Market] 1630 Ocean Park Blvd., Santa Monica, 310.399.8800, thymecafeandmarket.com. B & L daily, early D Mon.- Sat. American. No booze. AE, MC, V. **$ - $$ WHY** Of all the great westside hybrid café/markets that have popped up recently, this is the first that doesn't feel like a splurge, with most sandwiches and salads priced less than $10. **WHAT** Regulars come here for Chinese chicken salad; tomato, mozzarella and pesto sandwiches; and vegetable lasagnes to take home for dinner. The pain au chocolat is worth the morning splurge, but skip the café au lait—the price is oddly the same as a latte, and the brewed coffee isn't full bodied enough to stand up to the milk. **WHO** Santa Monica College students trying to decide whether to spend their lunch money on a Greek salad or a chocolate caramel brownie; moms with toddlers eyeing the red velvet cupcakes. 🥡

SOUTH BAY TO SOUTH L.A.

[Claire's at the Museum] Long Beach Museum of Art, 2300 E. Ocean Blvd., Long Beach, 562.439.2119, lbma.org. B Sat.-Sun., L Tues.- Sun. Californian. Beer & wine. AE, MC, V. **$$ WHY** One of the most civilized spots in Long Beach for lunch and weekend breakfast, with a dazzling view and good ladies-who-lunch food: crème brûlée french toast, salmon BLTs, chicken Caesars. **WHAT** Occupying the Arts & Crafts Elizabeth Milbank Anderson House on the museum grounds, with a lovely patio next to a huge, dynamic water sculpture and a killer view of the harbor, this is a great place to take out-of-towners for a California dreamin' lunch or weekend breakfast. **WHO** Museum-goers, date-lunchers, Long Beach State professors. ♥ 🍷 🥡 ☺ ♨

[Coffee Cup Café] 3734 E. 4th St., Long Beach, 562.433.3292. B & L daily. American. No booze. Cash only. **$ WHY** The perfect coffee shop, with properly cooked omelets, amazingly good vegetarian chorizo and great coffee. **WHAT** No one seems to mind waiting 45 minutes for a table in this cheery yellow diner on weekends, and not just because of the free while-you-wait coffee—the food is that good. From the vegetarian breakfast burrito and the lovely omelets to the oatmeal and

+ Lunch

🥡 VEGETARIAN ☺ KID FRIENDLY ☼ PATIO DINING 🚗 DELIVERY 🎉 PRIVATE PARTY

the banana pancakes, everything is fresh and delicious. **WHO** Young couples with babies and strollers, over-70 couples, neighbors running into neighbors—a real community mix. 🗺️🔖☺️

[Eat at Joe's] **400 N. Pacific Coast Hwy., Redondo Beach, 310.376.9570, originaleatatjoes.com. B & L daily, D Mon.-Fri. American. Beer & wine. AE, MC, V. $ - $$ WHY** Hearty diner breakfasts that are just what the hung-over Sunday-morning crowd needs to cure what ails them. The really hungry get the John Wayne omelet. **WHAT** Huge portions of straightforward American breakfast chow (omelets, home fries, biscuits and gravy) are served to gregarious groups seated at big communal tables lined with picnic benches. Good burgers at lunchtime. **WHO** Families and shaggy twentysomethings recovering from a few too many the night before. 🗺️🔖☺️

[Four Daughters Kitchen] **3505 N. Highland Ave., Manhattan Beach, 310.545.2444, fourdaughterskitchen.com. B, L & D daily. American. Beer & wine. AE, MC, V. $$ WHY** You've been surfing for hours and you're ready to stoke the engine with really good pancakes or a way better burger than you'll find elsewhere around here. **WHAT** A neighborhood hangout with wooden tables, lots of windows and flat-screen TVs, Four Daughters is home to well-prepared comfort food made with upscale ingredients. At lunch, the $12 Chinese chicken salad and $11 chipotle chicken sandwich are big enough for two. Stop in for a tap beer or sangria, read the paper over a very good latte, or just head out after each meal for another walk on the beach to work off the hearty food. **WHO** Local gal-groups in beach-walk wear, city workers, families and your more prosperous sort of surfer. ☺️

[Jongewaard's Bake N Broil] 🏛️ **3697 Atlantic Ave., Long Beach, 562.595.0396. B, L & D daily. American. No booze. AE, MC, V. $ WHY** To sit at the counter and revel in a perfect pot pie and, to keep the theme going for dessert, brownie pie with vanilla ice cream. If you can't stay, pick up some frozen pot pies to take home, and for your next summer party, order the French peach pie. **WHAT** The Bake & Broil (which is what everyone calls it) has been Long Beach's comfort-food destination for ages, and it remains as good as it's ever been. Handmade burgers, fresh strawberry pancakes, Mexican breakfast scrambles, hot turkey sandwiches, red velvet cupcakes better than at all those trendy cupcakeries... it's the diner food you remember from the happy childhood you probably didn't have. **WHO** Bixby Knolls locals and families who've been driving a distance to eat here for many years. 🗺️☺️

[Martha's 22nd Street Grill] **25 22nd St., Hermosa Beach, 310.376.7786. B & L daily. American. No booze. AE, MC, V. $ WHY** Very good breakfasts served outdoors overlooking the Hermosa Strand and the ocean. **WHAT** The parking's a nightmare, and you'll have to wait on weekends, but these are minor annoyances when faced with the reward of enjoying a glass of house-squeezed orange juice, a proper cup of coffee, very good fresh fruit and near-perfect eggs Benedict and omelets. A little bit of California heaven. **WHO** Volleyball players, bike-path cyclists, surfers and their dogs, who must wait patiently on the other side of the fence enclosing the patio. 📷🍷☺ ✿

[Mishi's Strudel] **309 W. 7th St., San Pedro, 310.832.6474, mishisstrudel.com. B Tues.-Sun., L Tues.-Sat., early D Tues.-Wed., D Thurs.-Sat. Hungarian. No booze. AE, MC, V. $ WHY** Fresh-baked strudel with Old World charm. **WHAT** This family-owned spot brings a taste of Hungary to the historic waterfront. Styled like a country café, Mishi's specializes in both sweet and savory strudels and crêpes. There are plenty of fruit-centric fillings, including apricot-almond and apple-walnut, as well as savory options, including spinach, mushroom and cabbage. Slow down and stay awhile with a cup of coffee or tea. 🍷🍽☺

[North End Caffé] 🏠 **3421 Highland Ave., Manhattan Beach, 310.546.4782, northendcaffe.net. B, L & D daily. American. No booze. MC, V. $ WHY** For the best breakfast in Manhattan Beach, and a terrific lunch, too—with a view of the ocean! The fries are worth the fat grams. **WHAT** Great coffee (try the one with a hint of orange peel) and excellent ingredients make this cheerful, always-busy little café the breakfast and lunch spot of choice in Manhattan Beach. It's located well north from the mobs near the pier, but that doesn't mean you won't have to wait for a table. Panini are a specialty, for breakfast and lunch, and they all feature quality produce on fresh baguettes. Try the egg-bacon-cheese, the pesto-brie or the Cuban. **WHO** Locals who can walk here and El Porto surfers. 🍽✿

[Pacific Diner] **3821 S. Pacific Ave., San Pedro, 310.831.5334. B & L Mon. & Wed.-Sun. American. No booze. MC, V. $ WHY** Hearty omelets, calamari and eggs, chicken-fried steak. **WHAT** Of San Pedro's several old-school breakfast diners, this is probably the most revered, more for its longevity and funky charm than its food—although the egg dishes go down just fine. **WHO** Cops, old longshoremen and assorted crusty San Pedro folks. 📷✿

[Uncle Bill's Pancake House] **1305 Highland Ave., Manhattan Beach, 310.545.5177, unclebills.net. B & L daily. American. No booze. AE, MC, V. $ WHY** The coffee's so-so, but the pancakes, omelets and potato dishes are all very good, and the vibe is Manhattan Beach happy. You're at the beach, you're eating banana pancakes, the weather's good... what's not to be happy about? **WHAT** As you can guess from the name, breakfast is the name of the game at this not-far-from-the-beach café, where the weekend crowds are considerable (unless you arrive before 8:30 a.m.) and the buttermilk pancakes are as good as you'd hoped. 📷☺ ✿

🍽 **VEGETARIAN** ☺ **KID FRIENDLY** ✿ **PATIO DINING** �car **DELIVERY** 🏠 **PRIVATE PARTY**

Coffee, Tea + Juices

Finding a decent coffee, tea or juice drink is easy in L.A.—in some areas you can't go more than a block without seeing a Starbucks, Coffee Bean or Jamba Juice (or all three). But instead, please explore the independent places found in almost every neighborhood. Here you'll find our favorites.

[ESSENTIALLY L.A.]
Aroma Café, Studio City (PAGE 238)
Café Corsa, USC (PAGE 231)
The Conservatory, Culver City (PAGE 240)
Funnel Mill, Santa Monica (PAGE 243)
Intelligentsia, Silver Lake (PAGE 232)
Intelligentsia Venice Coffeebar (PAGE 243)
Jin Patisserie, Venice (PAGE 244)
Jones Coffee, Pasadena (PAGE 236)
Lamill, Silver Lake (PAGE 233)
Langham Huntington Hotel, Pasadena (PAGE 237)
Royal/T Café, Culver City (PAGE 241)
Sanjang Coffee Garden, Silver Lake (PAGE 231)
Ten Ren Tea, Chinatown (PAGE 234)
Tierra Mia Coffee, South Gate (PAGE 247)
Tudor House, Santa Monica (PAGE 245)
Urth Caffé, Santa Monica (PAGE 245)

🏛 ESSENTIALLY L.A. ☺ LATE ♥ ROMANTIC 💲 VALUE 🔊 QUIET ♻ SUSTAINABLE

THESE CAFÉS AND BAKERIES
ALSO SERVE QUALITY COFFEE AND TEA DRINKS
AND WILL OFTEN MAKE THEM TO TAKE OUT:

3 Square Café & Bakery, Venice (PAGE 317)

Alcove Café & Bakery, Los Feliz (PAGE 300)

Amandine Patisserie, West L.A. (PAGE 317)

Belwood Bakery, Brentwood (PAGE 318)

BLD, Beverly/Third (PAGE 204)

Bloom Café, Mid-City (PAGE 204)

The Bookmark Café, Santa Monica (PAGE 222)

Bread & Porridge, Santa Monica (PAGE 222)

Bricks & Scones, Hancock Park (PAGE 205)

CaCao Mexicatessen, Eagle Rock (PAGE 79)

Café Tropical, Silver Lake (PAGE 209)

Clementine, Century City (PAGE 314)

Coffee Cup Café, Long Beach (PAGE 225)

Euro Pane, Pasadena (PAGE 308)

The Farm of Beverly Hills (PAGE 220)

Food + Lab, West Hollywood & Silver Lake (PAGES 205 & 210)

Frances Bakery & Coffee, Little Tokyo (PAGE 304)

Gelato Bar, Studio City & Los Feliz (PAGES 311 & 301)

Heirloom Bakery, South Pasadena (PAGE 309)

La Maison du Pain, Mid-City (PAGE 301)

Le Pain Quotidien, Pasadena, Brentwood &
Santa Monica (PAGES 214 & 224)

Little Flower Candy Co., Pasadena (PAGE 309)

Market on Holly, Pasadena (PAGE 215)

Marmalade Café, Malibu (PAGE 224)

Milk, Beverly/Third (PAGE 302)

Olive & Thyme, Toluca Lake (PAGE 218)

Proof Bakery, Atwater (PAGE 305)

Sweet Butter Kitchen, Sherman Oaks (PAGE 218)

Thyme Café & Market, Santa Monica (PAGE 225)

Village Bakery & Café, Atwater (PAGE 306)

VEGETARIAN ◎ KID FRIENDLY ✿ PATIO DINING ⊜ DELIVERY ⌂ PRIVATE PARTY

CENTRAL CITY

[Beverly Hills Juice Club] **8382 Beverly Blvd., Beverly/Third, 323.655.8300, beverlyhillsjuice.com. Mon.-Fri. from 7 a.m., Sat. from 10 a.m. MC, V. WHY** Cold-pressed apple-juice blends that are totally delish—try the apple strawberry or apple ginger. **WHAT** It's not really in Beverly Hills, but a harmless bit of false advertising is no reason to shun this teeny place, which specializes in cold-pressed fruit juices, wheatgrass, carrot juices and smoothie-like banana-based creations. **WHO** Healthful sorts on their way to Spinning or Pilates. ♻

[Cafecito Orgánico] **710 N. Heliotrope Dr., East Hollywood, 213.305.4484, cafecitoorganico.com. Sun.-Thurs. from 7 a.m., Fri.-Sat. from 9 a.m. AE, MC, V. WHY** Excellent organic coffee and a brief list of breakfast and lunch dishes. **WHAT** This offshoot of the first Cafecito Organico on Hoover also has a light menu and makes a perfect stop before ice cream at Scoops next door. The evolving menu usually has imaginative weekend brunch dishes, large, fresh salads and several sandwiches. Using sustainably grown, organic and free-trade South and Latin American coffee beans, the baristas pull a deft espresso. **WHO** LACC students and cyclists hanging out in the Hel-Mel "bicycle district." ♻🛍☺ ♻

[Chado Tea Room] **8422 W. 3rd St., Beverly/Third, 323.655.2056, chadotea.com. Daily from 11:30 a.m. MC, V. WHY** More than 200 varieties of tea, a tranquil setting and a yellow-coconut cake that you'll want to lie down in, because it's so hypnotically sweet and moist. **WHAT** It's really all about the tea—hundreds of teas, actually, from Darjeeling biodynamic green tea to intensely smoky Tarry Souchong, all properly brewed in a pot. A good selection of delicate sandwiches and pastries and a decadent afternoon tea menu make Chado a perfect stop for lunch or an afternoon pick-me-up. **WHO** Lots o' women, celebrating birthdays, taking their teens out for a treat and pausing for a shopping break. But men aren't afraid of the place. 🎫 ♪

[Insomnia Café] **7286 Beverly Blvd., Beverly/Third, 323.931.4943. Daily from 10 a.m. Cash only. WHY** A convenient location, comfy furniture and no-cell-phone policy make this a good spot for working or meeting someone, although parking can be tricky, and the WiFi's not free. **WHAT** This longtime caffeination station is a relaxed, friendly and very quiet place, with respectable coffee drinks and good snacks—and it's open until 1:30 a.m. **WHO** Screenwriters, freelance writers, students and a post-theater crowd. ☺ 🎫 ♪

[Sabor y Cultura] **5625 Hollywood Blvd., Hollywood, 323.466.0481. Mon.-Fri. from 6:30 a.m., Sat.-Sun. from 7:30 a.m. AE, MC, V. WHY** A friendly vibe, fairly easy street parking, free WiFi and skilled baristas. **WHAT** A double-wide storefront in Little Armenia, this spacious, inviting coffeehouse doesn't display the sort of Latin influences you might expect from its name. It's just an all-around good place to hang out over a latte, hot breakfast sandwich or frozen yogurt. Check for events: art openings, music, perhaps even flamenco dance. **WHO** A typical coffeehouse crowd, East Hollywood style. ☺ ♪ ☼

[Sanjang Coffee Garden] **101 S. Virgil Ave., East Hollywood, 213.387.9190. Mon.-Fri. from 8 a.m., Sat.-Sun. from 11 a.m. Korean. AE, MC, V. WHY** Coffee and tea drinks such as boba, Korean snacks, desserts and sandwiches. Drink prices are on the high side because many patrons stay for hours just ordering one drink. **WHAT** A lavish space catering to the Korean community features several heated outdoor areas, including one with a fire pit. All the amenities are provided, including free WiFi and blankets for snuggling by the fire, and it's open until 2 a.m. **WHO** Young Koreans—mostly smokers—and the occasional curious non-Korean. ☺ ☼

[Stir Crazy] **6903 Melrose Ave., Melrose, 323.934.4656. Mon.-Fri. from 7 a.m., Sat.-Sun. from 8 a.m. Cash only. WHY** A mellow (despite the name) hangout with good coffee and smoothies. **WHAT** A friendly neighborhood coffeehouse with free WiFi, lots of Laptop People, dogs (and smokers) on the patio and good coffee made until 1 a.m. on weekends. **WHO** Writers and locals who want to look like writers, tapping away on their MacBooks while sipping nonfat lattes. ☺ ☞ ☼

[T (Farmers Market)] **Farmers Market, 6333 W. 3rd St., Fairfax District, 323.930.0076, teashopla.com. Daily from 9 a.m. MC, V. WHY** Bypass the chains for this charming stall with hundreds of bulk teas, as well as tea drinks to enjoy in the Farmers Market bustle. **WHAT** Have a cuppa and a sandwich or take home a few exotic varieties of herbal and traditional teas. ☺ ☼

[Urth Caffé] **8565 Melrose Ave., West Hollywood, 310.659.0628, urthcaffe.com. Daily from 6:30 a.m. MC, V. WHY** Spanish lattes, tea lattes and all-around good drinks, most of which are organic and/or sustainably produced. Don't mind the poseurs and enjoy the coffee and excellent oatmeal or pumpkin pie. **WHAT** Sure, it's a Hollywood scene, and the parking is terrible, but you could do far worse in this 'hood for coffee, tea and/or a light meal. The baristas are skilled, the products are good, and the patio is a fine place to catch up with an old friend. **WHO** Actors, screenwriters and assorted pretty people—a stereotypical L.A. crowd. ☺ ☝ ☼

EASTSIDE

[Café Corsa] 🔖 **2238 S. Figueroa St., USC, 213.746.2604, cafecorsala. com. Mon.-Fri. from 7 a.m. MC, V. WHY** It's the least pretentious—and least expensive—place in town to enjoy coffee brewed by individual

+ Juices

cup in a Clover machine. **WHAT** Hidden in a strip mall between Staples Center and USC, this place is a total find for coffee lovers. It has a good and often-varying selection of fair-trade beans from around the world, a talented barista and a Clover machine, which allows aficionados to sample all sorts of coffees for as low as $2 a brewed cup. **WHO** The coffee-savvy from Downtown, USC and West Adams. 🖼️♻️

[Café de Leche] **5000 York Blvd., Highland Park, 323.551.6828, cafedeleche.net. Daily from 7 a.m. Cash only. WHY** This youngish café is everything that this gentrifying neighborhood promises to be: accessible, affordable and full of adorably attired babies. **WHAT** At the corner of York and Avenue 50, this is a perfect little coffeehouse in a neighborhood that needed it. The menu is small, but everything is delicious (try the jalapeño bagels). There's a fantastic selection of organic teas, as well as the expected lattes and mochas—and an amazingly creamy hot chocolate that's full of spices. A row of little tables is perfect for laptops, and there are enough outlets for them all—plus free wireless. **WHO** Twentysomethings working at their laptops and indie parents with cute indie children. 🖼️♻️🕐

[Cafecito Orgánico] **534 N. Hoover St., Silver Lake, 213.305.4484, cafecitoorganico.com. Mon.-Fri. from 6 a.m., Sat.-Sun. from 7 a.m. MC, V. WHY** A mellow alternative to Silver Lake's over-caffeinated coffee scene. **WHAT** Housed in a faux-lighthouse building on none-too-gentrified Hoover Street, this place started selling organic fair-trade beans at local farmers' markets before opening the café. With free WiFi, a large covered patio and baked goods from Echo Park's Delilah Bakery, it's a funky and calm place for a cappuccino or the special house Cafecito, made with steamed milk and sugar cane juice. All the freshly roasted beans are available by the pound. ♻️🕯️

[Coffee Table] **2930 Rowena Ave., Silver Lake, 323.644.8111, coffeetablebistro.com. Daily from 7 a.m. AE, MC, V. WHY** Because the front patio and back porch are spacious, and the menu is broad enough for any time of day. **WHAT** This Silver Lake stalwart offers not only a full range of coffee drinks but also hearty breakfast burritos, a decent burger, salads and desserts. **WHO** Silver Lake moms, screenwriters jousting over power outlets, and dog owners. 🌿🕐🕯️

[Intelligentsia Coffee] 🔒 **3922 W. Sunset Blvd., Silver Lake, 323.663.6173, intelligentsiacoffee.com. Daily from 6 a.m. AE, MC, V. WHY** A very serious approach to coffee, but without the snobbiness seen at some other one-cup-brewed-at-a-time joints. **WHAT** Silver Lake's intelligentsia—those who can afford your higher-end coffees, that is—belly up to the bar or snag a Sunset Junction patio table to linger over aromatic, beautifully prepared drip coffee or espresso drinks. **WHO** Silver Lake cool people—and isn't everyone who lives in Silver Lake cool? ♻️🕯️

[Kaldi] **3147 Glendale Blvd., Atwater, 323.660.6005, kaldiatwater.com. Mon.-Fri. from 6:30 a.m., Sat. & Sun. from 7 a.m. MC, V. WHY** Smaller than the South Pasadena location, this funky coffeehouse offers free WiFi and sidewalk tables that are prime for people-watching. **WHAT** This is the place to come for sturdy cappuccinos and plenty of other coffee and tea permutations, but don't come hungry—food selections are minimal. **WHO** Trendy young couples and families from hipsterfying Atwater. 📷 ☼

[Lamill] **1636 Silver Lake Blvd., Silver Lake, 323.663.4441, lamillcoffee. com. Daily from 7 a.m. AE, MC, V. WHY** For an obsessive approach to perfect coffee, made in a Clover or tableside via Chemex, served in the swankiest coffee shop in town. Excellent cold-brewed iced coffee, too. **WHAT** Is it a coffeehouse or a restaurant? The answer seems to be the latter, thanks to the menu by consulting chef Michael Cimarusti (Providence). But you can still come here just for a cup of hand-brewed coffee or a meticulously crafted latte, though you'll have to order it from a waiter instead of at a counter, and you'd better not be in a rush. If you're a serious coffee person, you've probably already been here. If you're not, it's probably not worth it just for a cup of coffee—but it might be worth it for a foodie lunch. **WHO** People who can order a $7 cup of coffee and live with themselves. ☼

[The Novel Café] **811 E. Traction Ave., Little Tokyo/Arts District, 323.621.2240, novelcafe.com. Mon.-Fri. from 7 a.m., Sat.-Sun. from 8 a.m. AE, MC, V. WHY** Good-enough Groundworks coffee, a hang-as-long-as-you-like vibe and a location in the hip Arts District. **WHAT** This ahead-of-the-curve Arts District coffeehouse is an offshoot of Venice's expanding Novel Café. It's scruffily pleasant, staffed by heavily tattooed young folks, and it has a big menu of wraps, pastries and salads—although we stick to the coffee and do our eating on the next block at Wurstküche. **WHO** Rocker-artist loft kids and a few casual-Friday types getting their dogs out of the loft for a walk. 📷 🐾 ☼

[Oaxacalifornia Juice Bar] **Mercado La Paloma, 3655 S. Grand Ave., USC, 213.747.8622, mercadolapaloma.com. Daily from 8 a.m. Mexican/Oaxacan. MC, V. WHY** Delicious licuados, smoothies and juices. **WHAT** In Mercado La Paloma, a nonprofit community center with restaurants, shops and meeting spaces, this Oaxacan stand makes very good juice drinks that go beautifully with the food from the famed Mo-Chica and the excellent Chichen Itza. Homemade ice creams, too. **WHO** Latino families and USC students from the neighborhood. 📷 ☺

[Primera Taza] **1850 1/2 1st St., Boyle Heights, 323.780.3923, primerataza.com. Mon.-Sat. from 7:30 a.m., Sun. from 8 a.m. MC, V. WHY** A place to hang in bitchin' Boyle Heights. **WHAT** This funky, rather cramped coffeehouse is emblematic of the gentrification of Boyle Heights (in case you didn't know, it's the new Echo Park, which

🥬 **VEGETARIAN** ☺ **KID FRIENDLY** ☼ **PATIO DINING** � **DELIVERY** 🎩 **PRIVATE PARTY**

in turn was the new Silver Lake only yesterday), thanks in part to the newish Metro station out front. It has all the essentials: free WiFi, art-for-sale on the walls, occasional live music and the expected coffee drinks, smoothies, pastries and light dishes. Try the Taza de Mocha, a latte made with Mexican cocoa. **WHO** Boyle Heights cool people and east Downtowners making the trek over the 1st Street bridge. 🗺️ ☺

[Swörk] **2160 Colorado Blvd., Eagle Rock, 323.258.5600, sworkcoffee. com. Daily from 6 a.m. AE, MC, V. WHY** Dark-roast Truck Driver blend, free WiFi and kids' drinks like the Princess Potion. **WHAT** More than a decade ago, this corner storefront with an Ikea-style décor brought good coffee, free WiFi and a stylish yet family-friendly vibe to Eagle Rock, which has since gone on to become a shabby-chic hip spot. **WHO** Moms and dads drawn by the irresistible combo of strong caffeine and a kids' play area; loyal locals with laptops or screenplays to read. ☺ ☼

[Ten Ren Tea] 🏛️ **727 N. Broadway, Chinatown, 213.626.8844, tenren. com. Daily from 10 a.m. Chinese. AE, MC, V. WHY** Bulk teas, ginseng and hot teas, iced teas and iced milk teas to sip in the shop. **WHAT** This Chinatown branch of the international tea company has a loyal following for its bulk teas from around the world: green, jasmine, black, Pouchong, Ti Kuan, organic teas, flavored teas and more. Take a break and sit down with an iced bubble (*boba*) tea or a pot of King's Tea. 🍵

[Tropical Zone Ice Cream & Juice Bar] **Grand Central Market, 317 S. Broadway, Downtown, 213.617.2233. Daily from 9 a.m. Cash only. WHY** This vintage juice bar is a throwback to the days when fruit juices were considered exotic health foods. **WHAT** This venerable stand offers a large selection of juices, including tropical fruits, and smoothie combinations at reasonable prices. There's ice cream, too. **WHO** Grand Central Market's endless parade of Downtown office workers, Latino shoppers and dutiful citizens on jury duty. 🗺️ ☺

[Urth Caffé] **451 S. Hewitt St., Little Tokyo/Arts District, 213.797.4534, urthcaffe.com. Daily from 6:30 a.m. MC, V. WHY** Spanish lattes, tea lattes and all-around good drinks, most of which are organic and/or sustainably produced. And did we mention free guarded parking? In the heart of Downtown's Arts District, no less? **WHAT** It's pricey and sometimes too crowded, but when you factor in the free parking, free WiFi and high-quality food (try the turkey burger and pumpkin pie), you could do far worse Downtown. The baristas are skilled, the bakery is good, and the patio is a pleasant place to talk shop. **WHO** Young Downtowners who look like they'd live in Santa Monica. 🌀🍃☼

SAN GABRIEL VALLEY

[Au 79 Tea Spirit] **1635 S. San Gabriel Blvd., San Gabriel, 626.569.9768. Daily from 12 p.m. Asian. MC, V. WHY** A huge selection of tea drinks and bobas; we love the lavender infusion. **WHAT** A happening Taiwanese tea and boba hangout, with a TV blaring by day, music playing by night and very good tea drinks all the time. **WHO** Young Taiwanese hipsters in animated conversation. ☺ ☺

[Bean Town Coffee Bar] 45 N. Baldwin Ave., Sierra Madre, 626.355.1596, beantowncoffeebar.com. Daily from 5:30 a.m. MC, V. **WHY** Because it makes you want to move to Sierra Madre just to make this place your local coffeehouse. **WHAT** This just might be the perfect coffeehouse—robust java, funky-but-comfortable furniture and a terrifically diverse crowd. All that plus bluegrass and folk music on the weekends, WiFi, board games, sidewalk tables and homemade baked goods. **WHO** Book clubbers, retirees, moms with strollers, teens, dogs. ▦ ☺ ☼

[Buster's] 1006 Mission St., South Pasadena, 626.441.0744, busterscoffee.com. Mon.-Fri. from 6:30 a.m., Sat.-Sun. from 7 a.m. Cash only. **WHY** Lime rickeys, Fosselman's ice cream and gentle baristas. **WHAT** A few steps from the Gold Line, this colorful neighborhood hub offers prime people-watching from a handful of sidewalk tables. Or grab an inside table (upstairs or down) to sip a latte or savor a scoop of mint chip. **WHO** School kids, commuters, local loft-dwellers and music fans (performances on weekends). ☺ ☼

[Chado Tea Room] 79 N. Raymond Ave., Old Pasadena, 626.431.2832, chadotea.com. Daily from 11:30 a.m. MC, V. **WHY** More than 200 varieties of tea, and a yellow-coconut cake that you'll want to lie down in, because it's so hypnotically sweet and moist. **WHAT** An afternoon tea room with an English look, knowledgeable servers, full high-tea service and many good teas. **WHO** Lots o' women, celebrating birthdays, taking their teens out for a treat and pausing for an Old Town shopping break. 🍴

[The Coffee Gallery] 2029 N. Lake Ave., Altadena, 626.398.7917, coffeegallery.com. Mon.-Fri. from 6 a.m., Sat.-Sun. from 7 a.m. MC, V. **WHY** You can hang out as long as you like, and the private room is great for a committee meeting. **WHAT** Maybe it's not the best coffee in town—and the service is often bizarrely slow—but there's something endearing about this appealingly scruffy place anyway. For one thing, the live music in the separate concert room is often amazing. **WHO** A cast of Altadena characters, from local politicians to aging hippies to moms 'n kids. ▦ 🍴 ☺ ☼ 🏠

[Fresh Roast] 308 S. San Gabriel Blvd., San Gabriel, 626.451.5918. Daily from 7:30 a.m. MC, V. **WHY** Roasted on-site coffee, in bulk or to drink here, prepared by the Chinese-American owner, Jimmy, who's brought his passion for coffee to a neighborhood that needed it. Great prices, too. **WHAT** This coffee roaster, coffeehouse and juice bar is a

+ Juices

🥬 **VEGETARIAN** ⊙ **KID FRIENDLY** ☼ **PATIO DINING** 🚚 **DELIVERY** 🏠 **PRIVATE PARTY** real find, run by a friendly guy who wants everyone to love coffee as much as he does. Fresh-roasted beans are just $8 a pound; espressos and lattes are carefully made; and the juice selection (coconut, orange, sugarcane) is seductive. Best of all, each cup of brewed coffee is made to order—Jimmy doesn't believe in having coffee sit around. Try the Vietnamese coffee. 🗺️ ☼

[Intelligentsia Pasadena] **55 E. Colorado Blvd., Old Pasadena, 626.578.1270, intelligentsiacoffee.com. Mon.-Fri. from 6 a.m., Sat.-Sun. from 7 a.m. Beer & wine. AE, MC, V. WHY** A multi-purpose café with indie cred in the midst of corporate Old Pasadena. **WHAT** Of course, it has its own pour-over coffees, a gleaming espresso machine and practiced baristas. But this new location, in a historic brick building furnished with reclaimed church pews and electric blue walls, also has a beer and wine bar with a thoughtful selection of pours. Eagle Rock Brewery supplies on-tap selections like Stimulus, a beer brewed with coffee, while small plates of cheese, charcuterie, pasta, tacos and more are available for grazing. With pastries and desserts too, this groovy temple of caffeine is good to go from early morning till 10 p.m. **WHO** Caltech and Art Center students and serious shoppers.

[Jameson Brown Coffee Roasters] **260 N. Allen Ave., East Pasadena, 626.395.7585, jamesonbrown.com. Mon.-Fri. from 7 a.m., Sat. from 8 a.m. MC, V. WHY** First-rate house-roasted beans or coffee to drink on-site in a spacious, peaceful setting. **WHAT** Can't find a seat at Jones? Then head to this fine coffeehouse, which also roasts its own beans (they're excellent) and has a lot more room to hang out than its west Pasadena competitor. Founded by Fuller Seminary folks, it has a community focus, free WiFi and an almost studious vibe. **WHO** Fuller Seminary and Caltech students, seniors meeting friends, and creative types looking for a place to write or think... with coffee. 🍵

[Jones Coffee] 🏛️ **693 S. Raymond Ave., Pasadena, 626.564.9291, thebestcoffee.com. Mon.-Fri. from 6:30 a.m., Sat.-Sun. from 8 a.m. AE, MC, V. WHY** The best latte on the eastside, great house-roasted beans and frequent live music. **WHAT** One of Pasadena's premier coffee roasters (the other is Jameson Brown), Jones has a globe-hopping selection of roasted beans (including organic choices) as well as green beans for home-roasting and offerings from the proprietors' Guatemalan coffee plantation. And the espresso drinks are exquisitely crafted. Extras include baked goods from Euro Pane, tamales on Fridays, regular live music and, on Wednesday evenings in summer, a great food truck confab. **WHO** Writers, moms, artists, Caltech and Art Center profs and students, Huntington docs... everyone who's anyone in Pasadena. 🗺️☼☼

[Kaldi] **1019 El Centro St., South Pasadena, 626.403.5951. Mon.-Fri. from 7 a.m., Sat.-Sun. from 7:30 a.m. AE, MC, V. WHY** An authentic and appealing slice of European-style café life, right in the middle of Small Town, U.S.A. **WHAT** The sultry purple neon sign beckons passersby into this popular hangout in a handsome old brick building across from the library. On the menu: well-made espresso drinks and sunny sidewalk tables, but not much to eat. **WHO** Students and game players who favor the outdoor tables; freshly coiffed patrons of the salon next door; errand-runners and library patrons. 🎵 ☼

[Langham Huntington Hotel] 🏠 **1401 S. Oak Knoll Ave., Pasadena, 626.585.6218, pasadena.langhamhotels.com. Thurs.-Sat. from 1 p.m. AE, MC, V. WHY** A proper silver tea service, heavenly scones and, for those who must, good Champagne. **WHAT** The swankiest afternoon tea east of Beverly Hills is served in the lobby lounge at this lovely Pasadena landmark. White linens, formal service, tiered trays of scones, sandwiches and pastries all reassure one that the barbarians are safely on the other side of the gates. The price may cause a heart attack, but what a way to go! **WHO** Blue-blood grandmothers taking their granddaughters to tea. ♥ 🎵 ☺

[Peet's Coffee & Tea] **605 S. Lake Ave., Pasadena, 626.795.7413, peets.com. Daily from 5 a.m. AE, MC, V. WHY** Major Dickason's blend. **WHAT** If you must drink at a chain, this estimable Bay Area institution is the one to pick. The coffee drinks are robust and made by actual baristas, the take-home beans are addictive and thoughtfully ground, and all the locations were carefully chosen to showcase Peets' outdoor tables in lively, people-watching neighborhoods. Delectable baked goods, too. **WHO** Parents after drop-off at Pasadena's nearby Polytechnic School; Lake Avenue shoppers; Caltech profs; homesick Northern Californians. 🎵 ☺ ☼

[Perry's Joint] **2051 Lincoln Ave., Pasadena, 626.798.4700, perrysjoint.com. Mon.-Fri. from 8 a.m., Sat. from 10 a.m. MC, V. WHY** Can't beat the soundtrack—great jazz on the stereo. **WHAT** A sophisticated, spacious spot, Perry's is a terrific place to hold small business meetings or to work on your laptop (free WiFi). Good coffee, tasty sandwiches and Dreyer's ice cream. **WHO** The hipper sorts of Northwest Pasadenans, after-school kids and employees of local nonprofits. 🖃 🎵 ☺

[Scarlet Tea Room] **18 W. Green St., Pasadena, 626.577.0051, scarlettearoom.com. Tues.-Sun. from 11 a.m. Beer & wine. AE, MC, V. WHY** A serene afternoon tea service with delectable scones and the best strawberry jam around. **WHAT** Tea-party groups (no, not that kind of Tea Party) meet here for the peaceful, gilt-trimmed setting and handy Old Pasadena location. If you can't make it for the finger sandwiches, check out the surprisingly happening dinner scene (live jazz on weekends). Good happy hour, too. **WHO** Teen girls, women celebrating birthdays and, at night, date couples. ♥ 🎵

🥬 VEGETARIAN ☺ KID FRIENDLY ☼ PATIO DINING 🚐 DELIVERY 🏮 PRIVATE PARTY

[Ten Ren & Tea Station] **154 & 158 W. Valley Blvd., San Gabriel, 626.288.1663; 111 W. Garvey Ave., Monterey Park, 626.288.2012; tenren. com. Daily from 10 a.m. Chinese. AE, MC, V. WHY** A good range of teas, delicious fried tofu and tasty taro balls. **WHAT** This tea-dealing chain is part retail store, part Chinese tea room. You can buy bulk green, jasmine, black, Pouchong, flavored, organic and pretty much any kind of tea, or sit down next door with a properly brewed cup or a refreshing boba. 🗺️☺

[Zephyr Coffee House & Art Gallery] **2419 E. Colorado Blvd., East Pasadena, 626.793.7330, zephyrcoffeeandart.com. Mon.-Sat. from 8 a.m., Sun. from 9 a.m. Cash only. WHY** A place to join the regulars and settle in with newspaper or laptop. Often-worthwhile music on weekend nights. **WHAT** This hidden gem is a Craftsman cottage suffused with Zen-like beauty and calm. Comfy sofas, tree-shaded patio tables and a menu that includes tasty crêpes. **WHO** Art students, hookah smokers on the side patio, and the sort of Pasadenan who sends her child to a co-op nursery school and grows her own tomatoes. ♥☼

[Zona Rosa Caffé] **15 S. El Molino Ave., Pasadena, 626.793.2334, zonarosacaffe.com. Mon.-Sat. from 7:30 a.m., Sun. from 9 a.m. Mexican. Cash only. WHY** Heavenly Mexican hot chocolate to sip in the charming and romantic upstairs room. **WHAT** Tiny and vividly colorful, this coffeehouse has Mexican flair and a prime location next to the Pasadena Playhouse. In summer they host live music in the adjacent alley. **WHO** Shoppers, strollers, readers and theater-goers—in addition to the Playhouse next door, there's an art-house Laemmle multiplex and the great bookstore Vroman's just around the corner ♥ 🎵 ☼

EAST VALLEY

[Aroma Café] 🏛️ **4360 Tujunga Ave., Studio City, 818.508.0677, aromacoffeeandtea.com. Mon.-Sat. from 6 a.m., Sun. from 7 a.m. MC, V. WHY** Well-made iced lattes, cappuccinos and chai drinks to drink on a patio of tremendous charm. **WHAT** Owned by the same folks behind Alcove in Los Feliz, this café/coffeehouse/bookstore is in a fetching old cottage with a lovely enclosed brick patio. The menu is extensive, but it's fine to just have coffee. Partial table service (order at the counter) can be spotty and a little full of attitude, and you'll have to wait at peak times, but the coffee, food and setting are usually worth it. **WHO** Studio City beautiful people, including lots of writers. ♥🖤☼

[Coffee Roaster] **13567 Ventura Blvd., Sherman Oaks, 818.905.9719, thecoffeeroaster.net. Mon.-Sat. from 7 a.m. MC, V. WHY** Roasted on-site beans sold by the pound, and robust coffee drinks to take away or drink in the tiny café. **WHAT** This longstanding Valley shop roasts beans to sell both retail and wholesale. That's its main business, but it also makes lattes, mochas and brewed blends.

🏛️ **ESSENTIALLY L.A.** ☺ **LATE** ♥ **ROMANTIC** 🗺️ **VALUE** 🎵 **QUIET** ☼ **SUSTAINABLE**

[M Street Coffee] 13251 Moorpark St., Sherman Oaks, 818.907.1400, mstreetcoffee.com. Mon.-Fri. from 7 a.m., Sat.-Sun. from 8 a.m. MC, V. **WHY** Nice people, good organic coffee, smoothies and chai, copies of the *L.A. Weekly* and free WiFi. **WHAT** A bright yet soothing space done in earth tones makes for a comfortable spot to sit with a cappuccino or an iced chai latte. Interesting art-for-sale, too. **WHO** Writers, artists, friends meeting to chat quietly and assorted Starbucks refugees. ☼

[Priscilla's Gourmet Coffee] 4150 W. Riverside Dr., Toluca Lake, 818.843.5707, priscillascoffee.com. Mon.-Fri. from 6 a.m., Sat.-Sun. from 7 a.m. AE, MC, V. **WHY** A lovely, relaxed neighborhood hangout with good cinnamon streusel. **WHAT** We wish the coffee were better, but we forgive Priscilla's any faults. It still has a lot more personality than Starbucks. Free WiFi, amusing industry eavesdropping and good coffeehouse snacks. **WHO** TV writers, production people, beautiful actress/moms—the usual Toluca Lake crowd. ☺ ☺ ☼

WEST VALLEY

[Java Groove Coffee House] 14310 Victory Blvd., Van Nuys, 818.785.6593, javagroovecoffee.com. Mon.-Sat. from 8 a.m. MC, V. **WHY** Perfectly respectable Illy coffee drinks (lattes, americanos), teas and chai in a part of the Valley that is woefully short on indie hang-outs. **WHAT** A fine, all-around coffeehouse with the usual offerings: coffee drinks, smoothies, bagels, panini, free WiFi and, for an extra treat, Belgian waffles. ☺ ☼

[Peet's Coffee & Tea] 18973 Ventura Blvd., Tarzana, 818.401.0263, peets.com. Mon.-Fri. from 5 a.m., Sat.-Sun. from 5:30 a.m. AE, MC, V. **WHY** True neighborhood coffeehouses are as rare as cool summer days in the West Valley, so Peet's is the next best thing—or the best thing, depending on how hooked you are on Major Dickason's Blend. **WHAT** If you must drink at a chain, this estimable Bay Area institution is the one to pick. The coffee drinks are robust and made by actual baristas, the take-home beans are addictive and thoughtfully ground, and the Ventura Blvd. location is prime for people-watching. Delectable baked goods, too. ☺ ☼

WESTSIDE: CENTRAL

[American Tea Room] 401 N. Cañon Dr., Beverly Hills, 310.271.7922, americantearoom.com. Mon.-Sat. from 10 a.m., Sun. from 12 p.m. AE, MC, V. **WHY** A beautiful space with both a retail operation and a tea room in the heart of Beverly Hills. **WHAT** Beverly Hills is the obvious location for a tea boutique of this quality and price level. Indulge in brewed tea and lovely petits fours at the counter, shop for a swank gift for a tea-loving friend, or take home a tin of a rare blend.

Coffee, Tea + Juices

🍃 **VEGETARIAN** ◎ **KID FRIENDLY** ☼ **PATIO DINING** 🚐 **DELIVERY** 🎉 **PRIVATE PARTY**

WHO BevHills matrons, tourists from around the world and tea buffs with full wallets.

[The Conservatory] 🏠 **10117 Washington Blvd., Culver City, 310.558.0436, conservatorycoffeeandtea.com. Mon.-Sat. from 7 a.m. AE, MC, V. WHY** Subtle, artful roasting in a low-key yet cool environment where the bean is king. Seriously good cocoa, too. **WHAT** The on-site roasting makes this a coffeehouse for aficionados. Fans sing the praises of the nuanced brews and drive happily from the Valley or beyond just to buy a pound. The location, across the street from Sony Studios, is a convenient place to caffeinate before a pitch meeting. **WHO** Culver City locals, studio musicians, screenwriters and anyone with business at that big movie studio across the street. 🔷 ☺ ☼

[Espresso Profeta] **1129 Glendon Ave., Westwood, 310.208.3375, espressoprofetala.com. Daily from 7 a.m. MC, V. WHY** Just when you think Westwood is nothing but chains, you find this charming spot with rich, creamy espresso pulled by people who love it. **WHAT** In an atmospheric 1927 brick building in the heart of the Village, Espresso Profeta has it all: beautiful coffee drinks made from custom-roasted beans, food from Breadbar and Buttercake Bakery, free WiFi (but no power outlets) and comfy spots to hang out. It's not cheap, but it's worth it. **WHO** Your more sophisticated brand of UCLA student. 🍃 ☼

[Euro Caffé] **9559 S. Santa Monica Blvd., Beverly Hills, 310.274.9070. Mon.-Fri. from 7 a.m., Sat. from 8 a.m., Sun. from 9 a.m. Italian. MC, V. WHY** For true Italian espresso drinks made from a giant brass R2-D2 machine, with good panini and baked goods, too. **WHAT** This small caffé is authentically Italian—which means no hanging around with your laptop for hours. Instead, drink your carefully pulled espresso or glass of Valpolicella (it's an enoteca, too) or eat your caprese salad at one of the three sidewalk tables or five indoor tables, and then move on. **WHO** The local Italian expat community, all of whom seem to show up when Italian soccer is on TV, mixed with women who've had work done and men of a certain age who know their way around a tanning booth. 🍃 ☼

[Paddington's Tea Room] **355 S. Robertson Blvd., Beverly Hills, 310.652.0624, paddingtonstearoom.com. Daily from 11 a.m. English. AE, MC, V. WHY** For either a proper British afternoon tea service or a more substantial high tea, both of which feature the Royal Blend from Fortnum & Mason and lovely finger sandwiches and scones with Devon cream. **WHAT** The stuffed-animal-phobic may get itchy (Paddington Bears are everywhere), but everyone else will enjoy the charm of this English tea room. Kindly women pour tea, and in back is a shop stocked with such British must-haves as Cadbury chocolate and looseleaf teas. **WHO** Ladies who take tea, grandmas treating grandchildren, and birthday celebrants. 🍃 ☺

🏠 **ESSENTIALLY L.A.** ☺ **LATE** ♥ **ROMANTIC** 🍃 **VALUE** 🍃 **QUIET** 🔷 **SUSTAINABLE**

[Paper or Plastik] 5772 W. Pico Blvd., Pico-Robertson, 323.935.0268, paperorplastikcafe.com. Daily from 7 a.m. MC, V. **WHY** It's business in the front and party in the back at this industrial-chic café that's equal parts coffee shrine and performance space. **WHAT** This small, subdued place serves impeccable brews by Intelligentsia and Ecco along with sweet and savory treats from Auntie Em's and Breadbar. On the mezzanine level, a shop stocked with Moroccan vases and artisanal Eastern European wares overlooks a large dance studio that husband and wife Yasha and Anya Michelson have transformed into a hub for emerging artists with dance classes, film screenings and performance salons. Turkish coffee with a hip-hop ballet? Naturally. **WHO** Coffee snobs, writers slaving away at their latest masterpiece and an eclectic mix of dancers, comedians, filmmakers and performers. 🖼️ ☼

[Royal/T Café] 🍴 8910 Washington Blvd., Culver City, 310.559.6300, royal-t.org/cafe. Daily from 10 a.m. Japanese. AE, MC, V. **WHY** For an L.A. take on a Japanese maid café, with very good, carefully presented matcha and milk teas and lovely tea-friendly sandwiches, Japanese dishes and pastries, served with performance-art flair. **WHAT** Royal/T provides the most singular tea experience you can possibly imagine, blending underground Japanese geek culture with English high-tea conventions, served by waitresses done up in French maids' costumes (a wee bit creepy in that *Lolita* way), set in the midst of a 10,000-square-foot collection of contemporary Japanese art. It's the strange and fascinating vision of collector/owner Susan Hancock, and you really must experience it. **WHO** Artists, collectors, tea ritualists and the curious. 🍴

[Urth Caffé] 267 S. Beverly Dr., Beverly Hills, 310.205.9311, urthcaffe. com. Daily from 6:30 a.m. MC, V. **WHY** Organic coffee, excellent teas and good food with a vegetarian/vegan emphasis. **WHAT** Except for the Lamborghinis parked out front and $200 T-shirts being worn by patrons inside, you could be at any of the other Urth locations. **WHO** Beautiful people, in a Beverly Hills way. 🌿🍴☼

WEST OF THE 405

[18th Street Coffee House] 1725 Broadway, Santa Monica, 310.264.0662. Mon.-Fri. from 7 a.m., Sat. from 8 a.m. Cash only. **WHY** Homemade rugelach and 50-cent refills. **WHAT** This adorable historic brick building, complete with homey outdoor patio, has a folksy, East Bay/East Village vibe (but no, Bob Dylan does not own it, local rumor mill notwithstanding). **WHO** Young moms, students, writers and people without cell phone addictions (there's an outdoor-calling-only policy). 🌿☺☼

[Abbot's Habit] 1401 Abbot Kinney Blvd., Venice, 310.399.1171, abbotshabit.com. Daily from 6 a.m. MC, V. **WHY** Mellow vibe, good coffee, amusing people-watching. **WHAT** Try for a coveted sidewalk table

---

🌿 **VEGETARIAN** ☺ **KID FRIENDLY** ☼ **PATIO DINING** 🚗 **DELIVERY** 🏠 **PRIVATE PARTY**

at this funky (think Berkeley in the '70s) place in the heart of ultra-hip Abbot Kinney. Or check out the two inside rooms, where you can grab a sandwich or settle in for the afternoon with a laptop or sketchbook. **WHO** A happy mix of upwardly mobile Venice homeowners and hippie stoners. ♻ ☺ ☼

[Balconi Coffee] **11301 W. Olympic Blvd. #124, West L.A., 310.906.0267, balconicofeeecompany.com. Daily from 10 a.m. MC, V.** **WHY** To sit in front of a row of siphons, sip coffee and talk to the owner about the body, flavor and other qualities of every coffee he offers. Try the latte flavored with crushed almonds. **WHAT** Why would a coffeehouse not open until 10 a.m.? Owner Ray Sato says because in the early morning, people are just slamming their coffee and hurrying on. He wants his patrons to relax and give their cup o' joe their full attention. And they do, sampling meticulously prepared coffee brewed from a variety of organic, local and/or fair-trade beans. The Japanese-influenced setting is serene, and there's free validated parking. **WHO** People who obsess over their beans. ☼

[Café Bolivar] **1741 Ocean Park Blvd., Santa Monica, 310.581.2344, cafebolivar.com. Mon.-Fri. from 7 a.m., Sat. from 9 a.m. Cash only.** **WHY** It's the perfect place to sit and finish your novel (the one you're reading or the one you're writing), while sipping coffee and eating some addictive *arepas* (stuffed cornmeal patties). **WHAT** This friendly, relaxed place is a real find in a sleeper Ocean Park neighborhood. It's got an open, modern look and warm Latin music on the stereo, along with excellent coffee and delicious lunches (grilled chicken sandwich with roasted pepper pesto, a true Spanish *jamón serrano*, a vegan torta). Free WiFi, too. **WHO** Art lovers and poets drawn to the openings and readings that occasionally liven things up; friends looking for a good spot to catch up. ▦ ◗ ☺

[Caffè Luxxe] **925 Montana Ave., Santa Monica, 310.394.2222, caffeluxxe.com. Mon.-Fri. from 6 a.m., Sat.-Sun. from 6:30 a.m. AE, MC, V. WHY** Each cup is a work of art. **WHAT** This place makes the best cappuccino in Santa Monica (calm down—Intelligentsia is in Venice). The setting is serene and European, with high ceilings and framed mirrors. Only espresso drinks are served (no brewed coffee), along with a few high-quality baked goods. But when the drinks are this good—the espresso creamy and almost sweet, the milk steamed with artistry and precision—who needs more? **WHO** Serious coffee lovers. ♻

[Dragon Herbs] **315 Wilshire Blvd., Santa Monica, 310.917.2288, dragonherbs.com. Daily from 11 a.m. Chinese. AE, MC, V. WHY** For adviser-designed herb tea drinks that just might cure what ails you. **WHAT** All sorts of Chinese herbs and teas are served at the tonic bar in this retail herb emporium. Tell the folks here what you're seeking (more energy, less weight, fewer hot flashes), and they'll fix you up with a drink that just might help. **WHO** The seriously health conscious.

[Funnel Mill] 🔒 **930 Broadway, Santa Monica, 310.393.1617, funnelmill.com. Mon.-Fri. from 9 a.m., Sat. from 10 a.m. MC, V.** **WHY** Siphon coffee and cold-water-infusion iced coffee, made with quality beans—you can taste the layers of flavor in the Sumatra Mandheling like a good bar of chocolate. **WHAT** Coffee is taken very seriously at this soothing spot, where a waterfall burbles and people work quietly on laptops (free WiFi). You can choose from a global menu of coffee beans to have ground and brewed in a glass siphon at your table, or explore the exceptional collection of teas, including an authentic Indian chai and fresh ginseng. Know that there are no take-out drinks, and expect to wait a good ten minutes while your coffee brews—it's worth the wait. The four-coffee sampler tray is a great way to expand your java palate. **WHO** Studious sorts who love the quiet, but mostly people who are *really* into their coffee or their tea. 🍵

[Groundwork] **2908 Main St., Santa Monica, 310.392.9243, lacoffee. com. Mon.-Fri. from 6 a.m., Sat.-Sun. from 7 a.m. AE, MC, V.** **WHY** For house-roasted organic coffee, properly robust, to take home by the pound or order in a cup. **WHAT** Don't expect to hang out in this minia-ture storefront—it's a place to buy good whole beans to take home or a tasty brewed cup or latte to take with you. 🌱☕

[Infuzion Café] **1149 3rd St., Santa Monica, 310.393.9985, infuzioncafe.com. Mon.-Fri. from 6:30 a.m., Sat. from 7 a.m., Sun. from 8 a.m. MC, V.** **WHY** Delicious "infuzions," friendly people. **WHAT** This tiny coffeehouse just north of the Promenade draws a local, non-tour-ist crowd all day long. There's free WiFi, but the tables are too small to allow for hours of leisurely Facebooking. The coffee's fine, and the café's signature "infuzions"—fruit-based iced-blended drinks—are delicious. **WHO** Local office workers and shoppers, who line up at peak hours. 🌱☕

[Intelligentsia Venice Coffeebar] 🔒 **1331 Abbot Kinney Blvd., Venice, 310.399.1233, intelligentsiacoffee.com. Sun.-Fri. from 6 a.m., Sat. from 7 a.m. AE, MC, V.** **WHY** So you can be greeted by your own personal barista. **WHAT** When this offshoot of the Chicago-by-way-of-Silver-Lake coffeehouse opened on Abbot Kinney, you'd have thought the Obamas themselves were pulling espressos from the Synesso machines. Coffee geeks walk into this light-filled industrial space and begin hyperventilat-ing at the sight of the Mazzer grinders and array of contraptions, from Si-phon to Chemex—but the gentle guidance of their personal barista soon calms the feverish excitement. Said baristas escort each guest through the space, guiding him or her to the station that best suits his or her desires (espresso, brewed, pressed). Yes, it's dreadfully precious, but the coffee is damn good. Seating is on uncomfortable stadium-style benches.

+ Juices

🍃 **VEGETARIAN** ☺ **KID FRIENDLY** ☼ **PATIO DINING** 🚗 **DELIVERY** 🎩 **PRIVATE PARTY**

WHO The sort of people who can argue about whether the overtones in a particular brew suggest cherries or tamarind. ♲

[Jin Patisserie] 🏠 **1202 Abbot Kinney Blvd., Venice, 310.399.8801, jinpatisserie.com. Tues.-Sun. from 11 a.m. AE, MC, V. WHY** Very good coffee and infused teas, sublime chocolates and scones to accompany them, and a lovely garden patio on which to enjoy it all. **WHAT** This elegant patisserie showcases owner Kristy Choo's meticulously crafted works of chocolate art, which go down well with a cup of coffee or tea. **WHO** The most refined of Abbot Kinney's cool crowd take tea and pastries on Jin's serene enclosed patio. ♥ 🍵 ♲ ☼

[The Legal Grind] **2640 Lincoln Blvd., Santa Monica, 310.452.8160, legalgrind.com. Mon.-Fri. from 9 a.m., Sat. from 10 a.m. MC, V. WHY** Where else can $45 buy you "coffee & counsel"—a cuppa joe and twenty minutes of legal consultation? **WHAT** Corporate law was a grind, so Jeff Hughes combined his desire to become a "people's lawyer" with his love of a good coffeehouse to create this unusual place. You can drop in or make an appointment to get legal help with your latte. 💲 🍵

[Newsroom the Espresso Café] **530 Wilshire Blvd., Santa Monica, 310.319.9100. Mon.-Fri. from 8 a.m., Sat.-Sun. from 9 a.m. AE, MC, V. WHY** Tasty oat bran muffins and other healthy treats. **WHAT** This friendly café is well located in central Santa Monica, just a short walk from the Promenade. The coffee drinks are carefully made, and the food is actually good for you: veggie burgers, quesadillas, organic salads. Try to score a table on the patio. 🍵 ♲ 🌿 ☺ ☼

[Peet's Coffee & Tea] **2439 Main St., Santa Monica, 310.399.8117; 1401 Montana Ave., Santa Monica, 310.394.8555; peets.com. Daily from 5 a.m. AE, MC, V. WHY** Major Dickason's blend. **WHAT** If you must drink at a chain, this estimable Bay Area institution is the one to pick. The coffee drinks are robust and made by actual baristas, the take-home beans are addictive and thoughtfully ground, and the people-watching is superb. **WHO** Main Street shoppers, after-beach coffee seekers, Ocean Park neighbors who walk over for a jolt. ☺ ☼

[Tanner's Coffee Co.] **200 Culver Blvd., Playa del Rey, 310.574.2739. Mon.-Fri. from 6 a.m., Sat. from 6:30 a.m., Sun. from 6:45 a.m. MC, V. WHY** The best coffee in the area, not to mention free WiFi, a few choice sidewalk tables and a great location in a secret beach neighborhood in Playa. **WHAT** Tanner's is the community hub for this great little beach village, which has resisted the glam gentrification of neighboring towns. It is serious about its coffee but is otherwise relaxed. **WHO** Surfers, LMU students and Playa residents. ♲ ☺ ☼

[Tudor House] 🏠 1403 2nd St., Santa Monica, 310.451.4107,
thetudorhouse.com. Mon. from 10:30 a.m., Wed.-Sun. from 9 a.m. English.
AE, MC, V. **WHY** Steak and kidney pie, welsh rarebit, trifle and full tea
with scones and tea sandwiches. There's also a shop full of British
imports. **WHAT** Santa Monica used to have a thriving British community, and the Tudor House has been there for some 40 years. Inside, it
resembles a British auntie—a bit dowdy but terribly cozy. **WHO** Tea-
sipping ladies and British ex-pats longing for clotted cream. ☺

[UnUrban Coffee House] 3301 Pico Blvd., Santa Monica,
310.315.0056. Daily from 7 a.m. MC, V. **WHY** Excellent double-shot cappuccino and highly entertaining evening performances. **WHAT** "Death
Before Decaf" is the motto at this neighborhood café, and the baristas
deliver the goods. As for the décor, think first apartment for theater
majors—walls painted red and purple, old movie-theater seats and velvet
drapes in bold colors. There's also free WiFi, plentiful tables and evening
music and spoken-word performances. Note that the lease is tenuous, so
it could disappear at any time. **WHO** A young, artsy, funky set. 📺

[Urth Caffé] 🏠 2327 Main St., Santa Monica, 310.314.7040, urthcaffe.
com. Daily from 6:30 a.m. MC, V. **WHY** Organic coffee, excellent teas
and good food with a vegetarian/vegan emphasis. **WHAT** Robust coffee, loose-leaf teas and tasty café fare for health-conscious, environmentally aware, Prius-driving westsiders. On sunny days the outdoor
tables are as prized as seats at the Oscars. A quintessential L.A. place.
WHO Hip Match.com blind-daters, girlfriends catching up, and all
sorts of beautiful Santa Monicans. 🌿📺☀

SOUTH BAY TO SOUTH L.A.

[Aguas Tijuana's Juice Bar] 8744 Washington Blvd., Pico Rivera,
562.949.7333, aguastijuanas.com. Daily from 7 a.m. Mexican. MC, V.
WHY For wonderful juice drinks—try the strawberries and cream
made with fresh berries, the piña or the escamocha. **WHAT** This friendly juice and smoothie bar makes 11 drinks daily (papaya, watermelon,
strawberry/banana, horchata), plus mixes smoothies and custom drinks
to order. Ingredients are fresh, and the place is spotless. Tortas are
offered, too. 📺☺

[Aroma di Roma] 5327 E. 2nd St., Long Beach, 562.434.6353,
aromadiroma.com. Mon.-Fri. from 5:30 a.m., Sat. from 6 a.m., Sun. from
6:30 a.m. AE, MC, V. **WHY** Good coffee, perfectly foamed lattes, breakfast pizza, lunchtime panini, a locals' vibe and Italian soccer on TV.
WHAT Second Street's best coffeehouse is a real neighborhood hub,
where friends are always running into one another while ordering a
latte or a gelato. Good Italian food (panini, salads), very good coffee

Coffee, Tea + Juices

🍃 **VEGETARIAN** ☺ **KID FRIENDLY** ☼ **PATIO DINING** �Delivery **DELIVERY** 🏠 **PRIVATE PARTY**

and an appealing atmosphere both inside and on the sidewalk patio.
WHO Neighbors who can walk here from their adorable Belmont
Shore bungalows. ☺ ☼

[Catalina Coffee Company] **126 N. Catalina Ave., Redondo Beach,
310.318.2499, catalinacoffee.com. Mon.-Fri. from 6:30 a.m., Sat.-Sun.
from 7 a.m. MC, V. WHY** Roasted on-site coffee, a decent selection of
teas and an inviting, hang-out-for-a-while vibe. **WHAT** Outside is a
sunny patio with thatched umbrellas, but inside it's more literary than
beachy, with a fireplace, lots of books, comfy high-backed armchairs
and a flea-market-chic look. Redondo's star indie coffeehouse only
has pay WiFi, but everyone's busy reading, chatting or playing board
games anyway. **WHO** Everyone who's anyone in Redondo. ☺ ☼

[Hot Java] **2101 E. Broadway, Long Beach, 562.433.0688, hotjavalb.
com. Daily from 6 a.m. MC, V. WHY** A relaxed vibe, very good brewed
coffee (lattes and cappuccinos are unexceptional), pastries from Ross-
moor Bakery and free WiFi. **WHAT** Two airy, modern rooms and some
sidewalk tables provide lots of space for the regulars to hang out,
but even then, it can get full, especially in the evening. Improv and
standup comedy are extras. **WHO** An interesting mix of beach people,
gay neighbors and the laptop-obsessed. ☺ ☺ ☼

[Library Coffeehouse] **3418 E. Broadway, Long Beach,
562.433.2393, the librarycoffeehouse.com. Mon.-Fri. from 6 a.m., Sat.-
Sun. from 7 a.m. MC, V. WHY** Perfectly fine coffee, respectable pastries
and light meals, free WiFi and a very comfortable funky-chic setting
in a great neighborhood. **WHAT** A longstanding Belmont Heights
hangout, the Library is large and rambling, stuffed with pleasantly
shabby Victorian furniture and bookcases stocked with used titles
for sale. Settle in for a spell. **WHO** The young 'n quirky, often with a
goth-literary bent. ☺ ☞ ☼

[North End Caffé] **3421 Highland Ave., Manhattan Beach,
310.546.4782, northendcaffe.net. Daily from 8 a.m. MC, V. WHY** The
best takeout coffee in the area and, if you have time to sit down and
eat, very good food, too. **WHAT** This isn't really a place to sit with just
a cup of coffee and linger—the people waiting for a table for breakfast
or lunch will look daggers at you—but it's a great place to get a first-
rate coffee drink to go. And what's your rush? You might as well sit
down and have some beignets and fresh berries to go with your latte.
WHO Locals who can walk here and El Porto surfers. ☜ ☺ ☼

[Planet Earth – Eco Café] **509 Pier Ave., Hermosa Beach,
310.318.1888, planetearthecocafe.com. Mon.-Fri. from 7 a.m., Sat. from
8 a.m. MC, V. WHY** Well-made organic, fair-trade mochas, lattes, teas
and chai drinks, tasty food (including vegan options) and interesting
music on the stereo. **WHAT** As you might guess from the name, this

place has a sweet, beach-hippie vibe, a devotion to all things organic and sustainable, and friendly owners who know how to make coffee properly. If only it stayed open past 6 p.m.... **WHO** A beach crowd grateful for a green, indie alternative to the coffee chains. ✪ ✎ ☺ ✪

[Portfolio Coffeehouse] **2300 E. 4th St., Long Beach, 562.434.2486, portfoliocoffeehouse.com. Mon.-Fri. from 5:30 a.m., Sat.-Sun. from 6:30 a.m. AE, MC, V. WHY** Excellent espresso, properly foamed cappuccinos, free WiFi and a stylishly studious vibe. **WHAT** The hub of life in the Broadway Corridor neighborhood, Portfolio wraps around the corner of 4th and Junipero near some fun vintage shops. The back room is filled with headphone-wearing people on laptops; the front room is chattier and has PCs to rent for a buck for ten minutes. Forgot your laptop? Pick up one of the smart magazines for sale. Expect superb coffee, good breakfast panini and baked goods, and lunch dishes that go beyond the coffeehouse basics. **WHO** Grad students, high-school girls with creative haircuts and black Converse sneakers, hip seniors... a diverse bunch. ☺ 📖 🎵 ✎ ☺

[Tierra Mia Coffee] 🏠 **4914 Firestone Blvd., South Gate, 323.563.3948. Mon.-Sat. from 6:30 a.m., Sun. from 7 a.m. 6706 Pacific Blvd., Huntington Park, 323.589.2065; tierramiacoffee.com. Daily from 7:30 a.m. AE, MC, V. WHY** Authentic Cuban café con leche, heavenly mochas, lattes infused with horchata and all-around superb coffee. **WHAT** These suave and handsome spots, each with comfy leather chairs and intoxicating aromas, take their coffee — and their beans — very seriously, buying them from organic, artisanal roasters and handling them with care. But there's a sense of whimsy that cancels out any pretension, as witnessed by the Rice and Beans, an horchata-flavored blended espresso drink sprinkled with crushed coffee beans. **WHO** The coolest people in South Gate and Huntington Park. ☺

+ Juices

Food That's Fast

Hungry and in a hurry? You'll have no trouble resisting the Del Taco urge when you see the astonishing range of L.A.'s offerings, from ramen houses to food trucks, burger joints to rib shacks, falafel stands to pizzerias.

ALSO CONSIDER THESE
SPEEDY GOURMET-TO-GO PLACES:

Artisan Cheese Gallery, Studio City (PAGE 291)

Auntie Em's, Eagle Rock (PAGE 303)

Café Surfas, Culver City (PAGE 294)

Clementine, Century City (PAGE 294)

Food + Lab, West Hollywood & Silver Lake (PAGES 286 & 210)

Gallegos Mexican Deli, Mar Vista (PAGE 295)

Gjelina Take Away, Venice (PAGE 395)

Joan's on Third, Beverly/Third (PAGE 286)

Julienne, San Marino (PAGE 290)

Larchmont Larder, Hancock Park (PAGE 287)

Ma 'n Pa's Grocery, Long Beach (PAGE 359)

Marmalade, Santa Monica & Malibu (PAGES 296 & 224)

Mozza 2 Go, Melrose (PAGE 288)

Nicole's Gourmet Foods, South Pasadena (PAGE 290)

The Oaks Market, Hollywood (PAGE 288)

Olive & Thyme, Toluca Lake (PAGE 292)

Porta Via, Pasadena (PAGE 291)

Recess, Glendale (PAGE 291)

🏛 ESSENTIALLY L.A. ☺LATE ♥ROMANTIC 💵VALUE 🔕QUIET ♻SUSTAINABLE

[ESSENTIALLY L.A.]

Angelo's Italian Deli, Long Beach (PAGE 278)
The Apple Pan, Rancho Park (PAGE 272)
Bay Cities Italian Deli, Santa Monica (PAGE 275)
Banh Mi My Tho, Alhambra (PAGE 263)
Bludso's BBQ, Compton (PAGE 278)
Cemitas Poblanas Don Adrian, Van Nuys (PAGE 270)
Cemitas Poblanas Elvirita #1, Boyle Heights (PAGE 256)
The Coop Pizza, Cheviot Hills (PAGE 272)
Dumpling House, Arcadia (PAGE 264)
El Parian, Pico-Union (PAGE 257)
El Pique Taco Truck, Highland Park (PAGE 257)
El Pollo Imperial, Long Beach (PAGE 279)
Falafel Arax, Hollywood (PAGE 251)
Guisados, Boyle Heights (PAGE 258)
Honey's Kettle, Culver City & Compton (PAGES 273 & 280)
Jack's Classic Hamburgers, North Hollywood (PAGE 268)
Jay Bee's, Gardena (PAGE 280)
Jody Maroni's, Venice (PAGE 276)
King Taco, Mt. Washington (PAGE 258)
Let's Be Frank, Culver City & beyond (PAGE 273)
Lotería Grill, Farmers Market (PAGE 252)
Mama's Hot Tamales, Westlake (PAGE 259)
Marukai Pacific Market, Gardena (PAGE 281)
Pavich's Brick Oven Pizzeria, San Pedro (PAGE 281)
Philippe the Original, Chinatown (PAGE 260)
Pollos a la Brasa, Koreatown (PAGE 253)
Santouka, Mar Vista (PAGE 277)
Señor Fish, Eagle Rock & Downtown (PAGES 261)
Shinu Rang-Olke Rang, Mid-City (PAGE 253)
Shisen Ramen, Torrance (PAGE 283)
Taco Zone, Echo Park (PAGE 261)
Tommy's, Westlake (PAGE 262)
Tops, Pasadena (PAGE 267)
Vito's Pizza, West Hollywood (PAGE 255)
Yuca's, Los Feliz (PAGE 255)
Zankou Chicken, various locations (PAGES 267 & 274)
Zelo Cornmeal Crust Pizza, Arcadia (PAGE 268)

Food
That's Fast

 VEGETARIAN KID FRIENDLY PATIO DINING DELIVERY PRIVATE PARTY

CENTRAL CITY

[Authentic Korean Dumplings] **698 S. Irolo St., Koreatown, 213.480.1289. L & D daily. Korean. Cash only. $ WHY** For the steamed King dumpling (a big daddy filled with beef or pork and either leeks, kim chee or rice noodles), the pan-fried dumplings and the kim chee dumplings. **WHAT** This Koreatown shack (really—it's an actual shack) lives up to its name and serves authentic dumplings, but they're as much Chinese as they are Korean. They're cheap, tasty and served in an instant. 🖼️ ☺ ✪

[Best Fish Taco in Ensenada] **1650 N. Hillhurst Ave., Los Feliz, No phone, bestfishtacoinensenada.com. L & D daily. Taqueria. Cash only. $ WHY** It's a place of tremendous simplicity: you got your hot-from-the-fryer fish tacos ($1.50) and your shrimp tacos ($2), and you can buy a canned soda or fresh horchata ($1) to drink. That's it. And you get your tacos one at a time. **WHAT** This seriously funky taqueria is run by a guy named Joseph, who jokes and flirts and sometimes lays down the law with the steady stream of customers—the law mostly being that you can't take the tacos to go. Some have dubbed him the Taco Nazi, but he's doing it for a good reason—if you don't eat these little bits of heaven right away, they turn into a soggy mess. 🖼️ ☺ ✪

[Cactus Taqueria] **950 Vine St., Hollywood, 323.464.5865. B, L & D daily until midnight. Taqueria. MC, V. $ WHY** *Birria* (goat), chorizo, al pastor and delicious *camaron* (fried shrimp), all served as tacos and paired with a good salsa and marinated-veggie bar. **WHAT** Your basic taco joint, except the choices are better than the norm; you can eat at a picnic table outside or take your tacos back to work. **WHO** Cops, Hollywood eccentrics and workers from the many local studios, post houses and production-related small businesses. ☺ ✪

[Carney's] **8351 Sunset Blvd., West Hollywood, 323.654.8300, carneytrain.com. L & D daily until midnight or 1 a.m. (to 3 a.m. Fri.-Sat.). American. Beer & wine. AE, MC, V. $ WHY** A tasty turkey burger, good hot dogs and all-around decent fast food served until 3 a.m. on weekends at modest prices—in a high-priced neighborhood. Oh, and free parking! **WHAT** An L.A. classic on the Sunset Strip, Carney's is a standard fast-food joint in an atmospheric old train car plopped in a parking lot. The chili's on the bland side, and the fries are just okay, but the burgers and dogs are totally satisfying, and the people-watching is superb. **WHO** Sunset Strip crawlers. ☺ ☺ ✪ 🚗

[Cassell's] **3266 W. 6th St., Koreatown, 213.480.8668. L Mon.-Sat. American. MC, V. $ WHY** For old-school burgers—large, flat, on big, plain white buns—that many people find delicious and comforting and others find too, well, old-school and bland. Everyone loves the potato salad, though. **WHAT** With roots going to 1948, Cassell's is one of L.A.'s culinary landmarks. The Cassell family no longer runs it, but it

still boasts house-ground, high-quality meat, homemade mayo, excellent lemonade and an addictive, subtly spicy potato salad. Best of all: They'll cook your burger rare if that's how you want it.
WHO Longtime customers from Wilshire Boulevard and downtown's insurance and real estate offices. 📝😊☼

[Dino's Chicken & Burgers] 2575 W. Pico Blvd., Mid-City, 213.380.3554, dinoschickenandburgers.com. B, L & D daily. American. Cash only. $ **WHY** Orange-red chicken marinated in a chile-laced sauce and grilled, resting on a bed of fries deliciously imbued with chicken juice. **WHAT** Despite the name, it's not about the burgers at this very modest stand; the half-chicken plate has achieved near-legendary status among connoisseurs of cheap eats. 📝😊

[El Chato] Olympic Blvd. at La Brea Ave., Mid-City, elchatotacotruck. com. D Mon.-Sat. Taqueria. Cash only. $ **WHY** Al pastor tacos at midnight. **WHAT** All the meats that go into the tacos and burritos are good, but the real reason people line up every night is for the pork al pastor, among the best in taco-truck land. **WHO** Latino families and the young and restless, refueling between clubbing and bar-hopping. 😊📝

[El Matador Taco Truck] Western Ave. at Lexington Ave., Hollywood. D nightly. Taqueria. Cash only. $ **WHY** Juicy, carefully prepared tacos al pastor and carne asada for just a buck, with a robust salsa roja that has a hint of habañero. **WHAT** This is the best taco truck in Hollywood, usually open from sunset until at least 2 a.m. and often bearing a line. **WHO** Local Latinos and after-club party people. 😊📝😊

[Falafel Arax] 🔖 5101 Santa Monica Blvd., Hollywood, 323.663.9687. B & L daily, D Mon.-Sat., early D Sun. Middle Eastern/Armenian. Cash only. $ **WHY** The best falafel in town, crisp on the outside and tender within. Succulent schwarma, too. **WHAT** This tiny diner has been attracting falafel addicts for more than 25 years, and the lines still haven't abated. 📝🔖

[I Panini di Ambra] 5633 Hollywood Blvd., Hollywood, 323.463.1200, thepaninilady.com. B, L & early D Mon.-Sat., early D Sun. Italian. MC, V. $ **WHY** Focaccia with *cipolle* (onion) or rosemary and potato; panini with prosciutto and provolone. You can also get the house-made focaccia to go. **WHAT** A little storefront on the gentrifying stretch of Hollywood Boulevard that's home to Sabor y Cultura is run by a lovely Italian woman, whose focaccia is the key to the two main dishes: by-the-slice pizza and grilled panini. Opt for pizzas with the lighter toppings, so they won't overwhelm her focaccia. You can eat here at a few tables or take it to go. 📝🔖

[JNJ Burger & Bar-B-Q] 5754 W. Adams Blvd., Mid-City, 323.933.7366, jnjbar-b-queandburgers.com. L & D Mon.-Sat. American.

🔖 VEGETARIAN ⊙ KID FRIENDLY ☼ PATIO DINING 🚗 DELIVERY 🎩 PRIVATE PARTY

Cash only. **$** **WHY** Exceptionally tender and tasty pork and beef ribs and pulled pork, smoked by Jay Nelson with oak and almond woods. **WHAT** A shack in the best sense of the word, JNJ is indeed a burger joint, but that's not why you come here. You come for the honest-to-goodness barbecue: tender pork ribs, hefty beef ribs and juicy hot links (pass on the brisket); extras include great collard greens and sweet potato pie. **WHO** Culver City studio folks sneaking away from their vegetarian lunch meetings for some ribs. 📷 ☺ ☼

[Joe's Pizza] **8539 W. Sunset Blvd., West Hollywood, 310.358.0900, joespizza.it. L & D daily. Pizzeria. Cash only. $** **WHY** Really tasty thin crust, New York–style pizza (just enough sauce and cheese, no crazy toppings) for eating in or to go—and delivery is free. **WHAT** Joe Vitale of *the* Joe's Pizza on Bleecker Street first tackled Santa Monica, and when he met with success, he opened this pizzeria on the Sunset Strip. Besides the classic pies, you can get a few heroes and pastas. But it's really about the slices. **WHO** WeHo locals grateful for a place to get a great slice for just $2.75. ☺ 🥄 ☺ 🚗

[Lotería Grill] 🏛 **Farmers Market, 6333 W. 3rd St., Fairfax District, 323.930.2211, loteriagrill.com. L & D daily. Taqueria. Beer at neighboring stall. MC, V. $ - $$** **WHY** Tacos with chicken mole, mushrooms, cactus or squash, huevos rancheros for brunch and stunning aguas frescas made from fresh fruits or jamaica flowers. **WHAT** This stand turns out some of the best Mexican food for miles around with a creative Mexico City–style flair. For more of a sit-down meal with the same food and the best margaritas in town, try Lotería Hollywood or Studio City. **WHO** Screenwriters and other Farmers Market regulars. 📷 ☺ ☼

[Moishe's Fine Middle Eastern Cuisine] **Farmers Market, 6333 W. 3rd St., Fairfax District, 323.936.4998. L & D daily. Middle Eastern. Cash only. $ - $$** **WHY** Quality falafel at a treasured spot in the old section of the Farmers Market. **WHAT** Don't worry about the impatient counter ladies—once you get past the ordering and into the eating, the falafel sandwiches at this gem are extraordinary, wrapped in super-thin pita, dolloped with great tahini dressing and served with ripe tomato and lettuce. And don't miss the savory bulgur pilaf and the *muhammara* (walnut/pomegranate/pepper dip). 📷 🥄 ☺ ☼

[Papaya King] **1645 Wilcox Ave., Hollywood, 323.871.8799, papayaking.com. L & D daily to 3 a.m. Hot dogs. Cash only. $** **WHY** Small, juicy hot dogs, just like the New York original. **WHAT** Pink's has competition in the line-up-for-hot-dogs department with the arrival of this New York hot dog icon, which draws huge crowds at night. Pass on the beefier but soggier jumbo dog in favor of the small, juicy, peppery original. The curly fries are generic, and we don't quite understand the devotion to the papaya juice drink, but these are tasty dogs indeed. **WHO** By day, ex New Yorkers; by night, young folks getting in some calories between club stops.

[Phillips Bar-B-Que] **2619 Crenshaw Blvd., Mid-City, 323.731.4772; 4307 Leimert Blvd., Leimert Park, 323.292.7613. L & D Tues.-Sun. Barbecue. MC, V. $ - $$$** **WHY** Pork ribs and rib tips, a bit chewy, properly smoky and full of flavor; try the mixed sauce. **WHAT** This local chain of South L.A. takeout-only rib joints has its rabid followers and ornery detractors; we're somewhere in the middle, believing for one thing that even so-so ribs are still a gift from the gods. These are saucy and substantial, not as tender as some but quite tasty. Call ahead to order or you'll have a long wait. **WHO** A constant crowd of fans waiting for their ribs and jockeying for one of the few seats.

[Pink's] **709 N. La Brea Blvd., Hollywood, 323.931.4223, pinkshollywood.com. L & D daily until 2 a.m. (to 3 a.m. Fri.-Sat.). Hot dogs. Cash only. $** **WHY** Old-school hot dogs of every conceivable topping combo, creatively named for celebrities and movies. **WHAT** These aren't the best wieners in town, but Pink's is still a must-stop for visitors and L.A. newbies, just to soak up the atmosphere and watch the tourists from all over the world. There's always a line, but the people-watching is half the fun. **WHO** Tourists, teenagers, Hollywood oddballs.

[Plancha, A Taco Joint] **8250 W. 3rd St., Beverly/Third, 323.951.9911, planchatacos.com. L & D daily, to 1 a.m. Fri.-Sat. Taqueria. AE, MC, V. $** **WHY** Just because you enjoy retail therapy on 3rd Street doesn't mean you want to spend $30 for lunch. And sometimes you want a great taco. **WHAT** Pete White paid his dues (25 years!) at Poquito Mas, and at his solo venture he uses farmers' market produce and quality seafood and meat to produce some of the best tacos around. There are burritos, quesadillas and fajitas, but really, it's all about the tacos. For carb-watchers, there's a grilled tilapia taco with a butter lettuce cup. We're besotted with the Tiger Tacos, a trio of plump, garlicky shrimp nestled in a corn tortilla, a light meal in itself for $3.25. For five bucks you can get three grilled steak, chicken or al pastor "street tacos," the best deal on 3rd Street. **WHO** Shopkeepers, fashionistas, neighbors with baby strollers.

[Pollos a la Brasa] **764 S. Western Ave., Koreatown, 213.387.1531. L & D Wed.-Mon. Peruvian. Cash only. $** **WHY** Where else can you get a Peruvian-style chicken cooked over real wood in the middle of a sea of Korean eateries? **WHAT** Come here for deeply flavored roast chicken that reflects the smoky flavor from cords of wood piled outside the tiny restaurant. The addictive spicy *aji* (garlic) sauce is the perfect foil to the crispy chicken skin.

[Shinu Rang-Olke Rang] **1032 Crenshaw Blvd., Mid-City, 323.935.2724. L & D Mon.-Sat. Korean. AE, MC, V. $** **WHY** The truck-

VEGETARIAN · KID FRIENDLY · PATIO DINING · DELIVERY · PRIVATE PARTY

stop rule: All those people in the line snaking out the door at lunchtime know that these are some of the best Korean dumplings around. **WHAT** Beautifully crafted Korean dumplings are gems at this modest café, whose name, roughly translated, means "All Family Restaurant." They're hand rolled and cut, and the taste and texture are noticeably better than the machine-made kinds. Order them deep-fried, boiled, steamed or in soup. 🗒️ 😊

[Singapore's Banana Leaf] Farmers Market, 6333 W. 3rd St., Fairfax District, 323.933.4627, farmersmarketla.com. L & D daily. Malaysian. MC, V. $ **WHY** Straightforward and satisfying Malaysian curries, salads and rendang chicken, presented with more flair than you'd expect of a Farmers Market stall. **WHAT** Melding the flavors of China, Thailand and even India, Malaysian cooking is richly spiced but not hot, sweet but not sugary, and this order-at-the-counter spot in the Farmers Market represents the cuisine very well, especially given that everything is less than $10. 🥄 😊 ☼

[Tinga] 142 S. La Brea Ave., Beverly/Third, 323.954.9566, tingabuena. com. L & D daily. Mexican/Taqueria. Cash only. $ **WHY** Mexican dishes with a jolt of traditional flavors in a casual, eco-friendly storefront café. **WHAT** Tinga's owners were inspired by Santa Barbara's deceptively casual La Super Rica. Their thick corn tortillas also have a house-made heft, with cochinita pibil pork tacos as spicy as advertised. Taco plates, quesadillas, burritos and tortas made with steak, short ribs and marinated chicken show a deft hand with seasonings. Tangy *elote* — roasted corn with Mexican cheese and chiles — is a worthy side dish, and for dessert there's Mexican chocolate pot de crème, giant coconut macaroons and wedding cookies. Don't miss the fresh aguas, like mint limeade. Tableware is compostable, and quality ingredients make the highish prices more palatable. ☼ 😊

[Tomato Pie Pizza Joint] 7751 1/2 Melrose Ave., Melrose, 323.653.9993, tomatopiepizzajoint.com. L & D daily. Pizzeria. MC, V. $ - $$$ **WHY** All the standards (plus an excellent white pie), along with calzones, subs and pasta dishes. **WHAT** Flavorful New York–style pies are sold at this modest shop with two locations, each of which has friendly service and efficient delivery. 😊 🚙

[Village Pizzeria] 131 N. Larchmont Blvd., Hancock Park, 323.465.5566, villagepizzeria.net. L & D daily. Pizzeria. Beer & wine. AE, MC, V. $ - $$$ **WHY** Garlic rolls as addictive as cigarettes but not quite as bad for you, as well as good salads and great pizza by the slice or the pie. **WHAT** The lucky folks who live in Hancock Park can get this pizza delivered whenever they like; the rest of us have to find parking on Larchmont and a seat in this typically crowded little spot. The reward is a first-class New York–style pizza, certainly one of the better in L.A. All the varieties are good, but the simple cheese is pure nirvana. The branch on Ivar and Yucca in Hollywood has takeout, a little seating and curbside delivery. **WHO** Marlborough girls and Hancock Park regulars. ☺ ☼ 🚙

[Vito's Pizza] 🏛 **846 N. La Cienega Blvd., West Hollywood, 310.652.6859, vitopizza.com. L & D daily (to midnight on weekends). Pizzeria. Beer & wine. AE, MC, V. $ WHY** Vito's has L.A.'s best crust. **WHAT** Carefully crafted, hand-tossed, New York–style pizzas with top-quality ingredients; try the signature white pie or the Terra Firma with the works. ☺ ☺ ☼ 🚙

[Woody's Bar-B-Que] **3446 W. Slauson Ave., Mid-City, 323.294.9443, woodysbarbquela.com. L & D daily. Barbecue. AE, MC, V. $ - $$ WHY** Tasty, meaty pork ribs (they're better than the beef ribs), tender chicken, chicken links and greens; if you don't want your meat covered in sauce, ask for it on the side. **WHAT** Vying with Phillips as L.A.'s king of down-and-dirty takeout rib joints, Woody's smokes good-quality ribs and chicken and pairs them with a potent and spicy sauce; there's also a milder sauce option.

[Yuca's] 🏛 **2056 Hillhurst Ave., Los Feliz, 323.662.1214, yucasla.com. L & early D Mon.-Sat. Taqueria. Cash only. $ WHY** The carnitas burrito of your dreams, and great cochinita pibil, too. **WHAT** Not many 100-square foot taco stands in a liquor-store parking lot can boast a James Beard award, but Yuca's can. Since 1976, Socorro Herrera and her daughter, Dora, have been the queens of Hillhurst, turning out fantastic tortas, tacos, burritos and, on Saturdays, Yucatan-style tamales. It's an aggressively carnivorous place—they won't even make a cheese quesadilla for vegetarians. There's a sit-down branch at 4666 Hollywood Blvd. **WHO** Construction workers, grandmas, tattooed musicians—a wonderful L.A. mix. 📱 ☼

EASTSIDE

[Al & Bea's] **2025 E. 1st St., Boyle Heights, 323.267.8810. B Mon.-Sat., L & D daily. Taqueria. Cash only. $ WHY** A basic place for basic food: L.A. burritos that are cheap, juicy and delicious. **WHAT** For decades, this utilitarian stand has served as a hub of Boyle Heights life. Located near Mariachi Plaza, the Metro station and Hollenbeck Station, it's where everyone in the 'hood goes for a burrito, to eat here or take to Hollenbeck Park. Don't bother with anything but the specialties: a bean and cheese burrito, with either red or green chile, or the combo burrito, basically the same thing but with meat added. **WHO** Kids, cops, construction workers and old guys who've been coming here forever. 📱 ☺ ☼

[Berlin Currywurst] **3827 W. Sunset Blvd., Silver Lake, 323.663.1989, berlincurrywurst.com. L & D daily. German. AE, MC, V. $**

Food That's Fast

🌿 **VEGETARIAN** ☺ **KID FRIENDLY** ☼ **PATIO DINING** 🚙 **DELIVERY** 🎩 **PRIVATE PARTY**

WHY Berlin's favorite street snack pops up at Sunset Junction, with a simple menu of saucy sausages and killer fries. **WHAT** Choose from pork, beef, chicken or tofu all-natural sausages and select a heat level of sauce. After they're grilled and sliced, the sausages are topped with an organic curry-flavored tomato sauce; you can add extra flavors like garlic or fruit for more variety. Fries are cooked extra dark—we add sautéed onions for maximum effect. With large photos of Berlin on the wall and weathered wooden tables and chairs, Berlin Currywurst packs a lot of Euro atmosphere into one small snack stop. Sit on the small patio or roam Sunset Junction with your sausage snack. **WHO** Hungry hungry hipsters. 🖼️ ☺ ☼

[Brownstone Pizza] **2108 Colorado Blvd., Eagle Rock, 323.257.4992. L & D daily. Pizzeria. MC, V. $ WHY** Huge, floppy New York-style pies and hearty traditional pasta dishes. Eat your pizza quickly—they get soggy if they sit around, and they don't take home well. **WHAT** Huge, ultra-thin-crust pizzas are served in a basic store-front setting. The pies and slices can be taken to Colorado Wine next door for a fun *vino con pizza* evening. 🖼️ ☺

[The Bucket] **4541 Eagle Rock Blvd., Eagle Rock, 323.257.5654, thebucket1935.com. L & D daily. American. Beer & wine. MC, V. $ WHY** Hefty, juicy (okay, greasy) burgers with the secret Bucket sauce. **WHAT** A good selection of beers (some by the pitcher), football on TV and a funky outdoor patio add to the laid-back vibe at this historic, dive burger stand. Live large (or not for long) and try the Cardiac burger (two half-pound patties, cheese, deep-fried bacon, ham and much more) or the less gut-busting green-chile burger. **WHO** Hungry-boy Oxy students, sports fans and young families. 🖼️ ☺ ☼

[Cemitas Poblanas Elvirita #1] 🏛️ **3010 E. 1st St., Boyle Heights, 323.881.0428. L & D daily. Mexican. Cash only. $ WHY** The cemitas carnitas and the cemitas with chicken in black mole are two of the best sandwiches in L.A.; the quesadillas filled with such things as squash flowers and mushrooms are also excellent. **WHAT** This hybrid restaurant-sandwich shop is a sit-down place, but we're putting it in Food That's Fast because it's really a place to get a quick sandwich—one of the best sandwiches you'll ever have in your life. The specialty is Mexican cemitas, made on soft, toasted buns that are filled to the bursting point with carnitas, milanesa beef, roasted chipotle, avocado, various cheeses, salsas and more. Save room for just one taco arabe, a sort of a tortilla wrap filled with fantastic bits of pork, and bring quarters for the jukebox. **WHO** Ebullient Latino families. 🖼️ ☺

[Chimu] **Grand Central Market, 324 S. Hill St., Downtown, 213.625.1097. L & D daily. Peruvian. MC, V. $ - $$ WHY** Ceviche, pollo alla brasa, seco de cordero and Peruvian soul food served from a take-out counter next to Grand Central Market. **WHAT** If you're skeptical

🏛️ ESSENTIALLY L.A. ☺ LATE ♥ ROMANTIC 🖼️ VALUE 🔊 QUIET ♻ SUSTAINABLE

about lunch counters with only stone tables and metal seats glued into the ground, keep in mind there's a former Lazy Ox Canteen sous chef (Mario Orellana) behind the stoves and a restaurateur (Jason Michaud) who's also a sustainability fanatic backing the enterprise. From these humble digs, they dish out food that's simultaneously sharp and subtle, layered with flavor and served in hearty portions at amazing prices. A hidden treasure. **WHO** Harried *L.A. Times* staffers contemplating their paper's decline, office workers looking for something new, Peruvian expats craving a taste of home. ♻ ☺ ✿

[Chin-Ma-Ya of Tokyo] 123 Astronaut Ellison S. Onizuka St., Little Tokyo/Arts District, 213.625.3400, chinmayaoftokyo.com. L & D daily. Japanese. AE, MC, V. $ **WHY** Brothy and flavorful ramen with lots of add-on toppings, like enoki mushrooms, bamboo shoots, bean sprouts and boiled eggs. **WHAT** This joint in the back of Weller Court serves some of Little Tokyo's best ramen. There are seven kinds, but it's the tan-tan men that keeps us coming back. The noodles are chewy, and the soup is creamy, spicy, salty and nutty all at the same time. It comes with ground beef and spinach, but don't be afraid to throw on extra toppings. Fun-loving waiters also add to the lively atmosphere. **WHO** Ramen fanatics tired of the wait at nearby Daikokuya. 🗇 ☺

[Daikokuya] 327 E. 1st St., Little Tokyo/Arts District, 213.626.1680, daikoku-ten.com. L & D daily. Japanese. Beer & wine. MC, V. $ **WHY** For 50 cents they'll add extra pork fat to your soup base. Need we say more? **WHAT** It's not as fast as we'd like, because of the lines of ramen addicts who slow things down at peak times. But the flavorful pork broth served at this dive is worth the wait. And you won't stay long, because hungry people will be staring at you to hurry up and finish. Night owls note that it's open until midnight during the week and 1 a.m. on weekends. ☺ 🗇

[El Parian] 🏠 1528 Pico Blvd., Pico-Union, 213.386.7361. B, L & D daily. Taqueria. Beer. Cash only. $ **WHY** The best carne asada in the history of mankind, served on pressed-to-order tortillas. Remarkable *birria* (kid), too. **WHAT** Pay no mind to the graffiti and the bars on the windows, and step inside this friendly spot for gorgeous, grilled-to-order birria and carne asada, served in huge tacos, in burrito form or to go by the pound. Unlike at many taquerias, cold beer is served, and there's free parking in back. **WHO** Pico-Union locals and a few adventurous Downtown office workers. 🗇 ☺

[El Pique Taco Truck] 🏠 Parking lot at York Blvd. & Ave. 53, Highland Park. L & D daily. Taqueria. Cash only. $ **WHY** Meltingly tender al pastor and savory chorizo tacos and burritos, served late into the night. **WHAT** One of L.A.'s finest taco trucks lives in the parking lot of the car wash at the corner of York and Avenue 53, and it has a devoted following. The al pastor is smoky and richly spicy, the carne asada is

Food
That's Fast

🍴 VEGETARIAN ☺ KID FRIENDLY ✿ PATIO DINING 🚐 DELIVERY 🏠 PRIVATE PARTY lean and savory, and the chorizo is addictive. **WHO** Workers from the car wash that shares this parking lot, Highland Park neighbors and Mexican *fútbol* fans (the truck bears its allegiance to Chivas). ☺ 🗊

[Guisados] 🏠 2100 E. César Chávez Ave., Boyle Heights, 323.264.7201, guisados.co. L & D daily. Mexican/Taqueria. MC, V. $
WHY It's everything a modern taquería should be—adaptive and inventive yet traditional and classic. **WHAT** Guisados was born from the minds behind Cook's Tortas, and here they channel the creativity of Cook's into homey stews and braises swaddled in sturdy, rough-hewn tortillas. The menu is forever changing, but keep an eye peeled for the tacos of smoky chicken tinga, deeply caramelized steak picado, earthy and subtly sweet mole and delicate *calabacitas*, a sort-of succotash of corn, zucchini, tomato, onion and a few crumbles of cheese.
WHO Lunching business folks and young families. 🗊 ☺

[Hana-Ichimonme] 333 S. Alameda St., Ste. 303, Little Tokyo/Arts District, 213.626.3514. L daily, D Mon.-Tues. & Thurs.-Sun. Japanese. Beer & wine. MC, V. $ **WHY** *Champon*, a robust, spicy broth with seafood and lots of noodles. **WHAT** This Little Tokyo warhorse has been turning out good, inexpensive ramen for years, and it's still going strong, despite the decline of the little mall it's in. A handy spot for a quick bite Downtown. **WHO** Japanese-American regulars and Downtown partiers looking for a quick, cheap, tasty meal. 🗊 ☺

[India Sweets & Spices] 3126 Los Feliz Blvd., Atwater, 323.345.0360, indiasweetsandspices.us. L & D daily. Indian. AE, MC, V. $ **WHY** Cooked-to-order southern-style treats, including pancake-like uttapam, spongy steamed idli dumplings and crispy crêpe-style dosa with *sambar*, a tart lentil stew. **WHAT** Vegetarian street food and the Indian snack fare *chat* are the main draws at this branch of this California mini-chain, which offers takeout as well as a dining room with communal tables. Check out the vivid orange signs trumpeting the specials, and be prepared for some intense chile heat. **WHO** Indian families and eastside food adventurers and vegetarians. 🗊 🖐 ☺

[Juanita's] 20 E. Olvera St., Downtown, 213.628.1013. L & D daily. Mexican. MC, V. $ **WHY** For the best taquitos around, and a place to eat on Olvera Street that isn't a tourist trap. **WHAT** This plain-jane stall in the middle of Olvera Street has a few tables and downright delicious taquitos. You can also get pan dulce, enchiladas and a few other things, but most everyone gets the taquitos. **WHO** Your savvier tourists and longtime regulars, sometimes picking up a few dozen taquitos for a party (call ahead). 🗊 ☺ ✿

[King Taco] 🏠 1118 Cypress Ave., Mt. Washington, 323.223.2595, kingtaco.com. B, L & D daily. Taqueria. Cash only. $ **WHY** Famously savory, just-greasy-enough meats, especially carne asada and carnitas, served in very good tacos, burritos and sopes. **WHAT** The mothership of the King Taco empire, this is an L.A. classic, with great carne asada tacos and kickass salsa roja. Order at the counter, snag a patio table, and pick up lots of napkins. ☺ 📷 ☺ ☼

[Mama's Hot Tamales] 🔒 **2122 W. 7th St., Westlake, 213.487.7474, mamashottamales.com. L daily. Mexican. MC, V. $ WHY** Indulge in these tamales not only because they're delicious, but because they're making L.A. a better place. Good coffee, too, and a gallery showcasing local artists. **WHAT** Sure, the tamales from every region of Mexico and Central America are wonderful, and yes, the café is a colorful community center, but this nonprofit is really about doing good: providing job training and business skills for low-income local women. Have a quick lunch in the café or pick up a few to take back to the office. **WHO** West Downtown workers, artists, Koreatown residents. 📷 ☺

[Mendocino Farms] **Citibank Building, 444 S. Flower St., Downtown, 213.627.3262; California Plaza, 300 S. Grand Ave., Downtown, 213.620.1114; mendocinofarms.com. L & early D Mon.- Fri. Modern American. AE, MC, V. $ WHY** Never the same old brown-bag lunch. **WHAT** When a former Lucques line cook moves to the sandwich line, quality ingredients follow. The roast chicken with herb-marinated goat cheese and ancho-cranberry chutney on Dolce Forno wheat is as good as it sounds; the albacore with citrus aioli and green apples on buckwheat you'll want to dissect and recreate at home. Cramped patio tables make it more takeout friendly. **WHO** Cubicle workers out for a few minutes of sunshine. ☺

[Metro Balderas] **5305 N. Figueroa St., Highland Park, 323.478.8383. L & D daily. Mexican. MC, V. $ WHY** Mexico City–style antojitos and some of L.A.'s finest carnitas. **WHAT** Metro Balderas may derive most of its menu from the street snacks of Mexico City—crisp, massive huaraches and chile-dipped pambazos—but it's renowned for its sublimely porcine carnitas. It goes whole hog on the weekends with specific cuts, including rib, kidney, ear, nose, tongue and the famed uterus. Each is its own universe of textures— pork cooked in its own fat until the edges crisp and the flesh almost dissolves with tenderness. Try the taco *surtido* (a mix of all those odd cuts) or the meciza, a pile of pork shoulder loaded into a supple tortilla. **WHO** Highland Park locals and far-flung pork lovers. 📷

[The Oinkster] **2005 Colorado Blvd., Eagle Rock, 323.255.OINK, oinkster.com. L & D daily. American. Beer & wine. AE, MC, V. $ WHY** For "slow" fast food that's really tasty: pulled pork, rotisserie chicken, burgers, Belgian fries, fresh salads and monster cupcakes. **WHAT** A former drive-through got a near-complete makeover but still retained its '60s A-frame goofiness. The gimmick is fast food prepared the slow way, with quality ingredients—a burger joint for people who read

Cook's Illustrated and want a craft beer with their pulled-pork sandwich. **WHO** Oxy students and tastefully tattooed Eagle Rock parents with their adorably outfitted kids. 🖼️ ☺ ☼

[Orochon Ramen] **123 S. Onizuka St., Little Tokyo/Arts District, 213.617.1766. L & D daily. Japanese. MC, V. $ WHY** To give your taste buds a jolt with ramen that comes in nine levels of spiciness. **WHAT** The ramen is tasty and the soup is flavorful, but what Orochon is famous for is its spicy challenge. The levels range from seven (no spice) to one (extremely hot), then moves up to "special number" one and two (unimaginably mouth-on-fire, tears-running-down-your-face hot). Those brave enough to finish a special number two bowl of ramen (broth included) get a place on the Wall of Fame. The wait can be long and the restaurant is small, but if you want ramen adventure, this is the place to go. **WHO** Spicy food lovers, USC students and locals looking for a face-sweating challenge. 🖼️ ☺

[Philippe the Original] 🏛️ **1001 N. Alameda St., Chinatown, 213.628.3781, philippes.com. B, L & D daily. American. Beer & wine. AE, MC, V. $ WHY** Marvelously soggy dip sandwiches (beef, lamb, pork), which Philippe's claims to have invented. **WHAT** We've been coming to Philippe's since we were knee-high to a wooden stool, and there's nothing we love more than sitting on a wooden stool in this 1908 order-at-the-counter, sawdust-on-the-floor landmark. The french dips are delicious, the wine by the glass is surprisingly good, and the counter ladies wear fetching little hats. What's not to adore? **WHO** A marvelous array of Angelenos: miniature Chinese ladies, strapping cops, big-shot politicians, down-on-their-luckers who scraped together enough for a sandwich and a cup of the famed ten-cent coffee. 🖼️ ☺

[Pitfire Pizza Company] **108 W. 2nd St., Downtown, 213.808.1200, pitfirepizza.com. L & D daily. Pizzeria. Beer & wine. AE, MC, V. $ WHY** Neopolitan-style pizzas (try the burrata), well-filled panini and good salads, plus delivery Downtown. **WHAT** Although it's a sit-down café, and a perfectly fine one, this is a handier place to know about for takeout and delivery, especially because it can get mobbed at lunch. (Note that lunchtime delivery orders need to be in by 11 a.m.) The individual pizzas are very good, the crusts thin but with enough bite, and the grilled panini are just as tasty. **WHO** Students, gallery explorers and Caltrans and City Hall toilers. 📞 ☺ 🚗

[Pollo Campero] **1605 W. Olympic Blvd., Pico-Union, 213.251.8594, camperowest.com. B, L & D daily. Guatemalan. AE, MC, V. $ WHY** So legendary that food historian John T. Edge included it in his seminal book, *Fried Chicken*. **WHAT** Forget the Colonel and check out this branch of the Guatemalan chain famous for its achiote-pepper-crusted chicken. Biscuits, slaw, fried plantains and a nice salsa bar round out the accompaniments. **WHO** Guatemalan ex-pats happy to no longer

🏛️ **ESSENTIALLY L.A.** ☺ **LATE** ♥ **ROMANTIC** 🖼️ **VALUE** 🔔 **QUIET** ♻ **SUSTAINABLE**

have to lug this *pollo* back in their suitcases. 🖫😊

[Ricardo's Fish Tacos] **1400 N. Virgil Ave., Silver Lake, @rickysfishtacos. L Sat.-Sun. Taqueria. Cash only. $ WHY** Excellent Baja-style fish tacos. **WHAT** Ricardo (better known as Ricky) has had to move his weekend street stand around, but lately he's been consistently in the parking lot at the Kimarge Salon—and there are even tables in the shade! He makes just one thing, fish tacos ($2.50), and they're terrific, the fish fresh from the fryer and the tortillas warmed to order. This is the real thing, made by an Ensenada native. **WHO** Farmers' market shoppers and surfers pining for Baja. 🖫

[Schodorf's Luncheonette] **5051 York Blvd., Highland Park, 323.258.8040, schodorfs.com. L daily. American. No booze. MC, V. $ WHY** Healthy, tasty sandwiches (on baguettes or ciabatta), served quickly by nice people who are working hard to run a sustainable operation. **WHAT** This wee, minimalist lunch and takeout spot is just what Highland Park needed, and it's being rewarded with good business. Quality salads, well-built sandwiches (try the Italian), Mexican and vintage sodas, and a few spots to sit and enjoy it all. **WHO** Highland Park gentrifiers and workers from York businesses. 😊🛍😊

[Señor Fish] 🦪 **4803 Eagle Rock Blvd., Eagle Rock, 323.257.7167, senorfish.net. L & D daily, B Sat.-Sun. Taqueria. AE, MC, V. $ - $$ WHY** Scallop enchiladas, seafood quesadillas, homemade salsas and heavenly beans, all of which you can eat in a setting of unusual (for a taqueria) charm. **WHAT** A fetching old bungalow with a stone fireplace and tree-shaded patio (it's very Berkeley) is home to L.A.'s most acclaimed seafood-focused taqueria. **WHO** Oxy students and their professors, with lots of new-era Eagle Rock yuppies mixed in. 🖫😊☼

[Señor Fish] **422 E. 1st St., Little Tokyo/Arts District, 213.625.0566, senorfish.net. L & D daily. Taqueria. Full bar. MC, V. $ - $$ WHY** Grilled-scallop tacos (make sure to order the grilled, not fried), fish tacos and decadently cheesy seafood quesadillas. **WHAT** This taco-stand-gone-upscale (complete with a bar) is home to very good seafood tacos, burritos and quesadillas, which you can eat on a most pleasant walled patio. Be prepared for a line at lunchtime. Parking in the next-door 24-hour lot is just $3 with validation. **WHO** Workers from the local warehouses, residents of the local lofts, and visitors to adjacent Little Tokyo. 🖫😊☼

[Taco Zone] 🦪 **Vons parking lot, 1342 N. Alvarado St., Echo Park. D nightly from 7 p.m. Taqueria. Cash only. $ WHY** Simple, perfectly grilled pork, beef and chorizo tacos. **WHAT** Some love the carne asada, others prefer the *lengua* (tongue), but all agree this truck parked outside the Vons market on Alvarado grills up some of the best meats in the area. Come anytime after 7 p.m., but expect crowds later in the evening,

Food
That's Fast

🛍 **VEGETARIAN** ◎ **KID FRIENDLY** ☼ **PATIO DINING** � **DELIVERY** 🕯 **PRIVATE PARTY**

when hungry clubgoers start congregating. **WHO** Echo Park families and fashionably attired young folks. ☺ 🗵☺

[Tacos Baja] **5385 Whittier Blvd., East L.A., 323.887.1980. L & D daily. Taqueria. Cash only. $ WHY** A top contender for L.A.'s best fish tacos. **WHAT** Still called by its former name, Tacos Baja Ensenada, this stylish lime-green former burger stand turns out seemingly weightless battered fish tacos whose textural contrasts of crunchy cabbage, crackly battered fish and tart, rich crema are an epiphany. A tiny ceviche bar serves blends of marinated seafood and tostadas splashed with lime and cilantro. **WHO** Families, taco perfectionists and anti-fried-food militants who'll break their own rule at this acclaimed spot. 🗵

[Tacos El Korita] **E. Olympic Blvd. at Herbert Ave., East L.A.. D nightly (to 2 a.m. weekends). Taqueria. Cash only. $ WHY** Tortillas *hechas a mano* (handmade) right on the truck are paired with good meats and either a smoky salsa verde or intense salsa roja. **WHAT** A taco truck's gotta be good to make it in this neighborhood, and El Korita is good, really good. Tortillas pressed to order, right on the truck—need we say more? **WHO** Pilgrims coming from as far away as the Valley, and families from just around the block. ☺ 🗵☺

[Tacos Tumbras a Tomas] **Grand Central Market, 317 S. Broadway, Downtown, 213.620.1071, grandcentralsquare.com. B, L & early D daily. Taqueria. Cash only. $ WHY** Great Michoacan tacos that are so big you have to eat them with a knife and fork. **WHAT** This hugely popular stand in Grand Central Market serves the biggest tacos in town, so big that they come with an extra full-size tortilla so you can turn it into two tacos. All the meats are expertly seasoned; we're partial to the chicken. Very good tortas, too. **WHO** Latino immigrant shoppers, jury-duty lunch-breakers and, on weekends, day trippers. 🗵☺

[Tomato Pie Pizza Joint] **2457 Hyperion Ave., Silver Lake, 323.661.6474, tomatopiepizzajoint.com. L & D daily. Pizzeria. MC, V. $ - $$$ WHY** All the standards (plus an excellent white pie), as well as calzones, subs and pastas. **WHAT** Flavorful New York–style pizzas are turned out at this modest shop with a few locations, each of which has friendly service and efficient delivery. 🗵☺🚗

[Tommy's] 🏠 **2575 Beverly Blvd., Westlake, 213.389.9060, originaltommys.com. B, L & D 24 hours daily. American. Cash only. $ WHY** For the chili burger and chili dog that have captivated three generations of Angelenos. **WHAT** It's a rite of passage for every self-respecting young Angeleno—drink too much, stay out too late, and then go to Tommy's at 3 a.m. for a greasy chili burger. We prefer the chili dog, but we're getting too old for Tommy's anyway. **WHO** The drunk, the hungry and the possessors of cast-iron stomachs. ☺ 🗵☺

[Two Boots] 1818 W. Sunset Blvd., Echo Park, 213.413.2668, twoboots.com. L daily, D nightly (to midnight Sun.-Thurs., 2 a.m. Fri.-Sat.). Pizzeria. MC, V. $ **WHY** Echo Park's first real pizza parlor comes with Cajun-via-New York flavor, and you can even get a slice to go. **WHAT** This acclaimed New York pizzeria picked Echo Park for its first western outpost, making locals happy with hearty pies with slightly sweet crusts, bearing such whimsical names as the Big Maybelle and the Cleopatra Jones. Toppings are considerably broader than most pizzerias, including crayfish, shiitake mushrooms and tasso ham. Delivery to the adjacent Echo music club. **WHO** Teens, families, clubgoers who like the late hours. ☺ 🚗

SAN GABRIEL VALLEY

[Banh Mi My Tho] 🗐 304 W. Valley Blvd., Alhambra, 626.289.4160, banhmimytho.com. B, L & early D Tues.-Sun. Vietnamese. Cash only. $ **WHY** Some of the San Gabriel Valley's best Vietnamese sandwiches come out of this tiny Alhambra mini-mall deli. **WHAT** A to-go operation with friendly counter service, Banh Mi My Tho packs a lot into a minuscule storefront: a half-dozen types of banh mi sandwiches, hot Vietnamese broken-rice and noodle-based meals, snacks like meatballs on a stick, packaged Vietnamese desserts and drinks. It focuses on the basics—charbroiled pork, shredded chicken and a deli special piled high with pâté and cold cuts, all stuffed with vegetables, cilantro and jalapeños and priced so low you'll want to take home a whole bag of them. 🗐

[The Counter] 140 Shoppers Lane, Pasadena, 626.440.1008, thecounterburger.com. L & D daily. American. Beer & wine. AE, MC, V. $ - $$ **WHY** For a generous, messy, not-inexpensive burger (Angus beef, turkey, chicken, salmon or veggie), prepared in a nearly infinite number of ways. Also terrific are the sweet-potato fries, crisp onion rings and thick shakes. **WHAT** Have a hankering for a burger with jalapeño jack cheese, carrot strings, a fried egg and apricot sauce? You can get just that in this outpost of the fast-growing, Santa Monica-born modern diner chain—in fact, you can get 312,120 possible combinations, including a simple cheeseburger. The beef is Angus, and they'll at least try to cook it on the rare side if you ask. **WHO** BMW-driving men and their iPod-wearing spawn. 🗐 ☺

[Dog Haus] 105 N. Hill Ave., Pasadena, 626.577.4287, doghausdogs. com. L & D daily. Hot dogs. Cash only. $ **WHY** Serious dogs served on grilled King's Hawaiian bread. **WHAT** These are solid, substantial hot dogs, often topped with bacon and/or chili. Skip the heavy, bland El Mariachi, but consider the BLAST dog, with bacon, lettuce, avocado, tomato and serrano chili, and by all means try the tater tots. A license for beer was in the works as we wrote this. ☺ ☼

🗐 **VEGETARIAN** ☺ **KID FRIENDLY** ☼ **PATIO DINING** 🚗 **DELIVERY** 🏮 **PRIVATE PARTY**

[Doña Rosa] **577 S. Arroyo Pkwy., Pasadena, 626.449.2999, dona-rosa. com. B, L & D daily. Taqueria. Full bar. AE, MC, V. $ - $$ WHY** Although it's a taqueria swank enough that you could take Nancy Reagan there, Doña Rosa is not phony, as evidenced by its excellent huevos con chorizo, hearty pozole and, most of all, its acclaimed pan dulce of every type. **WHAT** How the food can be so good here and so, well, less than good at its parent, the El Cholo in the Paseo, is hard to fathom. So just ignore the family tree, step up to the counter, and order a sope al pollo made with a freshly griddled masa cake. How they got a liquor license at an order-at-the-counter place we'll never know, but the superb $4 margaritas ($2.50 on Tuesday, Thursday and Friday, and $3.75 for a huge double) are the best deal in Pasadena. 🗺🍴☺☼

[Dumpling House] 📖 **921 S. Baldwin Ave., Arcadia, 626.445.2755. L & D daily. Chinese/Dumplings/noodles. MC, V. $ WHY** Good, cheap dumplings and other Shanghai dishes that you can eat here or have made quickly to take out. The scallion pancakes are even more essential to order than the dumplings. **WHAT** A little more downmarket than nearby (and much more famous) Din Tai Fung (*see Restaurants*), this friendly café and takeout joint is also known for its *xiao long bao*, the soup-filled dumplings that are the great addiction of Shanghai cooking. These are good ones, richly flavorful and with skins that are satisfyingly doughy but not too heavy. Also try the cumin lamb and, most essentially, the beef rolls, the epitome of fried comfort food. 🗺☺

[El Taquito Mexicano] **490 N. Lake Ave., Pasadena, 626.356.9411, eltaquitomexicano.com. B, L & D daily. Taqueria. MC, V. $ WHY** Sopes made with fat masa cakes, richly flavorful beans and tender chicken; all the meats (carne asada, lengua, carnitas) are good, too. By day you can eat in the plain but roomy café, by night at the taco truck. **WHAT** The women in this kitchen turn out some of the best Mexican food in the SG Valley, at rock-bottom prices. Night owls head for their cash-only taco truck, which is parked in the Nishikawa auto-repair shop lot at 510 S. Fair Oaks—it's open until at least midnight during the week and 3 a.m. on weekends. **WHO** Day laborers, contractors and in-the-know businesspeople fleeing their Lake offices. ☺ 🗺☺☼

[The Hat World Famous Pastrami] **491 N. Lake Ave., Pasadena, 626.449.1844, thehat.com. L & D daily. American. MC, V. $ WHY** Really good, salty pastrami; long, thick fries, preferably doused with chili and cheese; and cold horchatas and Orange Bangs. **WHAT** Sparkling clean, featuring retro graphics and a constant background chant of "pastrami burger, pastrami burger," this cute little checkerboard place with a grandiose name has preserved the stripped-down ethos of fast food and the SoCal car culture that spawned it. 🗺☺

[La Estrella] **502 N. Fair Oaks Ave., Pasadena, 626.792.8559, la-estrellarestaurant.com. B, L & D daily (until 2 a.m. weekends). Taqueria.**

📖 **ESSENTIALLY L.A.** ☺**LATE** ♥**ROMANTIC** 🗺 **VALUE** 🍴**QUIET** ☼ **SUSTAINABLE**

Cash only. **$** **WHY** Fried (Baja-style) fish tacos, ceviche and al pastor tacos and burritos. **WHAT** A vividly colorful stand that looks like it should be in a Mexican beach town, La Estrella has a crowd day and night. We prefer the meat dishes at El Taquito Mexicano, but the fish tacos are winners. ☺ 📷😊 ☼

[Lola's Peruvian] **230 N. Brand Blvd., Glendale, 818.956.5888, lolasperuvianrestaurant.com. L & D Tues.-Sun. Peruvian. Beer & wine. AE, MC, V. $ - $$** **WHY** Profoundly addictive crisp-skinned chicken, one of the most delicious in town, marinated in citrus juice, garlic and chiles and spit-roasted over a wood fire. **WHAT** A friendly Peruvian café with amazing roast chicken and fries, as well as good seafood dishes, including ceviches. Make sure to try the Peruvian chile sauce with your chicken. **WHO** Brand Boulevard shoppers and Glendale residents running in for a chicken to go. 📷😊 ☼

[Los Tacos] **1 W. California Blvd., Pasadena, 626.795.9291, lostacospasadena.com. B, L & D daily. Taqueria. Cash only. $** **WHY** Savory carnitas and carne asada, Baja-style red-snapper tacos and good vegetarian tostadas and burritos. **WHAT** A cheerful, friendly taqueria with a nicer-than-the-norm setting (comfortable booths) and excellent tacos, burritos, menudo and horchata, all at low prices. They also do a fine job catering parties. **WHO** Huntington Hospital workers, Art Center students, moms 'n kids. ☺ 📷🥄😊 ☼

[Lucky Boy] **640 S. Arroyo Pkwy, Pasadena, 626.793.0120. B, L & D daily. American/Mexican. Cash only. $** **WHY** Amazing breakfast burritos holding at least a pound of bacon, as well as all the burger-stand classics. **WHAT** A traditional burger joint with concrete tables outside, Formica tables inside and an army of hard-working guys in the tiny short-order kitchen. The breakfast burrito has its own Facebook fan page. **WHO** Young and hungry men, and all of Pasadena. 📷😊 ☼

[Mamma's Brick Oven Pizza] **710 S. Fair Oaks Ave., South Pasadena, 626.799.1344, mammasbrickoven.com. L & D daily. Pizzeria. MC, V. $** **WHY** Tasty thin-crust pizzas served by the (large) slice or whole pie, to eat inside or on the patio or to get delivered. Make sure to get a couple of garlic knots, too. **WHAT** Lots of locals swear by Mamma's white pizza, but we find it too sweet and prefer the margherita, the shrimp or just plain cheese. Nice people man the busy counter. **WHO** South Pas High kids and small-business guys. 📷😊 ☼🚐

[Mario's Italian Deli & Market] **740 E. Broadway, Glendale, 818.242.4114, mariosdeli.com. L & early D Mon.-Sat. Italian. AE, MC, V. $** **WHY** Superb and generous ten-inch Italian subs made before your eyes on fresh bread. While you're there, pick up some prosciutto, burrata and delicious, cheap homemade marinara sauce to take home. **WHAT** Every day around 11:30, the crowds start to gather at the long

🥬 **VEGETARIAN** ◎ **KID FRIENDLY** ☼ **PATIO DINING** 🚐 **DELIVERY** 🏠 **PRIVATE PARTY** glass deli case, waiting to place their order for one of the famous subs. (It looks like total chaos, but there is a system, so take a number.) Pastas are so-so, pizzas aren't bad, but it's the sandwiches you come for, especially the prosciutto, the lemon turkey, the meatball and the chicken parmigiana. They're as good as the best in Brooklyn. Really. **WHO** Hungry working men, most of whom take the sandwiches out, because the seating is limited. 📝

[Mediterranean Delight] 126 S. Brand Blvd., Glendale, 818.543.3272. L & D daily. Mediterranean. MC, V. $ **WHY** For a quick bite before or after a movie that's homemade and delicious. Free delivery, too. **WHAT** Tasty Mediterranean fast food—kebabs, falafel, roast chicken, fresh mahi mahi, hummus—is served inexpensively by a husband-and-wife team. In a mall spot where you'd expect a soulless chain, real people and real food thrive! **WHO** Glendale shoppers and moviegoers. 📝☺🚗

[Pondok Kaki Lima] 1200 Huntington Dr. , Duarte, 626.357.0907. Sat. 10 a.m. - 2 p.m. Indonesian. Cash only. $ **WHY** Indonesian street food in its natural habitat. **WHAT** Set up in a parking lot behind a Duarte motel, Pondok Kaki Lima is one of L.A.'s brightest beacons of Indonesian cooking. The weekly food fair is a collection of a handful of vendors, most of which specialize in a single dish, even if they serve more. Some focus on skewers of sweet, charred pork, others on long-simmered curries and entire meals wrapped in banana leaves. Sip a durian shake and stop by the nearby brick-and-mortar Indonesian market on the way out. **WHO** All corners of the Indonesian diaspora, a few well-traveled surfers and curious eaters from across the Southland. 📝

[Señor Fish] 618 Mission St., South Pasadena, 626.403.0145, senorfish.net. L & D daily, brunch Sat.-Sun. Taqueria. AE, MC, V. $ **WHY** Scallop enchiladas, seafood quesadillas, homemade salsas and heavenly beans. **WHAT** The generic strip-mall setting doesn't have a tenth of the charm of its Eagle Rock sibling, but the shrimp tacos and other Mexican taqueria dishes are every bit as good. **WHO** South Pasadena shoppers fortifying themselves for a trip to the always-crowded Trader Joe's across the street. 📝☺

[Slaw Dogs] 720 N. Lake Ave., Pasadena, 626.808.9777, theslawdogs.com. L & D daily. Hot dogs. MC, V. $ **WHY** West Virginia may have figured out a long time ago that cole slaw goes good on a hot dog, but here in California it's a revelation. **WHAT** You can create your own dog from the many varieties and toppings, but you won't do better than the house-designed versions, which are actually good salads on top of pretty good sausages. Try the Caesar Dog (chicken sausage and Caesar salad), the Thai Slaw Dog (spicy peanut-coconut satay dressing, cilantro-carrot slaw, crushed peanuts and Sriracha aioli) or, perhaps best of all, the Picnic Dog, a char-broiled Vienna beef link, barbecue sauce, onion rings, potato salad and a pickle. Is it an unusual combination that seems obvious, or an obvious combination that seems unusual? Who cares! You'll scarf it down in three minutes flat. Choose the onion rings over the underseasoned Belgian fries. 🖼️ ☺ ☼

[Tito's Market] 9814 E. Garvey Ave., El Monte, 626.579.1893. B & L Tues.-Sun., early D Tues.-Sat. Argentinean. AE, MC, V. $ **WHY** Huge hoagie-style sandwiches with Argentinean flair (meaning lots of meat); try the steak milanese. **WHAT** You'd never think to stop in this ordinary-looking little market in a strip mall if you happened along Garvey, but inside is an Argentinean market and deli that turns out extraordinary sandwiches, both made to order and ready to take out. **WHO** A diverse mix that reflects the community. 🖼️

[Tops] 🏛️ 3838 E. Colorado Blvd., East Pasadena, 626.449.4412, theoriginaltops.com. B, L & D daily. American/Mexican. MC, V. $ **WHY** The Kobe burger, made with American Kobe beef, smoked mozzarella, caramelized onion, tomato, mixed greens and herb mayo on a ciabatta bun, attracts burger buffs from as far away as Woodland Hills. **WHAT** This born-in-1952 fast-food institution has been spiffed up for a new era, with gleaming tile and shiny tables. The food is generous and beautifully prepared; its Kobe burger, pastrami, turkey burgers, tuna melts, hand-cut fries, tortilla soup and bacon-and-egg sandwiches are as delicious as we hope they'll be in every roadside diner but almost never are. **WHO** Middle-aged, middle-class working men, students and burger-joint foodies on a quest. ☺ ☼

[Zankou Chicken] 🏛️ 1415 E. Colorado Blvd., Glendale, 818.244.2237; 1296 E. Colorado Blvd., Pasadena, 626.405.1502; zankouchicken.com. L & D daily. Lebanese. AE, MC, V. $ **WHY** Intensely aromatic rotisserie chicken, the skin soaked just right with salt and seasonings. **WHAT** The spits never stop spinning at Zankou, which turns out hundreds of richly flavorful chickens a day, either to eat here or take home. Once the chicken drops below the finger-melting temperature (which takes a while), you tear it up and stuff it in a pita with a schmear of the white garlic sauce, and enter poultry heaven. 🖼️ ☺

[Zeke's Smokehouse] 2209 Honolulu Ave., Montrose, 818.957.7045, zekessmokehouse.com. L & D daily. Barbecue. Beer & wine. AE, MC, V. $ - $$$ **WHY** Baby-back ribs to dream about: smoky, succulent, with a nice char and light crust, and they take out beautifully. Excellent brisket, too. **WHAT** Zeke's is a multi-denominational shrine to the art of the barbecue, with chefs channeling some of the country's most renowned pit masters and turning out Kansas City, Memphis, North Carolina and Texas styles. Their sauces are masterful blends of hot, sweet, tangy and salty. Eat in or take out. **WHO** Locals, families and 'cue fans from both Valleys. ☺ ☼

Food
That's Fast

🥬 **VEGETARIAN** ☺ **KID FRIENDLY** ☼ **PATIO DINING** 🚗 **DELIVERY** 🎩 **PRIVATE PARTY**

[Zelo Cornmeal Crust Pizza] 328 E. Foothill Blvd., Arcadia, 626.358.8298. L Tues.-Sat., D nightly. Pizzeria. Beer & wine. AE, MC, V. $ - $$ **WHY** Unusual and very good pizza made with a cornmeal crust that's almost like a good hush puppy, crunching with each bite. Try the one with pancetta and red onions. **WHAT** A tiny, cheerful café flagged with market umbrellas and small outdoor tables, serving unusual and delicious pizza by the slice or whole. Worth a drive. 🖼️ ☺ ✿

EAST VALLEY

[Amir's Falafel] 11711 Ventura Blvd., Studio City, 818.509.8641. L & D daily. Israeli. AE, MC, V. $ **WHY** For some of the city's finest Israeli-style falafel, served in an accessible mini-mall spot near Universal City. **WHAT** A good, quick place serving freshly fried, pillowy falafel sandwiches; chicken and beef schwarma; and flavorful side dishes, including spicy carrot salad, tabbouleh, eggplant and cabbage salads. Be prepared for a line at lunchtime. **WHO** Hurried workers from local production companies, post houses and CBS Radford. 🖼️🔖

[Jack's Classic Hamburgers] 11375 Riverside Dr., North Hollywood, 818.761.4599, jacksclassichamburgers.com. L daily, D Mon.-Sat., early D Sun. American. Cash only. $ **WHY** Great bacon-chili-cheeseburgers, classic burgers sparked with fresh jalapeños and slightly healthier turkey burgers (which we fatten up with bacon). **WHAT** In a parking lot next to the 170 Freeway is the best burger stand in the Valley, home to fresh, quality hamburgers, crispy skinny fries, good onion rings and tasty chili. 🖼️ ☺ ✿

[Ohana BBQ] 11269 Ventura Blvd., Studio City, 818.508.3192, ohanabbq.com. L & D Mon.-Sat. Hawaiian. AE, MC, V. $ **WHY** The "Supah" salad is indeed super, topped as it is with grilled chicken, and the dessert shave ices are the best. **WHAT** The Hawaiian word for delicious is "ono," and that certainly applies to the Korean-influenced menu at this family-run spot. The Wiki Wiki noodle stir-fry (the Korean *chap chae*) is loaded with meat and vegetables, and the bibim bap features brown or white rice with veggies and a choice of barbecued pork, chicken, beef or tofu mixed with a sweet-hot chile sauce. Juicy beef short ribs and spicy pork ribs, too. 🖼️ ☺

[Pitfire Pizza Company] 5211 Lankershim Blvd., North Hollywood, 818.980.2949, pitfirepizza.com. L & D daily. Pizzeria. Beer & wine. AE, MC, V. $ - $$ **WHY** Neopolitan-style pizzas (try the burrata), well-filled panini and good salads (with farmers' market ingredients), plus delivery in a large area. **WHAT** Although it's a sit-down café, and a good one, this is a handy place to know about for takeout and delivery, especially because it can get mobbed at dinnertime. The modern individual pizzas are very good, the crusts thin but with enough bite, and the grilled panini are just as tasty. **WHO** NoHo hipsters. 🍷 ☺ ✿ 🚚

🏛️ ESSENTIALLY L.A. ☺ LATE 💜 ROMANTIC 🖼️ VALUE 🔔 QUIET ✿ SUSTAINABLE

[Poquito Mas] 3701 Cahuenga Blvd., Studio City, 818.760.8226, poquitomas.com. L & D daily. Taqueria. AE, MC, V. $ **WHY** Shrimp tacos San Felipe, the carne asada burrito and a particularly good salsa bar. **WHAT** The original Studio City location of this ten-store mini-chain long ago outgrew its parking lot, but patrons still throng to the tiny Baja-themed storefront with a minuscule outdoor eating area. Same menu and more spacious digs at the newer locations in Burbank, NoHo, West L.A., Sunset Strip, Torrance, Valencia, Chatsworth and Woodland Hills. **WHO** At the original location, hungry grips, best boys and Foley artists, along with the occasional celebrity. ☺ ☼

[Ramen Jinya] 11239 Ventura Blvd., Studio City, 818.980.3977, jinya-la.com/ramen. L & D daily. Japanese. MC, V. $ **WHY** On a coolish day there's nothing better than a big bowl of Jinya's aromatic *tonkotsu* ramen, laden with toothsome noodles and sliced pork belly. **WHAT** A Jonathan Gold rave put this ramen house on the foodie map, despite its location in a dark corner of a Studio City strip mall next to Marshall's. The soup's a bit pricey, but this ain't your ordinary ramen—and one bowl easily serves two. **WHO** Trend-followers, families with kids, and Marshall's shoppers. 🛍 ☺

[Smoke City Market] 5242 Van Nuys Blvd., Sherman Oaks, 818.855.1280, smokecitymarket.com. L & D daily. Barbecue. Beer & wine. AE, MC, V. $ - $$ **WHY** Beef ribs the size of small cudgels, smoked to fork-tenderness. **WHAT** This order-at-the-counter café specializes in Texas-style barbecue: smoking ribs, brisket and chicken over an oak fire all night. Everything is imbued with rich, smoky flavor, so ease up on the sauce and savor the meat, served on butcher paper with a slab o' white bread to soak up the juice. To wash it all down? Shiner beer from Shiner, TX, of course. **WHO** Hungry guys (and, it must be said, a few gals, too). 🖼 ☺

[Tacos La Fonda] NW corner of Vineland Ave. & Vanowen St., North Hollywood. D nightly. Taqueria. Cash only. $ **WHY** Tortillas made fresh on the truck, juicy carne asada and excellent salsas, especially the smoky, spicy roja. **WHAT** Some of the best tacos in the Valley are handed through the window of this truck, which takes up residence in the car wash parking lot in the evenings. **WHO** The usual assortment of taco-truck people: local families, big hungry twentysomething men and high school kids. ☺ 🖼 ☺

[Tacos Texcoco] Laurel Canyon Blvd. & Vanowen St., North Hollywood. D nightly. Taqueria. Cash only. $ **WHY** Good, classic tacos and burritos at astonishingly low prices. **WHAT** An old-fashioned, tow-style taco wagon festooned with a vivid mural depicting the legend of the volcanoes turns out delicious carne asada and carnitas tacos. **WHO** Really frugal taco hounds—these cost just 80 cents! 🖼 ☺

Food
That's Fast

🌿 VEGETARIAN ☺ KID FRIENDLY ☼ PATIO DINING 🚗 DELIVERY 🎩 PRIVATE PARTY

WEST VALLEY

[Amer's Falafel] 17334 Ventura Blvd., Encino, 818.995.6332, amersfalafel.com. L & D daily. Middle Eastern. AE, MC, V. $ - $$
WHY They do crispy right—even to the point of packaging takeout falafel in a separate paper bag to preserve that lightning-fast fry.
WHAT The falafel doesn't hit the oil until you order, and the result is a revelation: thin, ultra-crisp exteriors with succulent steaming insides. Go with a sandwich, or, better yet, order as a plate so you can sample the side dishes, including meaty roasted mushrooms or eggplant in tomato sauce.

[Asal Bakery & Kabob] 20008 Ventura Blvd., Woodland Hills, 818.436.2353, asalbakery.com. B, L & D daily. Persian. No booze. AE, MC, V. $ **WHY** To watch your order of *sangak*, a floppy, chewy, yard-long sesame-encrusted flatbread, pulled from the oven in front of you.
WHAT Co-owner Reza Abdollahi once owned a flour mill back in Iran, and this expertise is no doubt why legions of fans willingly take a number and line up. The kebab menu looks familiar, but that bread, soaked in juices from the well-seasoned kebabs or slathered with thick cream and honey at breakfast, is crazy-making. Have it with a grilled game hen or with a bowl of vegetable-laden soup. Then check out the bakery cases filled with butter-rich cookies. **WHO** Neighborhood Persians crowding in at every hour. Mealtimes can be a madhouse, but the line moves quickly.

[Bill & Hiroko's] 14742 Oxnard St., Van Nuys, 818.785.4086. B & L Mon.-Fri. American. Cash only. $ **WHY** The best old-school stand burger in the Valley. **WHAT** 84-year-old Bill Elwell has been making burgers on his vintage grill in this dumpy part of Van Nuys for decades, and something about the seasoning of the grill and Bill's technique makes for the perfect fast-food burger, complete with orange cheese and a grilled white bun. If you're a big eater, splurge on the $4.25 double.
WHO Devoted fans who return thrice weekly and try to snag a seat close to the grill, so they can watch Bill work his magic.

[Cemitas Poblanas Don Adrian] 14902 Victory Blvd., Van Nuys, 818.786.0328. L daily, D Mon.-Sat. Mexican. Cash only. $ **WHY** For the *cemitas poblanas*, like a hefty burger, only better. **WHAT** This shop next to a laundromat draws big crowds for its *cemitas poblanas*, astonishingly large and delicious sandwiches that sell for just $4. The basic sandwich starts with a large, toasted round bun layered with avocado, creamy fresh panela cheese, the meat of your choice, red onion, herbs and either roasted red jalapeño or a scorching chipotle purée. Fillings include barbacoa, juicy pollo adobado, pickled beef tendon, pork loin milanese (pounded thin and pan fried) or the house special, *cecina*, marinated cured beef. **WHO** Homesick families from Puebla, and newbies who've discovered this L.A. street-food-of-the-moment.

[D'Amores Pizza] **7137 Winnetka Ave., Canoga Park, 818.348.5900, damoresfamouspizza.com. L & D daily. Pizzeria. Beer & wine. AE, MC, V. $** **WHY** For light, flavorful, even healthy thin-crust pizza—it's technically Boston style, but it's almost identical to the best by-the-slice pies in New York. Eat here, take it out or call for delivery. **WHAT** Delicious thin-crust pizza is sold by the slice or the pie at this casual café in the depths of the Valley. Owner Joe D'Amore, a Boston native, imports water from Massachusetts to make his dough, and he says the higher mineral content of the water makes the dough less wet and helps the crust hold up without becoming cracker-crisp. Purists stick with the plain cheese, but the pizza bianco is also a winner. ☺ 📷 ☺ 🚚

[Fab Hot Dogs] **19417 Victory Blvd., Reseda, 818.344.4336, fabhotdogs.com. L daily, D Mon.-Sat. Hot dogs. Cash only. $** **WHY** For a ripper and tots. **WHAT** New Jersey native Joe Fabrocini missed the "rippers" (hot dogs deep-fried until their casings burst) of his youth, so he brought them to Reseda, and Jersey boys and girls make the trek to this little storefront from all over in gratitude. You can get your dog grilled or steamed—or turkey or veggie if you must—but rippers are the thing to get, possibly heaped with the house-made mustard relish or chili. The fries are fine, but trust us, you want the tater tots. 📷 ☺

[Italia Bakery & Deli] **11134 Balboa Blvd., Granada Hills, 818.360.2913, italiabakeryanddeli.com. L & early D Mon.-Sat. Italian. MC, V. $** **WHY** First-rate Italian sandwiches that would hold their own in New York. **WHAT** This well-stocked market and deli gets slammed at lunchtime, so consider phoning in your order for a sandwich made on either a hard or soft roll, both made on-site. Locals have been coming here for years and swear by their favorites—some say sausage is the best, others say the eggplant parmigiana, still others the fresh turkey and provolone. We like 'em all. Make sure to take home some focaccia for later.

[Panos Char Broiler] **16045 Victory Blvd., Van Nuys, 818.780.4041. B, L & early D daily. Greek. Cash only. $** **WHY** All-around excellent fast food: tender, tasty gyros; crisp falafel; savory souvlaki; pita or regular burgers; good fries. **WHAT** This long-established dive serves great, cheap Greek-Medi-American comfort food, and it serves it fast. Hours can be inconsistent, so don't be shocked if it's closed. 📷 🥢 ☺ 🚚

[Pita Pockets] **9127 Reseda Blvd., Northridge, 818.709.4444. L & D daily. Israeli/Middle Eastern. MC, V. $** **WHY** Laffa wraps heaped with lemony hummus and any number of savory, delicious fillings. One of the best sandwiches in the West Valley. **WHAT** The heart of this strip-mall spot is the round oven for baking *laffa*, the bubbly, doughy, completely addictive naan-like bread that is made fresh for each order. A cook spreads the warm laffa with hummus and then adds your choice of good things—chicken or lamb schwarma, falafel, grilled

🥬 VEGETARIAN ☺ KID FRIENDLY ☼ PATIO DINING 🚚 DELIVERY 🍴 PRIVATE PARTY

vegetables—as well as lettuce, onions, tomatoes and sauce. Try it once, and you'll be back for another soon. 🗐🥢☺☼

[The Stand] **17000 Ventura Blvd., Encino, 818.788.2700, thestandlink. com. L & D daily. American/Hot dogs. Beer & wine. AE, MC, V. $ WHY** The Chicago dog, the Downtown L.A. dog and the killer barbecue bacon cheeseburger. Don't miss the $1 dog on Monday evenings. **WHAT** The hot dog stand of your dreams, the Stand purveys an array of dogs, sausages and burgers with every topping you've ever fantasized about. And neon pickle relish, too! **WHO** Local families and others jonesing for a nitrite fix. 🗐☺☼

WESTSIDE: CENTRAL

[The Apple Pan] 🗋 **10801 W. Pico Blvd., Rancho Park, 310.475.3585. L & D Tues.-Sun. American. Cash only. $ WHY** Flat, flavorful steak burgers and hickory burgers wrapped in paper, as well as fries and homemade pies, are the mainstays of this landmark counter-only joint. **WHAT** With more than six decades of cooking burgers and pie in the same charming 1940s diner, with servers of the same vintage, the Apple Pan is always busy, but worth the wait. Don't dawdle—the waitresses aren't shy about wanting to turn their seats. ☺

[Beverly Falafel] **8508 W. 3rd St., Beverly Hills, 310.652.1670. L & D daily. Middle Eastern. MC, V. $ WHY** The house falafel plate with smoky baba ganouj. **WHAT** Neon-lit and cosmopolitan, this Beverly Center–adjacent eatery features garlic-marinated chicken breast, lamb chop plates and well-balanced falafel—crispy on the outside, creamy within. **WHO** A polyglot clientele, judging from the overheard Korean, Russian and Tagalog languages and accents at lunch. 🗐☺

[Bibi's Warmstone Bakery & Café] **8928 W. Pico Blvd., Cheviot Hills, 310.246.1788, bibiswarmstone.com. B, L & D Sun.-Fri. Middle Eastern/Israeli. AE, MC, V. $ WHY** Amazing savory treats baked in a stone oven: *sambusak* (Israeli calzone), pizzas and Jerusalem bagels, the thin, savory circles sold by vendors outside the ancient city's walls. **WHAT** Although it bills itself as a bakery first, Bibi's is a find for westsiders seeking something quick to eat that's both deeply delicious and not junky. Everything that comes out of the stone oven is wonderful, from the stuffed, sesame-encrusted pitas called toastees to the pizzas and individual quiches. **WHO** Kosher-keepers and devoted regulars who don't care about kosher but appreciate great food. ☺🗐

[The Coop Pizza] 🗋 **10006 National Blvd., Cheviot Hills, 310.837.4462, justmog.com/coop. L & D Tues.-Sun. Pizzeria. Cash only. $ WHY** Superb New York–style pizza, by the slice or the pie. **WHAT** Is this the best New York–style pizza in town? Many think so, and it's certainly on our very short list. There's no seating, just a stand-up counter with room for two to eat a slice or wait for a pie; Cheviot/Palms locals get delivery, and others happily drive a ways for takeout. Note that it's usually closed by 9:30 p.m., sometimes earlier if the kitchen runs out of dough. **WHO** Regulars who get this pizza far more often than is probably good for them. 🖥️🚚

[Falafel King] **1010 Broxton Ave., Westwood, 310.208.4444. L & D daily. Middle Eastern. MC, V. $ WHY** Decades of experience give this UCLA hangout (recently moved to a smaller spot down the street) the upper hand in fast yet healthy food. **WHAT** Great falafel, but also a wide selection of Middle Eastern salads to stuff in pita sandwiches, and schwarma, too. **WHO** A college and date-night crowd. 🖥️🐾☺

[Honey's Kettle Fried Chicken] 🏠 **9537 Culver Blvd., Culver City, 310.202.5453, honeyskettle.com. L & D daily. American/Southern. AE, MC, V. $ WHY** The chicken, of course—whole bird, combo meal or even in an individual pot pie. **WHAT** The chicken is justly famous, lightly battered and spectacularly juicy. But there's more to Honey's than those golden birds. From the freshly squeezed lemonade to the small fruit pies and buttermilk biscuits, a meal in this cream-and-gold dining room is a treat. And don't forget to eat your vegetables; they're skewered, kettle-cooked and delicious. ☺

[Jeff's Gourmet Sausage Factory] **8930 W. Pico Blvd., Pico-Robertson, 310.858.8590, jeffsgourmet.com. L & D Mon.-Thurs. & Sun. Kosher/American. MC, V. $ - $$ WHY** House-made, globally inspired sausages and excellent thick-cut pastrami. **WHAT** True to its name, Jeff's is more sausage factory than eatery. But if you opt not to buy your links by the pound, the kosher kitchen cranks out over a dozen sausage sandwiches, including a coriander- and nutmeg-laced South African boerewors, spicy Moroccan merguez and veal bratwurst. There are burgers and wraps, too, but the true secret is the pastrami, which may be the closest thing to Langer's in town. **WHO** Kosher corridor residents and westside sausage seekers.

[Lamonica's NY Pizza] **1066 Gayley Ave., Westwood, 310.208.8671, lamonicasnypizza.com. L & D daily until midnight (to 2 a.m. Fri.-Sat.). Pizzeria. Cash only. $ WHY** For delicious New York pizza, best eaten plain, by the slice and immediately. **WHAT** Your basic stand with thin-crust pies that have the proper balance of cheese to sauce to crust. Pizza heads argue constantly about whether this is proper New York pizza, but we don't care. This is L.A., and Lamonica's tastes good. **WHO** Bruins and Westwood cruisers. ☺ 🖥️🐾☺🚚

[Let's Be Frank] 🏠 **Helms Ave. between Washington Blvd. & Venice Blvd., Culver City, 888.2333.7265, letsbefrankdogs.com. L Wed.-Sun. Hot dogs. Cash only. $ WHY** Because there's no guilt—well, almost no guilt—involved in enjoying these all-natural, grass-fed beef hot dogs

🐾 **VEGETARIAN** ☺ **KID FRIENDLY** ☼ **PATIO DINING** 🚚 **DELIVERY** 🏠 **PRIVATE PARTY**

with organic accoutrements. It elevates the hot-dog cart to a haute level. **WHAT** Even a Prius-driving liberal Democrat can feel good about this swank cart parked near the old Helms Bakery building at lunchtime. Not only are the hot dogs, brats and Italian sausages artisanally produced, but they taste great and have just the right snap. Extras include organic sauerkraut and delicious grilled onions. It also has a little trailer, which cruises L.A. and parks consistently on Thursday evenings at Silverlake Wine (2395 Glendale Blvd.) to feed the tipsy masses after wine tastings. And with a $650 minimum order, they'll come to your next event. **WHO** Furniture shoppers and carefully rumpled families pushing $400 strollers. 🛒 ☺ ☼

[Paloma Selestial Taco Truck] Overland Ave. at Pico Blvd., Century City. L daily. Taqueria. Cash only. $ **WHY** *Cemita poblana de milanesa*, a Mexico City–style sandwich with thin-sliced, breaded beef, avocado and chipotle; good carnitas tacos, too. **WHAT** Also known as Tacos Wamu, this truck sets up lunch shop in the Chase (formerly Washington Mutual) parking lot every day, moving to the Pep Boys lot at Pico and Manning in the later afternoon. It's a reliable truck with respectable, consistent taco-truck fare. **WHO** Century City workers who don't want to spend $12 for a sandwich at the mall. 🛒

[The Stand] 2000 Avenue of the Stars, Century City, 310.785.0400; 1116 Westwood Blvd., Westwood, 310.443.0400; thestandlink.com. B & L Mon.-Fri. Hot dogs. AE, MC, V. $ **WHY** The "Loaded" dog, or any of the specialty hot dogs, such as the Chicago and the Downtown L.A. **WHAT** An alternative to Century City's pricey restaurants, the Stand has become a lunchtime mainstay for local office workers who appreciate a good hot dog. 🛒 ☺

[Zankou Chicken] 🏛 1716 S. Sepulveda Blvd., Westwood, 310.444.0550, zankouchicken.com. L & D daily. Lebanese. AE, MC, V. $ **WHY** Intensely aromatic rotisserie chicken, the skin soaked just right with salt and seasonings. **WHAT** The spits never stop spinning at Zankou, which turns out hundreds of richly flavorful chickens a day, either to eat here or take home. Once the chicken drops below the finger-melting temperature, you tear it up and stuff it in a pita with a schmear of the white garlic sauce, and enter poultry heaven. 🛒 ☺

WEST OF THE 405

[Abbot's Pizza Company] 1407 Abbot Kinney Blvd., Venice, 310.396.7334, abbotspizzaco.com. L & D daily. Pizzeria. AE, MC, V. $ **WHY** Huge slices of bagel-crust pizza to eat on the spot (the simple tomato-basil is best), or whole pizzas for takeout or delivery. **WHAT** The young folks just barely managing the $1,500 rent on their Venice dumps would starve if it weren't for the constantly replenished racks of by-the-slice pizza. Eat your slice at the narrow counter or at

🏛 ESSENTIALLY L.A. ☺ LATE ♥ ROMANTIC 🛒 VALUE 🔔 QUIET ♻ SUSTAINABLE one of the highly prized outdoor tables. **WHO** Shaggy students and fake-shaggy (i.e., $100 haircuts) Abbot Kinney shoppers. 🖼🍴☺🚗

[Baby Blues BBQ] **444 Lincoln Blvd., Venice, 310.396.7675, babybluesvenice.com. L & D daily. Barbecue. Beer & wine. AE, MC, V. $ - $$$ WHY** Memphis-style, slow-cooked, dry-rub ribs, both baby-back and long-bone. Also try the North Carolina-style pulled pork and the superb pork 'n beans, made with that same pork. **WHAT** A relaxed corner café with friendly people and a cheerful vibe. Eat here or take it out—and they deliver, too. **WHO** Venice carnivores—that's right, not everyone in Venice is vegetarian. ☺🚗

[Barney's Burgers] **Brentwood Country Mart, 225 26th St., Santa Monica, 310.899.0133, barneyshamburgers.com. L & D daily. American. Beer & wine. MC, V. $ WHY** Flashback to the 1980s with spicy curly fries (great) and burgers topped with anything you want, served al fresco at the Country Mart. **WHAT** Solid, if not brilliant, beef and tur-key burgers. The fries, variety of burger toppings, and outdoor tables (perfect for messy tots) are the draw. **WHO** After-school snackers, young families, and too-cool-for-school teenagers. ☺ ✿

[Bay Cities Italian Deli & Bakery] 📖 **1517 Lincoln Blvd., Santa Monica, 310.395.8279, baycitiesitaliandeli.com. L & early D Tues.-Sun. Italian. Beer & wine. MC, V. $ WHY** The Godmother sub and the meat-ball sandwiches. **WHAT** This large Italian deli and grocery store is *the* westside destination for huge subs, especially the Godmother—a mas-sive heap of Genoa salami, mortadella, capicola, ham, prosciutto and provolone on a house-baked roll. Get your sandwich to go or eat it out front. **WHO** East Coasters hungry for a taste of home. ☺

[Bravo Pizzeria] **2400 Main St., Santa Monica, 310.392.7466, bravosantamonica.com. L & D daily until 1:30 a.m., to 3:30 a.m. Fri.-Sat. Pizzeria. Beer & wine. MC, V. $ - $$$ WHY** Bravo nails the crust-sauce-cheese balance equation. **WHAT** Bravo specializes in very good thin-crust pizza, with a richly flavorful sauce and just the right amount of cheese. Service is spotty, but they deliver. **WHO** Main Street revelers who buy by the slice and locals who take whole pies home. ☺ ☺🚗

[The Counter] **2901 Ocean Park Blvd., Santa Monica, 310.399.8383, thecounterburger.com. L & D daily. American. Beer & wine. AE, MC, V. $ - $$ WHY** For a generous, messy, not-inexpensive burger (Angus beef, turkey, chicken, salmon or veggie), prepared in a nearly infinite number of ways. Also terrific are the sweet-potato fries, crisp onion rings and thick shakes. **WHAT** Have a hankering for a burger with jalapeño jack cheese, carrot strings, a fried egg and apricot sauce? You can get just that in this concrete-and-glass modern diner—in fact, you can get 312,120 possible combinations, including a simple cheese-burger. The beef is Angus, and they'll at least try to cook it on the rare

🌿 **VEGETARIAN** ☺ **KID FRIENDLY** ✿ **PATIO DINING** 🚗 **DELIVERY** 🎩 **PRIVATE PARTY**

side if you ask. This is the original; branches are popping up around town. **WHO** BMW-driving men and their iPod-wearing spawn. 🔲 ☺

[Falafel King] 1315 3rd St. Promenade, Santa Monica, 310.587.2551. L & D daily. Middle Eastern. MC, V. $ **WHY** A rare reasonably priced yet tasty place to eat on the Promenade. **WHAT** Good falafel, but also a wide selection of Middle Eastern salads to stuff in pita sandwiches— and schwarma, too. 🔲🔲☺ ☼

[Hole in the Wall Burger Joint] 11058 Santa Monica Blvd., West L.A., 310.312.7013, holeinthewallburgerjoint.com. L & D Mon.-Sat. American. BYOB. Cash only. $ **WHY** Cute knotted pretzel buns, house-made pickles and BBQ-style ketchup. **WHAT** This tiny burger joint may be nearly impossible to find (look for the Winchell's on Wilshire just east of the 405), but it's worth the effort. Longtime caterer Bill Dertouzos says he got tired of paying a fortune for top-quality burgers at fancy joints, so he opened this place. All the toppings on his $8 half-pound burger (beef, turkey or veggie) are house-made, and an order of fries (regular or sweet potato) will set you back just $2. Call ahead and your order will be ready in ten minutes, or grab one of the counter stools or "patio" tables (really more of an outdoor garage) and sip free Kool-Aid while you wait. 🔲🔲 ☼

[Hot Dog on a Stick] 1633 Ocean Front Walk, Santa Monica, hot-dogonastick.com. L & D daily. Hot dogs. Cash only. $ **WHY** For a hot dog. On a stick. **WHAT** Now found in malls across the nation, this goofy chain started right here on Muscle Beach in 1946. A good amusement when you have out-of-town guests. **WHO** Tourists, bike-path cruisers and little kids taking a break from the beach playgrounds. 🔲 ☺

[Hungry Pocket] 1715 Pico Blvd., Santa Monica, 310.450.5335. L & D daily. Middle Eastern. MC, V. $ **WHY** The best falafel on the westside, and good gyros and schwarmas, too. If you like it fiery, ask for the fresh hot sauce. **WHAT** This no-frills counter joint boasts low prices, friendly owners and light, crunchy falafel. Juices are hand-squeezed (try the apple), and the lamb schwarma is dreamy. **WHO** SMC students, local high school kids and Sunset Park neighbors. 🔲🔲☺ ☼

[Jody Maroni's] 🏛 2011 Ocean Front Walk, Venice, 310.822.5639, jodymaroni.com. L & D daily until sunset. American. AE, MC, V. $ **WHY** For the best fast food on the Boardwalk. **WHAT** Now found in markets across the country, Jody Maroni's sausages were first served at this little stand in the late '70s. There's nothing like a brat with grilled onions and peppers on a sunny summer day. **WHO** The circus of humanity that prowls the Venice Boardwalk. 🔲 ☺

[Joe's Pizza] 111 Broadway, Santa Monica, 310.395.9222, joespizza. com. L & D daily. Pizzeria. Cash only. $ **WHY** Very good thin crust, New

York–style pizza (just enough sauce and cheese, no crazy toppings) for eating at an outdoor table or to take out. **WHAT** Joe Vitale of *the* Joe's Pizza on Bleecker Street found success with this Santa Monica location, his first branch. ☺ 🔖 ☺ 🚙

[La Playita] **3306 Lincoln Blvd., Santa Monica, 310.452.0090. B, L & D daily. Taqueria. Cash only. $ WHY** Because this is one of the rare East L.A.–style taco stands on the westside, with delicious shrimp ceviche and carne asada burritos. **WHAT** A bare-bones taco stand with a couple of picnic tables and very good taqueria chow. **WHO** Latino working men and savvy locals from south Santa Monica. 📷 ☼

[Mendocino Farms] **4724 Admiralty Way, Marina del Rey, 310.822.2300, mendocinofarms.com. L & D daily. Modern American. AE, MC, V. $ WHY** First-rate sandwiches to eat here, take back to work or take to the beach. **WHAT** When a former Lucques line cook moves to the sandwich line, quality ingredients follow. The roast chicken with herb-marinated goat cheese and ancho-cranberry chutney on Dolce Forno wheat is as good as it sounds; the albacore with citrus aioli and green apples on buckwheat you'll want to recreate at home. 🔖

[Pitfire Pizza Company] **12924 Washington Blvd., Mar Vista, 424.835.4088, pitfirepizza.com. L & D daily. Pizzeria. Beer & wine. AE, MC, V. $ - $$ WHY** Neopolitan-style pizzas (try the burrata), well-filled panini and good salads (with farmers' market ingredients), plus delivery in Mar Vista, west Culver City and parts of Venice, Playa Vista and West L.A. **WHAT** Technically this outpost of the small local chain is in Culver City, but it's really Mar Vista or east Venice, and it's an area that needed a good pizza-and-salad café. Although it's a sit-down café, with a nice patio and a beer and wine license, this is also a handy place for takeout and delivery. The modern individual pizzas are sometimes overcooked but generally very good, the crusts thin but with enough bite, and the grilled panini are tasty. **WHO** Playa Vista families and east Venice twentysomethings. 🔖 ☺ ☼ 🚙

[Reddi-Chick] **Brentwood Country Mart, 225 26th St., Santa Monica, 310.393.5238. L & D daily to 8 p.m. American. Cash only. $ WHY** For a greasy-like-you-know-you-want-it half chicken covered in a mound of fries. **WHAT** North Santa Monica kids are practically raised on this simple, tasty rotisserie chicken, which you order from a window and either eat on the sunny brick courtyard patio in the posh Country Mart, or load into your Range Rover to take home. **WHO** Santa Monica and Brentwood families delighting in a simple, messy meal that costs less than they usually pay for valet parking. 📷 ☺ ☼

[Santouka] 🔖 **Mitsuwa Marketplace, 3760 S. Centinela Ave., Mar Vista, 310.391.1101, santouka.co.jp. L & early D daily. Japanese. Cash only. $ WHY** The shio ramen with *chasu* (pork), which will have you ordering seconds. Come to think of it, all the ramens will. **WHAT** This little place in the Mitsuwa food court with fake food on display may not look promising, but the broths are rich and wonderful, filled with meaty noodles and topped with quality ingredients. Aromatic, hearty and deeply satisfying. 💵 ☺

[Tacomiendo] 11462 Gateway Blvd., West L.A., 310.481.0804. L & D daily. Taqueria. MC, V. $ **WHY** Fat, warm handmade tortillas, a good salsa bar and perfectly fine meats. **WHAT** You can eat in or take out from this friendly strip-mall taco joint, best known for its fresh tortillas. A good spot to know about in a taqueria-poor part of town. **WHO** Regulars stopping by for a satisfying, inexpensive lunch. 💵 ☺

[Tacos Por Favor] 1406 Olympic Blvd., Santa Monica, 310.392.5768. B & L daily, D Mon.-Sat. Taqueria. Beer. AE, MC, V. $ **WHY** Tender *birria* (baby goat), generous carne asada and carnitas tacos, acclaimed chorizo-cheese tacos and restorative menudo on weekends. Watch out for the fiery salsas. **WHAT** This friendly, capacious taqueria manages to be both healthful (fresh tomatoes, lean meats, no lard) and authentic. **WHO** At lunch, a long line of people from nearby low-key entertainment-industry and tech businesses. 💵 🔖 ☺

SOUTH BAY TO SOUTH L.A.

[Angelo's Italian Deli] 🏛 190 La Verne Ave., Long Beach, 562.434.1977. L Tues.-Sun. Italian. Beer & wine. AE, MC, V. $ **WHY** For huge, exceptionally tasty sandwiches made from impeccable Italian cheeses, meats and seasonings. **WHAT** For a fast meal you won't forget, skip Belmont Shore's chain places and head to this tiny market and deli for a sandwich (grilled or not) filled with things like fresh mozzarella, prosciutto, turkey, broccoli, roasted peppers and fresh basil. There's nowhere to eat, so take it to the nearby beach or back to work. One sandwich will feed two with gusto. Another branch just across the OC line in Seal Beach. **WHO** Beach picnickers, neighbors and loyal followers coming from as far as Downey.

[Bludso's BBQ] 🏛 811 S. Long Beach Blvd., Compton, 310.637.1342, bludsosbbqandcatering.com. L & D Tues.-Sun., early D Sun. Barbecue. AE, MC, V. $ - $$ **WHY** Serious Texas-style barbecue that doesn't disappoint. **WHAT** Bludso's proclaims itself to be "a lil' taste of Texas," but there's nothing small about these flavors. There aren't any diminutive dishes, either: This storefront joint is a purveyor of hearty, meat-heavy barbecue in the style of the Lone Star State. And though it's relatively new compared to some of the Compton classics, it's already a powerhouse known for its brisket—but that doesn't mean you should discount the ribs and links. Finish up with a giant slice of red velvet cake or some cool banana pudding. **WHO** Well-traveled barbecue fiends and families picking up extended-family-size meals. 💵 ☺

[Busy Bee Market] **2413 S. Walker St., San Pedro, 310.832.8660. L & D Mon.-Sat. Italian/American. Cash only. $** **WHY** A sandwich institution of stomach-stretching proportions. **WHAT** Busy Bee earns its reputation on both quality and quantity: the locally famous deli is home to a cast of hulking sandwiches. It's a no-frills place, a convenience store that happens to house a great sandwich counter. The cold subs are plenty filling (mortadella, tuna, prosciutto and the like), but the hot sandwiches (meatball, turkey pastrami, roast beef) are even better. **WHO** Hungry locals and belly-busting fans from far and wide. 📝

[Dave's Burgers] **3396 Atlantic Ave., Long Beach, 562.424.3340. L & early D Mon.-Sat. American. Cash only. $** **WHY** Excellent and inexpensive turkey burgers, cheese dogs and hearty hamburgers. No fries, but you can manage with the little bags of chips. **WHAT** A burger shack in the parking lot of a gas station, with made-to-order fast food that's better than most. 📝 ☺ ✿

[El Burrito Jr.] **919 Pacific Coast Hwy., Redondo Beach, 310.316.5058. B, L & D daily. Taqueria/American. Cash only. $** **WHY** For good, hearty breakfast burritos, burgers and chiles rellenos that go down very well after a surf session or a run on Torrance Beach. **WHAT** There's a constant crowd at this cheap, reliable Mexican-American fast-food stand. Unless you're a 16-year-old who just surfed for four hours, get the junior-size burrito—the regular size will hit you like a ton of bricks. **WHO** Teens from South High, surfers, stoners and contractors taking a break from remodeling fancy PV houses. 📝 ☺

[El Pollo Imperial] 🏠 **5991 Atlantic Ave., Long Beach, 562.612.3315, elpolloimperial.com. L & D daily. Peruvian. MC, V. $ - $$** **WHY** A vast, seafood-driven Peruvian menu all available from a drive-through. **WHAT** El Pollo Imperial inherited its fast-food trappings from a shuttered KFC. You can dine comfortably inside on inexpensive rotisserie chicken or a nice rendition of *seco de cordero*, an herb-laced lamb stew. It's also surprisingly skilled when it comes to seafood. Sample it all with the *festival de mariscos*, four dishes (wonderful ceviche, a heap of fried squid, octopus and potatoes, saffron-stained seafood paella and a lightly fried fish filet bathed in garlicky gravy) united on one plate. Everything on the menu (even the cioppino-like *parihuela*) can be had from the drive-through—just call ahead. **WHO** North Long Beach's food-loving working class. 📝 ☺

[El Taco Loco No. 3] **1465 Magnolia Ave., Long Beach, 562.437.6228. B, L & D 24 hours daily. Taqueria. MC, V. $** **WHY** An honest taqueria that capably handles the classics. **WHAT** El Taco Loco No. 3 earned its number as part of a loosely affiliated South Bay chain. This location is particularly true to the taqueria tradition: fresh-made tortillas, all the meat (offal and otherwise) that you could want and late hours (it is, in fact, open 24 hours). Tripe tacos are a specialty, but

🌿 **VEGETARIAN** ☺ **KID FRIENDLY** ✿ **PATIO DINING** 🚗 **DELIVERY** 🍴 **PRIVATE PARTY**

perhaps even better are the *buche* tacos stuffed with hunks of lightly fried pig stomach. There's a small but potent selection of salsas and a tub of blistered peppers. **WHO** Neighboring families and workers streaming in off the 710. ☺ 📷 ☺

[Havana Sandwich Company] **229 Main St., El Segundo, 310.640.0014, havanasandwich.com. L & D Mon.-Sat. Cuban. AE, MC, V. $ WHY** Classic *cubanos*, plus, for those who like to push the envelope, creative variations like spicy jerk chicken and corned beef. The Mediterranean—roasted pork and feta cheese—is truly outstanding. **WHAT** These uncommonly well-crafted cubano sandwiches transcend their ingredients (roasted pork, ham, Swiss cheese and a loaf that's crunchy outside and soft within) when grilled into hot, juicy masterpieces. Bonus: free delivery. 📷🚗

[Hawkins House of Burgers] **11603 Slater St., Watts, 323.563.1129. L & D daily. American. Beer. MC, V. $ WHY** Truly behemoth burgers that value quality as much as quantity. **WHAT** Hawkins House of Burgers is perhaps best known for its man-versus-food portions, particularly the Hawkins Special: three beef patties, cheese, bacon, chili, onions, tomatoes, lettuce, a fried egg, pastrami and a hot link. But the burger stand-cum-convenience store is just as renowned for the thorough char on its patties, its juicy hot links and its peppery pastrami. Want to shave off some calories? Try the Whipper, which downsizes the Hawkins Special to two patties, pastrami and a hot link. **WHO** Watts locals and burger hounds from all over L.A. 📷 ☼

[Honey's Kettle Fried Chicken] **2600 E. Alondra Blvd., Compton, 310.638.7871. L & D daily. American/Southern. AE, MC, V. $ WHY** The chicken, of course—whole bird, combo meal or even in an individual pot pie. **WHAT** The chicken is justly famous, lightly battered and spectacularly juicy. But there's more to Honey's than those golden birds, which you can take away or eat here. From the freshly squeezed lemonade to the small fruit pies and buttermilk biscuits, a meal in this cream-and-gold dining room is a treat. And don't forget to eat your vegetables; they're skewered, kettle-cooked and delicious. 📷 ☺

[Jay Bee's] 🔒 **15911 S. Avalon St., Gardena, 310.532.1064, jaybeesbbq.com. L & D Mon.-Sat. Barbecue. MC, V. $ - $$ WHY** Tender, just-fatty-enough pork ribs, pulled-pork sandwiches, rib tips, brisket and cornbread, to eat at the one picnic table or to take home—except most people can't wait until they get home and rip into the ribs in the car. **WHAT** Barbecue fans can (and do) argue for days, weeks, even years about whose ribs are best, and it often comes down to personal taste. Jay Bee's, however, has the considerable distinction of winning a Chowhounds blind taste test. Other than the generic cole slaw, the food at this takeout shack is really, really good—worth a detour.

🔒 ESSENTIALLY L.A. ☺ LATE ♥ ROMANTIC 📷 VALUE 🔇 QUIET ♻ SUSTAINABLE

[The Local Place] **18605 S. Western Ave., Torrance, 310.523.3233. L & D daily. Hawaiian/Asian. AE, MC, V. $ WHY** For island-style sweet-salty chicken and plantation-style bone-in chicken, both accompanied by potato-macaroni salad and rice. **WHAT** Local food, Hawaiian style, means Euro-Asian fusion fare, and this place does it well. It's ultra-modern in looks but owned by the family behind the old-school King's Hawaiian Bakery next door.

[Los Muchachos] **118 Pier Ave., Hermosa Beach, 310.372.3633, losmuchachoshb.com. L & D daily, to 2:30 a.m. Fri.-Sat. Taqueria. Cash only. $ WHY** Tasty chicken or carnitas tacos, vegetarian burritos and guac 'n chips, just a block from the beach. **WHAT** A short stroll from the Hermosa Pier, this tiny stand makes the best fast food around. You can eat your tacos at the counter or at one of the teeny tables or, better yet, take it back on the beach for a picnic. Good vegetarian choices. **WHO** Surfers, skaters and beach walkers.

[Marukai Pacific Market] **1620 W. Redondo Beach Blvd., Gardena, 310.464.8888, marukai.com. B, L & D daily. Japanese. MC, V. $ WHY** For one of the best food courts in town; don't miss the toasted honey butter bread from MamMoth Bakery, the udon from Gen-Pei and the yakitori from Shin sen Gumi. **WHAT** The market's cool, but the real reason to come to this Marukai is the food court, which is resplendent with good, cheap, fast food: udon, gyoza, yakitori, bento boxes, sushi (the weakest thing here) and, to top it off, cream puffs from Beard Papa's.

[Maui Chicken] **29217 S. Western Ave., Palos Verdes, 310.732.1886; 2100 Redondo Beach Blvd., Torrance, 310.715.6284. L & D Mon.-Sat. Hawaiian. MC, V. $ WHY** For a superior execution of the traditional Hawaiian plate lunch... oh, and for that bacon-fried rice. **WHAT** Muted tropical colors add a nice note to an attractive setting in which to enjoy grilled sesame-splashed salmon, shrimp or orange roughy with seared asparagus, as well as the customary rice and macaroni salad (this one comes with potato chunks). Or go all out and order the poke with cubed raw tuna and roasted sesame oil.

[Pavich's Brick Oven Pizzeria] **2311 S. Alma St., San Pedro, 310.519.1200. L & D daily. Pizzeria/Croatian. MC, V. $ - $$ WHY** Distinctly unique Croatian pizzas that are among the best in L.A. **WHAT** There's no room for interior dining, but that's a necessary sacrifice—Pavich's allots most of its square footage to an enormous brick oven. And it's with that oven that owner Zdenko Pavic is able to craft truly excellent thin-crust pies. The marquee pizza is the Croatian, a wonderfully flavorful creation topped with smoked beef, roasted bell peppers, red onions, olives, mushrooms and a sprinkling of feta. There are also great brick-oven-baked calzones and Croatian specialties like stuffed cabbage and *pljeskavica*, a sandwich morphed into a burger of

Food
That's Fast

VEGETARIAN KID FRIENDLY PATIO DINING DELIVERY PRIVATE PARTY

sorts by adding roasted bell peppers, lettuce, tomatoes, onions, pickles and garlic sauce. **WHO** Neighbors strolling in for their weekly piece and pizza seekers from as far away as Ventura. 📷🥢😊☼

[Phillips BBQ] **1517 Centinela Ave., Inglewood, 310.412.7135. L & D Mon.-Sat. Barbecue. AE, MC, V. $ - $$$ WHY** Pork ribs and rib tips, a bit chewy, properly smoky and full of flavor; try the mixed sauce. **WHAT** This local chain of South L.A. takeout-only rib joints has its rabid followers and ornery detractors; we're somewhere in the middle, believing for one thing that even so-so ribs are still a gift from the gods. These are saucy and substantial, not as tender as some but quite tasty. Call ahead to order or you'll have a long wait. **WHO** A constant crowd of fans milling around the parking lot, waiting for their ribs.

[Porky's BBQ] **937 Redondo Ave., Long Beach, 562.434.9999, ribs123.com. L & D daily. Barbecue. MC, V. $ - $$ WHY** Top-notch pulled pork, plus other barbecue standards. **WHAT** Descended from the now-shuttered Porky's in Inglewood, this rib joint stepped right into the region's relative barbecue void, offering hefty ribs, crisp fried chicken, worthy brisket and its signature dish, pulled pork. Unlike the wispy, flavorless strands of meat found at other spots, this pulled pork is as it should be: in tender, juicy hunks. It's available as a plate (with the usual sides) or in a sandwich so thoroughly stuffed with meat that it makes hand-held eating a mere fantasy. The Long Beach location doesn't have much seating, but for that, there's a newer, bigger branch just across the Vincent Thomas Bridge (362 W. 6th St., San Pedro). 😊

[Rasraj] **18511 S. Pioneer Blvd., Artesia, 562.809.3141, rasraj.com. L & D Tues.-Sun. Indian. MC, V. $ WHY** They keep the ovens fired up all day, so everything's fresh and hot. **WHAT** This Gujarati-style *chat* (snack) and *mithai* (sweets) shop in Little India packs 'em in with a menu featuring vegetarian *thalis* (combo plates), curried dishes and a marvelous array of fresh goodies — all made from ground grains and beans — that include crispy chips, noodles, pancake-style dosa and uttapam, steamed buns (*idli*) and dozens of varieties of sweets. 📷🥢😊

[Roots Gourmet] **6473 E. Pacific Coast Hwy. , Long Beach, 562.795.7668, rootsgourmet.com. B, L & D daily. Latin American. MC, V. $ WHY** Latin-inspired café cuisine with a marina breeze. **WHAT** This strip mall café satisfies at all hours. At breakfast, it's spiced Mexican coffee with coconut oatmeal or baked french toast stuffed with mascarpone. A mother-daughter duo have transformed the family's roots into a vast, vegetarian-friendly, pan-Latin menu. At lunch, that means tamales stuffed with green chilies and cheese or vegan-friendly Colombian empanadas. There's a porky Cuban sandwich alongside a sandwich of tofu, mushrooms and onion jam. Dinner is mostly takeout, perhaps turkey albondigas soup and a rotisserie chicken with caramelized plantains. **WHO** Health-conscious café dwellers. 🥢☼

[Shisen Ramen] 🏠 **1730 W. Sepulveda Blvd., Torrance, 310.534.1698. L & D daily. Japanese. Beer & wine. AE, MC, V. $ WHY** Fantastic *paiko* (fried pork in curry spices) and owners so fanatical about quality that they won't let you take the noodle soup to go—they don't want to ruin the ramen's bite by letting it sit too long in the hot broth. **WHAT** Come here for imported Japanese ramen meticulously cooked and served in the style of China's Sichuan province. There's a generous array of noodle dishes and toppings that range from fried chicken chunks to fresh clams. 📺

[Taqueria La Mexicana] **3270 E. 4th St., Long Beach, 562.433.6389. L & D daily. Taqueria. Cash only. $ WHY** Memorable carne asada burritos, a good vegetarian burrito, excellent tortas and vibrant watermelon agua fresca. **WHAT** Long Beach's best taco joint is this bare-bones stand with an order window, indoor and outdoor seating and damn fine carne asada. A local treasure. 📺🍴☺☼

[Valentino's Pizza] **975 Aviation Blvd., Manhattan Beach, 310.318.5959, valentinospizza.net. L & D daily. Pizzeria. AE, MC, V. $ WHY** Excellent Brooklyn-style pizza (thin-crust) sold by the slice here or delivered promptly by the whole pie. **WHAT** Former New Yorkers (yes, plenty of them live in MB) say this is the closest thing to home in L.A., and indeed the crust has that not-soggy-yet-floppy-enough-to-fold-in-half consistency so essential to a New York pie. You can get red-sauce Italian dishes, but most regulars get pizza, to go or delivered, because there are only a couple of tables. 📺☺🚗

[Woody's Bar-B-Que] **475 S. Market St., Inglewood, 310.672.4200, woodysbarbquela.com. L & D Mon.-Sat. Barbecue. AE, MC, V. $ - $$ WHY** Tasty, meaty pork ribs (they're better than the beef ribs), tender chicken, chicken links and greens; if you don't want your meat covered in sauce, ask for it on the side. **WHAT** Vying with Phillips as L.A.'s king of down-and-dirty rib joints, Woody's smokes good-quality ribs and chicken and pairs them with a potent, spicy sauce; there's also a milder sauce option. Unlike at the Slauson branch, there are a couple of places to sit outside, but most folks take their ribs to go.

[Yaya's Burgers No. 2] **3202 E. Gage Ave., Huntington Park, 323.581.2383. L & D daily. Mexican. Cash only. $ WHY** Because there's so much more to the Mexican sandwich than carne asada–filled rolls. **WHAT** Seventy variations of the DF-style torta is an idea that might seem as gimmicky as popcorn-flavored ice cream. But each torta here is as precisely constructed as anything from a four-star kitchen. Choosing the best one is impossible, but the Dagwood-esque Tepic-K, aka the chile relleno torta, tops our list: this Baroque construction, loaded with avocado, a translucent smear of beans and crema, holds a chile relleno, roasted and stuffed with melty Oaxacan cheese, *and* a hefty slice of roast pork leg. 📺☺

Food
That's Fast

🍴VEGETARIAN ☺KID FRIENDLY ☼PATIO DINING 🚗DELIVERY 🏠PRIVATE PARTY

Gourmet-to-Go

You don't feel like having pepperoni pizza or bad Chinese takeout—you want something really good to take home after work, bring to a party or turn into a Hollywood Bowl or beach picnic. From humble but meticulously made tamales to elegant salads and cheese platters, the food in the pages that follow will fulfill your take-away needs.

[ESSENTIALLY L.A.]

Antica Pizzeria, Marina del Rey (PAGE 294)
Brent's Delicatessen, Northridge (PAGE 293)
Carrillo's Mexican Deli, Canoga Park (PAGE 293)
Claro's, San Gabriel & La Habra (PAGES 290 & 297)
Clementine, Century City (PAGE 294)
Food + Lab, West Hollywood (PAGE 286)
Gjelina Take Away, Venice (PAGE 395)
Joan's on Third, Beverly/Third (PAGE 286)
Julienne, San Marino (PAGE 290)
Mama's Hot Tamales, Westlake (PAGE 289)
Marmalade, Santa Monica (PAGE 296)
Mozza 2 Go, Melrose (PAGE 288)
Nicole's Gourmet Foods, South Pasadena (PAGE 290)
The Oaks Market, Hollywood (PAGE 288)
Olive & Thyme, Toluca Lake (PAGE 292)

ESSENTIALLY L.A. LATE ♥ ROMANTIC VALUE QUIET SUSTAINABLE

**MORE QUALITY TAKEOUT CAN BE FOUND
IN FOOD THAT'S FAST AND SHOPS.
HERE ARE SOME FAVORITES:**

Angelo's Italian Deli, Long Beach (PAGE 278)
Bay Cities Italian Deli & Bakery, Santa Monica (PAGE 275)
Beverly Glen Marketplace, Bel-Air (PAGE 365)
Broome Street General Store, Silver Lake (PAGE 355)
CaCao Mexicatessen, Eagle Rock (PAGE 79)
Cheebo, Hollywood (PAGE 56)
Cube, Melrose (PAGE 356)
Erewhon, Beverly/Third (PAGE 365)
FarmShop, Santa Monica (PAGE 223)
Froma on Melrose, Melrose (PAGE 357)
India Sweets & Spices, Atwater & Canoga Park (PAGE 358)
Jons Marketplace, many locations (PAGE 366)
Koreatown Galleria Market, Koreatown (PAGE 366)
Koreatown Plaza Market, Koreatown (PAGE 359)
Larchmont Wine & Cheese, Hancock Park (PAGE 370)
Liborio Market, Koreatown & Downtown (PAGE 366)
Maui Chicken, Torrance & Rancho Palos Verdes (PAGE 281)
Mendocino Farms, Downtown & Marina del Rey (PAGES 259 & 277)
Mercado Buenos Aires, Van Nuys (PAGE 360)
Mitsuwa, West L.A. & Torrance (PAGES 367)
Naples Gourmet Grocer, Long Beach (PAGE 361)
Olio Pizzeria, Beverly/Third (PAGE 207)
Owen's Market, Century City (PAGE 361)
Pitfire Pizza, Downtown, Culver City, NoHo (PAGES 260, 277 & 268)
Pollos a la Brasa, Koreatown (PAGE 253)
Porky's BBQ, Long Beach (PAGE 282)
Samosa House, Culver City (PAGE 362)
Santa Monica Seafood, Santa Monica (PAGE 350)
Smoke City Market, Sherman Oaks (PAGE 269)
Sweet Butter Kitchen, Sherman Oaks (PAGE 218)
Tito's Market, El Monte (PAGE 267)
Vallarta Supermarket, various locations (PAGE 367)
Woody's Bar-B-Que, Mid-City & Inglewood (PAGES 255 & 283)

Gourmet
To Go

VEGETARIAN KID FRIENDLY PATIO DINING DELIVERY PRIVATE PARTY

CENTRAL CITY

[The Deli at Little Dom's] **2128 Hillhurst Ave., Los Feliz, 323.661.0055, littledoms.com. B, L & D daily. Italian. AE, MC, V. $ - $$ WHY** Fresh pasta, marinated white beans, farro with grilled vegetables, and panna cotta—everything you need to fake-cook an Italian dinner at home. **WHAT** The folks behind the neighboring trattoria Little Dom's run this tiny takeout deli, with its winning 1940s look and its small glass case filled with eggplant caponata, delicious roasted brussels sprouts, cheeses, chocolate truffles… all the essentials (except wine) of Los Feliz life. Most people get their fresh pasta or warm panini to go, but there are a few places to sit—and espresso drinks, of course.

[Food + Lab] 🏛 **7253 Santa Monica Blvd., West Hollywood, 323.851.7120, foodlabcatering.com. B, L & D daily. American/Austrian. AE, MC, V. $ - $$ WHY** Fantastic sandwiches, excellent espresso, lovely patios both front and back, and all sorts of good food to take home and pretend you made. **WHAT** Nino Linsmayer and his mom, Esther, built a successful business as caterers before opening this café and gourmet-to-go market, so they came into the business already knowing how to make crowd-pleasing food. They have a devout following for their sandwiches (Austrian meatloaf, prosciutto with ricotta and honey, veggie-pesto), salads, soups and breakfast dishes, made with organic ingredients. They're Austrian, which explains the Viennese coffee and lovely strudels. **WHO** Mostly neighborhood locals, including people who actually walk here. 🏛🕯☼

[Greenblatt's Deli] **8017 W. Sunset Blvd., West Hollywood, 323.656.0606, greenblattsdeli.com. L & D daily until 2 a.m. Deli. AE, MC, V. $ - $$ WHY** Hefty deli sandwiches, potato knishes and famed matzo ball soup, to eat there or take out until 2 a.m. Free parking and $5 delivery in the area, too. **WHAT** Part wine store, part eat-in deli, part takeout spot, Greenblatt's has been a cherished Sunset Strip destination for decades. Have a restorative bowl of soup here and take some more substantial food home for later. **WHO** Sunset Strip partiers who need some good food to take home after a big night out. 🕯🚗

[Joan's on Third] 🏛 **8350 W. 3rd St., Beverly/Third, 323.655.2285, joansonthird.com. B, L & early D daily. Modern American. AE, MC, V. $$ WHY** Wonderful sandwiches (turkey meatloaf, pressed chicken, bacon and brie), lots of prepared salads (the lentil is particularly good), elegant cheese and charcuterie platters and famed cupcakes. **WHAT** Originally a caterer, Joan McNamara gradually expanded her business into a café, gourmet market and upscale takeout operation, and each facet has met with tremendous success. From the picnic baskets to the the office lunches to the daily takeout dinner entrées, Joan's food is uniformly excellent. Note that service on the café side can be erratic at busy times. **WHO** Chic women picking up a few things for a dinner party, and friends meeting for lunch, including a fair number of famous folks. 🐾

[Larchmont Larder] **626 N. Larchmont Blvd., Hancock Park, 323.962.9900, larchmontlarder.com. B, L & early D Mon.-Sat. American. AE, MC, V. $$ WHY** "Humpday" dinners, a complete family meal for four for $40 to $52, and Monday pasta dinners for less than $40 for four. **WHAT** Katie Trevino brings her business savvy, gregarious personality and network of Hancock Park friends to this gourmet takeout place in a handsome restored bungalow, and partner Michael Beglinger brings his decade of cooking experience, including the demanding job as executive chef for Wolfgang Puck Catering. The result is a homey yet elegant place to sit down for a lunchtime sandwich, buy the kids a cherry chocolate chip muffin after school, or order a spread for a dinner party. **WHO** St. Brendan's and Marlborough families picking up meatloaf and braised swiss chard because the swim meet ran late. 🐾☺☼

[Little Next Door] **8142 W. 3rd St., Beverly/Third, 323.951.1010, thelittledoor.com. B, L & D daily. French/Mediterranean. AE, MC, V. $$ - $$$ WHY** Rustic pastries and breads complement the pâtés and terrines, jewel-like salads, imaginative sandwiches and savory tarts. **WHAT** Gold-framed mirrors, cobalt-blue walls and a marble bar give this Parisian-style shop/café a glamorous atmosphere. Carefully chosen beers and wines, foodie gifts and house-made jams round out the collection of spiffy eat-in or takeout dishes. **WHO** French ex-pats lounging over pain au chocolat and cappuccino, fashionable young shoppers from the 3rd Street boutiques.

[Locali] **5825 Franklin Ave., Hollywood, 323.466.1360, localiyours. com. Daily. Modern American. AE, MC, V. $$ WHY** Locali is the opposite of Famima—instead of convenience foods imported from Japan, the emphasis is on locally sourced edibles from some of our favorite producers. Don't miss the Ruby Jewel ice cream sandwiches—they may come all the way from Portland, but they rock. **WHAT** Locali packs a lot of interesting products into a tiny storefront, and they're all either sustainable, organic and/or local: wine, beer from Dales Bros. and the Bruery, sandwiches and salads from M Café, Carmela Ice Cream, La Guera Tamalera tamales, prepared food from vegan suppliers, frozen foods, coffee and snacks. Books, shopping bags, water bottles and other tchochkes for the green lifestyle are stocked as well—even a handy countertop compost bin. Local delivery via bicycle! ☺🐾🚚

[Luna Park] **672 S. La Brea Ave., Miracle Mile, 323.934.2110, lunaparkla.com. L Mon.-Fri., D nightly, brunch Sat.-Sun. Modern American. AE, MC, V. $$ - $$$ WHY** Free delivery, online ordering and easy takeout of such good things as Cobb salad, grilled artichokes, mac

Gourmet
To Go

🐾 **VEGETARIAN** ☺ **KID FRIENDLY** ☼ **PATIO DINING** 🚚 **DELIVERY** 🏠 **PRIVATE PARTY** 'n cheese with broccoli, chic pizzas and grilled half chicken with a warm arugula salad. **WHAT** This shabby-chic San Francisco transplant delivers its reasonably priced, modern-American comfort food in the Miracle Mile area, and it also does a lot of takeout. The famed make-your-own s'mores don't travel well, but the blackberry-chocolate pie sure does. **WHO** Wilshire office workers picking up food for a lunch meeting and Hancock Parkers getting dinner on their way home from work. 🖼️📱🚗

[Monsieur Marcel] Farmers Market, 6333 W. 3rd St., Fairfax District, 323.939.7792, mrmarcel.com. B & L daily, D Mon.-Sat., early D Sun. French. AE, MC, V. $$ **WHY** Everything you need for *le pique-nique*, plus a full menu of French classics that can be ordered to go. **WHAT** This large gourmet shop and café filling a corner of the Farmers Market has every kind of French cheese imaginable, along with charcuterie, an amazing olive selection, baguettes, chocolates, wine and more. Alas, there are no prepared foods in the glass cases, but the adjacent café will whip you up some takeout (quiches, salade de chèvre chaud, roast chicken, great garlic fries).

[Mozza 2 Go] 🏛️ 6610 Melrose Ave., Melrose, 323.297.1130, mozza2go.com. L & D daily. Italian. AE, MC, V. $$ - $$$ **WHY** All the things you love about Pizzeria Mozza, without having to fight for a table. Great for Bowl picnics and office lunches. **WHAT** If you want your friends to think you're a great cook, just call up this take-out offshoot of the Mozza restaurants and order a tricolore salad, white-bean bruschetta, Mario's lasagne and butterscotch budino, and transfer everything to your own dishes. The small, swank shop has some pastries and Italian packaged goods, but everything else must be ordered at least an hour in advance. The pizzas are exactly as wonderful as in the pizzeria, but be warned that they won't hold up as well if they travel far. You can pick up yourself or spring for the delivery fee. 🌀📱🚗

[The Oaks Market] 🏛️ 1915 N. Bronson Ave., Hollywood, 323.871.8894, theoaksgourmet.com. B, L & D daily. Modern American. AE, MC, V. $ - $$ **WHY** All the yuppie-foodie essentials: pizzas cooked in a wood oven, beet salads, barista-pulled espresso made from beans roasted on site, fresh-squeezed celery juice and rare sodas, all of which you can enjoy on the patio or take to your Holly-wood Hills pad—or the Hollywood Bowl. **WHAT** The Oaks is really more of a gourmet-to-go emporium and café than a market, although its retail wine selection is impressive. You order at the counter, but this is no short-order sandwich shop: The menu runs to Belgian waffles, smoked fish plates, baby arugula salads, a great short-rib sandwich, lobster club sandwiches and wood-fired pizzas. It's all good. 📱☼

[Real Food Daily] **414 N. La Cienega Blvd., West Hollywood, 310.289.9910, realfood.com. L & D Mon.-Sat., brunch Sun. Vegan/American. AE, MC, V. $$ WHY** Organic vegan food prepared in a kosher kitchen—and it actually tastes good. You can order takeout, have them make party platters or get lunch or dinner delivered. **WHAT** Real Food's meat- and dairy-free fare includes many dishes that take out well or work for small parties. Try the salad platters, the lentil-walnut pâté and the cold sesame noodle salad. Your call on whether to try the tofu cheesecake. (We passed.) **WHO** Hollywood vegans and good-looking sorts who are just trying to eat more healthfully. 🌿🥡🚗

EASTSIDE

[Mama's Hot Tamales] 🏛 **2122 W. 7th St., Westlake, 213.487.7474, mamashottamales.com. L daily. Mexican. MC, V. $ WHY** Indulge in these tamales not only because they're delicious, but because they're making L.A. a better place. Good coffee, too, and a gallery showcasing local artists. **WHAT** Sure, the tamales from every region of Mexico and Central America are wonderful, and yes, the café is a vividly colorful community center, but this nonprofit is really about doing good: providing job training and business skills for low-income local women. Order a big bunch of tamales for your next party, or pick up a few to take back to the office. **WHO** West Downtown workers, artists, Koreatown residents. 🏛

[SugarFISH] **600 W. 7th St., Downtown, 213.627.3000, sugarfishsushi.com. L & D daily. Sushi. AE, MC, V. $$ - $$$ WHY** Takeout or eat-in sushi from the "Sushi Nazi" Kazunori Nozawa of Sushi Nozawa in Studio City—without the high price tag or quite the same creative combinations. Perfect to pick up before you head home after work. **WHAT** Nozawa has traded his omakase at the flagship restaurant for pre-set "Trust Me" combinations (hamachi nigiri, tuna sashimi with scallions) that are less expensive but just as fresh at these more laid-back quick joints (besides this, there's one in Brentwood and one in the Marina). The takeout is cleverly packaged and includes his famed "firm" nibbling instructions, so it almost feels like the Sushi Nazi himself is glaring over your shoulder at home.

[Tiara Café] **127 E. 9th St., South Park/Fashion District, 213.623.3663, tiara-cafe-la.com. L daily, brunch Sat.-Sun. Modern American. AE, MC, V. $$ - $$$ WHY** Downtown's best pizza, which holds up well in a take-out box, plus other goodies to take back to the office for lunch. **WHAT** This pink fashionista café has an adjacent mini-mart and gourmet-to-go counter, which is sadly open only until the early afternoon. Call ahead and they'll make you a fabulous pizza or salad to go. Worthy vegan and vegetarian options. **WHO** Fashion designers and their assistants picking up lunch. 🌿🥡

Gourmet To Go

🌿 **VEGETARIAN** ⊙ **KID FRIENDLY** ☼**PATIO DINING** 🚗 **DELIVERY** 🏛 **PRIVATE PARTY**

SAN GABRIEL VALLEY

[Claro's] 1003 E. Valley Blvd., San Gabriel, 626.288.2026, claros.
com. B & L Mon.-Tues. & Thurs.-Sun. Italian. AE, MC, V. $ - $$
WHY Prepared take-home dishes like lasagne and ravioli, huge and
delicious sandwiches, savory sausages, take-and-bake pizzas and a
bakery case lined with breads, cannoli and Italian cookies. **WHAT** This
old-school Italian market and deli has been around since 1948, starting
here in San Gabriel, and it now has five other locations. (This was
once an Italian-immigrant neighborhood, which is hard to imagine in
this Chinese era.) The deli offers sandwiches, sausages, antipasti and
hot dishes. Good for a takeout dinner for one or a party for a dozen.
WHO Third-generation loyalists and people proud of their Sicilian
blood, even if it's only a little.

[Julienne] 2649 Mission St., San Marino, 626.441.2299, juli-
ennetogo.com. B, L & early D Mon.-Sat. Modern American. AE, MC, V.
$$ - $$$ **WHY** Everything you need for a gracious picnic, dinner
party or pantry-stocking, plus lots of irresistible extras, from fleur de
sel finishing salt to an array of travel and food books that cooks and
Francophiles in particular will find delightful. **WHAT** This spectacular
gourmet-to-go shop has a freezer full of dinner-for-two entrées and a
deli case bountifully stocked with salads and main courses that might
include Tuscan meatloaf, red-onion crusted salmon, butterfly pasta
with lemon and chives, and couscous salad with toasted pine nuts
and cinnamon. The bakery case is justly famed, and the refrigerated
dips, dressings and sauces are lifesavers for time-pressed party-givers.
Nicely edited selection of wines, too, as well as gifts and books for
food lovers. **WHO** People with Sub-Zeros to fill—and lots of zeroes on
their bank balance.

[The Kitchen for Exploring Foods] 1434 W. Colorado Blvd.,
Pasadena, 626.793.7218, thekitchen.net. L & early D Tues.-Sat. Modern
American. AE, MC, V. $$ **WHY** When you invited eight for dinner and
forgot you had to be at a lacrosse match and don't have time to cook.
WHAT Pasadena's top caterer also has a great to-go section, where you
can pick up something good just for you for dinner, or order a lasagne
to feed a dozen for a last-minute gathering. **WHO** Everyone who's
anyone in Pasadena and the eastside.

[Nicole's Gourmet Foods] 921 Meridian Ave., South Pasadena,
626.403.5751, nicolesgourmetfoods.com. B & L daily, D Thurs. French. AE,
MC, V. $ - $$ **WHY** Great selection of sandwiches, salads, charcuterie
and, of course, cheese, along with an excellent array of frozen goods
and pantry staples. Call a day ahead and Nicole will make you a gorgeous quiche or a proper potato gratin. **WHAT** It all started with the
cheese, and that's still a prime take-home item, but the deli case also
beckons with pâtés, olives, French lentils and other delicacies. The

freezer case is stocked with an array of baking and hors d'oeuvre offerings, from croissants and quiches to miniature beef Wellingtons and empanadas. Wines are well priced and interesting.

[Porta Via Italian Foods] 1 W. California Blvd., Pasadena, 626.793.9000, portaviafoods.com. L daily, early D Mon.-Sat. Italian. AE, MC, V. $$ **WHY** Salumi platters, lasagnes, grilled salmon, amazing eggplant caponata, design-your-own salads and picnic boxes for Rose Bowl tailgate parties or outdoor concerts. **WHAT** Glass cases hold grilled baby lamb chops, quality prosciutti and salumi, eggplant involtini, simple pizzas and many more Italian lovelies to take home for dinner or parties. At lunchtime, west Pasadenans meet over salads and generous grilled panini. High-quality food at not-outrageous prices. **WHO** Lacrosse moms taking a break from Julienne. 🍴☼

[Recess] 1102 N. Brand Blvd., Glendale, 818.507.0592, recesseatery. com. B & L daily, early D Mon.-Sat. Mediterranean/modern American. BYOB. AE, MC, V. $ - $$ **WHY** Beautiful salads, sandwiches, pizzas and other goodies to take out or eat here. **WHAT** A former Patina chef decided he wanted to do his own thing in his own neighborhood, and the result is this popular café and gourmet-to-go spot. Breakfast brings takeout croissants or eat-in eggs; lunch and dinner mean prosciutto and mozzarella sandwiches, ahi tuna salads and lovely cheese pizzas. **WHO** North Glendale folks thrilled that they don't have to drive to Pasadena. ☼🍴

EAST VALLEY

[Artisan Cheese Gallery] 12023 Ventura Blvd., Studio City, 818.505.0207, artisancheesegallery.com. L daily. Modern American. AE, MC, V. $ - $$ **WHY** For the duck confit sandwich, made with Breadbar's ciabatta, Le Marechal cheese and a fig spread. People drive across town for this sandwich. **WHAT** Call ahead or stop by to order cheese platters for a party or one of the superb sandwiches—the duck confit is most famous, but we're also terribly fond of the grilled cheese, the portobello mushroom with goat cheese, and the bacon, cheddar and apple. Order an assortment for your next party. 🍴🚚

[Caioti Pizza Café] 4346 Tujunga Ave., Studio City, 818.761.3588, caiotipizzacafe.com. L & D daily, brunch Sat.-Sun. Pizzeria. AE, MC, V. $ - $$ **WHY** Superb salads (try the Humble Salad, a romaine wedge with bacon, goat cheese and roma tomatoes), Caioti's rightly famed individual pizzas and delicious pastas and sandwiches; call ahead and your takeout order will be ready. **WHAT** Ed LaDou may have shuffled off this mortal coil, but the California pizza he invented (that's right, it was LaDou, not Puck) lives on in this casual, noisy café, which does a good job with to-go orders. 🍴🍴☼

Gourmet
To Go

🍴 VEGETARIAN ☼ KID FRIENDLY ☼ PATIO DINING 🚚 DELIVERY 🏛 PRIVATE PARTY

[Marmalade] 14910 Ventura Blvd., Sherman Oaks, 818.905.8872, marmaladecafe.com. B, L & D daily. Modern American/French. AE, MC, V. **$$ WHY** A vibrant range of prepared dishes, salads and baked goods to take out. **WHAT** This Valley branch of the Marmalade mini-empire is an eat-in café but also has loads of tempting choices for takeout. Salads range from herb chicken ravioli in pesto to roasted beets with oranges and candied walnuts in rosemary vinaigrette; panini and bakery treats are numerous; and take-home entrées run to such things as chicken enchiladas, vegetable lasagne and poached salmon with sour cream and dill.

[Olive & Thyme] 🏠 4013 Riverside Dr., Toluca Lake, 818.557.1560, oliveandthyme.com. B, L & D Mon.-Fri. Modern American. Beer & wine. AE, MC, V. **$$ WHY** Gourmet takeout or eat-in fare of a quality never before seen in the Valley, at prices that are more Brentwood than Burbank. **WHAT** Restaurant investors Melina and Christian Davies pined for a gourmet shop/café close to their Toluca Lake home, so they created this spacious place, which satisfies all cravings, from Intelligentsia coffee and baked goods from Valerie Confections (the salted caramel croissant is flaky bliss; the white chocolate coconut cake makes us weak in the knees) to salads and sandwiches for lunch and early dinner (superb curried chicken salad, a succulent braised short-rib sandwich with horseradish crème fraîche) and a well-curated array of cheeses and artisanal foodstuffs. We're besotted. ☼

[Tashkent Russian Deli] 5340 Laurel Canyon Blvd., North Hollywood, 818.752.7222. Daily. Russian. MC, V. **$$ WHY** All manner of prepared dishes, including zaftig home-baked breads. **WHAT** Attached to Tashkent Produce is a tiny sliver of a kitchen where babushkas cook all day, producing fabulous takeout borscht, stuffed cabbage, lamb stew, baked chicken with pilaf and more from an ever-changing roster of homey goodies. Check the freezer for frozen dumplings and the deli case for a wonderful array of buffet-worthy sausages, cured fish and cheese. You may never cook again. **WHO** Mostly Russian mamas who'd rather get a manicure than cook.

[Village Gourmet Cheese & Wine] 4357 Tujunga Ave., Studio City, 818.487.3807. L daily, early D Mon.-Sat. Modern American. AE, MC, V. **$$ WHY** Good last-minute party food from the freezer case— spinach-pesto puffs, gorgonzola-fig phyllo rolls—as well as order-in-advance party platters (cheeses, crudités, caprese, caviar). Intelligently filled gift baskets, too. **WHAT** A convenient spot for all your high-end culinary essentials, from roasted-pepper-and-pesto sandwiches and chicken-apricot salad to good party foods and prepared foods, both fresh and frozen. The wine and cheese selections are smart, though not cheap. **WHO** Regulars picking up some lasagne or frozen pasta for dinner, and folks putting together Hollywood Bowl picnics. 🍷

WEST VALLEY

[Bauducco's Italian Market] **2839 Agoura Rd., Westlake Village, 805.495.4623, bauduccorestaurant.com. B, L & early D daily. Italian. AE, MC, V. $ - $$ WHY** House-made Sicilian bread, either to take home or to have the deli make into a chicken-parmesan or sausage sandwich, as well as good pizzas, lasagnes and Italian prepared dishes. **WHAT** Fabulous Sicilian bread and rolls are baked on the premises at this 40-year-old family business, where the deli cases are amply stocked with house-made sausages and salumi, both imported and domestic. The voluptuous sandwiches, pizzas and prepared foods to take home are very good—and if you don't want to take it home, there's a restaurant, too. 🚚

[Brent's Delicatessen] 🏠 **19565 Parthenia St., Northridge, 818.886.5679, brentsdeli.com. B, L & D daily. Deli. AE, MC, V. $$ WHY** Very good deli, delivered anywhere in the greater L.A. area for a large group, or to pick up for a small one. **WHAT** Brent's fleet of vans scurry around the Valley and the L.A. side of the Santa Monicas every day, delivering trays of deli sandwiches, smoked fish, raw veggies and lemon bars to offices, schools and home gatherings. It turns out lean meats, fresh breads, pretty fruit plates and a memorable whitefish salad, all at fair prices. For smaller orders, call ahead and it'll be ready for you to pick up. **WHO** Deli fans who need to feed a group for a meeting, a bridge party or a memorial.

[Carrillo's Mexican Deli] 🏠 **19744 Sherman Way, Canoga Park, 818.887.6118, carrillostamales.com. B, L & D daily. Mexican. MC, V. $ WHY** Great tamales, which you can either order online to be shipped or pick up at the deli or the factory (1242 Pico St., San Fernando, 818.365.1636). All the Mexican classics are first-rate. **WHAT** The atmosphere isn't much to speak of, so many regulars get this delicious food to take home—or, in larger quantities, to feed a party. The homemade tamales are righteous—get a few no matter what else you order—and you can feed a family on the $15.55 takeout special, which includes a pound of tender carnitas and sides of rice, beans, salsa and homemade tortillas. 📋

[Follow Your Heart Market & Café] **21825 Sherman Way, Canoga Park, 818.348.3240, followyourheart.com. B, L & D daily. Vegetarian/ vegan. AE, MC, V. $ - $$ WHY** Colorful, flavorful vegetarian and vegan cooking; many of the soup and main dishes (enchiladas corazón, spinach lasagne, spanakopita) take out very well. **WHAT** The '70s live on at this good-hearted natural-foods café and market, which was founded in 1970. But the food has kept up with the times, and it's all fresh and appealing. You can pick up staples from the market and takeout food from the café in back. **WHO** Vegetarians, vegans and seekers of healthful, organic foods. 📋♻️🍃

Gourmet To Go

🍃 **VEGETARIAN** ◉ **KID FRIENDLY** ☼ **PATIO DINING** 🚚 **DELIVERY** 🎩 **PRIVATE PARTY**

WESTSIDE: CENTRAL

[Café Surfas] 8777 W. Washington Blvd., Culver City, 310.558.1458, cafesurfas.com. B & L daily. Modern American. AE, MC, V. $ - $$ **WHY** Lovely pressed panini, Kobe beef burgers and creative salads, to take away or eat here. Try the smoked venison hot dog with Maytag blue cheese cream. **WHAT** The café next to famed restaurant-supply store Surfas serves predictably chic breakfast and lunch fare, and it's also a fine place to get food to take away, from daily soup specials to platters of high-end cheeses. **WHO** Kitchen-supply junkies shopping next door. ☺

[Clementine] 🏠 1751 Ensley Ave., Century City, 310.552.1080, clementineonline.com. B & L Mon.-Sat., early D Mon.-Fri. American. AE, MC, V. $$ - $$$ **WHY** Delicious updated feel-good food, like sloppy joes, saucy BBQ pork, soups and vegetable lasagne, to feed two people or a crowd. **WHAT** In addition to being one of L.A.'s more popular caterers, Annie Miler also runs this café, bakery and takeout place. Some dishes, like sandwiches and breakfast items, are served on an individual basis; others are sold by the pound (brisket) or the tray (lasagne). Call ahead for curbside pickup and your food will be placed in your car for you. Good Bowl and picnic boxes, too. 🏠

[Food] 10571 W. Pico Blvd., Rancho Park, 310.441.7770, food-la.com. B & L daily., D Mon.- Fri. Modern American. AE, MC, V. $ - $$ **WHY** The neighborhood is grateful for this gourmet market, café, takeout spot and caterer. Call ahead for excellent picnic baskets or party platters. **WHAT** It's not just the neon-red paint that makes this West Pico storefront stand out—the quality of its takeout and café fare has won it the devotion of many locals. You'll pay more than $10 for a sandwich—slow-roasted grass-fed beef tenderloin on a baguette, for instance, or cilantro tofu with grilled corn relish, avocado and tomato on five-grain bread—but the ingredients are top drawer. 🏠

[L'Epicerie Market] 9900 Culver Blvd., Culver City, 310.815.1600, lepiceriemarket.com. B, L & D daily. French/Californian. Beer & wine. AE, MC, V. $$ - $$$ **WHY** A French-accented restaurant, wine bar and deli that works for takeout as well as brunch, lunch, tapas or drinks. **WHAT** Chef Thierry Perez's latest Culver City venture combines a wine shop, gourmet-to-go and a full-service menu offering everything from crêpes to polenta with veal brains. Hard-to-find French products like mustard, candies, cheese and jam are fun to browse.

WEST OF THE 405

[Antica Pizzeria] Location changing, Marina del Rey area, anticapizzeria.net. L & D daily. Pizzeria. AE, MC, V. $$ **WHY** Brilliantly balanced pizza with that elusive char on the underside of the crust, as well as many other worthy Italian dishes, all of which are delivered

🏠 ESSENTIALLY L.A. ☺ LATE ♥ ROMANTIC 📷 VALUE 🔇 QUIET ♻ SUSTAINABLE in the Marina/Venice area. **WHAT** Alas, Antica lost its lease just as we went to press, but we are keeping it in the book because we have faith that it will have a new home by the time you read this. Chef and Naples native Peppe Miele was the first U.S. resident accepted into the Associazione Verace Pizza Napoletana, and he follows its strict rules on baking methods (wood-burning ovens) and dough (just flour, natural yeast and water). The result: small pizzas that taste utterly fantastico. 🍷�

[Cha Cha Chicken] 1906 Ocean Ave., Santa Monica, 310.581.1684, chachachicken.com. L & D daily. Caribbean. MC, V. $ **WHY** Chicken roasted and coated with an addictive sweet-fiery jerk sauce and served with all the trimmings, for less than it costs to park at the neighboring Casa del Mar hotel. **WHAT** This cheap, lively, riotously colorful outdoor joint does a brisk phone-ahead takeout business and is also popular for its party packages for 15 people or more. Its signature Jamaican jerk chicken is the centerpiece; accompaniments include black beans, rice, fried plantains and salad. 🟡

[Gallegos Mexican Deli] 12470 Venice Blvd., Mar Vista, 310.391.2587, gallegosmexicandeli.com. B & L Mon.-Sat., D Mon.-Fri. to 7 p.m. Mexican. AE, MC, V. $ **WHY** Fresh tortillas (this place started as a tortilleria some 60 years ago), lovely homemade tamales (try the chicken chile verde), substantial burritos and very good to-go trays of enchiladas, chile verde, carnitas and barbacoa. **WHAT** The Gallegos family has been making tamales and other good Mexican dishes in L.A. since 1945, and they're still going strong. You can eat here, but many get takeout or take advantage of the local delivery. **WHO** Generations of loyal fans, many of whom drive across town for a big order of tamales to go. 🟡🍷🚗

[Gjelina Take Away] 🏛 1429 Abbot Kinney Blvd., Venice, 310.450.1429, gjelina.com. L Mon.-Fri., D nightly, brunch Sat.-Sun. Modern American. Beer & wine. AE, MC, V. $$ - $$$ **WHY** The same excellent, expensive rustic-elegant food as at neighboring Gjelina, ready to take out in ten minutes. **WHAT** It can take six weeks to score a reservation at Venice's hottest restaurant, Gjelina, but now with GTA (Gjelina Take Away) next door, you can take the food back to work or home or even to the beach. The morning baked goods and breakfast sandwich are superb, as are the pizzas (lamb sausage) and salads (panzanella). Great coffee, too. **WHO** A constant crowd of Venice cool people. 🍷⚪

[Javan] 11500 Santa Monica Blvd., West L.A., 310.207.5555, javanrestaurant.com. L & D daily. Persian. AE, MC, V. $$ **WHY** Tasty kebabs, delectable little grilled lamb chops, saffron rice and other Iranian dishes, delivered to your door. **WHAT** Javan's classic Iranian food takes out well and is good for a small dinner or a buffet party. Pass on the salads in favor of the kebabs, lamb chops and delicious

🍷VEGETARIAN ⚪KID FRIENDLY ⚪PATIO DINING 🚗DELIVERY 🏛PRIVATE PARTY

lentil-based *ashjoe* soup. **WHO** Well-heeled Brentwood and West L.A. people getting delivery for the family or a casual dinner party. 🚗

[Lemon Moon] Westside Media Center, 12200 W. Olympic Blvd., West L.A., 310.442.9191, lemonmoon.com. B & L daily. Modern American. AE, MC, V. $$ **WHY** Gorgeous but unpretentious takeout food from star chefs Josiah Citrin (Mélisse) and Raphael Lunetta (JiRaffe); prices aren't low, but there's free validated parking in the underground structure. **WHAT** If we had one of those high-paying studio jobs that so many in this neighborhood have, we'd pick up takeout from here every day. Lots of the regulars take the rock shrimp ceviche, spicy Korean noodle salad or miso salmon back to the office for lunch, but many of these dishes keep well for dinnertime, too. **WHO** Entertainment-industry folks who work in this building or nearby. 🔖

[Marmalade] 🏛 710 Montana Ave., Santa Monica, 310.395.9196, marmaladecafe.com. B, L & D daily to 7 p.m. Modern American/French. AE, MC, V. $$ **WHY** A vibrant range of prepared dishes, salads and baked goods to take out. **WHAT** This flagship of the Marmalade mini-empire doesn't have the seating of its siblings but has loads of tempting choices for takeout. Salads range from herb chicken ravioli in pesto to roasted beets with oranges and candied walnuts in rosemary vinaigrette; panini and bakery treats are numerous; and take-home entrées include chicken enchiladas, vegetable lasagne and poached salmon with sour cream and dill. **WHO** Longtime loyal locals.

[Monsieur Marcel] 1260 3rd St. Promenade, Santa Monica, 310.587.1166, mrmarcel.com. B, L & D daily. French. AE, MC, V. $$ **WHY** Straightforward bistro food, some of which (escargots, quiches, salads, cheeses) takes out well. If you have time, sit for a spell with a glass of wine and have fun watching the Promenade parade. **WHAT** Occupying the former newsstand smack in the middle of the Promenade, this Gallic market, wine bar and café is a good, if pricey, place to get food to take home or to the office. Check the chalkboard for the daily offerings. ☼

[Real Food Daily] 514 Santa Monica Blvd., Santa Monica, 310.451.7544, realfood.com. L & D daily, brunch Sun. Vegan/American. AE, MC, V. $$ **WHY** Organic vegan food that actually tastes good. You can order takeout, order party platters or get lunch or dinner delivered. **WHAT** Real Food's meat- and dairy-free fare includes many dishes that take out well or work for small parties. Try the salad platters, the lentil-walnut pâté and the cold sesame noodle salad. Your call on whether to try the tofu cheesecake. (We passed.) **WHO** Santa Monica's many vegans and flexitarians. ♻🔖🚗

[SugarFISH] 4722 Admiralty Way, Marina del Rey, 310.306.6300; 11640 W. San Vicente Blvd., Brentwood, 310.820.4477; sugarfishsushi.

com. L & D daily. Sushi. AE, MC, V. $$ - $$$ **WHY** Takeout or eat-in sushi from the "Sushi Nazi" Kazunori Nozawa of Sushi Nozawa in Studio City — without the high price tag or quite the same creative combinations. The Marina location has curbside service for people hustling to catch a plane. **WHAT** Nozawa has traded his omakase at the flagship restaurant for pre-set "Trust Me" combinations (hamachi nigiri, tuna sashimi with scallions) that are less expensive but just as fresh at these more laid-back strip-mall joints (one in Brentwood, one in the Marina). The takeout is cleverly packaged and includes his famed "firm" nibbling instructions, so it almost feels like the Sushi Nazi himself is glaring over your shoulder at home. **WHO** Just-landed Angelenos grabbing takeout on their way home from LAX or Brentwood and Marina locals popping in for takeout or a quick bite.

SOUTH BAY TO SOUTH L.A.

[Claro's] 🔖 101 W. Whittier Blvd., La Habra, 562.690.2844, claros.com. B & L Mon.-Tues. & Thurs.-Sun. Italian. AE, MC, V. $ - $$ **WHY** Prepared take-home dishes like lasagne and ravioli, huge and delicious sandwiches, savory sausages, take-and-bake pizzas and a bakery case lined with breads, cannoli and Italian cookies. **WHAT** This old-school Italian market and deli is a branch of the mothership in San Gabriel, which has been around since 1948. The deli offers sandwiches, sausages, antipasti and hot dishes. Good for a takeout dinner for one or a party for a dozen. **WHO** Third-generation loyalists and people proud of their Sicilian blood, even if it's only a little.

[Olives Gourmet Grocer] 3510 E. Broadway, Long Beach, 562.439.7758, olivesgourmetgrocer.com. B & L daily, D Mon.-Fri., early D Sat.-Sun. Modern American. AE, MC, V. $ - $$ **WHY** For a food-lover's home away from home, not to mention a good place to pick up a rotisserie chicken for dinner or a platter for that potluck. **WHAT** This clean-lined store is as much a deli as a grocer, with a terrific sandwich counter, a salad bar, an olive bar and a different dinner-to-go every night: perhaps chicken and dumplings on a Sunday, or pan-seared salmon with rice and roasted broccoli on a Wednesday.

[Olives Gourmet Grocer] 5000 E. 2nd St., Long Beach, 562.343.5580, olivesgourmetgrocer.com. B, L & early D daily. Modern American. AE, MC, V. $ - $$ **WHY** Food for every need, from breakfast panini to party platters. **WHAT** Twice the size of its Broadway parent, this Belmont Shore Olives is as much a deli and gourmet-to-go place as a grocer, with a pizza oven, grilled panini, traditional sandwiches, a salad bar, an olive bar and a different dinner-to-go every night: perhaps chicken milanese or flatiron steak with roasted red potatoes and grilled vegetables. There's a seating area if you want to eat in. **WHO** Passionate foodies from all over Long Beach and Seal Beach.

Gourmet To Go

🥬 VEGETARIAN ◎ KID FRIENDLY ✿ PATIO DINING 🚗 DELIVERY 🏮 PRIVATE PARTY

Bakeries + Sweets

Look here for bread bakers, cupcake makers and cake decorators, as well as chocolates, ice cream and more.

[ESSENTIALLY L.A.]

21 Choices, Pasadena (PAGE 306)

Big Sugar Bakeshop, Studio City (PAGE 311)

Breadbar, Beverly/Third & Century City (PAGES 300 & 314)

Brooklyn Bagel Bakery, Westlake (PAGE 304)

Carmela Ice Cream, Pasadena (PAGE 307)

Coolhaus, Culver City (PAGE 314)

Donut Man, Glendora (PAGE 307)

El Gallo Bakery, East L.A. (PAGE 304)

Euro Pane, Pasadena (PAGE 308)

Fosselman's, Alhambra (PAGE 308)

Huckleberry, Santa Monica (PAGE 319)

Jerry's Soda Shop, Canoga Park (PAGE 313)

Jin Patisserie, Venice (PAGE 315)

L'Artisan du Chocolat, Silver Lake (PAGE 304)

La Brea Bakery, Miracle Mile (PAGE 301)

La Mascota, Boyle Heights (PAGE 305)

Little Flower Candy Co., Pasadena (PAGE 309)

Littlejohn's English Toffee, Fairfax District (PAGE 302)

Partamian Armenian Bakery, Mid-City (PAGE 302)

Patisserie Chantilly, Torrance (PAGE 322)

Porto's, Glendale & Burbank (PAGES 310 & 312)

Scoops, Mid-City (PAGE 303)

Susina Bakery, Beverly/Third (PAGE 303)

Valerie Confections, Silver Lake (PAGE 306)

QUALITY BAKED GOODS ARE
ALSO FOUND INSIDE THESE CAFÉS OR SHOPS:
Aroma Café, Studio City (PAGES 216 & 238)
Bauducco's Italian Market, Westlake Village (PAGE 293)
Bay Cities Italian Deli & Bakery, Santa Monica (PAGE 275)
Black Cat Bakery, Fairfax District (PAGE 204)
Café Tropical, Silver Lake (PAGE 209)
Claro's, San Gabriel & La Habra (PAGES 290 & 297)
The Conservatory, Culver City (PAGE 240)
Doña Rosa, Pasadena (PAGE 264)
FarmShop, Santa Monica (PAGE 223)
Froma on Melrose, Melrose (PAGE 357)
Homegirl Café, Chinatown (PAGE 210)
Howie's Ranch Market, San Gabriel (PAGE 365)
I Panini di Ambra, Hollywood (PAGE 251)
Jongewaard's Bake N Broil, Long Beach (PAGE 226)
Julienne, San Marino (PAGES 214 & 290)
Koreatown Galleria Market, Koreatown (PAGE 366)
Le Pain Quotidien, various locations (PAGES 214 & 224)
Liborio Market, Downtown & Koreatown (PAGE 366)
Little Next Door, Beverly/Third (PAGE 287)
Ma 'n Pa's Grocery, Long Beach (PAGE 359)
Market at Santa Monica Place (PAGE 359)
Market on Holly, Pasadena (PAGE 215)
Marmalade, various locations (PAGES 292, 296 & 330)
Marukai Pacific Market, Torrance (PAGE 281)
Nickel Diner, Downtown (PAGE 212)
Olive & Thyme, Toluca Lake (PAGES 128 & 292)
Olives Gourmet Grocer, Long Beach (PAGE 397)
Owen's Market, Century City (PAGE 361
Real Food Daily, W. Hollywood & Santa Monica (PAGES 289 & 296)
Recess, Glendale (PAGE 291)
Simplethings Sandwich & Pie, Beverly/Third (PAGE 207)
Sweet Butter Kitchen, Sherman Oaks (PAGE 218)
Thyme Café & Market, Santa Monica (PAGE 225)
Urth Caffé, various locations (PAGES 231, 234, 241 & 245)

Bakeries
+ Sweets

🦞 **VEGETARIAN** ☺ **KID FRIENDLY** ☼ **PATIO DINING** 🚗 **DELIVERY** 🎩 **PRIVATE PARTY**

CENTRAL CITY

[Alcove Café & Bakery] **1929 Hillhurst Ave., Los Feliz, 323.644.0100, alcovecafe.com. Daily. American. AE, MC, V. WHY** Strawberry whip cake, banana cream cake and truly superb chocolate chip cookies. **WHAT** For every two people who are ordering a meal to enjoy on the oh-so-charming patio or in the old Craftsman house, there's another person just getting something sweet to take away. The cupcakes are nothing special, but the chocolate chip cookies are well worth the calories, as is the See's Candy Bundt Cake. **WHO** Writers, musicians, costume deisgners, blind-daters and Los Feliz women sporting subtle tattoos and Kingsley-clad preschoolers. ☺ ♥▨☼☃☺ ☼

[The Bagel Broker] **7825 Beverly Blvd., Beverly/Third, 323.931.1258, bagelbroker.com. Daily. Deli. AE, MC, V. WHY** All the traditional bagel varieties and variations, like blueberry or cheese jalapeño, are baked daily. Order them by the bag, or have a bagel sandwich or bagels and lox on the premises. **WHAT** Bagel connoisseurs and New York transplants say this basic mini-mall deli in the heart of the Fairfax Jewish district is one of the few places in L.A. to get something approaching an authentic bagel.

[Beard Papa's] **Hollywood & Highland, 6801 Hollywood Blvd., Hollywood, 323.462.6100, beardpapa.com. Daily. Japanese/French. MC, V. WHY** Two words: cream puffs. **WHAT** The craze that has swept Japan is now in L.A., with branches popping up like Pinkberries once did. The obsession is over fat balls of choux that are baked all day long, and when you order yours, an employee fills it with sweetened cream (vanilla, chocolate, green tea, pumpkin), dusts it with powdered sugar, and off you go. **WHO** Food faddists who've just gotta try it. ☺

[Bennett's Ice Cream] **Farmers Market, 6333 W. 3rd St., Fairfax District, 323.939.6786. Daily. Ice cream. Cash only. WHY** For seasonal flavors like rose, for Rose Parade season, and pumpkin in the fall, and original creations like Fancy Nancy (coffee with bananas). **WHAT** Old-fashioned ice cream in dozens of flavors—no gelato here—is made on the premises behind viewing windows at this folksy Farmers Market stand. Bennett's also owns the Refresher soda-pop stand in the market and bottles its own sodas, including Spicy Hot Cola. **WHO** The marvelous cross-section of humanity that fills the Farmers Market each day. ☺ ☼

[Breadbar] ▤ **8718 W. 3rd St., Beverly/Third, 310.205.0124, breadbar. net. Daily. American. AE, MC, V. WHY** Hand-crafted whole-grain and country breads. excellent croissants and tarts, as well as breakfast, sandwiches and salads. Don't miss the Alpine cheese bread. **WHAT** Baker Eric Kayser first won the hearts of Parisians (no easy thing for a bread baker) and then came to conquer L.A. here and in Century City. The patio fronts bustling 3rd Street, with more tables inside the chic industrial space. A display case runs the length of the café, showcasing pastries and colorful tarts. He also hosts regular pop-up restaurants at night; check the website for details. **WHO** Serious bread eaters and the 3rd Street café crowd. ☼

[Diamond Bakery] **335 N. Fairfax Ave., Fairfax District, 323.655.0534. Daily. Deli/Kosher. Cash only. WHY** Kosher challah, delicious rye and heavenly cheesecakes. **WHAT** So maybe you have to wait a while, and maybe the fellow behind the counter could be a little less brusque. But these are the things one must endure to get a rye bread this good. Since you had to wait so long for your rye, you might as well get some chocolate chip rugelach. And maybe a cheesecake. **WHO** People who wouldn't pay $5 for a cupcake at gunpoint. 🖅

[Froyo Life] **1924 Hillhurst Ave., Los Feliz, 323.667.9900, froyolife. com. Daily. Yogurt. MC, V. WHY** Dulce de leche frozen yogurt, free WiFi and delivery. **WHAT** Want to see a cool, subtly tattooed, wedge-wearing junior studio exec leap up and down like a kindergartener? Invite her to Froyo Life, which has developed a rabid cult following in Los Feliz. The yogurts, both of the sweet-and-creamy and tart varieties, are well made, the toppings are extensive and quality, and the place is fun. Other locations in Montrose, Hermosa and Beverly Hills. **WHO** An obsessed crowd of 20something regulars. ☺ ☺ ☼ 🚗

[Gelato Bar] **1936 N. Hillhurst Ave., Los Feliz, 323.668.0606, gelatobar-la.com. Daily. Ice cream. AE, MC, V. WHY** Classic and seasonal flavors, ranging from a superb dark chocolate gelato to an amazing pear sorbet, served with excellent coffee and espresso. **WHAT** Home-made gelati in fun flavors from Gail Silverton, sister of L.A.'s culinary queen Nancy Silverton, in a colorful shop on happening Hillhurst. When you've had enough of the light stuff at Froyo Life, come here for the real thing. **WHO** The Los Feliz intelligentsia.

[La Brea Bakery] 🔒 **624 S. La Brea Ave., Miracle Mile, 323.939.6813, labreabakery.com. Daily. American. AE, MC, V. WHY** For its famous crusty baguettes and hearty artisanal loaves speckled with nuts, herbs and olives. **WHAT** The original bakery home of former Campanile pastry chef Nancy Silverton still has some of the best bread in town—and it's wholly different in quality from the grocery-store brand bearing the same name. **WHO** Tourists checking it off their list and locals grabbing a baguette for dinner.

[La Maison du Pain] **5373 W. Pico Blvd., Mid-City, 323.934.5858, lamaisondupain.net. Closed Mon. French/American. AE, MC, V. WHY** Kalamata olive bread, plain and chocolate croissants, macarons and traditional Parisian baguettes with a crisp crust that shatters to reveal light, soft bread. **WHAT** No, it's not the House of Pain, it's the House of Bread, as well as the House of Tarts, Quiches and Cakes. It's both a sweet little café with very good breakfast and lunch goodies and a take-away bakery with lovely breads and sweets. ☺

[Littlejohn's English Toffee] 🏛 **Farmers Market, 6333 W. 3rd St., Fairfax District, 323.936.5379, littlejohnscandies.com. Daily. Confections. AE, MC, V. WHY** Buttery, crunchy, chocolatey English toffee that is impossible to stop eating. **WHAT** Good God, how we love this English toffee, the highlight of our childhood visits to Farmers Market. It's made fresh throughout the day and sold in hunks or in tidier sticks. Good almond bark and honeycomb, too, but that's not why you come here. **WHO** Wide-eyed children and chocolate-addicted women who stash their purchases in their purses and then nibble on the toffee furtively, so the calories don't stick. ☺ ☼

[Mashti Malone's Ice Cream] **1525 N. La Brea Ave., Hollywood, 323.874.0144, mashti.com. Daily. Ice cream. AE, MC, V. WHY** The Mashti ice cream sandwich: your choice of ice cream stuffed between crisp wafers. **WHAT** Come here for Persian-style ice creams in inspired flavors that are as poetic sounding as they are delicious: orange blossom with pistachios, creamy rosewater, herbal snow, lavender, rose sorbet with sour cherry.... ☺

[Milk] **7290 Beverly Blvd., Beverly/Third, 323.939.6455, themilkshop. com. Daily. Ice cream/American. MC, V. WHY** The grasshopper ice cream sandwich, banana-peanut malt, creative cakes like Blue Velvet, and handmade shave ice (try the dulce de leche). Oh, and the vanilla-bean ice cream bar dipped in superb dark chocolate. **WHAT** This charming, airy sweets spot is beloved by the neighborhood for its good ice cream and desserts, its sidewalk tables, and the fact that it's open until 11 on weekends. The counter is piled with an array of tempting baked goods, and there are treats to take home in the cooler case. **WHO** Hancock Park moms picking up expensive but fantastic ice cream cakes and Beverly Boulevard date-nighters sharing shakes and sundaes. ☺

[Panos Pastry] **5150 Hollywood Blvd., Hollywood, 323.661.0335, panospastry.com. Daily. Armenian/French. AE, MC, V. WHY** Superb baklava of every variety, as well as the full range of French and Armenian pastries. **WHAT** An elegant temple of French and Armenian delicacies, done up in marble and mirrors. There's another branch in Glendale. **WHO** Baklava junkies and brides-to-be looking for a beautiful cake.

[Partamian Armenian Bakery] 🏛 **5410 W. Adams Blvd., Mid-City, 323.937.2870. Daily. Armenian. AE, MC, V. WHY** Devotees drive an hour for their *lahmajune*, aka Armenian pizza. **WHAT** This longstanding center of Armenian food culture in L.A. is now owned by two Mexican bakers—the devoted employees to whom Abraham Partamian left the business in his will. The lahmajune is as good as ever, and it does the heart good to see this place carry on so well. **WHO** Armenian-American famlies who've been coming here (often from great distances) for three generations, as well as lots of local lahmajune junkies. 📷 ☺

[Scoops] 🔒 **712 N. Heliotrope Dr., East Hollywood, 323.906.2649. Daily. Ice cream. Cash only. WHY** For ice cream and sorbet flavors you won't believe: chocolate-jasmine, cashew-ricotta, peanut-butter-celery-and-raisin, strawberry-lychee and many more; the roster changes daily. We adore the more mainstream Brown Bread, a vanilla ice cream with caramel and Grape-Nuts. **WHAT** Tai Kim isn't a vegan who wishes he could eat ice cream—he's a passionate lover of gelato-style ice cream (a little lighter than true gelato) who wants everyone to enjoy it, including dairy-free vegans. He's come up with dozens of recipes for fantastic regular and vegan ice creams and sorbets, and in the process made his little East Hollywood joint a major foodie destination—and now he has a new location in Palms, too. **WHO** Adventurous ice cream lovers. 📷 ☺

[Susina Bakery] 🔒 **7122 Beverly Blvd., Beverly/Third, 323.934.7900, susinabakery.com. Daily. American. AE, MC, V. WHY** Croissants for breakfast, quiches and such salads as dried cherry and brie for lunch, picnic boxes and lavish cakes—try the chocolate peanut butter mousse or berry blossom. **WHAT** Exquisite tarts and pastries are laid out in glass cases in this European-style bakery, with tables for enjoying sweets up to 11 p.m. ♥

[Sweet Lady Jane] **8360 Melrose Ave., Melrose, 323.653.7145, sweetladyjane.com. Daily. American. AE, MC, V. WHY** Gorgeous cakes, breakfast pastries and cookies that taste as good as they look. **WHAT** This is L.A.'s high-end birthday-cake central, turning out superb Almond Roca, chocolate mocha praline, passionfruit with apricot, triple berry, even red velvet cakes. They're no bargain, though, and the service can be less than warm. But the cakes are so good that no one really minds. **WHO** Fred Segal–clad moms on birthday-cake patrol and neighborhood lunchers.

EASTSIDE

[Auntie Em's Marketplace] **4616 Eagle Rock Blvd., Eagle Rock, 323.255.0800, auntieemskitchen.com. Daily. American. AE, MC, V. WHY** Dreamy scones, over-the-top coconut cupcakes, a great selection of domestic cheeses and a freezer full of take-home dishes. **WHAT** Julienne for the pierced-nose set, Auntie Em's is a one-stop food-lovers' haven—part café, part gourmet-to-go, part caterer and part bakery. From the bakery operation in the restaurant, you can special-order a red velvet cake or take home some amazing chocolate cupcakes, scones and muffins. **WHO** An Eagle Rock mix, from Oxy professors to tattooed Highland Park performance artists. ☺ ✿

Bakeries + Sweets

🌿 VEGETARIAN ◎ KID FRIENDLY ✿ PATIO DINING 🚗 DELIVERY 🎪 PRIVATE PARTY

[Brooklyn Bagel Bakery] 🏛 **2217 W. Beverly Blvd., Westlake, 213.413.4114, brooklynbagella.com. Daily. Deli. Cash only. WHY** Properly boiled and hearth-baked bagels, more compact and pleasingly dense than most in town, made fresh all day. **WHAT** Between Downtown and Koreatown lies one of L.A.'s most New York of businesses, a busy bakery with an equally busy retail outlet. Try the blueberry or the poppyseed, and don't miss Bagel Happy Hour (3 to 6 p.m.), when they're all half off. **WHO** Wholesale customers (coffeehouse and café owners), homesick New Yorkers and bagel devotees from across L.A. 📑

[El Gallo Mexican Bakery] 🏛 **4546 Cesar E. Chavez Ave., East L.A., 323.263.5528, elgallobakery.com. Daily. Mexican. Cash only. WHY** Life-changing, melt-in-your-mouth buttery crescent rolls (*cuernitas*) that are to supermarket pan dulce what La Brea is to Wonder Bread. **WHAT** When owner Jesus Huerta's mom started this bakery in 1949, she was determined to mimic the pan dulces she'd grown up with in Mexico. She played around with ingredients, eventually hiring Mexican artisans who helped her get it just right. Today, the variety is huge, including esoteric and difficult-to-make specialties. Free samples for the kids, great coffee and festive holiday goodies, like Day of the Dead breads. **WHO** Old-line East L.A. families and legions of pan dulce devotees with a palate for subtly sweet, yeasty treats. 📑 ☺

[Frances Bakery & Coffee] **404 E. 2nd St., Little Tokyo/Arts District, 213.680.4899. Closed Sun. French. AE, MC, V. WHY** Cakes that are remarkably moist and delicious without being overly sugary; the chocolate hazelnut, green tea–chocolate and cheesecake are all stars. Sit and stay for a cup of very good coffee or afternoon tea. **WHAT** The Japanese-American baker who runs this longtime cake heaven is French in spirit and in baking technique, as evidenced by his lovely croissants, quiches and, especially, his superb cakes and handmade chocolates. The good stuff vanishes fast, so come early. **WHO** Longtime regulars in on the secret.

[L'Artisan du Chocolat] 🏛 **3364 W. 1st St., Silver Lake, 213.252.8721, lartisanduchocolat.net. Closed Sun.-Mon. Chocolatier. AE, MC, V. WHY** Chocolates and truffles made in Silver Lake with skill and taste. If you're adventurous, try the Aztec (with apricot and three chiles, including habañero) or Kalamata olive; if you're a classicist, have the straightforward truffle or the dark chocolate ganache with coffee bits. **WHAT** Master chocolatier Whajung Park and her husband, Christian Alexandre, turn out some of L.A.'s most sophisticated chocolates at this hidden spot near Beverly and Virgil, in what's now the "chocolate ghetto" (Valerie Confections is on the block). Some of the best creations are the most exotic, but the traditional chocolates are suave and delicious, too. **WHO** Regular customers buying lovely gift boxes.

🏛 ESSENTIALLY L.A. ☺ LATE ♥ ROMANTIC 📑 VALUE 🔇 QUIET ♻ SUSTAINABLE

[La Adelita] 1287 S. Union Ave., Pico-Union, 213.487.0176. Daily. Latino. MC, V. **WHY** Fluffy, ethereal tres leches cakes. **WHAT** An excellent Mexican and pan-Latin operation that bakes soft bolillos, pretty fruit tarts, tortillas and delicious cakes, most notably the tres leches cakes. Next door is a worthwhile café offering dishes from all the Central American countries. It also has a small shop in the Grand Central Market Downtown. **WHO** Pico-Union locals. 🖼️☺

[La Mascota Bakery] 🏠 2715 Whittier Blvd., Boyle Heights, 323.263.5513, lamascotabakery.com. Daily. Mexican. MC, V. **WHY** The signature *bolillos* (white rolls) are a must-have for sandwiches, but the *quesadilla Salvadoreña* (sour cream-parmesan coffee cake sprinkled with toasted sesame seeds) and the house-made tamales are the secret gems here. **WHAT** This large bakery has been family run for more than 50 years, and it's still turning out some of the best classic Mexican pastries in town. Most pan dulce fans take their goodies to go, but there are a handful of patio tables for a quick bite and a bench out front where you can watch the tamale cooks in action. **WHO** The local postman, kids stopping by after school, and old-timers who have been coming for decades. ☺

[Lark Silver Lake Cake Shop] 3337 W. Sunset Blvd., Silver Lake, 323.667.2968, larkcakeshop.com. Daily. American. MC, V. **WHY** Caramel cake, coconut cake, chocolate chip oatmeal cookies, a very fine sea-salt caramel cupcake and a homey apple pie. **WHAT** This Silver Lake mainstay makes good, reasonably priced cupcakes, special-occasion cakes, cookies (including Mexican wedding cookies), vegan cupcakes and pies. 🖼️☺

[Pazzo Gelato] 3827 Sunset Blvd., Silver Lake, 323.662.1410, pazzogelato.net. Daily. Ice cream/Italian. AE, MC, V. **WHY** The always-rotating gelato flavors include a deep, concentrated pistachio that's sometimes paired with espresso, a mango-cayenne sorbet, mascarpone and European yogurt. Intelligentsia coffee is also served. **WHAT** Silver Lake residents and gelato fans from a distance fill this popular dessert shop, which does a big after-dinner business (it's open until 11 during the week and midnight on weekends). **WHO** Little kids who already have their favorites to young couples on dates looking for something new to try. ☺ ☺

[Proof Bakery] 3156 Glendale Blvd., Atwater, 323.664.8633, proofbakeryla.com. Closed Mon. French. AE, MC, V. **WHY** Sophisticated pastries, excellent coffee and fresh bread in a fast-transforming neighborhood. **WHAT** Though owner Na Young Ma is a Glendale native, Proof has a Parisian look, with marble-topped tables and chocolate-colored walls. Pastries strike the right balance between rustic and refined and rank with some of the best in the area. All things meringue are invariably good, from pistachio meringue cook-

Bakeries + Sweets

ies to meringue tarts topped with orange curd or passionfruit. The savory side is represented by gruyère-chive biscuits and airy cheese gougères. Cognoscenti Coffee handles the java, with pour-overs and cappuccinos made with San Francisco's beloved Four Barrel coffee. **WHO** Actual French ex-pats with adorable babies, Atwater Farmers' Market shoppers. ☺

[Valerie Confections] ⌂ **3360 W. 1st St., Silver Lake, 888.706.1408, valerieconfections.com. Daily; Sun. at the Hollywood Farmers' Market. Confections/chocolatier. MC, V. WHY** Four words: Blum's Coffee Crunch Cake. **WHAT** Luxurious truffles, chocolate-dipped toffee squares, square, tiered wedding cakes clad in candied rose petals, exquisite petits fours and house-made preserves are artfully arranged in the front of this commercial-kitchen space, which offers, in the See's tradition, a silver sample tray to welcome visitors. For many Angelenos, the main attraction is the Classic Cake Collection, re-creations of famous bygone L.A. desserts—owner Valerie Gordon is a food-history buff who's constantly researching at the Central Library. She sources from local growers wherever possible, leads seasonal canning classes, caters, and does elegant weekend teas at the American Tea Room in Beverly Hills. Cakes need to be ordered ahead. **WHO** Angelenos seeking the glory days of L.A. desserts.

[Village Bakery & Café] **3119 Los Feliz Blvd., Atwater, 323.662.8600, thevillagebakeryandcafe.com. Daily. American. MC, V. WHY** A non-sceney neighborhood breakfast and lunch spot with fresh baked bread and pastries. **WHAT** If the expensive, trendy brunches of Silver Lake and Los Feliz are too much to bear, head to neighboring Atwater, where the Village Bakery & Café has a case of homey baked goods and the room to enjoy them. It's also one of the few spots on the eastside to find fresh bread. At breakfast, Brian's Special Scramble piles bacon and eggs atop a potato pancake, parmesan and tomato, and brioche french toast is made with house-baked bread. Lunch brings sandwiches and salads; save room for a bacon-maple scone or a fluffy coconut cupcake. Sourdough rounds are the best of the bread choices. **WHO** A smattering of hipsters, parents with tots. ☺

SAN GABRIEL VALLEY

[21 Choices] ⌂ **85 W. Colorado Blvd., Old Pasadena, 626.304.9521, 21choices.com. Daily. Yogurt. AE, MC, V. WHY** Delicious in-house yogurt creations (especially the organic fruit ones in summer, like peach crumble) and a dazzling array of mix-in options to pair with the French vanilla or Valrhona chocolate. **WHAT** Known for its exuberantly friendly staff and a line that typically stretches outside the door, 21 Choices actually offers untold thousands of possible combinations for its custom-made, mix-in frozen yogurts. Give 'em snaps for their sustainable packaging and products. **WHO** Packs of Pasadena teens, families, date-nighters and, at least once a week, a gaggle of great-looking firefighters (they get to park the hook-and-ladder in the red outside). ☺ ♻☺

[Berolina Bakery] **3421 Ocean View Blvd., Glendale, 818.249.6506, berolinabakery.com. Closed Sun.-Mon. American/French. MC, V.**
WHY Limpa bread as it's meant to be baked, along with artisanal loaves and daily specials ranging from sunflower to potato-dill.
WHAT A toe over the Montrose line, this shop has been baking tasty Northern European and Scandinavian goodies for more than two decades. The owners (he's Swedish, she's Belgian) specialize in breads, including limpa, Black Forest, Swiss Farmer and rye-currant loaves. Other treats include croissants, Danish and buttery tortes.
WHO Sensible folks from La Cañada, Glendale and Montrose, who pick up something to go or have a nosh on the sidewalk patio. ☞

[Bulgarini Gelato] **749 E. Altadena Dr., Altadena, 626.791.6174, bulgarinigelato.com. Closed Mon.; hours may vary. Ice cream/Italian. MC, V. WHY** Amazing gelati and sorbetti, with such flavors as Sicilian pistachio (the addiction of many), cherimoya, peach-moscato and zabaglione. **WHAT** Leo Bulgarini and Elizabeth Foldi were so obsessed with gelato that they apprenticed in Sicily before coming up with their flavors, which attracts lots of pilgrims way up here in Altadena. Make your next party a hit by hiring their mobile gelato cart. **WHO** Road-trippin' gelato aficionados and local moms 'n kids, many of whom come here several times a week. ☺ ☼

[Carmela Ice Cream] 🏠 **2495 E. Washington Blvd., East Pasadena, 626.797.1405, carmelaicecream.com. Daily. Ice cream. MC, V.**
WHY Simply one of the best ice creams in L.A., flavored with locally grown flowers and herbs. **WHAT** It's well worth seeking out either Carmela's off-the-hipster-track shop or its farmers' market stands for luscious ice cream made with Clover organic cream. Salted caramel hits the apex of the creamy-meets-salty craze, and the fruit flavors, from strawberry-buttermilk to lemon-basil sorbet, sing with fresh, tangy notes. Coffee, cupcakes, ice cream sandwiches and cake pops are also available. A bit pricey, but a small cup is plenty satisfying. ☺

[Donut Man] 🏠 **915 E. Route 66, Glendora, 626.335.9111. Daily 24 hours. American. Cash only. WHY** Warm glazed doughnuts sliced open and filled with fresh strawberries in season—one of the most rewarding foods you will ever eat, served 24 hours a day. **WHAT** This Route 66 landmark has two claims to fame. The first is its burger-bun-size, hole-less glazed doughnut, which is sliced in half and filled with local strawberries (in spring and early summer) and fresh peaches (in summer), each in a just-sweet-enough syrup. The second is the Tiger Tail, a twisted glazed doughnut swirled with chocolate. The Tiger Tail is wonderful, but if you visit in strawberry or peach season and don't get one of those doughnuts, we can no longer be friends. **WHO** Junkies who drive from as far as Orange County, especially in strawberry and peach seasons. ☺ ☺

[Dr. Bob's Ice Cream] P.O. Box 2250, Pomona, 909.865.1956, drbobsicecream.com. By appt. Ice cream. Cash only. **WHY** Small-batch ice creams with a 16% butterfat content and incredibly good flavors, especially Really Dark Chocolate, lemon custard and, at Christmastime, peppermint. **WHAT** Robert Small, aka Dr. Bob, is a professor at Cal Poly Pomona who turned his love of ice cream into a booming business. You can stop by the plant on the Pomona Fairgrounds property, but there's no real retail operation—instead, look for his ice creams at Gelson's, Vicente Foods, Surfas, Bristol Farms, Olives, Bay Cities, Market Gourmet, Julienne or Howie's Ranch Market. **WHO** Only the most diehard fans call the factory and stop by with a cooler and dry ice when in the Pomona area, and count us among those diehard fans.

[Euro Pane] 🏠 345 E. Colorado Blvd., Pasadena, 626.844.8804. Daily. American/French. MC, V. **WHY** The croissants of your dreams, not to mention the best chocolate cake around, and substantial breads, too, many made with whole grains. **WHAT** Sumi Chang learned her craft in France and with La Brea's Nancy Silverton, and her two bakeries are now the most acclaimed in the San Gabriel Valley. The newer location is much larger and more attractive than the original a few blocks east. It focuses more on whole-grain breads and baked goods, but you can get the fabulous French-style croissants at either café. The original is at 950 E. Colorado Blvd., 626.577.1828. **WHO** Pasadena's intelligentsia read their *New Yorkers* over pains aux chocolats or lunchtime pressed sandwiches. ☺ ♪ ☼

[Fosselman's] 🏠 1824 W. Main St., Alhambra, 626.282.6533, fosselmans.com. Daily. Ice cream. Cash only. **WHY** The retro-charm of old-fashioned banana splits, chocolate malts and grab-it-while-you-can seasonal flavors, especially the fresh peach. **WHAT** Its ice cream is on just about every "best of" list around, but Fosselman's remains at heart an old-fashioned, family-run parlor that draws diverse crowds to its modest brick storefront. Although seasonal flavors like eggnog, licorice and fresh peach beckon, the regular ice cream and sherbet menu also is dazzlingly varied, from real vanilla and white chocolate chip to green tea and dulce de leche. And the shakes, malts and hot fudge sundaes are just like you remember them—maybe better. **WHO** Whole families—from infants to grandparents—along with much of the San Gabriel Valley on hot summer nights. ☺

[Goldstein's Bagel Bakery] 1939 N. Verdugo Blvd., La Cañada, 818.952.2457; 412 N. Santa Anita Ave., Arcadia, 626.447.2457; goldsteinsbagelbakery.com. Daily. Deli. AE, MC, V. **WHY** Large, chewy

bagels that are boiled and baked, and good bagel wraps, too.
WHAT New Yorkers may criticize, but these are excellent bagels by
California standards, and both branches have drive-through windows
for people who need a dozen assorted bagels—stat! **WHO** During the
week, folks rushing to work or taking a turkey-wrap lunch break; on
weekends, dads picking up bagels for the family. ☺ ☼

[Heirloom Bakery & Café] **807 Meridian Ave., South Pasadena,
626.441.0042. Daily. American. AE, MC, V. WHY** A dessert case packed
with dreamy retro desserts, including Hostess-never-had-it-so-good
chocolate cupcakes. **WHAT** Heirloom's first-rate breads and baked
goods, fine sandwiches (try the Cuban) and excellent salads (especially the Cobb) have made it one of the most popular breakfast and
lunch spots in South Pasadena. The setting is stylish, hip and friendly,
and the appealing patio is a magnet for just about everybody in town
on weekend mornings. **WHO** Outside: parents and their colorfully
clad toddlers sharing space with dogs and their well-behaved owners.
Inside: local business and creative types. ☺ ☼

[Little Flower Candy Co.] 🔒 **1424 W. Colorado Blvd., Pasadena,
626.304.4800, littleflowercandyco.com. Closed Sun. Confections/American.
AE, MC, V. WHY** Divine salt caramels and other gift-worthy candies,
as well as delicious bran muffins, pretzel rolls, cookies and gorgeous
cakes to order. **WHAT** Known for her national line of handmade sea-
salt caramels, Christine Moore has livened up this stretch of Colorado
Boulevard with a friendly bakery, confectionary and café. Great for
to-go sweets, or for a relaxed latte and scone or lunchtime pressed
sandwich, gorgeous salad or the best quiche in Pasadena. **WHO** West
Pasadena moms and the Euro Pane crowd. ♻ ✈ ☺

[Mignon Chocolate] **6 E. Holly St., Old Pasadena, 626.796.7100,
mignonchocolate.com. Closed Mon. Chocolatier. AE, MC, V. WHY** Espres-
so-caramel chocolates with the subtlest hint of sea salt, and dozens of
other superb chocolates, from the traditional to the inventive.
WHAT The meticulously crafted, classic French-style chocolates, made
in the Terpoghossian family's Van Nuys kitchen and displayed in this
swank little shop, are deeply delicious; we're already addicted to the
ones with the liquid caramel centers, and the dark chocolate with
ginger and lime sea salt is remarkable. Beautiful gift boxes, too. The
other location (315 N. Verdugo Rd., Glendale) is larger and serves coffee to go with your truffles.

[Mr. Baguette] **8702 Valley Blvd., Rosemead, 626.288.9166,
mrbaguettesandwiches.com. Daily. Vietnamese/French. MC, V. WHY** As
close to an authentic Parisian baguette as you can get in California.
WHAT As the name suggests, baguettes are the focal point, either to
take home or as part of the tasty *banh mi* (Vietnamese-French sandwiches) made here. These are not robust like the ones at La Brea—

+ Bakeries
+ Sweets

they're airy on the inside and intensely crusty on the outside, so they'll make a mess all over your table, just like in Paris. **WHO** Locals grabbing a sandwich for lunch and home cooks picking up baguettes for dinner.

[Old Sasoon Bakery] 1132 N. Allen Ave., Pasadena, 626.791.3280. Daily. Armenian. AE, MC, V. **WHY** A wonderland of Armenian baked goods. **WHAT** There are some two dozen savory specialties at this family-run shop, like tangy zaatar-rubbed flatbreads and tender, doughy pockets stuffed with spicy sujuk and cheese. All are baked to order, including the magnificent *khachapuri*, an oblong Georgian pizza topped with four kinds of Middle Eastern cheeses and an egg. There are sweets, too—flaky phyllo treats like baklava and pistachio-studded "nests." Old Sasoon satisfies morning, noon and night. **WHO** Flatbread fanatics and loyal locals. 🗒

[Panos Pastry] 418 S. Central Ave., Glendale, 818.502.0549, panospastry.com. Daily. Armenian/French. AE, MC, V. **WHY** Superb baklava of every variety, as well as the full range of French and Armenian pastries. **WHAT** An elegant temple of French and Armenian delicacies, done up in marble and mirrors. This is an offshoot of the original Hollywood location, and the pastries are just as good. **WHO** Baklava junkies and brides-to-be looking for a beautiful cake.

[Pie 'n' Burger] 913 E. California Blvd., Pasadena, 626.795.1123, pienburger.com. Daily. American. Cash only. **WHY** The best pecan pie anywhere and a host of dreamy meringue pies, including banana. **WHAT** For some reason most Pasadenans think of Pie 'n' Burger as a great place for breakfast or a lunchtime burger. But the name starts with "Pie" for a reason: These pies would make Mrs. Callender rend her garments in jealousy. If you have your heart set on a particular one, order in advance, but the kismet of seeing what's there is part of the joy. Keep an eye out for the new Pie 'n' Burger truck, which is cruising all over L.A. **WHO** Clever entertainers who don't bake and, during the holiday season, a rush of desperate pie-seekers. 🗒 ☺

[Polkatots] 720 N. Lake Ave., Pasadena, 626.798.3932, polkatotscupcakes.com. Daily. American. MC, V. **WHY** Dulce de leche cupcakes, either regular size or mini. **WHAT** This spot hidden in a low-end strip mall on an unfashionable stretch of Lake Avenue rocketed to fame when its dulce de leche cupcake won the 2009 L.A. Cupcake Challenge. It deserved the win; we're not even cupcake fans and yet we cannot resist these caramel-y treasures. All the cupcakes are good, and the cupcake cakes are birthday-party faves, but all we care about are the mini dulce de leches. ☺

[Porto's] 🏛 315 N. Brand Blvd., Glendale, 818.956.5996, portosbakery. com. Daily. Cuban/American. AE, MC, V. **WHY** The ornate tiered wedding

---

🏛 **ESSENTIALLY L.A.** ☺ **LATE** ♥ **ROMANTIC** 🗒 **VALUE** 🔇 **QUIET** ♻ **SUSTAINABLE**

cakes are award winners, and the Cuban sandwiches are worth driving across town for, as many do. **WHAT** This huge, gleaming café and bakery, founded by Cuban immigrants in the '60s, displays a gorgeous and staggeringly diverse array of goods. Where else can you find Cuban bread, all-American cheesecake and the guava/cheese strudel called *refugiado* all under one roof? ☺

[Sarkis Pastry] **1111 S. Glendale Ave., Glendale, 818.956.6636, sarkispastry.com. Daily. Armenian/Middle Eastern. AE, MC, V. WHY** For a terrific range of Middle Eastern sweets, notably the brioche-looking tahini cookies, the hand-rolled baklava, the layered bread pudding and the macaroons. **WHAT** The first Middle Eastern bakery in Glendale, Sarkis is one of the focal points of Glendale's Armenian-American community. Glass cases are packed with all sorts of beautiful and delicious things. There's another branch at 1776 E. Washington in Pasadena. **WHO** A devoted and longstanding eastside clientele. ☺☺

[Sasoun Bakery] **625 E. Colorado Blvd., Glendale, 818.502.5059. Closed Mon. Armenian. MC, V. WHY** For excellent *lahmajune* (Armenian pizza), cheese boreks and tahini cookies. **WHAT** This meticulous bakery turns out savory Armenian goodies, from cheese breads to the famed pizza-like addiction called lahmajune. Everything is very fresh. Another branch on Santa Monica in Hollywood. **WHO** Armenian-Americans and others who've discovered its superb lahmajune. ☺

EAST VALLEY

[Big Sugar Bakeshop] 🏠 **12182 Ventura Blvd., Studio City, 818.508.5855, bigsugarbakeshop.com. Daily. American. MC, V. WHY** Heavenly American desserts, from the ubiquitous cupcake (they're good) to more interesting things, like an astonishing cinnamon cake studded with Red Hots, the Reverse Chocolate Chip Cookie and the rich seven-layer bars topped with coconut. **WHAT** Lisa Ritter has become a demi-goddess in Studio City for her wonderful desserts, from apple-pie bars to cheesecakes. The brownies and seven-layer bars are great to take to a party, and the friendly, family-oriented shop has good foodie gifts, too. **WHO** Studio foodies and after-school moms and kids. ☺

[Gelato Bar] **4342 Tujunga Ave., Studio City, 818.487.1717, gelatobar-la.com. Daily. Ice cream/Italian. AE, MC, V. WHY** Classic and seasonal flavors, ranging from a superb dark chocolate gelato to an amazing pear sorbet, served with excellent coffee and espresso. **WHAT** Homemade gelati in fun flavors from Gail Silverton, sister of L.A.'s culinary queen Nancy Silverton, in a handsome Italian-country café setting. A real find on the most picturesque block in the Valley (also home to Caioti and Aroma Café). **WHO** Tujunga strollers and shoppers. ☺

Bakeries + Sweets

🍽 VEGETARIAN ☺ KID FRIENDLY ☼ PATIO DINING 🚗 DELIVERY 🎉 PRIVATE PARTY

[Martino's Bakery] **335 N. Victory Blvd., Burbank, 818.842.0715, martinosbakery.com. Closed Sun. American. AE, MC, V. WHY** The historic and utterly addictive tea cakes, glazed square mini-cakes (blueberry, buttermilk or cranberry) that are wonderful for breakfast or a midnight snack. **WHAT** Founded as a pie bakery by Victor and Eva Martino in 1926, Martino's switched to making wholesale doughnuts during WWII until it came up with the "tea cake," a cupcake predecessor, in 1945. It's still making them, now in this new bakery/café, and they're as good as ever. Buy a lot—the first few will be gone by the time you get to your car. **WHO** Generations of Angelenos who grew up on Martino's tea cakes. ☺

[Natas Pastries] **13317 Ventura Blvd., Sherman Oaks, 818.788.8050, nataspastries.com. Daily. Portuguese. MC, V. WHY** For the *nata*, Portugal's famous pastry—a custardy filling in puff pastry that's particularly cherished at Christmastime. Good espresso, too. **WHAT** This little Valley shop specializes in the very good sweets from Portugal, including the namesake *nata*, Portuguese sweet bread, and wonderful mini coconut-lemon cupcakes and mini cheesecakes. And now it's also serving a fine Portuguese breakfast and lunch in an adjacent dining room. **WHO** Portuguese ex-pats and regulars who have become addicted to the *malassadas*, delicious little sugar-ball doughnuts. ☺

[Porto's] 🏛 **3614 W. Magnolia Blvd., Burbank, 818.846.9100, portosbakery.com. Daily. Cuban/American. AE, MC, V. WHY** The ornate tiered wedding cakes are award-winners, and the Cuban sandwiches are worth driving across town for, as many do. **WHAT** This offshoot of the Glendale original founded by Cuban immigrants in the '60s displays a gorgeous and staggeringly diverse array of goods. Where else can you find Cuban bread, all-American cheesecake and the guava/cheese strudel called *refugiado* all under one roof? ☺

[Rocket Fizz] **2112 Magnolia Blvd., Burbank, 818.846.7632, rocketfizz.com. Daily. Confections. AE, MC, V. WHY** It's hard to imagine a confection or soda this place doesn't have, and the cheerful and friendly surroundings will make you want to linger awhile. **WHAT** A retro candy and soda lover's paradise in the heart of Burbank, Rocket Fizz stocks more than 500 varieties of soda and even more kinds of classic and rare candy in a space decorated with vintage rock concert posters and even older tin signs. There's a patio out back where you can enjoy your Sky Bar and cold bottle of Grape Crush. This is now a fast-growing franchise, with locations in Pasadena and throughout the Valley. **WHO** Kids, candy geeks and a pre-movie crowd. ☺ ☼

[Studio Yogurt] **12050 Ventura Blvd., Studio City, 818.508.7811, studiofrozenyogurt.com. Daily. Yogurt. Cash only. WHY** For a side-by-side of chocolate and peanut butter yogurt. **WHAT** A good froyo shop; the toppings are limited (i.e., fruit is frozen), but the house-developed flavors are often tasty. Huge portions, modest prices. **WHO** A constant line out the door of starlets, teens, seniors and families. 🍴😊☼

[Zaatar Factory] **2909 N. Glenoaks Blvd., Burbank, 818.859.7353, thezaatarfactory.com. Closed Mon. Middle Eastern. AE, MC, V. WHY** Savory Lebanese breads that are hearty enough for a meal. **WHAT** This Burbank bakery turns out an array of deliciously different breads and one lightly sweet specialty, tahini bread. The perfect Lebanese breakfast, *khachapuri* (a filled bread) are made to order with eggs and sausage or cheese. It's hard to choose between football-shaped cheese burek, triangular spinach-stuffed burek or *manaeesh*, a round flatbread topped with the tangy thyme, marjoram and sumac mixture known as *zaatar*. Try one of each as they come out of the oven, and take home some spicy lahmajune, topped with beef and peppers, for later.

WEST VALLEY

[Bea's Bakery] **18450 Clark St., Tarzana, 818.344.0100, beasbakery. com. Daily. Deli/kosher. Cash only. WHY** For *hamantaschen* (three-sided filled cookies), black-and-white cookies, rugelach and cakes that would make your Bubbe happy. **WHAT** A longstanding West Valley destination, this traditional Jewish bakery does a booming business in cookies, cakes, rye breads and challahs. Be prepared for a wait, but it's worth it. **WHO** Dutiful Jewish sons and daughters picking up something to take to their mother's house for dinner. 🍴😊

[Jerry's Soda Shoppe] 🏛 **De Soto Pharmacy, 20914 Roscoe Blvd., Canoga Park, 818.341.9515. Closed Sun. Ice cream. MC, V. WHY** The best ice cream soda in L.A., if not the world. **WHAT** Set inside a pharmacy that sells a Cronenbergian array of medical devices, this retro-style soda counter serves a fantastic array of ice creams: Lappert's, Cascade and Fosselman's (including our fave, chocolate-dipped strawberry). But what we love most is how they use that ice cream: A frosty mug is dipped in chocolate sauce, filled with Lappert's vanilla, soda water and chocolate syrup, then topped with whipped cream, chocolate sprinkles and a maraschino cherry. It's a work of art. **WHO** Fans who drive 20 miles just for an ice cream soda. 😊

WESTSIDE: CENTRAL

[Bluebird Café] **8572 National Blvd., Culver City, 310.841.0939, bluebirdcafela.com. Closed Sat.-Sun. American. AE, MC, V. WHY** For cupcakes that are just as good or better than Sprinkles's, for considerably less money. **WHAT** House-baked goodies are served at this little café or can be ordered at the counter to take home—but don't think you can eat one of these moist, rich red velvet or chocolate cupcakes in your car without making a huge mess. Delicious scones, too. **WHO** Culver

Bakeries + Sweets

City studio workers and neighbors.

[Breadbar] Westfield Century City, 10250 Santa Monica Blvd., Century City, 310.277.3770, breadbar.net. Daily. American. AE, MC, V. **WHY** Hand-crafted whole-grain and country bread and excellent croissants and tarts, as well as breakfast, sandwiches and salads. Don't miss the Alpine cheese bread. **WHAT** Besides being a fine bakery, this offshoot of the 3rd Street original is a terrific place to have breakfast or lunch. Baker Eric Kayser first won the hearts of Parisians (no easy thing for a bread baker) and now his superb breads show up in some of L.A.'s finest restaurants. He also hosts some of the city's hippest pop-up restaurants. **WHO** Chic Century City folks. ☼

[Buttercake Bakery] 10595 W. Pico Blvd., Rancho Park, 310.470.6770, buttercakebakery.com. Closed Sun. & Mon. American. AE, MC, V. **WHY** For tender layer cakes and cookies that are the stuff of childhood dreams. **WHAT** Home-style cakes, cupcakes and mini-cupcakes done to perfection: German chocolate, coconut, red velvet, and of course, vanilla buttercake. You'll also be tempted by criss-cross peanut butter cookies, bundt cakes and creamy cheesecakes that taste like they were baked in your mom's kitchen. Inscriptions on cookies and cakes at no extra charge. **WHO** People who believe there really is a Betty Crocker, and cupcake connoisseurs seeking true butter flavor and tender crumb. ☺

[Clementine] 1751 Ensley Ave., Century City, 310.552.1080, clementineonline.com. Closed Sun. American. AE, MC, V. **WHY** Grown-up homemade granola, cookies and seasonal pies. **WHAT** This all-American bakery and caterer makes simple sweets the way you always hoped yours would turn out: flaky berry pie, tender buttermilk strawberry shortcake and delicious thumbprint cookies. A good café menu, too. **WHO** Business types on lunch break and locals lingering over coffee and cookies. ☺ ☼

[Coolhaus] 8588 Washington Blvd., Culver City, 310.424.5559, eatcoolhaus.com. Daily. Ice cream. MC, V. **WHY** To enjoy an archi-tectural ice cream sandwich without having to chase a truck around town. **WHAT** After a couple of years of success with its modern-day ice cream truck, this vendor of insanely thick ice cream sandwiches named (and designed) in honor of Frank Gehry, Richard Meier and other architects now has its own café. The décor pays homage to both modern architecture and food trucks, the coffee is from San Francis-co's Blue Bottle, and the ice cream sandwiches are dreamy. ☺

[Dolce Forno Bakery] 3828 Willat Ave., Culver City, 310.280.6004, dolcefornobakery.com. Closed Sat.-Sun. Italian. AE, MC, V. **WHY** Wonder-ful fresh filled pastas (in five-pound bags), Italian country breads (ciabatta, focaccia, noci, panini rolls), tiramisu and special-occasion cakes. **WHAT** Celestino Drago, one of L.A.'s star Italian chef/restaurateurs, runs this bakery to supply his own places and other Italian eateries; retail customers can shop here during the week. It's best to call a day in advance for your order, because not much is kept in stock for walk-ins. **WHO** Chefs, shop owners and some retail customers.

[Edelweiss Chocolate Factory] **444 N. Cañon Dr., Beverly Hills, 310.275.0341, edelweisschocolates.com. Daily. Chocolatier. MC, V. WHY** The dark chocolate Caramellow (with marshmallow and caramel) and the milk chocolate–coconut Snocap will have you bursting into songs from *The Sound of Music*. **WHAT** Beverly Hills's premier chocolatier since the 1940s is as good as ever, especially the chocolate-covered marshmallows, which the original owner invented and which remain big sellers today. The truffles aren't so hot, but the carefully made retro-Swiss chocolates in the See's vein are good. ☺

[Jin Patisserie] **Intercontinental Hotel, 2151 Ave. of the Stars, Century City, 310.789.6485, jinpatisserie.com. Closed Sun. Chocolatier/French. AE, MC, V. WHY** For delicate, sculpturally gorgeous chocolates and pastries that taste as good as they look. **WHAT** After conquering Abbot Kinney with what may be L.A.'s most refined and serene chocolate shop and tea garden, Kristy Choo has branched out with this white-and-Lucite gallery-style shop in the Intercontinental. Same incredible chocolates and quality tea and coffee in a more modern setting.

[K Chocolatier] **9606 Little Santa Monica Blvd., Beverly Hills, 310.248.2626, dianekronchocolates.com. Daily. Chocolatier. AE, MC, V. WHY** For jewel-like (and jewel-priced) Swiss-style chocolates of good flavor and great beauty. **WHAT** Owner Diane Krön takes credit for inventing the chocolate-dipped strawberry back when she ran Krön Chocolatier in New York in the '70s; now she's returned from retirement to run this swank little Beverly Hills shop. If you take out a second mortgage, you can go wild with the milk mousse au chocolate, the crispy Teddy Bear chocolates and the dark-chocolate mints. **WHO** People pulling up in their Bentleys to pick up a hostess gift.

['lette Macaron] **9466 Charleville Blvd., Beverly Hills, 310.275.0023, paulettemacarons.com. Closed Sun. French. AE, MC, V. WHY** Parisian-style macarons, displayed like objets d'art, in the shop formerly known as Paulette (they dropped the "Pau" after a trademark tussle). **WHAT** French macarons are not the dumpling-style macaroons (normally made of coconut) that we see in the U.S. These are light, tender-crisp sandwich-style cookies that look rather like colorful, miniature hamburgers, except the fillings are luscious ganache. Try the Sicilian pistachio, salt caramel and Madagascar vanilla. There's a new shop on Fair Oaks in Old Pasadena.

Bakeries + Sweets

🍃 **VEGETARIAN** ☺ **KID FRIENDLY** ❀ **PATIO DINING** 🚗 **DELIVERY** 🎉 **PRIVATE PARTY**

[Original Brooklyn Water Bagel Co.] **262 S. Beverly Dr., Beverly Hills, 310.786.7400, brooklynwaterbagels.com. Daily. Bakery/ deli. MC, V. WHY** Because Los Angeles needs better bagels, and it needs more of them. **WHAT** Backed by talk show maven Larry King, this small franchised chain has a gimmick: real Brooklyn water. The bulky bagels are boiled in it, making them dense and chewy in the best possible way. You can also make your own egg cream with real Fox's U-Bet chocolate syrup or pour an iced coffee with cubes made of frozen coffee. Forget about the rest of the menu—stick to bagels and cream cheese. **WHO** Transplanted New Yorkers, old Beverly Hills Jews, and carb addicts.

[Platine Sweet & Savories] **10850 Washington Blvd., Culver City, 310.559.9933, platinecookies.com. Closed Sun.-Mon. American/French. AE, MC, V. WHY** Customized, "couture" cookies, brownies and teeny pots de crème for parties and gifts, and impulse treats to take home for yourself. **WHAT** This cookie boutique occupies a commercial kitchen in frumpy west Culver City, with a tiny counter and no seating. Despite the spare setting, the product has all the preciousness of a Sprinkles—a daily assortment of such sweets as Platinos (like Oreos); Short Stacks (weird, über-precious mini "pancakes" with caramelized bacon and maple-orange glaze); and custom ice cream sandwiches made with Milk ice cream. Trendy bona fides include coffee from Lamill, caramels and marshmallows from Little Flower, and jams from Mark & Stephen's. **WHO** People who like their cookies sweet and who think nothing of paying $2 for a two-inch cookie. ☺

[Scoops Westside] **3400 Overland Ave., Palms, 323.405.7055, @scoopswestside. Closed Sun. Ice cream/vegan. Cash only. WHY** Westsiders can now sample L.A.'s most original ice cream flavors at the Palms offshoot of the Heliotrope store. Many are vegan. **WHAT** Food blogger Matthew Kang, a longtime acolyte of Scoops proprietor Tai Kim, picks up some wild and wacky flavors at the original East Hollywood store each morning and brings them to the lime-green Scoops Westside. The signature Brown Bread is usually available, but the other flavors are anyone's guess—anything from Asian-tinged varieties like pandan coconut and black sesame banana to Guinness chocolate and coffee cardamom. Some experiments work better than others, but Kang's enthusiasm is infectious, so it's worth trying them all to find one you love. Intelligentsia Coffee is also available. **WHO** Food bloggers and UCLA students. ☺

[The Sensitive Baker] **10836 1/2 Washington Blvd., Culver City, 310.815.1800, thesensitivebaker.com. Daily. American/vegan. MC, V. WHY** Just because you're gluten and dairy intolerant doesn't mean you have to tolerate bad baked goods. **WHAT** Located a couple of doors from butter- and flour-abundant Platine, this bare-bones kosher and vegan shop has figured out how to avoid those ingredients and still produce moist cupcakes with fluffy frosting, soft quinoa-cranberry cookies and fudgy brownies that will appeal to even the gluten tolerant. The most popular bread—made with brown rice flour and hemp nuts—has a nice, bready pull, and the almond-meal bagels are satisfyingly chewy. In the freezer case are eggy brioche rolls, good scones, hamburger buns and vegan mac 'n "cheese." Note that they ship locally and make birthday cakes. **WHO** People with good taste who need to avoid troublesome ingredients.

[Sprinkles Cupcakes] **9635 Little Santa Monica Blvd., Beverly Hills, 310.274.8765, sprinkles.com. Daily. American. MC, V. WHY** For rich and beautiful (if sometimes too sweet) cupcakes; try the dark chocolate, lemon and cinnamon. If you call your order in ahead, you won't have to wait in line. **WHAT** We don't get the cupcake frenzy, but if you're among the obsessed, you will make a pilgrimage here, if you haven't already. What started here has now become a national chain. **WHO** Glamour moms and personal assistants who don't mind waiting in line a half hour for a dozen cupcakes. ☺🚗

WEST OF THE 405

[3 Square Café & Bakery] **1121 Abbot Kinney Blvd., Venice, 310.399.6504, rockenwagner.com. Daily. German/American. AE, MC, V. WHY** Can you say pretzel bread? **WHAT** Hans Röckenwagner's sunny, modern café is also a fine takeaway bakery, known for its meaty, delicious pretzel bread, as well as its pretzels, cinnamon rolls, ginger scones, cookies and rye bread. It's not cheap, but the goods are very good. **WHO** Venice hipster foodies who stop by Jin to pick up chocolates after getting their pretzel bread and scones here. 🍴☼

[Amandine Patisserie] **12225 Wilshire Blvd., West L.A., 310.979.3211, amandinecafe.com. Closed Mon. French. AE, MC, V. WHY** Absolutely perfect croissants, lovely birthday cakes and a small but free parking lot in back. **WHAT** As much a café as a patisserie, Amandine is a fine spot for breakfast (french toast) and lunch (croque madame). Or just pop in to pick up some croissants, quiches or tartlets or to order a special-occasion cake. Desserts are lush without being overly sugary. ☼

[Angel Maid] **4542 S. Centinela Ave., West L.A., 310.915.2078. Closed Mon. American/Japanese. MC, V. WHY** Birthday cakes, tres leches cake, chocolate mousse cake and heavenly cinnamon rolls. **WHAT** An old-fashioned, family-run bakery in the heart of West L.A.'s Japanese-American community, with absolutely lovely desserts. **WHO** Longtime members of the local Japanese-American community, and everyone else in the know. 📷☺

Bakeries + Sweets

🌿 VEGETARIAN ☺ KID FRIENDLY ☼ PATIO DINING 🚗 DELIVERY 🎩 PRIVATE PARTY

[Angelato Café] **301 Arizona Ave., Santa Monica, 310.656.9999, angelatocafe.com. Daily. Ice cream/Italian. Cash only. WHY** Enough flavors and colors of gelato and sorbetto to cause you to change your mind for hours. **WHAT** This bright, cheery storefront displays Italian gelati lined up like keys on a never-ending piano in both Italian flavors (hazelnut, tiramisu) and only-on-the-Promenade variations (blue bubble gum, apple pie). **WHO** Tourists and locals with kids in tow taking a break from Promenade shopping. ☺

[Belwood Bakery] **11625 Barrington Ct., Brentwood, 310.471.6855, belwoodbakery.com. Daily. American/French. MC, V. WHY** Very good brioche, proper French croissants, mini baguettes and, for lunch, baguette sandwiches made to order. Excellent lattes, too. **WHAT** This family-friendly bakery is a community center in this upscale community, a place to meet for coffee, grab a sandwich for lunch, order a birthday cake or take the kids after school for a macaroon treat. (And the macaroons are a treat.) The French-style breads and sweets are equally good. **WHO** Teens from the Brentwood School and Archer School, their parents and neighbors, including famous faces. ☺ ☼

[Café Boulangerie] **804 Montana Ave., Santa Monica, 310.451.4998, thecakecollection.com. Daily. American/French. MC, V. WHY** Classic white sourdough in the San Francisco style—as good an example of the type as you can find in L.A. **WHAT** The remaining vestige of what used to be a large and thriving bakery in Venice, Pioneer is now a smaller Montana bakeshop that still makes the best San Francisco–style sourdough bread in town. The cakes and pastries are fine but unremarkable; come here for the bread, or a good sandwich made on the bread. ☺

[Churros Calientes] **11521 Santa Monica Blvd., West L.A., 424.248.3890, churroscalientes.com. Closed Mon. Latin American. MC, V. WHY** Do one thing and do it well. In this case, it's churros. **WHAT** The food is a wash, but the churros, served warm from the fryer, are to die for. These are nothing like the Mexican churros that dominate L.A.—these are Spanish churros. They're smaller, denser and more crisp, served with toppings and fillings like dulce de leche, guava and sweet condensed milk. The classic is "con chocolate," which comes with a bracingly hot cup of the thick, rich, cinnamon-tinged hot chocolate, but even plain, they're a treat. **WHO** Locals with a sweet tooth and cinephiles rehashing the latest indie drama playing at next door's Royal theater. ☺ ☼

[Compartes] **912 S. Barrington Ave. , Brentwood, 310.826.3380, compartes.com. Closed Sun. Confections/chocolatier. AE, MC, V. WHY** Superb bon bons, caramels, English toffee, truffles and single-origin chocolate bars with such exotic flavorings as smoked sea salt, pink peppercorns and even a summer Harry's Berries strawberry truffle. **WHAT** The 1950s-era Brentwood fixture famous for its chocolate-dipped dried fruits is now run by young chocolatier Jonathan Grahm of the Bonny Doon Vineyard family. He's created a little chocolate salon, with robin's-egg-blue banquettes and aromatic kaffir lime and pink lemonade trees on the patio. Besides the confections, you'll find proprietary gelati: chocolate, of course, but also fig-balsamic and vanilla-black pepper. Try the European-style drinking chocolate, often prepared with cinnamon and cayenne but no milk or cream. It's just thick, dark chocolate served in two sizes—a shot glass (enough for an intense buzz) or a mug (let's not even discuss the effects). ♥☺ ☼

[Emil's Swiss Pastry] 11551 Santa Monica Blvd., West L.A., 310.473.6999, emilsswisspastry.com. Closed Mon. French. AE, MC, V. **WHY** Pastries in the classic, buttery French/Swiss style: éclairs, napoleons, chocolate croissants, strudels and gorgeous fruit tarts. **WHAT** This venerable business is now run by a younger European couple (she's French, he's Austrian), and they're doing a wonderful job making classic European pastries and some worthy American ones, too, like the not-bad-at-all fat-free bran muffin. Find yourself a table, sip some good coffee and try the breakfast pastries, quiches, bread pudding or incredible apple strudel.

[Grom] Malibu Country Mart, 3886 Cross Creek Rd., Malibu, 310.456.9797, grom.it. Daily. Ice cream. AE, MC, V. **WHY** Fruit flavors that taste like they were just plucked from the earth and rushed straight to the mixer. **WHAT** Of the 8 billion gelaterias in Italy, Grom differentiates itself by an obsessiveness with ingredients—it doesn't use any old pistachios, for instance, it uses Syrian pistachios. Its dark chocolate is the darkest in town, and its melon gelato is a revelation. There's nowhere to sit, but you'll consume your little cup of heaven so fast you won't mind. **WHO** Malibuites who look too thin to actually eat high-fat gelato, yet here they are.

[Huckleberry Bakery & Café] 🔒 1014 Wilshire Blvd., Santa Monica, 310.451.2311, huckleberrycafe.com. Closed Mon. American. AE, MC, V. **WHY** Fabulous (and normal-size) chocolate chip, ginger and oatmeal-raisin cookies, as well as flaky tarts and perfect pastries. **WHAT** This cacaphonous, always-packed café is also a superb bakery, featuring the work of Zoe Nathan, who's also the pastry chef at Rustic Canyon. We're all so over cupcakes, but the mini chocolate ones are divine, and for once this is a bakery that doesn't make one-pound cookies too big for anyone to eat. **WHO** Impeccably groomed westside women who look like they've never eaten a cookie in their lives.

[Jin Patisserie] 🔒 1202 Abbot Kinney Blvd., Venice, 310.399.8801, jinpatisserie.com. Closed Mon. Chocolatier/French. AE, MC, V. **WHY** For delicate, sculpturally gorgeous chocolates and pastries that taste as good as they look. **WHAT** Former flight attendant turned pastry chef

Bakeries + Sweets

Kristy Choo's artful, investment-grade creations are as decadent as they are beautiful. Create a small box as a perfect hostess gift, or linger on the patio with a piece of chocolate cake or a couple of jasmine-scented truffles. **WHO** The most refined of Abbot Kinney's cool crowd take tea and pastries on Jin's serene enclosed patio. ♥ 🍸 ☼

[La Monarca] **1300 Wilshire Blvd., Santa Monica, 310.451.1114, lamonarcabakery.com. Daily from 6 a.m. Mexican. AE, MC, V. WHY** An authentic Mexican bakery with westside-friendly touches, lunch and coffee drinks. **WHAT** The Boyle Heights stalwart now has a bright and welcoming Santa Monica location, where a French pastry chef brings a lighter touch to traditional Mexican pan dulce, breads and cakes (tres leches, coconut-flan), with a no-lard policy. Shelves are packed with appealing things like guayaba-stuffed croissants and pineapple empanadas. Drinks include organic Oaxacan coffee with delicious add-ins like dulce de leche, cinnamon and Mexican chocolate. For a heartier breakfast or lunch, try chorizo quiche or a chicken mole sandwich. **WHO** Santa Monica bikers, walkers and stroller-pushers. ☺ ☼

[N'Ice Cream] **1410 Abbot Kinney Blvd., Venice, 310.396.7161. Daily. Ice cream. AE, MC, V. WHY** Excellent gelati and sorbets, made fresh daily by a Danish couple. **WHAT** The Nielsens use organic milk and fresh fruit in their melty, sticky ice creams, which are creative without being twee and richly flavorful without being too sugary. Try the sour cherry or mint chocolate chip gelato or the fruit punch. Good lattes and gelato shakes, too. **WHO** Damned adorable Venice youngsters and their tattooed, yoga-pants-clad moms. ☺

[SusieCakes] **11708 San Vicente Blvd., Brentwood, 310.442.2253, susiecakesla.com. Closed Sun. American. AE, MC, V. WHY** For excellent homestyle sweets: German chocolate cake, banana pudding with vanilla wafers, layer cakes, cupcakes, whoopie pies and lemon squares. **WHAT** This nostalgia-driven bake shop dressed in retro colors turns out desserts that owner Susan Sarich found on her grandmother's recipe cards. Several more locations, including Calabasas (23653 Calabasas Rd., 818.591.2223) and Manhattan Beach (3500 N. Sepulveda Blvd., 310.303.3780). **WHO** Locals stopping by to pick up birthday-party treats and sneak a cupcake on the side. ☺

[Sweet Rose Creamery] **Brentwood Country Mart, 225 26th St., Brentwood, 310.260.2663, sweetrosecreamery.com. Daily. Ice cream. Cash only. WHY** Ice cream pie, thick milkshakes, and amazing flavors like malted chocolate with hazelnut praline. **WHAT** Owned by the folks behind Rustic Canyon and Huckleberry Café, this Country Mart spot showcases seasonal, small-batch ice creams and sorbets that include ginger, strawberry, banana, grapefruit-mint and that haunting malted chocolate. It also offers upscale versions of childhood treats: homemade waffle cones, Valrhona fudge pops, and floats, sodas, shakes

🏛 ESSENTIALLY L.A. ☺ LATE ♥ ROMANTIC 💵 VALUE 🍸 QUIET 🌱 SUSTAINABLE

and sundaes. From the tulip dishes to red-clad barstools, they haven't missed a beat. There's even a little bowl of fleur de sel behind the counter for sprinkling *á la minute* onto caramel ice cream. ☺ ☼

[Vanilla Bake Shop] 512 Wilshire Blvd., Santa Monica, 310.458.6644, vanillabakeshop.com. Daily. American. MC, V. **WHY** The usual faddish cupcakes (red velvet, dark chocolate, vanilla bean) and beautiful whole cakes to order in advance—for true comfort, get the Mom's Birthday Cake, a yellow cake with milk-chocolate frosting that will leapfrog you back to the '50s. **WHAT** A small and stylish bake shop specializing in cupcakes to go (large or mini), tiny one-serving icebox desserts (key lime pie, Dirt Cake) and impeccably frosted whole cakes. **WHO** Chic Montana moms ordering party cakes. ☺

SOUTH BAY TO SOUTH L.A.

[Alpine Village Market] 833 W. Torrance Blvd., Torrance, 310.327.4384, alpinevillage.net. Daily. German. AE, MC, V. **WHY** Fresh pretzels that will have you yodeling the whole way home. **WHAT** Sausages may be the claim to fame at this kitschy Bavarian market, but the bakery is not to be neglected. It turns out a variety of sturdy, delicious German rye breads along with strudel, kuchen, tortes and wonderful fresh pretzels sprinkled with rock salt. **WHO** Tourists and Angelenos who have been making the trek here for 40 years.

[Alsace Lorraine Pastries] 4334 Atlantic Ave., Long Beach, 562.427.5992, alsacelorrainepastries.com. Closed Sun.-Mon. French. MC, V. **WHY** Superb petits fours, which hardly anyone makes anymore, as well as remarkable cakes, including the St. Honoré and the wedding cakes. **WHAT** Classically trained Austrian bakers make gorgeous special-occasion cakes here, but the little things are lovely, too, like the macaroons and double-chocolate cookies.

[Babette Bakery] 1404 Atlantic Ave., Long Beach, 562.218.8877, babettebakery.com. Daily. French/American. MC, V. **WHY** Properly Parisian baguettes (crisp outside, airy inside), more substantial sandwich breads, croissants and addictive oatmeal cookies. **WHAT** Known for its breads and for fruit tarts that are far lovelier than the neighborhood outside, Babette is a great and affordable find for breads, breakfast pastries and desserts (but skip the cupcakes in favor of the cookies and tarts). Good panini and breakfast sandwiches, too. **WHO** Chefs, insiders and local high school kids with really good taste. ☺ ☺

[Buona Forchetta] 1150 Gardena Blvd., Gardena, 310.532.8140, buonaforchetta.com. Closed Sun. except for will call. American. MC, V. **WHY** For some of our very favorite breads in town—yes, some of them are better than La Brea's. They manage to be light and yet

Bakeries + Sweets

🌿 VEGETARIAN ☺ KID FRIENDLY ☼ PATIO DINING 🚙 DELIVERY 🎩 PRIVATE PARTY

somehow substantial, crusty enough but not dry. The rosemary focaccia and sea salt rolls are fabulous. **WHAT** Suzanne Dunaway went big-time when she sold her bread bakery to Mrs. Beasley's, but she's still the hands-on baker, and her products are as good as ever. You'll find her moist, substantial rustico, baguettes, filoncinos and focaccias at the better markets throughout California, but it's fun to come to the mothership, where you get it super-fresh—plus they often have fun breads that you won't find in stores. Most products freeze beautifully. **WHO** Buyers from upscale markets, caterers, restaurateurs and fans who want to go straight to the source.

[Delicieuse] 2503 Artesia Blvd., Redondo Beach, 310.793.7979, icedreamonline.com. Open Fri.-Sun. Ice cream. AE, MC, V. **WHY** French-style sorbets, strawberry goats' milk ice cream and creamy, rich cinnamon or white peach ice cream—not to mention the profound romance of lavender ice cream made with crushed lavender petals. **WHAT** Now that this sophisticated ice cream is sold at Surfas, Whole Foods and Beverly Glen Marketplace, Angelenos don't have to trek to Redondo Beach, but the devout still do, at least on weekends, which is the only time it's open to the public. There's a sweet little café, too. **WHO** Chefs who don't want to make their own ice cream, locals in the know and aficionados from far and wide. ☺

[Grounds Bakery & Café] 6277 E. Spring St., Long Beach, 562.429.5661, groundscafe.com. Daily. American. AE, MC, V. **WHY** For the best bagels in Long Beach; good breads and muffins, too. **WHAT** Just-chewy-enough California-style bagels (that is, large and relatively light instead of small and dense) are the main draw at this large, open bakery and café; try the onion, the poppyseed and the pumpkin. Also worthwhile are the muffins, the sourdough breads and the various coffee brews. The brownies taste great but are ridiculously oversized. ☺

[Patisserie Chantilly] 🏛 2383 Lomita Blvd. , Lomita, 310.257.9454, patisseriechantilly.com. Closed Tues. French/Japanese. AE, MC, V. **WHY** Flawless French pastries with Japanese flair. **WHAT** Keiko Nojima's creations are as cross-cultural as they are classic: delicate and refined pastries that seamlessly balance tradition and intercontinental innovation. Take the mactha roll, for example, alternating layers of green tea chiffon cake and chestnut cream topped with sweet azuki beans. Or the fabulous cream puffs stuffed with either chantilly, chocolate, chestnut or black sesame cream. There are plenty of chocolate and seasonal treats for those with sweeter teeth. **WHO** Dessert lovers of all ages and any language. ☺

[Portugal Imports] 11655 Artesia Blvd. , Artesia, 562.809.7021, portugalimports.net. Closed Sun. & Mon. Portuguese. AE, MC, V. **WHY** A rare chance to savor the sweet side of Portugal. **WHAT** This Artesia store serves what amounts to lunch—sausage sandwiches and a weekend-only selection of salt cod dishes—but the main reason to make the trip here is the selection of Portuguese breads and pastries. Try the *queijadas*, little tartlets flavored with almond, pineapple, caramel, coconut, sweet beans, orange or a creamy custard. Above all else, make sure to grab a loaf of *massa sovada*, a sweet bread blessed with just a hint of cinnamon. **WHO** Expatriates hungry for a reminder of home and those curious about the tastes of the Iberian Peninsula.

[Powell's Sweet Shoppe] **5282 E. 2nd St., Long Beach, 562.434.6105, powellsss.com. Daily. Confections. AE, MC, V. WHY** An astonishing selection of Jelly Bellies, Pez dispensers, gummies, candy and gum from sentimental boomers' childhoods and, best of all, chocolate bars imported from the U.K. and Canada, where milk chocolate is much better than in the U.S. **WHAT** Willy Wonka is the patron saint of this place; there's a shrine to him, and the movie seems to run in a continuous loop in the back. Candy of every imaginable kind is sold here, from the retro (Squirrel Nut Zippers, Gold Nugget bubble gum) to the modern (green tea chocolates) to the mainstream (gummy everything). The chocolate truffle selection is just okay, but the gelati choices are good. **WHO** Kids, and lots of 'em. ☺

[Tropicana Bakery] **10218 Paramount Blvd., Downey, 562.806.8343, tropicanabakeryandcubancafe.com. Daily. Cuban. AE, MC, V. WHY** Sweet Cuban classics and worthy sandwiches and entrées. **WHAT** Like Porto's, Tropicana blurs the line between bakery and restaurant. It has lots of great pastries—rum-soaked raspberry tarts, éclairs sweetened with dulce de leche, empanada-like *pastelitos* stuffed with the likes of cheese and guava—all of which go down even easier with a sip of Cuban coffee. Equally good entrées include pork-heavy sandwiches that make great use of the bakery's fresh bread. ☺

Bakeries
+ Sweets

Shops + Services

Everyone knows about Trader Joe's, Whole Foods and Sur la Table; the challenge is to find the great individual cheesemonger, wine shop, produce market, tofu maker, ethnic market, delivery services, soda-pop shop and caterer. Here's where you'll find all the things a food lover seeks.

[ESSENTIALLY L.A.]

99 Ranch Market, San Gabriel (PAGE 365)
Andrew's Cheese, Santa Monica (PAGE 331)
Angeli Caffé Catering (PAGE 326)
Auntie Em's Kitchen Catering (PAGE 327)
Border Grill Catering (PAGE 327)
Brent's Delicatessen Catering (PAGE 327)
Central Library Culinary Collection, Downtown (PAGE 333)
Cheese Store of Beverly Hills (PAGE 332)
Cheese Store of Silverlake (PAGE 332)
Claro's, San Gabriel (PAGE 355)
Clementine Catering (PAGE 326)
E. Waldo Ward, Sierra Madre (PAGE 356)
Epicurean School of Culinary Arts, Melrose (PAGE 335)

🏛 ESSENTIALLY L.A. ☺ LATE ♥ ROMANTIC 💲 VALUE 🔊 QUIET ♻ SUSTAINABLE

Farmers Market, Fairfax District (PAGE 357)
Fish King, Glendale (PAGE 347)
Galco's Soda Pop Shop, Highland Park (PAGE 357)
Grand Central Market, Downtown (PAGE 358)
Guidi Marcello, Santa Monica (PAGE 358)
Harvey's Guss Meat Co., Miracle Mile (PAGE 348)
Hipcooks, Lincoln Heights & Pico-Robertson (PAGES 336)
Hollywood Certified Farmers' Market (PAGE 338)
India Sweets & Spices, Atwater & Canoga Park (PAGE 358)
Jennie Cook's Catering (PAGE 329)
Joan's on Third Catering (PAGE 329)
Koreatown Galleria Market, Koreatown (PAGE 366)
La Española Meats, Harbor City (PAGE 349)
Liborio Market, Downtown & Koreatown (PAGE 366)
Lindy & Grundy, Hollywood (PAGE 349)
Lucques/AOC Catering (PAGE 330)
Luna Garcia, Venice (PAGE 344)
Marconda's Meat, Farmers Market (PAGE 350)
Mitsuwa, Torrance (PAGE 367)
New School of Cooking, Culver City (PAGE 336)
Nicole's Gourmet Foods, South Pasadena (PAGE 333)
Penzeys Spices, Torrance & Santa Monica (PAGE 362)
Pie 'n Burger Catering (PAGE 331)
Ross Cutlery, Downtown (PAGE 346)
Santa Monica Certified Farmers' Market (PAGE 340)
Schreiner's Fine Sausages, Glendale (PAGE 351)
Silverlake Wine, Silver Lake (PAGE 372)
Six Taste Tours (PAGE 364)
Super King Market, Altadena & Eagle Rock (PAGE 367)
Super Home Mart, Chinatown (PAGE 345)
Surfas, Culver City (PAGE 345)
Tierra Miguel Foundation (PAGE 353)
Torrance Certified Farmers' Market (PAGE 342)
Vinh Loi Tofu, Reseda (PAGE 363)
Wally's, Westwood (PAGE 373)
Wine Expo, Santa Monica (PAGE 373)
Wine House, West L.A. (PAGE 373)
Wolfgang Puck Catering (PAGE 331)
Woodland Hills Wine Co. (PAGE 373)

Shops +
Services

VEGETARIAN ⊙ KID FRIENDLY ☼ PATIO DINING 🚚 DELIVERY 🏛 PRIVATE PARTY

CATERERS

[Alligator Pear Catering] **7901 Canoga Ave., 818.347.7860, alligatorpearcatering.com. WHY** Careful service and very good food. **WHAT** Abi Chilton's serene, easygoing personality comes through in the events, large and small, that her company caters. Everything is taken care of, and the modern American/Mediterranean food is delicious. Lots of good vegetarian recipes in the repertoire, too. **WHO** Academy of Motion Picture Arts & Sciences, USC, AFI, UCLA Anderson School, the Family Channel.

[Along Came Mary] **5265 W. Pico Blvd., 323.931.9082, alongcamemary.com. WHY** When it's not just a party you're throwing, but a production—and a lavish, meticulously staged, high-budget production at that. **WHAT** L.A.'s most famous caterer is known for extravaganzas that give new meaning to the word "extravaganza." If you're having 500 for your daughter's Super Sweet 16 or 1,000 for your film premiere, Mary's the one to call. **WHO** The Oscars, the Grammys, MTV, all the studios and a bunch of really rich people.

[Alyson Cook Gourmet Foods] **P.O. Box 45023, 626.791.9757, alysoncookgourmet.com. WHY** Very good food, ranging from modern American classics to Indian and Thai dishes. **WHAT** Cook is a longtime L.A. caterer who was classically trained in Europe and worked as a private chef for such folks as Carol Burnett and the Queen Mum. Now based in Pasadena, she's on the faculty at the California School of Culinary Arts and runs a solidly professional catering business that does weddings, dinner parties and the usual shindigs.

[Angeli Caffé Catering] 🔒 **7274 Melrose Ave., 323.936.9086, angelicaffe.com. WHY** Deeply satisfying rustic cooking at prices that might inspire you to entertain more. **WHAT** Evan Kleiman and her trattoria, Angeli, are known for irresistible Italian fare—small pizzas, bruschetta, frittura mista, roast chicken—but the catering operation can go beyond Italian to do Provençal, Indian, American, even Irish food. The universal theme is a homey rusticity and robust flavors. **WHO** A longstanding and loyal clientele of production companies, studios and hip L.A. businesses. 📷

[Atmosphere] **6941 Scarborough Peak Dr., 818.914.4179, atmospherecatering.com. WHY** From high-profile corporate events to candlelight dinners for two, Atmosphere delivers the goods, as attested by its repeat client list. **WHAT** French-born and French-taught chef Nicolas Rolland partners in the kitchen with German-born chef Erik Fischer, trained in classic French and German cuisine. Their exquisite food will have you poking around the kitchen well before your guests arrive. Dana Rolland, with a background in PR and restaurant management, maintains a robust client list and oversees the atmosphere for which the company is famed—and named.

[Auntie Em's Kitchen Catering] 🔒 **4616 Eagle Rock Blvd., 323.663.8688, auntieemscatering.com. WHY** Outstanding modern American party food, as organic as possible, with particularly memorable desserts. **WHAT** Before she opened her oh-so-hip bakery, café and store, Terri Wahl was a caterer specializing in production shoots. Nowadays she also feeds the cognoscenti at commitment ceremonies, 50th-birthday celebrations and publication parties. **WHO** Party-throwing Occidental professors, Silver Lake graphic designers, Highland Park gentrifiers and even Malibu wedding planners. 🔵🍷

[Boneyard Bistro] **13539 Ventura Blvd., 818.906.7427, boneyardbistro.com. WHY** These guys make damn good barbecue and damn fine party food. **WHAT** This Sherman Oaks restaurant has a thriving catering business as well. Chef Aaron Robins combines traditional, people-pleasing barbecue with a more modern approach to service and sides—so instead of generic cole slaw, with your ribs you can have such things as fire-roasted artichokes with ceviche, a vegetarian falafel salad and Thai-spiced crispy calamari.

[Border Grill Catering] 🔒 **445 S. Figueroa St., 213.542.1100, marysueandsusan.com. WHY** For vividly flavorful food that's full of L.A. style, with good party management to boot—and if you want something funkier, they'll send their taco truck. **WHAT** Mary Sue Milliken and Susan Feniger have been L.A.'s culinary divas since they founded City in the '80s; their Border Grill restaurants are both showcases of modern California-Latin cooking. From the margaritas to the ceviche tostaditas and legendary guacamole, this is great party fare. **WHO** Downtown offices, Santa Monica production studios and north-of-Montana homeowners. 🔵🍷

[Brent's Delicatessen] 🔒 **19565 Parthenia St., 818.886.5679, brentsdeli.com. WHY** Very good deli, delivered anywhere in the greater L.A. area. **WHAT** Brent's fleet of vans scurry all around SoCal every day, delivering trays of deli sandwiches, smoked fish, raw veggies and lemon bars to offices, schools and home gatherings. Lean meats, fresh breads, pretty fruit plates and a memorable whitefish salad, all at fair prices. **WHO** Deli fans who need to feed a group for a meeting, a bridge party or a memorial.

[Buckboard Catering Co.] **1386 E. Foothill Blvd., Upland, 909.608.7393, buckboardcatering.com. WHY** For authentic, crowd-pleasing Santa Maria barbecue, cooked at your site. **WHAT** Some parties demand the social consciousness of vegan cooking. Others cry out for the aroma of slow-grilled hunks o' meat. Buckboard puts on a traditional Central Coast barbecue, with tri-tip, beef ribs, chicken and the trimmings (cole slaw, pinquito beans, white-bread rolls). Very nice people bring the wagon-wheel grill to your site and take care of everything for a modest price. **WHO** Mostly businesses and families

Shops + Services

🍷**VEGETARIAN** ◉**KID FRIENDLY** ◌**PATIO DINING** 🚗**DELIVERY** 🏠**PRIVATE PARTY**

from the San Bernardino area, but they travel west.

[Clementine] 🔒 **1751 Ensley Ave., 310.552.1080, clementineonline. com. WHY** For Annie Miler's deeply comforting comfort food and her fabulous desserts. In fact, consider making your next event a Clementine dessert party. **WHAT** Workplace breakfasts and lunches are the specialty of this café/gourmet-to-go/catering operation run by chef Annie Miler, who worked at Campanile and Spago before finding success on her own. Her team can also cater a swell dinner party, but they'll contract out the serving staff. Particularly good for smaller events that don't require full party management.

[Elements Kitchen] **25 S. El Molino Ave., 626.440.0001, elementskitchen.com. WHY** For inventive (but not too risky) food and good party management. **WHAT** Onil Chibas is Pasadena's hippest caterer (and restaurateur, at Elements), with food that combines the comfort of American classics with lots of Asian and Latin influences. Passed dishes might include Vietnamese-style beef skewers with chili and lemongrass as well as Italian-style caprese skewers with fresh mozzarella. Good for dinner parties and mid-size shindigs. **WHO** The kind of eastsiders who'd throw a wedding at the Pacific Asia Museum or a bar mitzvah at the Pasadena Museum of California Art. 🖐

[Gallegos Mexican Deli] **12470 Venice Blvd., Mar Vista, 310.391.2587, gallegosmexicandeli.com. WHY** Delicious and affordable tamales, enchiladas, chile verde and other Mexican classics. **WHAT** The Gallegos family has been feeding Angelenos well for generations. If you're really on a budget, you can pick up trays of tamales, carnitas, beans and salsa from the deli, or if you can spend a little more, they'll bring everything to you and handle the service and clean up. Make sure to get some peach empanadas for dessert.

[Good Gracious Events] **5714 W. Pico Bvd., 323.954.2277, goodgraciousevents.com. WHY** One of L.A.'s most prestigious caterers, known for staging mega events. **WHAT** High-end parties put on by Good Gracious routinely end up in swank magazines, and it counts many celebrities and corporations on its returning-customer list. Lavish weddings, fashion events, awards ceremonies and launch parties are specialties. **WHO** The kind of players who want to see artist renderings of their events before they happen.

[Green Truck] **3515 Helms Ave., 310.204.0477, greentruckonthego. com. AE, MC, V. WHY** Fresh, organic salads, soups, wraps and sandwiches, served on-site for parties, shoots and meetings. **WHAT** This sustainable twist on the roach coach not only parks at different spots in L.A. each weekday, but it also caters. Not to worry about greenhouse gases—your ahi poke tacos, vegan sesame tofu wraps and sweet potato fries will arrive via a truck running on recycled vegetable oil.

🔒 ESSENTIALLY L.A. 🌙 LATE 💜 ROMANTIC 📷 VALUE 🔇 QUIET ♻ SUSTAINABLE

Great for casual outdoor functions, especially if your guests will be hemp-wearing vegetarians. 🌿🍴

[Happy Trails Catering] **207 S. Fair Oaks Ave., Pasadena, 626.796.9526, happytrailscatering.com. WHY** For a lovely and reasonably priced wedding or garden party, as well as carry-out platters of comforting modern American food (grilled tri-tip, white-bean chicken chili, Southern fried-chicken salad) for all sorts of events. **WHAT** Many a wedding has been held in this secret garden behind a brick storefront on the south end of Old Pasadena. Groups of up to 200 can celebrate under the massive old camphor tree; during the week, the garden is a serene spot for lunch. **WHO** Brides from all over L.A., as well as Pasadena folks who need good food for a graduation party, anniversary or memorial. 📷

[Jennie Cook's] 🏠 **3048 N. Fletcher Dr., 323.982.0052, jenniecooks. com. WHY** For richly flavorful and sustainably produced modern comfort food—for vegans and carnivores alike—at moderate prices. Ask about dinner parties in her kitchen. **WHAT** Jennie Cook's homey style of cooking suits her Pennsylvania Dutch roots—but the surprise is the commitment to sustainability and health. Her kitchen turns out great briskets and bacon-wrapped dates as well as sophisticated vegan and vegetarian dishes, and she's made a commitment to use local and organic goods and to run an environmentally responsible business. She's also become locally famous for leading the fight to make LAUSD serve healthier foods in schools. **WHO** Brides, bar and bat mitzvah celebrants, producers and opening-night party planners. 📷🌿🍴

[Joan's on Third] 🏠 **8350 W. 3rd St., 323.655.2285, joansonthird. com. WHY** For a pick-up or delivery dinner for 12 or a full-service catered affair for 120, with equally good modern American cooking. **WHAT** Joan McNamara started as a caterer and opened a companion café some years ago; the café and gourmet-to-go operation are now hugely popular. Her team's food and style work well for sit-down dinner parties and mid-size weddings; they also do a lot of delivered-food catering for business meetings and photo and commercial shoots. Good order-in-advance box lunches, too. **WHO** Lots of famous people, but Joan would never divulge their identities.

[Junior's] **2379 Westwood Blvd., 310.475.5771, jrsdeli.com. WHY** Deli platters for a meeting or a full-service spread for a party or, God forbid, a memorial. **WHAT** A 50-year-old Westwood landmark, Junior's is the best westside deli and a reliable source for deli catering, from pick-up orders to full-service events. **WHO** Westside Jewish families preparing to feed a crowd after a bris or a funeral.

[The Kitchen for Exploring Foods] **1434 W. Colorado Blvd., 626.793.7218, thekitchen.net. WHY** Excellent food stations for large

🌿 **VEGETARIAN** ◎ **KID FRIENDLY** ◎ **PATIO DINING** 🚚 **DELIVERY** 🏠 **PRIVATE PARTY** parties, as well as the full range of party services—and great gourmet-to-go goodies for that last-minute dinner party. **WHAT** If you've ever attended a big wedding, fundraiser or celebratory shindig in Pasadena and environs, you're likely to have enjoyed Peggy Dark's food. Her long-established firm, which has also catered many a Hancock Park and Los Feliz event, does a consistently good job, and the gourmet-to-go section is ideal for smaller parties. The menu is particularly strong in Mediterranean cooking. **WHO** Everyone who's anyone in Pasadena and the eastside. 🖐

[Lety's Catering Service] **627 Rosecrans Ave., 323.240.4719, lettyscatering.com. Mexican. WHY** For made-to-order tacos, the hit of any party. **WHAT** L.A. has hundreds of "taco ladies," but most are under-the-table businesses. Lety's is bigger than most, but not so big as to be inauthentic or overpriced. They'll send a taco lady (or taco guy) who will set up a salsa bar and all the fixings (rice, beans, cilantro, onions) and will grill chicken, carne asade and al pastor on site, for as little as $6 a head. **WHO** Savvy entertainers on a budget. 📷 ☺

[Lucques/AOC Catering] 🍴 **8474 Melrose Ave., 323.246.0978, lucques.com. AE, MC, V. WHY** Because you've always yearned to recreate Lucques's Sunday suppers in your own home, down to the little table setups of olives, bread, butter and fleur de sel. **WHAT** Run by Suzanne Goin's sister, Jessica, the catering arm of the Lucques/AOC/Tavern empire handles everything from intimate birthday dinners to large events, including flower arrangements and wine if you like. Professional and thorough, the staff (including a chef from one of the restaurants) leaves your house as they found it. **WHO** Cal-Med seasonal aficionados with extra cash in their pockets. Not cheap, but not outrageous either, and you get what you pay for.

[Marmalade] **710 Montana Ave., 310.828.3808, marmaladecafe.com. Modern American. WHY** For a highly experienced, professional catering operation that isn't over-the-top expensive. **WHAT** Marmalade was once a friendly little gourmet-to-go and catering operation in Santa Monica, and now it's a corporate enterprise. So you won't get the personal service of years past, but you will get a well-tuned operation and crowd-pleasing Italian-French-California food. You can also order smaller-party platters to pick up from this branch or any of the others, which include Malibu, Farmers Market, Sherman Oaks, Rolling Hills Estates and Westlake Village.

[Patina Catering] **400 S. Hope St., 213.814.3049, patinagroup. com. WHY** For an A-list event at Disney Hall, Descanso Gardens, LACMA or one of the other prime locations for which Patina is the exclusive caterer. **WHAT** High-end corporate, society and Hollywood events, held at in-demand venues like MOCA or at your Hancock Park mini-mansion, are Patina's specialties. Crackerjack service, elegant

French-California fare and not-insignificant prices. **WHO** USC, Center Theatre Group, L.A. Opera, Buena Vista Pictures and, most recently, the newlywed Duke and Dutchess when they visited L.A.

[Pie 'n Burger] 913 E. California Blvd., 626.795.1123, pienburger. com. American. **WHY** Cheeseburgers and peach pie with vanilla ice cream. **WHAT** Want to make your guests happy without spending a fortune? Serve them burgers and pie from Pie 'n Burger, Pasadena's revered diner. It caters for parties of 50 or more, either burgers (including veggie) and pie or barbecue chicken and tri-tip and pie, with the usual trimmings (including ice cream for the pie). **WHO** People with means who want to keep it casual and affordable.

[Versailles] 10319 Venice Blvd., Culver City, 310.558.3168, versaillescuban.com. **WHY** Garlic roast chicken, Cuban roast pork and the fixings, all of which makes for festive, inexpensive party food. **WHAT** Although it doesn't have a catering operation, this mini-chain is popular with on-a-budget entertainers for quantity takeout. A few orders of the famous marinated roast chicken, a few orders of the salty roast pork, some plantains, and a couple of quarts of black beans and white rice, and you've got a party. Branches on South La Cienega and in Encino and Manhattan Beach.

[Wolfgang Puck Catering] 6801 Hollywood Blvd., 866.491.1270, wolfgangpuckcatering.com. **WHY** For the celebrity cachet, of course, but also because Puck remains the standard-bearer in modern American cooking. **WHAT** L.A.'s original celebrity chef is now a national superstar, with restaurants, airport cafés and catering operations from coast to coast. His food is universally appealing, and the entire operation is completely professional. It's no bargain, but no one expects it to be. **WHO** A-list wedding planners, A-list corporations and, of course, the Governor's Ball after the Oscars.

CHEESE & CHARCUTERIE

[Andrew's Cheese Shop] 728 Montana Ave., Santa Monica, 310.393.3308, andrewscheese.com. Daily. AE, MC, V. **WHY** Cheeses and party platters from one of L.A.'s most passionate cheeseheads. **WHAT** This handsome cheese shop is the work of Andrew Steiner, ex of Patina. "This Place Stinks" is the store's tagline, a clue to its lighthearted approach to what is, in fact, a very serious resource for high-quality cheese. Wine, beer and cheesy accoutrements are also stocked.

[Artisan Cheese Gallery] 12023 Ventura Blvd., Studio City, 818.505.0207, artisancheesegallery.com. Daily. AE, MC, V. **WHY** Exotic cheeses from around the world, Fra' Mani salumi and great sandwiches. **WHAT** This small family-owned cheese shop sells an array of artisanal cheeses and charcuterie, along with some gourmet products.

Shops + Services

VEGETARIAN **KID FRIENDLY** **PATIO DINING** **DELIVERY** **PRIVATE PARTY**

Staffers encourage buyers to taste before buying, which means service can be v-e-r-y slow if it's crowded. Artisan Cheese also makes delicious panini. **WHO** Val cheesehounds who don't want to trek over the hill to the Cheese Store of Beverly Hills.

[Barney Greengrass] **Barney's, 9570 Wilshire Blvd., Beverly Hills, 310.777.5877. Daily. AE, MC, V. WHY** For one thing: smoked fish. **WHAT** As a deli, we've found better. But the quality of the smoked fish (sturgeon, salmon, sable) is A-number-one. Get a platter for your next party and be prepared for happy guests. **WHO** The rich, the beautiful and the smoked-fish-obsessed rich and beautiful.

[Cheese Store of Beverly Hills] 🏛 **419 N. Beverly Dr., Beverly Hills, 310.278.2855, cheesestorebh.com. Closed Sun. AE, MC, V. WHY** A selection of cheeses that is unmatched in Southern California. **WHAT** Since 1967, this tiny shop has purveyed the world's finest cheeses to the world's pickiest customers. An oasis of funky, cheesy aromas in the rarefied air of Beverly Hills, the Cheese Store is staffed with people who know their products and can discuss the finer points of fromage. There's also a good selection of wines. **WHO** Foodies, tourists and homesick Europeans.

[Cheese Store of Pasadena] **140 S. Lake Ave., Pasadena, 626.405.0050, cheesestorepasadena.com. Daily. WHY** L.A.'s passion for cheese spreads eastward, into a spacious gourmet shop facing Shopper's Lane. **WHAT** A solid collection of imported and domestic cheese is kept in a temperature-controlled cold room, so shoppers tell the counterfolk what they're in the mood to sample or choose from the cheese menu. Wine and cheese tastings are held in a private room, which can be reserved for parties. And it's not all cheese: there's an olive bar, charcuterie, dried pasta, olive oil and fresh baguettes. We just wish we could get a closer gander at the cheese selection. **WHO** Pasadena matrons, students with upscale tastes. 🏛

[Cheese Store of Silverlake] 🏛 **3926 W. Sunset Blvd., Silver Lake, 323.644.7511, cheesestoresl.com. Daily. AE, MC, V. WHY** The widest selection of cheeses east of the Cheese Shop of Beverly Hills, as well as a well-edited wine department, high-quality charcuterie, olives and other gourmet items. **WHAT** Owner Chris Pollan may seem gruff at first, but his passion for Europe and America's finest cheeses shines through once he starts talking cheese. Ask him about the shelf of foods sourced from his native Rhode Island. **WHO** Trendy young moms giving junior a taste of Taleggio, all stripes of Silver Lake residents stocking up for weekend dinner parties.

[Gioia Cheese] **1605 Potrero Ave., El Monte, 626.444.6015, gioiacheeseinc.com. Closed Sat.-Sun. Italian. WHY** Fresh burrata, made every single weekday, and other lovely soft Italian cheeses.

WHAT Vito Girardi is a third-generation cheesemaker and the man responsible for most of the burrata you see in L.A.'s best restaurants. It is our good fortune that he also sells to the public—not just burrata, but also mozzarella, ricotta, mascarpone, affumicata, scamorza and other suave Italian beauties. Each cheese is made to order, so you must call in advance. **WHO** Chefs from many of California's best Italian restaurants, and home cooks willing to drive for fresh cheese.

[Nicole's Gourmet Foods] 🔒 **921 Meridian Ave., South Pasadena, 626.403.5751, nicolesgourmetfoods.com. Closed Sun. French. AE, MC, V. WHY** A one-stop shop for French ingredients, plus an amiable café and legendary cheese selection. **WHAT** If it's French, Nicole carries it: pâtés, cheeses, duck confit, truffles, chocolates, wines, pastry-making ingredients, pastry shells, puff pastry, French butter, olives, foie gras, sauce bases, frozen quiches, sea salts, lavender... whether you want to cook a French meal or get a to-go French picnic, you'll find it here. **WHO** Serious French cooks and bakers, and eastsiders who don't want to trek to Surfas for their fix of Noel 72%.

[Wally's] **2107 Westwood Blvd., Westwood, 310.475.0606, wallywine. com. Daily. AE, MC, V. WHY** Cave-aged Swiss gruyère, Gioia's bocconcini, Paul Bertoli's charcuterie, Catalan sausages and, should the urge strike, Petrossian caviars. **WHAT** It has a big reputation for its wines, especially rare and high-end ones, but Wally's is also worth a trip for its high-quality international cheeses, its charcuterie and its terrific gift baskets, a Hollywood-agent staple during the holiday season. **WHO** Studio bigwigs, UCLA professors, Brentwood matrons.

COOKBOOKS

[Caravan Book Store] **550 S. Grand Ave., Downtown, 213.626.9944, hq.abaa.org/books/antiquarian/bookseller/1396.html. Closed Sun. WHY** Need we remind you of the importance of supporting a 58-year-old antiquarian bookstore that celebrates the printed page? **WHAT** Owner Leonard Bernstein (not *that* Lenny) focuses on all aspects of western American history including culinary (he was the one to get MFK Fisher's papers and books upon her death in 1992), with attention to the early L.A. experience. The Dickensian cubbyhole next door to Water Grill stocks used and rare books on food and wine, charitables, food ads and postcards, in addition to big Civil War and Western literature sections. If Bernstein doesn't have what you're looking for, he'll try to find it. **WHO** Jonathan Gold, Sting, chefs from the Biltmore up the block, and Downtown bike messengers.

[Central Library Culinary Collection] 🔒 **630 W. 5th St., Downtown, 213.228.7000, lapl.org/central. Closed Sun. & Mon. WHY** One of most extensive cookery collections in the entire country is right in our backyard, and it's free. **WHAT** More than 18,000 cookbooks, from

Shops + Services

🥬 VEGETARIAN ⊙ KID FRIENDLY ✿ PATIO DINING 🚗 DELIVERY 🏛 PRIVATE PARTY

14th-century manuscripts, the first Spanish-language cookbook, and 1,000 California cookbooks to Nathan Myhrvold's *Modernist Cuisine*. Plus a vintage menu collection, advertising ephemera, periodicals and photos. **WHO** Serious scholars to the average food-curious Joe.

[Cook Books by Janet Jarvits] **1388 E. Washington Blvd., Pasadena, 626.296.1638, cookbkjj.com. Closed Sun.-Mon.; hours irregular. MC, V. WHY** More than 30,000 used cookbooks, cooking magazines, booklets and books on wine, the restaurant business and anything remotely having to do with food. **WHAT** Cookbooks upon cookbooks upon cookbooks, all used and sometimes rare, are piled all the way up to the 15-foot ceiling and on every available surface. The bulk of the business is online, so don't expect a comfy hangout; chances are good that you'll need help finding what you want—and you will want a lot here. **WHO** Collectors and aficionados.

[Cookbooks Plus] **24267 Main St., Santa Clarita, 661.296.4455, cookbooksplus.com. Closed Sun. WHY** To score that near-mint copy of *The Silver Spoon*, or another highly collectible cookbook. **WHAT** Not enough foodies know about the treasure-trove of cookbooks tucked away in Santa Clarita, just a half-hour north of L.A. This is one of the last of an endangered species: the bricks-and-mortar cookbook shop. Mimi Hiller's store offers some 17,000 new and mostly used cookbooks. Some of the inventory is online, but if you're an addict like us, you'll want to visit and poke around. Stop in during the Old Town Newhall Farmers' Market on Thursdays from 3 to 7 p.m.—it takes place on the store's doorstep.

COOKING SCHOOLS

[A & J Cake & Candy Supplies] **2254 Rte. 66, Glendora, 626.335.7747, ajcake.com. Closed Sun. AE, MC, V. WHY** Who wouldn't want to learn how to make cluster candies, chocolate pizzas and marshmallow buddies? **WHAT** From the front, this strip-mall place on a lost stretch of Route 66 looks like nothing more than a place to buy candy molds, and in fact it is an excellent supply house for bakers and candy makers. But a lot more goes on behind those doors: classes in candy and cake making, for the novice to the experienced. Free candy-making demonstrations happen twice a month, and if you like what you see, you can sign up to learn how to make your own bon bons. The cake-decorating and fondant-making classes are also popular. **WHO** Gaggles of middle-aged women friends, and moms with their teenage daughters. ☺

[California School of Culinary Arts] **521 E. Green St., Pasadena, 866.230.9450, csca.edu. WHY** To get a professional culinary education without having to move to Hyde Park or Paris. **WHAT** First taking root in a small South Pasadena space, this school has grown faster than it can keep up with—it's sprawled over Pasadena (you see its uniformed student chefs everywhere) and now has a satellite next to the ArcLight in Hollywood. This is a demanding school that's affiliated with Le Cordon Bleu and is geared toward the full-time student seeking a degree in culinary arts, patisserie or management. The only part-time program is for patisserie and baking. **WHO** A mix of right-out-of-high-school kids and midlife career-changers.

[Chefs, Inc.] 10955 W. Pico Blvd., Cheviot Hills, 310.470.2277, chefsinc.net. **WHY** A good, all-around cooking school with particularly worthwhile classes for teens, workshops with some of L.A.'s top restaurant chefs and summer camps for kids. **WHAT** Leslie McKenna cooked at Valentino, was a private chef for celebrities and now runs an all-around cooking school on the westside. Her kitchens are roomy and well equipped but have a homey warmth that will make non-pros feel at ease. It's a great place to hold a party, team-building event or teen party, and the classes range from the very basics for home cooks to serious training for future pastry chefs. **WHO** Kids, teens, groups of friends and more serious chefs in the professional programs. ☺

[Chez Cherie] 1401 Foothill Blvd., La Canada, 818.952.7217, chezcherie.com. **WHY** Trader Joe's cooking classes. **WHAT** This small school has a number of good classes, from knife skills to cooking basics, but what lively and very funny owner Cherie Twohy is best known for are her single-session classes in making the most of Trader Joe's products. These $55 classes are fun and full of great pointers and ideas. **WHO** La Cañada and Pasadena moms.

[Epicurean School of Culinary Arts] 🛢 8500 Melrose Ave., West Hollywood, 310.659.5990, epicureanschool.com. **WHY** Excellent facilities, 25 years of experience and some really fun workshops. **WHAT** The focus here is split between serious professional training and terrific, and terrifically fun, workshops: Cupcake Couture, Braised & Beautiful and more. The workshops reflect current trends and styles (including sustainability) but aren't faddishly trendy. There's a newer campus in Anaheim. **WHO** A mix of aspiring professionals and people who just love to cook—or want to learn to love to cook. 🛢

[Glendale Community College] 1500 N. Verdugo Rd., Glendale, 818.240.1000, glendale.edu. **WHY** An extensive and affordable program offering certificates in culinary arts and restaurant management. **WHAT** Go ahead and spend $45K for a year at a fancy cooking school—or consider the professional program at Glendale College. It has wicked awesome kitchens, an accomplished faculty, a student-run white-tablecloth dining room and a practical, get-a-job focus.

[Gourmandise School of Sweets & Savories] The Market, 395 Santa Monica Place, Ste. 329 , Santa Monica, 310.656.8800,

🍽 VEGETARIAN ◔ KID FRIENDLY ☼ PATIO DINING 🚚 DELIVERY 🏠 PRIVATE PARTY

thegourmandiseschool.com. MC, V. **WHY** Quality cooking schools are like independent bookstores—distinctive and passionate about their mission. **WHAT** The focus is still on desserts, but savory classes, a pro series and team-building workshops are now offered at Clémence Gossett and Hadley Hughes's trendy-looking space on the new food court at Santa Monica Place. **WHO** Amateur and aspirational bakers.

[Hipcooks] 642 Moulton Ave., Lincoln Heights, 323.222.3663, hipcooks.com. **WHY** Convivial, downright fun classes that end in a meal and are designed to help regular people learn to throw something delicious together without freaking out. **WHAT** Monika Reti is as much a therapist as a cooking teacher, getting people to shed their inhibitions (and terror) about cooking for a date, throwing a dinner party or even following a recipe. Now that her home-style classes/parties have become wildly popular, she's opened a branch on Robertson, and is now so hip she has programs in Portland and Seattle. Classes end with a sit-down dinner with wine, making them a bargain at $55 a person ($65 on Robertson). Topics include Endless Summer Salads, Thai One On and My Big Fat Greek Cooking Class. Great for a party of friends. **WHO** Couples, singles and birthday-party groups.

[New School of Cooking] 8690 Washington Blvd., Culver City, 310.842.9702, newschoolofcooking.com. **WHY** One of the best consumer-oriented cooking-school programs in Southern California, with an underlying love of food and a general joie de vivre. Good summer kid and teen programs, too. **WHAT** Well established and very well run, the New School has a mouthwatering roster of classes for both the amateur and professional: Izakaya: Japanese Small Plates, Essential Knife Skills, Summer in Provence, Yeast Breads and the all-important class in Cupcakes. Acclaimed Thai-cuisine teacher Jet Tila is on the faculty, as are several other accomplished cooks and bakers.

[Simple Gourmet] 443-A S. Pacific Coast Hwy., Redondo Beach, 310.318.6484, simple-gourmet.com. **WHY** We're delighted to see serious schools for home cooks popping up once again all over the county. **WHAT** A "culinary event company," this is really a cooking school plus. In addition to quality avocational classes, it offers kids' camps, team-building events, private cooking parties, and catering.

[Sushi Chef Institute] 222 S. Hewitt St., Little Tokyo/Arts District, 213.617.6825, sushischool.net. **WHY** For a rigorous and rewarding approach to making sushi, run by a master chef. **WHAT** Chef Andy Matsuda is a highly regarded sushi master and teacher, and he and his team of chef/teachers run an excellent school. Its core is a professional program for aspiring full-time sushi chefs, but it also offers short-term intensive workshops in things like being a sake sommelier. Private lessons also available. **WHO** A multicultural mix, mostly of in-training or skills-updating professionals but also of avid amateurs.

DELIVERY SERVICES

[LAbite.com] 626.405.1101, 310.441.2483, 818.205.0500, 213.405.1500, labite.com. L Mon.-Fri., D nightly. AE, MC, V. **WHY** Home and office delivery from an extensive range of restaurants. **WHAT** This is the dominant restaurant-delivery business in town, with centers in Downtown, Pasadena, the Valley, the South Bay and on the westside. It's heavy on chain restaurants (Daily Grill, CPK, P.F. Chang's) but also represents some good individual places, from Bread and Porridge in Santa Monica to Delphine in Hollywood. There's a $6 to $7 delivery fee and a 4% "convenience" fee (for whose convenience?), and you need to tip the driver. 🚗

[Why Cook L.A.] 310.278.3955, whycookla.com. L Mon.-Fri., D nightly. AE, MC, V. **WHY** When you can afford to have food from Sushi Roku or Chaya delivered instead of pizza. **WHAT** This westside (Marina del Rey to Hollywood) delivery service works with a high caliber of restaurant, including M Café de Chaya, Josie, Jar and Street. There's a $25 minimum, a delivery charge ranging from $8 to $15 (studios are a flat $10), a 6% handling charge, and you need to tip, so this is not for the frugal. But the service is good, and you can eat very well indeed. **WHO** Studio folks and a work-through-lunch crowd. 🥢🚗

FARMERS' MARKETS

[About Certified Farmers' Markets (CFMs)]
With the explosion in farmers' markets, not all of which were created equal, here's how we gauge quality and integrity. CFMs are places for growers to sell their crops directly to consumers. They are neither outdoor convenience stores nor swap meets. Ask yourself: What's the ratio of crops to crap? Management's focus should be on farmers first, not cool hemp bags. You should see lots of seasonal produce displayed with pride by engaged growers and employees capable of answering your questions. The "certified" in CFM refers to farmers being state-certified about what they grow and bring to market. Growers can also be certified organic, but that's a different matter and way too complicated to get into here. California CFMs are required to group certified producers together, separate from any "non-ag" stalls. You can tell when a sketchy operation is filling in a weak mix by allowing resellers (i.e. peddlers of Chiquita bananas) into the non-ag section. Harder to spot are farmers who supplement their own produce with wholesale stuff. Clues for these problems: Is it in season, does it occur in nature here (banana chips, not so much), is everything cello-bagged or of super uniform size and color? Most importantly, does it look, smell and taste appetizing? Following are our favorite markets.

[Atwater CFM] Wells Fargo Parking Lot, 3250 Glendale Blvd., Atwater, 323.463.3171. Sun. 10 a.m.-2 p.m. **WHY** A low-key, compact market that's easy to navigate, well priced and doesn't start until 10 a.m., so

🥢 VEGETARIAN ⊙ KID FRIENDLY ☼ PATIO DINING 🚗 DELIVERY 🏠 PRIVATE PARTY

you can sleep in. **WHAT** Less of a scene than the nearby Silver Lake Saturday market, this market (from the same nonprofit that runs the great Hollywood one) has gained fans for produce from the South Central Farmer's Cooperative as well as from Jimenez Family Farms (beets, lettuces, summer berries, rabbit, goat and Marcie Jimenez's pies), Cam Slocum (the "eastside tomato king") and Asian growers catering to Filipino shoppers. Fresh eggs, grass-fed meats and a popular pupusa stand round out the offerings. The *pièce de resistance* is Big Mista's BBQ, run by the gregarious Big Mista, who cooks brisket, ribs, pulled pork and chicken on his rolling grill. His pig candy is the best thing that ever happened to bacon.

[Beverly Hills CFM] 9300 Block of Civic Center Dr., Beverly Hills, 310.285.6830, beverlyhills.org. Sun. 9 a.m.-1 p.m. **WHY** One of the wealthiest zip codes gets its small-town mojo on with annual pie and chili cook-offs. **WHAT** This midsize market has easy-breezy street parking, a good selection of organic vendors, and a Persian New Year celebration. A-list growers include Harry's Berries, McGrath Farm, Weiser Family Farms and Honey Crisp, which has exquisitely ripe summer fruit—their peaches brought Jeffrey Steingarten to his knees in his nationwide search for the best. Don't miss Westfield's avocados and the *condimenti al fresco* at Domenico's. **WHO** Affluent seniors, young families, chefs and a large Persian community.

[Culver City CFM] Culver at Main, Culver City, 310.253.5775, culvercity.org. Tues. 3-7 p.m. **WHY** A very good fish vendor (the same guy who's in Hollywood on Sunday), excellent cheeses and delicious fresh-ground peanut butter. Plus free parking in the city's structures. **WHAT** This afternoon/evening market draws both shoppers looking for organic produce and people looking to meet friends and graze from the many prepared-food vendors—check out the fresh coconuts at the Korean-food stand.

[Glendale CFM] Brand Blvd. between Wilson Ave. & Broadway, Glendale, 818.548.3155, downtownglendale.com. Thurs. 9:30 a.m.-1 p.m. **WHY** Shear Rock Farm heirloom tomatoes in the summer and greens in the winter, and Sunny Yasuda's Glassell Park backyard avocados and citrus. **WHAT** Although technically showcasing growers only (no prepared food to speak of), this 18-year-old city market doesn't have a lot of soul or variety. Its one long row of stalls doesn't invite socializing or lingering. There are, however, several standout farms. Just beware of out-of-season supplementing by others and "farm" stands reselling purchased, rather than home-grown, produce in the non-ag sections at the ends of the market.

[Hollywood CFM] 🏛 Ivar St. at Selma Ave., Hollywood, 323.463.3171, hollywoodfarmersmarket.net. Sun. 8 a.m.-1 p.m. **WHY** Excellent produce from McGrath's and Kenter Canyon Farms, among many others, as well as wonderful eggs and free-range chickens from Healthy Family Farms, a good fish vendor, a few bakers and a great source for naturally raised bison. Switch from beef burgers to bison burgers—you won't be sorry. **WHAT** One of the finest markets in the state, with a superb selection and lots always going on: cooking demonstrations, cookbook signings, tastings, kids' amusements and live music. Parking is a challenge; you'll probably have to pay. Better yet, take the Metro—the Hollywood and Vine stop is a block away. Well worth a trip. **WHO** Chefs, caterers, families pushing tank-size strollers and European ex-pats with baskets on their arms.

[La Cienega CFM] S. La Cienega Blvd. at W. 18th St., Pico-Robertson, 562.495.1764, lacienegafarmersmarket.com. Thurs. 2-7 p.m. **WHY** To support vendors like berry grower Frances Burciaga (Gutierrez Farm), who went from field hand to passionate farmer/owner. **WHAT** It's a veritable bounty: Scarborough greens, Tenerelli stone fruit, Polito citrus, Tamai corn and heirloom tomatoes, and Gonzaga Farms' Asian veggies, lemongrass, ginger, sugarcane, fresh chickpeas, jicama (Tess will show you how to peel it properly) and delicious citrus. The non-ag stalls are worth the trip, especially J.D's Louisiana BBQ (smoked tri-tip) and Carbon Grill Hawaiian BBQ's gorgeous plate lunch. Opened through a city program to bring produce to underserved communities, the market now offers a good mix to a diverse clientele. **WHO** Sikhs, Hassidim, carpool moms and Shuge Knight.

[Larchmont Village CFM] N. Larchmont Blvd. south of Beverly, Hancock Park, 818.591.8161. Sun. 10 a.m.-2 p.m. **WHY** Particularly good fruit vendors and bakers, with a respectable mix of seasonal produce, too. **WHAT** If you oversleep and miss the Hollywood market, head to this sweet little one on Larchmont. But if you want some of the fabulous unpasteurized fresh orange juice, don't get there too late—it always sells out.

[Long Beach Southeast CFM] Alamitos Bay Marina, Marina Dr. south of E. 2nd St., Long Beach, 866.466.3834, goodveg.org/LBSE.html. Sun. 9 a.m.-2 p.m. **WHY** Worth the drive for Lili Ying's greens and her cooking and medicinal advice: Dandelion greens are good for your liver! **WHAT** Laid out galley-kitchen-style along the Alamitos Bay Marina, this popular market is directly south of a weekly crafts and food fair. Look for Bautista dates; Maggie's Farm salad mixes; Weiser potatoes and summer melons; and , from Lili Ying, cilantro with roots attached, plump chrysanthemum leaves for grilling, and great summer cukes. There's always a long line at J & P Seafood, and folks swear by Sconeage Bakery's granola and scones. **WHO** Well-heeled Naples and Belmont locals *and* EBT (food stamp) customers.

[Mar Vista CFM] Grand View at Venice Blvd., Mar Vista, marvistafarmersmarket.org. Sun. 9 a.m.-2 p.m. **WHY** A great Sunday

Shops + Services

🥬 **VEGETARIAN** ⊙ **KID FRIENDLY** ☼ **PATIO DINING** 🚐 **DELIVERY** 🎉 **PRIVATE PARTY**

vibe at a serious market. **WHAT** This market has become an important westside gathering place (Councilman Bill Rosendahl held his swearing in here) and resource for quality ingredients. Chefs Mary Sue Milliken, Hans Rockenwagner and Raphael Lunetta shop here for their families, and local eateries like Curious Palate walk over to stock up from such top-notch growers as Givens, Tamai, Capay Organic and Fat Uncle Farm. Dog-sitting and bike valet services make life easy. **WHO** A lively Oaxacan community from south of the market, upscale film folks from the north, and chefs who live in the 'hood.

[Pasadena CFM] N. Sierra Madre Blvd. & Paloma St., East Pasadena, 626.449.0179, pasadenafarmersmarket.org. Sat. 8:30 a.m.-1 p.m. **WHY** A great market east of Hollywood. **WHAT** This popular market on the edge of Victory Park offers Harry's Berries, Bill's Bees (honeys), ABC Rhubarb (herbs and greens), Two Peas in a Pod (super sweet sugar snaps, shelling beans, cauliflower, berries),and Mike Taylor (spring and Maui onions, tomatoes, nasturtiums). Good flowers, too. Stop by the Culture Club 101 stall for a kombucha refresher or a lacto-fermented soda. The same group runs a smaller but still worthwhile market on Tuesday mornings at Villa Park, 363 E. Villa, in central Pasadena. **WHO** Parents stocking up while their kids play AYSO soccer on the neighboring fields.

[Santa Clarita CFM] College of the Canyons Parking Lot 8, Valencia Blvd. & Rockwell Cyn. Rd., Santa Clarita. Sun 8:30 a.m.-noon. **WHY** Live in Granada Hills, Valencia, or Castaic? Get quality close to home and save gas. **WHAT** Locals love this spacious suburban market so much they bring cookies to their favorite farmers. Among its virtues are easy parking, a relaxed atmosphere and a nice variety, including Harry's Berries, Canyon Meadow eggs, Bunny Tree veggies, ABC watercress and flowering chives, Pritchett stone fruit, and meat from Watkins Cattle Company, which is dedicated to the whole animal (need oxtails, beef heart or soup bones?). **WHO** Families from the north San Fernando and Santa Clarita Valleys.

[Santa Monica CFM: Arizona] Arizona Ave. & 3rd St., Santa Monica, 310.458.8712, santa-monica.org. Wed. 8:30 a.m.-1:30 p.m. & Sat. 8:30 a.m.-1 p.m. **WHY** Harry's Berries, Lily's Eggs, Weiser melons, Rutiz carrots, Coastal Farms tomatoes, Cirone apples and apricots, Redwood Hill cheeses, Tenerelli peaches, McGrath beets… you won't believe your eyes or your taste buds. **WHAT** One of the best and largest in the country, the Wednesday-morning market is pounced upon by the city's best chefs, as well as buyers who snatch up hot items and whisk them to LAX to fly to chefs around the country. But there's enough for everyone, including fruits and vegetables you've never seen before, which you can learn how to prepare—if you ask questions. High quality and dense crowds. The Saturday market is a little mellower and has a somewhat different mix of farmers. Also in town is a smaller market at Virginia Avenue Park (Cloverfield at Pico) on Saturday mornings, and the hugely popular Sunday-morning market on Main Street (see next listing). **WHO** Chefs so famous they wear hats and sunglasses, thousands of passionate food lovers, and lots of strollers.

[Santa Monica CFM: Main Street] **2640 Main St. at Ocean Park Ave. & 2nd St., Santa Monica, 310.458.8712, santa-monica.org. Sun. 9:30 a.m.-1 p.m. WHY** Kids' amusements, live music, great people-watching and very good produce. **WHAT** This sibling of the famous Arizona Avenue market is the social event of the week in south SanMo, where neighbors meet and families shop. It may seem to be more about the face-painting and music, but there's also some terrific food from the likes of Spring Hill Cheese, Munak Ranch (heirloom tomatoes), Olson Farms (stone fruit) and Röckenwagner (pretzel bread). **WHO** Tons of families and Ocean Park/Venice locals.

[Silver Lake CFM] **W. Sunset Blvd. at Edgecliff Dr., Silver Lake, 213.413.7770. Sat. 8 a.m.-1 p.m. & Tues. 2-7:30 p.m. WHY** For its strong sense of neighborhood—some Silver Lake backyard farmers sell their produce here. It's a particularly good market for gifts made by local craftspeople. In spring and summer, look for the guy who sells wonderful backyard-grown herbs. If you're hungry, hit the crêpes booth. **WHAT** This small morning market sees neighbors catching up over coffee at the good coffee stand, cooks buying produce and browsers looking through the jewelry and hippie-girl dresses. Much of the produce is from certified farmers (including Beylik tomatoes and Mai Yang's root vegetables and Asian produce), but not all, so pay attention where you shop.

[South Pasadena CFM] **Meridian Ave. at Mission St., South Pasadena, 626.403.2820, ci.south-pasadena.ca.us/about/farmersmarket. html. Thurs. 4-8 p.m. WHY** This is one of the greenest markets in town, because you don't have to drive—it's right off the Gold Line Mission stop. **WHAT** Formerly ho-hum (a half -dozen clown acts!), this market has become a star thanks to new, strong management, which has brought many new vendors as well as chef demos and food talks at the adjacent SoPas library. Look for Rancho Mi Familia, McGrath, Bernard Ranch, Yasutomi (low-acid Momotaro tomatoes), Suncoast (artichokes, asparagus, cauliflower), J & J (grass-fed beef) and Organic Pastures' dairy. Non-ag stalls of note include Carmela's ice creams and the Panini stand, former Röckenwagner bakers who make their own rolls for fresh-pressed sandwiches). Who needs a carnival when you have idyllic grassy areas where kids can romp and charming cafés where you can sip a post-market glass of rosé? **WHO** Students from nearby Cordon Bleu Culinary Academy, young couples shopping after work, artists, teens—an affluent mix of all ages.

🌿 **VEGETARIAN** ⊙ **KID FRIENDLY** ☼ **PATIO DINING** 🚗 **DELIVERY** 🎩 **PRIVATE PARTY**

[Studio City CFM] **Ventura Pl. at Ventura Blvd., Studio City, 818.655.7744, studiocityfarmersmarket.com. Sun. 8 a.m.-1 p.m.** **WHY** For a Sunday family outing. **WHAT** After 11 years, this mid-size market has made moves toward quality and crop diversity to become a solid resource. We just hope the new management continues on this path and junks the M&Ms sold in the middle of the market. Seek out Givens Organics (who knew celery could be this tasty?), Fresno Evergreen's Asian vegetables, the Grove Washington navels (*the* original navel oranges from 1876), Lily's Eggs, and fabulous dates from Davall, plus the usual prepared-food booths. **WHO** The Valley affluent and lots of families indulging in pony rides and moon bounces.

[Torrance CFM] 🏛 **2200 Crenshaw Blvd., Torrance, 310.618.2930. Tues. & Sat. 8 a.m.-1 p.m. WHY** Because Torrance loves its farmers, and you can feel the love. **WHAT** The jewel of the South Bay, this market runs on two days, Tuesday and Saturday. Saturday is bigger, but both have a tasty mix of seasonal produce, plus a strong Asian selection—Hmong grower Vang Thao's stand, for instance, is popular for fresh peanuts, bird chiles and bitter melon, as well as beautiful eggplants, basil and garlic. The community-focused offerings—breakfast, lunch (including Big Mista's great barbecue) and entertainment—are plentiful. **WHO** A diverse crowd, ethnically, culturally and age-wise. On Tuesdays it's mostly seniors, mommies with strollers and summer-camp groups doing scavenger hunts; Saturdays it's a grand mix.

[Venice CFM] **Venice Way & Venice Blvd., Venice, 310.399.6690, venicefarmersmarket.com. Fri. 7 a.m.-11 a.m. WHY** A full range of organic and/or local produce, as well as good eggs, a great berry guy and breads and sweets from a couple of skilled local bakers. **WHAT** Get up early to get the good stuff at this bustling, intimate Friday market, which packs a lot of good food into a compact park space.

[Yamashiro Garden Market] **1999 N. Sycamore Ave., Hollywood, 323.466.5125, yamashirorestaurant.com. Thurs. 5-9 p.m. WHY** Yamashiro's view, fun prepared foods, and a bar. **WHAT** It's not a certified market, and it's more about the prepared foods and the fab views than the produce, but it's worth knowing about for a festive Thursday-night outing, especially if you're entertaining tourists and don't want to eat at the overpriced restaurant. There's an outdoor wine and cocktail bar, prepared-food stands, live music and tables overlooking the dreamy twilight cityscape—oh yeah, and some vendors for fish, eggs and greens. Validated valet parking for just $2.

KITCHEN & TABLE SUPPLY

[Anzen Hardware] **309 E. 1st St., Little Tokyo/Arts District, 213.628.7600. Daily. WHY** Knowledgeable service and some of the best professional-grade knives in the city. **WHAT** Knives are the big draw—Wolfgang Puck, the Border Grill gals, Joe Miller and Gino Angelini are all customers. You'll find everything from $50 starter santokus to $3,000 handmade sushi knives. Anzen, which means safety in Japanese, opened in 1946; current owner Nori Takatani started working here upon his arrival from Hiroshima in 1954, which means he knows his stuff. Besides knives, the narrow shop is packed with everything you'd expect in a hardware store and more: tabi boots, Japanese metal hot-water bottles, fish scalers and Jell-O-mold boxes. **WHO** Downtown folk (including cops on the beat) and chefs.

[Bar Keeper] **3910 W. Sunset Blvd., Silver Lake, 323.669.1675, barkeepersilverlake.com. Daily. AE, MC, V. WHY** When you need not just one kind of absinthe spoon, but several. **WHAT** Given his name (and his gregarious personality), it was probably destiny that Joe Keeper would someday open a store called Bar Keeper. In the Sunset Junction 'hood that is Silver Lake's foodie bull's-eye, he's put together a drinker's head shop of wonderfully curated gifts and essentials, from glassware and shakers to books and vintage bar gear. Thanks to the new license, you'll also find an impressive selection of booze from artisanal producers, including Batavia Arrack, Willett bourbon, Del Maguey mescal and Crème de Violette. **WHO** The sort of people who know that there is such a thing as an absinthe spoon.

[Bargain Fair] **7901 Beverly Blvd., Beverly/Third, 323.655.2227. Daily. AE, MC, V. WHY** Total bargains on quirky and basic kitchenware and tableware. **WHAT** This cluttered discount store is always worth a stop. For one thing, you can pick up such essentials as chafing dishes and 99-cent tongs. And you might just find a Russian tea set that you can't live without and certainly can afford. Best of all, there's a great selection of glassware at almost-wholesale prices. **WHO** Savvy caterers.

[Charlie's Fixtures] **2251 Venice Blvd., Mid-City, 323.731.9023, charliesfixtures.com. Closed Sun. MC, V. WHY** Great prices on high-quality restaurant- and home-kitchen-supply goods, from huge walk-ins to tabletop broilers. **WHAT** This cluttered, open-to-the-public wholesaler and retailer has most of the best names in professional-grade kitchen appliances and tableware at some of the lowest prices in town.

[Dish Factory] **310 S. Los Angeles St., Downtown, 213.687.9500, dishfactory.com. Closed Sun. AE, MC, V. WHY** Sixty thousand square feet of china, glassware and new and refurbished heavy-duty cooking gear, all at unbeatable prices. **WHAT** This restaurant-supply warehouse is open to the public, and it's developed a loyal following for its dishware and flatware—firsts and seconds, all at great prices. Also notable is the very good glassware at 35 to 50% discounts by case quantity, and the refurbished mixers, refrigerators and ovens. **WHO** Restaurant managers, chefs, caterers and intrepid home entertainers looking for that extra case of wine glasses or a refurbished professional mixer.

Shops + Services

VEGETARIAN ◎ KID FRIENDLY ☼ PATIO DINING 🚗 DELIVERY 🎩 PRIVATE PARTY

[Heath Ceramics] **7525 Beverly Blvd., Beverly/Third, 323.965.0800, heathceramics.com. Daily. AE, MC, V. WHY** No need to drive to Sausalito to admire this handmade tableware. **WHAT** A partnership between Heath and longtime L.A. architect and potter Adam Silverman, proprietor of Atwater Pottery, the airy store includes gallery space for ceramic artists as well as plenty of display room for tableware, some kitchenware, a tightly edited book selection and an even smaller selection of foodstuffs.

[Intelligentsia Coffee] **3922 W. Sunset Blvd., Silver Lake, 323.663.6173, intelligentsiacoffee.com. Daily. AE, MC, V. WHY** Gleaming home espresso machines to drool over, and maybe even buy. **WHAT** Pasquini's got some competition now that Intelligentsia is selling gear for the home barista. The range isn't large, but it's smart and thoughtful, from $7,500 hard-plumbed La Marzocco espresso machines that are sturdy enough for a small café, to simple little machines that go for as little as $500. It also has good burr grinders, knock boxes and other accessories.

[La Tavola] **9859 Santa Monica Blvd. , Beverly Hills, 310.286.1333, latavolalinen.com. Closed Sat.-Sun. AE, MC, V. WHY** This most diverse and interesting array of rental table linens in town. **WHAT** The go-to place in L.A. for table linens. Fabulous fabrics, unusual designs, fun accessories and good service. **WHO** The best party planners and caterers in town.

[Luna Garcia] 🏛 **201 San Juan Ave., Venice, 800.905.9975, lunagarcia.com. Closed Sun. AE, MC, V. WHY** You can change the mood of your tablescape by mixing and matching shapes and colors the same way you put together outfits from your closet. **WHAT** This venerable Venice pottery studio produces and sells its own handmade, collectible, durable dinnerware, bowls and serving pieces, which come in wonderful satin matte colors. Look for finds in the "seconds" room, the party-like semi-annual sales and owner Cindy Ripley's unerring eye for accessories, many produced by her talented friends. This place is sort of like the Slow Food of tableware. **WHO** Longtime regulars and couples who want a hip, arty alternative to bridal registries.

[Pasquini Espresso Co.] **1501 W. Olympic Blvd., Pico-Union, 213.739.0480, pasquini.com. Closed Sun. AE, MC, V. WHY** For serious home-kitchen espresso machines—but you need to have a resale license to buy here. **WHAT** If you have a resale license or are working with a contractor or designer who does, come here to get a good deal on an ultra-high-quality home espresso machine/steamer/grinder setup that will have you making espresso as good as Intelligentsia's. If you don't have a resale license, call them up to find a retailer. **WHO** Hardcore coffeeheads.

🏛 ESSENTIALLY L.A. ☺ LATE ♥ ROMANTIC 💵 VALUE 🔇 QUIET ♻ SUSTAINABLE

[Rafu Bussan] **326 E. 2nd St., Little Tokyo/Arts District, 213.614.1181. Closed Wed. AE, MC, V. WHY** For Mac knives, gorgeous Japanese tableware and clever kitchen gear, sold by incredibly nice people. Watch for the twice-yearly sales. **WHAT** For a gift to please your food-loving friend, head to this wonderful store, where you'll find tableware, bento boxes, tea sets, cookbooks, sushi knives, bowls, cooking gear and more. A fun place to browse, and nice gift wrapping, too. **WHO** Chefs, restaurateurs and hip couples registering for their weddings.

[Star Restaurant Equipment] **6178 Sepulveda Blvd., Van Nuys, 818.782.4460, starkitchen.com. Closed Sun. MC, V. WHY** A huge array of home and professional gear and accessories, at middle-of-the-road prices but with high-end service. **WHAT** Need a proofing cabinet or a panini grill? Make the trek from Van Nuys to Star, and plan on spending at least a couple of hours browsing the mouthwatering array of appliances, gadgets, tools, tableware, furniture and fixtures. It's open to the public, and if they don't have it, they can order it.

[Super Home Mart] 🏠 **988 N. Hill St., Chinatown, 213.628.8898. Daily. AE, MC, V. WHY** Fun, often bargain-priced Asian and American tableware and kitchen goods in a central Chinatown location. **WHAT** Attractive, festive and practical housewares are the draw here, and the prices can't be beat. You'll find Chinese stuff, of course, from woks to steamers, but also Japanese sake sets, Italian coffeemakers and much more. Particularly good tableware and glassware. **WHO** Chinatown tourists and savvy shoppers from Downtown, Silver Lake and Echo Park looking for a cool gift. 🚗

[Surfas] 🏠 **8777 W. Washington Blvd., Culver City, 310.559.4770, cafesurfas.com. Daily. AE, MC, V. WHY** The ingredients and equipment for virtually every style of cooking in the world. **WHAT** This former restaurant supply store has morphed into a food-shopper's paradise complete with a little café. In addition to thousands of fresh, frozen and packaged gourmet food items, Surfas has equipment aisles devoted to a fascinating array of large-scale appliances and arcane cookware that you never knew existed but now need. The goods aren't cheap, but the quality and service are high. **WHO** Professional chefs and semipro foodies.

KNIFE SHARPENERS

[Gary's Knife Sharpening Service] **310.560.3258, garysknifesharpening.com. WHY** A sharp knife is a thing of beauty. **WHAT** Few things frustrate a cook more than a dull knife. Gary understands. Westsiders will find him and his sharpening tools at several farmers' markets, including Torrance, Culver City, Mar Vista and Beverly Hills; check his website for the schedule. If you don't live on the westside, not to worry—with a $40 minimum order, Gary and

🍃 VEGETARIAN ☺ KID FRIENDLY ☼ PATIO DINING 🚍 DELIVERY 🏛 PRIVATE PARTY his team make house calls; we let our neighbors know one of Gary's people was coming, and everyone brought their knives, scissors and gardening tools, so meeting the minimum was a snap.

[Kitchen Outfitters] **5650 E. 2nd St., Long Beach, 562.434.2728, kitchenoutfitters.com. Daily. AE, MC, V. WHY** For professional knife sharpening in Long Beach. **WHAT** Drop off your knives (standard, serrated, ceramic, Japanese) and shears by 2 p.m. on Monday, and you'll get them back sharpened and/or repaired by 5 p.m., thanks to the Perfect Edge mobile truck. While you wait, you'll have fun shopping for kitchen gear in this Naples store, and you can wander over to Naples Gourmet Grocer for something good to take home for dinner.

[Perfect Edge Knife Sharpening] **562.895.6567, perfectsharpening.com. MC, V. WHY** This isn't the cheapest sharpening service around ($5.10 to $25 per knife), but it's worth it just to get a look in the mobile workshop, a handy guy's dream come true. And the work is excellent. **WHAT** This mobile sharpening truck appears at a few places in Southern California, including Koontz Hardware (8914 Santa Monica Blvd., West Hollywood) on Tuesdays and Kitchen Outfitters (5666 E. 2nd St., Long Beach) on Mondays. The truck will also come to your house with a decent minimum order. Besides sharpening, it can repair broken knives, scissors and garden tools.

[Ross Cutlery] 🏛 **310 S. Broadway, Downtown, 213.626.1897, rosscutlery.com. Daily. AE, MC, V. WHY** For knife shopping, knife sharpening and to get to go inside the Bradbury Building. **WHAT** Made famous for its courtroom role in the O.J. murder trial, Ross is nowadays more known for its knife-sharpening services—and yes, it sharpens cuticle clippers and pocket knives. Plan on leaving your knives for a couple of days. And good luck resisting the temptation to buy a new blade from its fantastic collection, including ceramic knives. **WHO** Chefs with their beloved knives.

MEAT & SEAFOOD

[Alexander's Prime Meats] **Howie's Ranch Market, 6580 N. San Gabriel Blvd., San Gabriel, 626.286.6767, alexandersprimemeats.com. Daily. AE, MC, V. WHY** For some of the best prime beef in L.A. Consider going in with friends on a side of dry-aged beef.
WHAT Inside the winningly old-school Howie's Ranch Market is this superb purveyor of beef—it's mostly from Harris Ranch, and it's mostly prime. The butchers know what they're doing. The marinated meats, notably the chicken and carne asada, are good, too. **WHO** Seekers of the perfect steak.

[Bel Air Prime Meats] **2964 N. Beverly Glen Blvd., Bel-Air, 310.475.5915. Daily. AE, MC, V. WHY** The on-site smoker, the Harris

Ranch beef dry-aged on the premises and the homemade sausages. **WHAT** Part of the elite Beverly Glen Marketplace is this high-end butcher, known for its prime beef, veal chops and kebabs and other prepared meats. Good movie-star-spotting, too. **WHO** Bel-Air locals, for whom the price of prime, dry-aged beef is of no more significance than change for the parking meter.

[Carnicería Sanchez] **4525 Inglewood Blvd., Mar Vista, 310.391.3640. Daily. Mexican. MC, V. WHY** Pork shoulder, carne asada, marinated chicken, fresh salsas and a good taquería. **WHAT** The go-to carnicería for westsiders, Sanchez is in a little food-centric Latino neighborhood at Culver and Inglewood. The meats and marinades are very good.

[Crusty Crab] **Ports O' Call, 1146 Nagoya Way, San Pedro, 310.519.9058. Daily. AE, MC, V. WHY** Fresh, live crab—especially the unique-to-California coastal species. **WHAT** For more than 25 years, this has been crab central in San Pedro's Ports O' Call Village. Boiled, steamed or packed up live to cook at home, these succulent crustaceans are the stars at this family-run seafood market/restaurant. Long-time customers check the tanks to pick out their favorites, and they know how to pick 'em: The reds are the sweetest, while the browns have the largest claws.

[El Gaucho Meat Market] **2715 Manhattan Beach Blvd., Redondo Beach, 310.297.2617. Daily. Argentinean. MC, V. WHY** Argentineans know and love their meat, and the butchers here *really* know and love their meat. Great for Argentine cuts (like beef for a parrillada), as well as empanadas. **WHAT** This butcher, market and café will handle all your Argentinean needs, from dulce de leche, to Ricci mayonnaise, to such spices as aji molido, to soccer matches on the TV. There's also a bakery (decent medias lunas) and good sandwiches. But the real star of the show is the butcher counter. **WHO** Argentineans and meat lovers traveling from all over the westside.

[European Deluxe Sausage Kitchen] **9109 W. Olympic Blvd., Beverly Hills, 310.276.1331. Closed Sun. French. AE, MC, V. WHY** Cold-smoked beef that's hung over hickory coals for 72 hours, and the house-smoked, very lean (this is Beverly Hills) salumi. **WHAT** This shop smokes its own meats and sausages in a brick pit in the back, and the German-trained owners stock their cases with impeccably spiced veal wieners, chubby bratwurst, smoked beef tongue and more. For the home sausage maker, this is a great place to order hard-to-get casings and caul fat.

[Fish King] 🏠 **722 N. Glendale Ave., Glendale, 818.244.0804, fishkingseafood.com. Daily. AE, MC, V. WHY** Hawaiian opah, sashimi-grade ahi, lobster bisque and everything seafood. **WHAT** The premier seafood market on the eastside (or perhaps in all of L.A.), Fish King also carries a few non-seafood essentials (pasta, bread, marinades, some fresh vegetables and citrus) and a few prepared dishes, notably excellent soups. The guys behind the counter know their stuff, and the fish and shellfish are outstanding.

[Fisherman Johnny's Seafood Outlet] **10604 Ventura Blvd., Studio City, 818.762.2335, fjseafoodoutlet.com. Closed Sun. WHY** Lower-than-usual prices on an array of seafood items, and a super-friendly owner. **WHAT** Not a conventional seafood market, this is partly a resource for high-quality, low-priced frozen and fresh fish and seafood and partly a lunchtime café, where owner Johnny and crew make lobster tacos, sea bass burritos and grilled fish plates. Look for big bags of Carlsbad Aquafarm oysters and mussels, vacuum-packed yellowtail and swordfish and several kinds of smoked fish. 🖼 ☼

[Fisherman's Outlet] **529 S. Central Ave., Downtown, 213.627.7231, fishermansoutlet.net. Closed Sun. WHY** Come for the adjacent seafood café and stay to pick out more fresh fish to cook yourself for dinner. But bring cash. **WHAT** A good all-around seafood market with a large section devoted to cooked crab and shrimp of every size. Low prices, a respectable selection and counter guys who move fast and know their stuff. 🖼

[Grindhaus Sausage Shop] **5634 Hollywood Blvd., Hollywood, 323.462.6328, grindhausla.com. Closed Mon. MC, V. WHY** Artisanal sausage. Need we say more? **WHAT** This little storefront along a down-at-the-heels section of Hollywood Boulevard purveys all manner of sausage, from hearty venison and macho boar to flirtatious duck with cherries and semisweet chocolate, which is much, much better than it sounds. House-made pickles and mustards as well as specialty products (duck confit) round out the offerings. Check the Twitter feed (@grindhausLA) for daily sausage varieties. **WHO** Sausage geeks.

[Harmony Farms] **2824 Foothill Blvd., La Crescenta, 818.248.3068. Daily. AE, MC, V. WHY** Hey, they've got game! (Try the buffalo burgers.) The frozen turkey meatballs are great, too. **WHAT** Run by a goofy bunch of guys in butcher's whites, Harmony specializes in wild game and organic, free-range lamb, turkey, beef and chicken. Great for superb lamb chops and first-rate Thanksgiving turkeys and prices much lower than the fancy markets. 🖼 ♻

[Harvey's Guss Meat Co.] 🏛 **949 S. Ogden Dr., Miracle Mile, 323.937.4622, harveysgussmeat.com. Open mornings Tues.-Fri. WHY** Lamb from Colorado and the Napa Valley; Kurobuta pork; and prime T-bones and porterhouse steaks from the Midwest, dry-aged on site for 30 days. **WHAT** Considered L.A.'s finest butcher, Harvey Gussman runs a wholesale operation that also sells to the public. It's not a place to browse—call the day before to see if they have what you want and then place your order. **WHO** Chefs, caterers and savvy home cooks.

[Huntington Meats & Sausage] **Los Angeles Farmers Market, 6333 W. 3rd St., Fairfax District, 323.938.5383, huntingtonmeats.com. Daily. AE, MC, V. WHY** A vast array of homemade sausages, Nancy Silverton's hamburger blend and Wagyu (Kobe-style) beef. **WHAT** The Huntington sells Harris Ranch beef, American lamb and an impressive selection of pork cuts, hams, bacon, house-made sausages and such specialties as Moffett's pot pies. The butchers give good advice on cooking and grilling techniques, too.

[J & T European Gourmet] **1128 Wilshire Blvd., Santa Monica, 310.394.7227. Daily. Polish/Hungarian. AE, MC, V. WHY** Incredible Polish and Middle European charcuterie made on the premises. **WHAT** Polish-trained meat masters John Pikula and Ted Maslo turn out several types of hams, smoked and cured meats and a grand supply of garlicky kielbasa, wiejska, kabanos and other sausages. The freezer holds homemade dumplings and soups, and in the cold case you'll find smoked fish and European butters to go with the rye breads on the shelves. **WHO** Grateful Middle European ex-pats and kielbasa aficionados.

[Jim's Fallbrook Market] **5947 Fallbrook Ave., Woodland Hills, 818.347.5525, jimsfallbrookmarket.com. Daily. MC, V. WHY** Ground-in-house meats, Harris Ranch prime cuts, very good tri-tip and some wild game. They corn their own beef—try it. **WHAT** It looks like your basic corner mom 'n pop market, which is what it was when it started back in the '40s. But today Jim's is the West Valley's best source for quality meats and full butcher service. Fresh fish, too.

[La Española Meats] 🔒 **25020 Doble Ave., Harbor City, 310.539.0455, laespanolameats.com. Closed Sun. Spanish. AE, MC, V. WHY** L.A.'s only outpost for house-made Spanish charcuterie, plus imported oils, wines and more. **WHAT** Inconspicuously lodged in an industrial side street, La Española makes the most of its Harbor City location by using its warehouse space to produce excellent sausages— including five types of chorizo and two types of morcilla—as well as cured Spanish meats. The market stocks canned fish, cheeses, dry goods and desserts, and there's a small patio where you can enjoy a *bocadillo*—a sandwich stuffed with their own jamón serrano, chorizo, roasted peppers and manchego cheese—and the Saturday-only paella, which rightly requires a call ahead. 🚚 ☼

[Lindy & Grundy] 🔒 **801 N. Fairfax Ave., Hollywood, 323.951.0804, lindyandgrundy.com. Closed Mon. WHY** Conscientiously sourced, pasture-raised meat and poultry make it feel good to be a carnivore.

🌿 VEGETARIAN ⊙ KID FRIENDLY ☼ PATIO DINING 🚚 DELIVERY 🏠 PRIVATE PARTY

WHAT At this gleaming temple of sustainable meat, the cleaver flies as muscular, tattooed proprietor Erika Nakamura breaks down a whole lamb, and a massive bone rests on the butcher block ready to become marrow. Nakamura and partner Amelia Posada are serious about their providers and their preparations, smoking chickens and making bacon and charcuterie. One case holds the best American cheeses, and the variety of sausages is legion, from pork kim chee to "gateway" chicken and tofu to chicken-apricot. Be flexible—since this is small-producer stuff, you never know what they'll have in stock. **WHO** Pro chefs and serious home cooks who don't mind paying for top quality. ☁

[Marconda's Meat] ⌂ **Los Angeles Farmers Market, 6333 W. 3rd St., Fairfax District, 323.938.5131, farmersmarketla.com. Daily. AE, MC, V. WHY** Andouille, chorizo, Marconda's ready-to-bake meatloaf mixture and butterflied legs of lamb. **WHAT** Want to grill bistecca alla fiorentina? Come here to get a custom-cut porterhouse for that, along with anything you might want in the way of pork, lamb (aged three weeks) or sausage; consider the Montana-grown Piedmontese beef from a breed of cattle naturally low in fat. Friendly, patient butchers who have seen it all make shopping here a pleasure. **WHO** Everyone from famous chefs to little old ladies dragging their wooden Farmers Market carts and micromanaging their meat orders.

[McCall's Meat and Fish] **2117 Hillhurst Ave., Los Feliz, 323.667.0674, mccallsmeatandfish.com. Closed Mon. MC, V. WHY** An artisan shop that's opening our eyes to new cuts. **WHAT** The butcher case offerings read like a fine dining restaurant menu: Angus beef, Kurobuta pork, farmer-direct chicken and duck. Don't miss the well-edited fish selection, which is tweeted weekly. We love the quality and the mom 'n pop vibe from the chef-owners; of course, you pay for all this. **WHO** Hip Los Feliz cooks and bloggers swooning over the Prince Edward Island mussels.

[Peking Poultry] **717 N. Broadway, Chinatown, 213.680.2588. Daily. MC, V. WHY** For live ducks and chickens, slaughtered to order if you want—or the more conventional (very) fresh poultry. Also a fine selection of cuts of pork, whole fish on ice and live tilapia and crab. **WHAT** Poultry is the claim to fame, both live and butchered, but fresh fish and pork are also in abundance, all at astonishingly low prices. The smell is on the intense side of intense (live and not-live chickens, ducks, fish, shellfish and meat will do that), but the place is scrupulously clean. And there's a free parking lot right in front! 🖅

[Santa Monica Seafood] **1000 Wilshire Blvd., Santa Monica, 310.393.5244, smseafood.com. Daily. AE, MC, V. WHY** The great retail fish market Santa Monica has long depended upon, as well as a much-needed casual oyster bar, which had been curiously lacking in this oceanside city. **WHAT** This longstanding market has seafood galore, of course, along with beer, wine and everything you might want to rub beneath gills and between tentacles. Skip the café (you'll be wishing you grilled that fish at home or picked up the attractive to-go sushi and salads). But the oyster bar is worth a stop for an inexpensive glass of Prosecco and a changing selection of Fanny Bay, Kumamoto and other varieties.

[Schreiner's Fine Sausages] 🏠 **3417 Ocean View Blvd., Glendale, 818.244.4735, schreinersfinesausage.com. Closed Sun. German. MC, V. WHY** Sausage-making as fine art, and especially worth a visit Thursday through Saturday, when the butchers prepare fresh brats, bangers, Swedish sausage and apple sausage. **WHAT** Schreiner's house-made sausages and cured meats are shipped all over the country, and with good reason. In addition to the wondrous sausages that fill the enormous deli cases, the smokehouse also makes marvelous Canadian bacon and Black Forest ham infused with sweet hickory. All sorts of European groceries, too, including Hungarian noodles and German beer and wines.

[Seafood Paradise] **8955 Garvey Ave., Rosemead, 626.288.2088. Daily. MC, V. WHY** The most jaw-dropping array of live seafood swim in spotless tanks: striped bass, spot prawns, eel, catfish, conch, oysters, cultured abalone, even Taiwanese frogs. **WHAT** A large, clean space is lined with uniform-size tanks holding everything from the sea or rivers you could possibly want to eat—and if you can't find it live, you'll likely find it on ice. Prices are excellent on popular items ($9.99 for live Maine lobster), but you'll pay dearly for the rarities, like live Australian coral trout for $45 a pound. **WHO** Chinese-American home cooks planning a special feast, and some local chefs.

[Taylor's Ol' Fashioned Meat Market] **Howie's Ranch Market, 14 E. Sierra Madre Blvd., Sierra Madre, 626.355.8267. Closed Sun. AE, MC, V. WHY** High-quality marinated meats. **WHAT** Carnivores, rejoice: This is the place to go for prime and choice Midwestern beef, along with marinated meats: tri-tips, carne asada, pollo asada, butterflied legs of lamb. Vegetarians can be diverted by all the beautiful produce.

PRODUCE

[Auntie Em's Organic Produce & Delivery] **4616 Eagle Rock Blvd., Eagle Rock, 323.255.0800, auntieemsdelivery.com. AE, MC, V. WHY** A great option for organic produce delivery for those who aren't lucky enough to score a farm share. **WHAT** Terri Wahl and her team at Auntie Em's cruise several weekly farmers' markets on behalf of their customers, then assemble boxes of produce (and such extras as cheeses and, on request, prepared foods). These boxes are delivered weekly, biweekly or monthly, and the basic price is $42 for a small (good for two people for a week or so) or $62 (for a family of four). 🌱🍴🚚

Shops + Services

🌱 VEGETARIAN ⊙ KID FRIENDLY ☼ PATIO DINING 🚚 DELIVERY 🎩 PRIVATE PARTY

[Figueroa Produce] **6312 N. Figueroa St., Highland Park, 323.255.3663, figueroaproduce.com. Daily. WHY** Fresh produce and some quality grocery items for a Highland Park neighborhood that needed them. Don't miss the bargain grass-fed ground beef. **WHAT** Don't be put off by the location next to a 99 Cent store—this is local entrepreneurial spirit at its best. There's a good-size produce department with fresh stuff; other aisles are stocked with a mix of Middle Eastern, Latin, Asian and the usual-suspect-corner-store items, along with a number of gourmet guilty pleasures, such as Dr. Bob's Scharffen Berger chocolate ice cream and Jones's coffee. The owners are keen to know what the locals want stocked, so pipe up!

[Grow] **1830 N. Sepulveda Blvd., Manhattan Beach, 310.545.2904, growtps.com. Daily. MC, V. WHY** For produce as good as at the better farmers' markets, and not just produce: quality meats and poultry and great local-producer items like baby food, coffee and cookies. And did we mention the free delivery? **WHAT** If every neighborhood had a market like this, life would be perfect. Grow carries local produce, as organic as possible, with varieties you don't see at Vons: blood oranges, unusual varieties of plums, sunchokes, frisée and so on, plus things like Kurobuta hams and impressive party platters. Prices are fair, the people are nice, and they deliver in the South Bay. 🚙

[Hillside Produce Cooperative] **Glassell Park, hillsideproduce-cooperative.org. WHY** Free backyard fruit, vegetables and herbs from thoughtful urban farmers. **WHAT** Actress Hynden Walch started this nonprofit co-op, through which residents from Glassell Park, Silver Lake, Los Feliz and Eagle Rock drop off their excess backyard crops at a pre-set time and place, and Walch and volunteers bag up assortments that are then delivered to all the participants. It's all free, it's all intended to make the world a better place, and Walch's good work has inspired others to organize backyard-produce co-ops (including on the westside and in the Valley, Long Beach, Ventura and Merced). 📷 ♻

[L.A. Wholesale Produce Market] **1601 E. Olympic Blvd., South Park/Fashion District, 213.896.4070. Midnight-8 a.m.; closed Sun. WHY** For fresh, often very high quality fruits, vegetables and flowers at wholesale prices. **WHAT** Get up really early (or stay up really late) and bring cash to shop at ground zero for L.A. produce—everything from mass-grown romaine to organic, small-producer blenheim apricots. Make sure to check out Davalan, which has some of the best fruit here. You have to buy in case quantity, so unless you have a big family, go in with friends. **WHO** Mostly professional buyers for markets and restaurants, but regular citizens show up, too. ☺ 📷

[LOVE Delivery] **310.821.5683, lovedelivery.com. AE, MC, V. WHY** Quality, often-organic produce, delivered weekly to your house by very nice people. **WHAT** For a weekly fee, the LOVE folks will deliver a box of assorted seasonal fruits, vegetables and herbs; you can request certain produce and say which ones you don't want. The quality's about as good as at Gelson's or Whole Foods, and about as pricey, but the service is more convenient—and it can inspire you to try new things. 🛍️🚗

[Marina Farms] **5454 S. Centinela Ave., Culver City, 310.827.3049. Daily. AE, MC, V. WHY** If you can't hit a farmers' market, stop here for quality produce at low prices. **WHAT** It's a little hit-or-miss, but typically (in season) you'll find things like super-sweet pluots, ripe figs, baby carrots, Japanese eggplant, Persian cukes and other less-commonly seen produce.

[Tierra Miguel Foundation] 🏺 **760.742.4213, tierramiguelfarm. org. MC, V. WHY** You're supporting an organic, sustainable farming operation and getting first-rate produce, too. **WHAT** Part of the CSA (Community Supported Agriculture) movement, this nonprofit farm sells "farm shares"—you pay an annual fee to support the farm, and in return you get a case of exceptionally delicious fruits and vegetables every week or two. The produce is delivered to several drop-off spots around town, so you'll have to do some driving to get it. At this writing, there's a waiting list. 🌿🛍️

[Valley Produce] **18345 Vanowen St., Reseda, 818.609.1955, valleyproducemarket.com. Daily. Middle Eastern/Indian. AE, MC, V. WHY** Every herb, green or fruit you could ever want, at great prices. **WHAT** With a focus on Persian, Middle Eastern and Indian foods, this produce and grocery market has bargain prices on avocados, stone fruits and lettuces, along with a vast selection of Mediterranean spices, Indian teas, Middle Eastern breads and discounted olive oils. Be warned that on weekends, cart traffic moves as slowly as the 405 on Friday afternoon. Other locations in Simi Valley and Valencia. 🛒

SPECIALTY & SMALL MARKETS

[Alpine Village Market] **833 W. Torrance Blvd., Torrance, 310.327.2483, alpinevillage.net. Daily. German. AE, MC, V. WHY** Some of the city's best sausages, plus a chance to pick up some fresh German rye with your bierschinken. **WHAT** Sure, it looks like a kitschy Bavarian tourist trap from afar, but this market inside the Alpine Plaza is an outpost of fine, authentic sausage making. It has its own smoking facilities and turns out sausage several times a week—a freshness factor that means less salt is needed as a preservative. There's also an immense selection of salumi, as well as country paté, European-style hams and lowfat and low-sodium sausages. The bakery turns out German rye breads, strudel, kuchen and tortes.

Shops + Services

🛍️ **VEGETARIAN** ☺ **KID FRIENDLY** ☼ **PATIO DINING** 🚗 **DELIVERY** 🎉 **PRIVATE PARTY**

[Angelo's Italian Deli] **190 La Verne Ave., Long Beach, 562.434.1977. Closed Mon. Italian. MC, V. WHY** To wallow in the flavors of Italy. **WHAT** The size of this market, hidden just off Belmont Shore's 2nd Street, belies the wonderful things found inside: pizza dough, fresh burrata from Gioia, a dazzling array of olive oils and balsamic vinegars, dried and frozen pasta, cheeses, tinned anchovies and tuna, every sort of cured meat, fresh cannoli, olives, even an Italian antacid, which you'll need. Great sandwiches are made to take out. Another branch is just across the OC line in Seal Beach. **WHO** Home chefs and party-throwers who'll make a detour for good ingredients.

[Bangkok Market] **4757 Melrose Ave., East Hollywood, 323.662.9705. Daily. Thai. AE, MC, V. WHY** For everything needed to concoct a Thai feast, from fresh lemongrass, kaffir lime leaves and Thai basil to galangal and great deals on canned coconut milk and other essentials. **WHAT** The first place in L.A. to find exotic Thai ingredients is still owned by the family of popular local chef and culinary teacher Jet Tila. 🍽️

[Bangluck Market] **5170 Hollywood Blvd., East Hollywood, 323.660.8000. Daily. Thai. MC, V. WHY** All your Thai and Southeast Asian cooking needs packed into a small Hollywood market that shares a parking lot with the great Sanamluang Café—so allow time to stop for some pad see ew before or after you shop. **WHAT** Besides the expected range of produce and groceries needed to make Thai food, this little market has a great selection of inexpensive cookware and utensils, as well as products from Singapore and the Philippines. Look for the fresh kaffir lime leaves, palm sugar, tiny eggplants, curries, fish sauces and frozen banana leaves.

[Bangluck Market] **12980 Sherman Way, North Hollywood, 818.765.1088. Daily. Thai. MC, V. WHY** All your Thai and Southeast Asian cooking needs. **WHAT** Besides the expected range of produce and groceries needed to make Thai food, this packed market has a great selection of inexpensive cookware and utensils, as well as products from Singapore and the Philippines. Look for the fresh kaffir lime leaves, palm sugar, tiny eggplants, curries, fish sauces and frozen banana leaves.

[Bauducco's Italian Market] **2839 Agoura Rd., Westlake Village, 805.495.4623, bauduccosrestaurant.com. Daily. Italian. AE, MC, V. WHY** Housemade Sicilian bread, either to take home or to have the deli make into a chicken-parmesan or sausage sandwich, as well as good pizzas. **WHAT** Fabulous Sicilian bread and rolls are baked on-site at this 40-year-old family business, where the deli cases are stocked with house-made sausages and salumi, both imported and domestic. The voluptuous sandwiches, pizzas and prepared foods are good, and the shelves hold everything you need to cook *la bella cucina*—but if you don't want to cook, there's a restaurant, too. **WHO** Lunch-breakers stopping for a sandwich and shoppers staring at the deli case. 🚗

[Bay Cities Italian Deli & Bakery] 1517 Lincoln Blvd., Santa Monica, 310.395.8279, baycitiesitaliandeli.com. Closed Mon. Italian. MC, V. **WHY** The Godmother sub, the meatball sandwich, olives from the deli case and that red-checked-tablecloth Italian vibe. **WHAT** A classic Italian deli and grocery store, Bay Cities deserves the longevity award for making it in Santa Monica since the '20s. The deli packs 'em in for olives, salads and sandwiches, including the famous Godmother, a massive heap of Genoa salami, mortadella, capicola, ham, prosciutto and provolone. The aisles are lined with imported pasta, olive oil, vinegar, anchovies, cookies and wine. The bread's baked on-site, and if it isn't as good as those crusty loaves in Florence, it's a lot cheaper than a plane ticket. **WHO** East Coasters hungry for a taste of home.

[Bombay Spiceland] 8650 Reseda Blvd., Northridge, 818.701.9383. Daily. Indian. AE, MC, V. **WHY** Think of it as the Dal House—the variety of beans and lentils is extraordinary. **WHAT** For a warehouse-style Indian market, Bombay Spiceland is amazingly well stocked. Whether you're looking for turmeric root, medicinal neem leaves, Bollywood's latest video rental or a phenomenal selection of *dals*, the beans and lentils central to Indian cooking, chances are you'll find it here. And don't miss the *chevdas*, those Indian snacks in the glass case near the front door—they're junk-food tasty but actually nutritious. 🚗

[Broome St. General Store] 2912 Rowena Ave., Silver Lake, 323.570.0405. Daily. AE, MC, V. **WHY** Coffee, sandwiches and desserts to eat in the front yard of this old house, plus simple-chic kitchenware (new and vintage) and that quintessential Silver Lake necessity, Dude No. 1 Beard Oil. **WHAT** Where Zanzabelle and Freight once cohabitated is now a fetching food-focused general store and café. You can pick up retro glass carafes, Morris Kitchen ginger syrup, bloody mary mix, sandwiches and salads from Heirloom LA, treats (salted caramel croissants, cheddar-bacon scones) from Cake Monkey and Valerie, and coffee from Gimme! Look for events, like Fried Chicken Fridays. ☼

[Claro's] 🏠 1003 E. Valley Blvd., San Gabriel, 626.288.2026, claros. com. Closed Wed. Italian. AE, MC, V. **WHY** Prepared take-home dishes like lasagne and a vast selection of imported pasta, cookies, breads and hard-to-find items from Italy, like pasta machines and espresso pots. **WHAT** This well-stocked, old-school Italian market and deli has been around since 1948, starting here, and it now has five other locations. (This was once an Italian-immigrant neighborhood, which is hard to imagine in this Chinese era.) The deli offers sandwiches (huge and delicious), meats, antipasti and hot dishes. The perfect place to stock up for a party. **WHO** Third-generation loyalists and people proud of their Sicilian blood, even if it's only a little. 🚗

🍃 **VEGETARIAN** ⊙ **KID FRIENDLY** ☼ **PATIO DINING** 🚗 **DELIVERY** 🍴 **PRIVATE PARTY**

[Continental Shop] 1619 Wilshire Blvd., Santa Monica, 310.453.8655, thecontinentalshop.com. Daily. English. AE, MC, V. WHY This is L.A.'s supply depot for all things British, from taped TV shows and magazines to airline tickets and, yes, food. **WHAT** If you've got a craving for English bangers, a Cornish pasty or imported frozen Yorkshire pudding, head for the freezer in this tightly packed, slightly dowdy emporium. The cooler holds clotted Devon cream and packaged Stilton and Colby cheeses, and the shelves are filled with single-estate teas, shortbreads, jams, jellies, tinned biscuits and candy bars. **WHO** Homesick ex-pats and persnickety Anglophiles.

[Cookbook] 1549 Echo Park Ave., Echo Park, 213.250.1900, cookbookla.com. Daily. MC, V. WHY You're feeling nostalgic for Drucker's Store from *Green Acres*. **WHAT** A tiny, well-edited neighborhood mercantile selling gourmet pantry items is hard to find outside of Brooklyn or the Bay Area, but now Echo Park has Cookbook. Each week a changing roster of takeout foods centers around a cookbook — or you can buy the book and the ingredients, which range from specialty flours, grains, local fresh produce and organic dairy to Brooklyn Brine pickles and cult Mast Brothers chocolate. **WHO** Echo Parksters and displaced Brooklyn and Oakland food sceners. ♻

[Cube Marketplace] 615 N. La Brea Ave. , Melrose, 323.939.1148, cubemarketplace.com. Closed Sun. Italian. AE, MC, V. WHY For its fresh and dried housemade pastas, along with an array of high-end olives, cheeses, salumi, sauces, olive oils and vinegars. **WHAT** Originally called the Divine Pasta Company, this place is now a high-end café and marketplace that stocks more than 85 varieties of cheese; salumi from Salumi Salame, the Fatted Calf and Pio Tosini; an excellent selection of oils, vinegars, salts and syrups; and such foodie essentials as capers, fresh pesto and Laguiole knives. **WHO** The Eaters, the Shoppers, the Wine Bar Hoppers, but not so much the Cooks and the Dinner-Party Throwers.

[E. Waldo Ward] 🏛 **273 E. Highland Ave., Sierra Madre, 626.355.1218, waldoward.com. Closed Sun. AE, MC, V. WHY** Fantastic blood-orange marmalade, thin-sliced bread-and-butter pickles, pickled peaches, boysenberry jam and such modern creations as raspberry-chipotle sauce. **WHAT** This fourth-generation preserves maker still occupies the original family factory and citrus farm hidden in plain sight in impossibly atmospheric Sierra Madre. It does the soul good to see places like this not just surviving, but thriving (thanks to the internet and savvy management by the founder's grandson, Richard Ward, and his son, Jeff Ward). Worth a trek.

[Epicure Imports] 6900 Beck Ave., North Hollywood, 818.985.9800. Open to the public only for occasional sales. AE, MC, V. WHY Vacuum-packed fresh foie gras, French nut oils, whole French cheeses and some wine buys. **WHAT** Several times a year (get on the e-mail list) this wholesaler of gourmet imported products opens its doors to the public, permitting a sometimes-chaotic supermarket sweep through aisles of plus-size food items (three kilograms of Valrhona dark chocolate, anyone?). The real gold mine is the refrigerated storage room, where the imported cheeses, hams and smoked salmon live. Bring a jacket. **WHO** Hardcore food lovers.

[Farmers Market] 6333 W. 3rd St., Fairfax District, 323.933.9211, farmersmarketla.com. Daily. **WHY** To people-watch, graze, write your novel and experience L.A.'s great cultural stew pot. **WHAT** It's not easy to describe our love for this mostly covered outdoor market. The love affair began in childhood, when we begged our mothers for English toffee from Littlejohn's; continued through high school, when we would hang out at Du-par's for hours; and will no doubt carry on through our dotage, when we will join the other 90-year-olds meeting friends for coffee and doughnuts (at Bob's, of course). The produce isn't up to Santa Monica Farmers' Market standards, but no matter— from the tacos at Lotería, to the salade de chevre chaud at Mr. Marcel, to the peppermint-stick ice cream at Bennett's, we adore every inch of this place. **WHO** Everyone you can possibly imagine.

[Follow Your Heart Market & Café] 21825 Sherman Way, Canoga Park, 818.348.3240, followyourheart.com. Daily. AE, MC, V. **WHY** An all-around well-stocked natural-foods market with good quality products at somewhat lower prices than at Whole Paycheck. **WHAT** The '70s live at this good-hearted natural-foods café and market, which was, in fact, founded in 1970. Besides organic produce, whole grains and all the expected natural foods, you'll find homeopathic remedies, green cleaning products and some home-décor items. The café in back is good for a healthy meal or takeout food.

[Froma on Melrose] 7960 Melrose Ave., Melrose, 323.653.3700, fromaonmelrose.com. Daily. AE, MC, V. **WHY** It's one of the very few places in town to get the extraordinary (and expensive) jamón ibérico de bellota. **WHAT** This small, quality shop stocks top-tier products to assemble a luxe Hollywood Bowl picnic or pick up delicious sandwiches. The high-end charcuterie includes the famous La Quercia domestic prosciutto, chorizo, bresaola and soppressata. You'll also find raw-milk cheeses and caviar, and you can special-order almost anything, including Kobe beef.

[Galco's Soda Pop Shop] 5702 York Blvd., Highland Park, 323.255.7115, sodapopstop.com. Daily. MC, V. **WHY** Because it's a vast wonderland of fizzy drinks of every conceivable flavor, color and container—plus a seriously old-school candy counter. **WHAT** For underage drinking, no place in the world beats Galco's, which stocks more than 250 kinds of soda (as well as a good selection of global beer).

Shops + Services

VEGETARIAN KID FRIENDLY PATIO DINING DELIVERY PRIVATE PARTY

Looking for coffee soda, authentic Kickapoo Joy Juice or Guayaba from Brazil? Boy, have you come to the right place. You'll also find a strange and wonderful array of near-forgotten regional candy, including Owyhee Idaho Spuds, Mallo Cups, Chick-O-Sticks and bubblegum cigarettes. And it ships. **WHO** Hipster kids, nostalgic baby boomers, immigrants seeking a fix of homeland carbonation. ☺

[Grand Central Market] 🔒 317 S. Broadway, Downtown, 213.624.2378, grandcentralsquare.com. Daily. **WHY** Stands specializing in very cheap produce of reasonable quality, rows of dried peppers and tubs of prepared mole, candies and staples, as well as lots of lunch counters. Make sure to get a taco at Tacos Tumbras a Tomas. **WHAT** A throwback to when Downtown really was the center of L.A., Grand Central Market is both a trip back in time and a daily shopping and eating destination for locals. The vast indoor market is filled with stands selling produce, meat, snacks, juices and such lunchtime staples as tacos and teriyaki. **WHO** Immigrant Latinos from the neighborhood, a few Downtown-dwelling yuppies and, at lunchtime, hordes descending from surrounding offices and jury duty. 🗺

[Guidi Marcello] 🔒 1649 10th St., Santa Monica, 310.452.6277, guidimarcello.com. Closed Sun. Italian. MC, V. **WHY** It's like stepping into the neighborhood *negozio di alimentari* you frequented on your last trip to Italy. **WHAT** This family-run, 14,000-square-foot warehouse and teeny showroom teem with "*tutti prodotti tipici regionali*." It's all here and it's all Italian: excellent dried pastas (Spinosi! Columbro!); canned tuna, beans and San Marzano tomatoes; rice and faro; chocolates and nougat; wine and beer; olives and marinated mushrooms; and a nice selection of salumi, cheeses and butters. You'll even find gold-flecked truffle salt and honey. If you're having a party, check out the freezer case for bags of ready-to-heat arancini and stuffed zucchini blossoms. **WHO** Just about every L.A. Italian chef (Giada's a regular), and last time we were in, Oscar-winning screenwriter David Seidler was deep in conversation with the owner.

[Holland American Market] 10343 E. Artesia Blvd., Bellflower, 562.925.6914, 1dutchmall.com. Daily. Dutch/Indonesian. MC, V. **WHY** Come for the wooden shoes, stay for the sambal oelek. **WHAT** You could come here for the Dutch groceries (cheeses, herrings, pastries) that the name promises, but the bigger draw for many shoppers is the enormous stock of Indonesian foods. *Bumbus* (spice bases for curries) and chile-based sambals are on display, along with other goodies, such as the essential sauce ketjap, fermented shrimp and Indonesian laurel leaves.

[India Sweets & Spices] 🔒 3126 Los Feliz Blvd., Atwater, 323.345.0360; 22011 Sherman Way, Canoga Park, 818.887.0868; indiasweetsandspices.us. Daily. Indian. AE, MC, V. **WHY** The large selec-

🔒 ESSENTIALLY L.A. ☺ LATE ♥ ROMANTIC 🗺 VALUE 🔊 QUIET ♻ SUSTAINABLE

tion of rice, teas, frozen items and all the ingredients to make a world-class curry. **WHAT** Take a trip to India by way of Los Feliz or Canoga Park, exploring the rows of unusual chutneys and well-priced spices, then noshing at the popular vegetarian cafeteria—it's known for its house-made sweets, including several flavors of kulfi ice cream. **WHO** Indian families from miles around, and local hipsters who appreciate the reasonably priced steam-table curries and fresh dosas. 🍴🍶

[Koreatown Plaza Market] **928 S. Western Ave., Koreatown, 213.382.1234, koreatownplaza.com. Daily. Korean/Asian. AE, MC, V.** **WHY** An extraordinary variety of mild and spicy *panchan*—those small, flavorful side dishes at the heart of a Korean meal—plus validated parking. **WHAT** This contemporary market in a Euro-chic shopping mall features an impressive array of Korean prepared foods, notably panchan, including marinated crab, pickled baby cucumbers, spicy squid strips and garlic stem salad. Other standouts involve *mandu* (gyoza-type dumplings), fresh-frozen sea vegetables, and kim chee in its many forms—from the fiery hot stuff involving cabbage or "leek" (actually Chinese chive) to a cooling, salty variety made with white radish. The enormous meat department offers many cuts suitable for all kinds of Asian cookery.

[Locali] **5825 Franklin Ave., Hollywood, 323.466.1360, localiyours.com. Daily. MC, V. WHY** Locally sourced edibles from some of our favorite producers. Don't miss the Ruby Jewel ice cream sandwiches—they may come all the way from Portland, but they rock. **WHAT** Locali packs a lot of interesting products into a tiny storefront, and they're all either sustainable, organic and/or local—beer from Dales Bros. and the Bruery, sandwiches and salads made from local foods, Carmela Ice Cream, La Guera Tamalera tamales, prepared food from vegan suppliers, frozen foods, coffee and snacks. Books, shopping bags, water bottles and other tchotchkes for the green lifestyle are stocked as well—even a handy countertop compost bin. ♻🍶�CarDelivery

[Ma 'n Pa's Grocery] **346 Roycroft Ave., Long Beach, 562.438.4084. Daily. AE, MC, V. WHY** One of the finest small markets around, tiny and personal and packed with good things to eat. **WHAT** Oh, how we love this wee little market in an old house! There's the quality produce, of course, and the good meat and fish. And those amazing scones made by the French guy who sells them at the farmers' markets, and the baguettes made by Babette. Oh, and the stupendous homemade beef and turkey jerky. and the burgers to eat on the picnic table outside, not to mention the daily takeout entrées (Wednesday is fried-chicken day!). You'll pay for all this, of course, but it's worth it. **WHO** A devoted cadre of neighbors.

[The Market at Santa Monica Place] **395 Santa Monica Place, Santa Monica, 310.394.1049, santamonicaplace.com/market.**

Shops + Services

🍶 VEGETARIAN ⊙ KID FRIENDLY ☼ PATIO DINING 🚗 DELIVERY 🎩 PRIVATE PARTY

Daily. AE, MC, V. **WHY** For the chance to take home amazing edibles both decadent and divine—or eat them on the spot. **WHAT** More like Harrod's food hall or Eataly NYC than the familiar food court, this collection of shops will put your appetite on sensory overload: Primi al Mercato (from Piero Selvaggio of Valentino) offers fresh pastas in a dozen varieties, including squid ink, gluten-free and beet-stuffed. His adjacent Norcino Salumeria stocks more than 20 Italian cured meats—guanciale, arista, parmacotto—along with a dozen of the world's best cheeses. Get your custom blend of organic single-origin coffee at Groundworks, your small-batch ice cream in inspired market flavors at N'Ice Cream and Beachy Cream; your handmade chocolates at L'Artisan, your pretzels and soufflés at Röckenwagner's; and your locally sourced pantry ingredients, sandwiches and takeout meals at the Curious Palate. **WHO** Culinary hedonists with money to spend.

[Market Gourmet] 1800 Abbot Kinney Blvd., Venice, 310.305.9800, marketgourmet.biz. Daily. AE, MC, V. **WHY** A great place to find gourmet pantry items from around the world, from Australian marmite to Israeli olive oil. Ex-pats and returning travelers will delight at the nostalgic brands here. **WHAT** This quirky little market has an international focus and a great selection of imported goodies (check out the tapenades, ploufs, flours and Asian sauces), as well as fantastic homemade soup, a compact but diverse cheese area and imported teas and coffees. A fabulous place to put together a food-lover's gift basket.

[Mercado Buenos Aires] 7540 Sepulveda Blvd., Van Nuys, 818.786.0522. Daily. Argentinean. AE, MC, V. **WHY** Excellent meat dishes in the café, and quality Argentinean and South American goods in the market. **WHAT** Part deli, part butcher, part market and part restaurant, this place is all things to all Argentineans. The bakery cases hold wonderful pastries, both sweet and savory: spinach-cheese pie, ham torta and, of course, a variety of empanadas. Elsewhere, look for imported Spanish and Italian prosciutto, delicate chicken-vegetable roll, matambre, tongue in vinaigrette, Chilean sea salt and olive oil mayonnaise. **WHO** Who knew there were so many Argentineans in the Valley?

[Monsieur Marcel] Farmers Market, 6333 W. 3rd St., Fairfax District, 323.939.7792, mrmarcel.com. Daily. French. AE, MC, V. **WHY** High-quality cheeses, olives, wine, duck confit and every preserve and oil made by man, as well as some everyday grocery-store essentials.
WHAT This large gourmet market tucked into a corner of the Farmers Market offers one-stop shopping for Francophiles and, especially, cheese lovers—the cheese selection is dazzling. The selection of epicurean products is vast, including many private-label lines, and there's a good array of imported and domestic wines as well. Make sure to allow time for *dejeuner* at the adjacent outdoor café.

[Monte Carlo Deli] 3103 W. Magnolia Blvd., Burbank, 818.845.3516, montecarlodeli.com. Daily. Italian. AE, MC, V. **WHY** Prosciutto di Parma, fresh pizza dough, canned and marinated anchovies, excellent cold cuts. **WHAT** Despite adding a gelato bar and some tables at one end of the store, this venerable Italian grocery thankfully refuses to gentrify. It carries all the necessities of life, including Illy espresso beans, Italian sausage, Rustichella d'Abruzzo pasta, salt-packed capers, fresh basil, Grana Padano, mascarpone and biscotti. **WHO** Older native Italians and younger foodies.

[Naples Gourmet Grocer] 5650 E. 2nd St., Long Beach, 562.439.6518. Daily. AE, MC, V. **WHY** Cowgirl Creamery cheeses, Fra' Mani salumi, Breadbar breads, delicious boutique sodas and lots more gourmet goodies. **WHAT** The tiny neighborhood of Naples has its own little Zabar's in this market, stocked with the best American food products out there—from such places as Niman Ranch, Paul Bertolli, Dr. Bob and Little Flower Candy Co.—and a few carefully chosen imports, too. The deli makes great sandwiches, and the cheese and salumi platters show up at the best Long Beach parties.

[The Oaks Market] 1915 N. Bronson Ave., Hollywood, 323.871.8894, theoaksgourmet.com. Daily. AE, MC, V. **WHY** A very good and surprisingly affordable selection of wine, beer and retro and rare sodas, as well as an extensive gourmet-to-go menu. **WHAT** Despite its name, this "market" doesn't try to compete with Gelson's across the street for your upscale-grocery needs. Instead, it serves just a few niches by offering a large and good-value collection of wine and beer, a coffee and juice bar, a coffee roaster and a good selection of small-producer packaged foods, like Dewar's old-fashioned candy chews from Bakersfield, Humboldt Fog cheese and exotic oils and vinegars. Excellent café fare, too. 🖺

[Olives Gourmet Grocer] 3510 E. Broadway, Long Beach, 562.439.7758; 5000 E. 2nd St., Belmont Shore, 562.343.5580; olivesgourmetgrocer.com. Daily. AE, MC, V. **WHY** For a food-lover's home away from home, not to mention a good place to pick up a rotisserie chicken for dinner or a platter for that potluck. **WHAT** The Broadway store is a compact, clean-lined gourmet market with particularly strong offerings in charcuterie and cheese, sophisticated sandwiches, sauces and oils, and prepared dishes to take home. You'll also find an olive bar (natch), a salad bar and just enough staples. Fun cooking classes, too. The Belmont Shore shop is twice the size of its parent, allowing room for a cheerful eat-in café.

[Owen's Market] 9769 W. Pico Blvd., Century City, 310.553.8181, owensla.com. Daily. AE, MC, V. **WHY** For posh prepared foods and high-end groceries, delivered for westsiders. **WHAT** Mindy Weiss, a high-end event planner, turned this little market into a sort of foodie

Shops + Services

🖺 VEGETARIAN ☺ KID FRIENDLY ✿ PATIO DINING 🚗 DELIVERY 🏠 PRIVATE PARTY

boutique. Besides basic grocery-store staples, you'll find naturally raised Angus beef from Montana Legend, prepared foods from Pasadena's Kitchen for Exploring Foods, desserts from the Cake Divas, eco-friendly cleaning products and an organic salad bar. If you have to ask the price of the cupcakes, you can't afford them. 🚗

[Penzeys Spices] 🏛 **1347 4th St., Santa Monica, 310.917.5577; 21301 Hawthorne Blvd., Torrance, 310.406.3877; penzeys.com. Daily. MC, V. WHY** *Kala jeera* (black cumin) and French four spice, and knowledgeable staffers who can tell you what to do with them. **WHAT** This Wisconsin-based chain is the Grand Cru of spice shops. At both the newer Santa Monica branch and in Torrance, you'll find a dizzying selection of chile powder, cinnamon and pepper blends. The cute retro look in the baking area is a candyland of Indonesian and Vietnamese cinnamon, crystallized and powdered gingers and such hard-to-find specialty ingredients as *mahlab* (sour cherry pits). **WHO** Farmers' market shoppers, home bakers, chefs and pastry chefs.

[Petrossian] **321 N. Robertson Blvd., West Hollywood, 310.271.6300, petrossian.com. Daily. Russian/French. AE, MC, V. WHY** To pick up a great gift for a caviar lover—and it's not all $364-an-ounce Royal Sevruga stuff, either. **WHAT** This Euro-moderne West Hollywood outpost of the Parisian fancy-food emporium has a caviar-and-crème fraîche décor, 1950s Hollywood glam photos and two big communal tables in the shop for tasting the goods. Shimmering cases hold of Petrossian products: caviars, smoked fish, pâtés, Champagnes, chocolate truffles... all the essentials of life, at least for some people. ♥

[Roma Italian Deli & Grocery] **918 N. Lake Ave., Pasadena, 626.797.7748. Daily. Italian. AE, MC, V. WHY** Excellent Italian prosciutti, cheeses, sausages, salumi and gnocchi, sold with style and lots of sample tastes. **WHAT** Roma's fans are so passionate that they are almost a cult, and their leader is Rosario, who confidently proclaims his sandwiches, prosciutti and cheeses to be the best in the world. We're not sure about that, but they are damn good. Some swear by the inexpensive produce, but we don't. 🗺

[Samosa House] **11510 W. Washington Blvd., Culver City, 310.398.6766, samosahouse.net. Daily. Indian. AE, MC, V. WHY** One of the best-stocked Indian markets in town, with savvy owners who do their best to help customers hunt down elusive products. **WHAT** The Punjabi owners stock ingredients for all kinds of Indian cooking, and they pride themselves on offering such exotic and hard-to-find foods as fresh curry leaves. And if you're looking for tandoori paste readymade to smear on chicken or lamb before broiling, they've got it—part of its huge selection of "convenience" foods. The café offers an allvegetarian buffet, too.

[Savor the Flavor] 11 Kersting Ct., Sierra Madre, 626.355.5153, savortheflavor.net. Daily. AE, MC, V. **WHY** A terrific selection of gifts for food lovers; good samples, too. **WHAT** This storybook shop in storybook Sierra Madre specializes in edibles, with some tableware and cookbooks thrown in for good measure. They love building custom gift baskets or helping you decide between the Chardonnay brittle, blueberry-acacia gummy pandas, and locally made dry rub for meats. You'll find sauces, marinades, soup mixes, vinegars, cookies and sweets galore, some from their own label and some from Stonewall, Barefoot Contessa and Robert Rothschild. **WHO** Local ladies-who-shop and day-trippers exploring Sierra Madre.

[Selam Market] 5534 W. Pico Blvd., Mid-City, 323.935.5567. Daily. Ethiopian. MC, V. **WHY** Neophytes can get a taste of the authentic Ethiopian culinary experience, and seasoned cooks can find exactly what they need (including three kinds of cardamom and green coffee). **WHAT** The meats are cut specifically for Ethiopian dishes, and the spice blends—including berberé, awazé and Nit'kr k'ibé spiced butter—are made in-house. Also on offer in this butcher shop/deli/grocery store are peppers, fenugreek and teff flour, if you'd like try your hand at making your own injera bread. (Those less brave can buy the Ethiopian bread ready-made.)

[Spice Station] 3819 W. Sunset Blvd., Silver Lake, 323.660.2565, spicestationsilverlake.com. Closed Tues. **WHY** All manner of fresh and fragrant exotic spices and a tea annex, too. **WHAT** Hidden down a Sunset Junction passageway, Spice Station is filled with spices and dried herbs from around the world. With dozens of salts (ghost pepper salt!), chiles and colorful flavored sugars, the shop offers many ways to make cooking exciting, and the gift sets are handy. Check out the custom blends, including a smoky chile mix and Swimming Fish rub. More than 100 types of tea are sold in the annex next door. Another location at 2305 Main St., Santa Monica. **WHO** Adventurous home cooks, tea lovers.

[Teheran Market] 1417 Wilshire Blvd., Santa Monica, 310.393.6719. Daily. Persian/Middle Eastern. AE, MC, V. **WHY** Hard-to-find Persian and Middle Eastern ingredients at bargain prices. **WHAT** A great feta selection, unusual breads and baked goods, good spices and low prices on olives, fresh herbs and basmati rice draw cooks to this mid-size Middle Eastern market. Check out the Al Wadi hummus—it tastes like homemade. 🗺

[Vinh Loi Tofu] 🏠 18625 Sherman Way, Reseda, 818.996.9779, vinhloitofu.com. Daily. Asian. MC, V. **WHY** Fresh tofu made on-site, as well as some vegan grocery essentials, including soy milk, tofu pudding and packaged vegan foods. **WHAT** Kevin Tran is L.A.'s king of fresh tofu. Come here to buy the good stuff, and allow time to eat in

🍃 VEGETARIAN ⊙ KID FRIENDLY ✿ PATIO DINING 🚚 DELIVERY 🎩 PRIVATE PARTY

his amazing vegan Vietnamese café while you're there. **WHO** A steady stream of regulars, as diverse as they come: Asian chefs, vegan moms with toddlers in tow, bikers, women in hijabs. ⟳◗

SPECIALTY SERVICES

[Culinary Historians of Southern California] **630 W. 5th St., Downtown, chscsite.org. WHY** Support the L.A. Public Library through blast-from-the-past food adventures. **WHAT** This affiliate of LAPL supports the impressive Central Library Culinary Collection through such events such as Californio ranchero barbecues and Little India tours, and it hosts excellent free monthly lectures from historians and food trenders, including Andy Smith, Paula Wolfert, Charles Perry and Jonathan Gold on topics from medieval Arab cookery to the current Sriracha craze. **WHO** Gen-Y to octogenarian gastronomic enthusiasts, both professional and non.

[Kirk's Urban Bees] **323.646.9651, kirksurbanbees.com. MC, V. WHY** Doesn't everyone want to be a beekeeper? **WHAT** Like dog walking and closet organizing, beekeeping turns out to be a task that can be outsourced. Typically urban beekeeper Kirk Anderson removes unwanted swarms and moves them to a new home that wants them. Once moved, the bees stay in their adopted yards, and he maintains the hive, which consists of monthly visits and a honey harvest in June. He doesn't feed them corn syrup, artificial pollen, chemicals or medicines. You can also buy jars of his locally produced honey online, and take a beekeeping class if you'd like to learn how to do it yourself. ⟳

[Melting Pot Food Tours] **424.247.9666, meltingpottours.com. WHY** Warm-hearted tours for people who like to wander, explore and nosh. **WHAT** Sisters Lisa and Diane Scalia are friendly, energetic and hungry, so it fits that they've gone into the walking-tour business. Their repertoire centers around three three-hour tours: the original, which explores Farmers Market and ventures onto 3rd Street, one in Old Pasadena, and a new one in East L.A. They find the worthwhile places (in Old Pas, you'll visit mom 'n pop places, not the Cheesecake Factory), and they weave in history, architecture and culture.

[Six Taste] ⌂ **888.313.0936, sixtaste.com. MC, V. WHY** Enthusiastic tours of some of L.A.'s best ethnic-food enclaves, including Thai Town, Little Tokyo and the Chinese neighborhoods of the San Gabriel Valley. **WHAT** Jeff Okita and Alex Tao love L.A. and love to eat, and they've channeled those passions into seven tasting tours: Little Tokyo, Santa Monica, Hollywood, Thai Town, Downtown L.A. and two in the San Gabriel Valley, one focused on dumplings and the other on a more diverse range of Chinese food. The $65 walking tours are usually four hours and include tasting stops at very good spots. Tourists are the main market, but these are great for locals, too.

⌂ ESSENTIALLY L.A.　⟳ LATE　♥ ROMANTIC　▣ VALUE　♪ QUIET　⟳ SUSTAINABLE

SUPERMARKETS

[99 Ranch Market] 🔒 140 W. Valley Blvd., San Gabriel, 626.307.8899, 99ranch.com. Daily. Chinese. AE, MC, V. **WHY** Great prices and an amazingly varied selection of Chinese grocery items. Worth a trip for the noodle case alone. **WHAT** The Gelson's of Chinese supermarkets, except instead of having 60 kinds of breakfast cereal, 99 Ranch has 60 kinds of fish sauce. An absolute must-visit, with a dazzling array of Chinese (not so much Korean or other Asian cultures) produce, sauces, noodles, kitchenware and ingredients, as well as terrific (and terrifically cheap) live seafood. Branches in Monterey Park, Rowland Heights and beyond. **WHO** A pan-Asian clientele, including tourists, locals, bargain-hunters and cooks. 🖘

[Beverly Glen Marketplace] 2964 N. Beverly Glen Cir., Bel-Air, 310.475.0829. Daily. AE, MC, V. **WHY** For small-town service with big-city products, from fine wines and prime meats to frozen organic baby food and boutique-label chocolates. **WHAT** This swank little market doesn't have 50 kinds of toilet paper, but it has everything a Bel-Air resident might need, including artisanal cheeses and sushi. There's an espresso bar, too. **WHO** Movie stars and captains of industry, as well as their personal assistants and nannies.

[Bob's Market] 1650 Ocean Park Blvd., Santa Monica, 310.452.2493, bobsmkt.com. Daily. AE, MC, V. **WHY** Hand-cut steaks, house-made sausages and excellent prepared salads and sandwiches. The butcher will even custom make your favorite sausage if you bring in the recipe and buy at least five pounds of it. **WHAT** A throwback in the best sense of the word, Bob's has personal service, a quality butcher counter, an excellent deli, carefully chosen produce and a well-edited wine collection — and the prices aren't as high as you'd expect for an indie market. It serves as a community center in Ocean Park. **WHO** Ocean Park locals who know the employees by name. 🚗

[Erewhon Natural Foods Market] 7660 Beverly Blvd., Beverly/ Third, 323.937.0777, erewhonmarket.com. Daily. AE, MC, V. **WHY** The salad bar, the sushi bar, the soups and the competitive prices. **WHAT** Before Whole Foods stores were popping up like so many organic chanterelles in a rain forest, Erewhon ("Nowhere" spelled backwards, sort of) was selling natural foods. It stocks hormone-free chicken and organic eggs but sells no red meat; bulk grains, beans and dried fruits but nothing made with white sugar; and imported olive oils but nothing made with hydrogenated vegetable fats. A spotless, well-organized, new-age market with good prices. **WHO** Tie-dyed '70s relics meet glam vegan twentysomething development girls. 🖘😊🛒

[Howie's Ranch Market] 6580 N. San Gabriel Blvd., San Gabriel, 626.286.8871. Daily. AE, MC, V. **WHY** Three reasons: Old-fashioned service with a smile. Famed meats from Alexander's. And classic

🌿 VEGETARIAN ⊙ KID FRIENDLY ☼ PATIO DINING 🚗 DELIVERY 🎩 PRIVATE PARTY

goodies from Lisa's Bakery. **WHAT** This compact, all-purpose market is worth a detour. Look for the Harris Ranch beef, dry-aged prime cuts, excellent marinated poultry and carne asada, and locally made empanadas and tamales. The wine selection is very good, too. And it delivers! **WHO** Seniors who've been coming here for decades, and foodies coming from miles away. 🚗

[Jons Marketplace] **3667 W. 3rd St., Koreatown, 213.382.5701; 12122 Magnolia Blvd., North Hollywood, 818.985.4780; 1234 N. La Brea Ave., Hollywood, 323.962.2429; 18135 Sherman Way, Reseda, 818.758.3422; 1717 W. Glenoaks Blvd., Glendale, 818.244.2575; jonsmarketplace.com. Daily. AE, MC, V. WHY** The cheapest pita in town, a dizzying selection of Eastern European sausages and meats, fresh Middle Eastern cheeses and giant tubs of yogurt, as well as imported jams, candies and spices. The merchandise varies by the density of the ethnic groups in the area. **WHAT** This small chain specializes in ethnic groceries, primarily Middle Eastern and Latino items, depending on the neighborhood. They all have great delis and good produce (you might have to dig a little) at very low prices. 💲

[Koreatown Galleria Market] 🏛 **3250 W. Olympic Blvd., Koreatown, 323.733.6000, koreatowngalleria.com. Daily. Korean/Asian. AE, MC, V. WHY** Paradise for Korean food-lovers and cooks, right in the middle of a glitzy shopping mall. While you're in the mall, check out Ho Won Dang, which sells special-occasion cookies. Try the tiny yellow cookies (their color comes from pine tree pollen) and the crisp, fried cookies coated with crushed pine nuts. **WHAT** It's worth a trip to Koreatown just to shop in this vast supermarket, which stocks everything to prepare a Korean meal and is often bustling with demonstrations and tastings of dumplings, meatballs or fried noodles. The produce section is lush with greens, soy sprouts, a half-dozen types of Asian mushrooms, lipstick peppers and fat Korean zucchini. There's also a large section devoted to *panchan*, the side dishes served in Korean restaurants, as well as dinner-ready hot dishes, marinated meats, shelves of kim chee and gorgeous trays of sashimi. 💲

[LAX-C] **1100 N. Main St., Chinatown, 323.343.9000, lax-c.com. Daily. Thai. AE, MC, V. WHY** A remarkable selection of Thai ingredients, packaged foods, cookware, even furniture. **WHAT** Part supermarket, part Costco-style warehouse, this shabby place is the go-to destination in town for everything you could possibly need to cook Thai food, all at very low prices (including produce). You may have to buy in huge quantities, so consider sharing with a friend or two. On weekends the parking lot fills with street-food vendors. **WHO** Thai restaurateurs and home cooks exploring Asian cuisines. 💲

[Liborio Market] 🏛 **864 S. Vermont Ave., Koreatown, 213.386.1458; 1831 W. 3rd St., Westlake, 213.483.1053; liborio.com. Daily. Latino/Cuban.**

AE, MC, V. WHY The most wondrous array of Latin American foods: Brazilian manioc meal, dried Peruvian potatoes, Guatemalan mashed black beans, the Salvadoran coffee cake called *quesadilla*, squishy-sweet ripe plantains, Mexican chorizos and marinated meat and, during the holidays, great tamales from many regions. **WHAT** This pan-Latin market draws cooks and enthusiastic eaters looking for ingredients for the cuisines of Cuba, Brazil, El Salvador, Peru, Guatemala and the Yucatán and Campeche regions of southern Mexico, among others. The family-run Liborio—originally a Cuban market—has expanded substantially since it opened in the '60s and now features a bakery and a meat department that can sell you *lechón asado* (whole roasted pig) or ready-to-use pupusa fillings. 🖫

[Mitsuwa] 🏠 **21515 Western Ave., Torrance, 310.782.0335; 3760 Centinela Ave., West L.A., 310.398.2113; mitsuwa.com. Daily. Japanese. MC, V. WHY** The same great selection of Japanese foods as its siblings but with a huge 15-store food court/retail center next door. Pick up Japanese cosmetics, books or pottery and stay for dinner. There's even a fast-food Chinese restaurant (go figure). Did we mention the complimentary valet parking? **WHAT** Everything you need to stock your Japanese pantry, including 20-pound bags of rice and gummy candies galore. Grab-and-go products like sushi and seaweed salad are good, too. But if you have a question, good luck, unless you speak Japanese or find the one employee who speaks English. Look for a kind customer instead.

[Super King Market] 🏠 **2260 N. Lincoln Ave., Altadena, 626.296.9311; 2716 N. San Fernando Rd., Eagle Rock, 323.225.0044; superkingmarkets.com. Daily. AE, MC, V. WHY** Low prices, good service, impeccable housekeeping and an unusual combination of mainstream American supermarket goods and a dazzling array of international foods. **WHAT** In 1993, the Fermanian family opened an unusual supermarket in Anaheim and over time found great success, and they've expanded to L.A. with markets in Eagle Rock and Altadena. You'll find all your supermarket needs along with an incredible (and cheap) selection of Armenian, Greek, Middle Eastern and Latin American foods: fresh and aged cheeses, sauces, yogurts, grains, prepared meats and exotic produce that's sometimes a little over-ripe. Impressive bakery, extensive deli with fresh cheeses, and a beautiful nut bar. **WHO** The most wonderful L.A. mix: An Indian woman in a gorgeous sari, a Central American family with kids in soccer uniforms, young indie couples, little old Lebanese women walking so slowly that you want to scream…. 🖫

[Vallarta Supermarket] **13051 Victory Blvd., North Hollywood, 818.760.7021, vallartasupermarket.com. Daily. Mexican/Latino. AE, MC, V. WHY** An unending selection of Mexican and Latin American ingredients, plus great takeout. **WHAT** The 19 L.A. County branches of this

🥬 VEGETARIAN ☺ KID FRIENDLY ✿ PATIO DINING 🚗 DELIVERY 🎩 PRIVATE PARTY

regional chain have butchers that prepare your meat *corte al gusto* (cut with flair), as well as the largest selection of Mexican and Salvadoran cheeses (Oaxacan, requesón, asadero, enchilada) in town, a great bakery department, quirky Mexican products, candies and loads of bargain produce. This is the flagship store; other locations include Burbank, Canoga Park, East L.A., Northridge, Van Nuys, Baldwin Park and Sylmar. 📑

[Vicente Foods] **12027 San Vicente Blvd., Brentwood, 310.472.5215, vicentefoods.com. Daily. AE, MC, V. WHY** Excellent prepared and deli foods, pretty produce and a butcher that carries four kinds of beef: Kobe, Midwestern prime, certified Black Angus and hormone-free Angus. **WHAT** A family-owned market that's kind of like a small Whole Foods (and Whole Foods is just down the street), Vicente Foods has L.A.'s best selection of products (preserves, candies, condiments, baked goods) from small, local manufacturers. It's not cheap, but this ain't a cheap neighborhood, and surely you've earned that sushi and dark chocolate! **WHO** Moneyed locals who are happy to pay for the convenience, quality and service.

WINE & SPIRITS

[55 Degrees] **3111 Glendale Blvd., Atwater, 323.662.5556, 55degreewine.com. Daily; tastings Tues.-Sun. AE, MC, V. WHY** A terrific array of Italians and a brick-walled, candlelit basement tasting room that's become the hippest spot in Atwater every night from 5 to 10 p.m. **WHAT** This eastern outpost of Santa Monica's Wine Expo is an oenophile hot spot in suddenly hip Atwater. As in Santa Monica, the specialty is small-producer Italian wines at very low prices; Champagnes are also a focus, and you'll also find some good choices from Spain. **WHO** Young wine buffs from Atwater, Highland Park and Silver Lake. 📑

[Chronicle Wine Shop] **919 E. California Blvd., Pasadena, 626.577.2549, cwcellar.com. Daily. AE, MC, V. WHY** The proximity to Pie 'n' Burger adds to the eccentric charm of this wine emporium located in an old motel room. Sommelier Elizabeth Schweitzer knows her stuff but is unpretentious about it. **WHAT** This place is in a (quirky) world of its own. No high-end tasting room here, but the atmosphere, reminiscent of a plain-jane French *cave*, makes this place worth a trip. When the flag is up on California Boulevard, the staff is in. **WHO** Caterers, party planners and low-key aficionados. 📑

[Colorado Wine Company] **2114 Colorado Blvd., Eagle Rock, 323.478.1985, cowineco.com. Closed Mon. AE, MC, V. WHY** Fun and surprising wine bargains in an un-snooty atmosphere, with a great wine bar to boot. **WHAT** The slogan here is "Wine for everyone," and that's refreshingly evident in the large selection of bottles for less than $25 and the tastings, which feature generous pours for $12 to $15. (Bonus: Cheeses from Auntie Em's!) **WHO** Attractive, friendly people in an attractive, friendly space in the hip heart of Eagle Rock. 🖼

[Domaine LA] **6801 Melrose Ave., Melrose, 323.932.0280, domainela. com. Daily. AE, MC, V. WHY** Because you're tired of the same old, same old. **WHAT** Wine enthusiast Jill Bernheimer started selling wine online, then dove into retailing with this small shop, which has become a cult favorite. Her low-key friendliness has endeared her to many who find wine shopping intimidating, and she loves to seek out esoterica; on a recent visit she was offering several bottlings of *txakoli*, a Basque white that most stores haven't even heard of. This is the place to find bottles that will astonish your wine-geek friends, and to discover well-priced alternatives to the big names that dominate supermarket wine shelves. **WHO** Adventurous wine lovers.

[Du Vin Wine & Spirits] **540 N. San Vicente Blvd. , West Hollywood, 310.855.1161, du-vin.net. Closed Sun. AE, MC, V. WHY** For its selection of French and Italian wines as well as a surprisingly large number of half bottles. **WHAT** Tucked away behind an office bungalow is this tiny cottage, a Mecca for lovers of European wines. This is the spot to find a big-ticket gift for a wine aficionado, as well as to snag esoteric varietals and regions that will spark cocktail-party chatter. Picpoul, anyone? There's a nice selection of upscale spirits, too, as well as a handful of gourmet foods. **WHO** Design professionals (it's around the corner from the Blue Whale) and wine lovers from WeHo and Beverly Hills.

[The Duck Blind] **1102 Montana Ave., Santa Monica, 310.394.6705. Daily. AE, MC, V. WHY** The specials. Sometimes you can luck into a $15 wine for $5. **WHAT** Don't let the outside fool you—what looks like a standard grungy liquor store is actually a perfectly fine wine shop. Lots of $10 and $15 bottles, plus some good local and international brews. **WHO** Neighborhood loyalists—this place has been around for half a century. 🖼🚚

[Flask Fine Wines] **12194 Ventura Blvd., Studio City, 818.761.5373, flaskfinewines.com. Daily. AE, MC, V. WHY** A chic tasting bar (Thursdays and Fridays) and a smart choice of small-producer Californians. **WHAT** Excellent displays and some little-seen Californian and French wines make this a fun place to browse. The monthly specials can be very good values. **WHO** Local tasters and producers' assistants who were dispatched to fetch an emergency $250 bottle for a gift.

[Gerlach's Liquor] **1075 S. Fair Oaks Ave., Pasadena, 626.799.1166. Daily. AE, MC, V. WHY** Great buys on special wines (we've found swell Malbecs for $9), a small but thoughtful selection of French, Calfornian and Oregonian wines, and a terrific choice of port, sherry and dessert

🌿 **VEGETARIAN** ◎ **KID FRIENDLY** ☼ **PATIO DINING** 🚚 **DELIVERY** 🎩 **PRIVATE PARTY**

wine. **WHAT** It looks like your basic drive-up liquor store, but there's a lot more to Gerlach's than meets the eye. Brothers Lewy and Fred Fedail know their stuff, and they pack a lot of good wines into a small climate-controlled room. A devoted clientele asks for their advice and takes it. **WHO** Blue-blood Pasadenans, artsy South Pasadenans and working guys picking up a six-pack. 📝

[K & L Wine Merchants] 1400 Vine St., Hollywood, 323.464. WINE, klwines.com. Daily. AE, MC, V. **WHY** Great location, competitive prices and a parking lot. **WHAT** This terrific shop, a branch of the Bay Area–based retailer, sits in the shadow of the ArcLight and offers a superb selection of imported and domestic wines. It also boasts a well-edited shelf of single malts, small-batch bourbons, craft vodkas and digestifs. **WHO** Collectors who trickle in from the Hollywood Hills and Hancock Park.

[Larchmont Wine & Cheese] 223 N. Larchmont Blvd., Hancock Park, 323.856.8699. Closed Sun. AE, MC, V. **WHY** Savvy wine picks, delicious sandwiches and Michel Cordon Bleu smoked salmon. **WHAT** This tiny shop on pricey Larchmont Boulevard stocks a well-chosen array of bottlings at a fair markup. Wine guy Simon Cocks offers trustworthy advice and doesn't hesitate to steer customers toward the best values (the "wine of the month" is always a good buy). The deli's sandwiches are justifiably renowned. **WHO** Hancock Parkers catching up with each other about kids, vacations and remodelings.

[Los Angeles Wine Co.] 4935 McConnell Ave., West L.A., 310.306.9463, lawineco.com. Daily. AE, MC, V. **WHY** Drink globably, save locally. **WHAT** This warehouse-style merchant has spent years scouring the world for great deals, and it lives up to its motto: "Every wine in stock, always sale priced." Whether seeking a $95 Burgundy for $80 or a $40 Italian Sangiovese for $30, value hunters love the steals and deals. **WHO** Penny-pinchers come for the Under $12 Club— more than 100 selections, some under $5. tk check 📝

[Mission Wines] 1114 Mission St., South Pasadena, 626.403.9463, missionwines.com. Daily. AE, MC, V. **WHY** It's a nice spot to just hang out around wine. **WHAT** Former Patina sommelier Chris Meeske runs a charming, artisan-style shop that showcases handmade, distinctive bottlings at every price point. Wine education and pairing wine with food are specialties, and the frequent tastings have become a linchpin of South Pasadena's lively food-and-wine scene. The $10 and under bargains are always good. **WHO** People who wouldn't be caught dead buying wine at TJs down the street.

[Moe's Fine Wines] 11740 San Vicente Blvd., Brentwood, 310.826.4444, moesfinewines.com. Closed Sun. AE, MC, V. **WHY** Wine is more fun than software, so thank you, Moe, for quitting your day job

🏛 ESSENTIALLY L.A. ☺ LATE 💚 ROMANTIC 📝 VALUE 🔇 QUIET ♻ SUSTAINABLE to open this place. **WHAT** Scott "Moe" Levy's high-end neighborhood shop looks like a dream home cellar, with stained-wood wine racks, Riedel stemware and a carefully chosen array of $8 to $800 wines, many from small California producers. And it is a kind of home for Moe, who quit the software business to realize his wine-merchant dream. Some international heavy-hitters are featured as well, along with delightful house chocolates and nuts. **WHO** Well-heeled Brentwood regulars, many of whom stop by for the Saturday-afternoon tastings.

[Off the Vine] **491 6th St., San Pedro, 310.831.1551, offthevinewines. com. Closed Mon. AE, MC, V. WHY** For tasty, good-value bottles from the Santa Ynez Valley and the northern and southern Rhône. **WHAT** The selection is small at this tidy little shop, but it's creative and includes some very good specials. The focus is on just three regions: California's Central Coast, the Rhône and Spain. Regulars stop by for the Friday- and Saturday-night tastings, and party-planning beer lovers order kegs of local and import craft beers (Bitburger, Allagash, Bayhawk, Green Flash and many more). **WHO** South Bay food-and-wine buffs who are tired of Trader Joe's.

[Palate Food & Wine] **933 S. Brand Blvd., Glendale, 818.662.9463, palatefoodwine.com. Closed Sun. AE, MC, V. WHY** For an international (and local) selection of superb wines, chos en and sold by people who are brimming with enthusiasm. **WHAT** Behind the hip restaurant Palate is a retail wine shop run by sommelier Steve Goldun, who has amassed a reasonably priced collection of carefully made wines from California and around the world. For your next party, consider a wine and cheese tasting held at the cocktail tables between the wine shop and the restaurant's cheese cellar. **WHO** Eastside oenophiles who like hang out for a while to talk about wine.

[Red Carpet] **400 E. Glenoaks Blvd., Glendale, 818.247.5544, redcarpetwine.com. Daily. AE, MC, V. WHY** For an impressive array of hard-to-find California bottlings. **WHAT** If Red Carpet doesn't carry it, you'll probably have to trek to the westside to find it. Staffed by enthusiasts, this venerable store has a vast selection of wine, beer and premium spirits, as well as cigars and stemware. The tasting bar is a popular hangout on weekends and Tuesday evenings. **WHO** Collectors who don't mind paying a few bucks more for good service.

[Rosso Wine Shop] **3459 N. Verdugo Rd., Glendale, 818.330.9130, rossowineshop.com. Closed Mon. AE, MC, V. WHY** To discover obscure vintners your tasting buddies haven't heard of. **WHAT** Tiny Rosso doesn't try to compete with the big guys; instead, owner Jeff Zimmitti focuses on France, Spain, Italy and California, selecting the best-value wines that go well with food. The result is a user-friendly shop that's a great addition to north Glendale's gourmet gulch on Verdugo Road.

Shops +
Services

🍃 **VEGETARIAN** ☺ **KID FRIENDLY** ✿ **PATIO DINING** 🚐 **DELIVERY** 🏛 **PRIVATE PARTY**

Pick up a bottle to enjoy with an excellent dinner at Bashan next door.
WHO A younger breed of collector and enthusiast.

[Silverlake Wine] 2395 Glendale Blvd., Silver Lake, 323.662.9024,
silverlakewine.com. Daily. AE, MC, V. **WHY** For a well-chosen selection
at every price point. **WHAT** This female-friendly, no-attitude shop
showcases small-production wines from all over the world. And sometimes the best wine for your occasion might be a Pacific Northwest
microbrew, or even a handmade sake. Tastings are happening events;
Monday brings wines paired with cheeses from the Cheese Store of
Silverlake, and on Thursday nights, the Let's Be Frank truck parks out
front. In summer, don't miss the Friday-night wine-tasting-and-tour of
the Hollyhock House in Los Feliz. **WHO** Silverlake hipsters, but the
unhip are welcome, too.

[Topline Wine Company] 4718 San Fernando Rd., Glendale,
818.500.9670, toplinewine.com. Daily. AE, MC, V. **WHY** Premium wine
and spirits at not-so-premium prices. **WHAT** This no-frills shop in
an industrial section of Glendale has a decent wine selection at very
competitive prices. It's arranged warehouse-style, with stacks of cases,
and it's worth poking through the boxes to find the buried treasures.
Also check out the spirits room and the particularly good collection of
aperitifs. **WHO** Price-conscious aficionados from all over.

[Venokado] 7714 Fountain Ave., West Hollywood, 323.850.1600,
venokado.com. Daily. MC, V. **WHY** You need the perfect wine or the
perfect gift, and you don't have a vast budget or time to wander
through a mall. **WHAT** The trio of women who run this chic shop sell
a well-edited selection of wines and gifts (for yourself or for others,
including babies) relating to food, wine, entertaining and the good life.
The name says it all—a mashup of the Italian word for wine (*vino*) and
the French word for gift (*cadeau*). The ladies have gained a following
for their clutch gift, a sleek box containing a bottle of wine and an
intriguing, fun assortment of other items, for $45 and up. We always
leave with an armful of interesting bottles, many under $20.
WHO Style-conscious WeHo regulars and savvy commuters who regularly take Fountain across town.

[Vinatero Wine Shop] 6531 Greenleaf Ave., Whittier, 562.464.9463,
vinaterowineshop.com. Daily. AE, MC, V. **WHY** A well-chosen selection
of global wines and beers in historic Uptown Whittier. **WHAT** With a
truly international selection of wines and specialty beers, including
some on tap, Vinatero is a shopper's dream: a thoughtful staff, custom
gift baskets and a gift registry. And with daily wine and beer tastings,
it's almost as much a bar as it is a shop. **WHO** Whittier oenophiles and
beer geeks as well as those looking for a thoughtful gift.

[Wally's] 🔒 **2107 Westwood Blvd., Westwood, 310.475.0606, wallywine. com. Daily. AE, MC, V. WHY** For the phenomenal selection of hard-to-find trophy wines. **WHAT** Steve Wallace founded his West Los Angeles wine shop in 1968 and despite cramped quarters has built it into one of California's leading wine retailers. This is the spot to find rare and small-production bottlings from Napa, Burgundy, Bordeaux and other fine-wine regions. Partner Christian Navarro handles the care and feeding of the shop's stable of heavy-hitting collectors. **WHO** Studio bigwigs, UCLA professors, Brentwood matrons.

[The Wine Country] **2301 Redondo Ave., Signal Hill, 562.597.8303, thewinecountry.com. Daily. AE, MC, V. WHY** Stuff you won't easily find elsewhere. **WHAT** Owner Randy Kemner has long championed offbeat varietals, off-the-beaten-track regions and underappreciated importers. The result is a shop with an eclectic array of wines selected for their ability to complement food, with particular strength in aromatic whites, including German, Austrian and Alsatian bottlings. **WHO** South Bay enthusiasts of ABC—"anything but Chardonnay."

[Wine Expo] 🔒 **2933 Santa Monica Blvd., Santa Monica, 310.828.4428, wineexpo.com. Daily. AE, MC, V. WHY** Educated and refreshingly honest staff members, who also know their way around tequila and beer. **WHAT** Wine Expo started as a champagne specialty shop and has evolved into the westside's go-to source for Italian wines. Owners Ali Biglar and Robert Rogness cultivate relationships with Italian winemakers and ship back via their own import business to keep prices low. Almost as entertaining as the vast selection are the clever descriptions posted by the cases. Ditto the newsletter, which is a hoot. **WHO** Fans of *vino italiano*. 📝

[Wine House] 🔒 **2311 Cotner Ave., West L.A., 310.479.3731, wineaccess.com. Daily. AE, MC, V. WHY** For 18,000 square feet devoted to wine, beer and spirits. **WHAT** Arguably the best wine shop in L.A., the Wine House has it all: great selection, good prices, informed staff and even a little gourmet food section, so you can get a tin of caviar to go with that magnum of Cristal. A year-round program of classes makes it easy to improve your tasting skills and expertise. Also check out the cool automated tasting bar.

[Woodland Hills Wine Company] 🔒 **22622 Ventura Blvd., Woodland Hills, 818.222.1111, whwc.com. Daily. AE, MC, V. WHY** It's all about the Burgs. **WHAT** A connoisseur's Mecca, Woodland Hills Wine specializes in (sigh) Burgundies, but the selection of top wines from California, Bordeaux, the Rhône, Italy, Austria and Spain is worth the drive to the west Valley. Woodland Hills also direct-imports many hard-to-find bottlings, including some bargains. Staffers are highly knowledgeable and give good counsel. **WHO** Serious collectors as well as wine newbies.

Shops + Services

🍃 VEGETARIAN ☺ KID FRIENDLY ☼ PATIO DINING 🚐 DELIVERY 🎩 PRIVATE PARTY

🍴 Indexes

BY NEIGHBORHOOD

🍴 Index: A to Z